John Burrow is one of Britain's leading intellectual historians. He was professor of Intellectual History at the University of Sussex from 1981 to 1995 and Professor of European Thought at Oxford from 1995 to 2000. His earlier books include *Evolution and Society: A Study in Victorian Social Theory* (1966), *A Liberal Descent: Victorian Historians and the English Past* (1981), which won the Wolfson Prize for History, *Gibbon* (1984) and *The Crisis of Reason: European Thought, 1848–1914* (2000). He is a Fellow of the British Academy and an Emeritus Fellow of Balliol College, Oxford.

JOHN BURROW

A History of Histories

Epics, Chronicles, Romances and Inquiries from
Herodotus and Thucydides to the Twentieth Century

PENGUIN BOOKS

PENGUIN BOOKS

Published by the Penguin Group
Penguin Books Ltd, 80 Strand, London WC2R ORL, England
Penguin Group (USA) Inc., 375 Hudson Street, New York, New York 10014, USA
Penguin Group (Canada), 90 Eglinton Avenue East, Suite 700, Toronto, Ontario, Canada M4P 2Y3
(a division of Pearson Penguin Canada Inc.)
Penguin Ireland, 25 St Stephen's Green, Dublin 2, Ireland
(a division of Penguin Books Ltd)
Penguin Group (Australia), 250 Camberwell Road, Camberwell, Victoria 3124, Australia
(a division of Pearson Australia Group Pty Ltd)
Penguin Books India Pvt Ltd, 11 Community Centre, Panchsheel Park, New Delhi – 110 017, India
Penguin Group (NZ), 67 Apollo Drive, Rosedale, North Shore 0632, New Zealand
(a division of Pearson New Zealand Ltd)
Penguin Books (South Africa) (Pty) Ltd, 24 Sturdee Avenue, Rosebank, Johannesburg 2196, South Africa

Penguin Books Ltd, Registered Offices: 80 Strand, London WC2R ORL, England

www.penguin.com

First published by Allen Lane 2007
Published in Penguin Books 2009
1

Grateful acknowledgement is made to Michael Alexander for permission
to quote lines from 'The Ruin' and 'The Wanderer' from his translation
of *The First Poems in English* on page 221.

Typeset by Rowland Phototypesetting Ltd, Bury St Edmunds, Suffolk
Printed in England by Clays Ltd, St Ives plc

978-0-140-28379-2

www.greenpenguin.co.uk

Penguin Books is committed to a sustainable future
for our business, our readers and our planet.
The book in your hands is made from paper
certified by the Forest Stewardship Council.

Contents

PART III

Christendom

PART IV

The Revival of Secular History

PART V

Studying the Past

Great thanks, laud, and honour ought to be given unto the clerks, poets, and historiographs that have written many noble books of wisedom of the lives, passions, and miracles of holy saints, of histories of noble and famous acts and faites, and of the chronicles since the beginning of the creation of the world unto this present time, by which we be daily informed and have knowledge of many things of whom we should not have known if they had not left to us their monuments written.

William Caxton (1484)

Acknowledgements

My first debt is to Stuart Proffitt, for suggesting I write this book and for keeping his faith in it during a long period of gestation, as well as overcoming my hesitation about taking on such a comprehensive project. He has added to my debt and my gratitude by his guidance with drafts of early chapters and by his immensely thorough editing of the finished text, which produced many justified criticisms and fruitful suggestions, which have greatly improved it.

A number of friends have earned my warm thanks by reading some or all of the draft chapters. Their corrections have saved me from embarrassing errors, and their encouragement and advice have helped me keep my nerve when venturing into areas where I was a novice. My thanks are due to Stefan Collini, John Drury, Patrick Mullin, Mark Phillips, Larry Siedentop, Quentin Skinner, John Thompson, Frank Walbank, Patricia Williams, Donald Winch and David Wootton. I should like to thank reviewers who have kindly sent me corrections. For remaining errors of fact or judgement I alone am responsible.

Jane Wyatt has typed a long and in places inscrutable manuscript and borne with heroic patience and good humour with my many changes of mind. I am once again deeply indebted to her.

I am very grateful to them all.

Introduction

A History of Histories?

Why 'A History of Histories', or, more explicitly, why not 'The History of History'? History, even if we allow it to be in its broadest sense a single kind of activity, is nonetheless a highly diverse one. Plagues, invasions, emigrations; the foundation, working and development of constitutional arrangements and political systems; wars, external and civil, revolutions, changes in religion and culture, gradual or abrupt, the formation of various kinds of collective identity – confessional, national, ideological – providential history in the sense of the dealings of God with man: all these and much else are properly regarded as history. Some histories are virtually pure narrative; others are virtually pure, almost atemporal, analyses, being essentially structural or cultural surveys. History is contiguous with many other genres and lines of inquiry, from epic and myths of origin to various social sciences, and touching also biography, drama, political and moral polemic, ethnography, novels, inquests and judicial investigations. It was, so far as we know, Herodotus who first used the term *historia* (inquiry) for what we call history. A *histor* in Homer was someone who passed judgement based on the facts as a result of investigation, so the link between history and inquest is a very old one.

How can this variety be converted into a single historical narrative: 'The History of History'? There is one answer which is obvious, being to some degree necessary to a narrative. This is by establishing a terminus, an end to which the episodes of the story are in some sense subordinate and contributing, so that they become moments in a progression. In the case of the history of historical writing – a genre which did not exist until the twentieth century – it was inevitable, given the period and its historiographical culture, that this was most commonly and easily done by taking the present state of the subject (or what it was assumed to be) as the terminus. By the early twentieth century this present state was characterized, variously but with a fair degree of consensus, as pure or 'scientific' or (tacitly) as 'professional' history, all identified perhaps with 'the idea of history' or the study of the past 'for its own sake'. Professional history, in particular, was explicitly or simply by assumption associated with systematic archival research and the critical examination of sources, which had come to be thought of as constitutive of all serious history. Within this general consensus there could be differences of opinion, as for example between J. B. Bury and G. M. Trevelyan, over whether history was a 'science' or an 'art', and over how far, if at all, the historian in pursuit of his 'science' should be concerned to establish laws (anathema to R. G. Collingwood in his classic book *The Idea of History*, 1946). But despite these differences there was enough consensus to provide the basis for a selective grand narrative of the history of historiography, in which past historians were highlighted and assessed for their roles, necessarily partial, but helpful (or perhaps backsliding), in the general progression to the twentieth-century historian's views and approved practice. In this sense it was possible to write 'The History of History'.

I do not want to be understood as speaking simply in denigration of the assumptions underlying this possibility, as though of a past cultural episode. The central concerns – above all with history as truth-telling and, at least as an ideal, as free from bias – were already very old ones and, though shaken, are still in some sense with us, for those of us for whom a distinction between, say, history and imaginative fiction is still an important one. In this view Herodotus was taking an important step in distinguishing his own *Histories* from the work of the poets, and Thucydides, though he may have judged unfairly, was invoking relevant criteria when he sneered by implication at Herodotus as belonging with authors less concerned to tell the truth than to entertain the public. Some distance between the search for historical understanding and merely emotionally or polemically effective writing is still part of the self-image and intentions of the historical profession. Of course, in the history of historiography zeal for truth has been a spectrum rather than an absolute – truth mattered, fairly obviously, more to Polybius than to Livy – but someone who wholly and perhaps wilfully falls off the negative end of the scale, like Geoffrey of Monmouth (this is not the place to argue the individual case), counts rather as a parodist or imitator of history.

All this may be true, but it remains true also that establishing a grand narrative of the history of historiography, by adopting a twentieth-century professional consensus as its terminus, was an impoverishingly narrowing strategy to adopt, eliminating or sidelining many interesting and potentially illuminating questions about approaches to historical writing, and indeed to the past as such, current in former times. There is, for example, the whole large and fascinating question of the surely very diverse motives for writing history. What did people in the past find interesting in *their* past, and why did they? Which 'pasts' did it lead them to focus attention on, as well as shaping how they chose to present them, and how and why did these change over time or how did different answers to these questions in a single period reflect and express differences within the culture? Why did new genres of historical writing emerge? Surely not only or invariably as a result of an extension of a pre-existing 'scientific' curiosity, though that was sometimes a factor.

This book aims to provide answers to these questions. They have not been entirely neglected, and historians of historiography have been concerned to divide their subject in terms of genre as well as of method. But there is a balance to be redressed, as well as an allegiance to be proclaimed. I have tried to focus here on the question of the pasts that people have chosen for themselves and why, as well as on how they investigated and presented them. This may seem scarcely revolutionary, but like all chosen strategies it involves sacrifices. In particular, in grouping historians according to subject matter I have sometimes been cavalier with strict chronology – a lesson historians learned when they moved away from annals as the dominant form. So, for example, the 'Alexander' historians are treated here as part of the story of the Greek encounters with the Persian empire, even though the historians whose work is still extant wrote much later, under the Roman empire. Perhaps most controversially, consideration of the Bible and its influence on historiography is postponed until its impact on the Gentile world in the early Christian centuries, rather than being placed, as chronology dictates, between Egyptian and Babylonian historians and Herodotus.

So, 'A History of Histories' is intended to recognize the plurality of 'histories' and the interests embodied in them, and to disclaim the ambition to construct a single grand narrative with the present as its terminus, which I see not only as implausibly prescriptive but also as narrowing the possibilities of exploration. There are, however, some exclusions which are intended also to be suggested in the title, with its implied retreat from comprehensiveness. No attempt has been made to deal with historiography outside the European cultural tradition (to which Egypt and Babylon are taken to contribute), notably Arabic and Chinese examples. Such exclusions are merely concessions to limitations of space, time and the author's knowledge. Another exclusion perhaps needs more apology, because it is at least in some measure arbitrary and the line of demarcation is a wavering one. I have taken the term 'histories', though itself a generous one, as excluding biography and memoirs. In a book in danger of trying to include too much, I have thought this necessary, though the criteria are admittedly not always easy to apply: memoirs are clearly close kin to eyewitness history, and a 'Life and Times' proclaims itself a mixed genre.

A word must be said about the treatment of the individual histories, which of course vary enormously in density and complexity, as well as in their accessibility to the modern reader. It is reasonable to assume that most readers of this book will not have read many or most of the historical works it discusses; indeed, that is part of the book's justification. One, primary, task therefore is to try to give a sense of the experience of reading these histories and what may be enjoyable about them. For many, perhaps most, historians, history has been a leisurely art, often requiring many volumes. It is not exclusively devoted to narrative, but narrative has long been at the core of it. It is therefore not enough just to convey the historian's intentions and views: some attempt must be made to convey not merely the structure of the narrative, but also its texture and qualities. In that respect, histories – which also often incorporate surveys, disquisitions, arguments and analyses – also resemble novels. I have made an attempt here, therefore, to give a sense, where appropriate, of what an eclectic, multi-layered, many-toned project a dense historical narrative may be. In attempting to render histories' special qualities I have not only resorted to a good deal of quotation but have attempted, sympathetically and with an awareness of the periods when they were written, to convey the literary qualities which form a large part of the experience of reading them. But these appraisals are also to be seen within, and perhaps as contributing to an overall understanding of, a more general context: the aims of historians in a particular period, the conventions which shaped their writing, and the ways these changed. I have also attended to historians' relations to the sources which made their work possible and partly conditioned it, and also briefly to the question of the particular writer's reliability. Awareness of this is part of an understanding of historians and therefore of the experience of reading them; history can never be, by definition, a purely literary endeavour. I have not, however, made any systematic attempt to focus on particular errors, for which, in any case, I should lack the necessary knowledge. That is the business of modern historians of the period, and they need no help from me. Such a checklist would, in any case, be intolerably tedious to read.

Historiography is not only a (wide) genre in itself, exhibiting continuities and revivals as well as shifting focuses of attention. It is also a part of Western culture as a whole – at times a highly influential and even central part – as well as being obviously a receptacle for the concerns of that culture and influenced by its fluctuations. European societies at different times and with varying emphases have attached immense importance to versions of their pasts and to notions of historical development, as well as plundering historical writings for legendary, heroic, tragic and pathetic motifs and topoi for poetry, drama and painting (in the eighteenth century, 'historical' painting was regarded as the highest pictorial genre), and for exemplary, inspiring and minatory rhetoric. Ideas of history and of aspects of the past have intersected with and partly constituted ideas of religion, morals and politics. They have embodied authority, and provided means with which to challenge it. Above all, perhaps, they have provided focuses of allegiance, self-identification and 'memory' for ethnic, national, religious, political, cultural and social collectivities and so helped to constitute them. Versions of the past have been offered, sometimes obliquely but often with visible anxiety, as diagnoses of contemporary predicaments or malaises.

We are accustomed to think of the intellectual history of Europe in terms of the history of philosophy, of science and religion, of art, literature and of ideas of social order and political authority. But the history of ideas about the past, as expressed in historical writing, and how the present stands in relation to it, is also part of that history; this book aims to contribute to an understanding of it. Among its chief components are conceptions of the distinctiveness of European civilization, contrasted chiefly with the empires of Asia; ideas of republican virtue, embodied in early Rome, supposedly corrupted by conquest and luxury; and the myth of Eternal Rome as mistress of the world, which became transmuted into the idea of a Christian empire. The Bible contributed ideas of collective transgression, punishment and redemption. From the sixteenth century onward we find the idea, largely derived from the Roman historian Tacitus, of an early freedom of the 'Germanic' peoples, and of the existence of 'ancient constitutions', with a continuing authority in the present, which European countries allegedly derive from their invasion by the 'Gothic' barbarians. Eighteenth-century historical writing incorporated concepts of the progress of 'civil society', chiefly in association with commerce, and of the end of 'feudal anarchy' (or, in Marxist terms, the supersession of the feudal nobility by the hegemony of the bourgeoisie). The nineteenth century was the great age of the preoccupation with national identity, in association with ideas of national liberation and the creation of the nation state as the normal political form. This has passed on into the modern aspiration to give a voice to suppressed minorities. History, in other words, to name only the most prominent influences, has been republican, Christian, constitutionalist, sociological, Romantic, liberal, Marxist and nationalist. All these have left residues in subsequent historical writing; none at the moment dominates it.

I have therefore made a conscious effort not to treat the history of historiography in isolation, but to be aware of its place in the wider culture, of the cultural and political influences playing on it, and of the ways in which it fostered, transformed and transmitted them. 'A

History of Histories' can and should be more than a record of the achievements, strengths and weaknesses of historians and the schools and traditions to which they belonged. It is itself a historical enterprise, one of the ways in which we attempt to understand the past.

Prologue

Keeping Records and Making Accounts:
Egypt and Babylon

History – the elaborated, secular, prose narrative (all these qualifications are necessary) of public events, based on inquiry – was born, we can claim with confidence, in Greece between roughly 450 and 430 BC. If we want to add Thucydides' very different kind of history to that of Herodotus, who is sometimes spoken of as 'the father of history', then we must speak instead of the second half of the fifth century BC. Even with this extension, and with the qualifications built into the description of the genre, it is extraordinary that we can speak of so short a period for its abrupt genesis, yet it appears to be justified. It is equally astonishing that we can plausibly claim that neither historian was to be excelled for over two thousand years subsequently – until, in fact, changes in methods and types of history begin to make comparison unrealistic.

To see what is meant by claiming that Herodotus and Thucydides were, so far as we know, the first historians, we need to recognize some basic distinctions which separate their work from examples of what we may call perhaps 'proto-history' in the ancient civilizations of Egypt and Babylon. Herodotus himself paid tribute to the Egyptians for their preservation of knowledge of the past: 'by their practice of keeping records of the past, [they] have made themselves much the most learned of any nation of which I have had experience' (*Histories*, II.77). In fact he seems to have believed too readily what he was told in the temples of Egypt when conducting the historical inquiries he incorporated into the panoramic survey of the known world with which he prefaced his account of the great Persian invasion of Greece in the early fifth century BC. His own references to Egyptian history are notably garbled, in contrast to what he has to say of the civilization of Babylon, on which he is much more reliable. Yet, whatever it may have pleased the Egyptian temple servants to tell him – it is not clear that his acquaintance ranged far up the priestly hierarchy – Herodotus' compliment to the Egyptians was not misplaced. Modern Egyptologists can know much more than Herodotus about ancient Egypt precisely because so much of it, thanks to the early establishment of a centralized bureaucratic state and the use of durable materials for inscriptions, has been preserved. To this we may add the effects of a dry climate and a traditional habit of mind: the records so preserved go back more than two thousand years before Herodotus' own time, the mid fifth century BC. The Egyptians were indeed then the world's premier record-keepers. The distinction between historiography and recording – between the sense in which Herodotus was, so far as we know, the first historian and the learning of his Egyptian informants – is therefore one to give us pause. It is valid enough, though of course, like all such distinctions, it becomes a little less rigid as we examine it.

Record-keeping is, in origin, commercial and bureaucratic good practice; it is not an art. Many of the factors which have preserved so much of the Egyptian past existed also in the ancient civilization of Mesopotamia, with its records inscribed on stones and clay tablets and, for most of the greatest matters, on the walls of temples, tombs and palaces. Every modern historian understands what we are speaking of here – namely archives – and regards them as in some form indispensable, as Herodotus, who worked by interrogation of 'learned men', did not. The inscriptions were intended as records from the beginning: their endurance was deliberate, as that of casually collected documents is often not. It is only the humbler artefacts, such as inscribed clay tablets, which have survived inadvertently. Inscriptions being essentially records, this produces a kinship between their authors and Herodotus, who says, in his initial statement of intention at the outset of his *Histories*, that he wrote to preserve the memory of great deeds (below, p. 11).

The key difference, of course, is the word that Herodotus used to describe his work: *historia*, inquiry. His method of acquiring the information for his *Histories* was chiefly interrogation. When he questioned the Egyptian temple servants and guardians, he, who seems to have known only Greek, was at a remove from the documents in a way that a modern historian would not care for. But, for all the deficiencies or secretiveness of his informants, we recognize something like an intelligible relationship: it is that between historian and archivist. It was he who, in the service of a systematic inquiry, history, was interrogating them; not vice versa. Similarly, when he interrogated 'overseas' Greeks and perhaps 'native informants' for knowledge of other parts of the world, as he must have done, it was he who was the anthropologist or ethnographer. There was, to state the obvious, no Scythian ethnographer; those whom the Greeks called Scythians, of whose customs Herodotus wrote an extended account, were illiterate nomads living north of the Black Sea. We have therefore argued ourselves into the position of saying that, as far as we know, there were no Egyptian or Babylonian historians earlier than Herodotus. The Egyptians were, as Herodotus says, learned; respect for Egyptian wisdom was high and even exaggerated in Greece, where, for example, the Greek gods, under other names, were thought to have originated in Egypt. But the Egyptians were recorders, not historians.

So far so simple. As we shall see in Chapter 1, Herodotus' notion of systematic inquiry was not entirely unique in Greece in his time. The inquiries closest to his own seem to have been mainly geographical (including of course 'human geography'), a concern which is very evident also in Herodotus' work. But inquiry, systematic research, is not the only characteristic of historiography. Another is the rendering of the results of the inquiry into connected historical prose: narrative. There is in fact a route in the ancient world from recording to more or less extended historical narrative which blurs a little the distinction between recording and history that seems so firm when we attend only to the element of research.

The earliest writing seems, understandably, to have been concerned with practical transactions, and can be thought of either as part of the transaction or just as a subsequent record. Early public inscriptions, in the grandest contexts, recorded on the walls of temples, seem also to have taken on this transactional character, as the rendering of an account by the ruler of his stewardship on behalf of the god: his buildings erected, his gifts, and the toils and achievements, including victories, by which they were procured. Inventories are common. Other kinds of list include the earliest materials for systematic chronology –

king lists, for example – and are therefore crucial to the possibility of reliable large-scale history. Laws too, like the early so-called law codes of ancient Mesopotamia, are also essentially lists, in a way familiar, though much later, from the books of Leviticus and Numbers in the Old Testament from the end of the second millennium BC.

The connection between narrative and divine stewardship seems to lie in explanations. That is, to render an account, initially in the form of a list, can come to involve an explanation, which in turn may take the form of a more or less elaborated narrative. Historians are accustomed to insisting, perhaps rather combatively since it is their stock-in-trade, that an explanation may take the form of a narrative. They may be less keen on claiming an ancient kinship with account-ants, and through them to the earliest uses of writing: making lists. The conceptual overlap here, however, is still caught in the related meanings, indicated by prepositions, of the English word 'account', which itself recalls its origin in the act of counting. It makes good sense if bad style, with each repetition making a different point, to say, 'Please account for the errors in the accounts you have presented to the board by giving your account of how they were compiled.'

Narrative inscriptions which were also explanations and part of the rendering of accounts can be seen growing fuller and more circum-stantial and far more 'human' in their references to motives and action. Campaign narratives – with their natural climax in victories (or pretended victories) and hence conquests, subjection or capture of alien peoples, and the acquisition of spoil – are among the earliest extended narratives, and are also, of course, characteristically narra-tives of expeditions, like that of Xerxes in Herodotus, and, nearly two centuries later, the greatest of all campaign expeditions, that of Alexander, who took historians with him. This is an Egyptian account from the middle of the second millennium BC of a victory and its trophies:

His Majesty proceeded on his chariot to Kashabu, alone and without a com-panion, and returned thence in a short time bringing sixteen living Maryannu at the side of his chariot, twenty hands at the foreheads of his horses and sixty cattle driven in front of him. Submission was made to His Majesty by this town. Now as His Majesty was going south in the plain of Sharon,

4

he found a messenger of the prince of Nahrin carrying a clay tablet at his neck, and took him as a living prisoner at the side of his chariot . . . Arrival of His Majesty at Memphis with joyful heart like a victorious bull. Amount of plunder . . . (Gardiner, *Egypt and the Pharaohs*, p. 197)

Then follows an itemization, with numbers, of slaves, horses, chariots, weapons and musical instruments. Expeditions were also apparently conducted by the pharaohs in the quest for valuables such as minerals.

Another Egyptian form of narrative pattern is the onset of a period of confusion and disasters, brought to an end by the advent of a ruler who restores order. These narratives of deliverance – whose archetypal protagonist later, under Hebrew influence, became the Messiah figure – have had, like the campaign narrative, a long history in Western historiography, influencing the representation of such figures as the emperors Augustus and Constantine and, in English history, Queen Elizabeth I and William III. Thus some of the archetypal patterns of historical narrative were established as early as the inscriptions recording the deeds of the rulers of ancient Egypt, Mesopotamia and Asia Minor. In the Bible, the books of Exodus and Deuteronomy are essentially expedition and campaign narrative, which features also in the work of some of the greatest later historians.

Another way in which the rendering of accounts, in the form of vindication, elaborates itself into narrative seems to have been cultivated particularly among the Hittites. That is, a record was made to establish the justice of what had been done, and to refer the matter to divine arbitration. A leading authority on the Hittite empire, O. R. Gurney, describes a document of this kind as showing a highly developed political conscience. The more legalistic form of this kind of record-keeping, and the provision of a narrative on which judgement was to be based, concerned, naturally, the making and breaking of treaties. Treaties are the only documents to be transcribed at length by Thucydides, much of whose opening book is concerned with the rupturing of treaties which constituted the opening of the Peloponnesian War. The Hittites, a millennium earlier, had begun the practice of making the preambles to treaties into occasions for brief historical narratives explaining the treaties' origins; eventually the prefatory narratives became detached from the treaties and decrees and became free-standing annals, the chronicle being a presentation of the ruler's actions as an offering to the god.

The annalistic form of recording is found also among the Assyrians, as well as in early 'historians' in Greek city states, along with accounts of supposed mythological origins. It is not employed by Herodotus – a work on such a large scale would have made it unusable – but it shapes Thucydides' history of the Peloponnesian War, with a division of each year into summer and winter for greater precision. It was to remain a fundamental historiographical form to the end of the Middle Ages.

Mention of annals brings to the surface a troublesome issue for early historiography: the need to find widely recognizable ways of marking chronology. This was less of a problem in centralized dynastic states like Egypt and Babylon – which is not to say that early king lists were always as helpfully drawn up as they might have been: attempting to eliminate all trace of a discredited ruler was a common Egyptian practice, while the lengths ascribed to reigns are clearly absurd. But in Greece, with no central political authority or record-keeping, the problem was acute. The only pan-Greek institutions were the oracle at Delphi and the four-yearly Olympic Games, with their famous winning athletes, and the Olympiads were eventually used as chronological markers. Thucydides dated events from the onset of the war he was recounting. For Athens it was possible to use the periods of office of the archons, the chief officials of the *polis*, who held their posts for a year, though they may not have been easy to recall. The Romans from earliest times kept lists of the pontiffs, the chief priests, which served the same purposes as the names of the rulers of Egypt and Babylon. Some idea of the difficulties of establishing a common chronology can be seen in an example of Thucydides overloading:

The thirty years' truce which was entered into after the reconquest of Euboea lasted for fourteen years. In the fifteenth year, the forty-eighth year of the priestess-ship of Chrysis at Argos, the year when Aenesias was ephor at Sparta, and two months before the end of the archonship of Pythodorus at Athens, six months after the battle at Potidaea, just at the beginning of spring, a Theban force . . . (II.2)

One other form of proto-historiography which calls for attention is the counterpart, of wider application, of dynastic lists, namely the construction of genealogies, often with mythic alleged origins, with which the very early Greek city-state historians also seem to have concerned themselves. This interest in origins leaves occasional marks in Herodotus' *Histories*, though as usual he does not always believe what he hears. Self-extolling histories of the great clans seem to have provided materials for the early history of Rome and to have been valuable sources despite their inevitably self-serving character. A particular cachet attached to descent from a god, Heracles being a favourite, or from a hero of the Trojan War. The Romans managed both, by being descended from Aeneas of Troy, who was the son of Venus. A well-attested genealogy could be useful or even indispensable, as we see in the Old Testament Book of Nehemiah, where it carried qualification for ritual office, and a flaw constituted disqualification (Nehemiah 7:5, 64). Alexander believed, or wished people to believe, that he was descended from the god Ammon.

Secular historical prose narratives (setting aside both epic poetry and the Bible, the latter being left for consideration later with its impact on Christian historiography) in the ancient empires were emerging gradually from more basic forms of bureaucratic record-keeping, though it is still a long step – a leap, in fact – from these to the richly humane and artfully controlled extended narratives of Herodotus. There are campaign and expedition narratives, and what may be called redemption and vindication narratives, accounts of disasters and rebellions and subsequent restorations, and of breaches of trust suffered and avenged. There were also the beginnings, among the Hittites, of annals as a form of recording.

The most elaborate, circumstantial and continuous of the early campaign narratives, though they exerted no direct influence on later ones, can at least claim a kind of kinship with them. One such is the account of the pharaoh Tuthmoses III (1490–1436 BC) in the campaign which culminated, in the twenty-third year of his reign, in the battle of Megiddo, recorded on the walls of his additions to the Temple of Amon-Re at Karnak. It contains an account of a council of war, with dialogue, and what has been called the earliest full description of a decisive battle. Before the battle, a debate arises over which route to take. The counsellors are notably sycophantic, but clearly have their own ideas when invited to express their opinions: 'How can one go upon this road which is so narrow? It is reported that the enemy stand outside and have become numerous. Will not horse have to go behind horse, and soldiers and people likewise? Shall our own vanguard be fighting, while the rear stands here . . . ?' The temple walls also exhibit, as was common, lists of defeated peoples, together with depictions. The narrative can also be checked against other accounts. Here then, as in comparable if less full or less vivid accounts, we have something which is certainly narrative, but which we may hesitate whether to call historical or proto-historical. Although fuller and less formulaically bombastic than other examples, it is an account of an episode, though a highly important one. It does not exhibit individualized character depiction, a sense of historical perspective (in this respect being rather like the two-dimensional side-face Egyptian conventions of representation) or the surrounding architecture of a large-scale historical design. Much the same could be said, of course, of many chronicles over the next two thousand years. It could not be said of Herodotus.

PART I

Greece

I

Herodotus: The Great Invasion and the Historian's Task

As was to become customary, at the beginning of his work Herodotus tells us why he wrote it. It was, he says, 'so that human achievements may not become forgotten in time, and great and marvellous deeds – some displayed by Greeks, some by barbarians – may not be without their glory; and especially to show why the two peoples fought with each other'. In other words his history was a monument, a marker set down against the oblivion with which time threatens all human deeds. He was successful beyond all reasonable expectation. We are still reading his account of his great theme, the invasion of Greece two and a half thousand years ago, and a mere half century before he wrote it, by the Persian Great King and the immense polyglot army drawn from all parts of his empire. Herodotus also promises a little later (*Histories*, I.95) to tell us how the Persians under their ruler Cyrus (the Great) won their predominant position in Asia, and this promise too he fulfils before going on to his account of the invasion of Greece.

One point in his initial statement which is worth pausing on is the reference to recording the great deeds of barbarians (i.e. non-Greeks) as well as Greeks. We should look in vain in the Egyptian and Babylonian records for such even handedness. What we are reminded of is Homer, who, as Herodotus soon reminds us, had written of an earlier conflict between Greeks and an Asiatic people. Homer allows his readers/hearers to sympathize with Trojans as well as Greeks, and as much or more with Priam and Hector as with Achilles and Agamemnon. Herodotus does not comment on this feature in Homer, but seems to take it for granted. He accepts, of course, the historicity of the Trojan War, though he thinks that Homer, as a poet, shaped his narrative to his epic purpose, and he is willing to correct him from his own inquiries among the Persians and Egyptians and by his own common sense: Helen could not have been in Troy during the siege, because the Trojans would have handed her back if they could (II.120). Herodotus has a pretty good idea when Homer lived, placing it some four hundred years before his own time, which is the mid fifth century BC.

But far more important than Herodotus' acceptance of the basic historicity of the Homeric poems is their existence, for all Greeks, as a narrative model. When Herodotus in his preamble speaks of writing to preserve great and marvellous deeds from oblivion and giving them their deserved glory, he can hardly be unaware of stretching out a hand to the Homeric epic, which purports to do precisely that. Herodotus' narrative of the great conflict sometimes carries Homeric echoes which we shall have to consider, but more generally the pacing of the narrative, the immediacy of its re-enactments of events and presentation of character, its humanity and its inclusion of the earthy and mundane – more than in Thucydides and historiography subsequent to him – all invite the adjective 'Homeric'. It is, however, Homeric on a vast scale, and therefore looser and deliberately digressive, as well as based on painstaking inquiries, sometimes requiring suspension of judgement, all of which is alien to the epic tradition. Herodotus is a garrulous, highly personal and conversational writer, with no aversion to the first person; one meets him face to face, as it were, so that it is not difficult to imagine the readings he gave in Athens by which his work was apparently first made public. We know his opinions, and hear of his travels, the wonders he has seen, the stories told to him, and his not infrequent scepticism about them. We can even reconstruct a good deal of his religious views, though here he is sometimes reticent. He is almost as personal a writer as Montaigne.

He was born, apparently around the mid-480s BC, in the Greek colony of Halicarnassus on the eastern side of the Aegean, so he belonged to that part of the Greek world transplanted to Asia. As the disputed borderland of Greece and the Persian empire, this area was to play a significant part in his history. Since the territory had recently been incorporated in the Persian empire, Herodotus was born technically a subject of the Great King. Though there is ultimately no doubt where his sympathies lie, and it seems he could speak only Greek, he never speaks of the Persians with contempt and has no difficulty in making his narrative identify with them as required. Though he travelled extensively – the extent has been questioned by some – and later apparently migrated to Athens, where he is said to have been a friend of the tragic dramatist Sophocles, it is surely appropriate that a man of such cosmopolitanism should have been born not only in an area which had seen Greek intellectual life hitherto most vigorously flourishing but at the interface of two great cultures, and pretty much at the centre of the known world. The date of his death is not certain, but it is clear that he lived into the period of the Peloponnesian War, i.e. at least beyond 430 BC. He is therefore, according to the best estimates, a generation earlier than Thucydides, though a contemporary, measured by the dates of their respective births and deaths.

Herodotus lists some early instances of friction between Europe and Asia – mythic or legendary – including the voyage of Jason and his Argonauts to Colchis, on the Black Sea, and the theft of the Golden Fleece. Then he rapidly advances to historical times, with the Persian conquest of the Hellenized kingdom of Lydia, in what is now western Turkey, under its king Croesus. Croesus, who plays a large part in Book I (the division into nine books is not original), is the first historical character to appear. Overthrown as a ruler, so that his career vindicates the wise saying of the Athenian Solon that no man can be called happy till he is dead, Croesus, made wise by his reversal of fortune, becomes the counsellor of his conqueror, the Persian king Cyrus. We are also told of the legendary youth of Cyrus, who was saved by a shepherd from exposure as a baby (I.108–17), and of the supplanting of the ruling Medes by the Persians under him. Cyrus then goes on to overthrow Babylon (539 BC), of whose customs Herodotus provides a description (I.192–200), after giving the reader a kind of conducted tour of the city.

The great wall I have described is the chief armour of the city; but there is a second one within it, hardly less strong though narrower. There is a fortress in the middle of each half of the city [i.e. as divided by the river]: in one the royal palace surrounded by a wall of great strength, in the other the temple of Bel, the Babylonian Zeus. The temple is a square building, two furlongs each way, with bronze gates, and was still in existence in my time; it has a solid central tower, one furlong square, with a second erected on top of it and then a third, and so on up to eight. All eight towers can be climbed by a spiral way running round the outside, and about half-way up there are seats and a shelter for those who make the ascent to rest on. On the summit of the topmost tower stands a great temple with a fine large couch in it, richly covered, and a golden table beside it. The shrine contains no image and no one spends the night there except, as the Chaldaeans who are the priests of Bel say, one Assyrian woman, all alone, whoever it may be that the god has chosen. The Chaldaeans also say – though I do not believe them – that the god enters the temple in person and takes his rest upon the bed. There is a similar story told by the Egyptians at Thebes . . . (I.178–86)

When Herodotus visited Babylon it was approximately a century since the city had fallen to Cyrus.

Herodotus' next three books deal with the further expansion of the Persian empire into Asia under Cyrus' son Cambyses and his successor Darius. It is Darius who makes the first incursion into Europe, his army being turned back by the Athenian victory at Marathon (490 BC) (VI.110–17). But overall the advance of the Persian empire seems unstoppable as, after swallowing the Greek colonies and the Hellen-ized kingdoms of western Asia, it advances to the limits of the known world. It comes to include not only the ancient civilizations of Egypt and Mesopotamia but the barely explored territories of Libya and Ethiopia and the nomads of the Arabian desert and the northern steppes. The effect is similar to that achieved by Edward Gibbon more than two thousand years later in his *Decline and Fall of the Roman Empire*, as he successively introduces the peoples who will overwhelm the Roman world.

Herodotus, in Books II to IV, follows the tide of Persian conquest by giving geographical and ethnographic surveys of the conquered lands and peoples. These surveys make up a substantial part of his work, and we shall need to return to them later. As a preamble to the great invasion of Greece under the Persian king Xerxes, the Persian world domination, as it seems, is made visible in the great muster of the composite army that Xerxes assembles, which Herodotus describes in detail, identifying each people in the review, with its distinctive

appearance, clothing and weapons, beginning with the Persians themselves. The descriptions, and that of the accompanying fleet (VII.61–
100), are too long for anything but a representative excerpt:

The Assyrians were equipped with bronze helmets made in a complicated
barbarian way which is hard to describe, shields, spears, daggers (like the
Egyptian ones), wooden clubs studded with iron, and linen corslets . . . The
Indians were dressed in cotton; they carried cane bows and cane arrows
tipped with iron, and marched under the command of Pharnazathres, the son
of Artabates . . . Then there were the Caspians and the Sarangians, the former
commanded by Ariomardus, the brother of Artyphius, dressed in leather
jackets and armed with the *acinaces* [Persian short sword] and the cane bow
of their country . . .

And so it goes on, with the Arabians, the Ethiopians ('in their leopard
skins and lion skins'), the Libyans, the Phrygians, the Thracians in
fox-skin headdresses – the list is apparently endless. It seems as though
the whole known world is gathering, hundreds of thousands strong
(the numbers have predictably been much debated), to crush the small
city states of Greece – from the Nile and the Libyan desert, from the
rivers of what was later to be European Russia, and from Thrace west
of the Black Sea to India and beyond, as well as from Persia itself. A
local man, seeing the Persian host, cries out in his anguish that Zeus
has changed his name to Xerxes (VII.56).

Herodotus is in no doubt that Athens was the core of Greek resistance and suffered most, being directly in the path of the invaders.
The most crucial policy decision on the Greek side was that of the
Athenians not to defend the city but to retreat across the isthmus
to the Peloponnese and rely on their fleet to defeat the Persians.
The determining factor, in Herodotus' account, was Themistocles'
interpretation of the Delphic oracle, whose prophetess had declared,
enigmatically as usual, that 'the wooden wall only shall not fall.'
Some thought this referred to a thorn hedge which surrounded the
Acropolis, but Themistocles spoke out for those who interpreted the
wooden wall as a reference to the Athenian ships, and was believed.
Athens took the lead in the great sea battle of Salamis (480 BC), in
which the Persians lost their fleet which was a severe check for them
(VIII.78–96).

But the most memorable episode of the invasion, given full treatment by Herodotus, was a defeat for Greece: the sacrificial battle fought earlier the same year by the three hundred Spartans under their king Leonidas at the pass of Thermopylae, in which most were killed (VII.210–28). Spartans were forbidden by law to retreat. The column subsequently erected to their memory bore what is, in its terse simplicity, still probably, even in translation, the most moving of all military memorial inscriptions:

> Go tell the Spartans, stranger,
> That here obedient to their laws we lie.

Herodotus says that he has taken the trouble to learn the names of all three hundred 'who deserve to be remembered'. It is characteristic that he mentions some of the Persian dead by name, and their ancestry. It is from Herodotus too, though it may not originate with him, that we have, put into the mouth of Croesus, one of the most famous epigrams on war: that in peace sons bury their fathers, but in war fathers bury their sons.

Herodotus' portrait of Xerxes, who deals atrociously with Leonidas' corpse, contains odd contradictions, perhaps reflecting different traditions. In some moods Xerxes shows good sense and magnanimity, in others a wilful savagery. He commits a sin of hubris, Herodotus strongly implies, when he causes the Hellespont to be whipped as the punishment for destroying, in a storm, the bridges he had had built:

Xerxes was very angry when he heard of the disaster, and gave orders that the Hellespont should receive three hundred lashes and have a pair of fetters thrown into it. I have heard before now that he also sent people to brand it with hot irons. He certainly instructed the men with the whips to utter, as they wielded them, the barbarous and presumptuous words: 'You salt and bitter stream, your master lays this punishment upon you for injuring him, who never injured you. But Xerxes the King will cross you, with or without your permission . . .' In addition to punishing the Hellespont Xerxes gave orders that the men responsible for building the bridges should have their heads cut off. (VII.35)

Herodotus then goes on to give a technical description of how the bridges were rebuilt.

Xerxes' most atrocious act occurs when a servant to whom he owed much pleaded that the eldest of his five sons should be left at home: Xerxes has the son cut in half for the army to march between the two halves on its route. Yet immediately afterwards we have the episode in which he appears most sympathetic and human, when sitting on a throne of white marble he is able to view his whole army and fleet and suddenly, at the moment of his highest glory, he weeps. 'And when he saw the whole Hellespont hidden by ships, and all the beaches and plains of Abydos filled with men, he called himself happy – and the moment after burst into tears.' Asked why, he replies that he was thinking of the shortness of human life, and that 'of all these thousands of men not one will be alive in a hundred years' time' (VII.45–6). It is an extraordinary moment, at which, thanks to Xerxes, or Herodotus, the political distinctions between peoples and even, for us, the gulf between ancient and modern melt away in the contemplation of a common human lot.

But though the Persians are never dehumanized, the differences between them and the Greeks – political and moral – make up a powerful message which Herodotus was to convey to posterity and which many generations were to draw on copiously. From Book V onward Herodotus turns for much of the time to the affairs of the Greek city states and the relations between them. Books V and VI, in fact, are probably the most confusing and least satisfying for the reader, lacking as they do both the exotic folkloric charm of the earlier ones and the dramatic single narrative line provided later by the great invasion by Xerxes. Greek factionalism, moreover, is more untidy and multi-centred than the simpler politics of Persian autocracy. It is, however, in these books that the theme emerges which gives the climax of the work its wider political significance. The Athenians had, with Spartan help, liberated themselves from the family of tyrants which had ruled them, and under their leader Cleisthenes had established a democracy (I.59–64, V.62–9). Athens became for Herodotus the great protagonist of Greek freedom in opposition to eastern despotism. This contrast – which Herodotus increasingly makes apparent, and in which the other Greek states, and particularly Sparta of course, participate in varying degrees – was to be an immensely enduring one in Western historiography and political thought, setting liberty against servitude, law against the tyrants' will, frugality, hardihood and valour against luxury and timidity. In describing the effects on the Athenians of their recently acquired liberty, Herodotus propounds an idea that was to resonate down the centuries in historiography; it was applied also to the early Roman republic.

Thus Athens went from strength to strength, and proved, if proof were needed, how noble a thing equality before the law is, not in one respect only, but in all; for while they were oppressed under tyrants, they had no better success in war than any of their neighbours, yet once the yoke was flung off, they proved the finest fighters in the world. (V.78)

Another aspect of the East–West contrast, with a long future as a historiographical cliché, is attributed to Cyrus the Great, and quoted by Herodotus as almost the last words of the whole work: 'Soft countries breed soft men,' and have to suffer the rule of aliens. Warned by Cyrus, the Persians choose for preference to live in a rugged land, but the association in European thought and historiography conveyed by the phrase 'Asiatic softness' was to endure down to the nineteenth century. The East–West antithesis was to be highly significant for the Greeks and Romans. Through them it reached a particular pitch of intensity in the European Enlightenment, and it still echoes resonantly in nineteenth-century historiography and the literature of imperialism, and in this long tradition Herodotus is by no means the most biased and unqualified manipulator of it.

The difference in character of the last books from the earlier, more ethnographic, ones is mainly obvious in the greater coherence and dramatic force of the narrative of the invasion. But it also makes a difference that, though we still spend much time with the Persian King, we also spend much more than before on the affairs of Greece, and the contrast is inevitably marked. Instead of the claustrophobic, sycophantic, sometimes fearful atmosphere of a despotic court, where such discussion as there is consists of advice, which can be given privately as well as in conclave, we have the overt, vigorous, fiercely factional and disputatious public life of the Greek city states, conducted characteristically in public debate and expressed through speeches designed to sway opinion. Herodotus has used direct speech from the beginning, but its use is largely informal, conversational and designed to further immediate action; it is not oratory; it is easy to think of the more conspiratorial words being spoken in whispers. Consider, for example, the way Herodotus describes the conspiracy of Persian nobles who, suspecting their ruler, Smerdis the Magus, who is passing himself off as the son of Cyrus the Great, is an impostor, agree to kill him. Herodotus makes extensive use of direct speech. The future king Darius, who is elevated to the throne as a result of their success (in 521 BC), speaks his mind:

'Listen, all of you,' Darius replied, 'if you take Otanes' advice [to recruit more conspirators] . . . somebody is sure to seek advantage for himself by betraying us to the Magus. You ought really to have done this thing entirely on your own; but as you have seen fit to let others in on it, and have communicated your intentions to me, I have only one thing to say – let us act immediately. If we let a single day slip by, I promise you one thing: nobody will have the time to betray *me* – for I will denounce you all to the Magus.' (III.71)

It is only later that we come to the lengthier set speeches which seem to make up so much of Greek public life. This is one of the Athenian commanders, in a debate over whether to risk a battle against the Persians (which turned out to be the victory of Marathon), also urging immediate action. He invokes principle as well as practicality. The alternatives, he says, are

either to enslave Athens, or to make her free . . . Never in our history have we Athenians been in such peril as now. If we submit to the Persians, Hippias [the expelled tyrant] will be restored to power – and there is little doubt what misery must then ensue: but if we fight and win, then this city of ours may well grow to pre-eminence among all the cities of Greece. (VI.109)

It is tempting to speak proleptically and say that we are approaching the kind of historiography of which Thucydides' work is the archetype and was to set a pattern for historical writing for a thousand years. It is not quite that. The Greek speeches in Herodotus are more direct and less carefully wrought, cerebral and ostensibly dispassionate than the remarkable ones which constitute so much of the experience of reading Thucydides. Nevertheless, they represent a marked contrast with the earlier books, and help also to enforce the contrast which gives the last three their overall meaning: the contrast of two worlds, of freedom and despotism.

This contrast is part of the reason for the cultural shift in Herodotus' work, but it is reasonable to infer that there is another, less obvious, one. The events of the latest books are also the nearest to Herodotus' own time, and they take place in the world he lives in and knows best and whose language he speaks – the Greek world. There must have been a marked difference in the quality and reliability and accessibility of the oral traditions on which Herodotus chiefly relied, and in his ability to interpret them. Thucydides was to enjoy all these advantages and that of writing contemporary history. The result is a perceptible access of 'realism'. The often folkloric character of the stories Herodotus tells about Persia, especially in the earlier books, and the frequent references to prophetic dreams have fallen away. Of course the contrast is not absolute. The Greek world too has plenty of room for dreams, oracles and omens. Nevertheless, the contrast seems at once one between East and West, between despotism and freedom, and also between ancient and modern, where 'modern' means the open political life of the Greek *polis*.

But, though Herodotus' feet were planted firmly in the world of Greek culture and rational inquiry, his curiosity about ancient civilizations and remote and nomadic peoples means that his history also constitutes a kind of bridge between that world and the 'barbarian' world beyond. Apart from the narrative of the invasion, which is far more dramatically controlled, circumstantial and balanced than any prose work before it, the other distinctive quality of Herodotus' work is embodied in the extensive geographical and ethnographic surveys of the earlier books – digressions, as they came later to be called as they became common but generally less extensive in historical works. In Herodotus they are highly entertaining and readable, made so by his omnivorous humane and tolerant curiosity about the world and about humanity in all its aspects and variety. Herodotus was an anthropologist and geographer as well as a historian, but it is less easy to be sure how completely original he is in these sections of his work.

We are largely ignorant of Herodotus' Greek predecessors and contemporaries as writers or compilers of historical accounts and materials, but it is clear that there were some. Most of their work has been lost, but what we know of them, and the existing fragments, makes it unlikely that anything like another Herodotus lies beyond the horizon of our knowledge. The best-known and probably most noteworthy precursor, Hecataeus of Miletus (b. 549 BC), was a geographer, mythographer and ethnographer of the Mediterranean and the countries around it. He wrote surveys of Europe, Asia, North Africa (called by the Greeks Libya) and Ethiopia. The first map seems to have been the work of another Milesian, Anaximander. Hecataeus' knowledge certainly extended further west than that of Herodotus, who disclaims acquaintance with the western Mediterranean and the lands to the north, including the Tin Islands, i.e. Britain (*Histories*, III.115). Herodotus refers to Hecataeus several times in his work, sometimes as a historical agent ('Hecataeus the writer'), though he also makes a point of rejecting, decisively, Hecataeus' view – which became common – that the world was entirely surrounded by a great ocean, referred to simply as 'Ocean' (IV.36).

Our chief source for Herodotus' predecessors is the first-century author Dionysius of Halicarnassus, whose birthplace was also that ascribed to Herodotus. In him, and also in Plutarch, we have accounts of early events, from sources now lost, which sometimes match but sometimes differ from those of Herodotus. These precursors and perhaps contemporaries appear to have written accounts of peoples and cities, usually about their alleged origins. Another early writer known to us from excerpts in Dionysius is Hellanicus of Lesbos, who wrote an early history of Athens, mostly mythical, and also on the origins of peoples more generally – a kind of early universal history – and on the customs of the Egyptians, Persians and Babylonians. Whatever differences there may be in the quality of achievement, Herodotus' interest in such matters was therefore not held in isolation. Hellanicus seems to have been above all a genealogist, and included hopeful etymologies deriving the Persians from the Greek legendary hero Perseus, and the Medes from Medea, the bride of Jason. Altogether he seems to have been more uncritical than Herodotus, but they do not belong to utterly different mental worlds. It seems impossible to date their works relative to each other.

If Homer provided a precedent for the narrative component of Herodotus' work, another anticipation was the study of geography.

In looking at Thucydides we shall have to consider other influences, but so far we seem to find history rooted in epic and in geography. Herodotus' ethnographic information derives from his travels and his indefatigable questioning of local informants, to whom he often refers. He was helped, of course, by an already extensive Greek diaspora in western Asia (from which he himself came) and along the shores of the Black Sea. Reference to written documentation in Herodotus' *Histories* is absent, though he sometimes refers to artefacts he has seen – walls, buildings, above all offerings in temples, particularly Delphi, and their dedicatory inscriptions – as corroborative evidence:

Gyges was the first foreigner we know of, after King Midas of Phrygia, son of Gordias, to dedicate offerings at Delphi. Midas presented the royal throne from which he used to give judgement; it stands with Gyges' bowls, and is well worth seeing. (I.14)

There was a fire at Delphi which damaged some of the gifts of Croesus, king of Lydia. Herodotus helpfully tells us how to locate what remains:

There were also two huge mixing-bowls, one of gold which was placed on the right-hand side of the entrance to the temple, the other of silver, on the left. These also were moved at the time of the fire, and the golden one, which weighs nearly a quarter of a ton, now stands in the treasury of the Clazomenians, and the silver one, which holds over five thousand gallons, is in the corner of the ante-chapel. (I.51)

Even Thucydides made a little more use of documentation – particularly by transcribing treaties apparently verbatim – though the events he described were exactly contemporary, and eyewitnesses and participants, including Thucydides himself, therefore abounded. But Herodotus was above all the man who asks questions, and who makes journeys in order to ask them:

There were other things, too, which I learnt at Memphis in conversation with the priests of Hephaestus, and I actually went to Thebes and Heliopolis for the express purpose of finding out if the priests in those cities would agree in what they told me with the priests at Memphis. It is at Heliopolis that the most learned of the Egyptians are said to be found. I am not anxious to repeat what I was told about the Egyptian religion, apart from the mere names of their deities, for I do not think any one nation knows much more about such things than any other. (II.3)

He could not have been himself an eyewitness of the historical events he describes – he was a small child even at the time of the most recent – though on his travels he certainly makes use of his eyes. He is among other things, though only sporadically, a kind of travelling antiquary, reporting to the world the marvels he has seen: monuments were among the marvellous deeds of men, and well worth recording for their own sake. He was predictably impressed by Egypt and Babylon, giving, as we have seen, a particularly precise description of the latter (I.180–83). At one point he even makes the grandeur of the engineering works of the Samians a reason for attending to their history (III.60).

Above all, however, Herodotus used his ears, if only because most of the inscriptions he may have seen were in a script and language he could not read. He regarded himself as an auditor, a collector, recorder, sifter and judge of oral traditions about the recent or remoter past. He sometimes says that these traditions are incredible, but as a matter of principle he still accepts a duty to set them down: 'My business is to record what people say, but I am by no means bound to believe it – and that may be taken to apply to this book as a whole' (VII.152) or, again, 'Anyone may believe these Egyptian tales, if he is sufficiently credulous' (II.123). Oral accounts often differed, sometimes in manifestly self-interested ways in the versions of different peoples, and it was also his business to pick the better, giving his reasons, or to reconcile them, or to suspend judgement if he had to. His criteria of judgement are sometimes psychological, sometimes physical probability (including sheer physical impossibility). He can even rather grandly bring superior ethnographic knowledge to bear. The Greeks tell many thoughtless stories (Hecataeus also says this), one being that the Egyptians tried to sacrifice Heracles to Zeus but that he thwarted them by killing them all. This, Herodotus says, shows the Greek ignorance of Egyptian customs, since the Egyptians do not perform human sacrifices, and anyway if Heracles was just a man he could not have killed tens of thousands of people – though Herodotus adds, 'And now I hope that both gods and heroes will forgive me for saying what I have said on these matters!' (II.45).

Herodotus' descriptions of the manners and customs of the Persians and Babylonians in Book I set the pattern for the successive ethnographic surveys of each people that the Persians successively encounter. Herodotus lists conscientiously, sometimes amusingly, occasionally incredibly, what became the standard objects of ethnographic curiosity: clothing, diet, marriage and funerary customs, ranks of society, religious beliefs and practices, health and the treatment of disease. His own attitude throughout is tolerant and unshockable. As he says – it is one of the ways in which he anticipates Montaigne – every people considers its own customs best, even those customs most bizarre to others. The Greeks would be horrified at the idea of eating their dead parents; some Indians are shocked at the idea of not doing so but burning them instead (III.38).

Sometimes one has to suspect Herodotus of an artful shaping of his accounts. The Egyptians, who read from right to left and whose great river floods in summer and falls in winter, 'seem to have reversed the ordinary practices of mankind' – eating in the streets and relieving themselves indoors (which casts a light on Greek habits), the men urinating sitting down, the women standing up, and so on (II.35–6). After recording that the Persians never acted on a decision taken when drunk without reconsidering it when sober, one can see that it was irresistible to add that a decision taken sober was always reconsidered when drunk (I.133). Often his ethnography rings true or can be verified, as in a reference to what seems to be a survival of matrilineal customs, or to temple prostitution in Babylon, or to the custom of the magi in Persia of allowing the bodies of the dead to be rent by birds and dogs (I.140).

Apart from the Egyptians, Herodotus devotes most attention to the Scythians, who lived to the north of the Black Sea, and the characteristics he records of their treeless and townless life are familiar from many much later accounts: he describes nomadic mounted archers with their wagons, dependent on their cattle and drinking milk; scalping their enemies and hanging the scalps on their bridles, while the skulls are turned into drinking cups; taking vapour baths, swearing blood brotherhood, and burying great men with their households, horses and treasure (IV.16–82). We seem already to have a premonition of the Huns, Tartars and Mongols. But remote Scythia, not surprisingly, also offered even more exotic phenomena: a people bald from birth; goat-footed men; men who sleep half the year. Herodotus seems to accept the bald race, though he does not vouch for it, but he draws the line at goat-footed and hibernating men.

There is the same strain of fantasy at times in the zoology of remote places, and here Herodotus seems less critical than of bizarre anthropology, so that among sound(ish) accounts of crocodiles and camels we get winged snakes (Egypt), giant burrowing ants (India), and cattle which have to walk backwards because going forwards their horns stick in the ground (Libya); he certainly believed in the winged serpents, because he had seen their skeletons. He believes in the phoenix, though he has not seen it, but rejects as incredible the story that it carries its parent wrapped in a lump of myrrh, though whether because of the power–weight ratio he does not say (II.73). He tries to be as accurate as he can in his geography, though often against heavy odds. His longest disquisition on a natural phenomenon, a detailed examination of the flooding of the Nile, which is in its way impressive, leads up to one of his less happy guesses: the Nile floods in summer and sinks in winter because, in winter, storms blow the sun off course towards upper Libya (II.10–26); this is not merely wrong but not very cogent.

No discussion of Herodotus can avoid the vexed question, in antiquity at least, of his reliability and his alleged credulity and even lying. Of course he was sometimes misled or ignorant, and he shared beliefs of the ancient world we do not now hold (though this cannot be what his ancient critics, by far the fiercest, meant). He seems to have been particularly unfortunate with his informants in Egypt, so that scholars working on ancient Egypt now have a much lower view of him than those of Babylon and Persia, who regard him as a valuable authority. The accusations against him in the ancient world which, taken with the rival model provided by Thucydides, undoubtedly lowered his reputation, now seem to rest on the misunderstanding that he necessarily endorsed what he repeated, in so far as they are not merely malicious. A modern reader is more likely to be impressed by his critical sense and his frequent scepticism or suspensions of judgement, once allowance has been made for the ancient belief in omens, oracles and prophetic dreams, which Herodotus takes very seriously while recognizing that they could be manipulated. The fundamental issue seems to be one on which we are now likely to find Herodotus' work both sophisticated and valuable. As we have already seen, he saw it as part of his role to write down even stories to which he gave no credence at all. It was a duty to record what people said to him, while leaving the reader in no doubt of his own opinion.

Herodotus' own world, that of a Greek-speaking elite, was a highly literate one, though still mainly reliant on oral tradition for its knowledge of the past. Much of the rest of the world, outside the centres of civilization, was preliterate; even the Persian kings seem to have been illiterate. But it was clearly a world buzzing with rival oral traditions and orally transmitted, formulaic popular tales, with legends and accounts of mythic beasts, peoples and countries, with stories of foundlings, tests, tricks, subterfuges, riddles and prophetic dreams. Cyrus the Great is brought up by a shepherd who was commanded to kill him on the orders of his grandfather the king, who had had a dream that a vine sprang from his daughter's genitals and overspread Asia, and interpreted this as a threat to himself (there is an analogy with the Perseus story in Greek legend). Cyrus is later recognized as a prince by his royal bearing, and he himself has a similar dream about Darius, who succeeds Cyrus' son Cambyses on the throne (I.107–16, 209).

Darius himself, whom we have looked at as one of the conspirators against the magus who has usurped the throne, becomes king by a trick. After a debate among the conspirators over the merit of the three forms of government, monarchy, oligarchy and democracy – which is uncharacteristic of Herodotus' accounts of Persian history, and seems very Greek – they agree to leave matters to fate by mounting their horses on the outskirts of the city, 'and he whose horse neighs first after the sun was up should have the throne'. Darius, advised by a clever groom, uses a mare to establish a conditioned reflex in his stallion, and becomes king of Persia. 'His first act was to erect a stone monument with a carving of a man on horseback, and the following inscription: "Darius, son of Hystaspes, by the virtue of his horse and of his groom Oebares, won the throne of Persia." The horse's name was included.' Herodotus does not claim to have seen it (III.84–8).

The tributes collected by Cyrus as king lead Herodotus into a digression on the method of collecting gold employed by the Indians ('their semen is not white like other peoples''), who are indebted to ants ('bigger than a fox') which burrow into sand which is rich in gold. The ants chase the Indians, who are mounted on camels to escape them and also to carry the bags of gold dust (III.102–5).

It is only through formulaic stories such as that of the youth of Cyrus that we can reconstruct anything of the mental worlds and popular tastes of preliterate societies. We owe Herodotus a debt for his conscientious and unsnobbish recording of them, though the prigs who later wrote history in a more restricted and self-consciously dignified fashion seem to have failed to grasp what he was doing, despite his own declarations. Without possessing the concept, he ranks, among his other titles, as the earliest, or certainly one of the earliest, of self-conscious folklorists. He did not, of course, view folklore as a genre, except as part of his 'inquiries', but his ability to record with partially or wholly suspended belief is an aspect both of his omnivorous curiosity and of his general tolerance. When it lets him down and he becomes over-sceptical we notice it, as when he dismisses as incredible the story that Phoenician voyagers travelling west along the southern coast of west Africa found that they had the sun to the north of them, on their right (IV.42).

As for religious belief, it is clear that he was pious without being slavishly credulous. He frequently announces that he knows more than he thinks it proper to say. 'I have already mentioned the festival of Isis at Busiris; it is here that everybody – tens of thousands of men and women – when the sacrifice is over, beat their breasts: in whose honour, however, I do not feel it is proper for me to say' (II.61). Similarly we have 'In Athene's precinct at Sais is the tomb of one whose name I prefer not to mention' (II.170). Whether this proceeds from awe of the gods and a sense of unease at making them an object of inquiry, from a sense of decorum and a desire not to give offence, or from such knowledge having been imparted to him under pledge of secrecy is not entirely clear. Probably, taking the large number of his utterances on the subject together, it is a mixture of all three. As seems to have been common, he regards the gods of all peoples as the same, only the names differing, and holds that Greek knowledge of the gods derived originally from the Egyptians. But, though he is respectful and discreet, he remains worldly-wise; he believes emphatically in portents as divine warnings, in omens, oracles, the sacredness of temples and the penalties of sacrilege, as well as the punishments of hubris, but he also knows how vested interests can misinterpret and even manipulate these things. Even the priestess at Delphi could be bribed, as she apparently had been to tell the Spartans that they must help Athens to rid herself of her tyrants (VI.123). He also has a conception of divine providence and divine justice (see II.120 and III.108) and of a fate before which the gods themselves are powerless (I.91).

Apart from providing an example to later historians and much ethnographic information, Herodotus left a prose epic of Greece's deliverance – the deliverance of freedom from the threat of an imperial despotism – which became a staple of European collective memory. The end of his work sees Greece secure and triumphant, with Athens as its dominant power. In his successor Thucydides, whose work begins half a century later, we see Athenian hubris and the fierce rivalries and mutual suspicion of the Greek city states, combined with the factionalism of their internal politics, taking a self-destructive course which would eventually end their autonomy.

2

Thucydides: The *Polis* – the Use and Abuse of Power

Our constitution is called a democracy because power is in the hands not of a minority but of the whole people. When it is a question of settling private disputes, everyone is equal before the law; when it is a question of putting one person before another in positions of public responsibility, what counts is not membership of a particular class, but the actual ability which the man possesses. No one, so long as he has it in him to be of service to the state, is kept in political obscurity because of poverty. And, just as our political life is free and open, so is our day-to-day life in our relations with each other. We do not get into a state with our next-door neighbour if he enjoys himself in his own way, nor do we give him the kind of black looks which, though they do no real harm, still do hurt people's feelings. We are free and tolerant in our private lives; but in public affairs we keep to the law. This is because it commands our deep respect. (Thucydides, *History of the Peloponnesian War*, II.37)

This is the most famous passage in the funeral oration pronounced by Pericles, leader of the Athenian democracy, over Athenian soldiers who had died during the first year of the Peloponnesian War (431 BC). It is a long speech, and Thucydides presents it verbatim, according to his normal practice, to which we shall have to return later. In Pericles' speech Athens is made to stand for a peak of cultural as well as political achievement, and, thanks to Thucydides, the image purveyed has established itself permanently in the educated European collective consciousness. Thucydides was a realist, and there is a good deal in the oration which his history subsequently inclines us to qualify, but setting it out in this way enables him to present a eulogy of Athens and what it could be made to stand for without precisely endorsing it. It is a speech.

Pericles' speech – enhanced for modern readers by echoes, not accidental, in the Gettysburg Address – is an oratorical tour de force which appropriately ends with an exhortation to the Athenians not merely to rally to the defence of liberty and of their city, but to fall in love with it, while earlier it has presented Athens as worthy of love. The speech begins, like Lincoln's, with a disclaimer of any need of the dead for honour by the living: the former are sufficiently sanctified by their sacrifice. Like Lincoln, Pericles then invokes the ancestors of the city and their legacy, 'a free country'. We have just seen his elaboration of what that means, including what we should call the liberal claim that in private life the Athenians are 'free and tolerant'. Each is free to enjoy himself in his own way. It has been common over the past two hundred years to deny that ancient democracies had a concept of private as well as public liberty. It is difficult to sustain such a claim in the face of Pericles' oration.

Pericles presents the life of Athens as an ideal balance between private and public, and also between the cultural and the political. The Athenian citizen, it is said, is well informed about public affairs and brave in war, but also loves the beautiful and things of the mind. He enjoys a vigorous public life, of contests and festivals, but also grace and beauty in domestic life. Athenian life is marked by ease, openness and versatility, without softness, but also without the need felt by the Spartans (Athens's main antagonists in the war) for a perpetual, overstrained training for adversity, though Athenians are just as brave and patriotic. The Athenians' virtues have brought them their empire and the power it wields, about which Pericles is notably unapologetic: 'Our city is an education to Greece', and 'Future ages will wonder at us, as the present age wonders at us now' (II.40–41). If the latter is true it is, of course, partly because Pericles and Thucydides have made it so.

The full dramatic quality of this eulogy of Athenian power and greatness at the outset of the war which was to bring the city down was presumably not entirely apparent at the time Thucydides wrote it. It is difficult confidently to ascribe conscious dramatic irony to a good deal in the history, because of uncertainty about the moment of writing in relation to the unfolding of events. Certainly, however, hubris is a recurring theme, as are, from the outset, the hazards and vicissitudes of war, of which the Spartans are generally more aware than the overbold Athenians. What does seem wholly apparent is the art which leads Thucydides to treat Pericles' oration, placed as it is so near the outbreak of the war, so extensively. The occasion was not obviously a great one: a public rite of a common kind for men who had fallen in what was, by the later standards set by the war, little more than a skirmish. It hardly demanded such full and resonant treatment in itself. Speeches in Thucydides are often not short, but Pericles' – almost eight pages in a modern edition – is unusually long. This is not to say that Pericles did not probably say something along these lines: the event was too public, too local and too recent for complete licence. The question of the speeches in Thucydides is a vexed and fascinating one. Whatever their claims to authenticity, which are discussed below (pp. 37–8), they are an important and distinctive part of Thucydides' art as a historian, however at odds with modern notions of the historian's responsibilities.

Both morally and materially, Athens ended the Persian Wars as the dominant power in Greece, centre of a confederation which rapidly became referred to as its empire over dependent and tributary states. In the fifty years from the Persian invasion (and the conclusion of Herodotus' history) to the outbreak of the Peloponnesian War among the Greek states (and the beginning of Thucydides' history) Athens' grip tightened. Thucydides gives a brief account of this period – the so-called Pentecontaetia (because it covers fifty years) – as a preamble to his history of the war. Athens was a rich and powerful imperialist state, the greatest in Greece. As a democracy, it also tended to be the hope of democratic factions in other states, oppressed by local oligarchies, just as the oligarchs tended to look for support to Sparta, so that when war broke out, in 431 BC, it sometimes assumed, locally, an ideological character.

It was, Thucydides wrote, justifying his choice of subject, the greatest crisis in Greek history, a conclusion he presents as foresight, since he cannot have known at the outset – or when he began writing, which may not have been long after – that it would last so long or inflict so much suffering, which are two of his reasons for calling it great. It is clear that Thucydides was writing contemporary history, but it is not so clear exactly how close to the events was his 'writing up' of them. His history ends in mid-sentence, in 411 BC, presumably as a result of his death, when the war had still some years to run, whereas Herodotus' work, which ends soon after his own birth around the mid-480s, seems to end as he wished it to do.

Thucydides, who was a wealthy Athenian, was not merely an eye-witness but also participated in the war he describes – an unsuccessful general, who was banished from Athens for his failure, he records his own contribution drily and without comment. What he does comment on is the advantage to him as a historian of his exile on the other side, in the Peloponnese. It gave him, he says, leisure and a different viewpoint (V.26). This is not to say that he changed sides. Such exiles were not uncommon: Xenophon experienced the same, both in Persia and in Sparta. Thucydides continued to write about both sides with the same dispassionateness, recognizing the virtues of both Athenians and Spartans and their attendant weaknesses: the former bold, enter-prising, overconfident and rash, the latter conservative, moderate – Thucydides prized moderation – and cautious to the point of slug-gishness. Both commit what we should call atrocities, though it is those by the Athenians that tend to make more impression on the reader. That the war begins with Athens at the height of its power and wealth is part of what Thucydides recognizes as the greatness of his theme; it is a more fortuitous benefit to the dramatic quality of his history, though Thucydides takes full advantage of it, that the war culminates, though it does not quite end, with the catastrophe of the failure of the Athenian expedition to Sicily, by which the pride and power of Athens were humbled. Greatness is a recurring preoccu-pation with Thucydides, as indeed with other ancient historians after him. The expedition to Sicily was the greatest expedition, the siege of Syracuse the greatest siege, just as earlier the battle of Mantinea was the greatest battle (Books VI and VII; Book V, 63–74). It is tempting to the reader, perhaps against the grain of the way Thucydides' history as a whole was written, to see Athens as its tragic protagonist, brought down by overweening ambition and overconfidence – he certainly stresses these – and by the way the Athenians from time to time fail to take the opportunities for a lasting peace.

Thucydides' history is presented in the form of annals. This was an established convention, into which he introduced a refinement by dividing his narrative into six-month periods, marked by the seasons: 'when the corn was ripe' or 'when the corn was ripening' are common introductory clauses. We have already considered (above, p. 6) the difficulties that Greeks, in particular, had in marking the years in a generally recognizable way, since the four-yearly Olympiads were the only regular pan-Greek event; the admiration for winning athletes preserved their memory. As his work progresses, Thucydides dates events from the beginning of the war 'described by Thucydides the Athenian'.

The annalistic form for historical writing, which pre-dated Thucydides and which was to have a two-thousand-year currency after him, has developed a discouraging reputation among readers for unimaginative compilation, and was eventually superseded, in the eighteenth century, by more thematic kinds of organization. In Thucydides' case it is a framework, and does at times lead him to deal exhaustively with relatively minor events that a modern historian would probably abridge, but he also uses it with some freedom: we have already seen the at-first-sight-disproportionate attention given to Pericles' speech.

For Thucydides, the chief quality to be sought in writing history is certainty. He distinguishes his own work from that of the poets and also, it has been generally assumed, from Herodotus, who is implied though not named under the category of 'prose chroniclers, who are less interested in telling the truth than in catching the attention of the public, whose authorities cannot be checked, and whose subject-matter, owing to the passage of time, is mostly lost in the unreliable streams of mythology' (I.21). Reliable history must be contemporary history or nearly so, for authorities to be checkable by the historian; there is as yet no implication that they must be laid out for the reader. Reliable eyewitness testimony, either the historian's own or that of his informants, is indispensable.

Narrative is the primary way in which the historical truths Thucydides offers are shown to us. Thus, for example, his account of the origins of the Peloponnesian War is presented initially as a narrative of events and only later focuses on the considerations which weigh with the protagonists, which he sets out in the form of speeches. At first, in his account, the two great powers, Athens and Sparta, were edged towards war by the behaviour of their satellites and by the internal instability endemic in many Greek city states, divided by factions, whose inclinations to democracy or oligarchy led them to seek help from Athens or Sparta respectively against their political rivals or neighbouring states. A successful coup or local conflict could transform the local balance of power alarmingly for either Athens or Sparta, bringing the risk of intervention. The same situations tended to nullify attempts during the war to patch together a lasting peace. Thucydides deals with these in detail, especially during the truce described in Book V (28–32). Unpicking the results of recent hostilities to produce a settlement was, he makes clear, immensely complex and difficult. We may generalize the problem by saying that it was not (as in a war between two unified states) a matter of a rectification of a common frontier or an exchange of more remote possessions. The allies had their own interests, fears and ambitions, and their policies were liable to change and manipulation. The result was an unstable cat's cradle of alliances, obligations and resentments which had to be negotiated. Each stage of the fighting tended to add a fresh layer of complexity, of wrongs inflicted and undertakings unfulfilled.

Hence, as in the Balkans before the First World War, local instabilities or changes of alliance, or the threat of them, sent shock waves though the chain of alliances to the two great powers, neither of which could afford defections or the appearance of weakness, while both were subject to the temptations of fishing in troubled waters. This is a summary of the events Thucydides recounts in Book I (24–65) in Epidamnus, Corcyra, Corinth and Potidaea, until a general denunciation of the existing treaty between Athens and Sparta came to seem a reasonable response on the grounds that by these events it had already been broken. Thucydides retails the arguments in detail, though he regards them as superficial: 'The real reason for the war is, in my opinion, most likely to be disguised by such an argument. What made war inevitable was the growth of Athenian power and the fear which this caused in Sparta' (I.23). In the latter part of Book I, apart from a brief summary of events between the repulse of the Persian invasion and the outbreak of the new war (479–435 BC), the centre of the narrative moves to Sparta; the deliberations on war or peace, in which the Spartans are swayed, for or against, by closely argued appraisals of the situation, are presented by the ostensibly verbatim report of the debate.

The Corinthians approach the Spartans for aid because Athens has wrested control of Corcyra from them; they rebuke the Spartans for their inactivity. They are followed by an Athenian delegation, which happens incidentally to be in Sparta, and which is given permission to speak. Its members begin by reminding their auditors of the debt of Greece to Athens for its role in defeating the Persians, and defend the Athenians' acquisition of an empire. They are unapologetic about making the case for this in terms which the later nineteenth century (AD) christened *Realpolitik*. Athenian imperialism obeys the dictates of security, honour and self-interest. 'We have done nothing extraordinary, nothing contrary to human nature in accepting an empire when it was offered to us and then in refusing to give it up . . . It has always been a rule that the weak should be subject to the strong; and besides, we consider that we are worthy of our power.' The Spartans too once thought so, 'but now, after calculating your own interest, you are beginning to talk in terms of right and wrong' (I.68–78). Negotiations and further speeches follow, in which caution is more evident on the Spartan side, while the Athenians, including Pericles, strike a more confident and warlike note. The antithesis between interest and principle, and the subordination of the latter when vital political interests are at stake, is a recurring theme in Thucydidean speeches, as is the view that the possession of power confers the right to exercise it over the weak, and that this is normal behaviour. That is the way the world is. The best possible combination, the Athenian speech quoted above implies, is power exercised with moderation and realism. Also characteristically Thucydidean is the warning with which the Athenians conclude, calculated to appeal to Spartan caution, about the unpredictability of war. People approach war the wrong way round: 'Action comes first, and it is only when they have already suffered that they begin to think' (I.78). Later, Thucydides himself remarks that in both Athens and the Peloponnese 'there were great numbers of young men who had never been in a war and were consequently far from unwilling to join in this one' (II.8).

Once the war begins we have, of course, campaign narratives, in which the modern reader is likely to be particularly struck by the set form which battles seem to take and the ritual features which characterize the clashes between armies similarly trained and equipped, sharing the same culture and employing the same heavy-infantry tactics, and usually observing the same conventions and rules. These features included the preliminary speeches by the commanders to their soliders; the 'paeans' or battle songs as the armies advanced, which were so similar that Thucydides remarked that they could cause confusion between friend and enemy; the subsequent truce, arranged by heralds, to enable the bodies to be exchanged; the setting up of a trophy by the victors. In the battle accounts in Roman history, which are in some respects similar, these details, apart from the speeches, are absent, though the taking of the auguries and in some cases making propitiatory sacrifices remained important. One reason why truces for the recovery of one's dead were relatively easy was the absence of anything in the nature of 'hot pursuit', which in turn was attributable to the Greek deficiency in cavalry. The debacle of the Athenian army in Sicily, which was harried by Sicilian cavalry in a manner described vividly by Thucydides, was exceptional (VII.78–81, 85). The fate of the Athenians – cut off from escape by loss of command of the sea, tormented by hunger and thirst, and eventually herded as prisoners into the oven-like quarries of Syracuse – was uniquely terrible.

Sometimes we become sharply aware that we are reading an author who has seen warfare for himself. (Thucydides, incidentally, refers to the unsuccessful action which led to his own dismissal and exile without emotion or special pleading (IV.104).) His comment on generals' speeches to the troops on the brink of action has an old commander's blasé understanding as well as intellectual fastidiousness. Men in such circumstances, he says, 'do not bother to avoid giving the impression of using conventional language; instead they bring forward the kind of appeals that can generally be used on all occasions: wives, children, gods of the native land' (VII.69). The Greeks in this period fought in phalanxes, massed bodies of armoured spearmen (hoplites) many ranks deep. On the clash of the phalanxes he adds a telling detail:

It is true of all armies that, when they are moving into action, the right wing tends to get unduly extended and each side overlaps the enemy's left with its own right. This is because fear makes every man want to do his best to find protection for his unarmed side in the shield of the man next to him on the right ... The fault comes originally from the man on the extreme right of the front line, who is always trying to keep his own unarmed side away from the enemy, and his fear spreads to the others who follow his example. (V.71)

In such a remark the terror of phalanx warfare is vividly caught in the exposition of a technical detail.

For the modern reader, because the stylized element is not present and because civilians are involved, Thucydides' descriptions of sieges and the sacking of towns are perhaps more memorable than his battle scenes and dispel any notion that kinship among Greeks made their warfare any less pitiless. Thucydides was alert to engineering and technological matters, which makes his accounts of sieges and sea battles precise on such points. In his description of the siege of Plataea by the Peloponnesians, he describes the earthworks, the siege engines and the countermeasures of the besieged. Both sides treated captured towns with extreme harshness – the men typically massacred, the women and children enslaved.

Thucydides, though an Athenian, acknowledges that Athens was unpopular and was felt to have been tyrannical towards its client states, and that the Athenians were the more aggressive in their approach to the war. In the initial Spartan response to the Athenians there are criticisms of the volatility and even light-mindedness of the Athenians, which seem to chime with Thucydides' general appraisal and should be set against the evidence of Pericles' Funeral Oration: 'We [the Spartans] are not so highly educated as to look down upon our laws and customs ... We are trained to avoid being too clever in matters that are of no use – such as being able to produce an excellent theoretical criticism of one's enemies' dispositions, and then failing in practice to do quite so well against them' (I.84).

We have just encountered one of a number of difficulties with Thucydides' speeches: the question whether any of them, or the remarks in them, represent Thucydides' own opinions. Certainly one can identify a number of recurring preoccupations, of which moderation in the use of power is one, and strong assertion of the right to exercise power another. The speeches, of which Thucydides includes

many, have drawn much critical examination. They are highly characteristic. They seem also to have been very influential, since the insertion
– invention is one word – of speeches became a feature of ancient
historiography well into the Roman period, though none are quite
like those of Thucydides. There are speeches in Herodotus, but they
are less lengthy and less important, and are often more like parts of
conversations than formed orations. Thucydides' own justification for
interpolating them is notably ambiguous, and even self-contradictory,
though the speeches themselves are written with confident authority
and an extraordinary virtuosity of a particular kind which for the
most part has little to do with revealing the individual personality of
the speaker. They are a reminder, of course, that ancient Greece, and
Athens in particular, saw a golden age of public debate and persuasion.
It is a persuasive suggestion that Thucydides' speeches owe something
to the teaching and example of the Sophists, those professional adepts
in the arts of debate and argument, whose dialectical virtuosity seemed
an end in itself rather than, as practised by Socrates, a tool in the
search for truth.

Referring to the speeches, Thucydides says:

I have found it difficult to remember the precise words used in the speeches
which I listened to myself and my various informants have experienced the
same difficulty; so my method has been, while keeping as closely as possible
to the general sense of the words that were actually used, to make the speakers
say what, in my opinion, was called for by each situation. (I.22)

The two requirements may have little to do with each other, and the
second gives a wide licence to authorial interpretation – of which
Thucydides clearly took advantage, for it has been complained since
antiquity that the voice we hear is Thucydides' own. Though the
speeches do not usually reflect the personality of the speaker, Pericles'
Funeral Oration is one exception, and another seems to be the rasping,
no-nonsense philistinism and plain man's anti-intellectualism of the
Athenian demagogue Cleon, whom Thucydides clearly despised (he
proved an incompetent and cowardly commander), which carries a
sense of recognition of the type across two and a half millennia
(III.36–40).

Paradoxical as it may appear, it often seems that Thucydides reveals his own mind more fully in the speeches than in the narrative, though we can never be quite sure. He is not an intrusive narrator. He occasionally speaks in the first person, or passes a judgement, but there is little to compare with the conversational approach of Herodotus. Occasionally he enunciates principles, but compared with the majority of historians up to the end of the nineteenth century – when historians began to be ultra self-conscious about their objectivity – Thucydides' overt moral judgements are few and terse. There seems to be plenty of evidence that he was impatient with moralizing rhetoric – his speeches sometimes disclaim the use of it, not always consistently. From time to time he attempts to summarize the significance of a narrative of complex events, but probably less often than a modern historian would. It is therefore not implausible to say that it is when he is purporting to retail the words of others saying 'what was called for' that he speaks most directly to the reader. The fact that the speakers differ does not detract from this point, because as a historian Thucydides is concerned not to adjudicate between them in terms of right and wrong, but to register the feelings and considerations that animated the events. The speeches, therefore, are the historian's versions of these. They reveal what the bare events themselves, without elaborate commentary, could not: the motives, apprehensions, appraisals and even guiding principles at work in the actions of the protagonists, like the speeches in a drama. They are the occasions when the agents explain themselves to the reader.

The quality of reflection – Thucydides' – in these rigorously controlled appraisals is impressive. The speakers sometimes explicitly distance themselves from mere rhetorical pathos and denunciation, which is as though Thucydides is saying that what we are about to hear of were the real considerations. The most comprehensively analytic of the speeches read like the situation and policy-option 'appreciations' of an able diplomat or think-tank member, rather than the words of a popular orator. This may sometimes make them implausible as oratorical *pièces d'occasion*, but it makes them superbly illuminating as Thucydides' commentary on the narrative of events. They are not, as speeches in later ancient historians often were, just rhetorical exercises, but rigorously clinical argument, and Thucydides' history would be enormously impoverished and much more opaque without

them. For a typical example – not arresting or colourful, but characteristic of the cool, analytic manner found in many of the speeches in
Thucydides – consider the argument of Nicias, the Athenian general,
against mounting an expedition against Sicily, where the Athenians
have been invited to intervene in a local war. Nicias makes a number
of cogent points in his long but unsuccessful speech; here he is
reminding the Athenians that, despite current appearances, their rear,
in Greece, would be insecure if the expedition were to take place:

In going to Sicily you are leaving many enemies behind you, and you apparently want to make new ones there and have them also on your hands.
Possibly you think that the peace treaty which you have made gives you
security; and, so long as you make no move, no doubt this treaty will continue
to exist in name (for it has become a nominal thing, thanks to the intrigues
of certain people here and in Sparta); it will certainly not stop our enemies
from attacking us immediately, if in any part of the world any considerable
forces of our own should suffer a defeat. In the first place, they only made
the peace because of their misfortunes; it was forced on them, and in the
matter of prestige we had the advantage. Then also in the treaty itself there
are still a number of points not settled . . . (VI.10)

There are two sets of grouped speeches, presented in the form of
debate and dialogue, which raise moral as well as policy issues, and
which have become famous as 'The Mytilenian Debate' and 'The
Melian Dialogue'. Both oppose considerations of mercy and politic
leniency to political necessity and harsh retribution – genocide in fact
– inflicted on a conquered city. The Mytilenian Debate has a dramatic
urgency because an Athenian trireme has already been sent with orders
to kill all the Mytilenian men and enslave the women and children.
The debate is over whether to rescind the orders (which is done in the
nick of time). Cleon, the Athenian demagogue, distinguishes himself
by his harshness. The debate in fact shifts away from the immediate
issue to consideration of the virtues and vices of government by discussion. Cleon, in particular, not only argues that the Athenian empire
rests on strength, not goodwill, but goes on to criticize the Athenian
way of taking political decisions. The Athenians, he says, are too apt
to treat political decisions as a kind of prize for oratorical excellence:
the assembly applauds novelty, and behaves like a connoisseur of

debating skills. His case on this point is powerfully put and, echoing Spartan references to Athenian volatility, may have Thucydides' weight behind it, as Hobbes thought it did. In oratorical competitions of this kind 'the prizes go to others and the state takes all the danger for herself. The blame is yours, for stupidly instituting these competitive displays.' Political wisdom is something quite different and less articulate.

We should realize that a city is better off with bad laws, so long as they remain fixed, than with good laws that are constantly being altered, that lack of learning combined with sound common sense is more helpful than the kind of cleverness that gets out of hand, and that as a general rule states are better governed by the man in the street than by intellectuals. These are the sort of people who want to appear wiser than the laws . . . who, as a result, often bring ruin on their country. But the other kind – the people who are not so confident in their own intelligence – are prepared to admit that the laws are wiser than they are and that they lack the ability to pull to pieces a speech made by a good speaker; they are unbiased judges, and not people taking part in some kind of competition; so things generally go well when they are in control. We statesmen, too, should try to be like them, instead of being carried away by mere cleverness and a desire to show off our intelligence. (III.38, 37)

Cleon's point here is connected to the particular case for extreme ruthlessness only by a non sequitur that modern readers will find familiar: an ingratiating populism leading to a rejection of bleeding-heart humanitarianism. People 'despise those who treat them well and look up to those who make no concessions' (III.39), so that 'To feel pity, to be carried away by the pleasure of hearing a clever argument, to listen to the claims of decency are three things that are entirely against the interests of an imperial power.' The Athenians might as well renounce the will to empire and 'go in for philanthropy' (III.40).

He is answered by another spokesman, Diodotus. It is through words that decisions must be appraised (the merits or otherwise of the Sophists, as teachers of the art of persuasion, seem to be at the heart of this debate). Diodotus' measured defence would not be out of place in a Platonic dialogue. It is a defence not only of discussion and of leniency as a matter of policy – he disclaims any general appeal to compassion – but of political responsibility contrasted with a facile responsiveness to the fickleness of the crowd. The argument for deterrence by harshness, though it addresses the right question – Athens' interests – is flawed by ignoring human nature. People take risks, not expecting to be defeated, and pride and hope or 'some incurable master passion' ensure that they always will. In particular, a man acting as part of a community 'has the irrational opinion that his own powers are greater than in fact they are'. The Athenian assembly is not a court of law seeking justice, but is concerned with security, and here Diodotus introduces what often seems a key word in Thucydides: 'moderation'. The situation is complex. The democratic parties in other cities are favourable to Athens, but the indiscriminate punishment of the Mytilenians will unite them with the oligarchic parties in a common fear (III.42–8). Thucydides' own comments on the debate are sparse but presumably significant. Cleon was a man 'remarkable among the Athenians for the violence of his character' (III.36), and the first ship, bearing the orders for massacre, 'was not hurrying on its distasteful mission' (III.49).

The Melian Dialogue (V.84–116) is presented, uniquely, not in set speeches, but in much briefer assertions and rebuttals by respectively 'Athenians' and 'Melians', as in a play. The Melians have to decide on surrender or resistance to a besieging Athenian army. The Melians plead for their neutrality. The Athenians again rest the case solely on expediency:

We . . . will use no fine phrases saying, for example, that we have a right to our empire because we defeated the Persians, or that we have come against you now because of the injuries you have done us . . . And we ask you on your side not to imagine that you will influence us by saying that you, though a colony of Sparta, have not joined Sparta in the war, or that you have never done us any harm. Instead we recommend that you should try to get what it is possible for you to get, taking into consideration what we both really do think; since you know as well as we do that . . . the standard of justice depends on the equality of power to compel . . .

The Melians reply that all men have an interest in fair play, and all may one day find themselves in another's power. To the Melians' further point that they can still have hope if they resist, the Athenians' response is brutal: realistic hope depends on resources:

Do not be like those people who, as so commonly happens, miss the chance of saving themselves in a human and practical way, and, when every clear and distinct hope has left them in their adversity, turn to what is blind and vague, to prophecies and oracles and such things which by encouraging hope lead men to ruin.

The Melians assert that they place their trust in the gods, who are not indifferent to right and wrong, and in the Spartan alliance. The Athenians' reply takes a different view of the gods:

Our opinion of the gods and our knowledge of men lead us to conclude that it is a general and necessary law of nature to rule whatever one can. This is not a law that we made ourselves, nor were we the first to act upon it when it was made. We found it already in existence, and we shall leave it to exist for ever among those who come after us. We are merely acting in accordance with it, and we know that you or anybody else with the same power as ours would be acting in precisely the same way.

The dialogue continues in this way, with the Melians clearly hankering to return to the ground of moral justification and the Athenians refusing it to them. They warn, in particular, against the delusions grounded in 'honour' – a form of pride which leads to ruin. The safe rule is 'to stand up to one's equals, to behave with deference towards one's superiors, and to treat one's inferiors with moderation'. The Melians decide for defiance, with trust in the gods and the Spartans and pride in 'the liberty which our city has enjoyed from its foundation for 700 years'. In victory the Athenians do not practise moderation; the Melian men are killed, the women and children are enslaved, and the city is repopulated as an Athenian colony.

The rational, sophisticated manner in which projected genocide is discussed in these two debates makes it natural to look for Thucydides' own attitude. We have already noted a couple of clues, as well as his possible endorsement of Cleon's rebuke to Athenian intellectual flightiness. The 'Machiavellian' or, if we want to avoid anachronism, Sophists' theme that might is right is so prominent that it was clearly a preoccupation of Thucydides, and it is one to which no really effective reply – only a reminder of the fickleness of fortune – is made. It is not altogether clear whether this is because politics is special, in that the moral inhibitions of private life do not apply, as it seems to have been for Machiavelli and for another modern kindred spirit, Max Weber, but it may have been. As Weber says, in politics one necessarily sups with a long spoon. The emphasis on moderation also seems to call for attention. It is essentially rational, because the unforeseeable is a crucial part of politics and no course guarantees absolute safety any more than it promises absolute virtue. It is surely significant that, in his account of the constitutional experiments which later followed the temporary overthrow of Athenian democracy, Thucydides explicitly opts for a middle course in the notion of a mixed constitution (VIII.97).

The opposite of moderation was fanaticism, and the classic case of political fanaticism in Thucydides is the account of the civil conflicts that began in Corcyra (in 427 BC) and spread all over Greece. These represent political factionalism wholly out of hand and becoming, for the agents, an end in itself. The account of the factionalism in the city states, prompted by the war, describes the pathology of societies under extreme stress in which all the normal conventions and restraints have ceased to operate. Thucydides' depictions of the psychology of fanaticism among the Corcyreans (and later elsewhere) still resonate, and one is reminded of the – often hotly disputed – claim for a perennial human nature. The Corcyrean democrats, feeling themselves threatened, began a massacre of fellow citizens. According to Thucydides, this was the precursor of many future revolutions and calamities in the Greek states: 'The knowledge of what had happened previously in other places caused still new extravagances of revolutionary zeal, [with] . . . unheard-of atrocities in revenge. To fit in with the change of events, words, too, had to change their usual meanings': aggression became courage and moderation cowardice. 'Anyone who held violent opinions could always be trusted, and anyone who objected to them became a suspect.' To attempt to opt out of the plotting and counter-plotting was 'disrupting the unity of the party', and fervent party members felt confidence in each other as partners in crime. The one standard became the will of the party at any particular moment. Even rational self-interest was jettisoned: 'Revenge was more important than self-preservation.' Society became divided, and there was a deterioration of character throughout the Greek world. Peace could not be made, because oaths were worthless. With the ordinary conventions of civilized life overthrown,

> human nature, always ready to offend even where laws exist, showed itself proudly in its true colours, as something incapable of controlling passion, insubordinate to the idea of justice, the enemy of anything superior to itself ... Men take it upon themselves to begin the process of repealing those general laws of humanity which are there to give a hope of salvation to all who are in distress, instead of ... remembering that there may come a time when they, too, will be in danger and will need their protection. (III.82–4).

It comes as no surprise that the seventeenth-century English translator of Thucydides was Thomas Hobbes.

The mark of fanaticism is the pursuit of advantage without limit, the love of terror for its own sake. Those who, in Thucydides, rationally employ power to their advantage sometimes stress that their behaviour is normal, according to human nature. But human beings released from the ties of convention are creatures of irrational extremes. The line between ruthlessness and fanaticism is the distinction between the normal and the pathological. But the arrogance of power and its overestimate also lead states to rash enterprises beyond their resources, of which the prime example is the Athenian expedition against Sicily, and the representative individual the dashing young Athenian aristocrat Alcibiades, cunning politician and Olympic prize-winner in the chariot races. Rashness is the exaggeration of the Athenian qualities of confidence, boldness and enterprise. In Thucydides' account, it meets its nemesis in the failure of the ultimately disastrous invasion of Sicily (in 415 BC), which allegedly brings Athens down cataclysmically from the height of its power, and is described by Thucydides in unprecedented detail in Books VI and VII. The attention given to the Sicilian venture is a striking example of authorial initiative. The invasion was an attempt to strike at Sparta through its allies and through domination of the western Mediterranean. It was, Thucydides claims, the greatest expedition undertaken in the Hellenic world, and its failure gives these books, like the latter part of Herodotus, the familiar shape of hubris and nemesis.

At the centre of the decision to invade and the conduct of the invasion is Alcibiades as politician and general. He is the extreme case of a highly recognizable type in many ages: a brilliant, arrogant aristocrat with political ambitions and considerable eloquence and ability. His supposedly undemocratic ambition inspired distrust, and when an act of sacrilege was perpetrated in Athens – the mutilation of the herms, the phallic statues which stood at various points in the city – Alcibiades and his associates fell under suspicion. It is easy to see this desecration as a youthful, aristocratic prank, but it was magnified into a plot against the city's constitution. Alcibiades was recalled from Sicily, but, fearing for his life, fled first to Sparta and then to Persia. Such exile was not uncommon – Thucydides himself experienced it – but Alcibiades remained influential, playing off the Persians and Spartans against each other and eventually manipulating for himself a return to Athens. He had undeniable glamour, which is evident also in his appearance in Plato's *Symposium*. Thucydides said that 'most people became frightened at a quality in him which was beyond the normal and showed itself both in the lawlessness of his private life and habits and in the spirit in which he acted on all occasions' (VI.15).

Thucydides has a majestic description of the setting-out of the expedition. The population of Athens, torn by fear and hope, go down to Piraeus to see its departure, while Thucydides hard-headedly estimates its cost. Then,

When the ships were manned and everything had been taken aboard ... silence was commanded by the sound of the trumpet, and the customary prayers made before putting to sea were offered up, not by each ship separately, but by all of them together following the words of a herald. The whole army had wine poured out into bowls, and officers and men made their libations from cups of gold and of silver. The crowd on the shore also, the citizens and others who wished well to the expedition, joined together in the prayers. (VI.32)

The fleet so splendidly described earlier goes to its destruction in the sea battle of Syracuse. Thucydides is detailed in his accounts of sea battles and technology: the special rams fitted to the Syracusan ships (VII.36); the ships on the defensive forming themselves into a circle, a kind of floating stockade; the attempts at ramming, with the ships fouling each other in confined spaces; the chaos and confusion – 'the great din of all these ships crashing together was not only frightening in itself, but also made it impossible to hear the orders given by the boatswains', who were themselves distracted by attempting to ram while avoiding being rammed themselves from several directions (VII.70).

The decisive sea battle of Syracuse, which doomed the Athenian expedition, was witnessed by the two armies from land, shouting and cheering as though in a theatre. For the Athenians in particular, who knew that their own fate depended on the outcome, there was terrible anxiety as they followed its fortunes. They were too close to see the whole picture, so

some saw that at one point their own side was winning, and took courage at the sight and began to call upon the gods not to deprive them of their salvation, while others, looking towards a point where their men were being defeated, cried out aloud in lamentation, and were more broken in spirit by the sight of what was being done than were the men actually engaged in the fighting. Others were looking at some part of the battle where there was nothing to choose between the two sides, and, as the fight went on and on with no decision reached, their bodies, swaying this way and that, showed the trepidation with which their minds were filled, and wretched indeed was their state, constantly on the verge of safety, constantly on the brink of destruction. (VII.71)

The fate of the Athenian army, isolated and hopeless on the island without their fleet, was indeed terrible, and Thucydides vividly describes their sufferings on their final march, 'especially when they remembered the splendour and pride of their setting out and saw how mean and abject was the conclusion. No Hellenic army had ever suffered such a reverse' (VII.75). The survivors are taken as prisoners to the Syracusan quarries.

There were many of them, and they were crowded together in a narrow pit, where, since there was no roof over their heads, they suffered first from the heat of the sun and the closeness of the air; and then, in contrast, came on the cold autumnal nights, and the change in temperature brought disease among them. Lack of space made it necessary for them to do everything on the same spot; and besides there were the bodies all heaped together on top of one another of those who had died from their wounds or from the change of temperature or other such causes, so that the smell was insupportable. At the same time they suffered from hunger and from thirst. (VII.87)

It is important to stress Thucydides' achievements as a narrator, because his own programmatic statements about the value of history may have led them to be underrated. Thucydides is the first author to proclaim that history should be useful, and he makes the possibility depend on his famous claim that, human nature being a constant, what 'happened in the past . . . will, at some time or other and in much the same ways, be repeated in the future. My work is not a piece of writing designed to meet the taste of an immediate public, but was done to last for ever' (I.22). The contrast may be a sneer at Herodotus' public readings. But Thucydides is too much a realist – even a pessimist – for there to be any glib suggestion that, armed with historical examples, we will be able simply to avoid the errors of the past. Human nature, the narrative tells us, is too powerful and too perverse for this, and rational calculation is only one element in any situation. There can be no thought, when reading Thucydides, of history being superseded by a manual of political and psychological maxims derived from it.

Thucydides was surely right to claim that his history teaches, but it is arguable that he did not fully understand exactly how this was so, and it is hard to express this clearly even now. It must be a common feeling that one has learned something about human nature and human affairs from his work, and not just from noting examples and their didactic import. As Robert Connor points out, in reading Thucydides one has enlarged one's experience, encountering human nature in action, assimilating the emotional as well as intellectual impact the detailed narrative makes on us. This narrative is extended yet also terse, acutely analytical yet also sometimes impassioned, and vividly presented to the imagination, not through surface ornament but in the penetration with which the predicaments of the actors are measured. We are taught by it indefinably – as we are taught by concentrated experience – which makes any talk of 'lessons' seem uncomfortably superficial. The subject is indeed human nature, and at times the distance of almost two and a half thousand years can be made to seem to contract almost vertiginously. But this is not because of the formula that Thucydides may seem to be accepting: that 'laws' of social and political psychology may be inferred from examples. What he certainly understood is that examples are complex because circumstances are so, and responses to circumstances are complex also. Historians, one is glad to be able to assert, have generally done better than their programmatic formulations of their task have suggested, which is one reason why discussions of the nature of historiography based on such formulations are so inadequate. Thucydides, if we take his pronouncements too narrowly, is no exception. It is quite appropriate, while registering that he can be a stirring, poignant or horrifying narrator, to speak also of his work as analytic or, better, diagnostic. But diagnosis is an art, and it has been aptly suggested that Thucydides' approach to history owes something to the treatises of Hippocratic medicine. This was a practice and not just a theory, and involved detailed observation of symptoms as well as classification of conditions.

The former is much in evidence in Thucydides' own account of pathological phenomena in his famous description of the plague which broke out in Athens in 430 BC. He himself caught it and survived; many, including Pericles, died. Thucydides gives a highly detailed account of the symptoms and course of the disease, so that, as he says, it would be recognizable if it ever broke out again. His description – there was, of course, no explanation – is so detailed that it might be that of a professional physician. He also, however, makes no attempt to obscure the extreme suffering of the victims and the effects on the society of Athens. His account is a harrowing as well as exact one, and it is pathology in a double sense: the pathology of the disease itself and of a whole society disintegrating under its effects. Human art or science had no help to offer, and 'Equally useless were prayers made in the temples, consultation of oracles, and so forth; indeed, in the end people were so overcome by their sufferings that they paid no further attention to such things' (II.47). Those who tried to nurse the sick caught the disease; this caused such fear that many people died alone and unattended. Bodies lay in the streets and in the temples where people had gone for refuge.

The result, Thucydides says, was an unprecedented lawlessness. As in the later account of political terror in Corcyra, which we have looked at, Thucydides depicts here, for different reasons, the pathology not just of a disease but of a society in dissolution. Despairing of the future, people sought the pleasures of the moment without restraint. Honour – reputation – counted for nothing. 'The catastrophe was so overwhelming that men, not knowing what would happen next to them, became indifferent to every rule of religion or of law.' Proper funeral ceremonies – a matter of much importance, for example in war – were neglected. 'No fear of god or law of man had a restraining influence. As for the gods, it seemed to be the same thing whether one worshipped them or not, when one saw the good and the bad dying indiscriminately' (II.52–3). No one expected to live long enough to be subject to human justice.

Thucydides' account is an extraordinary rhetorical and analytic tour de force, as a description of a human society *in extremis*. We can only guess at the long-term effects of the experience on his own view of life and human conduct. It is characteristic of Thucydides that we should have been led to this account of human and social catastrophe by following his claim to have written a history which should be useful. As often in his work, the terrible is placed within a framework of observation and analysis which does not sterilize it but rather strikes one, in the circumstances, as a powerful act of intellectual will. Thucydides' view of human life and conduct is wholly unsentimental, but never 'scientifically' desiccated.

The obvious applicability of the pattern of hubris–nemesis to the greatness of Athens and the disaster of the Sicilian expedition inclines one to make an analogy with Greek tragedy. Any attempt to draw this in detail is probably misguided, but morally, though not formally, the suggestion is surely not altogether misplaced. Some of the formulations in which a modern critic, Northrop Frye, characterizes the essence of the tragic outlook can hardly fail to resonate with readers of Thucydides: 'Tragedy seems to elude the antithesis of moral responsibility and arbitrary fate, just as it eludes the antithesis of good or evil': in tragedy 'one finds a "Dionysiac" aggressive will, intoxicated by dreams of its own omnipotence, impinging upon an "Apollonian" sense of external and immovable order' (*Anatomy of Criticism*, 1957). The references are to Nietzsche's essay on the birth of tragedy, and Nietzsche's tribute to Thucydides – idiosyncratic though it is – catches much about him:

Thucydides and perhaps the *Principe* of Machiavelli are related to me closely by their unconditional will not to deceive themselves and so see reason in *reality* . . . One must turn over line by line and read his hidden thoughts as clearly as his words: there are few thinkers so rich in hidden thoughts. Sophist culture, by which I mean realist culture, attains in him its perfect expression – this invaluable movement in the midst of the morality-and-ideal swindle of the Socratic schools which was then breaking out everywhere . . . Thucydides was the grand summation, the last manifestation of that strong, stern, hard matter-of-factness instinctive to the older Hellenes. (Nietzsche, *Twilight of the Idols*, 'What I Owe to the Ancients')

Thucydides seems to embody all the qualities that Nietzsche admired and did not always manage to embody himself. It is easy to understand the admiration. Almost all historians except the very dullest have some characteristic weakness: some complicity, idealization, identification; some impulse to indignation, to right wrongs, to deliver a message. It is often the source of their most interesting writing. But Thucydides seems immune. Surely no more lucid, unillusioned intelligence has ever applied itself to the writing of history.

3

The Greeks in Asia

Xenophon: The Persian Expedition

When the men in front reached the summit and caught sight of the sea there
was great shouting. Xenophon and the rearguard heard it and thought that
there were some more enemies attacking in the front, since there were natives
of the country they had ravaged following them up behind, and the rearguard
had killed some of them and made prisoners of others in an ambush, and
captured about twenty raw ox-hide shields, with the hair on. However, when
the shouting got louder and drew nearer, and those who were constantly
going forward started running towards the men in front who kept on shouting,
and the more there were of them the more shouting there was, it looked
then as though this was something of considerable importance. So Xenophon
mounted his horse and, taking Lycus and the cavalry with him, rode forward
to give support, and, quite soon, they heard the soldiers shouting out 'The
sea! The sea!' and passing the word down the column. Then certainly they
all began to run, the rearguard and all, and drove on the baggage animals
and the horses at full speed; and when they had all got to the top, the soldiers,
with tears in their eyes, embraced each other and their generals and captains.
(Xenophon, *The Persian Expedition*, IV.7)

The soldiers' excitement was understandable, and to mark the spot
where the sea came into sight they put up a cairn of stones surmounted
by captured shields. For the small Greek army, which had found itself
apparently trapped in the heart of the Persian empire, to have fought
its way back through hostile countries to the south-eastern shore of
the Black Sea had immeasurably increased its chances of survival.
There might be boats to be had, and along the southern shore there

were Greek settlements which might be friendly or could be coerced. There were still vicissitudes to be encountered, but the Greeks had taken a great step towards their homeland. How they had found themselves in their desperate predicament and how they won their way home is the story Xenophon tells in what later became his most famous work, the *Anabasis*, or in its English title *The Persian Expedition*.

To understand it fully we need some understanding of the relation of the Greeks, after the end of the Peloponnesian War, to the great oriental empire whose invasion they had repulsed more than three-quarters of a century before. We also need to know something of Xenophon, who is not only the book's author but also its central character, who emerged, by his own account, as the army's leader. Towards the end of Thucydides' history, as a result of the exhaustion of the combatants, the Persians were beginning tentatively to throw their weight into the scales of the conflict. There was, however, no further full-scale invasion. Rather it was the Greek world which, as a result chiefly of the continuing superiority of Greek (and subsequently Macedonian) fighting methods, began to penetrate the Persian, and some Greeks, notably the rhetorician Isocrates, began to advocate and predict a Greek takeover of the Persian empire. This was the context for the work of Xenophon. He wrote a decidedly disappointing and most historians now think unreliable continuation of Thucydides' history, the *Hellenica*, but the chief source of his fame in the modern world, *The Persian Expedition*, really in a sense makes him the successor of Herodotus, on a much smaller scale, for it encapsulates in microcosm the relations between the Greek and Persian worlds.

Xenophon was born soon after the outbreak of the Peloponnesian War, into the Athenian gentry; his affection for his native city was dimmed by his distaste for its democracy. He was a disciple of Socrates (of whom he wrote an account), a soldier, and a country gentleman, in Spartan and in Persian territory. His works are eclectic: apart from the history of Greece in continuation of Thucydides and his work on Socrates, he wrote a work of pedagogical eulogy, *The Education of Cyrus*, which was much admired in antiquity; a book on the art of hunting; and *The Persian Expedition*. The last, it seems, was not popular until the time of Alexander, over half a century later.

The Persian Expedition is a military man's vindication of his own conduct and that of the force to which he belonged. It is an enthrallingly detailed, first-hand account. The army of ten thousand Greek mercenaries become stranded, deep in the Persian empire, by the death of their employer, Cyrus, a Persian prince, who had hired them to help him with his attempted insurrection (401 BC). They have to fight their way back to Greek territory, traversing parts of the Persian empire which are often rugged, inhospitable, barbaric and even savage. It is another parallel with Herodotus that the work contains a good deal of casual ethnography. Xenophon is his own hero – perhaps, alternative accounts suggest, to an excessive degree. The expedition forms a single drama with a single protagonist, the ten thousand Greek hoplite mercenaries, and its resolution is the safe return of most of them to the Greek, largely Spartan-controlled, colonial world of the Bosporus region, where Xenophon had unfulfilled dreams of founding a city.

Beset by enemies, Persian and barbarian, in Xenophon's account the Greek mercenary army essentially survives by its discipline and military technique. To preserve its cohesion is often Xenophon's chief concern. This cohesion is fostered by a sense of solidarity as Greeks, and the troops give each other crucial support at moments of crisis, going, for example, to considerable trouble and difficulty to recover and bury their dead, as Greeks always did. This quality sees them through the hazards of a hostile climate and terrain, and the ever-present need to extort the supplies to keep them going in the lands through which they pass, in which for the most part they are clearly regarded as no better than a plague of locusts. Xenophon is at pains in all this to bring out his own qualities of leadership and persuasion: he is not, until the very end, the acknowledged leader, but his account certainly makes him the star performer.

Eventually, in the passage quoted above, which readers (who included generations of English schoolboys) found unforgettable, the rear of the column, which contained Xenophon, hears a tumult from the vanguard: 'The sea! The sea!' This is really the book's climax, and the odds are now tilted towards survival. Reaching the Black Sea raises the hope – only partially fulfilled – of an easy passage back by sea to Byzantium.

There are still savage barbarians to be encountered, however, and also, as the shore becomes more civilized, the hostility of local Persian rulers, and even of Greek settlements which view the advent of the army with dismay, and of Spartan governors, the Spartans having succeeded the Athenians as the Greek colonial power in the region. To none of them is the arrival of so large a number of disciplined soldiers – without means of support, and with habits, of necessity, little different from those of a band of brigands – at all welcome.

The last part of the book, in which Xenophon is given the outstanding part as leader and chief negotiator, is taken up with the attempts of the army's leaders to recompense themselves, pay the troops, and find a new employer. Eventually, in 399 BC, they find one in Sparta, fortunately facing the onset of a new war in which the army could be useful. Xenophon himself was forced to give up the ambition he had formed to found a city on the Black Sea, and took service with Sparta, for which he was rewarded with an estate which enabled him to settle down as a country gentleman.

The Persian Expedition, then, relates an epic fighting journey and the achievement, against heavy odds, of a fortunate homecoming. It has therefore something like the dramatic shape of earlier, legendary expeditions – the voyage of the Argonauts; the Trojan War and Odysseus' tortuous wanderings – as well as being a microcosmic foreshadowing of the campaign expedition of Alexander across the Persian empire to the Indus. More like Xenophon than any of these in its first-hand authorial testimony and dramatic compactness is the account in more modern times, by the Spaniard Bernal Díaz, of the campaign expedition to and capture of Tenochtitlán (Mexico City) by the conquistadores in the early sixteenth century, later written into an epic account of the conquest by the New England historian W. H. Prescott. Xenophon's story is one of survival, not conquest, and is perhaps the easier to identify with for that. It is a story with a single collective actor, recounting a continuous sequence of events over only two years (401–399 BC), and therefore contrasts with those ancient histories (including Xenophon's own *Hellenica*) which, with a variety of scattered actions in various locations to record, are cast more or less of necessity into the annalistic mould.

Always present as a background to the action, to the successive challenges and hazards met by the army as it attempts to fight its way home, and the dissensions and debates these evoke at various stages of the march, is an intense awareness of the contrast between Greeks and Persians and between both and the other barbarians. The army takes its Greekness with it into the heart of Babylonia and the wastes of Kurdistan and Armenia not only in its hoplite equipment and tactics, which give it the edge in battle, but in its self-awareness and its pride in its Greek identity and superiority. And history, as so often, is called on to buttress pride and resolution. At a critical moment Xenophon, in his account, calls on the troops to recall the past achievements of the Greeks against the might of the Persian empire. 'Remember how the Persians and their friends came with an enormous army, thinking that they would wipe Athens off the face of the earth; but the Athenians had the courage to stand up by themselves, and they defeated them' (III.2). The prize of that victory was freedom. The Persian prince Cyrus has earlier congratulated his Greek mercenaries on their freedom and the strength they derive from it, when explaining why he has recruited them (I.7). Xenophon himself calls on the soldiers to shun a life of ease and luxury and 'these fine great women, the wives and daughters of the Medes and Persians', lest they should be weakened in their determination to win their way home (III.2). The contrast of Greek (later Roman and European) masculinity with oriental servitude, effeminacy and luxury was later to become familiar in a literature that stretched from the *Odyssey*'s tale of the lotus-eaters, through Roman denunciations of Antony's enslavement to an Egyptian queen and Marlowe's 'pampered jades of Asia', to Tennyson's and Kingsley's reworking of the theme in the context of later European imperialism.

In Xenophon's story the reference to freedom is more than rhetoric. When the mercenaries lose their employer with the death of Cyrus and later lose their original commander to Persian treachery and are faced with the alternatives of surrender or the long march home – over a thousand miles, without bases, supplies or cavalry – they behave like Greeks: that is, they deliberate and debate and come to a collective decision and elect new commanders. This army has been called 'a polity on the move'. It is also pious, and this matters to Xenophon, who seems conventionally so, in contrast to Thucydides and perhaps even to Herodotus, in whose piety there seems a touch of good manners. Because the omens are unfavourable, Xenophon, by his own account, keeps the army in suspense for agonizing days before engaging in an urgently desired action (VI.4). He is scrupulous in making sacrifices. The gods are given their traditional role as the guardians of oath-taking and treaties, and Greek piety in this respect is contrasted with Persian treachery. Along with sacrifices of thanksgiving for deliverance, to Zeus, Apollo and Heracles, the army holds athletic games – a supremely Greek and indeed Homeric touch – with racing and boxing. (In Herodotus the Persian king had expressed wonder at the Greeks competing only for wreaths.) This is its chief form of celebration of its survival. When it is objected that the ground is too hard for wrestling, the games' organizer shows complete lack of sympathy: 'All the worse for the man who gets thrown' (IV.8). Xenophon's work had all the qualifications for a cherished pedagogical text in the English public schools.

The character, possessions and diet of the barbarian peoples the army had successively to resist, intimidate and pillage were, of course, of urgent practical concern, but in Xenophon's description there is sometimes a note of Herodotean connoisseurship of the quaintness of the exotic. Some of the barbarians were troglodytes. The food mentioned – a vital matter – included a toxic drink made from honey, said to induce delirium and madness (perhaps a kind of mead), pickled dolphin, and dolphin fat used instead of olive oil. One highly Herodotean observation – perhaps so much so as to cast doubt on it as observation – is the alleged inversion of ordinary customs: 'When they were in a crowd they acted as men would act when in private, and when they were by themselves, they used to behave as they might do if they were in company' (V.4). On one occasion the Greeks seem to make themselves the exotic people, putting on for the Paphlagonian ambassadors what one can call a display of ethnic dancing – Thracian, Magnesian, Mysian and Arcadian, emphasizing the composite character of the army. Xenophon describes this in some detail, though when a slave girl, belonging to an Arcadian, dances the Spartan war dance, the Pyrrhic dance, he seems to regard this as too well known to need description (VI.1).

Xenophon, as an aristocrat, was an admirer of Sparta, and it was with the Spartans that he was eventually able to make terms on behalf of the army and of himself, but the tone of the work as a whole is Panhellenic. The army, while it contained a preponderance of Athenians, was a mixture, though the fundamental contrast is of course with non-Greeks. One reading of Xenophon's work has seen it as a kind of Panhellenic propaganda, in the vein of Isocrates, demonstrating how easily Greeks could overcome Persians and hence how easy it would be, as Xenophon clearly hoped, to found new Greek colonies in Persian territory. His book surely contributed to a Western sense of superiority to the Orient from the Enlightenment onward.

Though *The Persian Expedition* may reflect the outlook of the Greek Panhellenists, it was not Xenophon's most popular work in Greek antiquity, which preferred his Socratic writings and the tediously high-minded *Education of Cyrus*. Later, however, the *Expedition* became more popular, with an imperialist interest which culminated in the time of the 'second generation' of historians of the conquests of Alexander. These writers were a second generation in the sense that the works of the various historians who accompanied Alexander's expedition have all disappeared, except for borrowings and excerpts, leaving two notable historians in Roman times, centuries later, to rewrite the Alexander story. One of them, Arrian, makes Alexander recall to his men before the battle of Issus the feats of Xenophon's Ten Thousand, and this may indeed have happened. It is to Arrian and his fellow Alexander historian Curtius Rufus that we must now turn.

The Alexander Historians: Arrian and Curtius Rufus

The greatest of all subjects for an campaign-expedition narrative, Alexander the Great's invasion of Asia in 334 BC, also marked the culmination of the encounters between the Greek world, including Macedon, and the Persian empire. Though there were numerous attempts, no historical account, it seems, was able quite to capture the scale of events as Herodotus had done with the invasion of Greece by the Persians. This has to be partly guesswork, however, for none of the earliest, eyewitness, accounts has survived except in so far as they were incorporated in the work of later historians writing in the Roman period. Alexander himself is said to have envied his supposed ancestor Achilles for having Homer to commemorate his deeds, while he himself had no comparable memorialist. We have intact, moreover, only the later historians who based their accounts on the earliest ones, one of whom, Ptolemy, was not only one of Alexander's generals but one of the successors to his empire, in Egypt. The Greek historian Arrian, who, writing in the second century AD, is the best-known of the extant later historians, said that the lack of a great memorialist was Alexander's only misfortune, and that it was a pity that his exploits were less well known than the much smaller achievements of Xenophon's Ten Thousand. He was not entirely disinterested, since he was claiming the first rank in Greek literature as Alexander's chronicler and because of the scale of Alexander's achievements. Writing four hundred years later, however, he was necessarily dependent on his now lost predecessors.

Alexander had taken with him his own historian, Callisthenes, the nephew of Aristotle, whose narrative was curtailed when Alexander had him executed for conspiracy. Apart from a general, Ptolemy, other memorialists of the campaign included an engineer, Aristobulus, as well as humbler figures who contributed their accounts to the stock of Alexander literature. Most popular of all, in the centuries after Alexander, was the history of Cleitarchus, who was not an eyewitness, though a contemporary who had access to the evidence of participants. We know something of the work of all these from the use made of them by later writers, Plutarch (AD 45–c.120), and Diodorus of Sicily, whose *Universal History*, in the mid first century BC, devoted a book to Alexander's expedition. There is also the work of Arrian and his chief rival now, because his history has survived, though with lacunae, the only Latin historian among them, Quintus Curtius Rufus. Both of these last enjoyed distinguished careers in the Roman empire, Arrian (whose Latin name was Lucius Flavius Arrianus) as governor of Cappadocia and archon (magistrate) of Athens, while Curtius is thought to have been a senator and consul in the first century AD. Their aims as historians are somewhat different, and they are clearly sometimes following different traditions. As historians of essentially the same events, their work offers examples of the possibilities for historical narrative in the early Roman empire. Arrian is explicit that the sources he trusts are Ptolemy and Aristobulus and that he is confident, when they agree, that he has the authoritative account. Curtius (and also apparently Plutarch and Diodorus) follows something like a rival tradition, stemming from Cleitarchus. The differences exhibited by the respective histories not only preserve some of the contemporary versions of the Alexander story (at the cost of leaving a good deal undecided), but embody notably different ways of writing history.

Alexander himself, of course, is at the heart of both accounts, and there is a good deal in the major events and even in the reading of Alexander's character on which they substantially agree. But the historiographical personalities of Arrian and Curtius are entirely different. Arrian's is the more 'official' account: sober and measured. He seems to trust Ptolemy implicitly, saying that after Alexander's death he had no motive to flatter or suppress, though surely as a participant Ptolemy may have had some things to gloss over, while Aristobulus, Arrian's other main source, had a reputation for flattery. Curtius, perhaps reflecting Cleitarchus as well as his own taste, is more circumstantial, sensuous and dramatic – and, for the fastidious, vulgar. His portrait of Alexander, though ultimately more adulatory than critical, lays more stress than Arrian on Alexander's moral deterioration under the influence of good fortune, luxury and oriental notions of despotic power and semi-divinity. The contrast we found initially in Herodotus and more markedly in Xenophon between oriental 'effeminacy' and Greek (later Roman) hardihood and austerity was a heavily stressed one in the Roman period; indeed, as we shall see, the idea of oriental contagion became something like a general explanation of decadence.

Arrian, it seems, took Xenophon as the model for his *Anabasis Alexandri* (*The Campaigns of Alexander*), but Curtius' work (*The History of Alexander*) is the more 'literary', with obvious transpositions of topoi from Herodotus: the wise but disregarded counsellor of the Persian king, for example, is analogous to Croesus in Herodotus. Almost a quotation from Herodotus is the remark attributed to Alexander that the Persians had more men in their ranks but the Macedonians more fighters (Curtius, 4.14.5). Numerous echoes of Livy (whom we shall consider later) have also been identified. Curtius has a taste for ethnographic digressions, though Arrian's relative abstention from these is to some extent misleading, since he reserved his Indian material for a separate work, also extant. In general, however, drawn by a taste for the description of Persian gorgeousness and luxury, and the opportunities for moralistic disapproval these offered, Curtius gives rather more of the Persian perspective than does Arrian. Arrian's work, in fact, though less censorious, is too personalized and one-sided to be an account of a clash of civilizations. Curtius, however, rejoices in the chance to contrast Darius' Persian army, gleaming with purple and gold, and the Macedonian force, 'gleaming, not with gold, not with multi-coloured clothes, but with iron and bronze' (3.26). Effeminacy is a stressed note in the description of the Persian host. The fifteen thousand called 'the king's kinsmen' were 'dressed almost like women', and Darius himself had a gilded belt 'which he wore in the style of a woman' (3.14, 19). Wives, the royal children's nurses, concubines, eunuchs and camp followers bring up the rear.

There is nothing of this in Arrian, who contents himself with numbers and the discussion of tactics, on which Curtius is decidedly weak. Instead, Curtius likes drama and pathos, in the manner of the rhetorical and picturesque historians of his period. The fate of Darius' family is composed like a picture:

His mother commanded respect for her age as well as for her royal dignity, his wife for a beauty that even her current misfortune had not marred. The latter had taken to her bosom her young son, who had not yet turned six, a boy born into the expectation of the great fortune his father had just lost. In the lap of their aged grandmother lay Darius' grown-up but unmarried daughters, grieving for their grandmother as well as themselves. Around her stood a number of high-born women, their hair torn, their clothes rent and their former gracefulness forgotten. (3.24–5)

Both historians tell the famous story of Darius' mother taking Alexander's friend Hephaestion for Alexander, which Veronese turned into a sumptuous picture, but Arrian characteristically says that he will not vouch for it.

It is common ground, though with nuances of disapproval, with Arrian the more inclined to excuses, that Alexander was a man of extraordinary courage, energy and charm, with an ambition beyond all reason. His rages, during one of which, at a banquet, he murdered his friend Cleitus for showing insufficient respect, and was then wildly repentant, are part of his character. Curtius emphasizes his increasing weakness for debauchery, both alcoholic and sexual. The pernicious influence of Asiatic luxury and servility and the contagion of foreign ways have him in their grip. Curtius has him kill Cleitus in a drunken frenzy; Arrian glosses over this, and seems to transfer much of the blame to Cleitus himself. Curtius attributes the burning of the Persian kings' palace at Persepolis also to a drunken revel, and has Alexander incited to the deed by a prostitute, while Arrian treats it as an act of revenge for the past Persian ravaging of Greece.

Curtius eagerly recounts the traditional story of Alexander's sexual liaison with the Queen of the Amazons (6.24–32). Arrian will have none of it: Ptolemy and Aristobulus do not mention it, and anyway there were no longer any Amazons by then, though they had existed once (7.13). In general, Arrian's portrayal is the more political, but he mentions Alexander's weaknesses and deplores his adoption of Persian dress and manners, while admitting a political element in it. He also mentions the excess of Alexander's ambition, while Curtius dwells more on his human weakness. Typically, they approach differently Alexander's claims to divine descent. Arrian treats them as probably manipulative, but does not doubt Alexander's descent from the legendary heroes Heracles and Perseus. Curtius too equivocates over Alexander's claim to descent from the Egyptian god Ammon, whom the Greeks identified with Zeus and Curtius naturally calls Jupiter. Alexander either believed 'or wanted others to believe' in his divine ancestry (4.7.8). Accounts agree that Alexander's casting of himself as a type of his ancestor Achilles was part of his character. According to Arrian, he had felt a kind of rivalry with Achilles since childhood (7.14), though it is only Curtius who tells (with disapproval) the tale of Alexander's having his dead enemy Betis dragged by the heels around the city of Gaza in deliberate imitation of Achilles' treatment of Hector (4.6.29). Arrian tells the story (Curtius' account is lost) of Alexander's visit to Troy and his gift of his own armour to the temple, taking away with him weapons from the Trojan War preserved there. It was also said that he laid a wreath on the tomb of Achilles, while his friend Hephaestion laid one on that of Patroclus (1.12).

Where the two historians differ slightly is in their accounts of Alexander's journey across the desert, in Egypt, to the shrine of Ammon (Zeus, Jupiter). Arrian shows a scientific interest in the natural phenomenon of the oasis where the temple stood (3.4), and records Alexander's delight at receiving from the oracle (Arrian adds 'or so he said') the desired answer to his question, which was apparently whether he was destined to rule the world. Curtius makes allowance for the possibility that Alexander was manipulating the credulity of others, but implies that Alexander became himself ensnared by it, with bad results for his relations with his independently minded Macedonian followers, though Curtius also subscribes to the cliché (it is found in Polybius and Livy earlier) that 'Nothing exercises greater control over the masses than superstition' (4.10.7). His description of Alexander's visit to the temple of Ammon (4.7) is less scientific but more circumstantial and picturesque than Arrian's. He too notes the peculiar properties of the water of the oasis, which was said to be cold at midday and boiling hot at midnight, but gives in addition some interesting details of the cult:

The image worshipped as divine does not have the properties commonly accorded to deities by nations, it most resembles a navel and is composed of an emerald and other jewels. When an oracular response is sought, priests carry this along in a gilded boat from which a large number of silver cups hang on both sides, and married and unmarried women follow singing some artless song by which they believe an infallible answer is elicited from Jupiter. (4.7.23, 24)

Herodotus would have loved the navel, but probably been more circumspect about the possible genuineness of the oracle. Arrian seems reluctant to admit Alexander's superstitious complicity, but there is a good deal in the general consensus about him – ardent, unreflective, impulsive, obsessed with his own descent and destiny – which makes it likely. Arrian seems the more reliable of the two historians: he is more fastidious in what he refrains from describing in imaginative detail, and his accounts are cooler and more rational. Whether that was the best way to understand the mentality of Alexander is open to doubt, and no final adjudication is possible.

The Alexander traditions, if not altogether compatible, left a legacy of images and an archetype to which later rulers aspired and on which sculptors and painters drew. (Plutarch was probably their chief carrier: Curtius was ignored until the Middle Ages.) Julius Caesar and Augustus (as Octavian) both visited the tomb of Alexander, as Alexander had visited that of Achilles. The image of Alexander, the strikingly handsome, godlike young world-conqueror, influenced the iconography of the young Augustus and the young Napoleon. Jacques-Louis David's picture of Napoleon visiting his sick and wounded soldiers (whom he was about to desert) in the hospital at Acre bound together a triple image of Alexander visiting his wounded soldiers after the battle of Granicus (Arrian 1.16), of Christ healing the sick, and of Napoleon. It was a kind of irony that, later, Napoleon's Russian antagonist should have been called Alexander. The son of Antony and Cleopatra was also named Alexander. Alexander the Great, who bequeathed an enduring legendary heritage in both East and West, had really no need to envy Achilles, for

> Is it not passing brave to be a king,
> And ride in triumph through Persepolis?
> (Marlowe, *Tamburlaine the Great*, II.v)

The Alexander historians we have, writing four hundred years and more after the events, have inevitably the air of an epilogue, but it has been only though them, in the absence of their sources, that we could complete the theme which was so important for early historiography, the encounters of the Greek and Persian worlds. Consideration of the next great theme, though it is still treated by Greek writers, requires a retracing of steps to the second century BC, to the earliest historians of the rise of Rome.

PART II

Rome

4

Polybius: Universal History, Pragmatic History and the Rise of Rome

Polybius, a Romanized Greek of the highest class, set himself in the middle part of the second century BC to write, chiefly for his fellow Greeks, the story of the rise of Rome to dominion over the whole Mediterranean area. His focus was inevitably the long struggle between Rome and Carthage for the hegemony of the western Mediterranean, but his history also comprehended the successful assertion of Roman power over Macedon and Greece. Polybius' account covered the years 264 to 146 BC. The period 264 to 241, the time of the First Punic (Carthaginian) War, is in Polybius only a preamble. The core of the history is the second or so-called 'Hannibalic' War (after the Carthaginian general), from 218 to 202 BC. Polybius became friend and adviser of the Roman general Scipio, who finally destroyed Carthage in 146 BC, though by then Polybius had returned to his native Greece. The rise of Rome involved an irreversible shift of the world's political centre of gravity from Greece, Macedon and Asia Minor to Rome, and one of Polybius' objects was to educate his fellow Greeks in the realities of Roman world power.

Polybius was born in Megalopolis, in the Peloponnese, at the end of the third century BC (the exact date is not known). In 167 BC he, with other aristocratic Achaean Greeks, was transported as a hostage to Rome, where he became highly placed and influential. Like other famous exiled historians – Thucydides, Xenophon and, later, the Jewish historian Josephus – he benefited from the perspectives that exile provided. He returned to Greece towards the end of his life, winning the gratitude of his countrymen for the way he then acted a mediator with their Roman masters: when he died, in or around 118 BC, statues were erected in his honour. He was therefore not only a man of two worlds but, like other prominent ancient historians, a public man – a fact of whose advantages to the historian he was proudly, even arrogantly, convinced. Rather more rarely, his was a public career crowned with success.

As a historian, he is at first sight something of a hybrid. Most obviously, in his frequently proclaimed conception of the historian's task and methods, based on the notions of truth and usefulness rather than entertainment, he follows the example of Thucydides: rebuking an earlier historian, Phylarchus, for the imaginative embellishments of his narrative, designed to elicit the reader's sympathy and pity, Polybius declares that 'It is not a historian's business to startle his readers with sensational descriptions, nor should he try, as the tragic poets do, to represent speeches which might have been delivered [Polybius is notably restrained in his use of direct speech] . . . It is his task first and foremost to record with fidelity what actually happened' (II.56). Only by being true can history fulfil its mission of being useful. History is learning by vicarious experience, and its lessons are inferred from what has happened to provide guides for future conduct. Polybius resembles Herodotus more than Thucydides in the frequency with which he addresses the reader directly, but the effect is completely different: it is not Herodotus' confiding conversationality, but an insistent didacticism, a sleeve-plucking pedagogical concern that the lesson conveyed in his narrative shall not be overlooked.

But in speaking of Polybius' 'Thucydidean' insistence on the usefulness of history, we are ignoring what he chose to write about. Though the centre of Polybius' work is the narrative of a great war, the 'Hannibalic' War, his history as a whole has an almost Herodotean breadth and ambition of scale. Polybius has neither quite the epic quality nor the entertainment value of Herodotus, nor the brilliance of Thucydides – as indeed who else did? – but it is not inappropriate to speak of him as an heir of both. Polybius himself is scathing about merely monographic history (that is, history devoted to a single theme, in contrast to universal history), even though the history he places highest on the scale is political and military and based on travel and on direct or indirect eyewitness testimony. His insistence on scale reflects, for him, the conditions of a changed world. World history now has a central theme, the rise of Rome, and any history unrelated to this is necessarily petty and parochial. For Polybius, writers of such monographs are necessarily driven to picturesque adornments in order to disguise the essential poverty of their themes (VII.7). Polybius speaks of the unity of his theme and hence his history in terms clearly borrowed from Aristotle's conception of the unities in drama: 'How, when and why all the known parts of the world were brought under the domination of Rome is to be seen as a single action and a single spectacle, which has an identifiable beginning, a fixed duration and an acknowledged end' (III.1).

Like other ancient historians, then, Polybius has looked for and found the 'greatest' event of his day as the theme for his history. But this cannot be monographic, because its theatre is, to Polybius, no less than the known world. It is universal history – the first mention of a category that was to have much currency later, especially in the Middle Ages, when Christianity provided what was taken to be the universal theme.

My history possesses a certain distinctive quality which is related to the extraordinary spirit of the times in which we live, and it is this. Just as Fortune has steered almost all the affairs of the world in one direction and forced them to converge upon one and the same goal, so it is the task of the historian to present to his readers under one synoptical view the process by which she has accomplished this general design. It was this phenomenon above all which originally attracted my attention. (I.4)

Polybius was able to write a kind of universal history that was nonetheless eyewitness-based because his theme, which is the quite recent rise of Rome to world dominion, requires only a relatively short timescale. For example, unlike his successor Livy, who also traced the rise of Rome, he does not attempt to take his account back to the foundation of the city, and he is fairly dismissive about such antiquarian research (XII.25e, i). Rome's conquest of its Italian neighbours, which takes up the first part of Livy's work, is taken for granted, though the encounters of Rome with the Celtic Gauls are given more attention because Polybius regards them as a kind of training for Rome's later world role. But the actual rise of Rome to world power was, as Polybius stresses, in fact outstandingly swift – taking less than a century. Polybius' history, then, is able to be both comprehensive in scale yet to extend back little beyond living memory.

In speaking of Polybius, for convenience, as an heir of Herodotus and Thucydides, we are committing an act of drastic simplification and foreshortening. Herodotus and Thucydides had numerous heirs – more than we can know of. There were several attempts to continue Thucydides' history, one of which, by Xenophon, we have noted. Polybius, however, mentions Thucydides only once, and Herodotus not at all. But Polybius is in fact, for an ancient historian, exceptionally profuse in references to his predecessors – all of them now lost to us. As the convention was, his references to them are all critical – abusive would sometimes be the word – but they are highly valuable in lifting a corner on a lost and once clearly copious historiographical world. Querulous though Polybius' attitude towards it is, he clearly has an awareness of historical writing as a continuing and in a sense even cooperative activity: he remarks that he is confident that, should he die before completing it, his history would be taken up and completed by others. This is, of course, a way of saying that his theme is too great to be ignored, but it is also a tribute to the existence of a community of historians.

As his precursors in various ways, Polybius mentions Timaeus (at length in Book XII, and abusively), Ephorus, Phylarchus, Theopompus, Aratus, Philinus and the Roman historian, who nevertheless wrote in Greek, Fabius Pictor. All their works are now lost, but they are clearly for Polybius the historians in possession of the field of historiography that he intends to cultivate, and in some cases he is clearly following them – though critically. He is anxious to claim that none of them has properly seized the historiographical opportunities and that his own work is therefore a genuinely pioneering one: 'While various historians deal with isolated wars and certain of the subjects connected with them, nobody, so far as I am aware, has made any effort to examine the general and comprehensive scheme of events, when it began, whence it originated, and how it produced the final result' (I.4). We are hampered by knowing so relatively little about these writers, though Polybius is not our only source, but in general his claim seems justified. It is, however, all too easy to gain a false impression of ancient historiography by forgetting how much of it has failed to come down to us, which is why even Polybius' diatribes are useful. Herodotus, Thucydides and Xenophon have been preserved for us by the authority and popularity they early acquired, which ensured multiple copying and hence survival (though sometimes precarious) through the ensuing centuries. We can be reasonably sure that nothing of comparable quality has been lost – the ancient librarians showed good taste, in Alexandria and later in Byzantium – but among lesser historians substantial survival is the exception, complete extinction or survival at best in epitomes or collections of extracts being the norm. Copyists consulted the interests of readers, not those of posterity. Even Livy, who was to become Polybius' chief rival as historian of Rome, survives only in severely curtailed form.

The accidents – not entirely accidental – of extinction and survival may easily give us an oversimplified and distorted picture not only of the quantity but also of the kinds of history commonly written in the ancient world. Thucydides' example, a monograph of contemporary political and military history, was a powerful one and may have damaged the reputation of Herodotus, as did a waning sympathy with the folkloric elements which Herodotus carefully recorded. But Thucydides' history, itself not exempt from criticism in antiquity, was far from being the only kind for emulation. Even the assertion, based chiefly on the Thucydidean example, that ancient historiography made little use of documentary records is a significant overstatement in the case of Rome. Patriotism, devotion to Rome's ancient laws, and family pride (Fabius Pictor, one of the first historians of early Rome, was a member of the great Fabian clan) fostered antiquarian inquiries in a way only faintly foreshadowed in the Greek interest in genealogies and the foundation of cities and their local annals. We shall have to come back to this point later in considering Livy and his predecessors: the title of Livy's history, *Ab urbe condita*, 'From the foundation of the city', stakes out a bold and consciously un-Thucydidean claim.

We need some awareness of Polybius' predecessors if we are to try to assess his originality as well as his possible debts. In particular, we need to attend to the genre of 'universal history' and how far his predecessors anticipated Polybius in writing it. One of the matrices, as in the case we considered earlier of Herodotus' Ionian precursors, seems to have been the mixed genre, by our standards, of geography, ethnography, legend (origins) and history – we might now be tempted to use a term like 'area studies'. We are essentially concerned with the Mediterranean basin, and particularly with the western Mediterranean. Polybius knew, of course, that the Persian empire had extended far to the east and had had its own claims to be the world empire of its day, as Alexander's had been as its successor; but for him Asia had been, as we should say, 'done'. Rome, and Rome's expansion south and east, was where world history was now in the making.

Polybius scorned the efforts of his predecessors who had treated the western Mediterranean and Greece – Philinus, Fabius, Ephorus and Timaeus – for having failed to produce a unified history, offering instead separate accounts of adjacent countries and events, with no central organizing theme (I.4). Other historians received other dismissals – Phylarchus for picturesque invention, and Theopompus, a historian of Greece, for indecent language in describing the dissolute court of Macedon. Polybius was clearly a firm upholder of what came to be called 'the dignity of history', to use the English phrase coined in the eighteenth century (VIII.10). What earlier historians had failed above all to grasp was both the significance of the rise of Rome and the new historiographic opportunity it offered. Universal history has now for the first time become possible and Polybius intends to write it: 'From this point onwards history becomes an organic whole: the affairs of Italy and of Africa are connected with those of Asia and of Greece, and all events bear a relationship and contribute to a single end' (I.3). Polybius speaks like a historian with a vision, who has found in it his lifetime's work: 'Just as Fortune has steered almost all the affairs of the world in one direction and forced them to converge upon one and the same goal, so it is the task of the historian to present to his readers under one synoptical view the process by which she has accomplished this general design' (I.4). It is vital to the Greeks to understand what has happened, so that they may learn to live in a Roman world.

Polybius says that he takes as the starting point for his prefatory opening book the moment when the Romans first crossed the sea (to Sicily). He also hints at another reason, for this moment coincided with the point at which Timaeus' history leaves off, 'namely in the 129th Olympiad' (264–260 BC) (I.5), while the history proper begins at the time of the 140th Olympiad (220–216 BC). Polybius also marks the beginning of the establishment of Roman power in Italy by reference to Greek chronology, notably the conclusion of the Peloponnesian War and the decline of Sparta (I.6). The Romans, having hardened themselves in their local wars with the Samnites and the Italian Celts, were able to defend themselves against the invasion of King Pyrrhus of Epirus in 280 BC and subjugate Italy. Later (Book II) Polybius undertakes, rather uncharacteristically, a geographic and ethnographic digression on northern Italy and the cisalpine Gauls.

It was in Sicily that the Romans first came into conflict with the Carthaginians, and thus the detailed part of Polybius' narrative begins with the events of the First Punic War. He makes the usual claims for the greatness of his theme, in the length and vicissitudes of the Punic Wars and the pertinacity of the equally matched combatants. The two states 'were still [we shall have to return to the implied reservation conveyed by that last word later] at that time uncorrupted in their customs and institutions' and 'both received no more than moderate help from Fortune', another Polybian theme to be considered later (I.13). Polybius adds that the two historians who are regarded as authorities here, Fabius and Philinus, have both erred by exhibiting bias, towards Rome and Carthage respectively. Polybius aims to correct these biases: 'If history is deprived of the truth, we are left with nothing but an idle, unprofitable tale.' In fact it seems clear that he is following Fabius and Philinus closely (I.13, 14).

Although Rome's wars with Carthage form the narrative core of his work, Polybius is conscious of the responsibilities imposed by universal history: 'I . . . have set myself to describe what was happening in all the known parts of the world at once' (II.37). So he also deals with affairs in Greece, dominated at the time by two rival leagues of cities, the Achaean League and the Aetolian League (Polybius himself was an Achaean). Rome was drawn into Greek affairs through its invasion of Illyria, the latter being at the time in conflict with the Aetolians. With the ending of Book II Polybius has completed his preamble and is prepared for his grand theme: 'how, when and why all the known parts of the world were brought under the domination of Rome'.

One has to admire the ambition of Polybius' historical enterprise, and fundamentally he was right: the growth of Roman power was the salient fact of contemporary history. But it has to be admitted that Polybius' deliberate shifts of focus for brief periods, from Greece to Macedon, to Egypt to Spain, in order to fulfil his project of writing world history in an annalistic form, are disruptive and, for the non-expert, confusing. What really holds the work together, apart from the central narrative of the Punic Wars, is Polybius' authorial personality, marked by his recurring preoccupations with causality, comparison, constitutional factors, the lessons of experience, and the influence of fortune, which he groups together under the name of 'pragmatic history'. As historical narrative, one of its strengths – not surprising from the author of a lost book on tactics – is in its handling of military matters, which make up much of the whole. Here, unlike some other ancient historians, Polybius is precise and analytic, and inspires confidence. At the heart of the narrative of the Punic Wars is the protracted invasion of Italy by the Carthaginian general Hannibal, to whose extraordinary career and outstanding generalship Polybius pays full tribute.

As we have seen, Polybius follows Thucydides in his repudiation of history written merely to entertain. He is severe, for example, on Phylarchus for loading his narrative with picturesque imaginative detail:

In his eagerness to arouse the pity of his readers and enlist their sympathy through his story he introduces graphic scenes of women clinging to one another, tearing their hair and baring their breasts, and in addition he describes the tears and lamentations of men and women accompanied by their children and aged parents as they are led away into captivity. (II.56)

Polybius – prototype of the gruffness of the future professional historian – will follow only the austere path of historical truth. (There will presumably always be Phylarchans and Polybians.) We have an example of this austerity at a moment when it seems particularly repressive, in the account of Hannibal's army crossing the Alps, the most famous episode in the history (III.47–55). Picturesque historians, Polybius claims, contradict themselves by hailing Hannibal as a great and far-sighted general while being compelled by the requirements of dramatic narration to present the crossing as beset by appalling difficulties, and in order to resolve the contradiction they introduce the guidance of gods into 'what is supposed to be a factual history'. Polybius himself seems bent on vindicating Hannibal's calculation and on literally demythologizing his exploit. He has, he tells us, traversed the terrain to form his own impressions. But only a few paragraphs later we have tracks made impossible by an avalanche, pack animals falling over precipices, mules and horses stuck fast in snowdrifts – all the stage furniture of picturesque history. This is, perhaps, less a piece of backsliding in Polybius as a historian than testimony to the impossibility of presenting the passage of an army over the Alps, with or even without elephants, as a piece of ordinary military logistics: sometimes history just *is* picturesque.

The same is perhaps true of another moment of high drama, the Carthaginian capture of the city of Tarentum, to which Polybius does full justice: the conspirators inside the walls sending fire signals from an empty part of the city reserved (unusually, in antiquity, within the walls) as a cemetery, deserted but for the tombs; the Roman officers carousing; the entrance, in another part of the city, of a young man, known to the guards, with a dead boar, as though from a hunt, but followed by Carthaginian soldiers; the terror of the Tarentines and the massacre of the Romans (VIII.24–30). (Livy's account (XXXV.8–10), which makes more of the hunting ruse, is for once less dramatic.) Polybius could no doubt justify this by an interest in the stratagem employed, but stratagem and excitement happily coincide.

Excelling in the description of tactics and weaponry and their influence on military outcomes, Polybius devotes a whole section of his history (VI.19–42) to a systematic and extended description of the organization, tactics and equipment of the Roman army – a digression much admired in the Renaissance. His attention to relevant technicalities is also evident elsewhere, for example in his account of the naval warfare in Sicily, where he describes in detail the Roman invention of an offensive contraption known as 'the raven', attached to the ships' bows, and its decisive effects (I.22–3). He also praises the extraordinary ingenuity shown by the mathematician Archimedes in inventions designed to thwart the Roman besiegers of Syracuse (VIII.3–6). (It is, however, characteristically Livy's story which has Archimedes killed by a soldier when the city fell, while he was drawing diagrams in the dust.) Polybius' descriptions of the encounters of the Romans with the Celtic warriors of northern Italy offer a nice study in the diversity of weapons and tactics. The Roman javelin was effective against the Gauls partly because of the deficiencies of the Gallic shields:

The shield used by the Gauls does not cover the whole body, and so the tall stature of these naked troops made the missiles all the more likely to find their mark . . . The Roman shields, I should explain, were far better designed for defence, and so were their swords for attack, since the Gallic sword can only be used for cutting and not for thrusting. (II.30)

The Gallic swords had the further disadvantage of bending, and 'unless the men are given time to straighten them with the foot against the ground, the second blow has virtually no effect' (II.33). For the connoisseur of military hardware and its qualities, Polybius is exceptional in detail and clarity. His accounts of the crucial battles of Trasimene (217 BC) and, above all, Cannae (216 BC), by which Hannibal established his army in Italy, are convincing, without apparent exaggeration or rhetorical embellishment. It is noteworthy that while Polybius gives, as one might expect, the gist of the generals' addresses to the troops, he presents them in indirect speech. However, the number of speeches given verbatim increases towards the end of the history, when Polybius was much closer to events and even a participant in them.

Polybius' weakness, at least in our eyes, is not rhetorical over-elaboration but sententiousness. It being his creed that history must above all be written to be useful, he is as ready to adorn his campaign and battle narratives with useful tips as he is to offer advice on political matters. Sometimes, it has to be admitted, the result is platitudinous or even tautological. Polybius can assure us that human nature is fallible (II.7) and that we should not rely on a continuation of Fortune's favours (I.35), while for a general to be a coward or a fool is productive of damaging consequences. The tendency to tautology is exemplified in a claim such as that 'rashness, excessive audacity, blind impetuosity, vanity or foolish ambition' are exploitable weaknesses, where Polybius seems indifferent that the choice of nouns and adjectives, especially the latter, has already predetermined the outcome (III.81). More interesting and less trite are maxims which tempt one to apply the anachronistic adjective 'Machiavellian'. One such, for example, is the distinction Polybius makes between men who come to terms as a matter of yielding to circumstances and those who do so because their spirit is broken. The latter may be trusted, the former not (III.12). Another is the dictum that humanity after victory, as practised by Scipio, is good policy (X.36). More 'Machiavellian' in the vulgar sense is the endorsement of Scipio's employment of superstition to encourage his troops (X.11). Polybius' approval of the politic use of religion was more than occasional: it was one of his reasons for admiring the Roman state.

We have already seen that for Polybius history must above all be truthful, because only on the basis of truth can we distil from it the lessons of experience – painless ones, unlike those from direct experience – which constitute history's utility and justification. There are many references to Polybius' understanding of the historian's task scattered throughout his work, but the fullest account occurs in Book XII, which is wholly and almost obsessively devoted to castigating the errors of other historians, and above all of Timaeus. The attack contains a good deal that seems petty and pedantic, but the book as a whole gives a conspectus of contemporary attitudes to history, seen from Polybius' distinctive point of view. Timaeus, according to Polybius, is a man of book-learning and documents: 'he has quite neglected the business of making first-hand inquiries, which is the historian's most important duty.' Since the historian cannot be an eyewitness to everything, what remains is to question as many people as possible, and to exercise judgement on what he hears. Timaeus, however, is prey to accounts of dreams, prodigies and other superstitions. In setting down the speeches of generals and statesmen, he has first made up his mind what ought to have been said and has then composed imaginary speeches as though writing a rhetorical exercise: 'He has neither set down what was said nor the real sense of what was said.'

Because, in Athens, he had access to the works of other historians, Timaeus assumed he had the material for writing history. He belongs to the class of historians who haunt libraries and dwell among memoirs and records. Timaeus, according to Polybius, is – to invoke a term from Carlyle – the historian as 'Dryasdust'. Documentary sources are of some value, but wholly inadequate to write a history of recent events (XII.25e). For this one needs – enter Polybius – 'those who have played some part in affairs themselves'. Those without such experience, civil and military, are disabled from understanding affairs and hence incapable of instructing others in their lessons. 'It is in fact equally impossible for a man who has had no experience of action in the field to write well about military operations as it is for a man who has never engaged in political affairs and their attendant circumstances to write well on those topics' (XII.25h, g). The study of documents is therefore only third in importance to the historian, behind a knowledge of the relevant topography and practical experience. Timaeus, not an eyewitness to events, 'has preferred to employ his ears', which is the inferior way – and even in this Timaeus' method is inferior, since the ears may learn 'either by reading or by the examination of witnesses' and Timaeus has preferred the former (XII.27a). (It is interesting that Polybius regards reading as receiving information through the ears.) Polybius himself did not altogether disdain documents, such as the bronze tablet he had discovered which Hannibal himself had caused to be inscribed with the details of his forces: this was another form of eyewitness testimony, and 'I considered this to be an absolutely trustworthy piece of evidence' (III.33).

For Polybius, the relationship between history and the experienced man of affairs is reciprocal. The latter makes the best historian, but in turn the best-instructed man of action is one versed in the lessons of history. Polybius is one of the first we know of explicitly to regard history as a training for a political career, though he presents it as a common claim. All historians, he says, have asserted that 'the study of history is at once an education in the truest sense and a training for a political career, and that the most infallible, indeed the only, method of learning how to bear with dignity the vicissitudes of Fortune [*Tyche*] is to be reminded of the disasters suffered by others' (I.1).

In being concerned above all with the study of causes and their consequences, and with the rise of Rome as the central event to be explained, the two aspects of Polybius' historical writing, 'universal history' and 'pragmatic history', are not in conflict but complementary. It is only large-scale comparative history which affords the parallels on which the study of causes can be based (what J. S. Mill was to call 'the method of difference'): according to Polybius, 'by far the most important part of historical writing lies in the consideration of the consequences of events, their accompanying circumstances, and above all their causes ... All these tendencies can be recognized and understood from a general history', but not from monographic treatments (III.32).

Making a comparison with the method of observation in the practice of medicine, Polybius, in approaching the outbreak of the Second Punic War, draws distinctions between the beginning, the pretext and the cause. The cause is what shapes purposes and decisions, the beginning is what gives effect to them (III.6). In tracing causes, Polybius gives primacy, as one might expect him to, to the influence of laws and institutions, and above all, in the case of Rome, to its political constitution, to which a whole book is devoted (VI). In the long, hard struggle with the Carthaginians, the quality of the Romans – their patriotism, resolution and steadfastness – was tested to the utmost. It was moral qualities rather than material resources that, at critical moments, gave them ultimately the advantage. These qualities were fostered by Rome's laws and institutions. Roman customs were nurseries of public spirit – like, for example, the funeral rites and orations in honour of distinguished men: 'It would be hard to imagine a more impressive scene for a young man who aspires to win fame and to practise virtue' (VI.53–4). 'Virtue', as always in this way of thinking, means public virtue, the qualities proper to a man (*vir*). Polybius here goes on to tell the now well-known story of the heroic self-sacrifice of Horatius at the bridge, holding back Rome's enemies. This episode, also told by Livy (who makes Horatius survive), was used by Macaulay in his *Lays of Ancient Rome*. (This Horatius, Horatius Cocles, is not to be confused with Publius Horatius, whose story inspired Jacques-Louis David's painting *The Oath of the Horatii*.) As we have already seen, the manipulation of superstition through public religious rites was admired by Polybius: it was what 'holds the Roman state together', for the masses can be controlled only by mysterious terrors. Religious matters are treated in Rome 'with such solemnity and introduced so frequently both into public and into private life that nothing could exceed them in importance'. For Polybius the introduction of such beliefs and rites was a wise and politic measure by 'the ancients', and the moderns take great risks in rejecting them (VI.56).

The Roman state was tested almost to destruction by the great defeat by Hannibal at Cannae. It was, according to Polybius, only the 'peculiar virtues' of the Roman constitution that allowed it to surmount this crisis (III.118). The constitution was itself then in its prime, and according to Polybius 'a noble spectacle', while that of the Carthaginians was already declining (i.e. becoming more democratic). After Aristotle, and particularly with a strong revival from the Renaissance to the eighteenth century, Polybius was to become the foremost authority on the idea of the three types of constitution, and the cycle through which they pass as each pure form mutates into its corrupt counterpart (kingship into tyranny, aristocracy into oligarchy, democracy into mob rule) and then into its corrective opposite. Polybius subscribed to the view, particularly popular in England in the seventeenth and eighteenth centuries, that the cycle could be suspended, at least for a while, by a balance held between the three elements; for the English there was a particular resonance in the notion, proclaimed by Polybius, that the Romans arrived at their balance not by abstract reasoning but by trial and error (VI.10) – something the English Whig tradition never tired of ascribing to England, in contrast to the French.

Though, according to Polybius, the Roman constitution at the time of the Second Punic War was still at its optimum point, an inseparable feature of the concept of balance and its concomitant, corruption, was anxiety. Polybius sees no time limit to Rome's empire, but Rome's constitution 'will pass through a natural evolution to its decay', for 'each constitution possesses its own inherent and inseparable vice' (VI.9, 10). Before the lost battles of Trasimene and Cannae, says Polybius in one particularly pessimistic reference, the signs were already showing themselves in a demagogic tendency which led to the appointment of the wrong generals, a lurch toward an overbalance of the democratic element, and hence, 'the first step in the demoralization of the Roman people' (II.21).

Demagogy as a symptom of corruption and decline was directly linked to the theory of the cycle. The other main indication of both ills was a more traditional blight: luxury, often associated with foreign influences. As the Greeks had blamed the Persians, so the Romans, notably that stern moralist and historian of early Rome Cato the Censor, came to blame the Greeks. Polybius endorses this view. Luxury and ostentation are the price of conquest and empire, as when the riches of Macedon were brought to Rome (XXXI.25). Too much prosperity is dangerous. It is as though the old conception of hubris, which in Herodotus brought down King Croesus, byword for wealth, has acquired the anxieties of a rude agricultural community waxing rich and transforming itself through commerce and conquest. It was an anxiety which, derived by Renaissance historians, notably Machiavelli, from the Roman historians Sallust and Livy, passed on from them into the eighteenth century, where it was to inform Edward Gibbon's account of the fall of the Roman empire, the vast counterpart to Polybius' work two thousand years earlier. The corrupting political consequences of luxury and venality became a staple of opposition rhetoric in eighteenth-century England. It is again no accident that the period from the Renaissance to the eighteenth century was the heyday of Polybian influence on European historical and political thought.

Polybius, had he been able to reflect on it, would have ascribed Rome's fall not only to luxury, corruption and the loss of the balanced constitution, as did his remote successors, but, as he also ascribed Rome's rise, to Fortune. We can be sure of this, because there was no large-scale historical development which, for all his interest in mediating causes, he was not prepared to ascribe to Fortune. It was Fortune which decided on and brought about Rome's world dominion. Fortune 'steered almost all the affairs of the world in one direction and forced them to converge upon one and the same goal'. Rome triumphant was a tour de force on the part of Fortune, which had never before 'put on such a show-piece as that which we have witnessed in our own times', an achievement 'the most excellent and profitable to contemplate' (I.4). This sounds like the language of religion, and certainly Polybius seems to personify Fortune as a goddess. It was as such that she was hailed in the Middle Ages and the Renaissance. It is natural to speak of Polybius' 'Fortune' as a kind of divine providence. But elsewhere Polybius speaks of Fortune as one does of blind chance. Fortune disposes of events simply arbitrarily. Fortune as contingency is what is left as an explanation when human reason has exhausted its resources. It is reasonable, Polybius says, to attribute such unforeseeable contingencies 'to the work of a god or of chance' (XXXVI.17). But this conception of Fortune as contingency does not seem one that could plan and bring about such a long-term and immense phenomenon as the rise of Rome, which does not appear to defy human reason, since Polybius can enunciate its causes, and does, while admitting that at times the Punic Wars were a close-run thing. We have to conclude that Polybius' conception of Fortune, though certainly of great importance to him, was essentially incoherent.

Polybius wanted to instruct, not to charm, his readers. He stands among the historians who have tried to use history as the basis for what would later be called historical, or more frequently political, science. For such a science the eighteenth century, in particular, was to turn to Polybius himself. In his desire to find a central theme in history, in his relative detachment and concern with accuracy, as well as in his interest in drawing usable lessons from history, he is closer to being our intellectual contemporary than are the great Roman historians who came after him, Sallust and Livy, whose focus was moral rather than what Polybius called pragmatic. This perhaps benefits him less than one might expect among modern readers, compared with the passionate, even agonized, involvement in their own times of other ancient historians, with whom we can empathize. We have our own, more recent, instructors in the lessons of history: Machiavelli, Montesquieu, Hume, Henry Adams. But Polybius is their precursor. In embodying his concerns in a massive account of the central theme of his time, the rise of Rome, he made enduringly for himself a prominent and distinctive role in the history of historiography.

5

Sallust: A City for Sale

Gaius Sallustius Crispus (Sallust) wrote the works on which his reputation rests in the early 40s BC. The periods on which he wrote were recent. His fame rests on two short monographs of near-contemporary history; he also wrote a general history covering a decade of the 70s and 60s BC, but only fragments survive. In the ancient world and in the Middle Ages, Sallust was highly regarded both for the content of his histories and for his famously economical style, and he has been ever since. Tacitus admired him, as Sallust himself admired Thucydides, and St Augustine quoted him. His is an extraordinary reputation to rest on two short monographs on events that were arguably not of the first importance.

One was a colonial war in North Africa against the Numidian king Jugurtha at the end of the second century BC. Sallust makes the usual claim for his subject's importance – it marked, he says, the beginning of civil strife in the Roman world – but this is special pleading: the fame of the Jurgurthine War owes more to Sallust than his to it; it seems likely he was drawn to the subject because he himself had been governor of Numidia half a century later. His other subject, the conspiracy of Catiline to overthrow the consular authority in Rome by force (65–62 BC) was certainly noteworthy and has been immortalized not only by Sallust but also in four celebrated orations by Cicero, who was a consul during the critical period. Sallust claims the conspiracy represented a threat without parallel to the Roman republic, and was an enterprise of unprecedented wickedness and criminality. Certainly had it succeeded the consequences would have been far-reaching; it was a symptom of the instability and lawlessness which several times plunged Rome into civil war in the first century BC.

Sallust was himself a politician in that insecure world. The Jugurthine War was still within easy living memory when he was a young man; Catiline's conspiracy was a contemporary event, which Sallust described twenty years afterwards. Sallust was a client of Julius Caesar, who was suspected, probably unjustly, of complicity in the plot and it has been claimed, though without much credence, that *The Conspiracy of Catiline* was a propagandist account to exonerate Caesar. Though Sallust produced two case studies, rather than a continuous account, his works introduce the major figures in the political scene of the first half of the first century: the two political adventurers Marius and Sulla, who successively mastered Rome in its early decades, and conducted ruthless massacres and proscriptions (outlawing of political opponents). Both made their reputations in the Jugurthine War, and Sallust draws portraits of both, admiring their qualities and deploring their subsequent careers. There is no intimate portrait of Cicero, or of Pompey the Great, who is a peripheral figure in the *Catiline*, but Caesar is given a notable speech and a eulogy.

At the heart of the problem of the Roman state in the first century, as its contemporary historians generally recognized, was the growth of a plutocracy, fattened on the proceeds of conquest, which engrossed much of the land of Italy and farmed it with slave labour. This, and the length of service far from Rome which the empire required, caused a breakdown of the old military system of a citizen militia whose members in theory returned to their farms at the end of their service. Marius had recognized the new reality by greatly reducing the property qualification for service, creating, in effect, a largely professionalized army, dependent on its commanders for procuring its pay and pensions. This was realistic, but had dire consequences as the provincial governors who commanded large armies became semi-independent warlords whose troops' loyalty was to them rather than to the republic. Marius, Sulla and subsequently Caesar conducted what were in effect military takeovers, and Pompey threatened to do the same. At the same time, a significant political fissure, much to the fore in Sallust's account of his times, became evident between the old senatorial elite, determined to cling to its privileges and monopolize the greater offices of state, and 'new men' – Marius was the archetype – who won their way by ability and in some cases achieved great wealth, and who resented the arrogance of the old nobility.

Sallust, who in 52 BC became a tribune of the plebs, their official representative and a high authority, very clearly gave his sympathies to the new men and is eloquent in condemnations – in speeches, notably by Marius (*Jugurthine War*, 85.10–48), and in his own person – of the grasping selfishness of the traditional elite. His own official career seems to have been decidedly shady, which constitutes an ironic comment on his frequent and vehement denunciations of avarice and the low standard of public life: he was expelled from the Senate in 50 BC for alleged immorality, but Caesar supported his career. After serving Caesar as an officer in the civil war, in 45 BC Sallust was installed by him as governor of Numidia, where he became notorious for extortion. He retired from politics, after Caesar's murder, a very rich man. In his prefaces he extols the life of retirement and rejoices in his escape from the envy, backbiting and servility of public life. The true life of man – there is a Stoic or perhaps Platonic high-mindedness on display here – is the cultivation of one's intellectual powers and the pursuit of a worthy fame. The depiction of great deeds in writing history belongs to the best life, no less than the performance of them. His self-congratulation on his present tranquillity of mind, and on his impartial detachment and happiness at having escaped the sordid conditions of political advancement in a corrupted political state, may express a genuine relief – now he was rich – but at times one is driven to suspect the bitterness or at least ambivalence of the superseded politician in his denunciations.

Sallust shares with other contemporaries a deep pessimism: Roman public morality is in steep decline. He clearly admires some of the traditionalist attitudes associated with Cato the Censor (below, pp. 91–2), and he gives an effective speech very much in that vein to Cato's great-grandson of the same name (*Catiline*, 52.8–53.4). Sallust became a highly influential critic of luxury and avarice as the vices which had undermined the old Roman virtues of austerity and integrity, speaking disapprovingly, for example, of Asiatic indulgences and a taste, corrupting to the Roman soldiery, for statues, pictures and embossed plate (*Catiline*, 10.6); the reference to embossed plate carries conviction. He often focuses on something he must have known very well: the characters and weaknesses, especially the vulnerability to bribery, of public men. He shares the typical idealization of ancestral Roman public virtue; its decline is a recent and a humiliating contrast. His characterizations of the new manners are generally pointed and precise, even if surely exaggerated. His two monographs are centred on two rather different, though related, kinds of political vice, which are represented as virtually omnipresent: venality in *The Jugurthine War*, unprincipled ambition as a form of greed in the *Catiline*.

The Jugurthine War has two aspects: the overt and military, and the covert workings of political intrigue; it is the latter which is usually decisive, up to and including the capture, by treachery, of Jugurtha which brings the war to an end. Below the overt military operations, in which the Romans generally prevail, forcing the Numidians to adopt hit-and-run tactics in a manner characteristic of colonial wars, is a second, less visible, contest, nicely poised because of the venality of Roman senators and Numidian courtiers alike. In Sallust's account, the course of events is often dictated by who has successfully bribed whom: it is a world in which the corruption of individuals goes far towards controlling public affairs. Jugurtha, a client king whose methods of obtaining the throne have discredited him in Rome, devotes himself with considerable success to suborning the Senate by bribery and bringing a number of senators to serve his interests. Sallust's comment is 'The public good, as so often happens, was sacrificed to private interests' (*Jugurthine War*, 25.5). Meanwhile the Roman commanders sent to bring Jugurtha to heel bribe his aides and allies to betray him. But they themselves are not all immune. Of the consul sent to command the army Sallust characteristically comments that his good qualities were made useless by his avarice. Bribed, he agrees to a truce (28.2).

Sallust seems to choose as his spokesman at this point a tribune-elect, Gaius Memmius, a well-known opponent of the nobility, to whom he attributes a speech which Sallust says, in his habitual formula, 'ran somewhat as follows'. Denouncing the abuses committed by the clique of nobles to secure their own position, Memmius makes their corruption the crux of his attack:

What manner of men are they who have made themselves rulers of the state? They are evildoers whose hands are red with blood. Covetous beyond measure, and stained with guilt, they are none the less swollen with pride, and there is nothing that they will not sell: honour, reputation, natural affection, every virtue indeed – as well as every vice – is to them a source of profit. (31.16)

Memmius' speech reflects the enduring bitterness left by the events of the 130s and 120s BC, when the tribunes of the plebs Tiberius and Gaius Gracchus, having introduced radical measures to benefit the poor, were successively murdered – events to which Memmius clearly refers. It is likely to strike the reader that the passion he expends on the ostensible issue, how Jugurtha was to be treated, is excessive, but it is explained by the climate of intense hostility to the nobles. Sallust himself attributes the mob's animosity towards Jugurtha to class hatred rather than patriotism. This mutual political hatred is, as it were, the subplot of *The Jugurthine War*. Sallust traces it to the defeat of Carthage (146 BC). With no external threat, a salutary restraint was removed. Civil strife was the product of peace and prosperity:

The division of the Roman state into warring factions, with all its attendant vices, had originated some years before, as a result of peace and of that material prosperity which men regard as the greatest blessing. Down to the destruction of Carthage the people and the Senate shared the government peaceably and with due restraint, and the citizens did not compete for glory or power; fear of its enemies preserved the good morals of the state. But when the people were relieved of this fear, the favourite vices of prosperity – licence and pride – appeared as a natural consequence. Thus the peace and quiet, which they had longed for in time of adversity proved, when they obtained it, to be even more grievous and bitter than the adversity. (41.5)

The nobles abused their power, the people their liberty, 'every man snatching and seizing what he could for himself'. But the nobility held the advantage: 'The people were burdened with military service while the spoils of war were snatched by the generals.' However, when the day came 'when noblemen rose to power who preferred true glory to unjust dominion: then the state was shaken to its foundations by civil strife, as by an earthquake' (41.5); Sallust is referring to the Gracchi, murdered by the oligarchs. By their political murders and banishments, the intransigent nobles condemned themselves to live in fear. The resort to extremes, the reader is led to feel, is irreversible; one is reminded, perhaps rightly, of Thucydides' account of the breakdown of civil order in Corcyra.

As a sequel to Memmius' speech, Jugurtha – who has meanwhile been bribing the Roman officers left in charge in Numidia – is summoned to Rome. There he is protected from the fury of the people by one of the tribunes, whom he has bought. Ordered out of Rome by the Senate, he is made to exclaim apocalyptically, as he turns and looks back at the city, 'Yonder is a city put up for sale and its days are numbered if it finds a buyer' (37.3).

The campaign against Jugurtha in Numidia is dominated, according to Sallust, by the same motive: cupidity. The Roman commander, Aulus Albinus, chooses to besiege the town where Jugurtha's treasury was kept – not an unreasonable military move, one would have thought. Jugurtha, however, succeeds in corrupting Roman officers, even down to centurions, and this, by promoting treachery in the army, gives him a victory. The new consul sent to command in Numidia, Metellus, is unbribable, to Jugurtha's concerned astonishment. (The reader shares his surprise.) Jugurtha sends envoys on a mission of corruption, but the biter is bit when Metellus turns them by his inducements. Metellus is superseded by Marius, elected consul in 107 BC; he is an able commander, lowly born and intensely ambitious. Sallust, who had earlier praised his good qualities (63.6), deplores the arrogance which grows on him as consul, but gives him, nonetheless, one of the most effective speeches in *The Jurgurthine War* (85.10–48), contrasting his own merits and achievements with the inherited privileges of men of family, and presenting himself as a plain, blunt man of the people, without superficial elegancies:

I cannot, to justify your confidence in me, point to the portraits, triumphs and consulships of my ancestors. But if need be I can show spears, a banner, medals, and other military honours, to say nothing of the scars on my body – all of them in front. These are my family portraits, these my title of nobility, one not bequeathed to me, as theirs were to them, but won at the cost of countless trials and perils.

My words are not carefully chosen. I attach no importance to such artifices, of which true merit stands in no need, since it is plainly visible to all. It is my adversaries who require oratorical skill to help them cover up their turpitude. Nor have I studied Greek literature; I had no interest in a branch of learning which did nothing to improve the character of its professors . . . They call me vulgar and unpolished because I do not know how to put on an elegant dinner and do not have actors at my table or keep a cook who has cost me more than my farm overseer . . .

Marius was a successful general in Numidia, but the final act – appropriately – was a result of treachery and the scheming of Marius' deputy, Sulla. Jugurtha's ally, the Moorish king Bocchus, has second thoughts after two defeats. Sallust cannot resist adding 'perhaps, too, he sought the advice of some friends whom Jugurtha had omitted to bribe' (103.1). Bocchus betrays Jugurtha, who is taken captive to Rome, appearing in the triumph awarded to Marius.

In the decades following the conclusion of the Jugurthine War in 105 BC, the political situation in Rome markedly deteriorated as Marius and Sulla fought their bloody political and military battle for supremacy. This accounted for the intensely nervous political climate in which Catiline, a ruined aristocrat and would-be demagogue, plotted to overthrow the consuls and make himself and his followers all-powerful. The projected coup was brewing over several years (66–62 BC) – Sallust has been accused of some chronological inaccuracy here – before matters came to a head with a rising in central Italy led by one of Catiline's supporters in 63 BC.

For Sallust *The Conspiracy of Catiline* was another study in the corruption of Roman public life. Here the keynote is not venality, though Catiline and his friends are clearly greedy and instigated to revolt by financial ruin brought on by their extravagances (there is a practical role for 'luxury' here). The central impulse (for, being out of office, they have nothing to sell) is inordinate, unprincipled and lawless ambition. Ambition, unlike avarice, and venality, is not seen as ignoble in itself, but perverted to pure selfishness and loosed from all restraint it represents the greatest possible danger to the state.

As so often in Roman polemic and diagnosis, Sallust's denunciation is thrown into relief by idealization of the past. The republic, in its early days, according to him, had advanced with such extraordinary rapidity because, relieved from the constraint represented by a jealous monarch, men burned to distinguish themselves and acquire glory in the service of the state (*Catiline*, 7.4). (This argument was to become popular in the Renaissance.) Avarice was almost unknown, and virtue was held in high esteem. Frugality and piety were the norms. Such virtue brought its rewards in the form of conquests, culminating in the destruction of Rome's great rival, Carthage. But then 'fortune turned unkind' and converted Rome's success into disaster. Leisure and riches were fatal:

Growing love of money and the lust for power which followed it engendered every kind of evil. Avarice destroyed honour, integrity and every other virtue, and instead taught men to be proud and cruel, to neglect religion and to hold nothing too sacred to sell ... Rome changed: her government, once so just and admirable, became harsh and unendurable. (10.6)

Sulla's dictatorship gave licence to robbery and pillage. Wealth became everything:

As soon as wealth came to be a mark of distinction and an easy way to renown, military commands, and political power, virtue began to decline. Poverty was now looked on as a disgrace and a blameless life as a sign of ill-nature. Riches made the younger generation a prey to luxury, avarice and pride. Squandering with one hand what they grabbed with the other, they set small value on their own property while they coveted that of others. Honour and modesty, all laws divine and human, were alike disregarded in a spirit of recklessness and intemperance. (13.5)

Avarice and ambition became blended, and the greed of Catiline and his followers, whetted by luxury, assumed a directly political form. Catiline himself is presented as a study in frustrated ambition perverted to political crime.

His associates are, according to Sallust, a rabble of cut-throats, perjurers, bankrupt gamblers and spendthrifts – Sallust gives a list of Catiline's supporters in the Senate, who are not excluded from these categories. Catiline's influence is fatal even to the innocent. He was said to have killed his own son to curry favour with his mistress and to be marked with the signs of a terrible remorse; one is tempted, anachronistically, to speak of the portrait as Miltonic or Byronic:

His unclean mind, hating god and fellow man alike, could find rest neither waking nor sleeping; so cruelly did remorse torture his frenzied soul. His complexion was pallid, his eyes hideous, his gait now hurried and now slow. Face and expression plainly marked him as a man distraught. (16.4)

The absence of troops from Italy, because they were serving under Pompey in the East, and the presence of many discontented veterans seem to give Catiline his chance. Aristocratic Roman youths are drawn to him and into his conspiracy. He makes a speech in which, by emphasizing the narrowness of the oligarchic clique which monopolizes power (20.12), he represents his followers as the poor and dispossessed, 'whether our birth be noble or base', and promises his supporters everything from magistracies and priesthoods to cancellation of debts. Sallust makes amply clear the eclectic nature of Catiline's following: poor men and bankrupt aristocrats, Sulla's discontented veterans and his victims. In central Italy Catiline's lieutenant, Manlius, recruits the local brigands, while sons of noble families are detailed to murder their fathers (43.2). The city populace of Rome, Sallust suggests, were favourably disposed to anything promising a riot (39.5).

The last part of the *Catiline* is concerned with discussion of the punishment of the plotters when they had been rounded up. It chiefly takes the form of two speeches, respectively urging banishment and death, the first from Julius Caesar and the second from Marcus Cato, great-grandson of the censor. This gives Sallust the opportunity for a final set of references to the loss of ancestral virtues. Interestingly, he then singles out among the factors which had made Rome great 'the pre-eminent merit of a few citizens' (54.3). Rome was living now on the capital their actions had accumulated for it, and it was this alone which had so far saved it from the consequences of the poor quality of its modern generals and magistrates. In their contrasting but equally admirable qualities, the two speakers, Caesar and Cato, were notable exceptions to this. Sallust was a friend and supporter of Caesar, and owed him much; the encomium he pronounces is no surprise. In that of Cato, however, Sallust seems to pay his respects to old Roman austerity, of which the lavishly extravagant and manifestly ambitious Caesar was hardly an exemplar (53.5). It may be that in this way Sallust is hinting that Rome needs new men of splendid abilities, like Caesar, but also the ballast of old Roman virtues.

In focusing on the quality of public men, despite the disgust with the present and the seductions of the legends of republican virtue which may have led him to produce an overdrawn contrast, Sallust was displaying a characteristic hard-headedness, welcome compared with clichés (we shall find them in Livy) about the morality-sapping cultural miasma diffused by Greek bric-a-brac and effeminate Asiatic tastes. One does not always have to trust his judgement, of course, though it is not implausible that North African courtly intrigues, and for that matter those of the Roman Senate, could be notably corrupt. Sallust's attribution, in *The Jugurthine War*, of almost every action to avarice has an air of obsessiveness. But there is more to it than that. It is interesting that two very different sets of people, the courtiers of a semi-barbarian North African monarch and (many) Roman senators, are under the sway of the same passion of avarice. This might seem an example of the idea of a more or less uniform human nature spoken of by Thucydides and Polybius, but it cannot be, because in Sallust, as later in Livy, the Romans of former times were not like that at all. Whence, then, the modern similarity? Sallust does not try to unpack the paradox, but it is easy to imagine an answer which, accepting Sallust's versions of the Romans, both ancient and modern, invokes a kind of inverse relationship between a sense of public duty and selfish individualism. If that is accepted, then the individualism (venality) of the barbarian and the senator, though contemporary, actually belong to different historical epochs. The former, the argument assumes, has never had a sense of the *res publica* and its claims on him (though one might have thought personal loyalty might perform the same function). However, as Sallust says, the individualism of the corrupted Roman belongs to a society in which the hold of public duty and an idea of the republic has been eroded by an influx of new wealth and the unprincipled avarice it has fostered.

Sallust does not extend his analysis to barbarian corruptibility: barbarians are like that – unreliable – just as they fight or run away as seems expedient. (Sallust's geographical and ethnographical 'digression' on Africa is brief and jejune) (17.4–19.1.) Barbarians, one might say – Sallust cannot – are like the rabble Livy would later describe as making up the early population of Rome before Romulus and Numa forged them into a polity and gave them laws and a collective idea of the sacred (below, pp. 106–7). Corruption, then, is not just a perennial tendency of human nature but a cultural phenomenon and, when exemplified by Rome, a historical one. Sallust is here only a step away from something like a conception of cultural history – the conception which the great scholar Erich Auerbach claimed was precluded by the moralism of ancient historiography (*Mimesis: The Representation of Reality in Western Literature*, 1953). Of course a step can be a long one, and it is not altogether clear whether the example offered by Sallust's argument, or one might say his half-argument, tells for or against Auerbach's denial to the Romans of a sense of cultural change. Sallust goes halfway, but only halfway, towards it. However, it does not seem to be *moralism* which is closing off the possibility; rather, this is what is opening it up.

Sallust is a master of economical, lucid and dramatic narrative, and of acid if exaggerated comment. He has perhaps some of the weaknesses of the disillusioned retired politician – though prolixity is not one of them – embittered, it may be, despite his protestations, at the ending of his career. But he has eminently the strengths of the breed, above all a robust understanding of the motives of political men and their often disingenuous manipulation of political rhetoric. His denunciations of modern Roman corruption are powerfully impressive, and must surely have influenced Livy. His diatribes are part of the background to – and sometimes emerge explicitly in – the copious political literature devoted to luxury and the loss of public spirit from the Renaissance to the eighteenth century.

6

Livy: *From the Foundation of the City*

It was a practice of the ancient Greeks and Romans to ascribe their distinctive institutions to the wisdom of a founder, perhaps with divine guidance: Lycurgus in Sparta, Solon in Athens, Romulus and his supposed successor Numa in Rome. At one time Alfred the Great was credited with this role in England, inventing, among other meritorious institutions, the jury and the University of Oxford. But the Romans added something more. It is the conception of an accretive constitution, ancient and continuous, but modified piecemeal over a long period, rather as the English, in the nineteenth century, prided themselves as their predecessors had done, on the antiquity and continuity of their constitution; one of its great merits was its gradual evolution, from precedent to precedent.

In Rome, a profound institutional conservatism came to be accompanied by a recognition of a certain desirable pragmatism and flexibility, mediating between the cherished inheritance bequeathed from the past and the needs and demands of the present. The Romans never developed this as a guiding idea to the pitch of self-consciousness and sophistication it acquired in England; in fact there was no word for it. It is implied, however, in the conjunction of two ideas they undoubtedly did have: respect for ancestral custom, the old Roman way, and moderation or conciliation, which implied flexibility – making necessary and timely concessions to preserve the unity, the concord, between the different orders of society. A particular example which clearly mattered to Livy was the erosion, over time and accompanied by much ill-feeling and resistance, of the rule that only members of the hereditary senatorial order, the patricians, were eligible for the supreme executive posts, the two annual consulships, and other offices. The Romans came to realize, and Livy illustrated it, that their constitution had to be understood not just as a single foundational act, like that of Lycurgus in Sparta, but historically. As Polybius had put it, the Romans owed their constitution not to theory but to experience. They had arrived at the result achieved by the power of reasoning by the great Spartan legislator Lycurgus, but the Romans 'did not do so by means of abstract reasoning, but rather through the lessons learned from many struggles and difficulties; and finally, by always choosing the better course in the light of experience acquired from disasters' (Polybius, VI.10).

It is dangerous to generalize about ancient historiography, because so much of it is lost altogether, or known only by repute or fragmentarily, but it does seem that the Romans developed an attitude to their history which gave it, and particularly its earliest and most obscure years, a more profound significance than other peoples and cities attributed to their annals and foundation myths. With the growth of Rome's power, they came to dwell on the contrast between the humble beginnings of the city spoken of by the tradition – the huts of the shepherds clustering on the Roman hills in the eighth century BC and the rabble of runaways and vagabonds with whom Romulus augmented his foundation – and the world empire which Rome had won by the middle of the second century BC. Even Athens, the chief imperialist power of fifth-century Greece, had achieved no such dizzying eminence. Only the empire of Alexander did so (which drew Livy into an uncharacteristic digression: would the Romans have beaten him? (IX.17–10)); but Alexander's empire was an intensely personal achievement, and as rapid in its rise as in its dissolution. It was certainly not the product of qualities nurtured by a long tradition, or of a gradual, hard-won expansion, like that which, over some centuries, had made Rome master first of its immediate vicinity, then of central Italy and the whole Italian peninsula, and then, by victory in the long-drawn-out wars with Carthage, over the western Mediterranean, and finally over the western part of Alexander's empire, in Macedon, Greece and the Near East. This is the story which, with one hiatus, the extant books of Livy's history tell, up to the middle of the second century BC. By this time Rome's empire was a subject of awestruck contemplation, as it was still more in Livy's own time, the second half of the first century BC, the Age of Augustus.

Polybius, over a century earlier, had recognized the power of Rome as the central fact of the contemporary world, and other Greeks had written on Roman history, but for a Roman there was obviously in it also an invitation to patriotic pride, often accompanied by a nervous anxiety. Rome's achievement fostered a retrospective piety towards the ancient Roman virtues to which it was ascribed, but by the first century, when Livy was writing his history (from 30 BC onward), it had come to seem that there was a dreadful paradox in Rome's success: the qualities which had procured it had been subverted by the wealth and ease which it had brought.

This combination of pride and pessimism which is manifest in Livy is also evident in the work of his contemporaries the Augustan poets Virgil and Horace. The Romans were a great people, who had deserved their extraordinary fortune and perhaps the divine favour which had permitted it, but – the theme so strongly stressed by Sallust – the modern Romans were not the men their forebears had been. We have seen, in Polybius, what became commonplaces about the corruptive effect of luxury, but for a Roman a century and more later it was more than a sociological truth or warning; it had become a source of profound misgiving as well as of rhetorical denunciation.

A number of cultural streams originally fed the ancient tendency to exalt the past over the present and to think of change as degenerative. Polybius, as we have seen, manufactured out of Aristotle's typology of constitutions, in which each form had its corrupt antitype, a theory of constitutional change in which each successful form was essentially unstable, though the Roman constitution was best able to stave off eventual inevitable degeneration. But there was also a general tendency to exalt the past: Homer's heroes were stronger than four modern men. One of the chief impulses to the writing of history was, as Herodotus says (above, p. 11), to preserve the great deeds of earlier generations, which thereafter could be invoked for encouragement and emulation, as Xenophon's beleaguered army was reminded of the Greeks' victories over the Persians. Similar invocations of Roman achievements are, in Livy, a staple of the general's address of encouragement to his troops before battle. But the element of pessimism in

Roman pride had been less specific among the Greeks, as a sense, as we find it in Herodotus and Thucydides, of the fragility of good fortune and greatness, expressed in the formula of hubris followed by nemesis. We have seen earlier, too, the self-congratulatory contrast of Greek freedom, frugality and hardihood and Persian luxury, effeminacy and servility. But, as the Roman imperium extended to the Near East, Alexander was sometimes instanced as an example of the contagious nature of Asiatic luxury, notably by Livy. In luxury lay the seeds of corruption, and in corruption the seeds of downfall. In Livy, and in Sallust before him, the question of moral fibre, nurtured by war, weakened by peace and ease, became the core of Roman history.

The preoccupation with Roman virtue and the piety towards longstanding Roman institutions and traditions, whose loss Livy deplores, expressed a sense of present malaise, but they also constituted a powerful impulse directing attention to the earliest centuries of Roman history, when Rome's institutional foundations were laid and the Roman qualities of character were in their original purity. This attention focused on traditions, on legends of patriotic deeds, on foundation myths, and on what survived of records and annals: in short, it led to historical research and writing in the form of antiquarianism. The Greek cities had had their myths of divine or heroic foundation and their legendary genealogies, and some of their citizens had compiled annals. Hellanicus, in the fifth century BC, had written a general account of the foundation of the greatest cities, and apparently provided the first history of early Athens. Polybius identified this as one of the types of history, but also distinguished such parochialism from his own practice of universal history. Only in the case of Rome, he realized, did city-state history and universal history in the long run coincide. By the second century BC nothing that could be known about Rome was merely parochial, and antiquarians who began to study the early history of the city could presumably think of this as no petty task.

Livy tells us that most of the early records were destroyed by a catastrophic fire at the time of the city's occupation by the Gauls in 386 BC. The importance of this has been seen as debatable, but early records certainly seem to have been sparse. Livy is to a considerable extent aware of the fragility of the evidential basis for his accounts of the earliest centuries, and unapologetic about it. They have, he says, 'more of the charm of poetry than of sound historical record' (I.1), but he retells the legends with gusto, though with periodic expressions of scepticism and reluctance to choose between rival versions. In writing the early history of the city he had a number of precursors, on whom he drew, but most wrote near his own times. Livy's literary gifts and the survival of approximately a quarter of his immense history of Rome from the conventional date of the foundation of the city (753 BC in the Christian calendar) down to his own day, including the first ten books, have made his *the* history of early Rome for subsequent generations. (Livy's work is conventionally divided into units of ten books, known as 'decades'.)

Greek historians besides Polybius had written on the history of Rome, including its earliest period, though mostly not exclusively. One of these was Polybius' whipping-boy Timaeus, and his work would have been available to Roman historians. A Greek contemporary of Livy, Diodorus of Sicily, included Rome in his universal history, which he said should include the earliest traditions of peoples. Another Greek contemporary, Dionysius of Halicarnassus, wrote specifically on Rome. His *Roman Antiquities*, of which half survives, traced Rome's rise from its mythological origins, stressing the allegedly Greek character of the Romans.

Among Roman authors, the first prose historian of Rome was Fabius Pictor – frequently cited, not always uncritically, by Livy. Fabius Pictor wrote in Greek, though he came of a highly distinguished Roman family, the Fabii. Livy instanced him as an example of the distorting effect of family pride among historians. He flourished towards the end of the third century BC, and was a senator and perhaps a pontiff or chief priest. The Roman priesthood was not a caste set apart, but consisted of representatives of aristocratic families, qualified to perform ritual sacrifices. His history, now lost, traced the development of Rome from its supposed origins to his own day, and it is likely that a considerable part is preserved in substance in Livy and other historians. In his possible pontificate, and his apparently obtrusive family pride, we have two of the kinds of source in which facts and traditions from Rome's early history were preserved.

It was the custom each year for the pontiffs to have a record of events inscribed on a publicly displayed whitened board. When the board was wiped for another year, a transcription was made. At the end of the second century BC the pontifical annals were published as a chronicle, which seems to have run from around 400 BC, to which accounts purporting to cover the foundation of the city and its early history had been added. It is not known exactly what it contained. Another publication, of the proceedings of the Senate, was produced from the first century BC, as were records of notable speeches.

Another source of recording was the family pride of the most eminent Roman clans. Rome was a society much given to commemoration. We have seen (above, p. 79) Polybius' approval of the funeral orations in honour of distinguished men, as a nursery of civic virtue. Roman religion was domestic as well as civic, akin to ancestor worship; ancestral busts were preserved, and their features would have been familiar to their descendants. Some families like the Fabii and the Claudii had been long prominent in the republic. Other possible sources of this kind, so-called 'banquet songs', have been thought to commemorate notable men and deeds, and to have been used by probably the first Roman historian to write in Latin, Marcus Cato – Cato the Censor – of whom Livy's history provides a vivid portrait, as also does Plutarch later. Cato, though a plebeian, was consul in 195 BC. His frugality and austerity, his intense conservatism and his hostility to foreign ways made him an archetypal figure in Roman public memory. His *Origins*, which has survived only very fragmentarily, included a treatment of Roman history from its foundation legends to the Second Punic War.

Two other authors of histories of early Rome both wrote their narratives in verse: Ennius, who in the second century BC wrote eighteen books of annals from the foundation, and Varro, writing in the first century BC, whose history is completely lost. Both are sometimes cited as authorities. For an ancient historian, Livy is fairly profuse in naming his sources, because he wants to explain his difficulties in deciding between them, which often he does not. Apart from Fabius and Cato, he mentions an author of the second century from another distinguished family, Calpurnius Piso, and, nearer to his own time, Cornelius Nepos and Licinius Macer. The latter is mentioned particularly because of his discovery of a list of early magistrates on linen rolls held in the temple of Jupiter Moneta, running from around 445 BC.

Livy himself was essentially a literary artist applying himself to history, not an antiquarian scholar. The accounts of the first three centuries from the foundation, including the expulsion of the kings and the establishment of the republic, conventionally dated to 509 BC, with which Livy begins his second book, are essentially legendary, though they may have a substratum of fact preserved in tradition. As history, thanks to the work of his predecessors, we can begin to have more confidence in Livy's work from around the middle of the fifth century.

Livy's history, *From the Foundation of the City* (*Ab urbe condita*), was written in 142 books, of which 35 survive. Understandably, the early books cover much longer periods than those which follow, so that I–X cover almost four hundred years, down to the beginning of the third century, and deal, after the foundational and legendary period, with the establishment of Roman power in central Italy. The next books we have (XXI–XXX), dealing with the Second Punic War, cover only twenty-three years, and the remaining books extant, recounting the establishment of the Roman imperium in the eastern Mediterranean (XXXI–XLV), take fifteen books to narrate the events of only thirty-three years. The work as we have it ends in 167 BC, over a hundred years before Livy's own lifetime. The size of the whole work, including what is lost, is awesome. What survives is around two thousand pages.

It was the early books which made the greatest impression on subsequent generations. For the books on the Hannibalic War Livy seems to have followed Polybius quite extensively, without much acknowledgement, though Livy's account became better known. Livy was unashamedly a picturesque historian of the kind Polybius denigrated, though perhaps the most accomplished of them. He is, in fact, a very considerable prose artist. It is characteristic that we find some of the 'human interest' stories from the Punic Wars in Livy, not Polybius: the young Hannibal taking an oath, at his father's bidding, to be an implacable enemy of Rome (XXI.1), and Archimedes, rapt in the contemplation of a mathematical problem, killed by a soldier in the storming of Syracuse (XXXV.31). Livy also enjoyed the posthumous advantage of writing in Latin; in the West, more boys have learned Latin than Greek even from the Renaissance onward, and many, like myself, must have had Livy among their early assignments.

Unlike most ancient historians, Livy (Titus Livius) had no official career. He was born in Padua around 60 BC, and spent most of his life, which he dedicated to writing his history, in Rome. According to Suetonius, the historian of the first twelve emperors, he helped the young Claudius, the future emperor, with his own early literary efforts. He was known to Augustus, though in no way an intimate, and he takes his place now with the other great celebrators and critics of imperial Rome in the Augustan Age, Virgil and Horace.

His history seems to have been an almost immediate success. Together with the biographies by Plutarch, the first ten books, in particular, have supplied Europe subsequently with a repertoire of legend and folklore only slightly less familiar and vital than that of the Bible and Greek mythology. Livy records the legends as worthy to be preserved and known. Like Polybius before him, and like Virgil, he regards the greatness of Rome as in some sense preordained. It was 'written in the book of fate that this great city of ours should arise, and the first steps be taken to the founding of the mightiest empire the world has known – second only to God's' (I.3). Recognizing their frailty as history, he neither endorses nor rejects the old stories. There is no reason 'to object when antiquity draws no hard line between the human and the supernatural: it adds dignity to the past, and if any nation deserves the privilege of claiming a divine ancestry, that nation is our own' (I.1). Livy's attitude would be unfairly described as credulous, but it is certainly pious.

So the early books introduce us to these stories, some of them still familiar: the she-wolf's suckling the abandoned twins Romulus and Remus; the flights of birds as an omen of the brothers' kingship (birds were always important in Roman divination); Romulus' murder of his brother in the ensuing dispute. Livy, as seems to have become customary, combines the story of Aeneas, the refugee from Troy, with the Romulus story. Aeneas settled in Latium, and united the indigenous Latins with his Trojans; Romulus was in his line of descent. Tradition dated the foundation of the city to 753 BC. A steadily more extensive inclusiveness is a continuous theme in Livy's history.

Romulus makes Rome an asylum for runaways; the Sabine women are captured, so that henceforth, though there is enmity and a desire for revenge, Romans and Sabines are kin. Neighbouring peoples are steadily included within Rome's orbit, and the ultimate inclusion is the extension of eligibility for citizenship to the provinces (see VIII.14). With the extension of the empire there is the same pattern of assimilation, by conquest and adoption.

One of the most famous stories is that of the rape of Lucretia by the son of King Tarquin the Proud, leading to the expulsion of the Tarquinian dynasty and the ending of the monarchy (c.509 BC) (I.59). It was memorably used as a theme in painting, notably by Cranach (Lucretia's suicide) and by Titian (with a fiercely energetic rapist), and in Shakespeare's sensuous narrative poem. The expulsion of the Tarquins provoked war with the Etruscans, and in fact much of Livy's early history, after the dwellers on the seven Roman hills have been brought together, is concerned with wars with the adjacent cities and peoples, within a steadily expanding radius: Veii, only nine miles inland from Rome; Fidenae even closer; the Albans, Volscians, Latins, Etruscans, Aequians, Sabines; dealt with in later books are the Samnites and Campanians to the south. The Gauls, established in northern Italy, are the only people actually to enter the city of Rome. These conflicts, which can grow wearisomely repetitive, are diversified by what really mattered to subsequent generations – the legendary stories of Roman patriotic heroism and self-sacrifice.

Several such stories relate to the defence of the new republic against the attempt of the Etruscan king Lars Porsenna to restore the Tarquinian dynasty. Porsenna, in these stories, is, however, magnanimously disposed to honour Roman courage, even in the young Roman aristocrat, Gaius Mucius, who attempts to assassinate him. When foiled, Mucius boldly acknowledges his intention, and is not surprisingly condemned to be burnt to death. Declaiming 'See how cheap men hold their bodies when they care only for honour,' he holds his right hand in the flames as a demonstration of fortitude. Porsenna pardons him, and he is known thereafter as 'Scaevola' or left-handed. Porsenna also pardons a girl, Cloelia, who makes a reputation as a heroine by escaping when detained as a hostage. The Romans honourably give her back, and Porsenna, moved by her courage, even more honourably returns her. She was subsequently honoured in Rome by a public equestrian statue (II.13).

Other stories are more sinister, one even having echoes of human sacrifice. A great chasm having opened in the Forum and been deemed an evil omen, the soothsayers call for a sacrifice if the Roman republic is to last for ever. A young soldier, Marcus Curtius, puts on full equipment and rides his horse fearlessly into the gulf (VII.6); the story was dramatically illustrated in a painting by Benjamin Haydon, the English Romantic artist and friend of Keats and Fuseli – the horse looks understandably reluctant. More emotionally complex is the story, also told by Plutarch (where Shakespeare found it), of Coriolanus, the proud oligarch who, exiled from Rome, is appointed general of an invading Volscian army. Moved by the entreaties of his mother, Volumnia, and his wife and children, he turns back and Rome is saved (II.40). The story is actually one of the triumph of affection over duty (at least to the Volscians), which seems to have been endorsed only because it benefited Rome. The reverse is much more common: Roman patriotic zeal begot what almost deserves to be called a heroic subgenre of the victories of public duty over private feelings, or, to put it another way, of the state over the family. This was Roman 'firmness' or 'sternness'. The archetypal figure is Lucius Junius Brutus, the leader against the Tarquins and therefore the father of the republic. As consul, Brutus had to preside over the execution of his two sons for a conspiracy to restore the monarchy (II.5). A similar scene is enacted in Book VII (10), where Titus Manlius, son of the consul of the same name, wins a ritualized battle against the Latins by engaging in single combat, against the consuls' orders. He becomes a popular hero, but is nonetheless executed for his disobedience, at his father's orders. Least sympathetic of all such actions (and its outcome) is that of Publius Horatius, one of the three Horatii, brothers who fought the Alban champions, the Curatii, in what was again a highly ritualized though mortal combat. Horatius, the only survivor, meets his sister, who had been betrothed to one of the Curatii and is weeping for him, and in a rage kills her. At his subsequent trial the word of his, and the girl's, father exonerates him: a Roman daughter who could mourn an enemy deserved to die; Horatius is freed (I.26).

A different and more amiable kind of republican virtue, which also became exemplary, was embodied in the story of Cincinnatus, a former consul (460 BC), who fell into poverty and was reduced to working with his own hands on his three-acre farm. A crisis having arisen, it is decided that he is the man of the hour and must be made dictator, a temporary post of supreme power reserved for emergencies. Summoned by a delegation from the Senate, 'he told his wife Rocilia to run to their cottage and fetch his toga. The toga was brought, and wiping the grimy sweat from his hands and face he put it on.' Cincinnatus, having overcome the crisis, resigned fifteen days later. The story had a resonance in another new republic, in America, as a precedent for the president's reversion to the status of a private citizen after his term of office; there had been fears that Washington would make his presidency perpetual or even make himself king. Cincinnatus returned to his plough, or rather to his Virginia estate. Roman pseudo-nyms – Cato, Junius – were popular among authors of republican or at least oppositional pamphlets in eighteenth-century England as well as America. The collective pseudonym of the American Federalists was 'Publius', though their writing was coolly sociological compared with the straining for republican virtue in emulation of Rome among the French revolutionaries a little later. The most extreme egalitarian among these, Babœuf, adopted 'Gracchus' as his first name, after Tiberius and Gaius Gracchus, the second-century leaders of the plebs.

It is not surprising, in fact, that in late-eighteenth-century France inspiration was found in the legends of Roman public virtue and patriotism. Jacques-Louis David's painting *The Oath of the Horatii* (1785), depicting the three brothers holding up their swords and dedicating themselves to patriotic self-sacrifice while the women weep, was found uplifting; collective oath-taking was to be a significant part of the public theatre of the Revolution, of which David was to be the celebrator and in a sense the stage manager. The cult of patriotic virtue, already evident in the 1780s, was in part a reaction against rococo erotic depictions of Greek mythology, so that in a sense they and scenes from Roman history were in competition. Others of David's works, like *The Lictors bringing Brutus the Bodies of his Sons* (1789) and *The Intervention of the Sabine Women* (1799) – Livy tells the story of their mediation between their new husbands and their enraged families in I.13 – could have appeared earlier, but other paintings from Roman history had an immediate topicality in these years. David's *The Generosity of Roman Women* (1791), in which the protagonists make a patriotic sacrifice of their adornments to the needs of the state, actually inspired a group of Parisian women to do the same when the new French republic was threatened by a foreign invasion to restore the Bourbons, like the intervention of the Etruscans on behalf of Tarquin. David was not the only painter to be inspired by Roman scenes. Equally topical, for example, was Jean-Baptiste Wicar's 1789 sketch for a subsequent painting of *Brutus Vowing to Expel the Tarquins*.

Livy, perhaps more than any other ancient historian (unless Plutarch's *Lives* are counted as histories), bequeathed to Europe, from the Renaissance onward, the conception of history as moral teaching by examples. The Roman character, rather than, as with Polybius, foresight and the unique virtues of the Roman constitution (which, by the time Livy was writing, was manifestly not working properly), was at the heart of Livy's history. Threats to Roman austerity were the importation of foreign cults, leading to the neglect of the native gods; luxury; the love of novelty; and the craze for extravagant entertainments – all of which provoke Livy to eloquent denunciation. His exaltation of the old Roman ways was of course not at all singular. Augustus, for example, fretted about the integrity of Roman family life and the fertility of Roman matrons. It is characteristic that in Rome there were long-established public officials, the censors, charged with keeping Roman manners and morals in order. The appraisal of character also provided a focus for the oratory of the Senate and the courts and the marking of public occasions: in the eulogy (*laudatio*), often at funerals, and in the case for the prosecution, the invective, the formidable character assassination of which the supreme virtuoso had been Cicero.

Livy seems to have understood the relationship between national institutions (including religious rites) and national character as a reciprocal one, each supporting the other. The Spartans, in Livy's view, did themselves much harm when they abandoned the ancient institutions bequeathed to them by Lycurgus (XXXVIII.34, XXXIX.33–9). The Romans, in being true to their institutions, would be true to themselves. Reciting the details of an ancient custom, he adds that now 'the memory of every practice, religious and secular, has been effaced by our preference for all that is new and foreign in place of what is native and traditional' (VIII.11). Livy is that not unusual kind of commentator, in the heyday of empire, who holds simultaneously that dominion is won by strength of character and that the country is going to the dogs: 'Even the authority of parents over children is held cheap and of slight account' (XXVI.22). Symptoms of decay now abound, begun by the importation of the luxuries of Asia. Livy mentions bedspreads, tapestries, sideboards and female lutenists at banquets, while 'the cook, who had been to the ancient Romans the least valuable of slaves and had been priced and treated accordingly, began to be highly valued, and what had been a mere service came to be regarded as an art' (XXXIX.6).

In the earliest books of his history, apart from its strikingly pessimistic preface, to which we shall return, Livy is naturally concerned with origins rather than decay. He itemizes the establishment of familiar Roman institutions and customs, many, though not all, being ascribed to Romulus or to his successor, Numa, the supposedly divinely guided lawgiver, who corresponds to the Athenian Solon. Among the creations of the founding period are the religious rites and festivals (these are described in Ovid's *Fasti*); the dedication of temples, including the temple of Vesta and the institution of the Vestal Virgins; the corps of pontiffs and augurs (who take the omens); the Senate, the Census and the organization of the army; and the main public works: the draining of the Forum, the building of the Circus, and the installation of the Cloaca Maxima, the great sewer of the city. With the republic came the two annual consulships (henceforth available as a method of dating), the tribunes and other public offices.

The details obviously have to be taken on trust, as Livy has taken them, but there is a factual basis. He does not gloss over the poverty and primitiveness of the early inhabitants: there is mention of cattle-raiding as an occasion for war. The lowlier Rome's origins, the more astounding its rise. Aeneas, in Virgil's poem, has a vision of future greatness, contrasting with the rusticity and wildness before him. Livy acknowledges the cultural borrowings from the higher civilization of the Etruscans, including motifs thought of as distinctively Roman such as the 'curule' chair of the magistrate, the purple-bordered toga, and the twelve lictors, who subsequently became the bodyguard of the consuls. There is archaeological evidence for similar borrowings. Though the details of the early wars seem invented – the single combats, for example, and the ultra-patriotic sentiments uttered – Rome did establish its pre-eminence among the neighbouring peoples; the communities of shepherds on the Roman hills coalesced as a polity, with the Forum as the centre of civic life instead of a marsh.

Rome was subsequently able to assert a dominion over the peoples of central Italy more widely, and this certainly implies some combination of cohesion and toughness, of foresight and military organization and prowess, to which the self-esteem embodied in the early legends must have contributed. The Romans – so long as they were truly Roman, that is – could think of themselves as stern, steadfast, public-spirited, and devoted to their laws and traditions, for the legends told them so. Livy's brisk characterizations of the national traits of other peoples point the contrast: the Carthaginians are treacherous (XXI.4, XXII.7); Spaniards unreliable (like all foreigners) (XXII.22); Numidians oversexed (XXIX.23); Athenians easily suggestible (XXXI.44); Thessalians restless and given to rioting (XXXIV.51); Syrians servile (XXXVI.13); Gauls initially fearsome, but easily discouraged (XXII.2, XXVII.48). All very un-Roman – though Livy is always suspicious of mobs, and applauds the religious institutions of Numa for giving the population something to think about in an interval of peace when 'there was an obvious danger of a general relaxation of the nation's moral fibre.' Numa is seen as inculcating fear of the gods, and instituting the rites to placate them, as a social discipline (I.19–20). Steady Roman patriotism was a product of time and institutions, and even the period of the monarchy was valuable in shielding the populace – 'a rabble of vagrants, mostly runaways and refugees' – from the abuse of a premature liberty and ensuring that it would have to be hard-won. Patriotism, like the constitution, is a product of slow growth (II.1).

The two main threats to its continuance were of foreign origin: foreign luxuries and foreign cults. Luxury operated as a kind of sociological disease, affecting other peoples – the Carthaginians and the Gauls – as well as the Romans, and it had its particular and noted plague-spots: Capua in southern Italy and Boeotia in Greece, as well as

Asia as a whole. His army's stay in Capua was described as 'Hannibal's Cannae' (i.e. the equivalent of his own defeat of the Romans) – the army was never the same again (VII.32, 38). Boeotia was similarly fatal to the army of King Antiochus of Syria (XXXVI.2). Like a plague bacillus, the infection was brought back to Rome by the city's victorious armies – particularly after the conquest of Macedon, when enriched with the spoils of Alexander's empire, and so ultimately from Asia.

Foreign cults, the second insidious threat, were periodically forbidden by the Roman authorities, with Livy's approval. Alien, unauthorized rites were apparently pernicious in themselves (VI.30, XXXIX.16), but a particularly lurid episode was the detection and punishment of a covert Bacchanalian cult in 186 BC. Initiated by a Greek soothsayer and hierophant of secret, orgiastic, nocturnal ceremonies, involving promiscuous mingling of the sexes and even murder, it had already spread widely. Its exposure caused panic. It was said that more than seven thousand men and women were involved. Some were punished; others fled or committed suicide. In hindsight this gives an interesting foretaste of future attitudes to Christianity (XXXIX.8–18), but Bacchanalianism, though perhaps ineradicable in some form, had less staying power.

It has to be remembered in considering Livy's mention of events like these that the fundamental form of his history was annalistic, though his command of smooth, continuous, well-paced narrative is such that it is easy to forget this. Some events were recorded just because they happened, just as each year was marked by the consulships and any notable omens or prodigies. We may be grateful for Livy's residual annalistic inclusiveness, because it gives us episodes which provide sidelights, even amusing ones, on 'social history' which Polybius would have thought it beneath the dignity of history to record. Other ancient historians recorded exceptional natural events, such as earthquakes, partly as chronological markers, and noted supernatural events if their interpretation as portents and warnings influenced policy. Livy does too, but he seems to record ominous phenomena with particular relish and sometimes for their own sake: statues weeping or sweating, fallen or disfigured; showers of blood, stones or, on one more interesting occasion, meat (III.10); the untoward behaviour of birds and other creatures; monstrous births; a talking cow and a nodding Juno. Livy does not endorse the accounts of these events, but admits his weakness for them and regrets their neglect by modern historians: 'My own outlook, as I write about events in times gone by, becomes in some way old-fashioned' (XLIII.13). We can read this as an endorsement of historical empathy.

Among the flashes of social history, it is impossible to omit the great flute-players' strike of 311 BC. Angry at being forbidden by the censors to hold their usual feast in the temple of Jupiter, they downed instruments, leaving sacrifices to be performed without music. They won. Their right to their feast was restored, and they were allowed 'on three days a year to roam the city in fancy dress, making music and enjoying the licence which is now customary' (IX.30). More potentially serious was the case of the witty Vestal Virgin in 420 BC. She was exonerated of a charge of unchastity, but was ordered to amend her over-elegant costume and not to make any more jokes. Another overdressed Vestal, who in 337 was actually convicted of unchastity, was buried alive.

The question of women's dress brought women out on the streets in an unprecedented demonstration in 195 BC. The Lex Oppia, a sumptuary law imposed on women during the Punic Wars, was proposed for repeal, only for the repeal to be blocked by the tribunes. Women flooded the streets, not only from Rome but from outlying areas. This provoked Marcus Cato, byword for austerity and discipline, to an impressive speech given him by Livy (though his own, also extant, was different). It is a good example of a style of oratory: Livy's speeches, unlike Thucydides' speeches as situation reports, not only embodied a studied rhetoric but were supposed to reflect the characteristics and manners of the speaker. Cato's vehement speech is one in which a fearful misogyny leads on to a thin-end-of-the-wedge argument – what will they ask for next? – as well as characteristic praise of older and sterner times:

Citizens of Rome, if each one of us had set himself to retain the rights and dignity of a husband over his own wife, we should have less trouble with women as a whole sex. As things are, our liberty, overthrown in the home by female indiscipline, is now being crushed and trodden underfoot here too, in the Forum. It is because we have not kept them under control individually, that we are now terrorized by them collectively . . .

Our ancestors refused to allow any woman to transact even private business without a guardian to represent her; women had to be under the control of fathers, brothers, or husbands. But we (heaven preserve us) are now allowing them even to take part in politics, and actually to appear in the Forum and to be present at our meetings and assemblies! What are they now doing in the streets and at the street corners? . . . Give a free rein to their undisciplined nature, to this untamed animal, and then expect them to set a limit on their own licence! Unless you impose that limit, this is the last of the restraints imposed on women by custom or by law which they resent. What they are longing for is complete liberty, or rather – if we want to speak the truth – complete licence.

This leads Cato on to a more comprehensive denunciation of modern degeneracy as a result of luxury and foreign influences. The ironies of conquest are on full display:

As the fortune of our Commonwealth grows better and happier day by day, and as our empire increases – and already we have crossed into Greece and Asia (regions full of all kinds of sensual allurements) and are even laying hands on the treasures of kings – I am the more alarmed lest these things should capture us instead of us capturing them; these statues brought from Syracuse, believe me, were hostile standards brought against this city. And now I hear far too many people praising the ornaments of Corinth and Athens, and jeering at the terracotta antefixes [figures at the angles of the gables of temples] of the Roman gods. For my part, I prefer to have those gods propitious to us – as I trust they will be propitious if we allow them to remain in their own abodes. (XXXIV.1–4)

Cato's speech was followed by another, in rebuttal, and the law was repealed. The women had won.

An episode in 295 BC casts an unusual light on the long-standing friction between patricians and plebeians. Having married a plebeian and so become déclassée, the daughter of a patrician was barred by the patrician matrons from sacrifices at the shrine of Patrician Chastity 'in the cattle market by the round temple of Hercules'. The woman, showing spirit, set up an altar in her own home to Plebeian Chastity, and invited duly qualified matrons to the sacrifices. Unfortunately, Livy says, the new cult became discredited by the presence of women who, though plebeian, were apparently not matrons, or chaste (X.23).

The social discord between patricians and plebeians comes to the surface intermittently in Livy's history, even in the early books. The conflicts to which it gave rise were particularly menacing at moments of external crisis. There was as yet no professional army, and at such moments the plebeian citizen soldiers felt their power and sometimes exercised it, though – and this is Livy's main message – at the eleventh hour the Romans always learned to compromise and present a united front. As Livy shows, and at one point in particular acknowledges (VII.19), the conflict designated as being between patricians and plebeians was really two, more or less unrelated, conflicts, involving very different sections of the plebeian population. The problems of the poorer plebeians were chiefly those of debt and the difficulty of retaining their smallholdings as the rich became richer as a result of conquest (this was really the solid basis of the luxury argument) and, since patricians were debarred from commerce, sought to buy up land, which could be farmed by another product of conquest, slaves. Landholding and military matters were also intertwined. Soldiers returning home after service found their farms in disrepair and, struggling to pay the taxes the war had made necessary, fell into debt. Later the displacement of the smallholder, together with the huge extent of the empire, made the citizen soldier an unworkable idea and a professional army inevitable, but these problems were to come to a head in the first century BC, Livy's history of which is lost.

The problem of debt, however, is one to which he frequently returns. Huge resentment was caused by the fact that the debtor was bound to his creditors, being effectively enslaved, often after (or even arguably for) having served his city. The abolition in 326 BC of enslavement of debtors – long demanded – Livy calls 'a second birth' of the liberty of the Roman people (VIII.28). The demands for an agrarian law – a redistribution of public land (again swollen by conquest) and restrictions on the size of landholdings – rumbled on, though the greatest crises, associated with the names of the two tribunes of the people Tiberius and Gaius Gracchus, occurring in the later second century, lie beyond the extant books of Livy's history. The establishment of tribunes of the people, however, recorded by Livy, was a significant step for the plebs (II.23, 32, 53, 58; III.55; VI.31; VII.29).

The issue of the hereditary privileges of the patricians was not, as Livy admits (VII.19), of much interest to the poor smallholders, but only to rich and prominent plebeians. Only patricians – members of the early families of senatorial rank, and therefore a kind of hereditary caste, the fathers or *patres* (hence 'patrician') – could hold the highest offices of state, or were qualified to perform the religious rites attached to them. The religious duties in fact were made much of by patrician speakers attempting to hold back the pressure of the more notable plebeians for access to office, it being held to be impious for anyone not from the qualified families to perform them. Eventually, with much bitterness and strife, patrician hereditary exclusiveness became eroded: the first non-patrician consul was elected, according to Livy, in 366 BC (VII.1). The religious duties are vividly presented in a speech which Livy gives to a spokesman for the plebs, but this time it is the thin-end-of-the-wedge argument in reverse. By 300 BC the plebs had the right to consulships, censorships and triumphs from which they were formerly excluded. So much has been conceded, the speaker says; how can the rest be withheld?

What god or man can think it unbecoming if men whom you have honoured with curule chairs, the purple-edged toga, the palm-embroidered tunic, and with the decorated toga, the triumphal crown and laurel wreaths, whose houses you have marked out from the rest by the enemy's spoils fastened to their walls – if such men add the insignia of pontiffs and augurs? Shall the man resplendent in the robes of Jupiter Best and Highest, who has been carried through the City in a gilded chariot to ascend the Capitol, not be seen with sacrificial cup and augur's crook when with covered head he slaughters the victim or receives an augury from the citadel? (X.7)

Livy's attitude to these conflicts is to praise moderation and concili-ation, and to disapprove of mob behaviour and aristocratic arrogance and intransigence. However, 'true moderation in defence of political liberties' is difficult, because the latter can easily get out of hand. He takes pride in the fact that difficult changes were accomplished with a minimum of violence. Cohesion, harmony, is the great need. The supreme test of the solidarity of the Roman people is the aftermath of the disaster of Cannae (216 BC), when, with a Roman army destroyed and Hannibal at the gates of Rome – *Hannibal ad portas* – the Romans, in all their consternation and even panic, essentially keep their nerve and surmount the crisis in united fashion, not thinking of suing for peace: 'No other nation in the world could have suffered so tremendous a series of disasters, and not been overwhelmed' (XXII.54).

Livy, to say it again, was not a 'research' historian, and his social thought seems commonplace – which is another way of saying representative. He is above all a superb narrator. The speeches he gives his characters are cogent and artfully wrought, according to the rules of ancient rhetoric. It is not fanciful to think that in them we catch something of the thunder-roll of senatorial eloquence in the golden age of Roman oratory. Livy's qualities are not easy to illustrate, especially in a foreign language. They depend on expansiveness, and so do not take kindly to brevity and selectivity. In the many campaign narratives, though he is notoriously weak on tactics and topography, he is good, it has to be said, with weather – as in the test, almost as severe as the Alps, imposed on Hannibal's men by the Apennines:

Heavy rain and a violent wind right in their faces made progress impossible; they could not hold their weapons, and if they tried to struggle on, the wind spun them round and flung them off their feet. The strength of it made it impossible to breathe, so all they could do was to turn their backs to it, crouching on the ground. Then the sky seemed to burst in a roar of sound, and between the horrific thunderclaps lightning flashed. They were blinded and deafened and benumbed with terror. (XII.58)

This may not be exactly history, but it is arresting imaginative writing.

Of all the stories of Roman 'firmness', the one which most lodges in the mind, without the self-conscious declamatory style of such stories' usual protagonists or their uncongenial fanaticism, is the account of the Gauls' occupation of Rome in 386 BC. The story of the sacred geese, whose cackling alerted the sleeping guards on the Capitol to a night assault, has entered into European folklore, but Livy's main rhetorical effect is kept for the aged former magistrates who refused to place themselves as a burden on the garrison in the citadel on the Capitol (which held out) but chose to die in their houses. Putting on their ceremonial robes, they took their seats in their courtyards, in the ivory-inlaid curule chairs of the magistracy, and waited. When the Gauls entered, Livy says,

something akin to awe held them back at what met their gaze – those figures seated in the open courtyards, the robes and decoration august beyond reckoning, the majesty expressed in those grave, calm eyes like the majesty of gods. They might have been statues in some holy place, and for a while the Gallic warriors stood entranced; then, on an impulse, one of them touched the beard of a certain Marcus Papirius – it was long, as was the fashion in those days – and the Roman struck him on the head with his ivory staff.

The spell was broken, the barbarian killed him, and the others were butchered where they sat (V.41).

The aftermath of the Gallic invasion also allowed Livy the opportunity for one of his surely most deeply felt speeches, given to the (temporary) dictator Camillus. Rome itself lay devastated, but the neighbouring city of Veii had been captured and lay at Rome's mercy. A proposal was made to transfer the city there instead of laboriously rebuilding Rome. Camillus was opposed to this, and recalled the sacred sites and customs of Rome for his audience:

We have a city founded with all due rites of auspice and augury; not a stone of her streets but is permeated by our sense of the divine; for our annual sacrifices not the days only are fixed, but the places too, where they may be performed: men of Rome, would you desert your gods? ... Think, for instance, of Jupiter's feast: how could his couch be decked anywhere but on the Capitol? What of Vesta's eternal fires, or of the image preserved in her shrine as a pledge of Rome's dominion ... The Vestal Virgins have their place – their *own* place, from which nothing but the capture of the City has ever moved them; the Flamen [priest] of Jupiter is forbidden by our religion to spend even one night outside the city walls – yet you would make them, one and all, go and live for ever in Veii. Ah, Vesta! Shall thy Virgins desert thee? Shall the Flamen of Jupiter live abroad night after night and stain himself and our country with so deep a sin?

The speech turns into a eulogy of the city, of its growth and situation and the future prophesied for it (V.51–2). One is reminded here both of Virgil and of Pericles' love letter to Athens in the Funeral Oration; it is a tribute to Livy that he is not diminished by the comparisons.

We do not know what Livy's account of his own century was like, but his preamble to the whole work is deeply pessimistic. He professes to expect that his readers will want to hurry on to the latest times and to read of how 'the might of an imperial people is beginning to work its own ruin.' Livy feels the opposite. Absorbed in antiquity, 'I shall be able to turn my eyes from the troubles which for so long have tormented the modern world.' He invites the reader to contemplate 'the kinds of lives our ancestors lived' and Rome's rise, and then to

trace the progress of our moral decline, to watch, first, the sinking of the foundations of morality as the old teaching was allowed to lapse, then the rapidly increasing disintegration, then the final collapse of the whole edifice, and the dark dawning of our modern day when we can neither endure our vices nor face the remedies needed to cure them. The study of history is the best medicine for a sick mind.

In the past, poverty among the Romans went hand in hand with contentment.

Whatever the merits of its application here, the idea of long-term decline, the product of Livy's combination of patriotism and pessimism, is highly interesting as a conception of history, for it itself is an intrinsically historical one; in it the idea of a perennial human nature is superseded. The past was unlike the present not only in superficial, material terms, but morally and intellectually. They did things differently then, and thought and felt differently. Livy had a conception, though a negative one, of a distinctive culture of modernity, compounded of religious indifference, cosmopolitanism and a febrile love of novelty. He was in love with the past to an extent no historian before him seems to have been, despite the dedication of historians to preserving the memory of great deeds, because he was convinced that its virtues had been lost. He contemplated the past with yearning – *pace* Macaulay, who said the exact opposite of him – not with a sense of confident possession.

Livy's work became famous almost at once, though its length doomed its chances of survival *in toto*: copying was, understandably, of decades of books rather than of the whole work, which is why some complete decades survive and others do not. A new edition of the first ten books was made around AD 396, and it is to this that we owe their survival. Livy had understandably less to say to the early Christian centuries than to his contemporaries, but interest in his work never died altogether. Copying of the first ten books was carried out in the ninth century, and again in the early fourteenth century. Livy became a central figure of the Renaissance, with a famous commentary by Machiavelli in his *Discourses*, and he remained a staple of education for five centuries beyond that. The doyen of French intellectual life in the later nineteenth century, Hippolyte Taine, wrote a thesis on Livy for his *agrégation*, and the Victorian imperialist publicist Sir John Seeley began his career with an edition of Livy's first two books. Macaulay derived from him the inspiration for his *Lays of Ancient Rome*, and in early-nineteenth-century Germany, following the work of Friedrich Wolf on Homer, Barthold Niebuhr drew from the early books of Livy a Romantic conception of the creative, collective self-consciousness of the *Volk*. This, reapplied by David Friedrich Strauss to the Hebrews and the Bible, became one of the seminal and most disturbing thoughts of the nineteenth century. If the whole of Livy's work had been lost, though Polybius, Dionysius and Plutarch would have filled some of the gaps, the subtraction from the future culture of Europe would have been incalculable.

Sir Richard Southern, in his *The Making of the Middle Ages* (1953), recounts that in the monastery of Cluny around 1040 a list was made of the books chosen by the monks from their library for private study. Predictably, most chose works of the Christian Fathers, or biblical commentaries, lives of the saints, or books on ecclesiastical history or monastic discipline. The exception was one monk, out of the sixty-four, who chose Livy. One wishes it were possible to know more about him.

7

Civil War and the Road to Autocracy: Plutarch, Appian and Cassius Dio

Livy continued working on his history until his death in AD 17, but the later books which carried it down to his own times are lost. The chief surviving accounts of the period of the Civil Wars include Caesar's own narrative of his war with Pompey, while for the Second Civil War, between Caesar's murderers, Brutus and Cassius, and his avengers, Mark Antony and Octavian, which ended with the victory of the latter at the battle of Philippi in 41 BC, we have the accounts of three Greeks living in the first and second centuries AD: Plutarch, Appian and Cassius Dio.

Caesar's account is presented in his typically dry manner. Plutarch's, in his Lives of Brutus and Antony, is a very different matter, for his forte was to be vivid and inspiring. He has left a deep mark on subsequent European literature, particularly through the English translation (not from the original but from a French translation) by Sir Thomas North in the sixteenth century, which was used by Shakespeare for his Coriolanus, Julius Caesar and Antony and Cleopatra. Plutarch was also, with Livy, a profound influence on later ideas of Roman republican virtue, most notoriously in late-eighteenth-century France. He wrote essentially to entertain and to provide moral lessons, to compare the heroes of the Greek political tradition – such figures as Solon, Themistocles, Pericles and Alcibiades – with Roman ones such as Coriolanus, Cato the Censor, the Gracchi, Brutus and Antony. This intention and the arrangement of his work makes it impossible to deal fully with it in the present context. It is not the intention here to deal in detail with biography as a genre, and Plutarch's Parallel Lives as a whole is made unwieldy by being spread for essentially didactic purposes over the whole of antiquity, Greek and Roman, back to legendary times and down to the end of the Roman republican period. However, there are always times to make exceptions, and the Lives of Brutus and Antony are particularly useful here, since they deal with the crisis of the republic in a way that no surviving work of a major ancient historian does. Fortunately Plutarch's qualities as a writer can be illustrated from a sample of the *Lives*.

In using these two brief biographies (the 'Brutus' is some fifty pages, 'Antony' longer), Shakespeare followed Plutarch so closely, sometimes quoting the translation almost verbatim, that even for new readers they have an air of familiarity. Our Brutus is Shakespeare's Brutus, who is Plutarch's, and the same is true of Antony – though of course the prose works are more detailed. Plutarch's 'Brutus' begins with a contrast with Brutus' great ancestor (though his descent had been disputed), the father of the republic, Lucius Junius Brutus, who was hard and uncultivated. Marcus Brutus possessed an ideal temperament for the practice of virtue, being drawn to the inner life of self-cultivation but also able to respond to a call to action ('. . . the elements / So mix'd in him that Nature might stand up / And say to all the world, "This was a man!"' – *Julius Caesar*, V.v.72–4). We get more on his character, the school of philosophy to which he subscribed, the traits of his oratory in Latin and in Greek, his political principles, and his high-minded reason for attaching himself to the party of Pompey. Although of Pompey's faction, after Pompey's death he received Caesar's pardon and even his favour, including appointment to the governorship of Cisalpine Gaul, where he displayed a notable and unusual integrity and benevolence. However, he kept his distance from Caesar and was subject to the influence of Cassius, his brother-in-law and rival. Plutarch makes Caesar's suspicions of pale, lean men apply to Brutus as well as to Cassius.

Shakespeare was able to follow Plutarch almost step by step because the latter's work is so tautly constructed, dramatic and full of incident – almost, already, like a play, with, of course, the climax of Caesar's murder. Brutus is troubled by the solicitations of Cassius and of anonymous letters reminding him of his ancestry, and his wife is driven distracted to see him so troubled. Caesar, on the fatal day, reverses at the last moment his decision not to attend the Senate, and dies at the foot of Pompey's statue ('Et tu, Brute' is a post-classical invention). Cinna the poet suffers his poignant death by mistaken identity. The spectre that appears to Brutus and promises, correctly, to meet him again at Philippi was not invented for the Elizabethan groundlings, but provides Plutarch with a no doubt welcome macabre touch, though it is not explicitly identified with the ghost of Caesar, as in Shakespeare by Brutus and the stage direction. Cassius commits suicide as a result of a misunderstanding, and is eulogized by Brutus as the last of the Romans – 'The sun of Rome is set. Our day is gone' – the line given to Titinius in *Julius Caesar* (V.iii.64). Antony declares Brutus the only disinterested conspirator, though not necessarily over his body. The hangers-on are the familiar crew.

Plutarch's 'Antony', for him a long biography, is more diffuse and, until the death scene in Cleopatra's mausoleum, less dramatic, so Shakespeare has to do a good deal with description, like the famous speech by Enobarbus (himself an invention) on Cleopatra in her barge, which is a close poetic rendering of a piece of Plutarch's prose. A fifth of Plutarch's work is devoted rather remarkably to Antony's campaign against the Parthians, which Shakespeare dismisses summarily. Plutarch's reading of Antony's character is interesting though familiar: boisterous, boyish, humorous, extravagant; he is a good commander, but unmanned by his passion for Cleopatra, who, in Plutarch, though not all ancient writers, is devoted also to him (in Shakespeare, 'O Antony!' is almost her last word). Apart from the barge scene, the most striking direct transcription is the dying words given to her attendant, Charmian, when she is asked was Cleopatra's suicide well done: 'Very well ... and meet for a Princess descended from the race of so many noble kings' (North's translation; cf. *Antony and Cleopatra*, V.ii.325–6). Charmian's very last words, the wonderfully human and enigmatic 'Ah, soldier!', however, are pure Shakespeare.

Plutarch can be psychologically complex as well as vivid and dramatic, but one does not go to him for historical vision or explanation. When confronted with the general question of the transition from republic to empire, he is content, as was quite common, to leave matters to the higher powers: 'But the day of the Republic was past, it would seem, and so the gods, wishing to remove from the scene the destined master of the world, kept from Brutus the knowledge of his success, even though it almost reached him in time' ('Brutus', 47). Personal motives and actions, and the contingencies which beset individuals and are controlled by the gods (or Fate) for their inscrutable purposes, do everything.

To turn from Plutarch to his younger contemporary, and fellow-Greek, Appian is to meet a genuine historian – though a somewhat colourless one – with a historian's typical concerns. In the part of his general history of Rome dealing with the first century BC (now published as *The Civil Wars*) Appian has a great theme, and knows it: the progressive decline of the republic into political violence, gangsterism, civil war and chaos. His starting point in these five books is the murders of the people's tribunes Tiberius and Gaius Gracchus, in 133 and 121 BC respectively, when they attempted a land redistribution on behalf of the poor. This, according to Appian, marked the end of traditional Roman political moderation: 'No sword was ever brought into the assembly, and no Roman was ever killed by a Roman, until Tiberius Gracchus, while holding the office of tribune and in the act of proposing legislation, became the first man to die in civil unrest' (*Civil Wars*, I.2). The moral barrier once broken, violence escalates into the murderous strife between the factions of Marius and Sulla in the early first century, followed by the civil war between Caesar and Pompey in the mid-century. Appian considers the grounds of the popular discontent which underlies the outbreaks of class conflict – grounds which are manipulated by successful soldiers turned political adventurers and gangleaders: the monopolization of land in Italy by the rich, who create great ranches worked by slave labour, in place of the small freeholders on whom initially fell the burden of military service (I.7). Hence the critical issue of land redistribution, which brought violent civil strife to Rome itself. Under Gaius Gracchus, too, began what was to become an established practice, the distribution of free grain to each citizen from public funds (I.21). Appian later says that this drew the riff-raff of the provinces to Rome (II.20). Appian also deals with the vexed issue of the extension of Roman citizenship to the provinces (I.23, 34). Marius becomes the hope of the popular cause as the Gracchi had been, and Sulla's faction represents the interests of the senatorial class. Their rivalry degenerates into warfare even in the capital itself: 'In this way the episodes of civil strife escalated from rivalry and contentiousness to murder, and from murder to full-scale war; and this [Sulla's] was the first army composed of Roman citizens to attack their own country as though it were a hostile power' (I.60).

The account of Caesar's murder, of which Appian greatly disapproves, has none of the attributes of Plutarch's in 'Brutus', but is much fuller on the political context, though Appian too relies on Fate for a higher causality. Caesar went to the Senate on the fatal day despite the warning of the soothsayer, 'for Caesar had to suffer Caesar's fate' (II.116). Elsewhere we are told explicitly that 'it would seem that the divine will was interfering with public affairs to bring about change' (III.61).

There has been disagreement about how far Appian was a mere compiler of other men's work. It is possible to say with certainty, for example, that his account of Catiline's conspiracy derived heavily from Sallust, but in general the ancient habit of mentioning sources only in cases of disagreement makes it impossible to be sure. He is an uneven writer, sometimes very lucid, sometimes confusing, which encourages the idea that his sources may bear much of the responsibility for this. His authorial personality is also rather thin – an impression perhaps accentuated by the fact that we know very little about him other than that he was an advocate in Rome, practising in the times of Hadrian and Antoninus Pius in the second century AD.

The chief idiosyncrasy of Appian's final books is the enormously extended treatment he gives to the proscriptions of Brutus' and Cassius' alleged supporters, who were hunted down and murdered. 'Some went down wells, some descended into the filth of the sewers, and others climbed up into the smoky rafters or sat in total silence under close-packed roof-tiles' (IV.13). The sequence of vivid anecdotes of sacrifice, treachery, suicide, escape, capture and miserable death is clearly intended by Appian, or his source, to evoke pity and terror, and the stories are indeed gripping (IV.5–51). Appian claims that he himself investigated the death of the most celebrated of the victims, Cicero, on the spot, but the inordinate length of this section (more than a third of Book IV), which has been called 'Tales of the Proscriptions', may suggest that Appian, having found a good source, rather overdid it. He may also be copying Tacitus, who devotes time to the similar persecutions of the Roman aristocracy under Tiberius and Nero (below, pp. 133–4).

Rome had become ungovernable, and Fate, by implication, sanctioned the transition to the autocracy of Augustus. For a subtle account of how this was effected, we have to turn to another Greek, Cassius Dio.

Dio, born around AD 163, migrated to Rome as a young man from the Greek province of Bithynia, south-west of the Black Sea. He entered the Senate under the emperor Commodus, and later held a consulship, which by then, of course, was not at all the chief executive office it had been under the republic. He held governorships including the proconsulship of Africa, and a second consulship in AD 229. His *Roman History*, as was not uncommon, covered the whole period from Aeneas and Romulus to his own proconsulship. Of the eighty books of his *Roman History*, those for the period 68 BC to AD 46 have survived intact. The books on the principate of Augustus are not only almost complete but are the only substantial ancient narrative of the period from 32 BC to AD 14.

At the beginning of the period, with Brutus and Cassius dead, Mark Antony is now based in Egypt, having renounced his Roman wife, Octavian's sister Octavia, to live in Egypt with Cleopatra and his children by her. In an elaborate ceremony in Alexandria in 34 BC, Antony issued a deliberate challenge. He proclaimed Caesarion, Cleopatra's supposed son by Caesar, to be Caesar's legitimate heir – the title claimed by Caesar's nephew and adopted son Octavian – and divided the territories of the East between the boy and himself. This division, known as the Donations of Alexandria, became the greatest of Octavian's grievances (50.1). Antony was suspected of intending to hand over Rome to Cleopatra and to transfer the government to Egypt. In the propaganda war from Rome which ensued, directed against Antony, and in Octavian's speech to his troops before the decisive battle of Actium, there was some choice ethnic and misogynist abuse of 'the woman from Egypt', of Egyptian customs, and of Antony's adoption of them. For example, he follows the Queen on foot with her eunuchs, and wears an oriental dagger. The Egyptians are slaves to a woman (no woman ever did or could rule in Rome); it is a disgrace to Roman soldiers even to serve as her bodyguards.

Antony adopts mythological names for himself, and the Egyptians worship reptiles and beasts as gods (50.5, 24–5).

After the battle of Actium (31 BC) and the retreat of Cleopatra and Antony to Egypt, the story Dio tells of their end is mainly the familiar one, focused on Cleopatra's mausoleum, partly because her treasure had been stored there. Cleopatra is seen by Dio as wishing for Antony's death in order to make terms with Octavian (51.8, 10). Antony, having tried to kill himself, is lifted up into the mausoleum to die in her arms. Finding Octavian impervious, Cleopatra prefers to die rather than be led in his triumph in Rome; she dies regally, though the asp is mentioned only as one possible cause of death, the other being a poisoned pin (51.12–14). She and Antony are placed in the same tomb. (Plutarch's (earlier) account in his Life of Antony, used by Shakespeare, who here again includes translated quotations verbatim, is essentially the same, though rather more favourable to Cleopatra and much fuller of pathetic detail.) Octavian shows a politic clemency to the Egyptians, and views the body of Alexander the Great, touching the nose and accidentally damaging it. Offered a sight of the embalmed Ptolemy rulers of Egypt, he says he had wished to see a king, not corpses, and he refuses to enter the shrine of the bull-god Apis, saying he worshipped gods not cattle (51.16).

In Rome, the crucial step is taken of offering Octavian the tribunician powers for life: tribunes had personal immunity and important powers of veto. In the provinces, he begins to receive the honours of a god, while those paid to him in Rome, though stopping short of this, are exceptional. Cleopatra's effigy is carried in his triumph, with a display of her treasures; her ornaments, Dio says, now adorn the Roman temples, while she herself is represented in gold in the temple of Venus. Roman hostility had clearly contained a good deal of fascination. Games were held, wild animals were slaughtered, and the hippopotamus and the rhinoceros made their debuts in Rome (51.20–22).

Octavian had behaved with modesty and, by Roman standards, moderation. Book 52 deals with the consolidation of his power, after a long preamble in which he is said to ask for advice on the form of his government from Agrippa and Maecenas, who respond with long speeches respectively in support of a republic and of autocratic rule. One is reminded of the (uncharacteristic) Persian debate in Herodotus when, the throne being vacant, the successful conspirators are presented as considering, in highly abstract form, the same issue (Herodotus, *Histories*, III.80–82), and one wonders if Dio was remembering it. Agrippa's speech is highly abstract and platitudinous. Maecenas' advice relates more closely to Octavian's actual situation; he must, Maecenas says, retain power or perish. Maecenas makes a strong plea for ruling in association with 'the best men in Rome' and suppressing the licence of the mob (52.14–15). His advice, which corresponds closely to the course Octavian was to take, is to retain the republican offices as positions of honour but to reduce their powers and make sure that Octavian controls who holds them (52.20).

He advocates a professional standing army, rather than a citizen militia, and puts the central dilemma in a nutshell: 'We cannot survive without soldiers, and soldiers will not serve without pay,' and the need for troops would arise whatever the form of government (52.28). He proposes that they should be paid and pensioned from the interest produced by the sale of public lands and by regular taxation (an innovation). Rome is to be beautified and entertained with spectacles (52.30). Personal disrespect to Octavian should be ignored, and sharply distinguished from conspiracy, which should be dealt with by the Senate. Excessive indications of his status are to be avoided: 'No man ever became a god by vote' (52.35). Alien religions – an old theme this – should be suppressed; they are associated with secret societies and conspiracies. Sorcerers are to be banned, and – this was to be a later preoccupation – even philosophers are suspect (52.36). Octavian is warned against deceivers – another later concern, noteworthy in Tacitus, which Dio seems to make Maecenas anticipate. Power is best held in reserve and exercised with restraint, and external peace is preferable to war, though readiness for war must be kept up (52.37–38). Maecenas concludes prophetically:

If in reality you prefer the fact of monarchical rule yet fear the name of king as accursed, you need not accept that title but can still rule under the style of Caesar. If you need other titles besides, the people will give you that of Imperator, as they did your father Julius, and they will pay honour to your august status by yet another form of address. In this way you can enjoy to the full the reality of kingship without the stigma that attaches to that name. (52.40)

Dio, in writing this long speech, had of course the advantages of hindsight, and in addition to drawing on a knowledge of Octavian's subsequent policies (as Augustus) he must surely have had an eye on his own times. By comparison with the imperial monsters he had served, and survived (Commodus, Caracalla, Elagabalus), Augustus must have seemed a model monarch, as well as having the advantage of being a name of immense power and authority. Maecenas' speech falls into the long tradition of 'Advice to Princes' (sometimes with the implication of criticism of those who do not follow it) as well as holding up the example of a revered forebear. In this case the speech is represented as having immediate effect. Once again, in ancient historiography, one sees a speech used both to give a survey of a situation, with its opportunities and dangers, and supposedly to reveal – in this case perfectly plausibly – the thinking behind policies pursued. Octavian, in Dio's account, inclines to Maecenas' advice but, in a final refinement, introduces the advocated changes over a period, to avoid the dangers in attempting 'to change the natural proclivities of mankind at a single stroke'; he even leaves some to be accomplished by his successors (52.41). Dio is not averse to recording examples of deviousness in Octavian's policy of autocracy by stealth. Recognizing the nervousness of Antony's former supporters, Octavian gives it out that Antony's papers have been burnt, but actually takes care to keep some for possible future use (52.42).

For the following year (28 BC), in which Octavian was consul for the sixth time and also used for the first time the title 'Princeps' ('First'), Dio's fifty-third book gives a typically annalistic record of spectacles held and temples dedicated, including, at Agrippa's expense, the Pantheon, which survives. The centrepiece of the book, however, is Octavian's speech to the Senate renouncing all his offices and announcing his intention to retire into private life: all his actions, he claims, have merely been taken to save Rome from the dangers which threatened it (53.3–11). As intended, the effect when the Senate persuades him to change his mind is that he receives from it autocratic powers as though against his will. His first subsequent act is to double the pay of his bodyguard compared with that of the ordinary troops – 'So genuine', Dio says sarcastically, 'was his desire to lay down absolute power' (53.11). Octavian then engrosses for himself proconsular powers for ten years in all the provinces where more than one legion was stationed, giving him effective control of the army (53.12–13). Dio notes that, though the time limitation became a dead letter, it was subsequently the custom of emperors to celebrate each decade of their reigns, as though their sovereignty were thus renewed. At this time (27 BC) Octavian assumes the name Augustus, giving up, as too 'royal', his desire to take that of Romulus.

Seemingly quoting Tacitus, Dio has no doubt that what has occurred is the institution of a monarchy:

The entire conduct and direction of affairs depend on the wishes of the one man who holds power at the time. And yet in order to maintain the impression that this authority is derived from the laws and not from their own supremacy, the emperors have arrogated to themselves all the functions, together with their actual titles, attached to those offices in which power resided.

As *imperator* they have inherited the powers of the consuls; as censor (though the title eventually fell into disuse) they scrutinize morals; as Pontifex Maximus they are supreme in religious matters; the grant to them of the traditional powers of the tribunes (who continue to exist) gives them the right of the veto and of personal immunity, their persons being treated as sacred (53.17). In addition they have been set beyond the law (*legibus solutus*) (53.18).

Although Dio allows himself some sarcasm at the expense of the facade thus created, his overall verdict is that it had become 'impossible for the people to have lived in safety under a republic' (53.19). His only real complaint, interestingly, is as a historian. In the past, when all matters were brought before the Senate and the people, government was transparent: many people recorded what was done, so that the true version of events was publicly known. Now, crucial events are concealed from common knowledge: reports are misleading and cannot be properly investigated. In future he, Dio, will perforce follow the official versions, but will add his own opinion 'as I have been able – relying on the many details I have gathered from my reading, or from hearsay, or from what I have seen – to form a judgement which tells us something more than the common report' (53.19). His complaint is an important observation, from a historian whose access, in his own time, to the very highest circles of power would have given him ample opportunity to register the differences between the reality of political action and the versions presented to the public, but it had been preceded, as we shall see, by a similar complaint by Tacitus.

The chief remaining events recorded of Augustus' reign are the loss of the three legions commanded by Varus in Germany in AD 9, which gave Augustus perhaps his greatest shock (56.18–24), and the successive deaths of the younger members of Augustus' family, which pave the way for the accession of his stepson Tiberius. Dio mentions ('some people allege') the rumours which had been retailed by Suetonius linking Augustus' wife Livia to these deaths, and indeed to Augustus' own, and he neither endorses nor rejects them. His verdict on Augustus draws a sharp distinction between his conduct as Octavian under the necessities of the period of civil war and his rise to power and his later exercise of it; Dio's judgement of the latter is wholly favourable. Under Augustus the Romans enjoyed the best of all worlds: 'They were subjects of royalty without being slaves and citizens of a democracy without suffering discord' (56.43).

We know little about Dio's sources, though it is clear he knew the works of Tacitus and Suetonius and would have known Augustus' own autobiography. If we rely on impressions, he strikes the reader as a generally sober and trustworthy historian; he avoids excess of sentiment or partisanship, and is not unduly conventionally rhetorical, except perhaps in describing the battle of Actium. Unlike a Roman of the senatorial class like Tacitus, he has no perceptible nostalgia for the republic, but abhors, like Livy, the excesses of both tyranny and anarchy. His account of the way Augustus presents the facade of a republic while coverting it into an autocracy contributed to an image, particularly relevant to Opposition suspicions in eighteenth-century England, of the subversion of a free constitution by stealth. It was a double image, depicting both a sinisterly crafty ruler, undermining the constitution from within, whom an ill-intentioned monarch might emulate, and, equally plausibly, a wise and moderate statesman, bringing a golden age of peace and plenty to a city long distracted by civil strife.

8

Tacitus: 'Men fit to be slaves'

Edward Gibbon, in his earliest work, an *Essay on the Study of Literature* (1761), took Tacitus as his model for the 'philosophic historian'. Tacitus, he wrote, 'employs the force of rhetoric only . . . to instruct the reader by sensible and powerful reflections'. Gibbon's essay was in some respects consciously backward-looking. Tacitus' reputation was waning a little compared with the immense vogue he had enjoyed from the late sixteenth to the late seventeenth century, the European 'Age of Absolutism'. Gibbon's praise was part of a defence of humanist learning against the new 'philosophic' – we should say 'scientific' – spirit which condemned knowledge of the past as useless. The phrase 'philosophic historian' laid claim to a foothold in both camps, the humanist by the noun and the modern by the adjective. Tacitus was a good candidate for the title because he had recently been much admired as a political thinker, compressing the wisdom gleaned from history into epigrammatic form. Montaigne, another admirer, had expressed the sense of a link between his own times and those of the Roman historian, which does much to explain the attention paid to the latter: 'You could often believe that we were the subject of his narrating and berating' ('On the Art of Conversation', *Essays*).

It was, of course, commonplace to turn to the ancient world for parallels: Appian, for example, seems to have been widely read during the period of the French civil wars of the sixteenth century. It was natural for people in the Age of Absolutism to find much in Tacitus that seemed relevant to their own situations; drawing lessons from Tacitus seems also sometimes to have been a covert way of referring to the disreputable political wisdom purveyed by Machiavelli. Contemporary history and drama offered parallels which, to the well read, must often have seemed like reminiscences. Shakespeare's Richard III, for example, like Tiberius and Nero, wears a mask of humility and virtue until he achieves undisputed power, when he emerges as a bloodthirsty tyrant. Shakespeare's Iago is the ambitious, intriguing, tale-bearing lieutenant whose archetype could seem to be Tacitus' portrayal of Tiberius' henchman Sejanus. Shakespeare's contemporary Ben Jonson wrote a play on Sejanus (1603), while his *Catiline* (1611) was based on Sallust and Cicero. Modern monarchs and princes and their intimates dabbled in astrology and magic, as their counterparts did in Tacitus. The French queen mother Catherine de' Medici, to whom the St Bartholomew's Day Massacre was widely attributed, must readily have recalled to some the formidable and sinister imperial wives and mothers Livia and Agrippina; rumours of serial poisoning attached themselves to all three. Tacitus not only described such a world, but did so as a public man who clearly felt guilt for the compromises he had made to survive as a senator during the bloodstained reign of Domitian, as he explains particularly in the biography of his father-in-law, Agricola (*Agricola*, 3, 45).

Cornelius Tacitus was a boy in the time of Nero, and in the year of civil war in the Roman world, AD 69 – 'the year of the four emperors', which is covered by the extant part of his *Histories*. He seems to have produced these in the very early second century. They were followed by his other major work, the *Annals*, which covers, now with lacunae, the earlier period from Tiberius to Nero. His public career progressed under Vespasian and Titus, and after the death of Domitian (AD 96) he became consul in 97 and later was made governor of the province of Asia. In the preface to the *Histories* he celebrates the happy age into which he has lived following the death of Domitian – the age of Nerva and Trajan (*Histories*, I.i).

If the reign of Caligula and parts of the reigns of Claudius and Nero had not been missing from the *Annals*, and also the period AD 71–96 from the *Histories*, his works would have formed a continuous series covering almost the whole of the first century. The reigns of Claudius and Nero, as well as those of the other first twelve emperors, are of course extant in the Lives of the Caesars produced by his contemporary Suetonius. Suetonius' work is biographical rather than historical; he organizes his account around character traits rather than the sequence of events, according to the precedents set by the well-known genres of the panegyric and the invective, and also includes much that would have been thought too trivial for history. Tacitus' works also overlap with that of Cassius Dio, most notably on the principate of Tiberius. Dio's history continued until his own time, the early third century, but the later part now exists only as Byzantine summaries. Ignoring these, however, the line of major historians from Livy to Tacitus covers the last three centuries BC and the first century AD, from the consolidation of Roman power in Italy to the end of the first century of the empire. The gaps, in Livy and Tacitus in particular, are damaging, but we are fortunate to have so much. The *Annals* survived only in two medieval manuscripts, one of one part and one of the other.

Tacitus, then, wrote contemporary and near-contemporary history. He cites the testimony of eyewitnesses, old men when he was young, whose memories stretched back well into the time of Tiberius (*Annals*, III.16). He certainly used the memoirs left by Tiberius and Claudius and the published transactions of the Senate, to which, as a senator, he would have had easy access. At the beginning of the *Histories*, and also in his *Dialogue on Oratory*, Tacitus shows himself highly self-conscious about the changing formative influences, cultural and political, on oratory and the writing of history, associated with the ending of a republican form of public life and the advent of the empire. In the *Dialogue* we have, in contrasting speeches, the rudiments of a kind of literary or cultural history, with attempts at appraisal. At the beginning of the *Histories*, speaking of historians, Tacitus remarks that 'So long as republican history was their theme, they wrote with equal eloquence of style and independence of outlook,' but when 'the interests of peace required the concentration of power in the hands of one man, this great line of classical historians came to an end. Truth, too, suffered, in more ways than one. To an understandable ignorance of policy, which now lay outside public control, was in due course added a passion for flattery, or else a hatred of autocrats'. Dio (53.19) was to make the same complaint of the inaccessibility of the real causes of events. Tacitus shows an acute, even perhaps excessive, awareness of the difference between public profession and private motive, and speculates freely about motives. For his own claim to impartiality – a standard one, and not always plausible – he found at the opening of the *Annals* a formula which became classic: he had written, he said, without passion or partiality – '*sine ira et studio*'.

Montaigne, in noting Tacitus' biases, turns his perception of them into something like a compliment: one can see, he says, that Tacitus' judgements sometimes do not fit the evidence, because he has presented it without distortion ('On the Art of Conversation'). There is a good deal in this, especially in the presentation of Tiberius, the most striking of Tacitus' portraits. Tacitus does not discount the lurid rumours of sexual vices surrounding Tiberius' retirement on Capri, but he is less interested and circumstantial than Suetonius. Tiberius' public actions and sayings as reported by Tacitus seem almost always sensible, humane and even generous, and commendably if cynically down to earth and sane, indicating a positive dislike of imperial pretension and of flattery. These traits are, of course, not incompatible with bizarre sexual malpractices or, more importantly for the Senate, with lethal spasms of suspicion. The Senate, even while he is holding it up to contempt and derision, is almost always at the centre of Tacitus' picture; it was, after all, his own order. In his account, Tiberius is always seen as a darkly threatening, brooding presence, the enigma of whose character, guarded by his taciturnity and preference for seclusion, is always given the most unfavourable interpretation, in terms of hypocrisy and duplicity, even when his overt words and actions give no support to this; to the charge of hypocrisy these can offer no defence. Tiberius' reclusiveness, even his modesty, are proof for Tacitus of his moral turpitude and his need to conceal it; his silences, invisibility and sometimes enigmatic utterances are invested with malevolence and menace. How much justification there may have been for this interpretation it is now impossible to say, though it is certainly arresting and memorable, but the relentlessness of Tacitus' adverse judgements ends by arousing suspicion.

What survive with apparent certainty, as recorded by Tacitus, are Tiberius' actions and sayings. Tiberius, Tacitus does not dispute, lived frugally and unpretentiously. He was not miserly, and we are given numerous examples of his generosity in alleviating public and private misfortunes (*Annals*, I.75; II.37–48, 87; IV.64; VI.17). There are occasions when he shows clemency and compassion, or discountenances proceedings against individuals for disrespect to himself (I.74), as when he vetoes a prosecution for having melted down a silver statue of him. It was said that on leaving the Senate he exclaimed in Greek, 'Men fit to be slaves' (III.65). But Tacitus' view is that he was hostile to servility and freedom alike. He is seldom given full credit for his words and actions; they are always seen as the instruments of a deep, nefarious policy. His toleration of free speech, for example, was a way of discerning 'the truth which servility hides' (VI.38). Tiberius' rejection of the proposal of a shrine to himself in Spain seems a model of sanity: 'I am human, performing human tasks, and content to occupy the first place among men. That is what I want later generations to remember ... Marble monuments, if the verdict of posterity is unfriendly, are mere neglected sepulchres' (IV.38). But even this was interpreted, Tacitus records without dissent, as attributable to a sense of guilt or to poverty of spirit.

In his interpretation of Tiberius, Tacitus seems to waver between seeing a real deterioration of character and attributing the change to Tiberius' growing authority and diminishing need for concealment of his true nature. It has been suggested that ancient writers – one sees the same pattern in Suetonius – were inclined to see characters as fixed and to attribute the lapsing of virtues and emergence of vices only to the disappearance of dissimulation. Tacitus admits the evidence of Tiberius' earlier virtues, but emphasizes the deterioration. Nonetheless, the summary he provides of the earlier, 'good', part of Tiberius' rule amounts to an impressive tribute, indeed a description of a model government: freedom of discussion, the choice of worthy men for office, the due enforcement of law, and measures of public relief sponsored by the Emperor in cases of bad harvests. Officials were kept in check and not allowed to be extortionate. 'His estates in Italy were few, his slaves unobtrusive, his household limited to a few freedmen. Any disputes he had with private citizens were settled in the law courts' (IV.6). The great change coincided with the advancement of Sejanus. It is tempting, but perhaps unwarranted, to think that Tacitus may have sought to reconcile discordant accounts under the general rubric of hypocrisy.

Most of the *Annals* – in fact virtually all that is not concerned with the campaigns of Roman armies on the frontiers, in Parthia, Macedonia, Armenia, Germany and Britain – is focused on the relations between the Emperor and the Senate. Tacitus' attitude to the Senate is both scathing and solicitous. He is anxious to preserve whatever examples of merit, worthy of earlier generations, he can find. He subscribes to a standard view of history as the servant of morality: 'to ensure that merit is recorded, and to confront evil deeds and words with the fear of posterity's denunciation' (III.65). Nevertheless, he is sometimes prepared to allow piety, concern for a family's good name, to draw a veil over abject behaviour: 'They are dead, and I feel I owe it to their ancestors not to name them' (XIV.14). But in general the shifts to which servility is driven in its search for advantage, or at least for survival, are observed with the ironic contempt of a man who understands them perhaps only too well. Tiberius' well-known hostility to sycophancy adds a further twist: a show of independence was the only flattery left (I.8). Public conduct was conditioned by the anxious eye always kept on the ruler to judge its effect, so that, on the accession of Tiberius, the senators 'must show neither satisfaction at the death of one emperor nor gloom at the accession of another: so their features were carefully arranged in a blend of tears and smiles, mourning and flattery' (I.7). 'Political equality', as Tacitus almost redundantly observes, 'was a thing of the past' (I.2). Despite his recording of occasional examples of virtue and independence, sometimes incurring death, the world of high politics described by Tacitus is predominantly one of slanderous accusations, malicious prosecutions, spying and tale-bearing, hypocrisy and subservience.

Informing became a deadly blight on the age:

Friends and relatives were as suspect as strangers, old stories as damaging as new. In the Forum, at a dinner party, a remark on any subject might mean prosecution. Everyone competed for priority in marking down the victim. Sometimes it was self-defence, but mostly it was a kind of contagion, like an epidemic. (VI.7)

The atmosphere of suspicion and fear in Tacitus' narrative is greatly intensified by the crooked ambition and arbitrary power and cruelty of Tiberius' chosen lieutenant, Sejanus, commander of the Praetorian Guard.

At Rome there was unprecedented agitation and terror. People behaved secretively even to their intimates, avoiding encounters and conversation, shunning the ears both of friends and strangers. Even voiceless, inanimate objects – ceilings and walls – were scanned suspiciously. (IV.69)

Surveillance has since been enhanced by technology, but clearly its essential nature remains the same. Elsewhere, in the *Agricola*, speaking of his own experience of tyranny and the sense of shame it brought, Tacitus says, 'The worst of our torments under Domitian was to see him with his eyes fixed upon us' (45), which reminds the modern reader of the court of Stalin, just as Sejanus is reminiscent of Stalin's chief of police, Beria.

Eventually Sejanus overreaches himself and is murdered. The appalling ruthlessness of Roman political atrocity is pitifully caught in the plea of his young daughter:

They were taken to prison. The boy understood what lay ahead of him. But the girl uncomprehendingly repeated: 'What have I done? Where are you taking me? I will not do it again!' She could be punished with a beating, she said, like other children. Contemporary writers report that, because capital punishment of a virgin was unprecedented, she was violated by the executioner, with the noose beside her. Then both were strangled and their young bodies thrown on to the Gemonian steps. (V.6)

But the persecutions do not stop. For Tacitus, the underlying cause of Sejanus' rise to power was 'heaven's anger against Rome' (IV.1). He laments not only the fate of Rome but his own as its historian:

I am aware that much of what I have described and shall describe may seem unimportant and trivial. But my chronicle is quite a different matter from histories of early Rome. Their subjects were great wars, cities stormed, kings routed and captured. Or, if home affairs were their choice, they could turn freely to conflicts of consuls with tribunes, to land- and corn-laws, feuds of conservatives and commons. Mine, on the other hand, is a circumscribed, inglorious field.

But, he goes on, even the apparently insignificant is worth examining, because it often causes major developments, whether the country is a democracy, an oligarchy or an autocracy (a mixture of these, he adds, never lasts long). When there was a democracy, it was necessary to understand the mind of the people in order to control them; when the Senate was powerful the wisest experts were those who best knew its mind. Similarly,

now that Rome has virtually been transformed into an autocracy, the investigation and record of these details concerning the autocrat may prove useful. Indeed, it is from such studies – from the experience of others – that most men learn to distinguish right and wrong, advantage and disadvantage ... So these accounts have their uses. But they are distasteful. What interests and stimulates readers is a geographical description, the changing fortune of a battle, the glorious death of a commander. My themes, on the other hand, concern cruel orders, unremitting accusations, treacherous friendships, innocent men ruined – a conspicuously monotonous glut of downfalls and their monotonous causes. (IV.32–3)

One may also, Tacitus adds, excite animosity by mentioning the disgraced ancestors of the living, or the latter may see their own behaviour mirrored in that of others and be accordingly resentful, or be put to shame by glorious examples.

Tacitus' account of Caligula is missing, and that of Claudius severely truncated – what remains of it focuses chiefly on the treachery of Claudius' wives, Messalina and Agrippina. Tacitus invokes the authority of unnamed witnesses in recording this: 'What I shall tell is the truth. Older men have heard and recorded it' (XI.27). The earlier part of Nero's reign is similarly dominated by his mother, Agrippina, though foreign affairs and campaigns, including those in Britain, claim the usual share of attention accorded them in annals. The burning of Rome, of course, forms another episode. Nero's own scandalous behaviour finds new forms of excess, and populace and senators, and their wives and daughters, are seen as grossly corrupted by sycophancy and debauchery, with the Emperor as leader of the revels. Even the spread of Christianity – 'the deadly superstition' – to Rome itself is additional evidence of decadence: 'All degraded and shameful practices flourish in the capital' (XV.44). The climax – Tacitus' extant account stops short of the fall of Nero – is the persecutions which follow an unsuccessful plot. Tacitus describes a number of cases in detail, dwelling particularly on dignified suicides. Ever conscious of the effect on his readers, he laments that they may find the otherwise unremitting ignominy tedious: 'This slavish passivity, this torrent of wasted bloodshed far from active service, wearies, depresses and paralyses the mind' (XVI.14). But the ends of notable men deserve not to be ignored, and in any case their ignominy was not their fault but – again – heaven's anger with Rome. As he appreciates, it seems a far cry from the impulse, going back as far as Herodotus, to write history to preserve the memory of notable deeds.

It seems in Tacitus' account, in fact, that the last recourse open to a member of the senatorial class to show worth was in the manner of taking his own life. The moral antithesis here is the Stoic one, between the striving for a worthless power and the dignity of a well-conducted withdrawal from an intolerable life or from imminent execution. Freedom is found only in the liberation of death and, sometimes, in the belated frankness or defiance it releases. But Tacitus, while recognizing this, recognizes also the passivity contrasted with death on active service. Roman virtue, it seems, is no longer active, patriotic and political, but self-centred and, in Stoic terms, 'philosophic'. Its reward is not fame but merely escape; at best death takes place calmly, like the prototypical death of Socrates, in the company of friends, an intimate elite.

One motive to suicide, as Tacitus notes, is that it spares one's family the sequestration that followed conviction for treason: the concern for others was for family, not country. There is an ironic contrast here, though Tacitus does not make it explicit. Early examples of Roman 'firmness', recorded, notably by Livy, from Lucius Junius Brutus onward, characteristically involved the sacrifice of family-feeling to the service of the state – a moral victory for public law over ties of kinship, which we may think of as a crucial step in the development of an idea of the state and its claims. In the world of tale-bearing and despotic terror described by Tacitus, the Roman state seemed a nostalgic memory; personal traits in the emperor, or the accusations covertly fed to him, or malicious or sycophantic prosecutions in the Senate, prevail everywhere; for the victim, the citizen *in extremis*, personal and family interests are again predominant. Tacitus is surely well aware of this as marking the contrast between republic and empire – hence his lament over the task imposed on the modern historian.

The *Annals*, as we have them, break off in mid-sentence in AD 66. The *Histories*, which were actually written first, take up the account after Nero's death, in AD 68, and record, in much more detail than is common in the *Annals*, the events of AD 69–70. They continued until almost the end of the century, but the rest is lost. The year AD 69 was one of exceptional eventfulness, comprising civil wars and usurpations, four changes of emperor, and the eventual establishment of a new dynasty by Vespasian: the century-long dominance of the Julio-Claudians, established by Augustus, was at an end. Hence AD 69 became known as 'the year of the four emperors': Galba, Otho, Vitellius and Vespasian. Ultimate power rested for a while nakedly with the soldiery, and the conditions of the late republic were re-created in a highly condensed form. Three of the emperors had a power base in one of the military provinces, where each was proclaimed emperor by his troops: Galba in Spain, Vitellius in Germany, and Vespasian – who took longest to reach Rome – in the east, while Otho, an associate of Nero, was proclaimed by the Praetorian Guard in Rome in a kind of Neronian backlash against Galba. Hence Rome was involved in civil wars for the first time for a century.

Deploring this, Tacitus implies that the elevation of Galba, the first to be proclaimed, should have been accepted, though he recognizes that the eventual winner, Vespasian, was in many ways the worthiest of the contenders. For Otho, a partner in Nero's vices, and Vitellius, always spoken of as lazy and compulsively gluttonous, he has no use at all. Drawing the parallel with the late republic, he adds that Caesar and Pompey, Augustus and Brutus, had been honourable antagonists, while when Otho and Vitellius accused each other of wickedness and debauchery 'here at least both were in the right' (I.74). The successive usurpers, the response of the Romans to them, and the conduct of the soldiers provoke Tacitus to savage ironies and dismissive epigrams. On Galba, for example: 'So long as he was a subject he seemed too great a man to be one, and everyone would have judged him worthy to rule if only he had not ruled' (I.49). Vitellius is commemorated for 'the excessive and imprudent generosity with which he squandered both what was his to give and what was not' (I.52). It is easy to understand the impression made on the young Edward Gibbon and to see the marks of Tacitus' influence on some of the stylistic traits as well as on the attitudes of *The Decline and Fall of the Roman Empire*.

Tacitus registers the affronts to the dignity of Rome in the disturbances of AD 69 and the behaviour of the Praetorian Guard with an obvious sense of outrage which, even compared with the dreadful events he was to chronicle in the *Annals*, testifies to the settled character that the empire had nonetheless assumed:

Roman troops made ready to murder an old defenceless man who was their emperor, just as if they were set on deposing a Vologaeses or Pacorus [rulers of Parthia] . . . Forcing their way through the crowd, trampling the Senate under foot, with weapons ready and horses spurred to a gallop, they burst upon the Forum. Such men were not deterred by the sight of the Capitol, the sanctity of the temples that looked down upon them, nor the thought of emperors past and emperors to come. (I.40)

Despite the delinquencies which had disfigured it, the imperial title had become, it seems, what Augustus' word had claimed for it: august. The injuries done to the city as well as its people, and worst of all the burning of the temple of Jupiter on the Capitoline hill, are clearly felt by Tacitus with indignation that they were the work of Roman armies, who treated Rome itself, as they had treated the peaceful provinces through which they marched, with all the harshness of conquering invaders.

As described by Tacitus, the world of AD 69 has in fact become a world turned upside down: the soldiers, insubordinate to their commanders as well as to the emperors, become mobs, while the Roman mob becomes homicidal, and – a particular outrage – senators are alleged to have taken swords into the Senate house. Peaceful Roman towns like Cremona – founded, Tacitus ironically recalls, as a bulwark against the Gauls – and later Rome itself, are sacked by Roman armies. The Gallic provinces try to placate the soldiers who pass through them 'to secure peace in the absence of war' (I.63). When Vitellius enters Rome, he makes a speech 'as if he were addressing the senate and people of a foreign state' (II.90). In the capital, Tacitus says, the populace were so corrupted that they applauded the fighting as though watching a gladiatorial combat:

Close by the fighting stood the people of Rome like the audience at a show, cheering and clapping this side or that in turns as if this were a mock battle in the arena. Whenever one side or the other gave way, men would hide in shops or take refuge in some great house. They were then dragged out and killed at the instance of the mob ... The whole city presented a frightful caricature of its normal self; fighting and casualties at one point, baths and restaurants at another, here the spilling of blood and the litter of dead bodies, close by prostitutes and their like – all the vice associated with a life of idleness and pleasure, all the dreadful deeds typical of a pitiless sack. (III.83)

But Rome nursed a moral plague (Sallust's influence seems very evident here), infecting the armies with the taint of luxury, softness and indiscipline (as Capua and Boeotia, one could add, had once been blamed for doing; the centre of corruption was now the capital itself) (II.69). Tacitus describes the armies' excesses almost pathetically as 'quite un-Roman' (II.73). The soldiers, with whom power lay, were, he makes clear, themselves fickle, disorderly and confused as well as grasping. At one point what begins as no more than a drunken misunderstanding is construed by the Emperor (Otho) and the senators as a full-scale mutiny, in what becomes an episode of comic and ignominious terror. The Emperor's dinner-party guests, in a state of acute anxiety, but trying to be nonchalant, look to him for a cue. 'They eyed Otho's expression. As is the way of suspicious minds, although Otho felt alarm, he also inspired it.' He tells them to leave. This is the signal for a general stampede. Magistrates throw away their badges of office. The troops panic in turn, and rush the banqueting hall demanding that the Emperor show himself. 'The whole building was a hubbub of weapons and threats ... Their blind and panic-stricken frenzy, finding no single target for its anger, clamoured for a clean sweep of everybody.' Eventually Otho appears and cajoles them with 'tears and entreaties', and they return to barracks – 'but grudgingly and with bad consciences. Rome resembled a captured city the next day. The great houses were shuttered, the streets almost empty, the populace in mourning. The downcast glances of the troops displayed sullenness rather than regret' (I.81–2). In this confusion the successive emperors and claimants were less the directors of events than flotsam on their surface, bewildered, hesitant and passive. The abjectness of the Senate, frightened of the troops and anxious only to hedge against any possible outcome, is presented as pitiful. While Otho reigned and Vitellius advanced, some, in denouncing Vitellius, timed their invectives for moments of uproar when they could not be heard clearly or took care to be incoherent (I.85). Otho's own speech was unexpectedly restrained in its reference to Vitellius' supporters, which Tacitus is inclined to attribute to his speechwriter's anxiety to protect his own skin (1.90). (In the *Annals* (XIII.3), Tacitus says that Nero was the first emperor to employ a speechwriter.)

In a world turned upside down, vice became virtue, poverty a blessing, and wealth a curse, and Tacitus' irony was fully equal to the opportunities. The Senate, in pardoning three of its members convicted under Claudius and Nero for extortion, changed the charge to the less grave one of treason, since the latter, by misuse, had lost (for the Senate) its gravity (I.77). Soldiers with the Othonian army, when captured, claimed credit with Vitellius for causing a debacle which was actually the result of inefficiency. Vitellius took them at their word and 'acquitted them of good faith' (II.60). The wealth of one senatorial victim led to his will being set aside, while 'Piso's last wishes were respected because he was poor' (I.48). The same Piso, adopted as his heir (Caesar) by Galba, procured from his elevation only one advantage: that of being murdered before the elder brother to whom he had been preferred.

With Vespasian installed as the victor, affairs return to a shaken normality, symbolized, it seems, by the description of the ceremonies for the rededication of the restored temple of Jupiter, though there are already ominous remarks about the new Emperor's son Domitian, who was to succeed his elder brother Titus in AD 81. Much of the remainder of the work which is left to us is concerned with debates in the Senate, apart from Book V, which is devoted to a garbled and decidedly hostile account of Jewish history and religion, made topical by the campaigns of Vespasian and Titus against the Jewish rebellion described in detail by Tacitus' contemporary the Jewish historian Josephus. The modern reader can for once enjoy the sense of thinking he knows better than Tacitus, though it is interesting to see what slanderous legends were current.

Tacitus clearly does not know the Bible, already available in a Greek translation. Thus, in the account of the flight from Egypt on which, Tacitus says, most authorities agree, it is the Israelites who are expelled, on the recommendation of the god Ammon (Tacitus called him Hammon) as an act of purification to cure Egypt of a plague they carry (generally identified as leprosy). Moses, boldly declaring to the Israelites that their own god has deserted them, exhorts them to rely only on their own resources. He follows his own precept by discovering, as a result of observing the behaviour of some wild asses, a source of water in the desert. On the seventh day of their emigration the Jews expel the Canaanites from their land, where they build a city and a temple, whose shrine, in gratitude for their deliverance, contains an image of a wild ass, though elsewhere they are said to erect no images and to practise a purely spiritual monotheism. They devote not only every seventh day, marking the end of their exodus, but also every seventh year to idleness. Their new religion was prescribed by Moses, and its practices are sinister and revolting: they ban exogamy, practise circumcision, and teach contempt of the gods and of patriotism. We are given fairly accurate descriptions of the Jordan and the Dead Sea, and also a reference to a desolate plain once supporting great and populous cities. The Jews are a degraded nation, and their religion, despite being a spiritual monotheism, is 'super-stitious'. The description as we have it ends with a brief account of the siege and capture of Jerusalem by Titus.

Book V, then, was a classic digression of a conventional kind, and it is only the existence of another, fuller and more familiar, source which enables the non-specialist to be more critical of it than of other such ethnographic digressions in ancient historiography. Tacitus observed such conventions, though his manner – he seems to have admired Sallust most among his predecessors – in its famous terseness, its epigrams and ironies, is highly distinctive. In the *Annals*, of course, he accepts the responsibilities of the annalist, though the *Histories*, in devoting so much space to such a short period, has more the character of a monograph. In the *Annals*, in particular, consulships, portents and notable deaths are recorded as they occur, and large amounts of attention are paid to campaigns on the borders of the empire; indeed, Tacitus seems to regret that conservative imperial attitudes to further extension of the empire do not allow him more opportunities for such descriptions (*Annals*, IV.32). Occasionally one can see Tacitus self-consciously testing the limits of the annalistic form and looking towards a more thematic treatment: 'If I had not proposed to record each event under its own year, I should have liked to anticipate and recount immediately . . .' (IV.71). At another point he confesses to having merged the events of two summers and even to condensing, into one, campaigns conducted by two imperial governors over a period of years, 'since piecemeal description would cast a strain on the memory' (as, reading from a scroll, it would indeed have done) (XII.40).

Affairs on the frontiers also provide the themes for two famous works, published not as digressions but as free-standing monographs. One is the biography – essentially a eulogy – of his father-in-law, Agricola, governor of Britain, of which it includes an account. The other, probably owing much to the elder Pliny, is widely regarded as the outstanding ethnographic monograph to have come down to us from the ancient world, the *Germania*. It has certainly had the most profound subsequent influence. From the Renaissance onward, this work of Tacitus, as we shall see later, was to be a key text in the scholarly rewriting, from ancient sources, of the early history of the European nations, replacing the legendary genealogies which had typically traced them to heroic refugees from Troy. In the seventeenth century it became a crucial text in constitutionalist opposition to absolutism. Much was made of Tacitus' declaration that the Germans had no hereditary kingships, so that the barbarians of German stock, for example the Franks and Anglo-Saxons, who established national kingdoms in Europe on the ruins of the Roman empire, presumably had originally had none either: freedom was older than absolutism. From the nineteenth century onward, as the study of European prehistory became more accented towards the uncovering of the racial origins and characteristics of the various nations, much stress came to be laid, with eventually ominous implications, on Tacitus' casual claim that the German tribes had always inhabited Germany and were racially unmixed. Tacitus' own text, divorced from these later preoccupations, is an accomplished and vivid work, whose depiction of German manners is not, in its effect, an unfriendly one: the account of the simplicity of German life, and particularly of its uncorrupted sexual mores, has been read as an implied criticism of the very different manners of Rome. Tacitus sets the Germans' drunkenness, idleness and quarrelsomeness against their sexual temperance and chastity, independence, courage and loyalty.

Germany also figures notably in the *Annals*, as the chief external danger to Rome: the destruction of three Roman legions under Varus in the Teutoburger Wald by the German hero Arminius (to whom Tacitus pays generous tribute), just before Tacitus' work opens, was an immense shock. Tacitus picturesquely evokes the horror of the battlefield, with its debris of bones, as a later Roman army (under Germanicus) found it.

The scene lived up to its horrible associations. Varus' extensive first camp, with its broad extent and headquarters marked out, testified to the army's labours. Then the half-ruined breastwork and shallow ditch showed where the last pathetic remnant had gathered. On the open ground were whitening bones, scattered where men had fled, heaped up where they had stood and fought back. Fragments of spears and of horses' limbs lay there – also human heads, fastened to tree-trunks. In groves nearby were outlandish altars at which the Germans had massacred the Roman officers. (I.60)

The Germans were formidable adversaries, and the campaigns that Tacitus describes in the lower Rhine area and along the Danube were matters of vital concern, increased by the horror clearly evoked by the fearful terrain in which they were fought. In the *Germania*, Tacitus speaks feelingly of how unappealing the lands of the Germans are to anyone not born there, being 'covered either by bristling forests or by foul swamps' (5). Near the beginning of the *Annals*, Roman anxiety about these sensitive frontiers is greatly augmented by dangerous mutinies in the armies stationed there. In reading Tacitus' account here one has to remember that he wrote it immediately after treating, in the *Histories*, the civil wars of his own time, to whose outbreak the indiscipline and rapacity of the armies had largely contributed.

The situation half a century earlier was restored by the generalship of Augustus' grandson and Tiberius' nephew Germanicus, whose premature death soon afterwards plunged the empire into mourning amid strong rumours of poisoning. The peril represented by the mutinies and the difficulty in dealing with them are caught particularly by Tacitus in two notable speeches, one by a private soldier setting out the troops' grievances and the other by Germanicus, reproachful, scolding and placatory. Tacitus observes the convention of writing speeches, though his are often quite short; sometimes he puts them in indirect speech. Those of Germanicus and the soldier are given ostensibly verbatim. Under a despotism, a mutinous army becomes for a while a democracy, with all the volatility and instability of a democracy founded in grievances and without settled habits and traditions. Oratorical persuasiveness becomes again a vital political instrument.

Tacitus does not gloss over the hardships and injustices suffered by the soldiers, but Erich Auerbach warns us against interpreting the vividness of their recital as sympathy with the mutineers' demands. It is a product only of Tacitus' artistry, and the mutineers' leader, Percennius, who makes their case, is described as a former agitator in the theatre, which certainly conveys contempt. To Auerbach (*Mimesis*, ch. 2) Tacitus' speeches are 'sheer display'. One hardly suspects him, it is true, of endorsing Percennius' case: the mutineers represented a grave danger, and had to be suppressed. Yet the question of imaginative sympathy remains tantalizing. Auerbach admits that the rhetorical genre of writing speeches 'allowed a certain sympathetic entering into the thoughts of the supposed speaker'. The question remains how there could be both sympathetic understanding, for purely aesthetic purposes, and also none. Certainly for the modern reader, Percennius' speech is cogent as well as eloquent. Imaginatively, at least, Tacitus understands his case:

Old men, mutilated by wounds, are serving their thirtieth or fortieth year. And even after your official discharge your service is not finished; for you stay on with the colours as a reserve, still under canvas – the same drudgery under another name! And if you manage to survive all these hazards, even then you are dragged off to a remote country and 'settled' in some waterlogged swamp or untilled mountainside. Truly the army is a harsh, unrewarding profession! Body and soul are reckoned at two and a half sesterces a day – and with this you have to find clothes, weapons, tents, and bribes for brutal centurions if you want to avoid chores. Heaven knows, lashes and wounds are always with us! So are hard winters and hardworking summers, grim war and unprofitable peace. There will never be improvement until service is based on a contract – pay, four sesterces a day; duration of service, sixteen years with no subsequent recall . . . (*Annals*, I.17)

In response Germanicus stages a spectacular suicide attempt, which causes a revulsion of feeling, and when order has been restored the ringleaders are butchered. The soldiers, Tacitus says, not merely tolerated this but 'revelled in the massacre as though it purged them of their offences' (I.44).

The soldiers' case has at least been allowed to be forcibly put. The same is true of Tacitus' treatment of barbarians. Indeed, the tribute to Arminius amounts to a memorable obituary: 'He was unmistakably the liberator of Germany [the subsequent title 'liberator Germaniae' comes from Tacitus] . . . To this day the tribes sing of him. Yet Greek historians ignore him . . . We Romans, too, underestimate him, since in our devotion to antiquity we neglect modern history' (II.88). There is a touch of the sentiment of Kipling's 'The Ballad of East and West' about Tacitus' tribute, as Arminius is promoted into an international heroic Valhalla. Tacitus was alert to barbarians' courage and dignity, and even presents their reproaches to the Romans in memorable epigrams. The British leader Caratacus, taken captive to Rome, tells his conquerors, in a scene which became canonical in Victorian school room history, 'If you want to rule the world, does it follow that everyone else welcomes enslavement?' (XII.36). Tacitus often uses this last word for Roman conquest. He makes a German, denouncing Roman greed, memorably express his rejection of the terms offered: 'We may have nowhere to live but we can find somewhere to die!' (XIII.56). Again, in a phrase which has become canonical, in the *Agricola* the spokesman for the Britons before their decisive defeat is made to pass what, in reading it, can seem like a definitive judgement on Roman imperialism. Speaking of the Britons as 'the last of the free', he identifies the Romans as 'the only people on earth to whose covetousness both riches and poverty are equally tempting. To robbery, butchery, and rapine, they give the lying name of "government"; they create a desolation and call it peace' (30).

Tacitus' own judgements are often emphatic, but, taken overall, they are not simple. He sees, and regrets, a nobility of character in the republican period now largely lost, but he insists on recording modern exceptions and he deprecates, as in the case of Arminius, an exclusive adulation of antiquity. He recognizes that peace and security required the supersession of the republic by the empire, of whose aberrations and the servility they evoke he is the merciless chronicler. He satirically describes the sycophancy of the Senate, but admits he knows by experience the terror of being under a tyrant's eye and the near-impossibility of reconciling survival with the preservation of personal integrity. The price of survival in such circumstances is high and lasting, even when the tyranny is relaxed. Speaking of the terrible time of Domitian, he laments the lost years, the erosion of energy and integrity, suffered by himself and his generation:

Think of it. Fifteen whole years – no small part of a man's life – taken from us. Many have died by the chance happenings of fate; all the most energetic have fallen victims to the cruelty of the emperor. And the few of us that survive are no longer what we once were, since so many of our best years have been taken from us . . . (Agricola, 3).

So far as Rome is concerned, Tacitus' conception of moral decline, though real, seems less deterministic than some; he also speculates that changes in manners may go in cycles (Annals, III.54). He certainly regrets aspects of the past, but he is not a natural idealizer, just as his endorsement of Roman imperialism is hardly bland. Heaven, certainly, has been angry with Rome and has employed tyrants as its scourges – an idea that resurfaces in St Augustine. Rome's sufferings prove that 'the gods are indifferent to our tranquillity, but are eager for our punishment' (Histories, I.3). Still, the present is at least much better than the recent past, and he is thankful to have lived to see it: 'Modern times are indeed happy as few others have been, for we can think as we please, and speak as we think' – a tribute to the age of Nerva and Trajan, in which he was writing (I.1).

Tacitus is in one sense a stern moralist, denouncing the extremes of vice, which he attributes freely to individuals and to the Roman Senate and populace, as well as to emperors: sycophancy, malevolent suspicion, spying and false accusation, riot and cruelty. He subscribes emphatically to the view that the function of history is to foster virtue and to castigate vice by preserving examples of both (Annals, III.65; Histories, III.51), though compared with Livy, who shared this attitude, his examples are more often minatory than inspiring. (We do not, of course, know what Livy's would have been as they approached his own times.) Tacitus regards the hypocrisy inherent in the Augustan system – the preservation of the outward forms of a republican egalitarianism – as actually enhancing rather than mitigating the horrors of servitude (*Annals*, I.81), but there is no alternative, and in taking the consulship (in AD 97) he himself played a notable part in the charade.

These complexities, and perhaps a training in outward conformity, are aptly expressed as irony, of which Tacitus is a master. We have noted the affinity with him felt by Edward Gibbon, who, in *The Decline and Fall*, explored the same ambivalences and contradictions – including those of the apparently incompatible virtues of civilization and barbarism, as well as their inseparable accompanying vices. The moral and political world is neither pure nor simple. When Gibbon writes that the Greeks, in the heyday of the empire, had been 'long since civilized and corrupted' (II) or – it is almost a precis of Tacitus – that the Caledonians preserved 'their wild independence, for which they were not less indebted to their poverty than to their valour' (I), it is easy to fancy that Tacitus nods in appreciation, as Gibbon surely must often have done when reading Tacitus.

9

A Provincial Perspective: Josephus on the Jewish Revolt

When Vespasian, the last of the four emperors to be proclaimed in AD 69, was persuaded to stake his claim, he was commander of the Roman legions in Palestine, attempting to suppress the Jewish revolt which had begun three years earlier. He left his son Titus in command, and with him he left the former Jewish rebel commander in Galilee, Josephus, the future historian of the revolt. Taken prisoner by the Romans, Josephus had won Vespasian's favour by prophesying that he would become emperor; Josephus apparently had a reputation for accuracy in such matters. He was thus enabled to be present, with the Romans, at the siege of Jerusalem, undertaken by Vespasian and completed by Titus, of which he subsequently gave a detailed account. After the war, with his prophecy vindicated and Vespasian now emperor, he continued in favour and, with a pension and Roman citizenship, returned to a property in Rome, where he wrote four works, all extant.

The first, entitled *The Jewish War*, was a piece of largely contemporary history, of the war in which he had participated on both sides; Josephus wrote it, he said, to correct current errors and provide an authentic record. It was written first in his own language, Aramaic, and then translated into Greek. He had the benefit of access to the memoirs of Vespasian and Titus, who both apparently vetted his text. His later works, including a spare and self-serving autobiography vindicating his role in the war, were written in Greek. The other two concern not himself but his people. His *Jewish Antiquities* is a long precis and paraphrase of the Hebrew Bible, with minor omissions and additions, to which is added the subsequent history of Palestine down to his own times, which repeats and greatly amplifies the first third of

The Jewish War, to which it is a historical introduction, covering approximately two centuries.

The variations from the biblical text in *Jewish Antiquities* are sometimes the product of Josephus' own learning in Jewish law and traditions, but they also show anxiety to give no opportunities to foreign denigration. He omits, for example, the episode of the worship of the golden calf, presumably in order not to reinforce a current slander that the Jews worshipped animals (*JA*, III.99; see also Tacitus, above, p. 141).

Josephus was a Jewish scholar, a priest and a Pharisee. In view of his role in the war – which he ended, from a nationalist point of view, as a collaborator with the Romans – it is important to stress that, although he was no political radical, and deplored the rebellion and the behaviour of the nationalist leaders, whom he saw as fanatics and terrorists bringing misery to his people, he was nonetheless a proud and patriotic Jew, anxious that the Greek-speaking world should understand and respect Jewish law and customs. This comes out most clearly in his last, polemical, work, which acquired the title *Against Apion* (Apion being one of the Greek critics he attacked), in which he set himself to refute Greek slanders against Jewish beliefs and practices and dismissal of the antiquity of the Hebrew sacred records.

Despite his brief period as a rebel general, in the Roman empire Josephus was a peace-loving provincial, who made it his task to explain the affairs of his troubled province and his unusual and often slandered people to the Greek-speaking part of the empire – which included, of course, the Roman educated class. In his narrative of the war, though the Roman governor is not excused, the heaviest criticisms are for the Jewish intransigents, and not for the Roman commanders, his patrons Vespasian and Titus. We have no reason to suppose these criticisms did not represent his real views. Nonetheless, his account is given chiefly from a Jewish perspective: it is the suffering of the ordinary population, especially the inhabitants of Jerusalem, and the faction-fighting and criminal behaviour of the insurgents that draw his attention, while his lamentation over the destroyed city and its Temple is clearly deeply felt.

When considering, earlier in this book, the originality of Herodotus' project of 'inquiry', the obvious point was made that it was he who was the interrogator and describer of exotic peoples: such peoples neither interrogated Greeks for the same purpose, nor, except in their answers to Herodotus, portrayed themselves for a foreign audience. This now needs some elaboration, because Josephus, much later, is precisely such a self-referential historian and ethnographer, as in the digression in *The Jewish War* in which he explains the beliefs of the Sadducees, Pharisees and Essenes. In fact, not long after Herodotus, non-Greek writers had appeared who adopted the Greek fashion for ethnographic description and the writing of history and practised it reflexively; they did so, it seems, in imitation of Herodotus, so they were practising a Greek genre, as indeed was Josephus. In the third century BC the Roman historian Fabius Pictor (see above, p. 98) wrote the history of Rome from Romulus in Greek, thus presenting it to the Greek world. The third-century Egyptian priest Manetho, whose history of Egypt in Greek was well known in the ancient world, is one of Josephus' targets. Attacking him, Josephus contradicts the old legend, which was purveyed much earlier by Hecataeus and which we have seen in Tacitus, that the Hebrews were ejected from Egypt as lepers, rather than, as the book of Exodus recounts, extorting their release from a reluctant Pharaoh (*JA*, III.265).

In the Greek world, the idea of the presence among the Jews of wise philosophers, analogous to the Persian magi, also seems to have been current. It may be the beginning of an image which much later made the Hebrew Kabbala one of the key magical texts of the European occult tradition and gave King Solomon his role in Freemasonry. But for the next half dozen centuries the image stood, if it stood at all, instead of closer acquaintance. Though the Bible was available in a Greek translation, for the benefit of Greek-speaking Jewish exiles, before the end of the second century BC, and was, as we have seen, paraphrased in Greek by Josephus in the first century AD, it seems to have made little impression on the Gentile world except with the advent of Christianity (see below, for example p. 184), in which the relation to Judaic tradition was a serious issue. On the other hand, it is thanks mainly to Josephus' *The Jewish War* that we know more of Palestine in the first century AD than of any other part of the empire: in Josephus, a Roman province found a voice and spoke of itself and of the experience of Roman rule. A writer neither Greek nor Roman had exhibited his people to a wider world, within the conventions of Graeco-Roman historiography. We should know incomparably more about Roman Britain if there had been a similarly able British historian.

Josephus begins his long historical preamble to *The Jewish War* with the second century BC, when Palestine was contested territory between two of the successor kingdoms of Alexander's empire, Syria and Egypt. We are told of the Jews' successful assertion of their independence, led by the family of the Maccabees, after the Syrian king's desecration of the Temple had acted as a trigger for revolt. Josephus' narrative rapidly advances to the career of Herod the Great, who in the second half of the first century BC established himself in power by cultivating the favour of the Romans, now the dominant power in the region, and was recognized by them as king of the Jews in 40 BC, though Judaea itself was subsequently brought under direct Roman rule (in AD 6) under a Roman governor. Herod's successors were still local client rulers half a century later, and the most successful of them, Agrippa II, played a peripheral role (described by Josephus) on the side of Rome and the Jewish moderates in the war of AD 67–70. Herod the Great himself had been a consummate politician, managing brilliantly to negotiate the rapid and violent transitions in the Roman politics of his day, dealing successively with Pompey, Caesar, Cassius, Antony and Octavian (whom Josephus calls 'Caesar', as he does later emperors), and remaining fast friends with all of them; if this was time-serving, he seems to have raised it to the level of an art.

Josephus introduces us to Herod's copious building projects, in the restoration and improvement of the Temple, in other notable buildings inside and outside Palestine, and in the creation, on a previously fairly insignificant site, of Caesarea as a great Hellenistic city on the coast of northern Palestine. Herod's lurid and tormented domestic life is also put under close scrutiny by Josephus, who had access to Herod's memoirs. The sections concerned, and the struggles for the succession, are a tax on the reader's concentration, perhaps largely because the royal dynasty, prolific in slander and treachery, was parsimonious with names, making do chiefly with permutations of Antipas, Antipater, Aristobulus, Agrippa and, of course, Herod. Royal families, it is true, often behave like this, but it seems sheer wantonness on

Herod's part to have murdered his first wife, Mariamme, only to marry another also called Mariamme. Salome, the notorious daughter of Herodias (a variation enforced by gender), does not figure in Josephus, but she was clearly a chip off the old block. Her great-grandmother Salome (of course) not only incited Herod to kill his wife, but, according to her nephew, entered his bedroom and had intercourse with him against his will. It was that sort of family (*JW*, I.443, 499).

In the increasing friction between the Romans, with their client local rulers, and the Jewish population, the sanctity of the Temple is, in Josephus' account, a recurring source of tension. Pompey had violated the sanctuary to enter it with his officers, but had refrained from looting; Crassus, however, in 55 BC, had robbed the treasury. Herod, a Hellenized Edomite, not a Jew, provoked a riot in 5 BC by adorning the gate with a golden eagle. Some young men zealous for the observance of the Law – the point was apparently debatable – tore it down, and they and the rabbis who had incited them were ordered by Herod to be burnt to death. The emperor Caligula, almost half a century later, posed a grave threat of violence by his determination to have a statue of himself in the guise of Zeus set up in the Temple; the situation was saved only by his timely murder. Josephus' description of the state of Palestine in the period leading up to the rebellion which broke out in AD 66–7 offers a vivid and plausible picture of a country sliding helplessly into anarchy under the influence of false prophets, bandit warlords, communal hatreds and an unsatisfactory governor: 'The religious frauds and bandit chiefs joined forces and drove numbers to revolt – threatening with death those who submitted to Rome' (II.264). Some of the religious extremists regarded all secular authority as evil and illegitimate, and behaved accordingly. Inevitably, as well as murderous internecine conflict between various factions, there was much mutual provocation between the more firebrand nationalist and religious fanatics and the imperial power, compounded by inter-communal friction. In Caesarea a conflict arose between Jews and Greeks over a partially blocked access to a synagogue. When young Jews took action to clear it, some Greeks retaliated by placing a chamber pot in front of the synagogue and pretending to sacrifice over it; bloodshed inevitably ensued (II.289).

Florus, the Roman procurator, whose avarice is bitterly criticized by Josephus, made his contribution by raiding the Temple treasury for money, of which he may have been short. Confronted by civil disturbances in Jerusalem, he countered by encouraging what amounted to a Roman military riot, with looting and much loss of life, after which he withdrew to Caesarea. The hotheads bent on rebellion took possession of the Temple and made it their headquarters; at one point, before the beginning of the siege superseded internal conflict, one faction held the upper level of the Temple complex, another the lower, and they fought each other ferociously. A contingent of Roman soldiers, after being given terms of surrender, were slaughtered as soon as they disarmed, and respectable Jews fled the city if they could.

The siege of Jerusalem by the Romans is naturally the core of Josephus' history, but first – equally naturally perhaps, if egotistically – he devotes considerable space to the preliminary campaign in Galilee, where he himself had been appointed a Jewish commander; it was very short-lived, because the Romans were quickly victorious, and was hardly crucial. Josephus' version of his achievements there is not over-modest. He was, by his account, fearless, adroit and an excellent military organizer; he admired Roman drill, and writes an interesting digression describing it. He was, apparently, the hope of his people, vital to their morale, and his capture by the Romans was felt by them as a national disaster.

His account of his capture is ingenuous without being altogether convincing, and it has to be said that if he behaved worse than he said he did then he behaved very badly indeed. Making his escape from his defeated army, 'helped by some divine providence', he finds himself in hiding with forty companions. Discovered and offered safe conduct by the Romans, he intends to give himself up, but his companions protest at being abandoned and recommend suicide. Josephus gives himself a decidedly well constructed, somewhat academic speech condemning suicide in general, which not surprisingly fails to grip his audience. (Josephus' speeches given to others are also often more than usually implausible as products of the spur of the moment, under stress.) Josephus then suggests they draw lots to kill each other, the final survivor killing himself. This was the formula later adopted by the defenders of Masada, which Josephus knew of before he wrote, since he describes it. The others comply, killing and offering themselves to be killed according to the rules, until – 'shall we put it down to divine providence or just to luck'? – only Josephus and one other are left alive. Surrounded presumably by the corpses of the compliant, Josephus apparently persuades his companion that, though his idea, the concept is fundamentally flawed. They give themselves up (III.341–91).

After a spell in captivity, Josephus is freed to begin his career of collaboration and the enjoyment of Vespasian's favour as a result of his prophecy of the latter's future greatness; Josephus seems genuinely to have believed in his ability to foretell the future and to interpret prophecies and his own prophetic dreams. He experiences the siege of Jerusalem from a ringside if not altogether safe position – he is struck once by a missile from the walls – shouting to the besieged in their own tongue that resistance is useless – which he believed – and that they should surrender; he also mentions the information on conditions inside the city that he received from deserters. His role would have been described in later military language as 'propaganda and intelligence'. In judging his conduct here we have to remember (and there is no reason not to take his word) that he had opposed the war, thought the rebellion doomed, deplored its leadership, and participated in it against his judgement. Earlier on, he gives King Agrippa a long speech in which he harangues the Jews on the might of Rome and the futility of their resistance, and this seems to express Josephus' own feelings (II.242–404). He had himself visited and lived in Rome for a while. He had every motive for presenting the leaders of the insurgents in the city as murderers, thieves and fanatics, which he repeatedly does, denouncing their faction-fighting, their desecration of the Temple, their ruthlessness to ordinary citizens, and the uselessness of it all – the immense suffering and the utter devastation inflicted on the Temple and the city.

Josephus is at pains to explain that the Jews brought the devastation on themselves, and largely caused it. He speaks of their leaders as zealots, and the only positive quality he concedes them – even, as a Jew, takes pride in – is their extraordinary and indomitable courage. The final cataclysm is apocalyptically described:

While the Sanctuary was burning, looting went on right and left and all who were caught were put to the sword ... little children and old men, laymen and priests alike were butchered; every class was held in the iron embrace of war, whether they defended themselves or cried for mercy. Through the roar of the flames as they swept relentlessly on could be heard the groans of the falling: such were the height of the hill and the vastness of the blazing edifice that the entire city seemed to be on fire, while as for the noise, nothing could be imagined more shattering or more horrifying ... Yet more terrible than the din were the sights that met the eye. The Temple Hill, enveloped in flames from top to bottom, appeared to be boiling up from its very roots ... (VI.270–77)

In his summing up of the causes of the catastrophe, Josephus singles out particularly the irony that, while clear divine warnings were ignored, false prophecies and spurious messiahs were gullibly embraced: the Jews had, literally, misread the signs. Some Jews still holding out ask for a parley. Titus answers them in an implausibly long speech in justification of Roman policy and in condemnation of the wickedness of the Jews in taking up a hopeless cause. According to Josephus, Titus had earlier wished to spare the city and the Temple; now 'he gave his men leave to burn and sack the city' (IV.253), which they very thoroughly do, while systematically looting the Temple treasury; the Roman soldiers carrying off the sacred vessels depicted over the arch of Titus in Rome is one of our abiding images from the ancient world.

The destruction of Jerusalem makes an unsurpassable climax to Josephus' history, but there was room for two more notable set pieces. One is the Roman triumph of Vespasian and Titus, described in all its state and splendour. Most interesting, and apparently unusual, are the travelling tableaux, three or four storeys high, showing stages of the war: men in flight and in captivity, siege engines battering down walls, an army streaming inside the ramparts, temples on fire, and a blazing countryside. The fall of Jerusalem had clearly caught the imagination of the Romans. Afterwards, one of the rebellion's ring-leaders, Simon son of Gioras, a particular bête noire of Josephus, was executed in the Forum, and Vespasian deposited the treasures from the Temple – the golden table, the seven-branched candlestick and the rest – in his newly built temple of peace. The other set piece is the fall of the rock fortress of Masada, in AD 73, with the mass suicide of its defenders; no one seems to have played the role of Josephus and survived.

It was common for ancient historians to claim some superlative for their theme: 'the greatest' in some relevant category. Disregarding arithmetic – always dubious in Josephus anyway – few who reach the conclusion of Josephus' story of the war will feel inclined, emotionally speaking, to challenge his own melancholy superlative: 'No destruction ever wrought by God or man approached the wholesale carnage of this war' (IV.423–30). Ancient historians dwell much on the horrors of war, and Josephus' account is second to none in its manipulation of horror, with its descriptions of massacres, of suicidal intransigence prompted by nationalist and religious fanaticism, of ruthless terrorism directed towards peaceful populations, of fratricide between rival groups and their warlords, with sacred buildings used as strongpoints, and of the final, crushing intervention of the imperial power, driven beyond all patience and discrimination to its own atrocities and to wholesale destruction. It is a sobering reflection that if, among ancient historians' accounts of human savagery, that of Josephus is peculiarly harrowing, it is also peculiarly familiar.

IO

Ammianus Marcellinus: The Last
Pagan Historian

Ammianus Marcellinus has been spoken of as 'the lonely historian'.
He was a pagan Greek, writing in Latin towards the end of the fourth
century AD, in a now officially Christian world. From him back to
Tacitus, three centuries earlier, stretches something like a historiographical desert, devoid of substantial surviving histories of the first rank.
To some extent the appearance of a hiatus is a product of the accidents
of survival, or rather of extinction, of manuscript sources. As we have
seen, Cassius Dio continued his own Roman history down to his
lifetime, the end of the third century, but the latter part survives only
in a Byzantine summary. We have just over half of Ammianus' work,
which itself survived only in a single ninth-century manuscript. The
earlier part, which began at the end of the first century, more or less
where Tacitus left off, is lost, so his history is exclusively contemporary
by accident. The whole must have been an unbalanced work, since
the previous two and a half centuries were covered in only thirteen
books, while the remaining seventeen books cover only twenty-four
years (AD 354–78); it was not uncommon for works of history to
become denser as they reached their author's own times.

The historiographical desert was traversed fourteen hundred years
later by Edward Gibbon, whose *Decline and Fall* begins with the mid
second century; from the notes to his twenty-third chapter we can get
an idea of the difficulties it created. Gibbon used the extant summaries of Dio, and also other Greek historians: Herodian, Aurelius
Victor (concise) – whom Ammianus may have known – and Zosimus
(largely lost). He also used, with many complaints of its quality, but
without realizing that it too was a contemporary work, though it
purported to be otherwise, the Latin *Historia Augusta*, a sensationalist

compilation of imperial biographies. Gibbon's snorts of disgust with it are frequent: 'this wretched biographer'; 'a most inaccurate writer'. It is with evident relief that, though critical of his 'coarse and undistinguishing pencil', Gibbon arrives at the firm ground of Ammianus' history (XVIII, n. 5).

Ammianus came from Antioch and served in the Roman army. Eventually he retired to Rome, where he produced his history in the early 390s. The period covered in the last and surviving part of it, which contains the reigns of Constantius, Julian and Valentinian, was one that he was in a position to observe at first hand, and on which he could interrogate eyewitnesses, which he did. Since the earlier books are lost, the work now begins abruptly, in 354, without preamble. Constantine the Great has been dead seventeen years, and his son Constantius, the survivor of a struggle for the succession, is emperor, though he has called on his younger cousin Gallus, elder brother of Ammianus' future hero Julian, to be his Caesar, the name now used for the junior imperial partner. 'Fortune', Ammianus tells us – and for him this was no mere rhetorical flourish – has let loose imperial misdeeds on the empire. Gallus, on whom the spotlight falls, is violent and bloodthirsty and played on by rumour-mongers and spies; 'Men began to fear even the walls.' As often with Ammianus, we can suspect an echo, conscious or perhaps occasionally unconscious, of an admired author, in this case probably Tacitus. One of Gallus' exploits to keep himself informed is to wander in disguise in the streets of Rome at night (an imitation of Nero perhaps) – even, as Ammianus says interestingly, 'in a city where the brightness of the street-lighting made night as clear as day'. Gallus is incorrigible. He 'raised high the hammer of self-will' and was carried away by his passions 'like a rushing river to overturn the obstacles which lay in its path' (14.1). Violent passions are common in Ammianus, and so is a tumble of metaphors, either predictable or, sometimes, incongruous.

After a quick excursion to the Persian frontier and a digression on the habits of the Saracens (digressions are another frequent feature), Book 14 switches to the emperor Constantius, who is wintering in Arles and displaying the familiar imperial propensity to suspicion and arbitrary cruelty and susceptibility to flattery and slander. This traditional theme occurs three times, in fact, with Gallus, Constantius and, later, Valentinian, and is much the same in each case, forming a good deal of what might be called the 'politics' of Ammianus' history, alongside military accounts. Tumults in Rome over a wine shortage, however, trigger an excursus on the city of Rome itself – 'a city destined to endure as long as the human race survives' – and its inhabitants. The remarkable past and the immense idea of Rome are contrasted with, as Ammianus says rather apologetically, talk of riots and taverns. We get first a brief summary of Rome's rise, won by valour, and its maturity and age, categorized (following Seneca) like the ages of man. Now in old age the Roman people prefer peace and, like a wise parent, have handed over the government of the empire to its present rulers; this ingeniously manages to make Rome old and young and to incorporate a metaphorical defence of the transition from republic to empire. In any case, Rome is venerable not senile, 'accepted in every region of the world as mistress and queen; everywhere the authority of its senators is paid the respect due to their grey hairs, and the name of the Roman people is an object of reverence and awe' (14.6).

However, in Rome there is a minority which discredits the majority by a frivolous competition in wealth and display, aspiring to gilded statues, and flaunting embroidered garments and high carriages. (Cato the Censor is called on for his usual growl of disapproval.) As usual, we are told that the ancestors were frugal, modest in dress and fortune. So far, so traditional; but then we get a sudden and fascinating swoop into thinly disguised autobiography, a comedy-of-manners vignette of the treatment of a stranger by fashionable Roman society, anticipating eighteenth-century satirical – we should probably add 'neoclassical' – descriptions of the fickle, heartless politeness of 'the Town' as in Fielding's *Tom Jones* and Voltaire's *Candide*. The ingénu is first received as though he were a long-lost friend; next day he is not recognized and has to begin again. If, after years of association, he goes away for a while and returns, he will have to start yet again from the beginning. As someone to be invited he will rank behind racing drivers and gamblers and pretenders to esoteric knowledge, but invitations can be procured from the attendants by a bribe. Rich Romans race at full speed through the capital, the women in litters, attended by swarms of their slaves and eunuchs, for whom Ammianus has a particular abhorrence. It is the old theme of luxury set against Rome's ancient virtue and venerability, but presented with exceptional animation and circumstantiality and a strong suggestion of personal slights remembered; it clearly hurts particularly that on the occasion of a threatened famine, when foreigners were expelled from the city, no exception was made for professors of the liberal arts, but dancers and dancing masters were exempt. As always with Ammianus, too, one has to suspect the presence of literary models. He refers, without the name, to a 'comic poet' (Terence, apparently) (14.6).

In a later book (28.4) we hear of the extravagances associated with dinner parties and even picnics. The houses of the great

are the resort of idle gossips, who greet every word uttered by the great man with various expressions of hypocritical applause, like the toady in the comedy who inflates the pride of the boastful soldier by attributing to him heroic exploits in sieges and in fights against overwhelming odds. In the same way our toadies admire the beauty of columns in a high façade or the brilliant sight presented by walls of coloured marble, and extol their noble owners as more than mortal. Sometimes too at their dinner parties scales are called for to weigh the fish, birds and dormice that are served. The guests are bored to death by repeated expressions of wonder at the unheard-of size of the creatures, especially when some thirty secretaries are in attendance with writing-cases and notebooks to take down the statistics, and all that is wanting to complete the appearance of a school is the schoolmaster . . .

A journey of fair length to visit their estates or be present at a hunt where all the work is done by others seems to some of them the equivalent of a march of Alexander the Great or Caesar. If they sail in their smart yachts from Lake Avenius or Puteoli, they might be going after the golden fleece, especially if they undertake the adventure in hot weather. If a fly settles on the silk fringes of their garments as they sit between their gilded fans, or if a tiny sunbeam finds its way through a hole in the awning over them, they wish that they had been born in the land of the Cimmerians . . .

Arriving at the public baths with an entourage of fifty, the aristocrats shout peremptorily, 'What has become of our girls?' Then we get another descent into low life, with a fine list of proletarian nicknames – 'Hogshead', 'Sausage', 'Pig's Belly' and so on – whose holders spend their time in gambling, discussing the rival merits of charioteers, and hanging about under the awnings of theatres. Some features of life in a big city are apparently perennial, and Harry the Horse, Ikey the Pig, Feet Samuels and Last-Card Louie would quickly have felt at home. The requirements of satire and censure could sometimes override the dignity of history, for which Ammianus seems half to apologize. He is very conscious of the decorum of history, and in fact ends his work with an injunction to historians to use the grand style, but his control of it is wobbly.

We have to return to Gallus in the East, and his erratic and savage behaviour, described in Book 14; Ammianus mentions his love of gladiatorial shows as an example of Gallus' taste for cruelty. The Emperor begins understandably to prepare the way for Gallus' removal and the latter, 'like a snake wounded by a spear or stone' (14.7) – Ammianus' addiction to animal similes is another striking feature of his prose – begins a violent purge, after which Ammianus lowers the temperature with a digression on the eastern provinces. Back with Gallus again – who is now 'a lion who has tasted human flesh' (14.9) – officials are prosecuted, tortured, executed. He has to be dealt with, and, full of foreboding and with his sleep tormented by the spectres of his victims, he is lured back to Italy, where he is executed. Ammianus concludes this book with a set of reflections on divine justice, invoking Adrastia (the daughter of Jupiter), who was also called Nemesis, 'who punishes evil and rewards good deeds . . . Queen over all causation and arbiter and umpire of all events, she controls the urn from which men's lots are cast and regulates their vicissitudes of fortune.' The myths of antiquity, he adds, endowed her with wings to symbolize speed and a rudder in her hand and a wheel beneath her feet 'to signify that she runs through all the elements and governs the universe' (14.11). The book ends with famous examples from Greek and Roman history of sudden and extreme turns of fortune.

For us, since Ammianus' work as we have it begins abruptly, and Book 14 is an arbitrary starting point, there has been something to be said for illustrating the work's central characteristics by considering this book in some detail. There is much here to which the reader of the later books becomes accustomed: imperial suspiciousness and cruelty; the ethnographic and geographical digressions; the veneration for Rome's past and for the city itself, despite the satirical descriptions of its population; the piety towards the ancient gods; the literary self-consciousness and allusiveness and the parade of historical examples; the metaphorical excess in the writing and the addiction to wild-beast imagery.

One frequent interest, not brought out in this book, is Ammianus' belief in portents and divination, which he regards as a branch of knowledge, though an inexact one, open to abuse. Later (21.1) he gives a pious rationale for auguries: 'We do not owe auguries and auspices to the will of birds; they have no knowledge of the future, and no one would be such a fool as to say that they have. The truth is that their flight is directed by God . . . By these means a gracious deity loves to reveal impending events to men.' Like consulships, portents were often recorded by annalists as reference points. Ammianus follows the annalistic conventions, though not obtrusively, which accounts for some of the rapid switches in the narrative from East to West and back, though later he handles chronology more loosely and provides a semi-apology for doing so (26.5; 28.1). But his interest in portents and prophetic dreams is far more than a matter of convention. They could be said to be one of the themes of his work, and he marks out divination and augury as 'practices followed by worshippers of the old gods' (21.2). Julian was addicted to them and prided himself on his skill. The rise of the future emperor Julian is another note not sounded in the first extant book, though it was to be the core of Ammianus' work.

In Book 15 enters Ammianus himself – a transition he always marks by the use of the first person plural – on the staff of the general Ursicinus, who is sent by the Emperor to lure an imperial pretender into a trap. The pretender, Silvanus, is a victim of Constantius' suspiciousness and of false accusation, which has left him no alternative but flight or rebellion. It is characteristic of Ammianus that, confessing the fears of himself and his colleagues on their dangerous and not altogether honourable mission to deceive Silvanus, he should claim that they were consoled by a banal saying of Cicero's. Pretending to support the pseudo-Emperor, they suborn some of his soldiers and have him murdered. At this point Constantius, to pacify Gaul, advances Gallus' younger brother, Julian, to be Caesar and to handle a dangerous situation there – which he brilliantly does, by his talents and charm and the shining example of his character. Ammianus is sometimes critical of him, but he greatly praises Julian's military abilities, even though his final campaign, against the Persians, ended in disaster. Julian's appointment to Gaul leads Ammianus to an ethnographic digression, memorable for his account of the bellicosity of the Gaulish women: in a quarrel 'the woman, with swollen neck and gnashing teeth [barbarians in Ammianus do a lot of teeth-gnashing], swings her great arms and begins to deliver a rain of punches mixed with kicks' (15.12).

In Book 16 Ammianus celebrates Julian's pacification of Gaul and his frugal, self-disciplined and consciously self-improving character, and mentions his still-concealed piety towards the old gods. Ammianus also returns the narrative to the neurotic atmosphere of Constantius' court, and the intrigues of his sinister henchmen – some of them picturesquely named, like 'Paul the Chain' and 'Count of Dreams'. The chief diversification is the Emperor's state visit to Rome (AD 357) (16.10). This gives Ammianus the chance for a set-piece description and a tribute to the ancient city. Constantius in the procession holds himself rigidly and does not spit or rub his nose, which Ammianus finds remarkable and attributes to affectation. Constantius, on this, his first visit, is amazed by the sights: the Forum, 'that sublime monument of pristine power', and the shrine of Tarpeian Jupiter, 'beside which all else is like earth compared with heaven, or the buildings of the baths as big as provinces, or the solid mass of stone from Tibur that forms the amphitheatre, with its top almost beyond the reach of human sight, and the Pantheon, spread like a self-contained district under its high and lovely dome' and so on. Of the Forum of Trajan Ammianus says, 'Its grandeur defies description and can never again be approached by mortal men.' It is a remarkable picture of fourth-century Rome, almost on the eve of its fall, seen by a Greek from Antioch and a Roman emperor who was a stranger to it. Ammianus' Rome, though then intact, is of course more recognizable to us than earlier descriptions of the city.

Ammianus was in the East during Julian's campaigns in Gaul and Germany. His numerous battle scenes are an odd mixture of epic cliché, with rivers foaming with blood and arrows darkening the sky, and sharp and clearly first-hand observation, like the squalors of being besieged in the city of Amida by the Persians, his terror and concealment during the sack, and his fortunate if somewhat ignominious escape (19.8). He was also very scared of elephants. Clearly the result of personal observation too is the reference to the engineer, 'whose name escapes me', who was mangled out of recognition by the backwards discharge of a carelessly loaded catapult (24.4). Ammianus scrupulously follows Julian's military career, to the point where, under pressure from the solidiers, he usurps the title of emperor and undertakes a long march from Gaul into the Balkans to make good his claim, only to be forestalled by the convenient death of Constantius from fever (20).

For posterity the greatest interest in Julian's brief reign (AD 361–3) is his abortive attempt to reinstate the worship of the ancient gods. Ammianus was essentially in sympathy, so his criticisms of Julian's excess of pagan zeal are striking. One of Julian's edicts which Ammianus censures most strongly banned Christians from practising as teachers of rhetoric or literature (22.10). Julian's worship was unduly ostentatious: 'The victims with which he drenched the altars of the gods were all too numerous' (22.12), so that the troops were gorged with meat and demoralized, at huge cost. According to Ammianus, the number of the sacrifices Julian performed led him to be called 'Axe-man' – Ammianus was always alert to nicknames (22.14). Julian's enthusiasm embraced all non-Christian cults, so that he attempted unsuccessfully to rebuild the Temple in Jerusalem, and in Mesopotamia sacrificed to the moon according to the local rite (23.1, 3). Divination, on which he prided himself, became a kind of public craze (22.12); Ammianus disapproves of freelance soothsayers – as was traditional (Tacitus mentions it). It was a world, in any case, agog with suspicions of sorcery. Julian's intolerance also closed the great church at Antioch, in rage at the burning down, apparently accidentally, of the temple of Apollo (22.13). Julian's piety, like Ammianus' own, contained, naturally, a marked strain of antiquarianism. He acted, just as Ammianus wrote, consciously in the shadow of precedents and past authorities: Ammianus cites Thucydides and Polybius, as well as quoting Virgil and Cicero and examples from Greek and Roman history. Typically, Julian, attempting to revive the famous

Castalian spring as a source of prophecy, ordains that bodies buried there should be removed 'with the same rite as that used by the Athenians when they purified the island of Delos' (22.12). The reference is to Thucydides, an attempted reading back across almost a thousand years, and a testimony, fostered by a deliberate antiquarianism, to the cultural unity of the ancient world.

Julian's death, from a wound received in the disastrous Persian campaign of AD 363, is another such conscious tribute, full of reminiscences of the relevant canonical event, the death of Socrates. Julian expires discoursing with philosophers on the sublimity of the soul and forbidding his followers to mourn 'for a prince who was restored to heaven and numbered with the stars' (this was a Neoplatonic belief) (25.3). Paganism on its deathbed was pulling out all the stops. Ammianus' own paganism, though clearly devout, was of a more restrained and genial kind. In tacit contrast to Julian, he praises the toleration practised by the otherwise deplorable (Christian) emperor Valentinian, and speaks of 'the plain and simple religion of the Christians', which 'preaches only justice and mercy'. He has none of the prejudice shown earlier by Tacitus, while noting the atrocities the Christians practise on each other: 'no wild beasts are such dangerous enemies to man as Christians are to one another' (21.16, 22.11, 22.5). Ammianus gives the impression that men could differ about religion without harming or impeding each other, though in estimating the extent of his tolerance it must be remembered that he was writing under a Christian emperor.

Julian so dominates Ammianus' work that there is a natural tendency to regard the events recorded under his successors as an anticlimax, but in fact these included two of the most significant and ominous events in the later history of the empire: the permitted migration of the Goths across the Danube into Roman territory in AD 376 and the defeat and death of the emperor Valens in battle against the Persians at Adrianople in AD 378. Ammianus describes these, and is fully aware of the catastrophes they represent: the Goths immediately go on the rampage, and Adrianople, he says, is a disaster second in Roman military annals only to Cannae (31.8, 31.12–13). Of course he does not know these, as historians are now likely to see them, as stages in a rapid downward descent culminating in the sack of Rome itself in AD 410 and the loss of the western empire. For Ammianus, the empire, though passing through a time of great tribulations, was still the world's central fact, as Rome itself was the Eternal City. He can still speak without irony, referring to modern communications, of 'our great and glorious latter days' (21.10). The empire is so widely beset that it is 'as if the whole world were at the mercy of the Furies' (31.10), but we must not read more into this than was intended. The extent, if any, of Ammianus' historical pessimism has been a matter of debate, but it would be wrong to endow him, even obscurely, with foresight. He did not know that he was writing materials for a chapter in *The Decline and Fall of the Roman Empire*.

II

General Characteristics of
Ancient Historiography

Compared with the centuries which followed, ancient historical writing, from the Greeks to Ammianus, formed a single genre, which the Renaissance attempted to revive. Before continuing, it is worth trying to summarize what the characteristics were which made it an entity, with common standards, preoccupations and assumptions, especially as these have been subject to some misrepresentation.

Throughout the classical period, historians were intensely aware of their predecessors, Greek and later Roman, and of many more of them than we now have access to or even knowledge of, thanks to the vicissitudes of manuscript survival. Ammianus, the last of the classical historians, was among the most self-conscious of all in this respect, and cites precedents freely from what we think of, as he did, as the classical canon, both literary and historiographical. Although, annoyingly to us, it was not the normal practice to name sources, ancient historians clearly treated their predecessors and contemporaries not only as sources but as models, rivals and, it is tempting to say, colleagues, across the two languages and many centuries. They use, occasionally quote, and cite in cases of disagreement or uncertainty; they echo, plagiarize (though it was not thought reprehensible to do so), emulate, criticize, denigrate – all of this, no doubt, more often than we can be aware of – in a manner characteristic of a scholarly and literary community, in this case exceptionally long-enduring, of co-workers consciously aware of it and of their heritage. We noted Polybius' confidence that if he died before finishing his work others would take up and complete it; such continuations are an occasional feature of ancient historiography.

In this sense ancient historians are an even more coherent group than the poets or philosophers, though the former were bound to-gether by admiration for Homer and the latter characteristically belonged to 'schools'. Herodotus and Thucydides, though not all historians admired both, early achieved a pre-eminence comparable to that of Plato and Aristotle for philosophers. The transmission of their works, through centuries of transcription by hand, never hung by a thread, as did that of Polybius, Tacitus and others; nor was their work lost, like most of Livy's history. Because many authors have disappeared without trace, or exist only in fragments, many of the intellectual threads that bound this community together must be invisible to us or have to be the subject of guesswork. We can be reasonably confident that there has been a substantial correlation between merit, judged by both the copyists and ourselves, and survival, which is some consolation, but our sense of the collective life, as it were, of the ancient historians is irreparably damaged.

Some of the continuities, of course, were given by the continuities of Graeco-Roman culture and ancient public life more generally: the literary culture grounded in Homer and the Olympic pantheon, Greek philosophy, and the ethics of Stoicism. More directly relevant to historical writing are the rules for prose composition and oratory formulated by, and widely accepted from, the teachers of rhetoric, which have sometimes been thought to have exercised a baleful influence on history as accurate recording and which certainly exercised some constraint on what it was proper for historians to write about. Historical writing, as is made clear by the recipes for it propounded by Cicero, was above all a literary art, even if one with its own additional rules concerning truth-telling. Continuities in the frame-work of public life, which the historians chiefly attended to, and reflected, were provided, among other things, by a respect for oratory, indicated by the many invented speeches composed for their characters by the historians in the tradition established by Thucydides. Another continuity was the worship of the gods and a respect for their temples (paying attention to their foundation and occasional destruction), and for the venerated objects stored and displayed in them, which sometimes acted as mementos of significant events and were men-tioned by historians accordingly. Associated with this is the recording of portents and auguries, prophetic dreams and oracles, and supernatural or monstrous occurrences generally. It is tempting to see a steady 'secularization' in the historians' attitudes to these, but this is hard to do, though Livy, for example, deplores modern scepticism. The historians themselves range from pretty clear unbelief (Thucydides) to complete acceptance (Xenophon, Ammianus), but these examples do not suggest a steady trajectory.

Recording portents was part of the annalistic form which, from Thucydides onward, provided the frame for most works of history, though some historians treat it more freely than others: portents were recorded as part of the year's notable events, just as consulships continued to be recorded as chronological reference points long after they had ceased in Rome to be politically significant. Ethnographic and geographical digressions, pioneered by Herodotus, and the set-piece speeches which, as we have noted, were Thucydides' innovation (though he was criticized for making all his speakers sound alike) remained notable features of historical works. Both, especially the digressions, were freely used by Ammianus. The concentration on the events of public life, presented in an elevated style and with long, though sometimes conventional, accounts of military campaigns, is an enduring feature, but much that we would find of interest is excluded as beneath 'the dignity of history', to use the phrase Lord Bolingbroke in the eighteenth century (*Letters on the Study and Use of History* (1752), Letter 5.2) applied approvingly to Thucydides and Xenophon. This inhibition did not apply in the related art of biography, nor in ethnographic digressions. In the motives for the writing of history, the one announced by Herodotus, the preservation of the memory of great deeds, is an abiding one. The emphasis on the 'greatness' of one's theme – the greatest war, siege, conflict, achievement, city, empire – remains a constant from Herodotus onward, seconded, in some cases, by claims for one's immediate access to the events. Tacitus virtually apologizes for being unable to claim the former: it is a sign of the degeneration of Roman public life. Among the Roman writers, of course – and the view is shared by Polybius and Ammianus, though Greeks – the theme of the degeneracy of manners is also a constant, from Sallust to Tacitus.

The view, first articulated among the Romans, that the function of history is to inculcate virtue and castigate vice, through the presentation of examples of inspiring and ignominious behaviour, becomes standard. The rival, more intellectually formulated, Greek view that we find in Thucydides and Polybius, of the utility of history in offering examples of success and failure, practical wisdom and folly, takes second place to it. It was common throughout, of course, for history to be written after a distinguished public career, both political and military, which Polybius makes a *sine qua non*; the great exception is Livy. The interest in causality and in distinguishing different types of causes, again of keen interest to Thucydides and Polybius, is by modern standards low. What is of great interest, from Herodotus to Tacitus, as an explanation of success or failure and decline, is the moral fibre of a people, which forms a central theme in Livy and which, in the case of the Romans, is also acknowledged by Polybius. Typically, this interest and explanation are expressed in antitheses whose components vary but also display a certain congruity: primitive hardihood opposed to luxury; West to East (initially Greeks and Persians; later Romans and orientals or, chiefly, Greeks); freedom to servitude; past to present. The same basic opposition can be given an ethnic, military, political or historical dimension, often related to each other, as required. The contrast is often attended with adjectives suggesting masculinity and effeminacy: luxury and servility are unmanly. It was left to the Romans to convert them into something like a general conception of historical decline.

Of course the broad consensus about historical writing also accommodated disputes and, over time, notable shifts of perspective. Among the former, for which Polybius' polemics provide a good example, were the rival claims of truthfulness, whose importance for history was universally agreed in theory, and picturesque and appealing narration. Over time, the most obvious effect of the shift of focus from Greece to Rome is that the subject matter becomes more concentrated: a single city dominates the narrative, so that the historian does not have to switch, sometimes bewilderingly, from one city to another. The problems in establishing a common chronology were also greatly alleviated. On the debit side there is a perceptible loss of a characteristic Greek cosmopolitanism, a Homeric emotional even-handedness in dealing with the two sides of a conflict, between Greek cities or even between Greeks and Persians. Livy and Tacitus are hardly parochial writers – the theme of imperial expansion and the need constantly to return to affairs on the frontiers, as well as the ethnographic tradition to which Tacitus contributes (though Livy's barbarians are usually just stereotypes), ensured that. But, for Livy, Roman patriotism is overriding, and this issues, of course, in an antiquarian attention to the city's origins. Despite the existence of a genre of local histories (mostly lost), no Greek city seems to have paid its past such close and pious attention, leaving it generally to highly speculative genealogies and foundation myths. For this reason the contrast between past and present does not have the same function, while in Rome, from Sallust onward, a conception of long-term moral decline became established. Tacitus' writing under the empire (and the same may be true of Livy's lost books dealing with the last years of the republic) is clearly ambivalent, wistful for a lost past but not committed to the possibility of its recovery. Such wistfulness seems wholly un-Greek. The quality of Ammianus' nostalgia, if that is the right word, is harder to assess. His not always well-judged dippings into the bran tub of literary allusion, quotation and historical parallels can seem like gestures to a grander past, but he may just be showing off.

There are certain abiding popular misrepresentations – certainly misrepresentations if taken too generally and literally – which seem to recur in references by non-specialists to the general features of classical historiography; sometimes, it seems, these derive from taking Thucydides as being wholly representative, or from interpreting too crudely what he claims to be doing. In this way and by over-selective and uncontextualized quotation elsewhere, a number of myths, over-statements or half-truths about classical historiography can be too uncritically propagated. Though there is substance in some of them, all are false if stated as general truths without qualification. We can deal with them schematically:

1. *That all history was contemporary history.* This is up to a point true of early Greek historiography; as an account of Roman history, including that written by Greeks, it is not true at all. It is true of Thucydides, of Xenophon and of the earliest (though not the later) Alexander historians. Herodotus' history, disregarding the early references to legend and to Homer, stretched back some three-

quarters of a century before his own time. We should also not deny the title of historian to the Greeks who wrote of the foundation of cities and of the history of the Mediterranean area, particularly the latter. It is certainly not true of Livy, nor of the Roman antiquaries who preceded him, nor of his Greek contemporary Dionysius of Halicarnassus, whose work also began with the foundation of Rome, nor of Dio, whose history covered the whole history of Rome down to his own times in the second century AD but a great proportion of which has not survived. It is not even true of Josephus, if one puts his two major works together – the *Jewish Antiquities*, which begins with biblical history, with *The Jewish War*, which itself has a substantial opening section beginning two centuries before the war itself. Ammianus, as we have seen, is a contemporary historian accidentally, since his first books, covering the century and a half before his own time, are lost. Tacitus can just be regarded as a contemporary historian only if one allows the memory of the oldest living eyewitnesses to count as contemporary.

2. *That ancient historiography is exclusively political and military.* This is broadly true as a prescription and declaration of intent, though it excludes biography, which moves between the official and the intimate; the earliest biographies (Greek) seem to have been of philosophers and literary men. In history proper, the most obvious exception is the often very extensive ethnographic digressions, from Herodotus onward, which deal with physical appearance, beliefs, clothing, diet, hygiene, habits, as well as marriage and funeral customs. Even in the accounts of the historians' own societies one would have to define religious matters as political – not unreasonably perhaps – to make the generalization hold, which for a modern readership is misleading. There are also, as we saw in Livy, the incidental passages of social history occasioned by the annalistic form or by the censure, in both Livy and Ammianus, of modern manners: the terrible stories of the proscriptions, in Appian and Tacitus, with Roman aristocrats driven to flight or into hiding, give us glimpses of the interiors of houses, domestic habits, and the relations of slaves, faithful or vindictive, with their masters. An admittedly jejune social and economic history is also inescapably part of Livy's and Appian's recording of the social conflicts in

Rome, with their references to the depression and indebtedness of the small freeholder. Descriptions of aristocratic and proletarian misbehaviour, of rowdiness and rioting in the streets of Rome, and of plutocratic domestic luxury and lower-class fecklessness are common and often vivid in Sallust, Livy, Tacitus and Ammianus.

3. *That there was no conception of long-term historical change.* This is to some extent answered above in the discussion of 'contemporary' history, but it is worth elaborating, for if we mean literally a conception it is certainly not true of Thucydides, the most ardent advocate of contemporary history. He thought, as others did not, that it was not possible to write long-term history to the required standards of accuracy, but that is another matter. Near the outset of his history he gives a sketch, of a kind that became fashionable during the eighteenth-century Enlightenment, of the development of early Greek society 'from rudeness to refinement' (to use the eighteenth-century phrase) chiefly – another anticipation of the eighteenth century – as a result of commerce. No one would seriously claim this as one of Thucydides' major achievements as a historian, and it seems to have exercised no discernible influence, but as evidence that he was well aware that life in Greece had once been very different it is irrefutable. Polybius also gives a brief conjectural account of the origins of political society out of primitive beginnings in which human beings were little different from herd-animals (VI.5–7). Livy, similarly, knows very well that the Forum had once been a marsh, surrounded by the primitive huts of a shepherd population. Elsewhere he gives a thumbnail sketch of early human society as such, conceived in terms of what later came to be called 'the state of nature'. More subtly, as I have argued, the conception of a long-term deterioration in Roman character and manners is itself a conception of historical change, implying the emergence of fundamental differences that were more than merely material. Despite the long consensus on the conventions of historiography, and the near-consensus on its ends and methods, some writers even display an awareness that historiography itself is not unaffected by historical change. Polybius thought that with the rise of Rome a new kind of history, universal history, became possible. Tacitus, who wrote a dialogue in which styles of oratory are treated historically,

was conscious that the tasks of the historian and the manner in which it was possible to write had been reconstituted by the change from republic to autocracy. In such views the possibility of 'a history of histories' was at least logically present if not made conscious.

4. *That there was a notion that all change is cyclical.* This has in a sense been dealt with above, but it is still worth confronting it directly. It is true that among the Greeks, notably in Polybius, there is a conception, deriving from Aristotle's categorization of constitutions and their corrupt forms, of the dynamics of constitutional change which seems to imply a cyclical set of transformations. But not only was this view of constitutional change not universally subscribed to and deployed, the cyclical conception itself was not notably applied to other dimensions of life, though Tacitus, in passing, at one point wonders if it could be. (He speaks of it as though of a new thought, not a cliché.) Of course there was a widely diffused view, from Herodotus onward, that all prosperity and glory were held on a very uncertain tenure, but it is a long way from there to the more precise and technical conception of the omnipresence of cycles. Thucydides certainly did not expect Greek society to return to its earlier state, nor did Livy envisage a future for the Forum as a pasture for cattle (though if he had done so he would have been right). Sadly for him, there is no sign that he expected the Roman character to regenerate itself, or that Tacitus expected a return of the republic. On the other hand even the worst tyranny was ended by the death of the tyrant, and there is no suggestion of an institutionalized self-perpetuating tyranny such as Orwell envisages in his *Nineteen Eighty-four*.

It is sometimes implied that a cyclical view and the absence of a conception of long-term change were entailed by a belief in an unchanging human nature, which is indeed proclaimed by Thucydides and accepted by Polybius as grounds for asserting the usefulness of history. We have already looked at the inadequacy of this considered as an interpretative master key to Thucydides' work. In Polybius it is counterbalanced in its effects by his claim to discern in history the emergence of a great new fact: Rome's rise, and Fortune's intention to promote this from now on as the central thrust of universal history.

The relation between an idea of universal human nature and an awareness of social variability across space and time is conceptually a very complex one, which cannot be entered into here. It may be sufficient as an indication of that complexity to mention the case of Herodotus, who is at once broadmindedly cosmopolitan and fascinated by the cultural – and it is natural to say psychological – variety exhibited by the different peoples into which mankind is divided. Thucydides' abstention from ethnographic digressions and Polybius' circumspection with them seem to owe more to austerity towards history written to entertain than to any dogma about human nature. Herodotus, however, is an author who, with a touch of pathos or humour, can transcend in a second the gulfs created by cultural prejudice and by time, as in the description of the tears of Xerxes, yet can also dwell with a fascinated attention on the bizarre forms – to us and to the Greeks – that human nature can assume. The other distinguished ethnographer among the ancient historians, Tacitus, similarly, though to a lesser degree, sees the Germans both as comprehensibly and even sympathetically human and also as very unlike the modern Romans, just as he and Livy see the latter as mostly no longer like the Romans of old. The variety of human nature was in fact of the keenest interest to the ancient historians generally; Thucydides is the exception rather than the rule.

In this first section of this book much attention has been given to a handful of ancient historians, compared with the immensely larger number of historians to be considered (or, alas, ignored) in the sections to come. But the former remained unchallenged as historical models and authorities, and highly regarded as sources for moral and political wisdom, for approximately two thousand years, in a way that no other group of historians has been. This alone justifies extended attention, as does the fact, not universally true of even influential historians, that they are mostly highly rewarding to read.

PART III

Christendom

12

The Bible and History:
The People of God

The differences between biblical and biblically inspired and classical historical writing are manifold. The historical books of the former are not written as literary exercises in the leisure following a public career, and they are not bound to the rules of classical rhetoric. Though the Bible incorporates the grandeur and sublimity of myth and epic, as well as ecstatic song and personal lamentation, it is also often homely and earthy: nothing human (or divine) seems alien to it. Despite the incidence of prominent priests and patriarchs, kings and prophets, the scriptures are concerned essentially with a people, the children of Israel, in their relationship with their God and its vicissitudes through time; religion and history are inextricably intertwined, because God is not primarily the god of a perennial nature, but the mover of history. He is omnipresent in a way utterly different from the pious references to fate, justice and the will of heaven found in classical historiography.

Hebrew history is insistently providentially guided; the writing of it, even before Christianity, was regarded as directly inspired, so there are no comparisons of authorities or attempts to reconcile conflicting ones, no expressions of doubt or boasts of inquiry: the authority is God himself. Despite the presence within it of a recurrent pattern of sin and retribution, which, with redemption, is also its overall pattern, it is essentially linear and directional – far more so than is even the theme of the rise (and decadence) of Rome. It had a beginning (Adam, Noah and the promise to Abraham); it will have an end in the Apocalypse, which is foreshadowed in the part of the Bible designated by Christians as the Old Testament. So there is a beginning and an end: sin and then the Last Judgement, with salvation for some. These are linked logically as well as historically by Christ's Incarnation as the middle term between them, which from the eighth century became the pivotal moment for dating: without Sin, no History.

The Pentateuch, the first five books of the Hebrew scriptures, probably referring to events towards the end of the second millennium BC, was written down in the first half of the first millennium BC; it was gathered, in the second half, into the canon of the biblical books much as we have it today, but it made little impression on Gentile culture until the coming of Christianity. As the Septuagint (from the seventy-two translators), it was translated into Greek in Alexandria in the third century BC, for the use of Jewish exiles, but remained largely of interest only to them. It was expounded for the pagan world early in the Christian era by Philo of Alexandria and Josephus in the first century AD, but their impact was on Christians, not pagans. With Christianity firmly established, the authoritative Latin translation throughout the Middle Ages, the Vulgate, was provided by St Jerome (AD c.340–420).

Considered as a whole, of course, the Hebrew scriptures, which Christianity adopted as the Old Testament, are immensely hetero-geneous, comprising various genres of ancient literature: creation myth, national epic, wisdom literature, genealogies and king lists, songs and prayers, laws and detailed ritual prescriptions, prophecy and protracted warnings of divine wrath, often clothed in symbolism, though without the oracular sites prominent in the Hellenistic world. They also contain something like 'political history', especially in the books of Samuel, Kings and Chronicles. Yet on a wider view they have too an extraordinary narrative coherence, presenting a view of the fate of mankind and subsequently of God's Chosen People from the Creation and the expulsion from Paradise as a result of Adam's sin to the second beginning of mankind with Noah, after the Flood; then to God's promise of land and favour to Abraham, vindicated in the deliverance from Egyptian captivity; then the journey of the people through the wilderness under their great leader Moses, by whom they are handed down God's law. They conquer and settle their Promised Land, the land of Canaan. All this can be described as foundation myth merging into epic. In the ensuing books comes an apparent transition from priestly to kingly rule, with conflicts with neighbour-ing peoples akin to the Romans' fight for survival and the conquest of central Italy, but with exogamy and assimilation as a menace, not an achievement, because they threaten their monotheistic religion. The people transgress again, rather as the world's inhabitants had done before the divine punishment of the Flood; they suffer a second exile, this time to Babylon, under Nebuchadnezzar; the Temple in Jerusalem, the centre of their national cult of Yahweh, is destroyed. Their return from this exile, or 'captivity', and the rebuilding of the Temple are owed to the Persian Great King Cyrus, whose empire has succeeded that of Babylon as supposedly (though spuriously) prophetically described in the Book of Daniel.

This unity of theme, whose protagonist is the children of Israel and whose divine orchestrator is Yahweh, is no doubt the product of judicious editing and selectivity, with the part sometimes standing for the whole and significant events symbolically magnified and simplified. The Egyptian pharaoh of the first captivity, and Exodus, is unfortunately unidentifiable in the Egyptian records, but with the Assyrian and Persian monarchs Nebuchadnezzar, Cyrus and Darius, who appear from the end of 2 Chronicles and in Ezra, Nehemiah and Daniel, Hebrew history becomes integrated with the known history of the Mesopotamian world of the seventh and sixth centuries BC, and even datable. In Samuel, Kings and Chronicles we have Near Eastern kingly and priestly history on a small scale, given world-historical significance by the interventions and presiding will of Yahweh. In the narratives, constructed with great maturity for their period, there are vividly drawn political agents, court intrigues and dynastic struggles – as well as innumerable wars (described with less sophistication, because Yahweh's inclination is the deciding factor) – depicted sometimes in richly dramatic terms comparable with Homer. Together they represent a historiography that can stand comparison with the Persian sections of Herodotus, though crucially without the element of 'inquiry'; instead, in Ezra, there is an attention to documentation which modern historians would approve of. Ezra and Nehemiah, in the fifth century BC, are recognizably priestly historians and scribes writing a kind of contemporary history and quoting sources. With the subsequent history described in the uncanonical books of the Maccabees, we enter the world described later by Josephus, after his epitomization of the Bible in *Jewish Antiquities*, and embark on the theme which would continue to the very end of the Jewish state in the first century AD, of the resistance of the Israelites to their Hellenizing rulers in defence of their religion and the purity of the Temple.

Judaism became a matter of vital interest in the Gentile world with the diffusion of Christianity. The classical heritage was too strong for the Bible ever entirely to monopolize the historical consciousness of Gentile Christians, but for something like a thousand years, and in many contexts for much longer, it was to become central to it. From the fifth century AD onward most writers were content to take their Roman history in the form of digests, with which they were duly provided, while the classical historians, with the notable exception of Sallust (who was both moralistic and brief), became largely ignored or even unknown.

The impact of the Bible on Christian conceptions of history, from the earliest Christian centuries to the nineteenth, was radical and pervasive. It was not only that the sin of Adam, the Incarnation and the Last Judgement framed all history. The fact that biblical history presented the dealings of God with his Chosen People in something like a recurrent pattern of transgression, punishment and deliverance meant that the same pattern could be expected to be repeated so long as history lasted: history presented a recurring series of types and situations within the historical macrocosm of primal sin and final judgement. Christendom naturally took to itself the role of the Chosen People. Subsequently this role proved to be of almost infinite application, to any nation or sect which, abetted by its chroniclers, chose to assume it: the people's faith, greatness or sufferings, the divine favour or the chastisement visited on it, demonstrated the equation. Given the notion of repetition, the Bible made available as roles in contemporary history a gallery of memorable characters and deeds: warrior, rebel, judge, prophet, great king (or tyrant), ensnaring or patriotically homicidal women, all for recognition by the historian or adoption by the agents themselves and their eulogists or detractors. As Gibbon said, recording one set of such applications, which became at some times common currency of public abuse, 'The characters of Eve, of the wife of Job, of Jezabel, of Herodias, were indecently applied to the mother of the emperor [Valentinian II]' (*Decline and Fall*, XXVII).

But above all the Bible offered an archetypal pattern, repeated many times, of covenant with God and entry to the Promised Land, of collective transgression and its punishment by devastation, exile, captivity, followed by deliverance and return, symbolized by the rebuilding of Jerusalem and the Temple. It is a pattern, it may be noted, which makes human beings the prime movers of history only through their transgressions: transgression is their role in the historical dynamic, though there is a subsidiary one for the instruments of punishment, whether tyrants or barbarians, and for the individual bringers of deliverance – types of Moses and the Messiah. It hardly needs saying that in secular history collective misbehaviour (particularly infidelity and fornication), destruction, oppression and occasional better times, or at least the promise of them, as well as successful migrations, have been common enough to make the pattern frequently recognizable. It was up to a point recognized in pagan history too: the pharaoh who restored order to troubled times was a stock figure in Egyptian inscriptions, as was the early lawgiver in Greek and Roman legend. Augustus was the Roman archetype of a prince of peace, whose advent could be mythically represented as the return of the goddess of justice, Astraea, to earth; she was all too often a *dea abscondita*. But in Judaeo-Christian thought Moses and Christ himself became the archetypal deliverers, as David was the successful warrior king, prophet and songmaker. In pious and courtly rhetoric such monarchs as the emperors Constantine and Charlemagne, Queen Elizabeth and William of Orange, and a good many others, were allowed by their adulators and commentators to awaken the resonances of providential salvation history.

The adoption of the Hebrew scriptures as the Old Testament by Gentile early Christians may not seem inescapable; after all, they claimed to have superseded the original Chosen People, as the children of a new covenant. In some respects the Old Testament was even potentially embarrassing, as was the behaviour of the Olympians in Homer, and in both cases one response was to allegorize the more disreputable episodes, after which the Old Testament could furnish suitable material for pious meditation. One very notable exception was Marcion, a Christian scholar of the second century, for whom the Jewish God was creator of the wicked world and was not the same as God the father of Jesus. He refused the allegorical option in treating the Old Testament, and so found Yahweh ethically unacceptable. He was excommunicated in AD 144. But Gentile Christians needed the Hebrew Bible. They needed its prophecies, alleged to be of Christ, to vindicate the claim that he was the Messiah; they also felt a need to rebut the charge that Christianity was a recent innovation, a parvenu religion (Eusebius, *History of the Church*, 1.3–4). The Old Testament provided Christianity's ancestral title deeds. Once adopted, it offered a satisfying, comprehensive interpretation of human history and a rich repertoire of symbolic identifications applicable to subsequent history, now widely seen as a drama which Providence continued to inscribe, its characteristic ways of proceeding being starkly and awfully revealed by God's earlier dealings with his Chosen People.

Since the Hebrew scriptures were requisitioned to provide a prophetic series of figures or types of Christ as the Messiah – Moses, Joshua, David and others – as well as apparent actual prophecies, the habit of looking for such types, along with new identifications of God's elect, became readily transferred to modern history. We have to be a little careful. Not all analogies with biblical characters amount to what is specifically typological or figural thinking, nor are such identifications entirely unprecedented. Some are just analogies, applied often in flattery or contempt, and characters from pagan history could also be invoked as prototypes. Josephus had very aptly compared Moses to Solon and Romulus. More polemically, in the sixth century Gregory of Tours combined Roman and scriptural allusion when he called King Chilperic 'the Nero and Herod of his time'. In classical times, self-identification with figures from legend and history seems to have been common, as Alexander the Great identified and vied with, and may have imitated, Achilles. The emperor Caracalla was obsessed with Alexander himself, and had a picture produced, one half of whose face was Alexander's while the other half was Caracalla's. Sometimes, with the figural habit of mind ingrained, semi-identifications could be made on the basis of names. Henry VII's son Arthur was hailed as a revenant in this way.

But figural thinking proper, as it became current in patristic thinking from the second century AD, required the attribution of a specified providential role for which the Bible, and even Christ, provided the archetype. In this way the salient events of biblical and Jewish history could be recycled as interpretations of subsequent events, in polemic, eulogy or historical commentary. The fall of Jerusalem in AD 70 became such an archetypal event, and Josephus' account of it was much read by Christians. It powerfully affected Christian imaginations as early as the New Testament itself, where Jesus is made to prophesy it: 'There shall not be left one stone upon another, that shall not be thrown down' (Mark 13:2, cf. Luke 21:6, 24). The catastrophe raised crucially the question why God had allowed it – and in a way that evoked a response in terms of sin, judgement, prophecy and deliverance.

Punishment entailed the need for deliverance and implied a deliverer. The counterparts, in the Christian era, to the figural anticipation of Christ in the Old Testament were the deliverer monarchs and leaders of later times, just as new Israels, chosen, sinful and chastised, also identified themselves through their prophets.

We shall see shortly how Eusebius gave a biblical and messianic aura to the emperor Constantine as a divine instrument and deliverer of God's people. The earliest British history – though it is more jeremiad than history – is a biblically phrased account of the sins and consequent sufferings of the Britons at the hands of the barbarians after the withdrawal of the Roman legions in AD 410. This was the *Ruin of Britain*, by the sixth-century monk Gildas. He presents the Britons' disasters in biblical terms as a divine chastisement for transgression, while he hails the martyr St Alban as a Joshua, himself – again the name ('Jesus' in Greek) helps – taken as one of the types of Christ. Other such parallels could be more encouraging. Bede, taking his cue from Gildas, saw his own people, the English, as the instruments of God's justified wrath against the Britons, and hence as a chosen people. As the greatest Catholic (i.e. non-heretical – most barbarians were Arian heretics) modern people, the Franks seem to have received encouragement from the papacy to see themselves as the new Israel – though the point has been argued. Protestant Bible-reading in the vernacular gave new impetus to such ways of thinking in the sixteenth and seventeenth centuries. In sixteenth-century England the preface of the *Acts and Monuments* of John Foxe, better known as Foxe's *Book of Martyrs* and a key Protestant text, spoke of the recently crowned Queen Elizabeth as the new Constantine; the latter had become a standard type of the Messiah as deliverer. In Foxe's modern martyrology the English were God's elect people, an idea powerfully present in the next century among the Puritan opponents of Charles I, encouraging their intractability. Many Protestant sects were to see themselves as seeking to build the New Jerusalem, an aspiration passed on to the secular utopians of the nineteenth century. The Puritan colonists of New England in their new land naturally drew on the same conception. John Winthrop, the first governor of Massachusetts, spoke of them as having made a covenant with God; the Spanish conquerors of Mexico, a century earlier, had on their first sight of Montezuma's capital hailed it as 'the Promised Land', just as Martin Luther King's dream promised it to his people five and a half centuries later. The soldier historian of the Spanish conquest, Bernal Díaz (below, p. 426), was prompted by the siege and destruction of the Aztecs' capital to recall the fall of Jerusalem.

Of course such rhetoric tended to be the currency of historical agents, of sects and colonizers, rather than of reflective historians and chroniclers, but the latter were not immune. They generally held aloof from the prophetic, millenarian speculations prompted by the Hebrew and Christian eschatologies and keys to world history, most notably the spuriously prophetic dreams in the Book of Daniel and the Revelation of St John the Divine. These influenced historical schemata like that of the twelfth-century prognostications of Joachim of Flores (1135–1202). Joachim's threefold division of the epochs of history, which included a strong prophetic element, was based on the Trinity: the epochs of the Father, the Son and the Holy Spirit, which would be the last. Eusebius, the first church historian, whom we must look at shortly, disapproved of millenarian speculation. But the biblical archetypes and imagery could colour secular descriptions, even without full commitment to the biblically grounded providential scheme. Ancient historiography, for example, records many catastrophic sieges and destructions of cities, but Josephus' account of the fall of Jerusalem reached a new pitch of intensity and lamentation, which seems to owe something to the Hebrew prophetic tradition. The prophets were the unsurpassed, as well as inspired, connoisseurs and experts in divine wrath, in the iniquities and faithlessness of peoples and their dire punishment:

> For, behold, the Lord cometh forth out of his place, and will come down, and tread upon the high places of the earth.
>
> And the mountains shall be molten under him, and the valleys shall be cleft, as wax before the fire, and as the waters that are poured down a steep place.
>
> For the transgression of Jacob is all this, and for the sins of the house of Israel . . .
>
> Therefore I will make Samaria as an heap of the field . . .
>
> And all the graven images thereof shall be beaten to pieces, and all the hires thereof shall be burned with the fire, and all the idols thereof will I lay desolate. (Micah 1:3–7)

Such admonitions, in the English of the Authorized Version, left an indelible impress on imaginations nurtured on the Bible; Josephus' *Jewish War* also provided popular Protestant reading.

Hear Thomas Carlyle's peroration at the end of his *The French Revolution* (1837), fusing in his unique fashion prophetic, iconoclastic fervour and satire:

> Imposture is in flames, Imposture is burnt up: one Red-sea of Fire, wild-billowing, enwraps the World; with its fire-tongue, licks at the very Stars. Thrones are hurled into it, and Dubois Mitres, and Prebendal Stalls that drop fatness . . . Higher, higher yet flames the Fire-Sea; crackling with new dislocated timber, hissing with leather and prunella. The metal Images are molten; the marble Images become mortar-lime . . .

Carlyle was exceptional in the energy with which he could exploit the apocalyptic mode, but in secular history it was revolution which, more than any other theme, invited it. For the early Christians, however, the vital concomitant of judgement and condemnation was the promise of salvation brought by Christ. For the church historian Eusebius this promise was typified in contemporary history by the conversion to Christianity of the emperor Constantine and the deliverance of the Church from persecution.

13

Eusebius: The Making of Orthodoxy and the Church Triumphant

In the early fourth century the Christian Church endured intermittent periods of imperial persecution, with their crops of martyrdoms, the last and severest of which ended only in AD 312 with the conversion of the emperor Constantine and the transformation of the Church's position from persecuted sect to its eventual privileged status. Few great historical transitions have been more sudden. But the Church had been constructing itself since apostolic times, over almost three centuries, and, as expectations of an imminent apocalypse waned, it was beginning to become conscious not only of its present and future but also of its past.

The notion of the Church as the new community of the elect, and its commitment to teaching and evangelization, gave a crucial importance to the question of its identity and purity; as the generation of the Apostles slid further into the past, it became essential to distinguish and defend the authentic tradition. Questions of historical continuity were vital, especially before the earliest formulations of doctrine from the fourth century by councils of the Church, which provided reference points. It was essential to demonstrate continuity with the Old Testament prophecies, with the testimony of the Apostles and the lines of descent from them of Christian bishops, and with the teachings of those who had become established as authorities, as Fathers of the Church. These continuities were necessary to weed out heresies, spurious books, ecstatic false prophets and enthusiasts, and deviant interpretations of the sacred writings. Orthodoxy had to be forged in the face of competing zealotries and of the intellectual problems posed by the assimilation of Greek – above all Platonic – intellectual traditions to those of the Hebrew sacred writings and the Gospels. There were formidable difficulties in interpreting complex texts recognized to be at least in part symbolic. The question of the unity of the Church was essentially the same as that of its continuity; it has to be remembered that by the time of Constantine's conversion the ministry of Christ was as distant as the death of Louis XIV from ourselves. The Acts of the Apostles had in a sense laid the foundations for what was now explicitly attempted: a first history of the Church, and it was provided in the early fourth century by Eusebius, bishop of Caesarea.

Eusebius was a Greek, born probably in Caesarea, in Palestine, of which he became bishop in the early 260s; he lived to see the Church severely persecuted (AD 305–12) – his own teacher was one of its martyrs – and then delivered by the conversion of the emperor Constantine; he was a notable participant in the Council of Nicaea (AD 325), where he met and supported Constantine. Nicaea defined the nature of Christ so that the followers of Arius, for whom Christ was not of the same nature as the Father but subordinate to him, became heretics. Eusebius, who has been suspected of having Arian tendencies, seems to have prized the unity of the Church above all else; he treated the formula adopted at Nicaea as definitive. At Caesarea, Eusebius was heir to the great biblical commentator Origen (c.185–c.254), who pioneered symbolic and typological readings of the Bible. Eusebius' own reading of even secular history was highly providentialist – understandably in someone who had witnessed what must have seemed the miracle of the Emperor's conversion immediately following the most severe and protracted persecution in the history of the Church. Constantine's conversion became for Eusebius almost like a second Incarnation, and Constantine was clearly God's representative on earth.

Besides his *History of the Church*, which covers the whole period from the birth of Christ to the time of writing in the 320s, and which was very soon to be translated into Latin, Eusebius was well known in the Middle Ages as the author of a *Chronicle*, epitomizing the history of the great peoples of antiquity down to the Romans, with an attempted interpretation, in parallel columns, of pagan and Hebrew chronologies. This was to be much drawn on for the preambles to medieval chronicles, being continued by St Jerome and sometimes therefore known as 'Eusebius–Jerome'. Part of its purpose for

Eusebius was to demonstrate the superior antiquity of the religion of the Hebrews – also a preoccupation of Josephus – over the others.

Eusebius wrote in another genre which was to achieve great popularity, Christian martyrology, an account of the recent great persecution in Caesarea. Martyrdom, prefigured in the crucifixion of Christ, with remoter precedents in the books of the Maccabees and the death of Socrates, became a central Christian preoccupation. Martyrs triumphed in the manner of their deaths, and were translated at once to heaven. Commemoration of them became an important feature of Christian liturgy, and accounts of their sufferings – often highly circumstantial, as they are in Eusebius – became, like the slightly later Lives of the saints, with which they overlapped, a form of popular Latin literature or what one might paradoxically call documented folklore. Martyrs corresponded in some respects to the heroes of pagan legend and history, but their deaths were self-chosen, they included a significant number of women, and their ends were not, ultimately, tragic but triumphant. The details of the physical agonies of martyrs, complementing those of Christ, were to be a rich source of Christian iconography. Martyrs and saints were influential citizens of heaven, and gifts and pilgrimages to their shrines would be a source of much wealth to the cathedrals and abbeys fortunate enough to possess their bodies or any fragments of their remains.

Eusebius' history was highly original in conception and became *the* history of the early Church, in the sense that his successors sought only to continue, not to supplant it. It had an entirely new subject matter, and reads quite differently from any classical history. Church history was inevitably heavily involved in polemic, in establishing the undeviating line of orthodox tradition and distinguishing it from the snares of heresy, inauthentic books and deviant interpretations. It also recorded the more notable episcopacies and martyrdoms. Jews, pagans and, above all, heretics are Eusebius' polemical targets, and he writes his history to confound them, with no claim, like that which had become standard in classical histories, to write without passion or partisanship: he wrote avowedly to establish and vindicate Christian orthodoxy. Compared with the classical writers of history, this may seem to put a greater distance between him and modern notions of historical propriety, but it also had the ironic result of bringing his practice closer to that of modern historians, just as the religious controversies of the Reformation were later to do. Because he writes not to entertain but to prove and to vindicate, he needs the authority of sources, and the question of which are to be treated as authoritative (though of course this is not just or even primarily a question of reliable witnesses) is crucial for him. Hence he quotes them, copiously, and sometimes reproduces others to discount their deviant interpretations. Indeed, without the library of which he was so proud, his book could hardly have been written at all. Hence he may be less of a historian than his classical predecessors, but he is more of a scholar – though certainly not a disinterested one.

One feature of his book, before it becomes a record of contemporary events, is a succession list of the bishops of the main Christian sees from apostolic times. As we have seen, succession lists of pharaohs, kings, pontiffs and consuls are among the earliest forms of historical recording. In Eusebius, of course, they are crucial in establishing the apostolic succession, as the institutional spine of orthodoxy. Another vital interest, analogous to it in the realm of doctrine, is the establishment and justification of the accepted canon of scriptural books – there were a number of additional candidates – and, alongside these, the acceptance of approved biblical commentators and the rejection of their heretical rivals. One way, therefore, in which Eusebius' book seems hardly a history at all is that, after the Incarnation and until the conversion of Constantine, there are, apart from martyrdoms and the inevitable apostasies under persecution, virtually no events. As one of Eusebius' modern commentators puts it, 'his history is peopled not by men or events but by those who wrote books.' The precedent was not so much classical narratives of political and military affairs as the Greek histories of philosophers and their schools. Often one feels one is reading a kind of select bibliography, with a polemical commentary and extensive quotations. Here he is on Clement of Alexandria:

Of Clement's works, the *Miscellanies*, all eight books are in my possession [there follows a list of titles] . . . In the *Miscellanies* he has woven a tapestry combining Holy Writ with anything that he considered helpful in secular literature. He includes any view generally accepted, expounding those of Greeks and non-Greeks alike, and even correcting the false doctrines of the heresiarchs, and explains a great deal of history, providing us with a work of immense erudition. With all these strands he has blended the arguments of philosophers, so that the work fully justifies the title of *Miscellanies*. (6.13)

This gives quite a good idea of the creation, from diverse materials, Christian and pagan, of a body of relevant Christian erudition. Eusebius himself speaks of the condemnations of heretics and their opinions as giving 'the names and dates of those who through a passion for innovation have wandered as far as possible from the truth' (1.1). The individuality of Eusebius' work lies therefore not in a manner of narration, but in what he chooses to record, and approve or condemn. He is, above all, making a record of the right and wrong paths, but he is content largely to let those who took them either speak for themselves or exist just as names and dates. This is not to say that his tone is dispassionate. The Devil is at work in the making of heresies, which are detestable impostures; heretical sects 'crawled like poisonous reptiles over Asia and Phrygia' (5.14).

Merely scholarly error is sometimes more gently treated, but the anatomy of false prophecy in Eusebius and his sources – much is quotation – is often vivid and precise, like his description of a pseudo-prophet in a state of unnatural ecstasy (5.17), and an account of the practices of a heresiarch in Antioch, who arranged 'for women to sing hymns to himself in the middle of the church on the great day of the Easter festival: one would shudder to hear them' (7.30). On the aids to orthodox devotion the sources can be rhapsodic: the bones of a martyr are 'more precious than stones of great price, more splendid than gold' (4.15).

It is in the recording of martyrdoms that Eusebius' work ceases to be a matter of disputes over words, and this gives a distinct character to the last three, contemporary, books, which are particularly devoted to the martyrs. Bookishness is put aside, and Eusebius, who in the establishment of orthodoxy can often seem a complacent writer, is provoked to a quasi-biblical eloquence – with again, of course, much quotation and allusion – by the contemplation of God's chastisement and of the Church's eventual victory:

The Lord in his anger [at the arrogance and quarrels of certain church leaders] covered the daughters of Zion with a cloud, and cast down from Heaven the glory of Israel . . . Everything indeed has been fulfilled in my time; I saw with my own eyes the places of worship thrown down from top to bottom, the inspired holy Scriptures committed to the flames in the middle of the public squares, and the pastors of the churches hiding disgracefully. (8.2)

Some behaved disgracefully, others heroically. The former are not identified, but the latter are named and glorified in a way that recalls one of the earliest impulses to historiography: that great deeds may not be uncommemorated.

Eusebius' writing also rises to the highest pitch of excitement when describing in detail the physical symptoms of decay suffered by the persecuting emperor Galerius:

[He] was pursued by a divinely ordained punishment, which began with his flesh and went on to his soul. Without warning suppurative inflammation broke out round the middle of his genitals, then a deep-seated fistular ulcer; these ate their way incurably into his innermost bowels. From them came a teeming, indescribable mass of worms, and a sickening smell was given off; for the whole of his hulking body, thanks to overeating, had been transformed even before his illness into a huge lump of flabby fat, which then decomposed and presented those who came near with a revolting and horrifying sight. (8.16)

The doctors were unable to bear the extraordinary stench. It is no wonder that Gibbon said that Eusebius described 'the symptoms and progress of [Galerius'] disorder with singular accuracy and apparent pleasure' (*Decline and Fall*, XIV, n. 37). The symptoms, in fact, bear a considerable resemblance to those ascribed by Josephus to Herod the Great. Those detailed by Eusebius with which God afflicted the last of the persecuting emperors, Maximin, are somewhat different but equally picturesque:

He was wasted by hunger, and the whole of his flesh was consumed by an invisible fire sent from God, so that all the contours of his former shape disintegrated and disappeared, and nothing but a collection of dry bones, like a phantom reduced by long years to a skeleton, was left, so that the onlookers could imagine nothing else than that his body had become the grave of his soul, which was interred in what was already a corpse and completely disintegrated. As the fever that consumed him blazed up ever more fiercely from the depths of his marrow, his eyes stood out of his head and fell from their sockets, leaving him blind. (9.1)

Maximin, perhaps not surprisingly, confessed his offences against Christ and was permitted to die.

God, having scourged his people, relents towards them. Constantine overcomes his co-emperor in battle in a manner compared by Eusebius to the destruction of the armies of Pharaoh in the Red Sea. In the account of Constantine's triumphant entry into Rome, the Emperor – 'God's friend' – is welcomed by the people as their deliverer and saviour, to the accompaniment of much quoting by Eusebius of biblical rejoicings, especially from the Psalms. Constantine and his son Crispus, 'holding out a saving hand to all who were perishing', are closely paralleled to God and his Son, while 'his adversary thus finally thrown down' (actually Maximin) seems a type of the Devil (10.9). Constantine is compared to Christ as miraculous healer: 'Taking the only Quickener of the dead as ally and co-worker he raised up the fallen Church, after first cleansing her and curing her sickness; and he clothed her with a garment' (10.4). Eusebius is referring to the rebuilt places of worship whose rededications he celebrates, and specifically to that of Tyre, for which he himself gave the oration, which he reproduces for us. Eusebius presents the deliverance of the Church virtually as a type of the final redemption. All dissensions between Christians fall away: 'There was one power of the divine Spirit coursing through all the members, one soul in them all' (10.3).

The deliverance of the Church is conflated in Eusebius with the reunification of the empire, the peace of the Church being, it seems, identical with the Pax Romana. Constantine and his son 'reunified the Roman Empire into a single whole, bringing it all under their peaceful sway, in a wide circle embracing north and south alike from the east to the furthest west'. Freed from their fear, men 'kept dazzling festival; light was everywhere, and men who once dared not look up greeted each other with smiling faces and shining eyes. They danced and sang in city and country alike . . .' (10.9). The empire and the Church are both healed, and there seems no significant difference between them. Eusebius not only draws on the Christian notion of redemption, but also stands at the end of a long tradition of the myth of Rome as the Eternal City and of the empire without end proclaimed by Virgil. It could never be a wholly Christianized idea, since for Christians history was to have an end in the Second Coming of Christ, but in Eusebius, who was notably cool towards speculations about the coming end (e.g. 3.39), it came as near as possible to being so.

Supplemented by St Peter's alleged martyrdom there, the myth of Rome and its enduring authority was to be exploited in the high Middle Ages by the papacy, through the conceptions of the canon lawyers, and was to be competed for by the Holy Roman Emperors. A century after Eusebius, it had been contested by Augustine. Confronting the clamour of pagans claiming that the sack of Rome by the Goths (AD 410) was a consequence of the rejection of the old gods and hence the fault of the Christians, Augustine, in his *City of God* (after AD 412), refused to identify God's people with any earthly community; the distinction between the earthly and the heavenly city was not an external one but referred to two different states of the soul, which would acquire their visible embodiments only with the Last Judgement. But Augustine cared enough about the argument advanced by the pagans to inspire his disciple Orosius to write his *Seven Books of History against the Pagans* (AD 417), to show that disasters like the sack of Rome had occurred at all periods in the past. Orosius made much of the occupation of the city by the Gauls, as described by Livy; the modern disaster was therefore not attributable to the abandonment of paganism. Orosius discharged his task in an epitome of world history – with special attention to Roman history – which, together with a similar and later epitome by Isidore of Seville, became one of the key works of the Middle Ages, being constantly drawn on for the general preambles to chronicles and local histories of all kinds. But Orosius also did more than Augustine can have intended, in a way that draws him closer to Eusebius' view of history than to Augustine's. Orosius, in fact, succumbed, more explicitly than Eusebius, to the myth of eternal Rome, and, like Eusebius, identified the Church with the fortunes of the empire.

There were two schemata current at the time for world history: the sequence of four empires derived from the prophetic dream recounted in the biblical Book of Daniel (2.31–44), which became highly influential, and the classical six ages of man, followed, for Christians, by an eternal Sabbath. Augustine adopted the latter, but made no use of the former; Orosius subscribed to both. In both of them the Roman empire figured as the last of the series, the final act of human history, to be followed only by the last days. It would remain, therefore, without a human successor, and would endure to the end of secular time. The empire figured prominently and not negatively in Orosius as part of the providential scheme. In particular, the Augustan peace was linked to the pivotal moment of the Incarnation – not only in time, but as the necessary condition for the spreading of the Gospel. The rise of the Roman empire was therefore part of the divine plan. The conversion of the barbarians in modern times was concomitant with the extension of the empire, of which Orosius accordingly approved: 'fall' is, despite the incursions of the Goths, not part of his conception of the empire's ordained role.

The fact that Christianity came to flourish under imperial patronage ensured that Eusebius' Rome-centred view of Christian history would prevail. The collapse of the empire in the West before the barbarian invaders did not displace the Eusebian–Orosian conception of universal history as one might have expected. The Pope in the city of Rome – where the tomb of St Peter, to whom Christ was supposed to have confided his Church, was located – and later the Merovingian kings and the Carolingian emperors, all had a strong vested interest in this version of the relation of Rome to Christianity. The eventual adoption in the West of the phrase 'Holy Roman Empire' only made explicit what had long been the dominant conception of Christian historiography.

14

Gregory of Tours: Kings,
Bishops and Others

It was a characteristic of medieval historical writing, compared with classical historiography, to be at once all-encompassingly universal and highly and unapologetically particular and local. Typically, a chronological account, more or less full or episodic, of the chronicler's parent institution or locality would be prefaced by an outline of universal history – often a mixture of biblical events with those of secular ancient history, drawn from Orosius or St Isidore of Seville (AD c.560–636), and the biblical-secular chronologies begun by Eusebius and continued by Jerome (above, p. 189). After that, more or less abruptly, the contemporary chronicle could begin, mainly local in focus but with occasional interpolations, quite often garbled, from the wider world of great events. In the West, after the deposition of the last Roman emperor in AD 476 there was no longer, as there had been ever since Polybius, a single dominating secular protagonist for history, the Roman empire. The western medieval empire – never except briefly under Charlemagne anything like universal – and the consolidation of the national kingdoms were yet to come. The *Liber Pontificalis*, the house chronicle of the popes, dealt initially with the local concerns of the bishop of Rome. In a politically fragmented world, whose chief binding agents were councils of bishops and the dynastic alliances of ruling families, almost all history was, on a greater or smaller scale, primarily local and was written accordingly; the most important form taken by record-keeping, as with the pagan Roman *fasti* (books of ceremonies and festivals) and pontifical annals, was the successions of popes, bishops and abbots and the chief events of the liturgical year based on the lunar calendar, into which narratives of heterogeneous contemporary events, often very brief, could be interpolated.

The ten ample books that constitute the *Histories* of Gregory, metropolitan bishop of Tours from AD 573 to 594, show the typical mixture of universal history in the first book, rapidly narrowing to the general affairs of Gaul after the Frankish invasions of the fifth century and to a localized contemporary chronicle in the last six books. However, the history of the previous century is unusually full, and the contemporary chronicle is exceptionally copious and vivid, strongly marked by the personality of its author, who displays some of the self-consciousness, though not the literary airs, of a classical historian. Gregory's life and the contemporary events he records were centred on, though not entirely confined to, the Loire valley. The Roman empire still existed, of course, in the East, and in its nearest embodiment in Italy, centred on Ravenna, but it was essentially peripheral. The Pope in Rome was more relevant but not particularly intrusive. The great monastic movement, particularly Irish, which criss-crossed Europe, transcending tribal and diocesan boundaries, belonged more to the seventh century than to Gregory's sixth. Generally the French metropolitans managed the affairs of their localities, meeting occasionally in conclave. Gregory, though he travelled widely in Gaul, never went south of the Alps or east of the Rhine. As a metropolitan bishop, he was at the centre of the world that concerned him.

He begins his work with a summary of world history based on the Bible, passing to the Incarnation of Christ and the general history of the Church, before proceeding quickly to Gaul, where he alights, still in his first book, at Clermont-Ferrand, his birthplace. For the modern reader the descent from the universal to the particular may seem precipitous, but it clearly seemed quite natural to Gregory, and is not untypical. His continuator – known, inauthentically, as 'Fredegar' – mentions in his prologue his preparatory reading in the chronicles (he identified Jerome, Isidore of Seville and Gregory himself) 'from the beginning of the world to the decline of Guntramn's reign'. What other chronological marker for the present could he have used? It is the reference also to the Creation – the mingling, in other words, of sacred and secular history – which makes his statement odd to us. Bede, writing in the same century (the eighth) in England and focusing on ecclesiastical history, which Fredegar largely ignores, solved the problem of chronological notation by dating forward and backward from the Incarnation, which historians have done ever since, despite the slight inconvenience of counting dates BC backwards. Gregory mingles secular and ecclesiastical history, 'the wars waged by kings and the holy deeds of martyrs', and defends doing so by the precedents of Eusebius and Jerome (II, preface). He will, he says, set down events 'in the muddled and confused order in which they occurred', and he does.

Gregory's concerns are misrepresented by the later entitling of his book *The History of the Franks*. Gregory was not a Frank, and his interest in them – chiefly their kings – seems largely incidental; it was because, as the rulers of sixth-century Gaul, they were inescapably there, but he has nothing like the interest in their destiny that, for example, Polybius had in the Romans who had conquered his people. His ethnic awareness and interest is generally minimal: he does not even mention that Gaul was a country of two utterly distinct languages, Latin and Frankish.

St Gregory himself, like many of the bishops of Frankish Gaul, was a Gallo-Roman aristocrat, from a family productive of senators, bishops and saints. He was brought up in Clermont-Ferrand in the household of his uncle St Gallus, bishop there from AD 525, and he eventually succeeded his cousin St Euphronius as bishop of Tours in AD 573. Sainthood seems to have been an informal *Légion d'honneur* of the sixth-century Gallic episcopate, and there was a marked dynastic element to it, despite the electoral process in the appointment of bishops; the process of papal canonization was not formalized until the twelfth century. The bishops were the defenders of Catholic orthodoxy and public morals, the leaders of their clergy and their people, and the administrators and trustees of the wealth of the Church, for the upkeep of buildings (in Tours especially the cathedral and shrine of St Martin) and the relief of the poor; they were necessarily the familiars – remonstrating, mediating, conciliating – of the Frankish kings. All these concerns marked out the themes of Gregory's history.

The cities of Gaul, under their aristocratic native bishops, remained in large measure the heirs of Roman administrative traditions, just as the heritage of Rome persisted in the vernacular Latin of Gregory and his congregations; it is not clear that he knew any Frankish, and he never refers to the language. He was not well instructed in the classical literary heritage, and he knew nothing of that of Greece. His apologies for his unpolished Latin are a little more than the customary humility, but he says he writes to be understood – not for him the artificial archaizing of some late antique writers. It has been plausibly held that his history is a kind of continuation of his pastoral work, an anthology of tales with a homiletic purpose. Among his other writings, to which he often refers the reader, are martyrologies, Lives of the Fathers of the Church and of St Martin of Tours, and a collection of miracles.

We have seen Eusebius recording martyrdoms. The prototypical saints' Lives, initiating a staple of medieval popular clerical reading, were Athanasius' *Life of Antony*, the fourth-century hermit beleaguered by picturesque demons in the Egyptian desert, which was soon translated into Latin, and, nearer home and later, Sulpicius Severus' largely fictitious *Life of St Martin* (c.403), which effectively initiated the cult of the saint at Tours, where the inestimable treasure of his bones was housed in the cathedral. Cult centres of this kind were a great source of miraculous cures, posthumously effected by the saint, guaranteeing his sanctity and influence with God and drawing a lucrative stream of pilgrims and donations. Saints' Lives were formulaic, retailing the saint's birth and origins, and dwelling on the holy and triumphant death, but largely reducing the intervening life to a succession of miracles, often echoing those recounted in the Gospels, and apparently often parasitic on earlier models of the genre, but also sometimes including transmuted stories from classical antiquity and Christianized folk tales. Like St Antony, the saint was characteristically beset by diabolic adversaries – though these were not necessarily temptations – and miracles were the armoury from which he drew to confound them. As moralizing entertainment we might compare them with Plutarch's *Lives* in the pagan world, but by comparison they are naively presented and generally unindividualized.

After death, saints' bodies characteristically refused to putrefy and gave off a sweet perfume – Gregory is enthusiastic about this – and they wrought miracles by contact with the relics, which included objects touched by the saint. Competition for relics was understandably keen. Gregory's story of the arrival of St Martin's corpse in

Tours gives an example. The men of Tours and the men of Poitiers, assembled at St Martin's deathbed, had disputed possession of the body:

The men of Poitiers said: 'As a monk he is ours. He became an abbot in our town. We entrusted him to you, but we demand him back. It is sufficient for you that, while he was a Bishop on earth, you enjoyed his company, you shared his table, you were strengthened by his blessing and above all you were cheered by his miracles. Let these things suffice for you, and permit us at least to carry away his body.' To this the men of Tours replied: 'If you say that we should be satisfied with the miracles that he performed for us, then admit that while he was with you he did more than in our town. If all his other miracles are left out of the count, he raised two dead men for you and only one for us . . .' They went on with their argument until the sun went down and night began to fall. The body was placed in the middle of the room, the doors were locked and he was watched over by the two groups. The men of Poitiers planned to carry off the body as soon as morning came, but Almighty God would not allow the town of Tours to be deprived of its patron. In the end all the men of Poitiers fell asleep and there was not one who remained on guard. When the men of Tours saw that the Poitevins had fallen asleep, they took the mortal clay of that most holy body and some passed it through the window while others stood outside to receive it. They placed it in a boat and all those present rowed down the River Vienne. (I.48)

They carried the body back to Tours in triumph along the Loire, 'praising God and chanting psalms'. The detailed touches of the window, the boat and the singing are typical of Gregory's anecdotal methods.

The acquisition of St Martin was a great moment, but for Gregory no circumstance was too humble or physically particular, no action too purely domestic, to be unworthy of narration if there was a moral or spiritual point to be made. There could be no question of his history being confined to political (or even political and ecclesiastical) events, because it is not clear that he had any particular concept of the political as a category. Apart from the combating of the Arian heresy, Gregory's world, even that of the ruling Merovingian dynasty and its rival rulers (perhaps 'chieftains' would be a better word than 'kings'), is a highly personal one, in the same way that the importance and wealth of the city of Tours derived largely from St Martin's body. Motives and conduct are particular to the individual and are hardly ever generalized except as pleasing or displeasing to God, and, unlike in some Christian histories, such as those of Gildas and Bede in Britain, it is characteristically individuals, not peoples, whom God punishes or favours. The second sentence of Gregory's preface refers, in mentioning the animators of the contemporary events he proposes to chronicle, to 'kings losing their temper'. There is no place here for abstractions like 'royal policy' or 'aristocratic resistance'. Great men behave much as small ones do – out of anger, cupidity, wilfulness, revenge. No such abstract concept as the blood feud among the Franks is mentioned: Gregory and perhaps his readers take it for granted. Even the saints, in Gregory's world, know how posthumously to avenge affronts.

Gregory begins his work with the memorable, and entirely accurate, reflection that 'A great many things keep happening, some of them good, some of them bad.' It is probably not misguided to read into this that we must not look to Gregory's history for an overall plot, though attempts have been made to impute one to him – such as a framework lifted from Old Testament history, the notion of the Franks as a people with a mission, or the idea of a steady decline of behaviour in Gaul from the time of King Clovis (d. AD 511) (e.g. IV.45). Though he goes on to speak of the quarrels of 'the inhabitants of different countries', and occasionally describes the behaviour of mobs, Gregory's protagonists are individuals. It is true that he speculates briefly about the origins of the Franks (II.9), the invaders of Gaul in the previous century, quoting an earlier Latin historian, now lost, and – in a rare case of generalization – about the origins of the 'long-haired kings' and the kind of kingship they possessed. (It was believed in Gregory's day that a Merovingian who had his hair shorn lost his eligibility for kingship.)

The most emphatically 'historical' single event in the history of the Franks, because it was also an event in the history of the Church, was the conversion of King Clovis to the Catholic faith – according to Gregory, with his whole army – in AD 496; the other barbarian peoples who overran the West had been converted to the Arian version of Christianity. Gregory, rather uncharacteristically, makes the obvious and usual analogy in such circumstances: with Constantine. The current Roman emperor gave Clovis the title of consul. The baptism forged the link between the Franks and the papacy that would, three hundred years later, be crucial to the emergence of a Frankish, Carolingian, western empire. After Clovis, however, the Frankish kings (there were four simultaneously in Gregory's time, thanks to the division of the inheritance), and their nobles, appear in his history not as figures of historic destiny but simply because they were the secular powers, the great men, of their day. They are able to do good, chiefly in the form of donations to St Martin's shrine, and, more often, harm, in their internecine wars, often indistinguishable from raids for plunder, with extortion and occasionally massacre visited on peaceful town and peasant populations. To Gregory, civil wars were a particular evil of the times, and he prays that they may cease.

The homicidal feuds within the dynasty, however, he records in deadpan fashion, shocking the reader by apparently treating them as normal, which they were. Merovingians, one comes to feel, just were like that. The reader is, of course, as Gregory presumably knows, sometimes registering the existence of the blood feud, but it does not occur to Gregory to categorize it as an institution of the Franks, so it looks like mere vengefulness or even motiveless ferocity. Gregory's account of and epitaph on Clovis – who has been spoken of as the hero of his history (he is hardly that) and who was certainly the greatest warrior king of the Merovingian line, establishing his rule over much of Gaul as well as embracing Catholic Christianity – are notable. Gregory drily recounts Clovis's behaviour, including his ogreish habit of unexpectedly bisecting people with his axe, and even seems to appreciate his gallows humour. After recounting Clovis's axe-work on two of his relatives, and his command to put a third to death, Gregory adds:

As soon as all three were slain Clovis took over their kingdom and their treasure [the kingdom was centred on Cambrai]. In the same way he encompassed the death of many other kings and blood relations of his, whom he suspected of conspiring against his kingdom. By doing this he spread his dominion over the whole of Gaul. One day when he had called a general assembly of his subjects, he is said to have made the following remark about the relatives whom he had destroyed: 'How sad a thing it is that I live among strangers like some solitary pilgrim, and that I have none of my own relations left to help me when disaster threatens!' He said this not because he grieved for their deaths but because in his cunning way he hoped to find some relative still in the land of the living whom he could kill. (II.42)

Yet Gregory's biblically phrased summary is that 'Day in day out God submitted the enemies of Clovis to his dominion and increased his power, for he walked before Him with an upright heart and did what was pleasing in His sight' (II.40). Great kings, like the prototype, the biblical David, who enjoyed God's favour, were admittedly not expected to be perfect, but – well! It mattered, of course, that detestation of the Arian heresy provided the only 'ideological' element in Gregory's history. He records, ostensibly verbatim, his own acrimonious debate with an Arian heretic (V.40) and also Catholic martyrdoms in Arian Visigothic Spain, which actually seem to have been very rare. He retails the sufferings of a Catholic girl who, forced to endure rebaptism as an Arian, cries out in defiance – and with a good recollection of a nice distinction bred from Greek philosophy – 'I believe the Father with the Son and the Holy Ghost to be of one substance,' before being consecrated to Christ by having her head cut off (II.2).

The Frankish kings are one element in Gregory's history, and at times it focuses on them and their often atrocious deeds. They do not, however, dominate the history. This can best be seen by a summary of his first four books; the later ones, when the history becomes contemporary and Gregory himself appears, are better dealt with thematically. In Book I, after a very short time with the Old Testament and the history of the Christian Church, we arrive at the conversion of Gaul, followed by the unedifying marital affairs of the first bishop of Clermont-Ferrand, and shortly afterwards by the death in AD 397 of St Martin, third bishop of Tours, with which the book ends. The framework of Gregory's book is, above all, episcopal history in the area of the Loire valley. The Franks make their entry in Book II, but most of the earlier part of that too is episcopal. However, the latter part of the book is dominated by Clovis, and ends with his death in AD 511. The next two books interleave Frankish and episcopal themes as Gregory has promised. Endearingly, he greets the opening of Book V, with which the era of his personal knowledge opens, with the words, 'Here, I am glad to say, begins Book V. Amen.' His own first appearance is a dramatic instance of a confrontation in which the Church, embodied as St Martin's shrine, with Gregory as its guardian, confounds the representative of royal Frankish power. The episode illustrates Gregory's way of telling a story, and so is worth quoting at length:

Next Roccolen marched on Tours, having received orders to do so from Chilperic . . . He pitched his camp on the further bank of the river Loire and sent messengers to me saying that I must expel Guntram from my church, for he was accused of having killed Theudebert. If I did not carry out his commands he would order the city and all its suburbs to be burnt to the ground.

Chilperic was one of the four Frankish kings, grandsons of Clovis, at that time. His half-brother Guntram had indeed killed Chilperic's son Theudebert in battle. Roccolen is presented to us without introduction. Gregory is defiant:

As soon as I heard this I sent a deputation to Roccolen to say that what he demanded had never been done down all the centuries from ancient times, and that it was quite unthinkable that the holy church could be violated; that if it were to happen it would bring small profit to him or to the King who had sent such orders; and that he would do better to shake in fear before Saint Martin the Bishop, whose miraculous power only the day before had made paralysed limbs straight [recorded by Gregory in his Life of St Martin]. Roccolen was no whit abashed. He pulled to pieces the church-house on the opposite bank of the Loire, in which he had his quarters. The building was nailed together: the men of Maine, who formed Roccolen's army, put the nails in their pockets and sneaked off with them, destroying the harvest and ruining everything else as they went. When Roccolen was committing these outrages he was punished by God, for he fell ill with jaundice and turned bright yellow.

Seeking recovery, Roccolen is carried to the church he had threatened to violate, but he remains ill and personally unforgiven. He was clearly really unregenerate, for

We were then in the holy month of Lent: and he kept on eating baby rabbits. He had earlier drawn up for the first day of March certain ordinances by which he planned to mulct and ruin the people of Poitiers. Twenty-four hours before that he died; and with him died his overweening arrogance. (V.4)

The next section begins, 'It was at this time that Felix, Bishop of the city of Nantes, wrote an abusive letter to me.' The ostensible occasion was a complex affair involving the murder of Gregory's brother Peter, a deacon, who was accused of murdering his own bishop, whose office he coveted. The real reason, according to Gregory, was that Felix, a greedy and arrogant man, coveted some church land in Gregory's see. He retorts in kind, giving us the best bit of his letter and adding, 'I will say no more for fear that you begin to think I am much the same myself.'

Gregory's work is not particularly egocentric or self-justificatory, but after the beginning of Book V the history becomes still more focused on Tours and his own diocese. Within it his range of attention is wide, and reflects the multifarious interests and concerns of a Gallic bishop as pastor of his people and clergy; at times reading him reminds one of the recollections of a magistrate or judge (which in a sense he was) of broad human sympathies, with a taste for gossip. Gregory was clearly a born raconteur, and no level of human life (except perhaps, as individuals, that of the peasantry, for whom he has only a generalized concern) was inaccessible to him: domestic slaves, artisans, contumacious nuns, impostors (a particular worry), drunks – including several bishops (one also mentally unbalanced) and an ascetic who became an alcoholic – and fornicating priests and abbots, as well as ferocious Frankish nobles like Roccolen and fratricidal monarchs, all people his stories.

The story of Roccolen exemplifies the tension between bishops like Gregory, determined to maintain the Church's rights, and the Frankish kings and their representatives, with their incessant raiding and feuding, in which the ordinary populace, to whom the bishops are pastors, is caught up. Roccolen was acting on the King's orders, in pursuit of a blood feud within the royal family, and also acting as a tax-collector, to give a misleadingly bureaucratic name to something so random and sporadic. Such confrontations of royal power with the Church's privileges were, of course, common, and not only in Gaul. Perhaps the most famous, immortalized in a dramatic painting by Van Dyck, was the refusal of the Archbishop of Milan, St Ambrose, to allow the sinful emperor Theodosius to enter his cathedral until he had sought forgiveness. What comes foremost in Gregory's account is that Roccolen is a bad, arrogant man, disrespectful to St Martin's shrine, and a meat-eater in Lent (his illness might surely have earned a dispensation – Gregory makes it sound as though he devoured the rabbits whole), as well as an extortionist. St Martin, however, can and does avenge affronts to his relics and his church; there are other instances. A not uncommon disease is attributed to divine intervention and punishment.

Miracles are a frequent preoccupation of Gregory's, but it has been plausibly argued that, though he can recognize them, he does not have anything like a precise modern definition of them as suspensions of a regular order of nature. Rather, the whole world witnesses all the time to God's power, but some aspects and events more strikingly and instructively than others, chiefly because of their obvious moral or spiritual import. Where a moral context is lacking, Gregory admits himself at a loss. Noting some exceptional astronomical behaviour, he assumes, as historians for the previous thousand years would have done, that it is a sign – but 'I have no idea what it all meant' (V.??) Given a morally relevant situation, however, timely cases of cirrhosis, such as Roccolen's, are clearly miraculous and proper for pious contemplation. God looks after his own, at least when they are as influential or have such a powerful patron as St Martin. Some miracles are more gratuitous than this, especially perhaps the fragrance associated with saints' relics, but these minister to faith and pious joy. Miracles confound the Devil, as well as the wicked men who are his agents. The constant metaphysical strife, waged partly by physical means, is not a walkover, however. The Devil also has exceptional powers, which is why impostors are so persuasive and dangerous. The Devil, it appears, afflicted a man of Bourges with a swarm of flies, which sent him mad. He became a wandering ascetic, dressed in animal skins, and 'In order to encourage him in his deception the Devil gave him the power of prophesying the future.' He set up as a prophet and eventually as Christ, and gathered a large following – part fanatics, part bandits. These were eventually attacked by some muscular servants of the Bishop of Le Puy, whom he had threatened; they killed the false Christ and dispersed his followers, some of whom never returned to full sanity. Such impostors, who acquire 'great influence over the common people', are a big nuisance. Gregory says, 'I saw quite a few of them myself. I did my best to argue with them' (X.25).

Gregory as raconteur can often remind the reader of later writers of (fictional) tales such as Boccaccio. The stories even tend to begin in the same ways, though more often as a preamble to murder or sometimes a miracle – and sometimes both – rather than to amorous intrigues, though these are not altogether absent. 'A certain merchant called Christopher travelled to the city of Orleans . . .'; 'At this time there lived near the town of Nice a recluse called Hospicius . . .'; 'A Breton Count killed three of his brothers . . .' These stories as often involve people otherwise obscure as they do the great. Every soul and therefore every wicked or good deed matters. When Gregory gives in his preface an entirely traditional reason for writing history, 'to keep alive the memory of those dead and gone, and to bring them to the notice of future generations', he may have been thinking chiefly of the 'great', especially martyrs and saints. But the later, contemporary, part of his history, which attends to many others who are not great, is perhaps better covered by what he goes on to speak of: 'the quarrels between the wicked and the righteous'. Martyrdoms had become rare, but of such quarrels there was no end, and all were, by definition, significant.

One striking feature of Gregory's writing is his confident sense of rapport with his readers, expressed in homely, confiding terms (though these may be exaggerated by translation from the Latin). At one point – one can envisage him scratching his head and clicking his tongue – he even apologizes for forgetting his chronicler's manners: 'I meant to tell you earlier on of a conversation I had with Saint Salvius, the Bishop. I forgot to mention it so perhaps you will not mind if I include it here' (V.50). His own feelings and judgements are not intrusive but are sometimes explicit – above all when, in a famous passage, he laments the death of young children from the plague: 'And so we lost our little ones, who were so dear to us and sweet, whom we cherished in our bosoms and dandled in our arms, whom we had fed and nurtured with such loving care. As I write, I wipe away my tears . . .' (V.34). He goes on to quote Job. Gregory has the ability, like

Herodotus, to annihilate historical time in contemplation of a common humanity. His anecdotes, typically several pages long, tend to be highly circumstantial and detailed, with invented or roughly recollected conversations, descriptions of what exactly people were doing at the moment of crisis, the prevailing weather, and the precise manner in which a murder or an assault was committed and the physical consequences. Only people's appearance is neglected. Apart from the required long hair, we have generally no idea what Gregory's Merovingian kings looked like, in contrast, for example, to Einhard's later description of Charlemagne; Einhard had learned from Suetonius. The larger context too, if there is one, is largely or wholly left to the reader to supply, while the agents, as we saw with Roccolen, are given little or no introduction. All this, of course, is consistent with a homiletic purpose. One can imagine some stories interpolated into a sermon for the moral, though Gregory is not generally an explicit moralizer: he is sometimes, in fact, remarkably abstemious in this respect.

This is episcopal history in a broad sense as well as at times a narrower one: Trollope with bloodshed. The more institutional concerns include disputed episcopal elections and a long account of a revolt in a nunnery, led by a daughter of King Charibert, who seems to exemplify the family traditions except that she does not actually murder anyone personally (though she does organize a gang of roughs who assault the prioress and fight the abbess's supporters in riots leading to deaths). The revolt is ended by violence, with rebellious nuns having their hair shorn – and, according to Gregory, in some cases also hands, ears and noses. It had been a vexatious affair, and he recounts it at considerable length (IX.38–43, X.15–17). This was exceptional, but disturbances of all kinds were the everyday currency of Gregory's life as a bishop. His tenth and last book ends with a list of the succession of the bishops of Tours, and brief descriptions of their deeds, before his final computation of the years (5,792) between the Creation and his own consecration as bishop in 'the fifth year of Gregory, Pope of Rome, the thirty-third of King Guntram and the nineteenth of King Childebert II'. The kings' names act as chronological markers, but it is the bishops who provide the list and the summarized deeds.

Medieval chronicles were frequently composite, one author, often anonymous, taking over from another to continue the record. Even where authors are identified, earlier ones are often epitomized (Orosius being a favourite, and later Isidore of Seville) as part of the compilation. Gregory, however, who seems to have an unusually acute sense of himself as author and of the integrity of his work, concludes with a plea that, while his successors are welcome to rewrite it in verse if they wish (so far as we know the offer was not taken up), they must above all leave the work in its entirety. He was fortunate: his work was highly popular, and was preserved and copied intact.

It was also, however, epitomized, together with a continuation of some seventy years after the end of Gregory's own work, in the chronicle which the Renaissance was to attribute to 'Fredegar'; the name has stuck. In all, albeit patchily, continuations took the chronicle into the Carolingian period, in the *Annals of the Realm of the Franks* (AD 741–827). These continuations, including Fredegar, are quite properly described as chronicles of the Franks: there is, that is to say, a focus, above all, on the Frankish courts and their wars, as well as an increasing stress on the Franks as a people, with further embroideries of their mythological origins. Fredegar's is the first work in which we find the long-lived claim of a Trojan ancestry, which of course made them kin to the Romans. It is worth dwelling briefly on Fredegar's chronicle, because it is typical in a way that Gregory's work is not, and it brings out Gregory's distinctive characteristics.

After the usual world-historical preamble and chronology – he acknowledges Jerome and Isidore – and the résumé of Gregory's books, Fredegar shuttles between the various Merovingian courts, with news flashes of world events, sometimes obviously seen through a fog of rumour. He is much more thematically consistent than Gregory, though also generally terser and secular in his interests, with little on bishops or the supernatural. There is, however, one episode to which he gives particularly extended treatment, which is of exceptional interest. It concerns the expulsion from Burgundy in AD 610, by the Merovingian king Theuderic, of the Irish St Columbanus, who, there and in Italy, exercised by his foundations an immense influence on the development of monasticism. Fredegar gives the domestic circumstances of the expulsion, instigated by the King's grandmother Brunechildis (Brunhild), who, not wishing to be outshone by a young queen, takes exception to Columbanus' admonition to the King to abandon his promiscuous ways and take a wife. The account of Columbanus hints warily at unused supernatural powers.

Brunechildis dominates part of Fredegar's narrative just as her sister-in-law and rival wicked queen, Fredegund, is ubiquitous in Gregory's last six books. Among the latter's numerous lurid crimes was the attempted assassination of Brunechildis, though it seems one of the more venial. Fredegund's exploits memorably include, in Gregory's account, slamming down the lid of a treasure chest on the neck of her daughter, who had annoyed her by referring to her low birth:

She leant on it with all her might and the edge of the chest pressed so hard against the girl's throat that her eyes were soon standing out of her head. One of the servant-girls who was in the room screamed out at the top of her voice: 'Quick! Quick! Mistress is being choked to death by her mother.' (IX.34)

After this, according to Gregory, relations between the two women deteriorated. Fredegund's son, King Chlotar, according to Fredegar, succeeded in catching Brunechildis, and after accusing her of the murder of no less than ten Frankish kings, and having her tortured, he had her led between the ranks of the soldiers on a camel and then tied to a wild horse, by which she was torn to pieces.

Fredegar is not often so colourful. Here he is, typically, in an example taken at random, at his most terse and annalistic:

In November this year [Fredegar dates by regnal years] Gundoald, supported by Mummolus and Desiderius, dared to invade part of Guntramn's kingdom and to destroy his cities. Guntramn sent to meet them an army under Leudegesil the constable and Aegyla the patrician. Gundoald took to flight and sought refuge in the city of Comminges, whence Duke Boso hurled him from the cliffs; and thus he died. (4.6)

Fredegar often breaks up narratives – of the pursuit of feuds, for example – for the requirements of strict chronology. As he tells us in his preface, 'chronicle is a Greek word meaning in Latin the record of the years' (a definition from Isidore of Seville's *Etymologies*), and he takes the obligations it imposes seriously: 'How this came about

I shall set down in the right year under its proper sequence.' His occasional brief interpolations or news flashes from contemporary world history – common in medieval chronicles – are sometimes startling, notably the report of the baptism of 'the emperor of Persia' and sixty thousand of his subjects, followed by the conversion of all Persia to Christianity: it seems like an echo of the conversion of Clovis.

'Fredegar', whoever he was, has nothing like the anecdotal art and human curiosity of Gregory. Gregory himself is hardly a great historian: he is too episodic, too uninterested in generalization and context, and takes too much for granted. But, to use a metaphor understandably favoured by commentators, he opens a window on vivid, varied and animated scenes, at different social levels, in sixth-century Gaul – all domesticated and made personal. There is nothing else like it.

15

Bede: The English Church and the English People

Augustine, who was to be the first archbishop of Canterbury, was dispatched by Pope Gregory the Great on a mission to the English, and arrived in Kent in AD 597. On his way northward from Italy, he and his retinue of monks broke their journey at Tours, in 596. Gregory of Tours, who had died in 594, thus missed wishing them well by just two years. But for that, one would be able to speak literally of Augustine passing through Gregory's present into the past which was to engage the attention of the first English historian, Bede (who knew Gregory's work), over a century later. Bede's history begins with the dealings of the Romans with Britain, the early progress of Christianity there, and the establishment of the Saxon, Angle and Jutish invaders in the later fifth century. But for him the history of the English as a people really begins with Augustine's mission and the foundation of the English Church, and this is the true starting point of his *Ecclesiastical History of the English People* (c.735).

Bede's history, like Gregory's – though it resembles it in little else – deals much with episcopacy, but whereas in Gaul the Christian episcopate was already established when the Franks arrived, and inherited much of the tradition of Roman rule in the towns, in England the kings of the various and shifting political entities into which the country was divided by the invaders were crucial to the success of the Christian missionary endeavour: their patronage almost guaranteed success; their hostility represented a severe setback. Bede is if anything even less interested than Gregory in secular history for its own sake, but kings play quite a different, and generally much more positive, role in his history. Bede also has a much more acute ethnic interest than Gregory: he distinguishes carefully between the various

213

peoples who composed the population of Britain, and he has a clear conception, surprising perhaps in view of their political divisions, of the Anglo-Saxon people as a whole, as 'the English'.

Bede's work occupied an exceptionally distinguished place among the histories of the various barbarian successors to Roman rule in the West, which are not really exemplified in Gregory's subsequently mistitled *History of the Franks*. Apart from Gregory's work and Bede's, we have also the *History of the Deeds of the Goths* by Jordanes (d. *c.*554), a history of the Goths and Vandals by Isidore of Seville (d. 636), consisting mainly of extracts, and the *History of the Lombards* by a Carolingian courtier and monk of Monte Cassino, Paul the Deacon (d. 799). The best account of the Huns comes from a Roman history by a fifth-century Greek, Priscus, whose work is largely lost but from which survives a fascinating description of a Roman embassy to Attila which Priscus accompanied. But the category of 'barbarian' history proves on examination to be more complex and heterogeneous than it might seem. Apart from the question of quality, where Bede stands in a class of his own, the authors and their purposes were disparate; while the Goths and Lombards were Arian heretics, their historians were Catholics, believers in the Trinity, which set a distance between themselves and the peoples they considered and also gave them interests and concerns which transcended ethnicity. Jordanes, though apparently he had Gothic ancestry, is emphatically a man of the eastern Roman world (though he wrote in Latin) and an admirer of the contemporary emperor Justinian, while Paul belonged equally emphatically to the world of Charlemagne, conqueror of the Lombards.

Bede, however, is writing about his own people, though in Latin, and he has no sentiment on behalf of the Roman empire, only for the Roman Church. He is conscientious in retailing (not always accurately) the main episodes in Romano-British history, but then goes on to distinguish the origins of the invading tribes and their settlement as a patchwork of realms (he speaks of provinces). These were those of the South, East and West Saxons, of Kent (settled by the Jutes), of East Anglia, Northumbria and Mercia (the Midland kingdom), as well as those of minor or subordinate kinglets. But he is freed from any nostalgia for Roman Britain not only by his own race, but by his manifest contempt for the Britons, including the quality of their Christianity. Of the four peoples and five languages (the fifth being Latin) of Britain, he speaks warmly though not uncritically of the Irish monks established in northern Britain (he usually calls them Scots); the Picts are shadowy and the Britons disreputable; the English are a chosen people. The scholarship of the last couple of decades has impressively answered the obvious question why Bede is so confident that the English are one people, despite political multiplicity much greater than in Gregory's Gaul (which had a single ruling dynasty, though its sovereignty was often divided). One particular source of this idea, before Bede, seems to have been Pope Gregory, who in his letters speaks of the 'gens Anglorum' (not 'Saxonum') as an entity for conversion. Why Gregory preferred eponymous Angles to Saxons seems unclear: the story of the famous papal pun ('not Angles but Angels') provoked by the sight of boys, presumably slaves, in the marketplace, which Bede retails as 'a story handed down to us by the tradition of our forebears' (II.1), embodies but does not explain the preference. What is absolutely clear, however, is that Gregory conceived from the outset that the Church to be established among the English was to be a single entity, with its primate at Canterbury, and that Bede was happy to follow him, not least in constant references to 'the English people'.

In a sense therefore, the English owe their existence as a people, or at least the recognition of it, to the papacy, and it was confirmed by Bede's history, which, in all Church matters – which form the core of his book – takes a wholly 'Gregorian' point of view. The precondition of that existence is Catholic orthodoxy and unity in subordination to the see of Canterbury. Bede's book is the history of the achievement of that unity, through the manner of the Christian conversion of England and the establishment of its Church, over the century follow-ing Augustine's mission and prior to Bede's work. Bede is as hostile to heresy as Eusebius or Gregory – he mentions particularly Pel-agianism, the British-born heresy that salvation was possible without grace, and Arianism – but they were not issues of his own time, any more than was paganism, at least among the educated and powerful. What exercises him is the dissidence of the Celtic, Irish strand of Christianity, established in much of Northumbria by the missionary efforts of Irish monks, over the date of the observance of Easter, and this is something to which he frequently reverts. Bede himself was an expert computator, so this was home territory for him, but what was most painful was the threat to unity.

Bede's history, then, is a history of the English people, but it is above all an ecclesiastical history. Kings, once converted, sometimes figure as model rulers with biblical overtones – partly, one assumes, *pour encourager les autres* in Bede's own time. The situation of the English, as, following Bede, we may call them, was, after all, like that of the Israelites when, after defeating the original holders, they were settling their land. Bede had written a commentary on the books of Samuel and Kings, and was used to providing a providential as well as allegorical gloss on the events of apparently secular and tribal history; his Latin, which he wrote admirably, sometimes echoes the language of the Latin Vulgate Bible. The English conquest, as the chastisement of the unworthy Britons – a theme he gets from the British Jeremiah, Gildas, writing around the second quarter of the sixth century – is part of God's providential design. The English are therefore God's chosen instrument for punishment of sin.

Bede (born *c.*673), who was entered into the recently founded monastery of Monkwearmouth, in Northumbria, at the age of seven, and spent his whole life there and in the nearby sister house of Jarrow, made himself into the most learned man in Europe, with an impressively varied list of authoritative writings to his credit, most copiously in biblical commentary, but also in the computation of time, and in hagiography, martyrology, hymnology and poetry. Besides the *Ecclesiastical History*, he wrote a history of the abbots of his monastery. The precondition of his learning was his access to the library, remarkable for its time, collected mostly by his abbot and mentor Benedict Biscop on travels in Italy and Gaul. Bede lived and worked in remotest Northumbria, but it was in ecclesiastical terms a vibrant and sophisticated place; Monkwearmouth had over six hundred monks by AD 710. By that time England was itself sending missionaries to Germany.

The reader who for the first time encounters Book I of Bede's *History* is likely to become aware of an authorial presence of great power and authority. Bede, one feels, is as reliable as he can be. This may be a slight exaggeration given the didactic moral purpose he has announced in his preface: to encourage good conduct by recording notable examples of goodness and wickedness. He is calm (except on heresy), measured, and apparently completely in control of his theme and his sources. He is generally chronologically lucid, being apparently the first author to date, as became normal, to and from the birth of Christ – an immense convenience. But he is also not slavishly tied to strict chronological sequence in the manner of an annalist, and he sees no objection to useful retrospect. He is scrupulous in giving his sources. Hagiography is prominent among them, and he records miracles with, presumably, a mixture of belief and homiletic purpose. As in Gregory, while some are genuinely 'impossible', others could be put down to timely good fortune: seas calmed, winds opportunely changing, ailments recovered from. Bede's miracles always have a moral or spiritual point, most usually the triumph of Christianity over paganism; they are, then, weapons in the war of gods, and of course the pagan gods are demons. He never recounts the fantastic merely for its own sake. But Bede's *History* is not only impressively controlled – at least until his own times, when it becomes more source-driven and less structured. It is also highly dramatic. The miraculous stories and the confrontations of Christian and pagan are brought vividly to life, as are the leading personalities, especially King Oswald, Bishop Aidan and St Wilfrid. It is not surprising that Bede's work, now regarded as the masterpiece of early medieval historiography, soon obtained a very wide currency on the Continent as well as in England.

His preface is in the form of a letter to King Coelwulf of Northumbria, to whom he sends his work at the King's request. Coelwulf is said eagerly to desire 'to know something of the doings and sayings of men of the past, and of famous men of our own race in particular'. History, Bede tells us in a formula by now standard, as it had been from Roman times, gives us good and bad examples to emulate and avoid. Then, exceptionally, Bede lists his main sources, just as a modern historian might do. Above all there is Abbot Albinus, who has transmitted to him through Nothelm, 'a priest of the church of London', ecclesiastical documents held at Canterbury. Nothelm, clearly a travelled man, has also himself been able to see and transcribe documents from the papal archives in Rome, including letters of Pope

Gregory the Great, all of which he has made available to Bede, who also acknowledges help from bishops and monasteries in various parts of the country. For Northumbria itself he is not dependent on any particular source, but 'on countless faithful witnesses', though he particularly acknowledges a debt to the Lindisfarne Life of St Cuthbert, which he has used in his own life of the saint and partly reused in his history.

The work proper begins, as Gildas had done, with a brief but accurate geographical survey of the British Isles. It is enthusiastic, and has been thought to show deliberate resonances with the idea of Paradise, before the Fall. The narrative begins, as so many histories of Britain have done since, with the invasion of Julius Caesar, which Bede dates at 60 years before the Incarnation and 693 from the foundation of Rome, thereby correlating Christian and Roman chronology. Bede claims that stakes driven into the bed of the Thames as part of the Britons' defences are still (700 years later) to be seen, and he describes them. He knows about the later, Claudian, invasion, but makes a hash of dating and explaining the Roman wall (on which Gildas is also misled), which he must have known well, and relating it to the Roman earthwork linking the firths of Forth and Clyde. There is no Boudicca. Instead, apparently from the *Liber Pontificalis*, there is a legendary British king, Lucius, who calls for Christian instruction in a letter to Pope Eleutherius (I.4). Persecutions of Christians in Britain under the empire are mentioned, particularly Diocletian's, and the death of the British martyr St Alban (AD 301) is recounted in detail, with the miracles attending his execution (I.7). Though unsound on the wall, Bede makes interesting reference to other surviving physical evidence of the Roman occupation: cities, lighthouses, bridges and paved roads (I.11). The eventual arrival of St Augustine's mission in Kent is the main event of Book I, but (citing Gildas by name as a source) Bede also devotes considerable attention to the cowardice, moral delinquency and spiritual inertia of the Britons: God justifiably punishes them, with the Saxons and other invaders as his chosen instruments (I.12–16). Bede is the first, but not the last, English historian to be anti-Briton.

In Bede's account of the invasions we first meet figures taken from Gildas and perhaps not entirely legendary, though it is impossible to tell. First of these is the British king Vortigern, who invites the incomers as military allies, which would have been common Roman practice; the 'Angles or Saxons' arrive in three longships. (The Goths also, according to Jordanes, migrated in three ships.) There are the Saxon chiefs Hengist and Horsa, whose claimed descent from Woden Bede records without comment. (There is nothing odd about the claim, which is found also in Frankish royal genealogies, but one wonders if Bede knows who Woden was. It may seem implausible that he did not, though he takes little interest in the details of paganism; but since he regards the pagan deities as devils it seems equally unlikely that he would have made no comment if he did.) Then we have mention of the British war-leader Ambrosius Aurelianus, again from Gildas, and his victory over the invaders at the (unidentified) Badon Hill. (Subsequent commentators tried to link him with a much later arrival in literature, Arthur, king of the Britons.) Bede's discrimination of the tribes as Angles, Saxons and Jutes has stood up well to archaeological investigation, and some of their divisions are perpetuated, of course, in the names of English counties such as Sussex and Essex, though Wessex has slipped from administrative recognition into a literary conceit in the armoury of tourist boards.*

For Bede, the chief hero of the conquest period, after St Alban, is the Gallic saint St Germanus of Auxerre (commemorated, like St Alban, by a place name: St Germans in Cornwall). Germanus comes to refute the Pelagian heresy rife among the Britons, and he does so – assisted by some notable miracles – despite the Devil's contriving a fall which breaks his leg; Bede compares him to Job (I.19). Germanus, undaunted by his injury, gamely insists on leading the British side to victory against a mixed pagan force of Picts and Saxons (I.20). But, despite this demonstration, the Britons are incorrigible, criminally failing in any missionary endeavour towards the newcomers. However, God 'did not utterly abandon the people he had chosen', and thus instigated Pope Gregory to dispatch Augustine and his monks

---

* The author of the 1955 translation of Bede cited here spoke of his work as 'a treasury of tales loved by every English child'. That would clearly be over-optimistic now, and perhaps it was then, but the author of this book attended, sixty years ago, a school in which the 'houses' were designated Angles, Saxons, Jutes and Vikings. It would now be fashionable to see in this an example of collective 'memory'; I have always suspected it was the headmaster's ironic comment on our level of literacy.

for their salvation (I.23). The foothold in Canterbury was allowed by the Kentish king Ethelbert, whose wife, Bertha, was a Christian Frank. But the fragility of a Christianizing enterprise dependent on dynastic politics is revealed when, in Kent, King Ethelbert, who had converted, is followed by apostate sons. Christianity was also insecurely established in Northumbria.

The initial conversion of Northumbria furnished Bede with several notable stories. One concerns the pagan high priest Coifi, who, after initially a somewhat pragmatic assessment of the Christian case ('If the gods had any power, they would surely have favoured myself, who have been . . . zealous in their service'), declares himself convinced and celebrates his laicization with the acquisition of arms, forbidden to a priest:

Thus equipped he set out to destroy the idols. Girded with a sword and with a spear in his hand, he mounted the king's stallion and rode up to the idols. When the crowd saw him they thought he had gone mad; but without hesitation, as soon as he reached the temple, he cast into it the spear that he carried and thus profaned it. Then, full of joy at his knowledge of the worship of the true God, he told his companions to set fire to the temple and its enclosures and destroy them. The site where these idols once stood is still shown, not far east of York, beyond the river Derwent, and is known today as Goodmanham. [It still is.] (II.14)

It has been pointed out that a spear was part of Woden's ritual, which Bede could scarcely have known, which seems to reinforce the story's authenticity.

A different style of argument, in the form of a parable, was provided by another of the Northumbrian chief men:

Your Majesty, when we compare the present life of man on earth with that time of which we have no knowledge, it seems to me like the flight of a single sparrow through the banqueting-hall where you are sitting at dinner on a winter's day with your thanes and counsellors. In the midst there is a comforting fire to warm the hall; outside the storms of winter rain or snow are raging. The sparrow flies swiftly in through one door of the hall, and out through another. While he is inside, he is safe from the winter storms, but after a few moments of comfort, he vanishes from sight into the wintry world from which he came. Even so, man appears on earth for a little while; but of what went before this life or of what follows, we know nothing. Therefore, if this new teaching has brought any more certain knowledge it seems only right that we should follow it. (II.13)

The vividness of the imagery of the warm and lighted hall, the centre of comfort and feasting, contrasted with the surrounding darkness and the uncharted wide world beyond, and the brevity of the sparrow's flight through it, has ensured this speech a deserved subsequent fame. It has the quality and the same kind of imagery and sensibility as that of Anglo-Saxon poetry in the vernacular:

> Bright were the buildings, halls where springs ran,
> high, horngabled, much throng noise;
> these many meadhalls men filled
> with loud cheerfulness: Wierd changed that.
>
> ('The Ruin')

> Where is the house of the feast? Where is the hall's uproar?
> Alas, bright cup! Alas, burnished fighter!
> Alas, proud prince! How that time has passed,
> dark under night's helm, as though it had never been.
>
> ('The Wanderer')

Poetry was one of Bede's many interests and there is later (IV.24) a digression on Caedmon, a monk of Whitby, discovering his poetic gift, which Bede clearly greatly appreciates and regards as miraculous.

Perhaps a more typical insight into pagan mentalities, which Bede does not generally attempt to penetrate, is provided by the story of the three pagan sons of the Christian king of the East Saxons, who demand, though unbaptized, to be given the consecrated communion bread administered to their convert father. The bishop explains to them the indispensability of baptism, to no avail:

The bishop answered, 'If you will be washed in the waters of salvation as your father was, you may share in the consecrated bread as he did: but so long as you reject the water of life, you are quite unfit to receive the bread of life.' They retorted, 'We refuse to enter that font and see no need for it; but we want to be strengthened with this bread.'

The bishop stands firm, and is expelled from the kingdom (II.5).

Christianity flourishes in Northumbria, however, under King Oswald (604–42). He erects a cross which becomes a site of cult, and many miracles are performed there. Oswald is a Christian because, in exile, he has been instructed by the Scots (Irish), who at his request send him Bishop Aidan from Iona; Aidan establishes his see, under Oswald's patronage, on the island of Lindisfarne, off the coast of Northumbria. This leads Bede on to the missionary efforts of the Irish in North Britain, which have predated those from Canterbury and which he treats in a notable, retrospective chapter on the conversion of the Picts by St Columba, in 565 (II.4). Bede speaks enthusiastically of the purity of life and love of God found in the Irish settlement of Iona, off the west coast of Scotland, but he deplores the mistaken view taken there on the date of Easter, which he attributes to the monks' isolation. Aidan, transferred to Northumbria but not being proficient in English, has King Oswald himself to translate for him. Bede is exceptionally warm in his commendation of Aidan's holy life and humility, which he contrasts with 'the apathy of our own times' (III.5). We learn from Bede's account of him that monks in the Irish tradition preferred to walk rather than ride, keeping their pedestrian habits when becoming English bishops, who generally kept more state. King Oswald gives Aidan a fine horse, which Aidan gives to a beggar (III.14, also IV.3). Oswald reproaching him for this, Aidan reads him a lesson on the greater value of a human being compared with a horse. Oswald, moved by his humility, begs his forgiveness:

At the bishop's urgent request, the king sat down and began to be merry; but Aidan, on the contrary, grew so sad that he began to shed tears. His chaplain asked him, in his own language, which the king and his servants did not understand, why he wept. Aidan replied: 'I know that the king will not live very long; for I have never before seen a humble king.' (III.14)

There is elsewhere a story of a Christian king killed by his kinsmen for forgiving his enemies, i.e. renouncing the ethics of the feud (III.22). Oswald in fact dies in battle with the pagan King Penda of Mercia (642), who had previously put an end to Edwin, the first Christian king of Northumbria. Oswald's sanctity is vouched for by posthumous miracles.

Aidan too, while still alive, performs miracles. Bede's obituary for him shows again, touchingly, his mixed feelings about Celtic monasticism. Aidan cultivated peace and love, poverty and humility, and used his priestly authority to check the proud and powerful, comforting the sick and relieving the poor. 'I greatly admire and love all these things about Aidan, because I have no doubt that they are pleasing to God: but I cannot approve or commend his failure to observe Easter at the proper time, whether he did it through ignorance of the canonical times or in deference to the customs of his own nation' (III.17). The wooden pillar against which Aidan leaned when he was dying was miraculously preserved in a fire; this motif of the wooden pillar has been seen as a folkloric one from the pagan cult of Thor.

Further successes for the Christian mission continue to be interleaved with descriptions of saintly lives in Bede's account. It is noticeable that Bede tends to prefer examples of the good for edifying purposes, while Gregory of Tours's preference – or perhaps just his experience – furnishes more of the opposite kind: it has been held more plausibly of Bede than of Gregory that he is an idealizer of earlier generations, in contrast with a less heroic and exalted present. The crux of his history is his account of the Synod of Whitby (AD 664), by which the vexatious question of the date of Easter is settled and the unity of the Church in Britain (except, of course, for the Britons) is secured. The synod was called and presided over by the Northumbrian king Oswy, another of Bede's model Christian kings, who followed the Irish method of computation, while his wife, instructed in Kentish (Roman) customs, observed the Roman one, so that one observed Lent while the other feasted – clearly an inconvenience, if no worse, in a royal household. At Whitby, for the first time, we meet the formidable figure of Wilfrid, a Northumbrian who has been to Rome and Gaul (we might be inclined to say Brussels) and has returned with strongly Roman (or Eurocratic) notions on Easter and the shape of the monastic tonsure; he emerges at Whitby as a spokesman for the Roman party.

Pace Bede, the issue of the date of Easter was not really a matter of Irish barbarism and rusticity; the case of the basis for computation could be argued either way, but Wilfrid has a strong argument, which he exploits very effectively, in the isolation of the Irish compared with the breadth of consensus and the tradition of the Church arrayed against them.

Our Easter customs are those that we have seen universally observed in Rome, where the blessed Apostles Peter and Paul lived, taught, suffered, and are buried. We have also seen the same customs generally observed throughout Italy and Gaul when we travelled through these countries for study and prayer. Furthermore, we have learnt that Easter is observed by men of different nations and languages at one and the same time, in Africa, Asia, Egypt, Greece, and throughout the world wherever the Church of Christ has spread. The only people who stupidly contend against the whole world are these Scots [i.e. Irish] and their partners in obstinacy the Picts and Britons, who inhabit only a portion of these two uttermost islands of the ocean. (III.25)

Bede is scrupulous in summarizing the arguments, but a fuller account of the technical issue is provided later in a letter from Bede's abbot, Ceolfrid (V.21). King Oswy, in his summing-up, makes much of the authority of the See of St Peter, and the power of the popes inherited from St Peter to bind and loose, and he decides for the Roman position. Some of the Irish, unable to accept the new practice, leave Northumbria to return to Iona, with some of Aidan's bones. Bede again pays tribute to the austerity of life in the Irish monasteries and the devotion they receive from their people, contrasting it with the inferiority of his own time: 'For in those days the sole concern of these teachers was to serve God, not the world, to satisfy the soul, not the belly' (III.26).

Bede's attitude to Wilfrid, with whose position he agreed, has been much discussed: the consensus seems to be that he respected but did not greatly like him, and gave him none of the affection he could not help feeling for Aidan. Wilfrid's stormy later career is alluded to by Bede: thanks to his dictatorial and uncompromising character, it included exile and even imprisonment before he was reinstated as a bishop, as well as missionary work in Sussex. Bede seems even to have glossed over some of its features – Wilfrid, for example, became extremely rich (IV.12–13, V.19).

After Whitby the Irish gradually fell into line everywhere (in the south of Ireland they had never been dissident, so the issue was not straightforwardly Celtic Christianity versus the rest). Bede cared deeply about the unity of the Church, and for him it was clearly a great moment when, in 716, even the intransigents in Iona accepted the Roman computation and tonsure:

This seemed to happen by a wonderful dispensation of God's grace, in order that the nation which had willingly and ungrudgingly laboured to communicate its own knowledge of God to the English nation might later, through the same English nation, arrive at a perfect way of life which they had not hitherto possessed. (V.22)

Earlier the high point of the history seems to have been reached at the opening of Book IV, when the new Archbishop of Canterbury, Theodore, dispatched by the Pope from Italy in 669, became 'the first archbishop whom the whole Church of the English obeyed', thereby setting the seal on the period of conversion and the establishment of a united episcopacy in England in close communion with Rome. It is perhaps this sense of a mission accomplished, as well as the greater volume of recent and contemporary testimony reaching him from all over England within the period of living memory, which makes Bede's last two books markedly more hagiographical. There is, for example, no mention of secular affairs after around 690; there had no need to be.

It is in this section of the book (IV.27–32) that Bede incorporates material from his own *Life of St Cuthbert*, who became, reluctantly, bishop of Lindisfarne. Bede's accounts are artfully composed, and hagiography and its incidentals can tell historians of the period much about the mentality which produced it, but the ordinary modern reader of Bede's last two books is likely to be fairly easily sated with holy deaths, visions of heaven and hell, potent relics, uncorrupted and fragrant corpses, and even the setting to rights of a distressed horse (a posthumous miracle of St Oswald) (III.9). The heroic age of conversion was over, but the individual heroism of the saints still did its work: the Church in England was doing well in its unceasing war with the demons.

Bede concludes, in 731, with a view of the present in Britain: a state of peace, secular and ecclesiastical (V.23). The Picts and Scots are Christian, docile and content. Only the Britons impotently nurse their resentments and preserve their own bad customs in respect to Easter.

But they have – clearly for their own good – 'been brought in part under the subjection of the English'.

As was said earlier, Bede has throughout his history tended to prefer to recount good examples rather than bad, and he has none of Gregory of Tours's candour about ecclesiastical scandals – disciplinary matters were a bishop's business, hardly a monk's, except within his own monastery. If we looked only at the conclusion of the history we might think him complacent. In fact a letter written towards the end of his life shows him deeply disturbed by the lethargy, worldliness and wealth of the contemporary Church in England. Nonetheless, granted foresight as well as hindsight, he would have had to agree, as to some extent he clearly did, that he had lived in fortunate times: the battles with pagan idols and Celtic obstinacy had been won in the previous century; the end of his own was to see the first incursions of the Northmen.

PART IV

The Revival of
Secular History

16

Annals, Chronicles and History

Annals and Chronicles

In 789 there is an ominous entry in the vernacular *Anglo-Saxon Chronicle*:

In this year King Brihtric married Offa's daughter Eadburh. And in his days there came for the first time three ships of Northmen and then the reeve rode to them and wished to force them to the king's residence, for he did not know what they were; and they slew him. Those were the first ships of Danish men which came to the land of the English.

Those three ships again! They were a portent of great damage to, among much else, the settled, scholarly monastic life that Bede had known, with its libraries and schools and riches. The Chronicle entries for the previous years record much internecine warfare; eventually the Danish invasions would play a part in the consolidation of a unitary kingdom, ruled, in the earlier eleventh century, by a Danish king (Cnut or Canute). Four years after the first entry on the Danes, the Chronicle records 'the ravages of heathen men miserably destroyed God's church on Lindisfarne [Aidan's], with plunder and slaughter.' The following year it was the turn of Bede's own monastery of Jarrow.

The bare entries of the vernacular Chronicle provide the record of these disastrous years. Bede's great achievement, popular and revered though it became – on the Continent as well as in England – had no remotely comparable successor for four hundred years. There was a hiatus, which *The Anglo-Saxon Chronicle*, terse though its entries are, especially the earlier ones, was left to fill. It was a remarkable enterprise, and at this point one unique in the whole of Europe. The

Chronicle seems to have been first compiled around the ninth century: the chronicler writing up 789 has hindsight. It was continued thereafter with copying and variations in a number of monasteries, so that the whole Chronicle runs from the landing of the Saxons in 494 to the end of the Anglo-Norman dynasty in 1154. Exactly when, where and why came the initiative for commencing it remains conjectural: Wessex, and a royal impetus, have been suggested; in its last years the centre of its production was Peterborough; King Alfred has been mentioned as its progenitor, and certainly with Alfred the entries become fuller and less purely annalistic, with campaign narratives extending over several paragraphs.

The differences between annals and chronicles, and between chronicles and histories, are a good example of quantitative change turning into qualitative. In individual cases, of course, and at the margins, the classification can become arguable, but the categories are pretty clear. *The Anglo-Saxon Chronicle* offers, over time, an example of annals mutating into chronicle, just as some diaries are merely lists of engagements and others can be regarded as contributions to literature and history. If annals sometimes grew into chronicles, annals themselves seem often to have grown from calendars, kept, of necessity, in monasteries, chiefly for calculating each year the date of Easter. A diversity of matter – portents, weather, local, national and even international events – might then be integrated or else inscribed in the margin. Deaths and successions of popes, bishops, abbots and kings were of particular interest, as were battles, fires and other disasters. For a typical example, chosen at random, we may take a thirteenth-century entry in the long-sustained Chronicle of Bury St Edmunds. It was, of course, originally in Latin:

1239. William Raleigh was elected Bishop of Norwich on 10th April. That horrible race of men known as the Tartars, which had once come swarming from remote fastnesses and overrun the face of the earth, laid waste Hungary and the neighbouring territories. On 18th June Eleanor, queen of England, gave birth to her eldest son Edward. His father was Henry . . .

The rest is Henry's genealogy back to Alfred, and we are given a cross-reference to an earlier genealogy for Alfred back to Adam. It is a rich entry: the Mongol (Tartar) invasions, the birth of Edward I, and the election of an East Anglian bishop. We would, of course, be much mistaken in expecting narrative; there are no thematic connections between the entries, except the birth and the genealogy. We should think instead of a newspaper whose timescale is the year, not the day. We are ourselves unperturbed by the most diverse news stories appearing in juxtaposition, with the conventional division into panels.

History as a genre, though often attending to the passage of the years as most classical historians had done, characteristically involves extended narrative, relevant circumstantial detail, and thematic coherence; the recording of facts is dictated by thematic, dramatic and explanatory considerations, rather than just chronological juxtaposition and convention. These distinctions were recognized in the twelfth century by Gervase of Canterbury. We may say that, as types, annals are disconnected, chronicles are episodic, history is ideally continuous; particular classifications can sometimes be disputable.

Though annals continued to be kept, chronicles and histories take us to the twelfth century. But before considering them we cannot ignore what flows in, given a chance, to supply the place of history for the next three hundred years: legend. The Britons, or Welsh, though they had a rich bardic literature, had so far as we know produced only two short and fragmentary histories between the fifth and the twelfth centuries, and certainly nothing like so coherent, authoritative, substantial and respected a work as Bede's. In the twelfth century an attempt was made to give them one: *The History of the Kings of Britain*, by a secular clerk, apparently based in Oxford, Geoffrey of Monmouth. With a problematic relation to possible earlier writings and to oral tradition, Geoffrey is full and circumstantial, above all on the dark years of the fifth century when even Bede is largely terse or silent: the era of the Saxon invasions. We can, in fact, no longer postpone speaking of Arthur, the great British hero king, as Alfred, three centuries later, became the English one. But while the contemporary narrative sources for Alfred – chiefly the vernacular Chronicle and Asser's Life of Alfred, whose authorship and date have been much debated – are meagre (the story of the cakes is a twelfth-century addition), knowledge of Arthur kept getting fuller and fuller. Alfred was to remain of interest, but from the twelfth to the seventeenth century, despite dissentient voices, there is no doubt who was the hero king enshrined in the national collective memory: it was Arthur.

Pseudo-History: Geoffrey of Monmouth

So far as we know, Arthur first appears in historical writing in the ninth century, a hundred years before Alfred, but already four centuries after he was supposed to have lived – which is a problem. The fifth-century British monk Gildas, who wrote of the Saxon invasions and who lived close to the time of Arthur's supposed flourishing, does not mention him, though as we have seen he does mention a Romano-British leader or *dux* called Ambrosius Aurelianus, who defeats the Saxons in a great battle, and Bede copies him. Arthur does not appear under his own name until the *History of the Britons* (c.830) by Nennius, who wrote in Latin but clearly knew Welsh and Welsh genealogies and traditions. Yet in Nennius Arthur, although a war-leader who wins battles against the Saxons, is still scarcely more than a name. It was Geoffrey of Monmouth, three centuries later still, who, from whatever legendary scraps or nothing but the name, launched Arthur on his career as great king and national hero, holder of a renowned court to which knights flocked.

Arthur's historical credentials, in fact, are thin almost to vanishing point, but his legend, like the stories of the Greek heroes and the *Iliad*, and Aeneas and Romulus in Rome, is a historical fact of a kind – and an important one, in the sense that it powerfully influenced or even dominated the picture many people in Britain, including the English, had of their past, particularly from the twelfth to the seventeenth century. Then, perhaps with more sensitivity to the difference between history and legend but with a willing suspension of disbelief, he figures notably in the nineteenth. After Geoffrey, the remains of Arthur and his queen, Guinevere, were 'discovered' by the monks of Glastonbury in 1191, and Arthur and his knights became central to the emerging ethos of chivalry, with a number of sub-legends, worked up in France and Germany, to inspire the creation of medieval orders of chivalry which aped Arthur's Round Table, like the fourteenth-century Order of the Garter created by Edward III. Preceded by a number of medieval romances, Sir Thomas Malory's *Le Morte d'Arthur* in the next century gave classic shape to the legends of Arthur for English readers; it was one of the first books selected for publication on Caxton's new printing press. In the sixteenth century Arthurian prototypes were a cult at the Tudor court; the Tudors were sometimes self-consciously Welsh, and Henry VII's first son was christened Arthur. Milton, in the next century, meditated an epic of Arthur before settling for Satan. Renaissance scholarship did some damage to Arthur's historicity, but, as we have said, from the seventeenth to the nineteenth century Alfred and the Saxons enjoyed a renewed vogue, largely for political reasons. The Victorian imagination divided its allegiances between the gentlemanly and romantic Arthur and the more populist image of Alfred; it is apt that the greatest Victorian poet to exploit the legends of Arthur was christened Alfred.

Without Geoffrey of Monmouth, the legends of Arthur – if they can be imagined – would have called for only a passing mention here at the most. Geoffrey's work, written in the 1130s, not only launched the Arthurian legend but did it in a manner which claimed, and in a number of respects plausibly claimed, to be history. The interest of Geoffrey's work is not exhausted by consideration of whether it has any factual basis. Geoffrey clearly knew what his contemporaries expected a history to be like, and was talented enough, free apparently from any danger of allowing his narrative to be dominated by its sources, amply to give it to them. Nennius' work alone could never have launched the legend: it is too genealogical, fragmented, incoherent and in many places bare – more a compilation than a history. It speaks more fully of Merlin than Arthur, and it also gives a more extensive account than Bede of the British king Vortigern and his uncontrollable Saxon allies Hengist and Horsa, all of which Geoffrey borrows and elaborates further. Geoffrey, though he understandably retails genealogies, remedies all Nennius' defects.

Geoffrey does not claim to be the author, but only to have translated into Latin from the Welsh 'a certain very old book' shown him by Walter, archdeacon of Oxford. Whether such a book, for which there is virtually no independent evidence, existed and, if so, what it may have contained are interesting but not crucial questions. If Geoffrey was only the translator, the problem of the sources for his assertions is merely transferred to the old book, though if this did exist the question of how old it was, i.e. how much nearer the alleged time of Arthur, would become important. The consensus seems to be that, though there may be traces of Welsh legend and genealogy, partly from oral tradition, in Geoffrey's work, it is essentially his creation. If it were true, it would certainly be a very remarkable part of what has been called the twelfth-century historiographical renaissance – remarkable not only for the important gap it purports to fill in historical knowledge of Britain, but also for the accomplished and assured manner of Geoffrey's narration. In one sense it deserved the popularity it achieved. It has, however, no known sources apart from some well-known (and some garbled) fragments of Roman history, and items from Gildas, Bede and Nennius. Much more damagingly, some of what it describes at length, notably Arthur's great victorious battle with the Roman procurator Lucius Hiburnus in Gaul, left no trace in Roman records and historiography: so great an event could not have been overlooked in a highly literate and historically self-conscious society.

About a fifth of Geoffrey's *History* concerns Arthur, though this proportion rises to a third if one includes Merlin, who, apart from arranging Arthur's conception, plays no part in the later story. The book begins with a foundation myth, along the lines of the *Aeneid*. Brutus, great-grandson of Aeneas (with a genealogy back to Noah), whom Gregory culled from Nennius, after somewhat Virgilian wanderings arrives with some Trojan followers and becomes the eponymous founder of Britain, at that time (as Bede says) called Albion, and inhabited only by giants. The most formidable of these, Gogmagog, is hurled into the sea, apparently off Plymouth, by the eponymous founder of Cornwall, Corineus. Geoffrey is fond of such etymologies; his greatest coup of this kind is the British king Lud (London, Ludgate). Geoffrey's work, though well constructed, is not evenly paced. What are sometimes little more than king lists are interspersed with extended narratives. Some of the more perfunctory kings have subsequently had niches created for them for reasons generally incidental to Geoffrey's purpose and chiefly on account of the memorability of their names: Gorbaduc (subject of one of the earliest English tragedies) and

Hudibras (the subject of a seventeenth-century satirical poem) both have walk-on parts in Spenser's *Faerie Queene*; there is King Coel – neither old nor merry; Cymbeline is unaccompanied by Shakespeare's Iachimo and Imogen; but King Leir appears with his whole family, with their usual names, and his story is as Shakespeare tells it, but with a happy ending – Cordelia becomes queen of Britain.

In Book VIII (of twelve) we arrive at familiar legendary territory with Merlin. His greatest feat, apart from contriving the conception of Arthur by some shape-changing work on Arthur's father, Uther Pendragon, is to transport the Giants' Ring (Stonehenge) from Ireland to Wiltshire as a burial place for British kings. Geoffrey, who is rather chary of the supernatural, makes the process sound more like engineering than magic: the King's men, understandably, are making a mess of it when Merlin arrives like a clerk of works who knows his business. Merlin's forte is actually prophecies, and Geoffrey provides them in Book VII, which was written independently and produced first as 'The Prophecies of Merlin'. It had a large vogue, not least because it hints at a future resurgence of the British or Welsh. Though there is hardly any room for doubt that it was seriously intended, it is so easily parodied that for the modern reader it is inescapably funny, not least in the bathos of the combination of high-flying animal symbolism with the homely names of the English counties: 'A Wolf will act as standard-bearer and lead the troops and it will coil its tail around Cornwall. A soldier in a chariot will resist the Wolf and transform the Cornish people into a Boar.' Significant beasts abound: the Ass of Wickedness, a Hedgehog loaded with apples, a bad-tempered Mountain Bull, the Dragon of Worcester, the Boar of Totnes, the Adder of London, and more. One has the impression Geoffrey could do this kind of thing in his sleep. Merlin tells Vortigern, perhaps redundantly for the reader, that the Red Dragon standing for Britain will be overrun by the White Dragon of the Saxons whom the King has unwisely welcomed, but 'the race that is oppressed shall prevail in the end'; it is a rather rare glimpse of history from a British perspective, the opposite of Bede's.

Geoffrey is rather more circumspect with the complementary later legend that Arthur is not dead but will return, as in the German myth of the Sleeping Kaiser. Geoffrey's account of Arthur's end is slightly ambiguous. After his last great battle with Mordred, Arthur is said to be 'mortally wounded'; he is not said to have died, but is reported to have been taken to the Isle of Avalon, mythically a place of healing, though later identified as Glastonbury, 'so that his wounds might be attended to'.

When Geoffrey was writing, the ideas of chivalry, which were to do so much to amplify and shape the Arthurian legend, and derived so much from it, had not assumed their later predominance. Apart from some exotica we will consider in a moment, his book is chiefly an apparently reliable account of Dark Age power politics. Arthur is a great king and commander, in the moulds of Caesar and Charlemagne, rather than the later knight errant. His wife is Guinevere, who is seduced by Mordred, Arthur's nephew, but there is no Lancelot and so no ideal of courtly love, which was soon to attach itself firmly to him. There is also no Holy Grail. Gawaine, Kay and Bedevere are there, and Arthur's sword is recognizable in its guise of Caliburn – though his spear, which, rather surprisingly to the modern reader, is called Ron, is not. There is no sword-in-the-stone. Arthur's court at Caerleon-on-Usk (Book IX) is of incomparable splendour, and sets the fashion for knights everywhere. Arthur also holds court in Paris after conquering Gaul. He additionally conquers the Picts, Norwegians and Danes (there seems to be some reminiscence of Canute ruling a great northern empire). Arthur is on the point of marching on Rome when he is recalled to deal with Mordred's treachery.

Arthur sometimes displays individual prowess, notably in giant-slaying (X.3, 4), and he measures the relative strength of the giants he has killed like a connoisseur. One, anthropophagous, giant has taken residence at the top of Mont Saint-Michel; another has a cloak made of the beards of the men he has killed. Such exploits read like intrusions from the world of *Beowulf* into the mode of Roman history which Geoffrey seems to be adopting for Arthur's campaigns; they may stem from separate, pre-existing legends adapted by Geoffrey. But meeting a challenge from Lucius Hiburnus, the Roman procurator in Gaul, Arthur seems to slip easily into Roman habits himself. He raises an army of 180,300 men – excluding foot soldiers, whom Geoffrey says were not easy to count. Rome musters a world-representative army of 400,160 men. In the ensuing battle, preceded by generals' speeches in classical fashion, the armies stood face to face

with javelins raised ... As soon as they heard the sound of battle-trumpets, the legion commanded by the King of Spain and Lucius Catellus charged boldly at the division led by the King of Scotland and the Duke of Cornwall, but the latter stood firm, shoulder to shoulder, and the Roman force was not able to break it. As the Roman legion persisted in its fierce attack, the division commanded by Gerin and Duke Boso moved up at the double. The Roman legion fought bravely, as has already been said, but this fresh division attacked it with a sudden cavalry charge, broke through and came into contact with the legion which the King of the Parthians was directing against the division of Aschil, King of the Danes ...

and so on (X.9–12).

It is very convincing, apart from the numbers perhaps. If only it convinced. Making allowance for the fact that we are reading Geoffrey in a modern translation, it is instructive to compare his with the account of the same battle (Sassy) by Malory in his *Le Morte d'Arthur* (1469), three centuries later:

Then the battles [divisions] approached and shove and shouted on both sides, and great strokes were smitten on both sides, many men overthrown, hurt and slain; and great valiances, prowesses and appertyces [conspicuous deeds] of war were that day showed, which were over long to recount and noble feats of every man, for they should contain an whole volume. But in especial, King Arthur rode in the battle ... (V.viii)

Arthur kills Lucius with his own hand. Geoffrey, in neoclassical mode, has room for troop dispositions and tactics, despite his reluctance to count foot soldiers. Malory's account is of a chivalric rough-and-tumble, brought to an end by single combat.

Geoffrey has a number of devices for conveying authenticity, some of them subtle. For example, when Leir's grandson by Regan becomes king, 'In his time it rained blood for three days and men died from the flies which swarmed' – a nice *faux-naïf* chronicler's touch. Nennius had a rain of blood, like many historians before him, including Livy, but no flies. Geoffrey also produces presumably spurious charters, but this was a common skill. He also makes chronological cross-references between biblical, Roman and his own British history, in the manner pioneered by Eusebius. Isaiah was prophesying while the British flies were swarming; Cordelia was coeval with Romulus and Remus, and Brutus the Trojan with Eli the judge in Israel.

What is one to make of all this: of Geoffrey's intentions and the spirit in which he wrote? They are not perhaps quite the same thing. British patriotism and a drive for ecclesiastical preferment – he tried two dedicatees – seem sufficient motive, but how did Geoffrey regard his own creation, as we assume it to be? It is perhaps not wrong, and certainly tempting, to use the word hoax, but whether Geoffrey was in his own mind a hoaxer seems more problematic. He was a parodist of near-genius, and a considerable imaginative writer. How far he may have convinced himself that what he wrote is what the records would have said if they were fuller, or existed, seems impossible to say. It has been suggested that his reputation would stand higher if he had presented his work openly as a literary epic, like the *Aeneid*. Perhaps. The notion of Geoffrey delighting in his own mischief tends to appeal so much to the modern sensibility, with its taste for literary hoaxes, concealed jokes, parody and the confounding of the genres of fact and fiction, that we should no doubt be wary of it. Geoffrey's skill and success may even seem to reinforce a postmodern scepticism about the truth claims of history: it looks like history, it smells like history, so why isn't it history? In fact – blessed word! – it suggests the opposite of scepticism. In the Renaissance the exposure of the so-called Donation of Constantine, conferring on the Pope the succession to the sovereignty of the Roman emperors in the West, gave rise to, or reinforced, scepticism about the documentary grounds of all history. But this was the wrong inference: the point was that it had been possible to demonstrate that the Donation was a forgery. Similarly with Geoffrey's work. It is not the same as that of the chroniclers who were his contemporaries, however ungainly, gullible, careless or biased they may sometimes have been, and we know why it is not: the concept of fraudulence logically presupposes that of authenticity. William of Newburgh, half a century after Geoffrey, said that *The History of the Kings of Britain* was all made up, 'either from an inordinate love of lying, or for the sake of pleasing the Britons'. Apart from Geoffrey's obvious quest for preferment, these are pretty much the alternatives. It is time to return to the terra firma of twelfth-century chronicle and history, even if it conceals pitfalls.

Secular History and Chronicle: William of Malmesbury's Modern History and the Scurrilities of Matthew Paris

The Anglo-Saxon Chronicle was unique in its time, and so, in his way, was Geoffrey of Monmouth. But chronicles were produced all over Europe in the Middle Ages. In France, as in England, a centralizing monarchy gave a focus for secular chronicles and created the possibility of a kind of national history. This was represented, above all, in France by the Grandes Chroniques de France, issued in the vernacular with royal sponsorship from the thirteenth century. To avoid giving a lifeless and perfunctory survey, however, it is necessary here to narrow the perspective to a single country. Accessibility to an English-speaking readership, if nothing else, suggests that the focus shall be England, which fortunately had a rich chronicle literature, of which a proportion has been translated from the Latin.

By the twelfth century the island of Britain had undergone five major transformations, all of them the result of incursions from the European mainland: invasion and conquest by the Romans, the Saxons, the Danes and the Normans, and conversion to Catholic Christianity, from Ireland and from Rome. Each had left a residue in the records: in Caesar and Tacitus, in Gildas and Bede, in The Anglo-Saxon Chronicle, and, most recently, in the late-eleventh- and twelfth-century accounts of the campaign of Hastings and the Norman Conquest. In the early twelfth century, when first-class chroniclers began to proliferate, the Conquest was only just receding from living memory, and the Anglo-Norman chroniclers included it as a matter of course. Some even seem to have been spurred to write by a divided inheritance and a sense of the massiveness of the transformation effected in the previous generation. For actual contemporary accounts we are less well off. The best prose account is that of the chronicler William of Poitiers, who is a eulogist of Duke William of Normandy. But in many respects the best record is a unique document, the Bayeux Tapestry.

Historically, the Tapestry covers much the same ground as William of Poitiers. It is still visible in its 230 foot by 9½ inch glory and splendidly displayed in the town of Bayeux where it was in all probability made, at the order of its bishop, William the Conqueror's brother, Odo of Bayeux. It is also a text, and not even in the fashionably metaphorical sense, for it carries a verbal narrative in Latin running across it. As an object of beauty, it is enhanced by the narrow horizontal bands, top and bottom, like marginal annotations, which contain rather heraldic-looking birds and beasts, and scenes of ordinary lives and deaths, realistically depicted.

The narrative itself begins with the dispatch to Normandy of Earl Harold of Wessex, on an embassy to Duke William from King Edward the Confessor. Harold is shipwrecked and captured by a local magnate, but is freed by William. They go campaigning together, and then Harold swears on holy relics his fealty to the Duke. Back in England, Edward dies and Harold, ignoring his oath to William, takes the crown. William prepares an army, lands in Sussex, and defeats the Saxons in battle; Harold dies with apparently – it has been disputed – an arrow in his eye. There are vivid scenes of contemporary life throughout: sea voyages; shipbuilding; hunting; porters with their burdens; soldiers foraging, preparing food, building a wooden fortress, and setting fire to a house from which a woman and her child are seen emerging. In the margins, the birds and beasts give way to small archers shooting and soldiers mutilated, dead, unceremoniously stripped of their armour. It is a dazzling and humane document, comparable in historical importance to Trajan's Column, but easier to inspect.

The Anglo-Saxon Chronicle, as one would expect, is woeful about the Conquest and treats it, as Gildas had done the Saxon one, as a punishment for sin. Then and later the Chronicle is more than usually sensitive to the sufferings of ordinary people. The slightly later Anglo-Norman chroniclers Orderic Vitalis, Robert of Jumièges, Henry of Huntingdon and William of Malmesbury borrow from the Chronicle (as well as from Geoffrey of Monmouth) and also, not improperly of course, from each other. Orderic and William were of mixed parentage, but all the chronicles treat Harold with respect. It is impossible to do justice to any of them by flitting between them. If a choice has to be made – and it has – it is the work of William of Malmesbury which suggests itself most strongly.

William, as his name implies, was a monk of Malmesbury Abbey in Wiltshire, of which he was librarian; like a number of monastic writers, he was the author of a history of his own abbey, as well as of Glastonbury. His *oeuvre*, though varied in the manner to which we have become accustomed, shows an exceptional concern for orderliness and thematic choice. Hence in his two largest works he treats secular and ecclesiastical history separately, in the *Deeds of the Kings of the English* (*Gesta Regum Anglorum*) and the *Gesta Pontificum Anglorum*. The latter is a kind of continuation of Bede. In the *Deeds of the Kings* he laments the long hiatus in the recording of the English past, except in the Chronicle (i.e. *The Anglo-Saxon Chronicle*) and declares it to be shameful. He also denounces what he calls the lies of the Britons. The most easily summarizable of his works, which here will have to stand, imperfectly, for the whole, is his work of contemporary history, the *Historia Novella* (i.e. 'Modern History'), which covers the years 1126–42, and is brought to an end by his death.

His preface to the *Deeds of the Kings*, however, explains his approach to the historian's task and sources. He has, he says, no warrant for the truth of 'long past transactions but the consonance of the times ... Whatever I have recorded of later times, I have either myself seen, or heard from credible authority.' More unusually, he is self-conscious about historical narrative and the need for thematic coherence. On Alfred, for example, he says, 'To trace in detail the mazy labyrinth of his labours was never my design,' for to give a recitation of his exploits 'in their exact order of time would confuse the reader'; William considerately summarizes. In his account of the Conquest – not very different from others – he takes on the responsibility of assessing its consequences, portraying the Saxon and Norman characters (respectively feckless and dissipated and calculating and frugal), and focusing particularly on the state of the Church at the time of the Conquest (bad). The point is not the adequacy of William's assessment, but his making the attempt. In the *Modern History* too he is prepared to defy strict chronology and 'to make into a parcel, as it were, the main points scattered through my text bearing on the conduct of Robert, earl of Gloucester, King Henry's son, and to present them in a recapitulation for the reader to evaluate'. The Earl of Gloucester was William's dedicatee and patron and also one of the dedicatees of Geoffrey of Monmouth's *History*.

As narrative, the *Modern History* begins with the ending of Henry I's reign and the disputed succession which follows. Henry's only legitimate son had died in the fateful sinking in the Channel of the vessel called the *White Ship* (1120). William laments this in the *Deeds of the Kings*: 'No ship was ever productive of so much misery for England, none was ever so widely celebrated throughout the world.' The events of the *Modern History* are those of the troubled reign (1135–54) of King Stephen and the civil war produced by the claim of Henry's daughter Matilda to the crown. Henry had made the nobles swear fealty to Matilda, but after his death many of them supported Stephen. It has to be admitted that William's promised recapitulation of the last part of King Henry's reign seems dispensable, concerning itself with the shamefulness of the fashion of long hair for men, a territorial dispute between the bishops of Llandaff and St David's, a disputed papal election, and a cattle plague: William here seems to have stepped into chronicle territory. But the rest of the *Modern History* is a fairly tautly constructed monograph on the civil war which follows the seizure of the throne by Stephen, count of Blois, aided by his brother the Bishop of Winchester, whom William knows. William addresses his monograph to posterity, in the preface to Part III, reverting to his point that the absence of a record is a disgrace: 'In the year of the Lord's Incarnation 1142, I am undertaking to unravel the trackless maze of events and occurrences that befell in England, with the aim that posterity should not be ignorant of these matters through our lack of care'; the chief lesson to be learned is the changeability of fortune, the mutability of the human lot.

For a comparable monograph on contemporary history one really has to go back to Roman times; William, like most medieval authors, was aware of Sallust and Livy, as well as knowing Virgil, Juvenal, Cicero and other classical writers. The story he has to tell is nothing less than that of the great crisis of the hitherto strong Anglo-Norman state; William points the contrast with the peace and security of Henry I's reign. *The Anglo-Saxon Chronicle*, on which William draws in the *Deeds of the Kings*, was eloquent on the sufferings of the populace as anarchy ensues and rival barons turn into no better than bandits:

1137. They oppressed the wretched people of the country severely with castle-building. When the castles were built they filled them with devils and wicked men. Then, both by night and day, they took those people they thought had any goods – men and women – and put them in prison and tortured them with indescribable torture to extort gold and silver.

Then the chronicler describes the torture. The same entry provides the famous remark that men 'said openly that Christ and his saints were asleep'. Then, in the manner of chroniclers, the subject switches to the building works of an abbot of Peterborough – the Chronicle was by now being produced there – and the alleged torture and blasphemous crucifixion by the Jews of Norwich of the child afterwards hailed as St William of Norwich. William of Malmesbury echoes the Chronicle on the suffering created by the civil war, but his forte is really high politics. Castle-building figures in the *Modern History* too, but chiefly as one of the stumbling blocks to peace. Bishops, presumably moved by the desire for security, have been building castles, contrary to canon law, and the King, violating the immunities of the clergy, has had some of them imprisoned. Both sides had a case, and William is good at presenting such dilemmas.

Although a monk, William was clearly also a man of the world, with acquaintances and sources among the great; he evidently went to a good deal of pains to inform himself of the inside of events. He is close to his patron, Matilda's illegitimate brother, the Earl of Gloucester, and also to the papal legate, Henry of Winchester. He also knows well Henry I's chancellor, a man of great power in the previous reign, Roger, bishop of Salisbury, and the local oppressor of William's abbey. Roger was, William says, 'conscious of his power and abused God's indulgence rather more than was proper for such a man', while greatly glorifying his see of Salisbury. His attempt on the independence of Malmesbury Abbey is turned by William into an elegant epigram. The Bishop had also tried to elevate his own priory of Sherborne into an abbey: 'Roger tried to turn abbeys into a bishopric, the property of a bishopric into an abbey.' (It reads better in Latin: 'abbatias in episcopatum, res episcopatus in abbatiam'. One feels like applauding.) The Bishop, under the new regime, falls from his high estate. William says, 'While to many he seemed pitiable, few pitied him,' adding 'which I myself am sorry for' (II.33).

The fortunes of the civil war fluctuate; Stephen, genial and kindly, is also weak; Matilda is headstrong and uncooperative (I.14–15). Allegiances are tested, repudiated, sway this way and that. William largely bypasses the military events and concentrates on the attempts at reconciliation, notably in the two councils called in 1139 and 1141 by the Bishop of Winchester, the papal legate, and the reasons for their failure. William attended the first of the councils. He clearly prefers Stephen personally, but blames him for his violation of the charter of liberties of the Church, to which he had agreed, and which William transcribes. Reckless men take advantage of Stephen's weakness, some coming as mercenaries from overseas to enjoy the pickings (I.18). In King Henry's reign, William says, foreigners came to England as refugees from strife at home; now they come for plunder (II.36). The unspoken threat behind the proceedings of the council is Stephen's possible excommunication for arresting bishops, but matters do not proceed so far – not only, William says, for lack of direct papal authorization, but also for fear of more violence (presumably against the Church) in England. William, one feels, understands the motives of public men biding their time, doing, he says, not what they would but what they could. The interests of the Church are clearly close to his heart, but he is not excessively judgmental, nor particularly cynical, though he clearly disapproves of Matilda – 'this virago' – his patron Robert of Gloucester's half-sister.

William knows of the second legatine council only by report. He laments that nothing had been achieved: 'So all this year [1141], whose tragedies I have briefly related, was ill-omened and almost mortal for England, which after thinking that it might now in some sort draw a breath of freedom, fell back again into misery, and thus, unless God's mercy sends a remedy, it will long remain' (III.59). The central event of this time was the escape of Matilda from Oxford, where she had been besieged. Other writers sensed the picturesque opportunity – she had been lowered from the walls before escaping across the snow. William does not. The outlines of the eventual solution to the conflict – Stephen's enjoyment of the crown for life and the succession of Matilda's son Henry, the future Henry II – are adumbrated in William's text, but he was prevented by death from seeing it implemented, so his history ends abruptly.

Since William mentions 1141 as ill-omened, it is perhaps worth repeating an event he records of the previous year: an eclipse of the sun on 20 March 1140, which, he says, 'was thought and said by many to presage disaster for King Stephen [he lost a battle]'. William adds that, at Malmesbury, 'at first men sitting at table . . . feared the primeval chaos; then, hearing what it was, they went out and saw the stars around the sun' (II.38). 'Then, hearing what it was' – an eclipse was still an omen, but it was also clearly reassuring to find it a recognized astronomical event.

William does not mute his criticisms of the great, but he speaks, generally, with decorum. Even the word 'virago' applied to Matilda, subsequently having only unfavourable connotations, could at least in classical Latin sometimes mean 'heroine' as well as 'mannish woman'. The great exception is made for Robert Fitz-Hubert, 'the cruellest of all men and also a blasphemer against God'. Robert has prisoners smeared with honey and then put in the glare of the sun to be tormented by insects (II.39). We are all glad when he is hanged. We may feel that William is sometimes discreet, but contemporary history, as he says, is particularly tricky. He is less inhibited in the *Deeds of the Kings*, sometimes offering vivid physical descriptions of kings in the manner of Suetonius and Einhard. William Rufus, for example, is florid (of course), pot-bellied and powerful, with differently coloured eyes. He is also bad. William of Malmesbury is also perhaps something of a snob. Some Londoners – a portent – came to the second Winchester council to make the case for King Stephen. The Bishop of Winchester describes them as 'magnates', because they have come from so great a city. William seems to regard them as gatecrashers; they claim to represent 'what they call the commune of London' (III.49) – William's 'quam vocant' has the effect of a raised eyebrow. The first London Chronicle would be produced half a century later, in 1188.

'Discreet' is not a word that could ever be applied to our next protagonist, Matthew Paris: he is populist, scathing, cynical, violently partisan, prejudiced and funny. Aware that his chronicle, of which his own manuscript copy survives, was full of indiscretions, he obviously tried subsequently to erase some of the most egregious. It was wasted labour. Not only were the erasures inefficient, the indiscretions were too many for him – bowdlerizing Matthew Paris was like trying to de-vein Gorgonzola. He is not a historian but a chronicler, but his episodic and heterogeneous *Greater Chronicle* is vivid, entertaining, and held together by a highly personal view of the world.

Matthew was born soon after 1200, and became a monk of the Benedictine abbey of St Albans. He compiled, as was common, a general history of the world from the Creation, incorporating the work of his predecessor in St Albans, Roger of Wendover, narrowing down to 1259. Matthew's own chronicle covers something over two decades, but it is still very large, including European as well as English events. Recognizing this, he epitomized himself, twice over, into a shorter chronicle on English history alone, and then an abbreviation of that. He also produced an appendix of documents, the *Liber Additamentorum*. Matthew's material remained heterogeneous, but the new orderliness was at work in him also. He wrote hagiographies, including a life of St Alban, in Anglo-Norman verse, and so obviously intended for the laity and women, but his *Greater Chronicle* is almost entirely mundane, though not unecclesiastical, in its interests. The eminent medievalist V. H. Galbraith called it 'the high-water mark of medieval historical writing in England' (*Kings and Chroniclers*, 1982).

Because the chronicle form, to which Matthew remained wedded, does not allow for extended narrative development, an attempt to give a flavour of the *Greater Chronicle* is bound to be largely a recital of Matthew's prejudices and snorts of indignation and disgust. Fortunately they are entertaining. His sympathies are popular in so far as they are not purely Benedictine, and he is consistently against authority – papal, royal and episcopal – especially when it attempts to exact money and ignores chartered and customary rights, particularly those of monasteries. He is sensitive to public opinion, and treats it, perhaps for the first time, as something to be reckoned with. Hostility to Henry III's foreign favourites was a theme of the time, and Matthew joins in enthusiastically, referring to 'hungry foreign nobles . . . with empty stomachs and open mouths gaping for the king's money' (27);

the last is a favourite image with him, and is applied also to the Pope.

Periodically Matthew reports briefly but sympathetically on Parliament's remonstrations against royal exactions and foreigners. His reporting is always colloquial and down to earth: the king 'lost his temper and said to his counsellors, "It is your fault that the magnates have been alienated from me. Look! I am on the point of losing Gascony and have been robbed of Poitou. My treasury is empty! What can I do?"' (64). King Henry is not only rapacious, but also parsimonious and without dignity. He takes the cross (i.e. vows himself to a crusade) merely as a money-raising device. He attempts to establish his own temporary fair in London, for the sake of the tolls, prohibiting other retail sales for its duration to the detriment of the tradesmen; the site is plagued with wind, tearing at the awnings, and rain, so that the merchants were 'cold, wet, hungry and thirsty . . . Their feet were dirtied by the mud and their merchandise spoilt by rain' (70). Matthew, a century after William of Malmesbury, writes with sympathy of the opposition of the mayor and commune of London to the King, though in monastic chronicles generally references to citizens and townspeople and their fractiousness seem to be disapproving. Matthew is not only hostile to foreigners and exacting great overlords: he has a Benedictine prejudice against the new mendicant orders, and is cynical about the motives of those who congregate in the new universities: 'The world is now become elated with pride and despises the religion of the cloister,' adding characteristically, 'aiming at despoiling the monks of their property' (110).

Except when he quotes papal and episcopal letters, which are naturally formal, none of the great are allowed to retain their dignity. Matthew describes with relish the behaviour of the Archbishop of Canterbury, Boniface of Savoy, the King's uncle. In 1250, visiting the church of St Bartholomew in London, and finding the canons showing a spirit of independence, Boniface falls into a rage, rushes at the sub-prior, and 'vigorously [strikes] that holy man, a priest and a monk, with his fist, as he [stands] in the middle of the church, truculently repeating the blows, now on the aged face, now on his grey-haired head, and yelling "This is how English traitors should be dealt with"' (148). He causes serious injuries, and the citizens of London, understandably enraged in their turn, cause a tumult. We seem to be back in the world of Gregory of Tours – or perhaps we have never really left it. Secular ecclesiastics get drunk and vomit; friars dress like lords and are used by the Pope as smooth-tongued extortionists (8) – Matthew disapproves of religious wandering about. Matthew has been called an early constitutionalist. This is not exactly wrong, but over-theoretical. He stands, certainly, for established rights of all kinds, though especially monastic ones; he is certainly sympathetic to the baronial 'opposition' and to the citizens of London, and is unimpressed by great autocrats. He sometimes reminds one of a modern tabloid editor: disrespectful, populist, xenophobic and anti-intellectual.

He was also, uniquely, a talented illustrator of his own work. His marginal illustrations are not cartoons, though they have something of their quality, but elegant, attractive, sometimes quaint coloured drawings of relevant objects and scenes, as well as purely decorative heraldic shields. Of course they do not have the delicacy and richness of some illustrated missals, Gospels and books of hours. They are like Matthew's writing, lively and demotic and sometimes macabre: a pillory, a purse (relevantly), a Franciscan, a Jew, maltreated prisoners, hangings, maps (including the Holy Land, with camel), a galley, a battle, a shipwreck, a collapsing building illustrating that old standby of the chronicler an earthquake, and martyrdoms (St Alban, Becket). Most unusual is the town band of Cremona, mounted, surprisingly, on an elephant; the city is relevant because of the ignominious part it played in the Italian resistance to the emperor Frederick Barbarossa, whose deeds seem to fascinate Matthew; they were the subject of a contemporary work by Otto of Freising. To read Matthew in an illustrated edition, with its birds, shields, satirical drawings and the bric-a-brac of contemporary life, adds considerably to the pleasure.

Two Abbey Chronicles: St Albans and Bury St Edmunds

Matthew Paris also wrote, in another common monastic genre, a 'Deeds of the Abbots' for his own house, St Albans. In his preamble, he provides for what was essentially conventual local history the same kind of rationale as was standard for national histories, with a twist at the end. It was done

> so that neither their good deeds nor indeed their bad ones will perish in the future times through oblivion and by this means not only will people now and in the future be incited to do good, but evil people will be deterred by fear of scandal. Furthermore, if any secular or ecclesiastical person has piously conferred benefits on this church, not only his name but the benefit itself . . . will be perpetuated without a thread of falsity.

Keeping a record of benefactions, not only those in kind but those in land and privileges, was a motive to recording the history of the abbey, as it was to the forging of charters. It gave greater security of possession of donations, which had often been made in a more customary and less documentary age and therefore lacked what was now increasingly required in cases of dispute, a written record. It also acted as a kind of inventory, and hence a guard against misappropriation.

Matthew's writing, as his frank prefatory remarks suggest, loses nothing of its saltiness and suspicion of authority by being turned inward: he is no more a respecter of abbots per se than of kings and archbishops. Hagiographer though he also is, and staunch defender of conventual rights, he is here easily recognizable as the author of the *Greater Chronicle*. His interests are ecclesiastical and mundane. The abbey suffers, for example, from that perennial menace the dodgy builder, who gives 'treacherous advice to add unnecessary, futile and excessively expensive ornaments', so that the abbot loses his nerve, the work is abandoned, and a wall falls down. To pay for the completion, the abbot sends 'a certain cleric called Amphibalus, whom the Lord had raised from the dead on the fourth day through the good offices of St Alban and St Amphibalus', on a preaching tour with the saints' relics, to raise money (15). Matthew seems to record this simply as a fund-raising technique, with no other comment. But the work still languishes. Eventually, however, a refectory, a dormitory and privies are completed. St Alban, as usual, can look after his own. When the abbey is threatened with losing a lawsuit, as a result of a charter forged by a treacherous monk who has been bribed by the other side, the traitor is discovered and exiled to the daughter house of Tynemouth, which seems, perhaps for climatic reasons, to have functioned as a sort of penitentiary. There, drunk and gorged, he meets his deserts by dying in the privy, calling out 'Take him, Satan!' There is a similar death in Gregory of Tours, perhaps in imitation of that of the heresiarch Arius, who was said to have died voiding his bowels. Of course people do die there. In the St Albans case, Matthew says that there were doubts whether the deceased merited Christian burial, but, to avoid a scandal, the brethren 'kept silent about many things' (18).

An abbey was a polity in miniature, in which endless friction and disputes were produced by the often uncertain division of power and customary rights between kings, bishops – we have seen the Bishop of Salisbury oppressing Malmesbury Abbey – abbots, conventual officials and the assisting cloister monks, and the abbey's tenants. The abbot was an autocrat, but in times of vacancy the monks became (under restrictions) an electorate, with the right of proposing candidates for royal ratification. The monk they were electing would be a great man, a magnate of the kingdom. Matthew gives a detailed account of the proper procedures for elections, and also of the proper conduct of abbots-elect. Conflicts with ecclesiastical and lay neighbours on land and rights of jurisdiction, use and tolls were fertile in lawsuits and even, on occasion, violence – usually confined to the abbey's servants, though not always. The lay enemy of St Albans, who had the charter forged, disputed the abbot's right to depose the prior of a church of which he himself was patron. He flourished the same or another charter, but also, less subtly, laid siege to the church as if it were a castle, threatening to castrate the new prior and the monks with him, who were reduced, according to Matthew, to the last stages of thirst and starvation. The abbey appealed to King John, who comes rather well out of the story, though we are told he hated the Earl. Exclaiming 'Ho! By God's feet who has heard of such things!', he intimidates the Earl's men into abandoning the siege (20).

Matthew offers all kinds of information on the internal affairs of the monastery, from the commissioning of paintings for the church and the acquisition of books for the library to the withdrawal of a customary allowance which had become used for boozing. The death of Abbot John, who had panicked over the affair of the overcharging builder, is recounted by Matthew not only piously but touchingly.

One of John's accomplishments had been that he was 'an incomparable judge of urine' (30), but his failing eyesight meant that he was unable to use this diagnostic skill on himself. The deaths and solemn obsequies of abbots were great occasions. Abbot John's farewell to his monks is genuinely moving, though Matthew also characteristically records his transgressions as he had promised, naming his flatterers and deploring his tyrannical use of exile to remote priories or 'cells' of the monastery as a punishment. The monks seek and obtain a charter prohibiting this from the next abbot, but he breaks it; one of the victims weeps and begs to remain at home among his brethren. Exile could in some cases apparently mean solitary confinement. It is another charge against the new abbot, William of Trumpington – a young man – that he prefers to dine with laymen rather than in 'the friendly society of the cloister' (49). Matthew is also free with his criticisms of the abbey's officials.

Abbot William, in other respects, seems not a bad sort, and among other benefactions he performs a highly meritorious act in obtaining – we are not told how – a rib of St Wulfstan from the Bishop of Worcester (19). Matthew, again according to his undertaking, is highly interested in recording acquisitions and embellishments, by commission or donation – images, paintings, the beautification of the altars, the strengthening of the church roof with lead. Abbots and monks, as well as laypeople, are among the donors. Matthew pays generous tribute to the painters and craftsmen responsible for the work, as well as to the quality of the gifts, though he also has to record the reprehensible and shocking theft, twice, of the Eucharist and its holy and jewelled gold and silver vessels from the church. At one point, recording a lay benefaction, Matthew gives what seems a premonitory glimpse of countless future entries in countless parish magazines, recording innumerable gifts of stoles, altar cloths and hassocks, piously fringed, crocheted and embroidered: 'Mistress Alice, the daughter of Henry Cocus, bequeathed a red silk chasuble, nicely worked with gold, to this altar' (50).

St Albans was a notable centre for the production of chronicles. We have already seen that Matthew continued the chronicle, from the Creation, of Roger of Wendover. The consecutive St Albans Chronicle continues to the year 1440 – more than two hundred years in the writing. Galbraith, in fact, speaks of 'the St Albans school of history' – Thomas of Walsingham, a St Albans monk, was a notable chronicler of the Lancastrian period. Other monastic centres of chronicle production were Worcester, Canterbury, Durham and Peterborough. One such centre, however, Bury St Edmunds, produced, like Matthew in the midst of the St Albans Chronicle, a gem among the prevailing worthy mediocrity, though one, unlike Matthew's, focused only on the affairs of the monastery.

At the end of the eleventh century the abbey of St Edmund had produced a Miracles of their saint, murdered by the Danes in 876, whose body it possessed. The document also traced the history of the abbey up to the dedication of its new church in 1094, as well as its running dispute over its autonomy with the Bishop of Thetford (a see later transferred to Norwich). As seems not uncommon, hagiography led to local history, just as the latter sometimes incorporated national history through outside pressure on the abbey's immunities, particularly from the King and particularly financial. Bury also produced an architectural history of the abbey and a continuation of its chronicle up to the second half of the thirteenth century, one of the notable events in which is a revolt by the young townsmen against the abbey in 1264. It also refers to the much more serious revolt in Norwich in 1272, in which the cathedral was set on fire and thirty or so servants of the monks were dragged out and murdered; the Bury chronicle estimates the number of citizens involved at over thirty thousand, including many women.

The gem of the Bury sequence, however, is the famous Chronicle of Jocelin of Brakelonde, which was given a permanent place in English literature when, soon after its publication by the Camden Society in 1840, Thomas Carlyle adopted it to stand for the past in admonitory contrast to the present in his tract for the times *Past and Present* (1842). It is to Carlyle's credit that he so early recognized Jocelin's quality, though his condescension is at times irritating. Jocelin's chronicle covers the last decades of the twelfth century (Henry II, Richard I) and continues into the early thirteenth, in the reign of King John. It begins, domestically, in the time of Abbot Hugh, who is old and feeble and who has let things get out of hand. Hence, though it is called a chronicle, Jocelin's work exhibits one of the archetypal themes of historical narrative: the aged ruler, chaos, a deliverer, and renovation. The abbot, and under him his deputy the prior, should have been responsible for maintaining all St Edmund's rights and liberties against its great neighbours, and against the King and the Pope, as well as ultimately for internal discipline. However, the abbey is going to ruin, piling up debts through its officers, chiefly the sacrist and the cellarer, who are out of control. The sacrist was responsible for the services of the church and its fabric, and for collecting dues from the towns-people, who were all tenants of the abbey. The cellarer was responsible for the purchase of provisions for the monks and guests, and for collecting revenues, in dues and kind, from the abbey's lands. The sacrist and cellarer were thus both responsible for raising and spending money (the distinction is therefore not the same as that between bursar and steward, though it has some similarities). There were ample opportunities for both to get into more debt, and they had done so, apparently from laxity and incompetence rather than peculation, each going his own way and becoming ever more hopelessly entangled with interest payments and further debts.

The old abbot dies, and there is an interregnum; the monks regularly pray for a new abbot – though, Jocelin ironically comments, if some had known who it was to be they 'would not have prayed so devoutly' (11). Jocelin's description of the ensuing election is a superb piece of writing, retailing with humour and immense vitality, with much use of direct speech, the whispering and lobbying and the airing of old resentments and prejudices and new anxieties and calculations as the monks approach their great decision. The election opens up divisions between the old and the young, the learned and the unlettered, and through Jocelin we can see suddenly revealed the qualities sought in an abbot and the jealousies, resentments and apprehensions by which the monks are swayed, as well as their individual dispositions: timid, proud, even cynical. Intellectual snobbery is countered by anti-intellectualism. One says, 'Abbot Ording was a good man and ruled the house wisely'; an unlearned man might make a good abbot, 'though he is not so perfect a philosopher as some others'.

To this another made answer, 'How may this be? How can he, a man who has no knowledge of letters, preach a sermon in Chapter, or on feast days to the people? How shall he who does not understand the Scriptures have knowledge how to bind and loose, seeing that "the rule of souls is the art of arts and the science of sciences"? God forbid that a dumb image should be set up in the Church of St Edmund, where it is known that there are many men of learning and of understanding.' Again another said of yet another, 'That brother is literate, eloquent and prudent, strict in his observance of the Rule; he has greatly loved the Convent, and has endured many ills for the possessions of the Church; he is fitting to be made Abbot.' And another replied, 'From all good clerks, O Lord deliver us; that it may please Thee to preserve us from all vexatious Norfolk disputants, we beseech Thee to hear us.'

Jocelin himself supports the intellectual side, though in his subsequent account he seems to reproach himself for youthful priggishness:

And I indeed, being a young man, 'understood as a child and spoke as a child', and I said that I would not agree to any man being made Abbot, unless he knew something of dialectic and could distinguish between false argument and true. And another, who thought himself wise, said, 'May God Almighty give us for our shepherd one who is a fool and ignorant, so that he will have to ask us to help him!' (12)

Jocelin's inexperience in elections leads him into an embarrassing indiscretion:

On one occasion I could not contain my spirit, but blurted out what I thought, thinking that I spoke to faithful ears, and I said that a certain brother was unworthy to be Abbot, though he had loved me and conferred many benefits upon me; and said I thought another worthy to be Abbot, and named a man whom I loved less. I spake as my conscience bade me, considering the common good rather than my own advancement, and I spoke the truth, as the sequel proved. And behold! one of the sons of Belial revealed what I had said to my benefactor and friend; for which cause to this day I have never either by prayer or gift been able to recover his favour to the full . . . and, if I live long enough to see the abbacy vacant once again, I shall take care what I say.

The argument sways this way and that. Some take counsel of their fears: a man apparently humble 'while he is in cloister, yet, if he chances to hold any office, he is apt to be disdainful, scorning monks and loving men of the world more than he should'. (This was also a theme in Matthew Paris.) Another candidate simply had a speech impediment.

Abbot Samson is elected, and, after an anxious wait, the King's assent is given. Samson, former sub-sacrist, becomes, by the suffrage of his fellow monks, a great man in the kingdom; the abbey dominates not only the town but its surrounding area, and is a direct tenant of the Crown, like the great lay nobles. As in Matthew's chronicle, much solemn attention is given to the embalming and funeral of the new abbot's predecessor, as well as to the installation of the successful candidate, when over a thousand people dine afterwards. Jocelin becomes the abbot's chaplain, and hence gets to know him intimately, and he shares this intimacy with the reader. Samson is a strong man, autocratic in his ways and a firm ruler, but also attractively human. He causes resentment by not having favourites, even from his former supporters. It is also resented when, clearly not trusting the sacrist and cellarer to do their jobs properly, he installs his own nominees – secular clerks, not monks – at their elbows, to see that the accounts are kept in proper order.

There were, as ever, ample causes of dispute, both internal and external, and Jocelin's chronicle is largely a record of them, great and small: with neighbouring lay magnates, with the Archbishop of Canterbury over jurisdiction, with the Bishop of Ely over timber, and with the townspeople over customary rights and dues, over dung and buildings, over an unauthorized mill (which Samson has demolished) and over catches of eels. Samson is in dispute with King Richard over the disposal of a ward of St Edmund whom the King wishes to marry to his own nominee. Samson stands firm, and it is the King who blinks first, subsequently behaving with some magnanimity. Samson has wrought a great renovation in the abbey's fortunes, but his relations with the monks become tense over such issues as the damage done by the abbot's fishpond to the monks' meadow, over dues from cows' pasture, and over the division of costs of hospitality – over whose guests were the abbot's charge and whose the monastery's. The cellarer was, as always, in the thick of things. Samson generally carries matters with a high hand, but he feels the cares of office and confides in Jocelin that he would have preferred to be a humble schoolmaster, which he had been before taking the habit, or a minor official of the monastery, rather than an abbot. There is a very touching scene when some of the opposition, in fear of the abbot's powers, capitulate, and Samson, victorious, dissolves publicly into tears at the acrimony which has invaded the house. The brethren, themselves now moved, weep also, and both sides exchange the kiss of peace.

The great set-piece description, over many pages, is of the opening of St Edmund's shrine and the reverent unwrapping of the body, following a fire which required renovation work. It is clearly a huge privilege for some of the monks to see and even touch their patron, and it causes some envy. Twelve monks, including the highest officers, were chosen.

So, while the convent slept, these twelve put on albs and, drawing forth the coffin from the feretory [shrine], they carried it and setting it on a table near the ancient place of the feretory, they made ready to remove the lid, which was attached and fastened to the coffin by sixteen very long iron nails ... The Abbot, therefore, standing close by, looked within and found first of all a silken cloth veiling the whole body, and after that a linen cloth of wondrous whiteness: and over the head was a small linen cloth, and beneath it a small cloth of silk, finely woven, like a nun's veil. And afterwards they found the body wrapped in a linen cloth, and then at last the lineaments of the holy body were revealed. Here the Abbot stopped, saying that he did not dare go further, to see the sacred flesh unclothed. Therefore taking the head between his hands, he said groaning, 'Glorious Martyr, Saint Edmund, blessed be the hour when thou wast born! Glorious Martyr, turn not to my perdition this my boldness, that I, a miserable sinner, now touch thee; thou knowest my devotion, thou knowest my intent.' And he proceeded to touch the eyes and the nose, which was very large and prominent, and afterwards he touched the breast and arms and, raising the left hand, he touched the fingers and placed his fingers between the fingers of the saint; and going further he found the feet turned stiffly upwards as of a man dead that self-same day, and he touched the toes of the feet and counted them as he touched them. (113–14)

After this high point there are further wrangles and reconciliations; the life of the monastery goes on. The last word, however, deserves to go to King John. After his coronation he visits the monastery, 'led thither by devotion and a vow that he had made'. Unfortunately, John's devotion comes cheap. 'We indeed believed that he would make some great oblation; but he offered nothing save a single silken cloth which his servant had borrowed from our Sacrist – and they have not yet paid the price. And he had received the hospitality of St Edmund at great cost to the Abbey, and when he departed he gave nothing at all to the honour or advantage of the Saint save some thirteen pence sterling . . .' (116–17).

St Edmund deserves to become the patron saint of all those who entertain royalty.

17

Crusader History and Chivalric History: Villehardouin and Froissart

Villehardouin's The Conquest of Constantinople

When, in 1187, Abbot Samson of Bury St Edmunds heard that the Crusader kingdom (Outremer) had lost Jerusalem to the Muslims, after eighty-seven years of Christian occupation, he put on a hair shirt and drawers and abstained from meat. Jerusalem had been the great prize of the First Crusade. Inevitably the Crusades, as the foreign events most exciting to Christians, found a place in chronicles. William of Malmesbury, in the *Deeds of the Kings*, gave considerable attention to Pope Urban II's proclamation of the First Crusade at the Council of Clermont in 1095, including documentation, and then took his readers on an excursus through Rome, Constantinople and Jerusalem, with descriptions. Matthew Paris, a century later, gave intermittent attention – which is the attention he gave everything – to the crusading of the German emperor Frederick II, whose career and dubious reputation (he was excommunicate when setting out on crusade) clearly fascinated him.

From 1096, when the first Christian forces assembled, the Crusades to the East covered a period of three centuries, and they not surprisingly affected European imaginations and sensibilities. As we shall see shortly, they also revived the earlier very common historical genre of the campaign monograph. The last example – by the Byzantine historian Procopius in the work entitled *The Wars* – had dealt with a campaign in Europe, mounted from Byzantium by the emperor Justinian to reconquer the Gothic kingdom of Italy for the Roman empire in the first half of the sixth century. (Procopius' other well-known work, *The Secret History*, is chiefly a hysterical and obsessive account of the sexual practices of the empress Theodora.) The Crusades were the first sustained effort of European expansion eastward, other than missionary endeavour (including Charlemagne's forcible conversion of the Saxons), since the time of Julian the Apostate's campaign in Persia in AD 363.

A crusade was, by definition, a pilgrimage, and a crusader acquired the merit and privileges of a pilgrim, including the remission of sins. Only a pope could grant this, so only a pope could proclaim a crusade, just as each individual could only become a crusader by taking a vow. There were to be many crusades, and not just in Asia Minor. They became a papal weapon in Europe too – against the Muslims in Spain, the pagans on the Baltic seaboard, the Albigensian heretics in southern France and northern Italy, and the popes' political opponents. They answered Stalin's later query 'How many divisions has the Pope?' Given a crusade, a good many – but only intermittently and temporarily. They were also like missiles, once launched almost impossible for him to control, as was vividly exemplified by the Fourth Crusade, which set out ostensibly for Jerusalem and ended by conquering Constantinople and much of the Greek Christian empire.

The background to Pope Urban's innovation in preaching the First Crusade was the increasing harassment of Christian pilgrims to the Holy Land by its Muslim rulers and the crumbling of Byzantine military resistance to the Turks, which led to calls for help. The motives of some of the crusaders seem to have included land-grabbing by themselves from the outset, and the setting-out of a crusade also tended to be associated with pogroms against European Jews – classed with Muslims as common enemies of Christ. Crusades also tended, not without reason, to be seen by the Byzantines in the light of invasions rather than assistance. Clashes and bloodshed were not uncommon, partly because the First Crusade, in particular – it might be better to speak of a flow of bands and individuals eastward rather than of a single entity – was badly organized and provisioned. Jerusalem fell to the crusaders, however – in 1099, to the accompaniment of sack and massacre – and a Christian king of Jerusalem was elected, though little more than first among equals.

There are several contemporary eyewitness accounts of the First Crusade. One of the most interesting, because of its perspective more than its intrinsic merits, is that by the daughter of the Byzantine emperor Alexius I, the *Alexiad* of Anna Comnena. It is a eulogy of her father, but it also provides an insight into Byzantine attitudes to the crusaders – numerous as the stars in heaven or the sands of the seashore – whom she calls Franks (the usual name), barbarians and also, most frequently, Kelts. Her animus against them, whom she calls treacherous and greedy, is understandable. One of the leaders, Bohemond of Taranto, had only recently been waging a war against the Greeks in Albania from his base in southern Italy. To Anna he was an unmitigated villain. Other leaders she refuses to name: the syllables of the names are too barbarous (10.x). The Pope, Urban's predecessor Gregory VII, is 'the abominable pope' (1.xiii). These judgements are understandable, but, though her work is well organized, they largely rob her of the historian's first requisite, curiosity, just as her portrait of her father the Emperor is repetitively eulogistic. It is a pity that the very accomplished and perceptive court history of the Byzantine statesman Michael Psellus ends in 1078, a decade before the crusaders began to arrive. Anna does, however, note the crusaders' self-destructive impetuosity: 'Kelts are indomitable in the opening cavalry charge, but afterwards, because of the weight of their armour and their own passionate nature and recklessness, it is actually very easy to beat them.' 'The Keltic race ... combines an independent spirit and impudence, not to mention an absolute refusal to cultivate a disciplined art of war' (11.vi). These comments were to remain valid down to the last, fatal, charge of the Frankish knights at the battle of Nicopolis in 1396, where their hopes were finally extinguished. The crusader settlements, amid a sea of hostile Muslims and Greeks, never attracted the Latin, Catholic immigration which could alone have secured them. Crusading was at times impressive, and to Byzantines and Muslims threatening, but it was always too intermittent, the enthusiasm too short-lived (as in a sense it was intended to be: the crusader's vow did not include settlement) for long-term security.

The most accessible account of the Fourth Crusade, which had been proclaimed by Pope Innocent III in 1198, is the work unabashedly and accurately called *The Conquest of Constantinople*, by Geoffroy de Villehardouin, who was a major participant in it. The eyewitness work produced by the Sixth, a generation later, the *Life of St Louis* by Jean de Joinville, has a vividness and humanity that Villehardouin lacks and is more enjoyable to read, but it is more personal memoir and biography than a general history, and the abortive campaign of the French king Louis IX in North Africa cannot rival in interest the extraordinary crusader attack on Constantinople. Villehardouin was in one sense superbly placed to write the history of the Crusade in which he played a prominent part. He accompanied it throughout, and was high in its councils, a number of times acting as envoy and negotiator – to the Venetians who carried the expedition in their ships, to the Greeks, and between warring lords among the crusaders themselves once they had carved out their territories. Only the Muslims lay outside his range, and indeed they play virtually no part in his book. (Alexius I had actually negotiated an alliance with them in fear of the crusaders.)

But his book suffers from the same handicaps as Anna Comnena's, whose prejudices, without knowing it, he echoes and reverses: Greeks are treacherous and not to be trusted. He is so identified with the strategic decision taken by the main body of the crusaders – essentially to support the Venetians in their war of acquisition of Christian territory across the Adriatic, and then to attack Constantinople – that opponents of it – like the Greeks who, essentially, are being invaded – are denied the exercise of historical understanding or even curiosity: they are simply saboteurs. He was, as one of the envoys sent by the intending crusaders to arrange transportation with the Venetians, actually an architect of the course they subsequently followed. Over-optimistic about the numbers to be given passage, the envoys contracted a huge debt to Venice, which the crusaders, who had to meet their own expenses, were unable or unwilling to pay. They therefore became subservient to Venetian designs on the Byzantine empire, the Venetians being bent at the very least on extracting trading privileges.

Some crusaders, understandably, wanted to keep clear of Venice, to cross the Adriatic from the Norman French base in southern Italy and to make their way directly to the coast of Syria. It was a legitimate point of view, but Villehardouin will have none of it, and even the predicament with which his book suddenly ends in 1207 (we do not know what happened to him), with the crusader lords fighting to defend their lands newly acquired from the Greek empire against the pressure of the Christian King Johanitza of Bulgaria and Wallachia, seems to give him no second thoughts. Nor, for that matter, does the crusaders' very thorough and destructive sack and devastation of Constantinople in 1204, and the division of its booty. He seems a classic example of the general – he was marshal of Champagne and later of 'Romania', the Latin conquests – whose conviction that his course was the right one overrides any concession even of goodwill to his opponents in strategy. He continually lumps together the diversity of dissident views as belonging to 'those who wished to break up the army', and he makes little distinction between those who went back to Europe, who may indeed have been seeking a way out, and those who went on independently to Syria, 'where they could do no good'. His self-serving account sometimes reminds one of Josephus, but the latter is incomparably the better narrator and analyst. For a military leader, Villehardouin can be unhelpful on tactics, with 'as God willed it' functioning as a frequent all-purpose explanation of success or failure. He sometimes refers to knights having won honour and distinction, in the manner of heralds reporting on battles and tournaments, and he records important deaths, but shaming seems to be an important part of his motive for recording. His lists of named backsliders are much longer than those of the meritorious; the former are always, in his unwearied litany, 'those who wished to break up the army'.

Villehardouin's history is written in the vernacular and in prose, though the vernacular was more often used for verse. It is a history, not a chronicle: a controlled monograph, beginning at an appropriate place, the preaching of the Crusade, rather than with the creation of Adam, and presented as a coherent continuous narrative. In that respect it recalls a number of ancient historians, though Villehardouin falls a good way short of them in execution, and the recollection seems to be ours rather than his. He has apparently no awareness of predecessors; his book lacks the conventional preface and its promises, and he has no literary airs, which is rather a relief after the agonizingly literary self-consciousness of Anna Comnena. In fact it is doubtful whether he could read or write, so his work was probably dictated.

In spite of the absence of a preface, his motives in composing it, however unselfconscious, are not hard to make out. He knows that the fall of Constantinople to the crusaders, in which he has played a part, was an extraordinary event – he calls it an achievement. In the absence of a preface there are no customary claims for the greatness of the events recounted, but he is fully aware of them: of the splendour of the city and the enormity of the crusaders' undertaking, even though it was ostensibly initially to restore an heir who had been deposed from the imperial throne. He is several times overcome by the size and grandeur of the fleet which carries the crusaders (though it was smaller than it should have been). He is not generally a picturesque writer, but the disembarkation arouses him to a kind of celebration: 'a most marvellous sight; knights and sergeants [men-at-arms] swarming out of the warships, numbers of sturdy war-horses taken out of the transports, countless fine tents and pavilions unloaded ready to pitch' (46). As for Constantinople itself, those who have not seen it cannot imagine that so fine a place exists. The crusaders

noted the high walls and lofty towers encircling it, and its rich palaces and tall churches, of which there were so many that no one would have believed it to be true if he had not seen it with his own eyes, and viewed the length and breadth of that city which reigns supreme over all others. There was indeed no man so brave and daring that his flesh did not shudder at the sight . . . Never before had so grand an enterprise been carried out by any people since the creation of the world. (59)

A description of the booty taken by the crusaders arouses him to similar wonder and hyperbole.

It is hard to say how devout Villehardouin is, despite the frequency of 'as God willed it'. Certainly his interest in ecclesiastical matters seems low. He mentions the Pope's disapproval of the attack on a Christian Adriatic city, but not the excommunication of the Venetians. He records dissension over its direction among the Cistercians with the crusade, but their leading dissident, the abbot of Vaux, who eventually makes his own way to Syria in disgust, is a deserter and 'a disgrace'. There is no mention of the installation of a Catholic patriarch in Constantinople and a Catholic chapter in the church of St Sophia, which aroused fierce resentment among the Orthodox Greeks. More surprisingly, his gloating over the booty of the city makes no mention of the immense number of relics, which were much prized and indeed commanded high prices in the West. Villehardouin mentions the Pope's indulgence as a motive for the crusaders, but Jerusalem as an object disappears very rapidly from his pages and does not recur. He records an interesting declaration, presumably not untypical, by a man deserting a ship returning from Syria to join the crusader army, who calls to his former associates as he leaves them, 'I'm going with these people, for it certainly seems to me that they'll win some land for themselves' (57). Villehardouin passes no comment on this not very pilgrim-like sentiment.

Froissart: 'Matters of great renown'

According to Villehardouin, some of the French knights who took the cross in 1199 and sent him and others to negotiate their passage with the Venetians were attending a tournament at Ecry, in his own province of Champagne. Tournaments resembled crusades in that, though for even more restricted periods, they brought together members of the knightly and noble classes, sometimes with an international dimension. As mimic warfare, sometimes lethal, they had some of the characteristics of real conflict, though crucially without archers or sieges: there were heralds to record and proclaim feats performed, much glitter and display, courtesy to opponents, and even vows, though of more idiosyncratic and even eccentric kinds than the crusading vow which turned a warrior into a pilgrim. They even seem to have influenced the ways in which actual warfare was reported and conducted, with much emphasis on the exhibition of individual prowess and thereby the acquisition of distinction and honour; we find several examples in Villehardouin. Among the informants for his history used by Jean Froissart, nearly two centuries later, seem to have been heralds, and some of his descriptions have what might be called a heraldic perspective, as a kind of scorecard. As combats with rules, tournaments – though sometimes productive of bad blood as well as actual blood, and even tumult and disorder – fostered the solidarity of the knightly class and both exemplified and encouraged notions of chivalrous behaviour, the conduct proper to a knight: foul strokes were dishonourable.

The idea of chivalry, as a code of conduct for the aristocratic warrior class, fostered by the clerical authors of the vernacular romances centred on Arthur and his knights, had been evolving since the twelfth century and reached its height in the fourteenth. As the central rite of chivalry, apart from the ceremony of knighting itself, tournaments mutated from the chaotic free-for-all – the melee – of the twelfth century (Matthew Paris records a number in the early thirteenth being cancelled for fear of disorder, as well as on account of that perennial English enemy of sporting events, the weather) into something increasingly lavish and ceremonial. The early melees must have been rather like early football matches between villages, with few rules, no clearly demarcated areas, and some deaths. Later the circumscribed area of the town square was preferred, with ordered sequences of individual combats, and stands for spectators, including ladies, and festivities to follow.

Like warfare, again, the tournament had its commercial side, since the valuable horse and armour of the vanquished became the property of the victor; something like 'professionals' existed among poor knights. In war, the prisoner, spared to be ransomed, was a negotiable commodity as well as a brother knight in misfortune; prisoners could be bought as a speculation on the ransom, rather like discounting bills of exchange. Chivalrous, that is courteous and fraternal, treatment of prisoners was another hallmark of class solidarity, which commoners did not benefit from.

Chivalry, as an articulated personal idea for the layman of knightly birth, stood at the confluence of several influences, of which we have just considered one. The ecclesiastical influence was seen chiefly in the ceremony of knighting, which came increasingly to resemble a religious rite, and in the oath sworn, to uphold justice and protect the weak. It was an oath-taking society: the central social bond was that between vassal and lord, established by an oath of fealty, and a disloyal vassal was held to be forsworn. It seems to have been common for crusaders to regard themselves as sworn vassals of Christ as their lord, whose honour was insulted by Muslim possession of the Holy Places. Vows also played a part in another source of chivalric ideas: the cult of courtly love, developed in the twelfth century chiefly in Aquitaine, which was both fostered by and reflected in the later elaborations of the Arthurian legends and in prose and verse romances. This represented an attempt, more female than ecclesiastical, to soften the manners of a warrior aristocracy. The devotion of the lover to his lady was a kind of vassalage. To be disloyal was to be dishonoured, while the knight's devotion was supposedly both an inspiration and a kind of purification, tested, like his courage, by ordeal. The vulgarized form of the ideal in the north saw the knight as lover exhibiting greater prowess, fighting better; we find examples of this idea, as we shall see, in Froissart.

Of course the gap, in both love and war, between ideal and reality could be very wide: sacking, looting, massacring were normal concomitants of fourteenth-century warfare, and Froissart's *Chronicles* shows them to us. The knight was often, like the crusaders with Villehardouin dividing the loot of Constantinople, still recognizably kin to the Frankish chieftain as brigand known to Gregory of Tours, and the motives for warfare remained much the same, alongside the desire for honour and reputation through a full scorecard.

Froissart was the supreme historian of fourteenth-century warfare seen in the chivalric mode, as well as of a good deal besides. His work has a few chronicler's features, of which one is his incorporation of the work of a predecessor, Jean le Bel, which he acknowledges and which largely makes up his book from 1327 (the accession in England of Edward III) to the early 1360s, when it becomes wholly his own; it ends in 1400, after the deposition of Richard II. Froissart is also not averse to including interpolated stories for no better reason than that he has been told them and likes them. But in general he is a master of fluent, controlled and relevant narrative, in which, constantly, there seems some influence from the fictional prose romances, often Arthurian, popular in his time. Conversations are frequently used to carry forward the narrative. Froissart's work is history, but he does not make a fetish of the historian's sobriety: one has sometimes the sense that the general direction of the truth will do, and he is slapdash with details. His is a free and easy narrative manner, which is highly readable and not at all pedantic. He wrote in the vernacular, clearly for a lay audience, and was first translated into English in 1523–5. Centred on northern France, England and Flanders, with excursions to Scotland, Gascony and Spain, his account is a panoramic view, from a particular and largely – but not exclusively – chivalric perspective, on his century. It is given focus and direction by the protracted conflict between the English and French monarchies, though it is not confined to this. It also incorporates revolts in Paris, London and Ghent, and the French peasant risings known as jacqueries. The Peasants' Revolt in England (1381) is given extended if not very confidence-inspiring treatment. The Black Death is merely mentioned, though the sect of the Flagellants to which it gave rise is described. The Papal Schism (1378–1417), deriving from the election of rival popes, receives some attention.

Froissart was born in the county of Hainaut around 1337, into a bourgeois family with an apparent involvement in the unchivalrous trade of moneylending. He was early drawn to the court of Edward III of England in the wake of his countrywoman, Edward's queen, Philippa of Hainaut, for whom he wrote an account of the recent Anglo-French wars in verse, for which he says he was rewarded well. He eventually returned to the Continent, though he paid a later visit to England, and, having taken orders, he died a canon of Chimay, near Liège, in 1405. In the preface to his *Chronicles* he tells us it was written at the request of his patron, Robert of Namur: 'In order that the honourable enterprises, noble adventures and deeds of arms which took place during the wars waged between France and England should be fittingly related and preserved for posterity, so that brave men should be inspired thereby to follow such examples, I wish to place on record these matters of great renown.' The references to posterity and providing examples were a standard formula, but the diction is the idiom of chivalry: 'honourable enterprises', 'noble adventures' and 'great renown' through bravery. It is no surprise when he then goes on to tell us that he has sought the acquaintance of great lords in France, England, Scotland, Brittany and elsewhere, among whom his inquiries have been made.

To place Froissart's work in a category of 'chivalric history', however, requires amplification, and even some qualification. Concepts of honour, prowess and courtesy are freely deployed, and we get plenty of examples of the class camaraderie of knighthood, as well as its commercial aspect. In the campaign that ended at Crécy (1346), some French knights, threatened with being slaughtered in a general massacre, call out to an English knight they recognize 'because they had campaigned together in Granada and Prussia [both places of authorized crusades] . . . in the way knights do meet each other'. They beg him to make them his prisoners, which would mean his protection. 'When he heard this Sir Thomas was delighted, not only because their capture meant an excellent day's work and a fine haul of valuable prisoners' (75). Sir Thomas's shining catch represented simultaneously the solidarity of the crusaders' old-school tie, the knight's duty to display mercy to the vanquished, and what the eighteenth century, celebrating the civilizing effect (the civic successor to 'courtesy') of international trade, would later call *le doux commerce*. In English, 'courtesy', a key component of chivalry, is only etymologically a half-step from 'courtly' (*courtois*, *höflich*), related to the manners of the court, just as 'chivalry', which largely faded away later, retains its original horsiness.

There is an amusing account, apparently given to Froissart at first hand, of an attempt to teach chivalry to the Irish, who were, it seems, recalcitrant to its values and customs. They do not fight in chivalrous fashion, taking no ransoms and running away when expedient (the inability of French knights, in particular, to distinguish between withdrawal and disgrace was a considerable tactical handicap). Eating their enemies' hearts, which the Irish are also said to do, is definitely not chivalrous. Froissart's informant is a pained English knight (named), who has undertaken to instruct four Irish kings in the knightly code – which includes table manners, though not the menu. They must sit at a separate table from their minstrels and dependants, and not share utensils with them. The kings become angry, apparently, when the hall furniture is rearranged to observe degree. It also has to be explained to them that they have been incorrectly knighted, with an unceremonious dubbing at the age of seven. Paedo-investiture will not do, and they will have to be re-knighted properly, rather as St Wilfrid insisted on Irish monks being re-tonsured. They must also learn to wear breeches. It is very like missionary work, unaided by miracles, and no sparrow appears to point a moral, though chivalry would presumably have required something of gaudier plumage. The Irish, after being taught 'the virtues and obligations of chivalry', are then, duly instructed and presumably breeched, knighted according to the proper rite by Richard II. Incidentally, though not bare-legged, the Germans too, according to Froissart, do not really understand chivalry as the English, French and Scottish do, and mistreat their prisoners (414–16).

Chivalry was, of course, a matter of honour and prowess as well as courtesy and humanity. Froissart is a connoisseur of knightly feats. In this respect the battle of Poitiers (1356) apparently excelled that of Crécy: Poitiers had more class – 'There were incomparably more fine feats of arms than at Crécy' (138). In both, it is true, Froissart acknowledges the crucial role of archery. At the sea battle of Winchelsea (1340) Edward III adopts the tactics of the tournament, treating his ship as both horse and lance: 'Steer at that ship straight ahead of us. I want to have a joust at it' (116). (The ships meet head-on, and Edward's is so badly damaged that it has to be abandoned.) As a royal command this ranks with that of the French king at Crécy, also in its way chivalric, when the Genoese crossbowmen in his army were retreating: 'Kill all that rabble. They are only getting in our way' (89).

Sometimes in Froissart, as was mentioned earlier, one catches echoes of the idea, derived from the ethic of courtly love, that being in love was a combat advantage. Sir Eustace d'Aubricourt performed fine feats of arms and was irresistible, 'for he was young and deeply in love and full of enterprise' (161). His is not the only example. Froissart adds that Eustace won great wealth by his deeds; presumably his love also prospered. On another occasion two knights, French and English, show personal animosity because they wear ladies' favours of exactly the same shade of blue; whether their suspicions are aroused is not specified.

In terms of the ethic and manners of chivalry, the centrepiece of Froissart's work is the conduct of Edward's son the Black Prince towards his captive the French king John the Good, made prisoner at Poitiers. The preamble is unseemly, the King being such a valuable prize that there is a fight over possession of him, with people of all sorts grabbing him and shouting 'He's mine' – almost, one feels inclined to say, as though he were a relic, which would also have had a market value. The King is understandably relieved to be taken into custody by the Prince, who that evening, at a supper for King John and his captive nobles, stages what can only be described as a kind of chivalric ballet:

He himself served in all humility both at the King's table and at the others, steadfastly refusing to sit down with the King in spite of all his entreaties. He insisted that he was not yet worthy to sit at the table of so mighty a prince and so brave a soldier as he had proved himself to be on that day. He constantly kneeled before him, saying: 'Beloved sire, do not make such a poor meal, even though God has not been willing to heed your prayers today. My noble father will certainly show you every mark of honour and friendship ... In my opinion you have good cause to be cheerful, although the battle did not go in your favour, for today you have won the highest renown of a warrior, excelling the best of your knights. I do not say this to flatter you, for everyone on our side, having seen how each man fought, unanimously agrees with this and awards you the palm and crown, if you will consent to wear them.' (144)

The French and English present all approve highly of the Prince's conduct and agree that 'in him they would have a most chivalrous lord and master.'

For the modern reader, at least, the pendant to this scene is Froissart's description of the massacre of the citizens of Limoges ordered by the Black Prince after its capture. For once Froissart forgets his aristocratic sympathies:

There were pitiful scenes. Men, women and children flung themselves on their knees before the Prince, crying: 'Have mercy on us, gentle sir!' But he was so inflamed with anger that he would not listen. Neither man nor woman was heeded, but all who could be found were put to the sword, including many who were in no way to blame. I do not understand how they could have failed to take pity on people who were too unimportant to have committed treason. Yet they paid for it, and paid more dearly than the leaders who had committed it.

There is no man so hard-hearted that, if he had been in Limoges on that day, and had remembered God, he would not have wept bitterly at the fearful slaughter which took place. More than three thousand persons, men, women and children, were dragged out to have their throats cut. May God receive their souls, for they were true martyrs. (178)

Froissart, a bourgeois himself, is consistently more sympathetic to townspeople than to peasants. He has no sympathy for the participants in the French jacqueries, the peasant uprisings against the higher classes, or for those in the English Peasants' Revolt in 1381. He gives allegedly verbatim an egalitarian sermon by their clerical leader, John Ball, which six centuries later seems very cogent, but Ball is 'crackbrained', the rebels 'wicked men', and their actions 'devilry' (212). He shows much more respect for the rebels in Ghent against the counts of Flanders; they are almost his own people, but their defeat, followed by their massacre at the battle of Coutrai (1302), is still 'greatly to the honour and advantage of all Christendom and of all the nobility and gentry' (350). Anything which threatened order and degree was wicked per se. Yet it is not invariably only in his comments on burghers that Froissart's sympathies seem reversed. He loves, of course, the flourish and display associated with chivalry – the silken pavilions, elaborate tableaux, royal entries, festivities, knighting and marriage ceremonies. But in recounting the French preparations for an (aborted) invasion of England, after describing the orgy of painting and embellishing of the ships, including gold leaf, he catches himself and adds 'and it was all paid for by poor people throughout France' (305–6). Froissart accepts, but it is not true to say that he endorses, the concomitants of glorious war, which he understands very well: looting, burning and devastation. 'So was the good, fat land of Normandy ravaged and pillaged by the English' – so effectively, in fact, that 'the very servants in the army turned up their noses at fur-lined gowns' (71).

There is in Froissart one striking example of bourgeois heroism, as well as the author's pity, in the famous final act of Edward III's siege of Calais, which is forced to capitulate by starvation. When it is announced that Edward will spare the inhabitants if six leading citizens will make their submission to him with halters around their necks and the keys of the town in their hands, six quickly volunteer. The pathos of the subsequent scene in which Queen Philippa pleads for their lives, eventually successfully, with her initially implacable husband greatly appealed to the Edwardians who set up a cast of Rodin's tableau of the wretched men's predicament, still visible on the Embankment in London. The townsfolk were expelled by Edward, who intended to plant the town with English, and Froissart again expresses pity, though it seems the expulsions may have been exaggerated.

It is interesting that the knights captured were released on parole, Edward declaring that 'they are gentlemen and I can trust them to keep their word' (109–10). The acceptability of the knight's parole was a function of the sanctity of the chivalric oath. The extreme of honourable and chivalrous behaviour in this respect was exhibited by the French King. Released to his own country after undertakings have been given, he finds that one of his followers has broken the conditions, whereupon he insists on returning voluntarily to his captivity in England, thereby, one assumes, having his tit-for-tat with the Prince. His arrival was predictably the occasion for great festivities. But parole applied only within the knightly class. When the young Count of Flanders was made captive by his bourgeois subjects, 'They watched him so closely that he was hardly able to go and piss' (99).

Froissart, then, was a writer at once courtly and earthy, chivalric but sometimes more widely humane, with the bourgeois sometimes peeping past the associate of knights and nobles. But of course it is as the historian of the world of chivalry that he is above all remembered, a reputation he would have embraced. There is a painting by the American-born history painter Benjamin West, in the age of George III, of Edward III crossing the Somme during the Crécy campaign; it is a subject taken directly from Froissart, and conveys very well the impression made on later generations by his work. The French disputed the crossing. Here is Froissart's description:

The two Marshals of England sent their banner-bearers forward, in the name of God and St George, and followed closely themselves. The bravest knights herded their horses into the river, with the best mounted in the lead. There were many jousts in the river, and many unhorsings on both sides, for Sir Godomar and his men defended the crossing bravely. A number of his knights, with others from Artois and Picardy, had decided not to wait on the bank but to ride into the ford and fight there in order to win greater distinction. So there was, as I have said, many a joust and many a skilled piece of fighting . . . The Genoese also did much damage with their crossbows, but the English archers shot so well together that it was an amazing sight to see . . . (80)

Froissart has no word of reproof here for the French knights who throw away their tactical advantage in possession of the bank and go down into the river in their search for 'greater distinction', though later, in his account of Crécy itself, he blames the pride and vanity of the French for their fatal indiscipline, 'for there were too many great lords among them, all determined to show their power' (86).

West's picture puts Edward himself centre stage and in midstream. There are some very small English archers doing their bit on an outcrop in the background. It is not realism; mud is unthinkable. It is Froissart's already partly idealized world, idealized still further by historical distance and the conventions of history painting, with none of Froissart's own occasional earthiness and realism. But the picture is in the highest degree animated and glittering. The focal point is the King himself, beneath his fluttering banner quartering the leopards of England and the fleurs-de-lis of France; the same quarters appear on his shield and surcoat, and his horse is similarly emblazoned. Heraldic devices served the purpose of identification: Edward seems quadruply insured against anonymity. But he makes a gallant and colourful figure, waving his battleaxe in a way that seems more debonair (another approved knightly quality), and encouraging to his followers, than menacing to the French already engaged, close on the further bank. The painting is a selective but not inappropriate evocation of the way Froissart often, though not invariably, sees his world. It is appropriate too, as George III observed, that it was to hang in Windsor Castle, where King Edward instituted the Order of the Garter, and which, according to Froissart, had been built by King Arthur (67).

18

From Civic Chronicle to Humanist History: Villani, Machiavelli and Guicciardini

The gatecrashing Londoners at the Council of Winchester (above, p. 245) were a portent. As cities grew, in wealth and population, and developed corporate institutions for self-regulation, corporate consciousness grew also, and produced record-keeping, just as it did in monasteries. We have looked at conventual chronicles, at national histories presented as the deeds of kings, and at vernacular history as the representation of the deeds of a chivalric warrior aristocracy. Town chronicles, also in the vernacular, came to express a similar self-consciousness, in their case that of the largely unlearned but literate burgesses – the merchants, financiers and employers of labour, chiefly in the various aspects of the cloth industry – who dominated town life. Theirs was sometimes a contentious and divided form of self-assertion, with substantial citizens set against nobles and over-lords and also against the lower grades of artisans with their own grievances. There were serious insurrections in the later 1370s and early 1380s in the major centres of population and urban prosperity and power: Paris, London, Ghent and other towns of Flanders, and Florence, which witnessed its first serious rising of the inferior artisans, the *ciompi*. Town life had flourished in central Italy, and manifested itself in Florence in city chronicles from the eleventh and twelfth centuries onward.

In central and northern Italy some cities became virtually auton-omous, essentially city states; the conflicts of popes and emperors, and the primarily German concerns of the latter, made imperial suzerainty increasingly nominal. The result was in some cases, most notably in Venice and Florence, the emergence of a republican form of internal politics and the political fragmentation of Italy into a number of mutually suspicious and hostile states, both of which had implications for the writing of history. This was also to be shaped by the revival of classical learning known as humanism, which from the fifteenth century onward incorporated a close attention to the manner as well as the content of exemplary Roman historians, particularly Livy. But the local situation was not that of the empire, nor of a national kingdom: it was rather that faced by republican Rome, with its early conflicts with the rival states which were its close neighbours, and its growing internecine class conflicts. As the eminent historian of the Renaissance Denys Hay put it, 'The Anglo-Saxon Chronicle, Malmesbury, the St Albans writers down to Matthew Paris, were, whether they knew it or not, writing the history of England . . . And so, in a less marked fashion, with France. But no works like that can be found in Italy' (*The Italian Renaissance*, 1977).

But city chronicles proliferated, and from them, in conjunction with the classical revival, emerged in Florence in the fifteenth century a way of writing history much more closely modelled than before on Roman practice, and a new way of reflecting on the lessons of history. It incorporated not merely the conventions of Roman historiography – Greek historical writing was still much less well known, though translations were beginning to be made – but also the substance of Roman and modern Italian history as a source of republican inspiration and political lessons. The most favoured classical historians were still those admired in medieval times, Sallust and Livy, until the great vogue for Tacitus began in the late sixteenth century. But the image of Rome assumed a different form from that current in the Middle Ages, focused not on the imperial city, the *urbs aeterna*, but on the struggling early republic to which the Romans of the first century BC had themselves looked back as a lost era of patriotic republican virtue.

Vernacular chronicle-writing implied not a certain detachment, as humanist history, with one foot in the classical world, was later to do, but the reverse: a close and intimate involvement in the life of the city, as the abbey chroniclers were involved in their own, smaller, communities. Monastic chronicles seem to have grown in some cases out of calendars; in the case of a lay, mercantile community such as Florence there were, instead, the family and business archives – they were the same thing – in which a literate laity recorded their affairs. These archives naturally came to incorporate public matters, with lists of office-holders and the interpolation of notices of general civic or even international events. In Italy, such public occurrences were events, such as wars, which involved the city with one or more neighbouring republic or principality; on a wider scale, the doings of popes and even of kings, crusaders, Turks and Mongols were of interest. In more local terms there was a kind of continuum between public life and the domestic and familial, with feuds between the greater families being a matter of acute public concern, since they were a frequent cause of disturbances, while family alliances were one of the keys to power. The tenure of public offices in Florence was very short, so rotation was rapid and participation wide; having held an office was an important mark of status for families as well as individuals.

There is a traceable evolution in Florence from private memoirs and family histories to vernacular chronicles and then to humanist histories of the Florentine polity. But the transition between the last two is more like a fracture, with the latter being superimposed on the former – as Machiavelli's history, written in the vernacular, incorporates sections from Villani's *Chronicle*, composed two centuries earlier, into a work which, overall, has a wholly different character and set of interests and is written for a different and more sophisticated readership. This transition which represents a rupture as well as continuity is of more than local significance: it was pregnant for European historiography generally, and represents a vital moment in its development. The humanist historian, distancing himself from the colloquial manner and the largely local though promiscuous interests of the chronicler, was set apart by his education, of which he was proudly conscious, by his constant (rather than occasional) awareness of his classical models, and by a stern sense of relevance imposed by what Machiavelli's contemporary Guicciardini called 'the laws of history'. A leading modern authority on Guicciardini, Mark Phillips, has shown how his unpublished works exhibit the transition we have been considering here in a single literary career: he wrote, among other things, a family history, from which grew a Florentine history; this was later supplemented by another, which represented an attempt at an ambitiously polished humanist history, with, for example, formal invented speeches, but also incorporating much documentary research. This remained incomplete and in draft. Guicciardini finally went on to the monumental *History of Italy* by which he is remembered.

To appreciate the change more generally, we first have to look more closely at what is by common agreement the most rewarding of the medieval Florentine chronicles, that by Giovanni Villani. It was written in the earlier part of the fourteenth century; Villani died in the Black Death, the European catastrophe which dominated the middle years of the century. He was a member of a minor but reputable commercial family with interests in banking and trading ventures. Within an overall framework of providential history, ultimately derived from Orosius (above, p. 195), which he took from a medieval papal chronicle, he traced the story of his city (he always uses the possessive: 'our') from what he supposed to be its origins to his own times; for the usual obvious reasons, the *Chronicle* becomes much more detailed the nearer it approaches the present. It is a mark of the communal character of his enterprise that it was continued after his death by his brother and nephew, as, in a monastery, it would have been continued by a younger monk. Initially prosperous, Villani was ruined by the establishment of a more democratic city regime after the overthrow of the brief foreign rule of the Duke of Athens (the title was a reminder of the Crusades), son of the King of Naples, in 1342–3. Before that he had served several times as one of the eight priors who sat, each for two months at a time, in the city's executive government, the Signoria.

Villani's *Chronicle* has no explanatory preface, but later in the work he provides what amounts to one. Pope Boniface VIII had proclaimed 1300 as a jubilee year (always good for the prosperity of Rome), with indulgences for pilgrims to the city of St Peter. Villani, as he tells us, was one such pilgrim; he pays tribute to the admirable organization of the provisions for the pilgrims' reception (VIII.36). Like Ammianus a thousand years earlier and Gibbon four and a half centuries later, he was greatly moved by the venerable grandeur of the city and was inspired, he tells us (like Gibbon), to the composition of the work to which his name is attached – though, again like Gibbon, he seems not to have begun writing for several decades. He was perhaps scarcely aware of the contrast, of which Gibbon makes so much in his circumstantial account of his work's conception, between the Rome of the republic and the Caesars and the clerical Rome of his own day. Viewing, Villani says,

the great and ancient things therein, and recalling the stories and the great days of the Romans [he mentions Virgil, Sallust, Livy and Orosius among others] and other masters of history, who write alike of small things and great [a good self-description, but hardly likely to appeal to some of the authors he cites], of the deeds and actions of the Romans, and also of foreign matters throughout the world, I myself, to preserve memorials and give examples to those which should come after, took up their style and design, although as a disciple I was not worthy of such a work. But considering that our city of Florence, the daughter and creature of Rome, was rising, and had great things before her, whilst Rome was declining, it seemed to me fitting to collect in this volume and new chronicle [the title his work was given] all the deeds and beginnings of the city of Florence . . . and in this year 1300, having returned from Rome, I began to compile this book, in reverence to God and the blessed John and in commendation of our city of Florence.

Florence was the daughter of Rome because, according to tradition, it had been founded by Julius Caesar. The humanists, with their surer grasp of Roman literature and history, were later to correct this, placing the foundation firmly in republican times – to Villani, Caesar was an emperor – some decades earlier, as a settlement for Sulla's veterans, as Sallust describes in his *Catiline*. But Villani also gives the foundation a wider context in the colonization of Italy. After a brief reference to the Tower of Babel and then the foundation of Florence's older rival Fiesole, on the hill above the river, by King Attat, Villani moves smoothly into familiar Virgilian territory with the emigration from Troy. Italian history is, as usual, overrun by vagrant Trojan émigré princes. After a short digression on the Roman eagle and the Florentine lilies as emblems – Villani was always interested in such insignia – we have the Romans building on the site of Florence a temple of Mars, their god, in black and white marble, which Villani clearly takes to be Florence's cathedral (which still stands). In an imperial persecution in AD 270 Florence acquires its first martyr, St Miniato, a hermit and son of the King of Armenia, who had migrated to Italy. Beheaded, the saint has his head replaced, so that he is able to walk up the hill to where his church now stands, before expiring and being buried. In due course the temple of Mars was consecrated and dedicated to St John, as Florence's cathedral, which, on account of the favourable astral situation at its foundation, was able to survive the devastation wrought by the Goths (I.32, 35). Villani is careful to tell us that heavenly influences do not absolutely bind human fate or human free will, but all the same . . . (III.1).

We are still in legendary times, for a little later we learn from Villani, or rather his sources, as news from abroad, of the birth of Merlin in Great Britain ('which is now called England') from a virgin. It was Merlin who ordained the Round Table of knights errant for King Uther Pendragon, descended from Brutus, grandson of Aeneas, and this was afterwards restored by his son Arthur, 'as the Romances of the Britons make mention' (II.4). In other chapters (10, 12, 13) we get a brief and essentially historical account of the Franks and their emancipation of Italy and the Church from the Lombards. Siena, Florence's chief rival after Fiesole, was first inhabited, we are told, by invalids accompanying the Frankish king Charles Martel, for 'Siena' derives from 'non sana', unwell. This leads up to the coronation and empire of Charlemagne, by whom, it is alleged, Florence was rebuilt (III.1). Villani in fact gives a detailed description of the rebuilding, comparing the result with the modern city and again invoking a favourable disposition of the planetary bodies, though he sadly traces the subsequent dissensions of the city to the original mixture in its population of 'the noble Romans and the cruel and fierce Fiesolans'; the alleged reception of the Fiesolans into the city (IV.6) sounds rather like the assimilations in early Roman history as described by Livy. From the twelfth century – which is rapidly reached after a certain amount of attention to the quarrels of the empire and the papacy in the eleventh – the *Chronicle* becomes much more substantial and circumstantial. The feuds and constitutional arrangements of the Florentines, and the defence of their liberties in the face of external threats, now take centre stage – though still with excursions elsewhere, and with an account of the origins of the strife between Guelfs and Ghibellines in Florence and of which great families embraced which cause (e.g. V.39). Florence was predominantly a Guelf (papalist) city, and

Villani's own sympathies were Guelf. The Ghibellines were supporters of the emperors.

There is something very attractive about Villani's civic pride and his obvious responsiveness to the city's topography and the physical texture of its life. He accepts and sometimes deploys as an explanation Sallustian commonplaces about the dangers of too much tranquillity and prosperity, as nurseries of pride and factiousness, yet he also cannot help showing his delight at their manifestations. In 1300

our city of Florence was in the greatest and happiest state which had ever been since it was rebuilt, or before, alike in greatness and power and number of people [30,000 is his estimate, with 70,000 men of military age in the whole territory controlled by the city] . . . whereupon the sin of ingratitude, with the instigation of the enemy of the human race, brought forth from the said prosperity pride and corruption, which put an end to the feasts and joyaunce of the Florentines. For hitherto they had been living in many delights and dainties, and in tranquillity and with continual banquets; and every year throughout almost all the city on the first day of May there were bands and companies of men and women, with sports and dances. But now it came to pass that through envy there arose factions among the citizens . . . (VIII.39)

Around 1300, the factions began to be called the Whites and the Blacks, so that there could, for example, be Black Guelfs and White Guelfs. The change to the new, apparently empty, categories seems a recognition that the feuds were essentially those of great families (whom Villani, as usual, names) and their adherents: Florentine faction-fighting contained class dimensions, of nobles against citizens and rich against poor. Villani's later books take up the descriptions of these factions and the tumults and bloodshed to which they gave rise. (These are also dealt with in Machiavelli's later *Florentine History*, with, as one would expect, a more probing political curiosity, though in no less detail but with less 'surface'.)

Villani's Florence is a city not only of factions and constitutional complexities but also of banners and emblems under which the citizens range themselves and to which, in moments of danger and tumult, they rally, summoned by bells to gather in militias and processions (e.g. VI.39). According to Villani, in the late twelfth century even the faction-fighting could at times be suspended in fellowship. Florentines allegedly became so used to their civil wars that 'one day they would be fighting and the next day they would be eating and drinking together and telling tales of one another's valour and prowess in these battles' (V.2).

Villani gives a detailed account of the constitutional changes made by the temporarily dominant Ghibelline faction in 1266 (VII.13). Attempting to appear even-handed, the Ghibellines appointed two temporary rulers (*podestà*) who were not imperial nominees but knights of an order called officially the Knights of St Mary but known as 'The Jovial Friars of Bologna'. Villani describes the robes and insignia of the order, but adds that it was short-lived, 'for the fact followed the name, to wit, they gave themselves more to joviality than to anything else'. Colleges were set up from the various trades guilds (trades and districts partly coincided) which were a persistent feature of the city's governing structure, though their numbers varied over time. Villani lists them and the emblems and colours they bore as banners: judges and notaries, cloth merchants, money-changers (who bore a standard depicting gold florins on a red ground), wool merchants (a white sheep), physicians and apothecaries, silk merchants and furriers. Later, inferior trades were incorporated, including butchers (a black goat), stonemasons and carpenters (saw and axe) and smiths (pincers) (VII.13). Villani's most memorable description of this kind is that of the civic totem, the *carroccio*, which the Florentines took with them in war against Siena in 1260:

The *carroccio*, which was led by the commonwealth and people of Florence, was a chariot on four wheels, all painted red, and two tall red masts stood up together on it, on which was fastened and waved the great standard of the arms of the commune, divided white and red, and may still be seen today in S. Giovanni [the cathedral]. And it was drawn by a great pair of oxen covered with red cloth, which were set apart solely for this ... This *carroccio* was used by our forefathers in triumphs and solemnities, and when they went out with the host, the neighbouring counts and knights [usually severely excluded from civic matters] brought it from the armoury of S. Giovanni and brought it to the piazza of the Mercato Nuovo, and having halted by a landmark, which is still there, in the form of a stone carved like a chariot, they committed it to the keeping of the people ...

It was given a bodyguard of the best soldiers, and acted as a rallying point. A month before it was to set out a bell tolled from one of the city gates without ceasing:

And this thing they did in their pride, to give opportunity to the enemy . . . to prepare themselves. And some called it Martinella and some the Asses' Bell. And when the Florentine host went forth, they took down the bell from the arch and put it into a wooden tower upon a car, and the sound guided the host. By these two pomps of the *carroccio* and the bell was maintained the lordly pride of the people of old and of our forefathers in their expeditions. (VI.75)

Machiavelli's view of the superiority of a citizens' militia to mercenary troops, presented as rooted in a nostalgic Roman republicanism, does not strike one as particularly visually imaginative. One can only speculate on the impression this passage might have made on his imagination and sensibility.

Another civic possession was the lions. Lions were also kept in the Tower of London, where they belonged to the king, but these were republican lions. One of them justifies his place in the *Chronicle* in time-honoured fashion, as a portent. 'A fine young lion', having been presented to the commonwealth by Pope Benedict VIII, was, remarkably, kicked to death by an ass, either in fear 'or through a miracle'. Those learned in matters of divination said this boded no good to the Pope, who shortly died (VII.62). The appearance of the other lion, in 1258, seems more gratuitous: a remarkable event is described by Villani because it happened. By the negligence of its keeper the lion escaped, terrorizing the citizens, and caught a boy, holding him between its paws. But it allowed the boy's mother to snatch him from it, 'and the lion did no hurt either to the woman or to the child [later called "Orlanduccio of the lion"], but only gazed steadfastly and kept still', which was to be attributed either to the innate nobility of the lion's nature or to fortune (VI.69). There was, however, a political footnote: when a member of the city's supreme government, which at that time had acquired a reputation for arrogance, 'took and sent to his villa a grating which had belonged to the lion's den and was now lying about in the mud of the piazza of S. Giovanni, he was condemned therefore to a fine of 1,000 lire for embezzling the goods of the commonwealth' (VI.65). This is a good example of republican mores – it is difficult to imagine Lorenzo de' Medici being fined for nicking municipal debris from the Piazza, or the episode being thought worthy of the attention of history. The telling of the story, at some length, serves very effectively to mark off Villani's kind of chronicle-writing from the humanist historiography which had arrived by the age of Lorenzo. It was not that Villani did not have wider views, but they were theological, astrological and apocalyptic, rather than comprehensively political and historiographical.

It is seldom that one is able to see the transition of genres – indeed, one can speak of it as the transition from the Middle Ages to the Renaissance – in such sharp focus as one can in passing in a century from Villani's *Chronicle* (though chronicles continued to be written) to the new humanist historiography written in Florence. This was presented in polished and learned Latin prose informed by a neoclassical political perspective and a sense of what historical writing in emulation of Sallust and Livy (which Villani had naively supposed himself to be doing) really involved. In the mid twentieth century Hans Baron hailed the work of the early-fifteenth-century Florentine humanist scholar Leonardo Bruni as seminal in this transition, speaking of 'something like a Copernican revolution' in which Bruni's *History of the Florentine People* was a major landmark (*The Crisis of the Early Italian Renaissance*, 1955). From this claim derives the term 'civic humanism', which a number of scholars have adopted to express the kind of republican political turn and Ciceronian moral outlook which Bruni's work has been taken to represent. John Pocock, in *The Machiavellian Moment*, has traced a long route for this attitude through Machiavelli and on to the polemics of opposition to the executive in eighteenth-century England and to the political thought of the American founding fathers and the United States Constitution. Certainly there came to be in Italy, and from the seventeenth century onward in other parts of Europe, a revival of interest in the concept of early Roman virtue and an identification with the Ciceronian idea of the active public life in the service of the state. More recent scholarly work has challenged Baron's claims for Bruni's unique originality and the importance of what Baron regarded as its political matrix, the threat to Florence's independence represented by the power and aggressive designs of the Duke of Milan, Giangaleazzo Visconti. Even if we do not take Bruni as a uniquely original Copernican figure, it is now accepted that in central Italy an articulated republican ideology established itself and found expression in humanist writings which changed the way that ancient Rome was seen and appealed to, most notably in Machiavelli.

Bruni himself was a notable scholar, being one of the earliest Italians to read Greek. He was highly successful in his attempt to re-create the manner of the ancient historians, and he read Thucydides and Polybius in the original when this was very rare. Machiavelli, a century later, though well educated, is not generally credited with any Greek at all; certainly, though he makes occasional references to Greek history (we know that he read Plutarch), Thucydides and Polybius are not the presence in his work that one might have expected in view of some of their affinities of temperament and interests. Bruni was the teacher of one of the greatest of all Italian humanist textual scholars, Lorenzo Valla, who made an unsatisfactory Latin translation of Thucydides. (The difficulties are great.)

Bruni was head of the Florentine chancery, the state secretariat, in which a century later Machiavelli would also serve. It had responsibility for correspondence with other states, so the humanist training in classical rhetoric was highly relevant. The term 'humanist' derived from the 'humanities' (*umanita*) component of the educational curriculum: essentially an education in Latin rhetoric based on close imitation of the most highly regarded ancient models, notably Cicero and Seneca, but also including Sallust, Livy and Virgil. It contrasted, therefore, with the training in law, theology and dialectics which had formed the apex of medieval education, when grammar and rhetoric were regarded as more elementary and were often based only on excerpts from ancient authors; Bede, for example, quotes Virgil, but it has been doubted if he knew his work except in extracts.

The rise in prestige of rhetoric was essential to what is spoken of as humanism, and with it came the intensive study, imitation and attempted recovery in their pristine state of the approved classical authors. From the time of Petrarch in the later fourteenth century, humanist scholars aspired not merely to learn from classical writers,

as their medieval predecessors had done, but to re-create the spirit
and manner and moral world of Cicero and Seneca. In a sense they
wished to *be* classical authors, imitating their eloquence and adopting
their values, and paying attention therefore to their letters and other
forms of self-revelation as well as to more public compositions;
Petrarch was said to have treated Cicero as an alter ego. As the art of
persuasion, rhetoric was valued in the Roman world as the essential
political skill. The value attached, in principle at least, throughout the
Middle Ages, to the ascetic, contemplative life, institutionalized in
monasticism and subsequently vigorously attacked by Machiavelli,
was superseded among the humanists by a Ciceronian and republican
endorsement of the active life in the service of the republic, with its
necessary qualities of nerve and will as well as of eloquence and public
spirit. The public life of the Italian republican city states in the later
Middle Ages – open, contentious, sometimes dangerous, exhibiting
sudden and violent reversals of fortune, which had to be mastered if
possible – both required and gave scope to these qualities.

Using earlier chronicles – including Villani – Bruni and others
rewrote the history of Florence, in Latin and in the humanist, Livian,
manner and from a humanist perspective inspired by republican
Roman history. It was not hard to see in the struggles of early Rome
with its neighbours an analogue with the conditions of Florence. This
emphasis on republican rather than imperial Roman history was in a
sense reversing the historiographical coup effected by Eusebius and
Orosius a thousand years earlier, when they made Augustus' and
Constantine's empire part of the providential Christian story, by treating (and welcoming) the empire as the necessary condition for the
spreading of the Christian message and the Christian Church. In the
East, the Christianized empire had lasted, in theory at least, ever since,
and it had been renewed, with papal sanction, by Charlemagne in the
West. By resorting to the beleaguered early Roman republic as a
model, humanism was not only reviving the ethics of public life as
expressed in Cicero, Sallust and Livy, with honour and fame as the
reward for service, but also raising the possibility of learning political
lessons, as advocated by Polybius for example, from Rome's success
in overcoming its rivals. The connection made explicit by Sallust (see
above, p. 90) between republican emulation in the pursuit of honour,

free institutions and the conquering energy exhibited by the Romans made Rome not the pivot of Christian history but an example and an inspiration. The message was particularly appropriate to Florence, whose civic freedom had been asserted *against* the residual imperial power, so that anti-Ghibelline sentiments were, as we learn from Villani, predominant, though not universal.

It was to be Machiavelli who notoriously took the humanist ethic of activity in the pursuit of glory to an extreme, refusing to blink at the incompatibility, when taken to such an extreme, with Christian principles, and even seeming to relish exposing it. It was also he who attempted to make the history of republican Rome, together with examples from modern history, into a basis for lessons of permanent political usefulness – systematically in the *Discourses on the First Ten Books of Livy* (completed in 1519), but also in places throughout his writings. His *Florentine History*, published in 1532, frequently reveals the same aspiration. Several of his predecessors in the chancery, after Bruni, had also produced such histories; Machiavelli presented his own to Giulio de' Medici, who had become Pope Clement VII. It represented a partial rehabilitation for him with the Medici, but he was never able to resume the official career he had lost in 1512 when the Medici had returned to power in Florence, overthrowing the republican regime for which he had worked and in whose service he had undertaken ambassadorial missions to France, Rome and the emperor Maximilian. He had also worked to create a militia which was supposed to free Florence from its dependence on mercenaries. His friend the historian Guicciardini also had experience in diplomatic missions on the Florentine government's behalf. This practice of keeping close watch on one's neighbours by accredited ambassadors was a new development, born of the tensions and anxieties created by the existence of a number of independent states in close, mistrustful juxtaposition, with constantly shifting intentions and alliances.

One product of this was the articulation by Guicciardini of a consciously held conception of the balance (*contrapeso*) of power between states, by which the independence of each might be preserved and none enabled to become too powerful. Among the important duties of an ambassador was to write reports (which subsequently became important sources for historians (below, p. 465)) – appraisals of the power and preparedness, the intentions, intrigues and struggles for influence, in the host state. Together with an education in the Latin classics as a training in rhetoric, and the study of the ancient historians, this was a highly appropriate preparation for writing contemporary and recent Italian history. Both Machiavelli and Guicciardini were clearly fascinated by the experience of diplomacy, though Machiavelli was the more confident in framing political generalizations for future application; Guicciardini was more sceptical, and wrote a critique of Machiavelli's *Discourses* along these lines. For the appraisal of the unique configurations of circumstances of which he saw politics as being made up, history was the ideal medium. Guicciardini's *History of Italy* – which is essentially what came to be called 'diplomatic history' – is accordingly immensely long and detailed. It was published posthumously in 1561, though written in the 1530s, and concludes in 1527.

Machiavelli's *Florentine History* alternates the treatment of internal and external affairs. In its later books it too is highly detailed, but the political scientist is always struggling to break free into general maxims and widescale comparisons, which he gives at the opening of each book. They are tailored appropriately to the themes revealed by the main events to be described, which are grouped into the category of a particular political problem and are considered generally before being recounted. These themes include why the internal divisions of Rome could be bridged by conciliation – a notable theme in Livy – and even added to the warlike spirit of the Romans, while those of the Florentines only enfeeble them (III); why the Romans were able to maintain their institutions with little change, while the Florentines are constantly changing theirs (IV); why states oscillate between order and disorder, to which the answer, provided first by Sallust, is that 'valour begets tranquillity, tranquillity ease, ease disorder, and disorder ruin. And conversely out of ruin springs order, from order valour, and thence glory and good fortune' (V). This leads on to a condemnation of the dangerously seductive and enervating effects of literary pursuits, much in the spirit of Cato the Censor, whose law expelling philosophers is favourably cited.

Book VI endorses the plundering habits of the states of antiquity; modern wars are, on the other hand, impoverishing, because the vanquished are spared and the spoils are taken by the soldiery – hence, in part, Machiavelli's campaigning against the use of mercenaries. Book VII opens with a warning against factions that was to echo down the centuries, particularly in eighteenth-century Britain and America, until in the nineteenth century constitutional opposition became respectable; Machiavelli makes the point that the more powerful the regime, the more opposition can be expressed only as conspiracy, which he acknowledges should form the preamble to Book VIII, which includes the famous (and recent) Pazzi conspiracy against the Medici in 1478, but he excuses himself on the grounds that he has dealt with the issue elsewhere, i.e. in the *Discourses*. In his subsequent account of the outcome of the plot, in which Lorenzo de' Medici himself was wounded and his brother Giuliano assassinated, but which nevertheless failed, Machiavelli the political connoisseur cannot refrain from itemizing the qualities required by the political assassin: coolness, courage and resolution, bred by long experience in affairs of life and death (VIII.5).

Connoisseurship and an irrepressible taste for maxims of advice, even to a cause we cannot imagine him in any way sympathetic to, is shown by Machiavelli also in his account earlier of the important insurrection of the poorer artisans, the *ciompi*, in 1378. A leading rioter offers his fellows advice in a speech which, though there may be an element of parodic exaggeration, bears strongly the stamp of the author:

That our old outrages may be forgiven us we must needs in my judgement commit new, multiplying offences, redoubling our burnings and pillagings, and endeavouring to enlist as many as possible as companions in our crimes. For when the offenders are many, none are punished; petty offences are chastised, but great and grave offences are rewarded; and where many suffer wrong, few seek to avenge it. For wrongs that touch all equally are borne with more patience than those directed against individuals. (III.13)

This is Machiavellianism for the lower classes. The speaker winds up with a general reflection on virtues punished and vices rewarded which makes one suspect Machiavelli of indulging in self-parody, or perhaps the expression of his real opinion under the safe fictional cover of a reported speech by a malefactor. The routes to wealth and power in the world are force and fraud. Those who fail to use them are the losers: 'The faithful servant is a servant always, and the good are always poor. None escape from bondage but the unfaithful and the bold, and none from poverty but the rapacious and dishonest.'

A good deal of the earlier part of Machiavelli's history is familiar from Villani, but Machiavelli brings out more clearly the roles of the papacy and the emperors in keeping Italy divided by their rivalry and hence permitting the de facto independence of the greater cities. He pays tribute, in fact, to the diplomatic skill with which the popes, originally dependent on the emperors, raised themselves to parity (I.9–11). Machiavelli adopts the classical practice of inventing speeches, introducing them by 'to this effect'. One of the most notable is allegedly delivered during the resistance to the Duke of Athens in 1343, when the populace rise and crowd into the piazza with home-made standards (the Duke having confiscated the previous symbols of freedom and corporate identity). One of the priors makes a long, defiant speech on the traditional freedom of the city, whose mementos are 'the seats of the magistracy, the standards of the free companies', which will not allow it to be forgotten (II.34). 'What is it that you can do', the Duke is asked, 'that will outweigh the delights of freedom and make men cease from longing to revert to their old condition?' One has to wonder in what mood of nostalgia, bitterness or hope Machiavelli wrote this celebration of civic freedom.

After the accounts of faction-fighting and constitutional changes in Florence, culminating in the rise of the Medici, Machiavelli turns (in Book V) to what is essentially skilfully told diplomatic history, which is given an ironic turn by his contempt for mercenary armies, whose leaders and troops alike are concerned only with their own interest and who change sides readily when it suits them. The result has been a state of neither peace nor war, without tranquillity but also without patriotism or valour: 'For the wars of Italy were brought to such a degree of futility as to be entered on without fear, waged without danger and ended without loss' (V.1). After a protracted and detailed narrative, in the Roman manner, of an apparently hard-fought battle between the Florentines and the troops of the *condottiere* Niccolò Piccinino, Machiavelli clearly enjoys giving the casualty list:

And in this great rout and protracted engagement, lasting from four in the afternoon to eight in the evening, one man only was slain, and even he perished not from wounds, or any blow dealt him in combat, but from being trampled on after falling from his horse. With such safety did men then fight; for all being mounted on horseback and sheathed in mail, and assured against death should he surrender, there was no reason why they should die, their armour protecting them while they fought, and surrender saving them when they could fight no longer. (V.33)

Though it deals much with relations between Florence and her neighbours, there is relatively little strictly military history in Machiavelli's *Florentine History*, though he wrote a treatise on *The Art of War*; there is certainly less actual fighting than in Livy. Machiavelli's treatment of external relations traces the constantly shifting pattern of alliances and the motives behind it. The professional commanders of mercenary armies, the *condottieri*, ostensibly employees, act sometimes like leaders of independent states, which several became. Machiavelli deals, with exemplary lucidity, with the calculations, threats, demonstrations, treacheries and covert dealings of the various relevant governments. One could reasonably call this 'ambassador's history'. In Book VI, for example, he gives a masterly account, too long to quote, of rival views in Florence on whether to favour the aspiration of the *condottiere* Francesco Sforza to the dukedom of Milan, showing how they are conditioned by a complex interaction of domestic political considerations and estimations of Florence's interests as a state (VI.23). He speaks admiringly in this respect of the successes achieved by Venice: 'It had been, as it were, the destiny of the Venetian republic to lose in war and gain in negotiating peace' (VI.19). Venice is cited by Machiavelli for the stability of its republican institutions. The Venetian republic as a political model was to be a legacy to the political discourse of the eighteenth century. In Machiavelli's brief digression on the early history of Venice, he speaks of it as a republic which, 'both for its institutions and for its importance, deserves to be celebrated beyond every other Italian state', though now (that is, in the 1520s) the Venetians live, 'like all the rest of the Italian princes, at the mercy of others' (I.28, 29).

Machiavelli can also admire the skill with which the popes, by adopting a kind of balance-of-power policy, have kept Italy divided, and he recognizes that this division is what has made the free development of the Italian states possible, though now it makes them hopelessly vulnerable to the intervention of the states beyond the Alps – 'the barbarians', as he and Guicciardini sometimes call them (I.23, 28). He is similarly ambivalent about the internal divisions in Florence. In so far as they proceed from emulation and avidity for public distinction he speaks of them, following Sallust, as a source of energy and strength. He draws a distinction between this and the creation of a faction by the distribution of favours and the exercise of patronage, which is objectionable and which has been characteristic of Florence, to its harm. This is a preamble (VII) to a consideration of the rise to power of Cosimo de' Medici, and clearly points at him.

Considering that Machiavelli wrote his *Florentine History* in a sense with Medicean encouragement, it is less sycophantic and more independent in its judgements than one feels entitled to expect, helped, of course, by the fact that the Medicean rulers were officially republicans. For example, in his concluding eulogy of Lorenzo de' Medici, with whose death the book ends, Machiavelli speaks favourably of Lorenzo's careful adherence to 'the simplicity of republican manners', despite the munificence of his patronage, and of his restraint in not seeking princely foreign marriages for his children. There is a bitter irony, however, in his account of the conclusion of the Pazzi conspiracy against the Medici. When the cry of 'Liberty' was raised, as in the past, there was no rallying to it, for 'the ears of the people had been stopped by the prosperity and bounty of the Medici, and liberty was no longer known in Florence' (VIII.8).

For Machiavelli, Lorenzo's death in 1492 marked a turning point, because, in Machiavelli's concluding words, 'Italy, remaining bereft of his counsel, found no resource in those who survived him either to satisfy or restrain the ambition of Ludovico Sforza, guardian of the Duke of Milan.' It was Ludovico, as Machiavelli's readers knew, whose invitation had led to the invasion by Charles VIII of France in 1494, from which both Machiavelli and Guicciardini dated the present abject state of Italy, at the mercy of foreign powers. Machiavelli spoke of the invasion as 'all these evil seeds, which . . . very soon ruined, and still continue to ruin, Italy'. For the elaboration of these consequences,

readers were able to turn, after its publication in 1561, to Guicciardini's *History of Italy*, which begins where Machiavelli's ends.

Francesco Guicciardini, more socially distinguished than his friend
Machiavelli, had served as an ambassador, to Spain in 1512–13, but
he both came of an eminent Florentine family and remained on good
terms with the Medici, so that under the two Medici popes, Leo X
and Clement VII, he rose very high in the government of the papal
possessions, as president of the Romagna and lieutenant general of
the papal armies and later governor of Bologna. After his fall from
power, when he devoted himself in his retirement, like many ancient
historians, to writing his history, he spoke with some irony of the
grandeur of his former state, referring to himself, as he does in his
history, in the third person: his fellow citizens would not have recognized him 'with his house full of tapestries, silver . . . surrounded by
a guard of more than a hundred landsknechts, with halberdiers and
other cavalry in attendance . . . never riding out with less than one
hundred or one hundred and fifty horse; immersed in governing
bodies, titles, "Most illustrious lords . . ."'. There was an irony in
Guicciardini's eminence in the papal service, for, as he makes clear in
the history, he was contemptuous of the abject state of the papacy
and the Church in Italy, and came to deplore the role of the former
in Italian affairs as pernicious. Privately he said that if 'the position I
have served under several popes [had not] obliged me to desire their
greatness for my own self-interest . . . I would have loved Martin
Luther as myself'. His account of the policies and characters of the
popes – written, of course, after his fall – is unsparing, though there
is no approval in his references to Luther.

Guicciardini's history is immensely long and covers only forty-four
years, from 1490 to 1534, so it is also immensely detailed – though
for the first time, by focusing entirely on the relations of states, he
was able to produce a work which considers Italy as a whole. Guicciardini's general characterization of historical change, in contrast to
Machiavelli's famous reiteration of the notion of a cycle of prosperity
followed by downfall, warns us of his commitment to the fine grain
of historical events and hence to multiple explanations, which he
indeed provides, though they mostly concern the intersection of many
motives, intentions, calculations, misconceptions, irrational impulses

and fleeting or enduring psychological dispositions; Guicciardini seldom offers one motive for an action when he can think of three or more. Human affairs, he says at the outset of his history, are mutable, 'not unlike a sea whipped by winds', and the reader of his work comes to feel the force of the analogy.

Guicciardini's commitment to the particular, to the uniqueness of each situation, has two important consequences. One, of which he is fully aware, is a warning against overconfidence in commentators and, more crucially, in statesmen: arrogance is folly. The second, which informs the whole of Guicciardini's history, is a commitment to explanation through narrative, through recounting the dense particularity of each important historical moment. (On this see Phillips, *Guicciardini*, pp. 121ff.) Close narration is indispensable, and Guicciardini provides it. But his history also has a general theme. That of Machiavelli's history, despite its attention to foreign affairs, is above all factionalism and the loss of civic liberty, though this is perhaps not as clear as it might have been made if the methods of Cosimo and Lorenzo de' Medici in manipulating the government and effectively ruling with a republican facade, though acknowledged by Machiavelli, had been traced in more detail. Guicciardini is also concerned for his city's liberty, which he understandably approaches as a rich oligarch, but the central theme of his history is determined by the period it covers and by its focus on external affairs: it is the tragedy, felt also by Machiavelli, but not traced by him, of foreign dominance of Italian affairs and the reduction of the Italian states to a condition of subservience. With extraordinary powers of organization, and clearly much research, though it is hardly exhibited, Guicciardini narrates in one after another episode of complex negotiations how this outcome has been arrived at. The only comparable historiographical achievements are the studies in the nineteenth and twentieth centuries of what came to be called 'the European states system'.

But Guicciardini's work, though precise, controlled and dignified, is also in its totality a lament, an aspect which sometimes surfaces in the narrative, and there are villains. These are the Italian rulers, among whom the popes figure prominently, whose reckless and short-sighted ambitions allow the tragedy to occur. Fortune is sometimes invoked, but, while rulers should take account of it, Guicciardini's account is not deterministic: it traces the consequences of human folly, in many guises. Guicciardini's passionate indictment of the narrow selfishness of the leaders of the Italian states is prompted by a sense that the tragedy need not have happened. Only Lorenzo, who stands as a contrast, and a memory, is lavishly praised – for his understanding of the necessity for an intra-Italian balance of power. Potential strong men emerge, notably Cesare Borgia (the subject of Chapter VII of Machiavelli's *The Prince*) and Pope Julius II, but they overreach themselves and fail. No Italian measures up to the magnitude of the danger; instead they help to aggravate it, sometimes in rashness, sometimes in ignorance. As a political actor and former ambassador, Guicciardini understands very well the contrast between surface appearances and the considerations that lie behind them, as well as the multiplicity of factors and pressures to be calculated and responded to, and the misconceptions and rumours which cloud judgement.

The initial French invasion in 1494 was actually short-lived, but it opened the gates and revealed the appalling military superiority and ruthlessness of the transalpine states. Nothing, Guicciardini sees, is the same again. The French fight to win, burning houses and refusing to take prisoners, and they employ terrifying new weapons with irresistible power, above all field artillery. Guns as siege weapons were well known and ponderous, but the French cannon, firing bronze balls, were rapid and manoeuvrable, drawn by horses, not oxen: 'They used this diabolical rather than human weapon not only in besieging cities but also in the field' (I). Such weapons 'rendered ridiculous all former weapons of attack which had been used by the ancients'. Guicciardini, in fact, is quick to note the developments of his own day which surpass the knowledge and techniques of the ancient world. He notes Venice's loss of the spice trade to the Portuguese, who sail around the southern coast of Africa direct to the Spice Islands, and the growth in the power of Spain. These voyages 'have made it clear that the ancients were deceived in many ways regarding a knowledge of the earth' (VI).

It seems appropriate that Guicciardini's own history, though in a sense humanist-bred, was not at all slavishly imitative of current models. He conforms to the convention of confecting speeches, which review policies and alternatives, but his own accounts of the complex webs of diplomatic relations are highly original; the cutting from one power centre to another is exceptionally rapid and at times, it must be admitted, bewildering. Guicciardini's technique is jagged, where humanist history is typically smooth and even bland. The power of Guicciardini's history is moral and intellectual; it is a tragedy presented as a tour de force in the organization of masses of detailed material and complex narrative. It is a challenge rather than a pleasure to read: there is point to the legendary story which tells of the prisoner who, made to choose between reading Guicciardini's accounts of the wars of Florence with Pisa or the galleys, after a few pages choses the galleys. Not since Thucydides had the interaction between a number of states – small, vulnerable, ambitious and fearful, sharing a common language and culture but varying in constitutions – been subjected to such close and coldly rational analysis. There is nothing of comparable complexity in Livy's accounts of the early Roman republic in its struggles for survival and expansion, though, it has to be remembered, Livy's descriptions, unlike Thucydides' and Guicciardini's, were not contemporary or even nearly so. In general, however, the difficulties in translating Thucydides and the humanist's requirement of models for Latin eloquence – together with Machiavelli's preoccupation (derived from Livy and Sallust) with republican morale, the successes it brought, and the dangers to it that those successes represented – ensured that it would be the Roman historians who would chiefly inspire the writing of history in the humanist tradition down to the eighteenth century.

PART V

Studying the Past

19

Antiquarianism, Legal History and the Discovery of Feudalism

'Studying the Past', the title of this last group of chapters, marks a new beginning: the use, from the sixteenth century onward, of the textual methods of Renaissance humanism to reveal and understand not only the works of ancient philosophers and poets but the European past, which from the later seventeenth century began to be called the Middle Ages. This technique was archival historical research, though that phrase did not become current until much later, and by this means, inquiries could be carried back beyond the memories of the historian, or of eyewitnesses, and freed from dependence on earlier historians and chroniclers. This was a great transformation, and we have to ask how it happened. Its importance for history was subsequently overlooked. Partly this was the result of focusing on what was, from the Renaissance, the dominant prescription for historical writing: imitation of the revered ancient models, which meant chiefly political narrative from which morals could be drawn. Partly also it was a matter of limited intentions and a relative lack of self-consciousness. In a good many cases, sixteenth- and seventeenth-century scholars, then spoken of as antiquaries, stumbled into archival research rather than adopted it as a programme for history, and their motives, as we shall see, were often political rather than what the nineteenth century, when an ideal of historical research was made explicit, approvingly came to call 'scientific'. In the eighteenth century such work was often denigrated and condescended to in comparison with elegant imitation of classical models, as uncouth, useless, pedantic and, given the state of many manuscripts, dirty and ungentlemanly.

The long-term result, even after attitudes to archival research had changed, was an undervaluing of the admittedly far from elegant or even readable results of the work of antiquaries and hence a distorted perspective on the history of historical studies. In particular, this encouraged an exaggerated view (with the full backing of its protagonists) of the acclaimed 'revolution' in historical methods in the nineteenth century, particularly in Germany. Germany certainly then took the lead, with state sponsorship, in creating institutions for historical scholarship and in establishing an education for apprentice historians in the emerging historical profession – above all in the famous Berlin seminar of Leopold von Ranke – with the critical use of primary sources as its defining ethic. This was immensely influential, but it is doubtful whether it counts as an intellectual revolution (see Chapter 25). A different emphasis has been made possible by the work of scholars over the past half-century. Therefore in this chapter we need to consider the work and motives of sixteenth- and seventeenth-century scholars, though their work is of a very different kind from the histories discussed in other chapters, since it consists not of available and potentially enjoyable narratives, but typically of commentaries on highly specific philological and antiquarian topics. It is essential, however, to have some idea of its consequences.

But before this we have to take further account of the most approved genre of historical writing in the period: political narrative written in emulation of the ancient historians. Guicciardini's *History of Italy*, though in the humanist tradition, is highly original. After this achievement, humanist narrative historiography for the next two centuries has been widely regarded as meagre in interest if not in quantity, leaving few if any monuments whose appeal transcends their period and the concerns of specialists. This may be a lazy judgement, but it is not one I am able to controvert. The humanist prescription for history was imitation of the best ancient models – most notably Livy – by a smooth eloquence and an exclusively political focus. History was a literary genre in which truth took second place to rhetorical effectiveness in the provision of inspiring examples of good and great conduct. This is, to a modern reader, not an appetizing set of prescriptions.

The fierce republican enthusiasm which had given early humanist history an edge, though it continued to inform European traditions of political thought down to the English, American and French revolutions, waned in historiography during the European Age of Absolutism. The office of historiographer royal (established in England in 1661) in France was held by some distinguished – and subversive – incumbents, from François Hotman in the sixteenth century to Voltaire in the eighteenth. William Robertson, whom we shall attend to shortly, was historiographer royal for Scotland in the mid eighteenth century. But the title is potentially a double-edged gift to Clio: patronage, but also the possibility of control. In Tudor England and in the France of Louis XIV, prudent historians got the approval of authority in advance when handling sensitive subjects. The reign of Richard II, who had been deposed, was a ticklish subject in the time of Elizabeth. A French historian, Nicolas Fréret, found himself in the Bastille in 1714 for indiscreet views on the Germanic – and hence Tacitean – character of Frankish society and a forthright dismissal of Trojan origins: Tacitus' *Germania*, a text newly available from the beginning of the sixteenth century, notoriously supported the absence of hereditary monarchy among the Germans. A Cambridge professor, Isaac Dorislaus – suspiciously a Dutchman, and therefore tainted by republicanism – had his lectures suppressed for the same offence a century before Fréret's misfortune, in 1627.

It will not do, of course, to dismiss the whole genre of humanist historical narrative as bland literary exercises in pedagogy and sycophancy. The author of the most exhaustive survey of humanist historical writing in sixteenth-century Italy has found it relatively free from obvious political censorship and warns against taking the pieties endlessly reiterated in prefaces entirely seriously as a guide to what lay beyond them (Fryde, *Humanism and Renaissance Historiography*). The growing vogue, in the later sixteenth century and all through the seventeenth, for Tacitus' *Annals* and *Histories* as the most admired model, rather than Livy, introduced a welcome diversification, though the enthusiasm for Tacitus also expressed itself in collections of maxims of political conduct: he was safer to cite than Machiavelli. Some historians and commentators aspired to a Tacitean epigrammatic brevity and subtle psychological portraiture – though Guicciardini could also be a source.

There was a particular fascination with dissimulation, as is sometimes revealed in memoirs of the period, which, being more covert, are sometimes more interesting than the histories. The *Memoirs* of Cardinal de Retz, one of the leaders of the Parisians in the disturbances during Louis XIV's minority in the 1640s, are wonderfully candid, for example, about the ways in which, as distributor of alms for the Archbishop of Paris, he had used his position to build up a political following. An interest in court motives and the contrasts between public profession and private intention were particularly apt to a modern age of absolutism, not altogether unlike the times in which Tacitus had lived, when, as he himself recognized, the conduct of government was curial rather than public and displayed in oratory; the *arcana imperii*, the closet secrets of despotic policy, exercised a fascination precisely because they were closed. Even in parliamentary early-eighteenth-century England Viscount Bolingbroke, who had himself headed a government, shared Polybius' snobbery towards mere scholars, who 'have seldom the means of knowing those private passages on which all public transactions depend . . . They cannot see the working of the mine, but their industry collects the matter that is thrown out' (*Letters on the Study and Use of History*, Letter 5). It was also true, however, in France at least, that public records of the past were becoming better organized and inspectable by recognized scholars, who were sometimes their keepers. The Valois and Bourbon rulers recognized the value of the past as a potential propaganda arsenal, as well as that of archives as a necessary practical resource, even if they had to be handled with care.

Two of the most interesting 'Tacitean' narrative histories of the period were both written in the early seventeenth century: Francis Bacon's *History of the Reign of King Henry VII* (1622) and the Venetian Paolo Sarpi's *History of the Council of Trent* (1619), the great church council which in 1545–63, in the wake of Luther's Reformation, had refurbished the weapons of the Catholic Church. Bacon's work broke no new ground in its employment of unpublished sources, though he used some; mostly he relied on the available chronicles. But his psychological portrayal of the King impressed itself, perhaps ineradicably, on subsequent generations: Henry is seen as avaricious, parsimonious, prudent, suspicious and secretive – there seem to be elements of Tacitus' Tiberius – though Bacon also allows for his better, humane, qualities. Sarpi is presented by his leading modern English commentator, David Wootton, as himself a lifelong arch-dissimulator, for he was a friar and, according to Wootton, a convinced atheist. In his account of the Council, which to Sarpi's dismay laid the foundations of the Catholic Counter-Reformation, Sarpi excels, in Tacitean–Guicciardinian fashion, in the dissection of psychology and motives and in describing the historical ironies by which all the agents find their hopes defeated. Wootton sees an additional originality in the depiction of how individuals are governed not merely by individual motives but by the collective interests they represent: bureaucratic necessity rules their actions.

Blandness was by no means always a feature of humanist historiography. The civil wars in later-sixteenth-century France produced a copious stream of contemporary histories of a highly partisan kind. But the greatest contribution of humanism to history in the sixteenth and seventeenth centuries was not neoclassical prescriptions for narrative historiography, but the application of the methods of humanist critical scholarship to the study of the past. Though its full effects, which are still with us, were not to be felt until the eighteenth century, this is such an important innovation that it requires closer attention, even though there is no single, much less readily accessible, work of the period in which the non-specialist reader can find its principles, applications and achievements epitomized. It is an expanding tradition of practice and its widening applications, rather than a corpus of enduring works, which is of interest.

As the early Christian centuries, culminating in the world-historical summary of Orosius, marked a new epoch in the conception of the past and the approach to it (above, p. 195) – an epoch which was to last for a thousand years and more – so we now have to consider the opening of the modern era in the study of the past. Though there have been changes since, particularly those associated with the establishment of a historical profession, which we shall have to look at later, there has been nothing of comparably transforming influence. The main novelty is expressed in the phrase we have already glanced at: 'the study of the past'. It is this phrase that we must now try to unpack.

The impulses to historiography to be found in Herodotus are investigative and commemorative, but the former is in the service of the latter. In a sense, all history beyond mere transcription must in some sense be investigative, more or less profoundly or superficially, but as we have seen, for a long period, and not least in humanist historical narratives, the commemorative aspect loomed larger. History was the retrieval and presentation of what deserved to be remembered, against the remorseless flow of time. For a long time there was relatively little sense that the past lay inert but potentially revivable until quickened by the researcher and historian, in documents and archives. Hence the recording and writing of history could seem like a contest with an otherwise all-enveloping oblivion. Now, however, though it would be another two centuries and more before its full potential was realized, the investigative impulse was becoming urgent, guided and controlled by the methods that humanists had been developing from the late fourteenth century onward.

Initially this essential characteristic of the historian's craft derived not from an impulse which it is altogether appropriate to call historical, but rather from the impulse to retrieve, admire, even to imitate. It is easier, initially, to call it literary and moral rather than historical, and it was applied chiefly to past documents – texts – which were in a broad sense literary, including the work of classical historians. The method was philological, and its chief purificatory agent in the search for the authentic text was the detection of anachronism. This was made possible only by a cultivated sense, the product of erudition, of what the grammar, style and diction of late-republican Latin (in particular) made it possible, or more importantly impossible, for an educated Roman or literary master to have written and meant. (The model prized above all was Cicero.) The most dramatic single demonstration of the power of critical scholarship to revise the past by the detection of anachronisms was its application not to a classical and literary text, but to a medieval and political one. It was the famous demonstration by the great early-fifteenth-century Italian humanist Lorenzo Valla that the document purporting to convey authority in the West from the emperor Constantine to Pope Sylvester, the 'Donation of Constantine', could not possibly belong to the fourth century AD and was therefore a medieval forgery. In the long run, even more far-reaching in its effects was to be the application of humanist critical techniques to the foundational texts of Christianity in the New Testament, notably by Erasmus in the early sixteenth century. But in general historiography the most influential and profoundly transforming development – initially in Italy in the fifteenth century, and flowering in France in the sixteenth – was to be their application to the corpus of Roman jurisprudence, the *Corpus Juris Civilis*, compiled in the reign of the emperor Justinian and handed down as authoritative ever since.

Humanist scholarship was a powerful solvent of received views of the past and versions of past texts. The texts the humanists prized from the ancient world, which included those of Roman law, were in their modern incarnations the products of centuries of transmission and transcription. They were therefore apt to be overlaid with well-intentioned but anachronistic commentaries, interpretations, interpolations and misunderstandings, as well as scribal errors and forgeries, which to the humanist scholar were the silt and encrustations beneath which could be glimpsed the pristine gold. The method of obtaining it was literary archaeology conducted with a moral and aesthetic passion for recovering and making available for imitation the literary manners and cultural and political values of the cherished period. The humanists therefore developed an acute sense of what might be called the pathologies of cultural transmission: the vicissitudes, misfortunes and well-intentioned ignorant maltreatment as well as deliberate manipulations (with no sense of guilt) to which the priceless wisdom and literary heritage of the ancients had for up to fifteen centuries been subjected.

The application of philological methods to the reconstruction, in due course, not merely of Roman literature but of Roman history and eventually of the more recent – though still often remote – European past generally was a process of extension and transference. The methods of humanist scholarship were naturally applied to the Roman law texts, and through them to a greater understanding of the Roman institutions to which the laws referred. Then outside Italy, and in particular in sixteenth-century France and half a century later in England, the practices of legal historical scholarship came to be applied to the barbarian and medieval antecedents of modern legal institutions and customs. How, with what motives, and with what eventual consequences for the future general understanding of the European past will be the questions to which the rest of this chapter is chiefly devoted.

To summarize at this point the first part of the argument: literary archaeology led to and provided the tools for legal archaeology, and legal humanism led in turn to the study not chiefly of events but of institutions, the most important of which in the Middle Ages, namely feudal institutions, were so pervasive as to constitute what the eighteenth century would come to call 'the state of society'. 'The state of society in the feudal age(s)', for example, is a common piece of eighteenth-century diction, but two centuries of energetic scholarship, mostly legal, were necessary to make intelligible what came to be so casually referred to. Concomitant with that scholarship were also the vastly increased dissemination of information of all kinds, including scholarly, following the invention of printing in the later fifteenth century, and the better organization of and access to archives, generally speaking (though there were still many obstacles). In these developments was to lie the future of historical studies, and indeed the very possibility of systematically 'studying the past'. Later we shall look at the long-term consequences for what, until the eighteenth century, remained relatively unaffected in its own humanist mould, imitative rather than investigative, overawed by its classical precursors: narrative historiography.

We begin, however, with the notion of legal humanism. Later, legal scholarship was to become notably entangled with and to be both stimulated and warped by political conflicts, particularly in England, but initially the application of humanist techniques to legal texts seems to have been prompted by the same enthusiasm for recovering and purifying the heritage of the Roman world that inspired humanism generally. But the consequences of this application in France, particularly centred in the middle and later years of the sixteenth century in the University of Bourges, were to be ironic. Inquiries conducted to uncover and apply the legal wisdom of the Romans, purged of the dross of medieval commentaries which had in fact been part of the process of the adaptation and application of Roman law in more recent societies, ended by identifying a Roman law so pure that it was in fact manifestly alien, the law of a past and different society. To purify turned out, unintentionally, to be to historicize and to distance in a disconcerting fashion. Some jurists bluntly faced this. In his

Anti-Tribonian (1567), François Hotman proclaimed that Roman law, being the law of another time and place, was useless to French jurisprudence; he focused attention instead on the study of native, customary law.

In fact the study of Roman law in humanist fashion made it historical in a double sense: not only was it made remote, but it was historically relativized. It was not an ideal, frozen in time, but was itself the product of a long legal history, during which Rome had itself altered greatly; it had been collected only at the end by Justinian's legists, who themselves seemed sometimes uncomprehending of what they were dealing with. There was, then, no single jurisprudential moment, permanently available, once recovered and returned to its original condition, for use in the present.

There was a parallel here with the disputes among humanists over the authority to be accorded to the works of Cicero: was the Latin of Cicero mandatory for all time? That it should be was recognized as an indefensibly extreme view and was mocked accordingly, but the problems of jurists were greater. Working with an ideal but arguably unduly restrictive model, it was possible to write Latin prose which could pass as that of the first century BC, though it was at the expense of the flexibility of the colloquial Latin which in some circles was still a living tongue, now stigmatized as barbarous. But even if the ideal legal model could be identified, lawyers could not avoid questions of its applicability to an intractable contemporary reality. The alternatives were to relegate Roman law to the status of a purely academic study or to face the necessities of adaptation such as the medieval glossators had faced in their day.

A consequence of making Roman law a historical phenomenon rather than a timeless model, and of the growing perception of stubborn realities, presumably of more recent origin, to which it could not be fitted, was the recognition that in large part the characteristic laws, customs and institutions of the modern nations must derive from these nations' barbarian ancestry, or at least have evolved since the establishment of the barbarian kingdoms, owing perhaps nothing to Rome and to imperial edicts. One possible inference was an exaltation of local customary law, as suited to the people or peoples who lived by it. This was Hotman's solution. The charge of barbarism, in a sense true, had to be faced down, and historical scholarly attention had to be refocused from Rome and the empire to – as we should say – the early and high Middle Ages. In discerning the alienness of much of the late-Roman codes, the sixteenth-century French jurists were in a sense discovering medieval history – though not yet by that name – and recognizing medieval Europe not merely as ignorant, barbarous and uncomprehending, but as creative. For jurists who wished to discern the origins and guiding principles of their own laws, the Middle Ages were fundamental.

There was a patriotic and even sometimes a populist dimension in this. Roman civil law, in the late-antique compilations in which it had been chiefly inherited, tended naturally to be markedly authoritarian. Roman-law maxims included the notorious 'Quod principi placuit legis vigorem habet' ('What is pleasing to the prince has the force of law') and the idea that the prince is 'legibus solutus' (not bound by the law). Customary law, on the other hand, tended to endorse inherited private and corporate rights and privileges: to be, in fact, feudal in character. Imperial and customary were in a sense antitheses – as were the rival versions, Trojan and barbarian, of the origins of the European peoples and monarchies. The Trojan connection, following the example set by Virgil, embodied in Brutus, Francus and other eponymous émigré Trojan princes, was a flattering one, linking the people concerned, through cousinship to Aeneas and common descent from Priam, to the Romans. In the early modern period, as humanist scholarship promoted an ever-increasing scepticism and eventual dismissal of legendary Trojan princelings unknown alike to history and to ancient literature, and as Tacitus' *Germania* became increasingly known and influential, the original 'freedom' of the Germans became launched on a long career in European historiography.

We must not, however, produce an oversimplified picture of humanist scholars scouring the prehistory of Europe with the detergent of philological method: their own works could provide new sources of confusion, and even new forgeries. Moreover it was not only the ubiquitous Trojans who had given kings and legendary inhabitants to pre-Christian, pre-literate Europe. All of them must in theory have been traceable back to Noah, and some were explicitly so, for the Bible, as well as Virgil's fiction and classical legend, was a major source for early history, providing giants (who seem to have been common) and near-relatives of Noah like his grandson Gomer, who became regarded as progenitor of the Gauls. The sixteenth-century antiquary John Bale had pre-Trojan Britain founded by Samothes, son of Noah's son Japhet, one of whose descendants, Druys, founded the order of the Druids. Imaginary genealogies were only reluctantly abandoned, partly because an assured grasp of the authentic classical canon was necessarily a work of erudition and time, and partly because the alternative, apart from the discovery of the *Germania*, was not so much new knowledge as a void. With the potential of archaeological delving still unrecognized – though the importance of artefacts (and particularly classical artefacts) as witnesses was beginning to be appreciated – virtually nothing could be known of the pre-Roman period in the past of the northern European nations. In the 1570s, in his history of Scotland, George Buchanan, an accomplished French-nurtured Scottish humanist, though a partisan and unreliable Protestant historian of his own time, the reign of Mary Stuart, was purveying with apparent confidence a list of forty legendary pre-Christian Scottish kings with such names as Thereus, Durstan, Mogallus and Athireo. He only reluctantly began to lose confidence in them after their rejection by the Welsh antiquary Humphrey Llwyd, who was scornful of Scottish pretensions, though himself happy with Geoffrey of Monmouth.

The world of sixteenth-century humanism was a copious and complicated one to find one's way around, even for the erudite, and particularly if we include works overlapping with narrative history – historical topographies, etymologies, 'universal histories' and even the beginnings of annotated bibliographies. It has become customary among modern scholars to distinguish strongly in this period and down to the eighteenth century between neoclassically modelled narrative histories and humanist antiquarian learning with no pretensions to elegance. It was a distinction which contemporaries themselves remarked, and on the historians' side it was reinforced with a good deal of abuse of useless, pedantic and uncouth learning. In his *Letters on the Study and Use of History*, Bolingbroke, whose historiographical models were the trinity revered by the humanists, Sallust, Livy and Tacitus, and who propounded the exiled statesman's view of history as made useful by the instructive examples it could yield, denounced scholars who made 'fair copies of foul manuscripts, give the signification of hard words, and take a great deal of grammatical pains' as mere under-labourers. Even with the most eminent of them – he mentions Scaliger, one of the greatest of Renaissance scholars – he is prepared 'to avow a thorough contempt for the whole business of these learned lives; for all the researches into antiquity, for all the systems of chronology and history'; he would rather make mistakes in these 'than sacrifice half my life to collect all the learned lumber that fills the head of an antiquary' (Letter 1). Now, however, we tend to find the humanist prescriptions for history depressingly imitative, while at least some of the admittedly often disorderly and miscellaneous work of the antiquaries is pregnant with reappraisals of the European past.

Ancestors mattered – even remote ones. Medieval Europe was a legalistic society in which, except specifically in contexts where Roman civil and canon law held sway, rights and therefore much of the structure of recognized obligations were characteristically justified by existing inherited title rather than philosophical principle. Sometimes the only witness to such entitlements was custom, through increasingly they came to seem insecurely grounded without documentary support – a powerful incentive to forgery, at least in the benign form of apparently guaranteeing what one did have rather than laying claim to what one did not.

At the highest political level, documents such as the spurious 'Donation of Constantine' could be powerful support for or even be deemed essential to a vital claim. We are told of Edward I of England circulating the monasteries, where such documentary 'memory' was most likely to be preserved, if only in the form of recorded custom, for support for his claim to the overlordship of Scotland; when he had the opportunity, he destroyed Scottish archives. In the sixteenth and seventeenth centuries, precedent-hunting and the search for documentary authority became, in some contexts, urgent, calling on the resources of modern interpretative skills and erudition, honed on the study of Roman law but increasingly applied to more recent national history. Given the powerful tendency to cast political claims and controversies into a legalistic mould, the appropriation and possession of an apparently authoritative version of the national past could be highly relevant. Some version of 'ancient constitutionalism' as political argument can be found in a number of European countries, including Scotland, where it was purveyed by Buchanan, and the Netherlands.

Historical–legal arguments were not, of course, the only ones. Biblical precedents, theological dicta, and even references to Aristotle's *Politics*, along with the lessons of experience and history, were also canvassed. The historical examples – particularly but not exclusively the Roman ones – could be treated in Machiavelli's fashion, as a storehouse of examples rather than of rights and precedents. But the sixteenth and seventeenth centuries, particularly in France and then, half a century later, in England in the period preceding the Civil War, were the great age of invocation of origins, precedents and long-established or immemorial rights in constitutional and political debate. Such arguments were naturally the province of lawyers, or at least of the legally trained, as many of the educated laity were. Although this mode of argument could sometimes produce only a fairly mindless sequence of citations, regardless of historical contexts, it became increasingly historically sophisticated. In some contexts, too, the legal–antiquarian passion, applied heterogeneously to various aspects of the past, bypassed political argument to become an investigation of origins and derivations conducted for its own sake, or from an impulse that was broadly patriotic rather than directly political.

Both patriotism and politics, in fact, were present in the legal–historical scholarship of sixteenth-century France, fusing in what came to be called 'Gallicanism', the assertion of the historic distinctiveness of the realm of France, independent of both papacy and empire. But Gallicanism could accommodate also, though by no means always, a kind of anti-royalist populism, in references to Tacitean and Frankish 'freedom' – which the word 'Frank' itself was held to embody. It was harder, obviously, to incorporate the Gauls, later the Gallo-Romans, in the story of an independent France, though attempts were made and there were Celticists as well as Germanists. The circumstances of later sixteenth-century France – plunged into civil war, massacres, political assassinations and a succession crisis – gave such historical ideas a polemical relevance. Religious conflict threatened to tear France apart. A number of the most notable jurists were Huguenots or at any rate moderates drawn to the party of patriotism and order, the Politiques. The extreme Catholic party, the Holy League, under the leadership of the family of the Guises from Lorraine and, in collaboration with Spain, holding a papalist, 'ultramontane' position, could be seen as representing the prospect of the de facto subjection of France to a foreign power. It was the great crisis of the French monarchy, as the first half of the seventeenth century was to be for the English one when supporters of parliamentary privileges and the royal prerogative searched the record offices, in Westminster and the Tower of London, for legal precedents – the earlier the better – for their respective positions. It was strongly disputed whether Parliament, including the House of Commons, which in fact owed its origin only to royal writ in the thirteenth century, was coeval with or even older than monarchy. The question of Saxon 'freedom' and its alleged continuity with the present, unaffected by the Norman Conquest, was, like the equivalent for the Germans of which it was an offshoot, launched on a historical career which carried it well into the nineteenth century. Even in Elizabeth's reign, Anglo-Saxon studies were patronized by Archbishop Parker in the hope that they would demonstrate that the Church in England had always been independent of Rome. It was a preoccupation analogous to aspects of French Gallicanism.

The most politically embattled of the French sixteenth-century jurists was François Hotman. In his *Franco-Gallia* (1573) Hotman unrolls precedent after precedent from the chroniclers, including Gregory of Tours and Fredegar, to show that the ancient kings of France were elected and could be deposed. For Hotman, the French Estates General were descended from the old Germanic assemblies. The evolution of Germanic custom also embraced the feudal bond. Some authors derived this ultimately from the institution of clientage in the Roman world, others from the Teutonic *comitatus* of the chief's immediate entourage, whose position later became secured by hereditary tenure of land on condition of military service, establishing the full feudal relationship.

One feature of the enthusiasm for custom and the history of law was that, though it encouraged an interest in antecedents, it could also accommodate the idea of a subsequent evolution and even be accompanied by a scepticism about the possibility of tracing remote origins. Seen in this way, the history of law could provide the basis for a new kind of national and indeed comparative history, encompassing customs, manners and even ideas. For example, the *Recherches de la France* (from 1560) of Etienne Pasquier (whose choice of the vernacular is striking) was professedly a search for the distinctive *ésprit* of France and was highly patriotic in inspiration. It was not a narrative history but a collection of monographs on different aspects of French culture, essentially philological in method, with commentaries on the history of words for institutions and customs. French authors in the period, notably Jean Bodin, were also making attempts in the direction of secular universal history, tracing a history of civilization from primitive origins; Bodin specifically cites Thucydides and attacks the Christian and medieval periodization of the Four Empires, derived from the Book of Daniel, which made Rome the last empire before secular time would give way to eschatology. The word 'civilization' itself was not coined (in France) until the later eighteenth century, so we have a construction like 'le temps ou a commencé la civilité' (Loys le Roy, 1575). The need was proclaimed, if not satisfied, for secular general history of religion, laws, customs and manners (*mœurs*), not provided by the classical historians.

There was no such rigorous reappraisal of the past in sixteenth-century England as was offered by legal humanism in France: that had to wait until the mid seventeenth century and the spur provided by the conflict of the Crown and Parliament. But antiquarian learning was vigorously pursued in Elizabethan England towards the end of the century, often under the influence of a patriotic enthusiasm, a kind of love affair with England and Englishness in which sixteenth-century English histories and chronicles played a notable part. After the accession of Elizabeth in 1558 on the death of her Catholic sister Mary, the story of English history was refurbished in a fashion that was Protestant, patriotic and providential. The greatest single influence seems to have been John Foxe's *Acts and Monuments*, which went through successive and enlarged editions until an eight-hundred-page folio, with woodcut illustrations, was published in 1570. Because its second half set out the record of Protestant martyrdoms in Mary's reign, which was the task with which Foxe had begun, it became known as Foxe's *Book of Martyrs*. But Foxe set these martyrs in a wider context of Christian and English history as a whole, which also became influential. For the facts in this he relied heavily on the Italian humanist Polydore Virgil's *History of England* (1535), which Foxe adapted to Protestant purposes in terms of a long struggle in which the Christian faith, grounded in the Bible and sometimes represented by a godly English monarch (Arthur, Alfred, Elizabeth), confronts first paganism (Saxons, Danes) and then the authority of the corrupt Church of Rome. After the sixteenth-century English translation of the Bible, Foxe's book has been spoken of as the greatest single influence on English Protestant thinking of the late Tudor and early Stuart period.

Following the Reformation, there was a strong desire to show that England had received the Christian revelation independently of Rome, and this involved a rehabilitation of the Christian Britons whom Bede had despised; the Britons were already fashionable owing to the cult of Arthur and the accession of the Welsh Tudor dynasty. The idea of an autonomous origin for English Christianity was fostered by Elizabeth's Archbishop Parker (1504–75), a notable patron of anti-quarian studies. The supposed visit to England in the first century AD of Joseph of Arimathea, one of Christ's disciples, and possibly even of Christ himself, derived from a medieval legend (part of the Holy Grail cycle), was appealing, and still echoes in William Blake's *Jerusa-lem* (1804–20). Protestant history required significant reappraisals. Henry II was the hero, not the villain, of his conflict with Archbishop Becket, defender of clerical privileges. Henry IV was not merely the usurper of his cousin Richard II's throne, but was condemned as persecutor of the Lollards, the English proto-Protestants of the fif-teenth century, who were patriotically credited with a seminal role in the European Reformation.

True Christianity had triumphed in modern times. The Tudor dyn-asty, having reconciled the nation after the Wars of the Roses and put an end to the Lancastrian usurpation of the Crown, had produced in Henry VIII the great vindicator of the rights of an independent English Church against the spurious claims of the papacy. His daughter Mary's reign (1553–8), however, had seen not only the persecution of the true Protestant faith but also the dominance of foreigners, the Pope and Mary's husband, King Philip of Spain, in English affairs.

Elizabeth's accession was therefore a providential deliverance not only of Protestantism but of the nation, which the scattering of the Spanish Armada in 1588 by 'the winds of God' confirmed. Foxe compared Elizabeth to the emperor Constantine (born in England and the son of a British Christian queen, Helena) as liberator and protector of the Christian Church, and himself to the historian Eusebius. Religious truth and national independence were bound together, while England was the major Protestant power in Europe. It was obvious that the English were a Chosen People, and English history a providential story of national and religious independence. The Elizabethan chroniclers John Stow and Ralph Holinshed (drawn upon by Shakespeare) popularized this version of the nation's past and role, much assisted by cheap printings in convenient, readily portable octavo volumes. Stow's *Summary of English Chronicles* (1565) and Holinshed's *The Chronicles of England, Scotland and Ireland* (1577), which was influenced by Foxe, were highly successful publishing ventures.

Patriotic history was given solidity and depth by patriotic antiquarianism. Fine private libraries and manuscript collections were formed by Parker, Lord Burleigh, Elizabeth's chief minister, and Sir Robert Cotton, and these later came to form the bases of public, university and college libraries. The Elizabethan Society of Antiquaries, composed largely of lay gentry with, as was common, some legal training, was evidence of a cooperative spirit which made such holdings accessible by fellow scholars.

Another aspect of the patriotic antiquarian impulse was the appearance of the great topographical surveys of England, whose precursor was John Leland's *Itinerary* (not published until 1710). The land itself and the evidence it bore of its history became objects of loving attention and investigation. The two strands, Protestant providential history and topographical antiquarianism, were not wide apart. Leland's disciple John Bale (above, p. 309) became a radical Protestant and Foxe's mentor. The most fully achieved topographical work was William Camden's *Britannia* (1586). Other notable publications in this vein were William Lambarde's *Perambulation of Kent* (1574), the first known county history, and John Stow's remarkable *Survey of London* (1598–1603).

As a scholarly genre, topographical antiquarianism had had

European predecessors – particularly Florio Biondo, whose *Italia Illustrata* dated from the mid fifteenth century. A more immediate model was the map-making with in-depth scholarly historical surveys which is known as chorography, and whose sponsor was the great Flemish map-maker Ortelius, who encouraged Camden's work. After Camden, with the monasteries gone, the patrons of local history in England were inevitably the gentry, who had an overriding preoccupation with genealogies. But tenures and the names and histories of offices were of interest, and from this sprang the work on the history of tenures by the great antiquaries of early Stuart England John Selden and Sir Henry Spelman, which was also to throw light on the early history of Parliament.

Feudalism, as the possible critical break between Roman customs and those of the barbarian kingdoms, inassimilable to Roman civil law, was of peculiar interest in sixteenth-century France. Hotman wrote a treatise on feudal tenures (*De Feudis*, 1572). Such endeavours involved working back from more modern times, looking in particular at changes in legal terminology and trying to make out if they were superficial changes of nomenclature or pointed to real changes in practices. In his classic study of the beginnings of the historical study of law in seventeenth-century England, and its consequences, *The Ancient Constitution and the Feudal Law*, John Pocock showed half a century ago how, although the early-seventeenth-century English lawyers focused attention on legal precedent and documentation, their addiction to notions of an immemorial common law and an immemorial constitution inhibited proper historical investigation of the kind the French jurists had pursued so effectively. In France the legal situation was complex, with no single common law, with a distinction between the areas of customary law and those of written law (the *pays du droit écrit*), and with a larger presence of Roman law. This complexity had acted as a spur to sophisticated historical investigation to trace the respective strands, and even to the beginnings of a comparative approach to law. England, by contrast, was parochial and self-satisfied, and the legal reverence for the authority of the past was essentially *un*-historical: English law was what it had always been, a perennial and therefore in a sense timeless body of custom.

The breakthrough, in Pocock's highly persuasive account, was chiefly to be found in Sir Henry Spelman's work on the history of feudal tenures, beginning with his *Glossarium Archaeologicum* (1626). The feudal tenures revealed by this were distant not only from the institutions recognized in Roman law, but also from those of recent times. The multifaceted character of feudalism, to use the modern term, made it particularly well adapted to stand for the character of a whole type of society. Its central relationship was at once legal and social, military and economic, accompanied in its maturity by an ethic of loyalty and honour, all perpetuated through inheritance. It was at once a way of organizing military force, a social hierarchy, an ethos and what Marx would later call a mode of production.

Some of this was, of course, as yet more implicit than explicitly conceptualized. Spelman's method was, as usual, philological. In form, as was common for such antiquarian inquiries, his work was a dictionary or glossary of terms for usages, ranks, offices, customs, tenures and so on, arranged alphabetically like an encyclopedia. It firmly rejected Brutus and legendary Trojan origins. English law, Germanic and Anglo-Saxon in origin, and the feudal relationship were the product of an evolution, an adaptation of barbarian custom to new circumstances of settlement on the land and its hereditary transmission. The *feud* or *feudum* had been, in fact, the key to English law as a whole; Parliament, as the House of Lords, was originally the council made up of the king's tenants-in-chief, i.e. those with no feudal superior between themselves and the Crown, attending as one of their obligations to the feudal lord; the House of Commons, not mentioned in Magna Carta (1215), could not therefore have been in existence before the thirteenth century. Spelman also knew that the feudal relationship had declined, though he had no account of this. As Pocock puts it, 'The feudal revolution in English historiography was to impose on English history the division into pre-feudal, feudal and post-feudal periods which has ever since characterized it.' The great public crisis of Spelman's lifetime, the Civil War between Parliament and King, culminating in regicide, confirmed the conception of a post-feudal, modern period, for the regicide was not an act of the barons but of the House of Commons, which essentially arrogated sovereignty to itself.

The most general inferences from this for an overall conception of history were drawn by James Harrington in his *Oceana* (1656). Harrington was a republican, and he produced a kind of optimistically republican schematization of general history, whose most modern part rested on the view that the monarchy had been overthrown not by the feudal tenants-in-chief but by the independent gentry represented in the House of Commons, who were now the decisive power in the commonwealth. From the vantage this provided, Harrington produced a remarkable retrospective summary – not a narrative – of general European history, with Roman republicanism as its starting point, modern freeholder republicanism as its present state, and the feudal relations based on a distinctive form of land tenure, which Harrington called 'the Gothic balance' (between king and barons, with the people as a makeweight), as the pivot. The key to his history is the distribution of landed property, which is the basis of all power. The engrossing of land by the rich, unchecked by the attempts of the Gracchi to impose redistribution by agrarian laws, had destroyed the Roman republic in destroying the basis of its citizen armies. The emperors depended instead on a hired professional soldiery who became increasingly 'Gothicized'. In due course the military benefices distributed as the rewards for service became hereditary and conditional on future service; this was the essence of the feudal tenure of land and military vassalage and hence of the Gothic balance, with the people as subordinate tenants of feudal overlords.

Harrington treats the decline of the balance, initially in favour of the king, as recent, citing, from Bacon's *History*, Henry VII's legislation against private armies of retainers. Crucial also, in his account, however, is a diffusion of landownership among the gentry following the dissolution of the monasteries, creating thereby a powerful class of independent freeholders, outside the feudal hierarchy. The opportunity thus exists for a revival of a freeholder republic with a citizen militia. Pocock sums up Harrington's *Oceana* as 'a Machiavellian meditation on feudalism'. Of course Harrington's account of the decline of feudalism is not acceptable to modern scholars; his terminology differs from theirs, and his monocausal scheme is crude. Nonetheless it is possible to make out here the general characterization of the course of European history, and some of its causes, which, with modifications and fits of restlessness, historians have mainly lived by ever since. Though Harrington's scheme is less comprehensively ambitious than the earlier tentative moves towards secular universal history (including social and cultural history) among the French, it is more specific and fully achieved. The key had initially been that of custom, and subsequently the conception of feudal tenure as an institution which had had a beginning and an end, even if both, and particularly the latter, were still obscure. Harrington provided an overview firmly based on what the eighteenth century would freely call 'the state of society', the most significant changes in which – not the sequence of the Four Empires – would be the successive turning points of the historical story.

20

Clarendon's *History of the Rebellion*: The Wilfulness of Particular Men

The exaltation of the Tudor monarchy and the cult of Queen Elizabeth among the chroniclers during her reign is so marked that the subject taken by England's greatest seventeenth-century historian, Edward Hyde, earl of Clarendon (1609–74), 'the Great Rebellion', as he called it, has almost the appearance of a paradox. Yet there is a continuity of a kind. Though the breakdown of relations between King and Parliament from the 1620s to the 1640s was fed by fiscal and constitutional tensions, a powerful underlying as well as often overt theme in it was the idea of an 'incomplete' religious revolution. Elizabethan historiography's incorporation of the idea of the English as a Chosen People was not a piece of complacency: it was implicitly a call to action, to the fulfilment of an exacting, divinely imposed role. Despite their discontent with the compromises of the Elizabethan church establishment, the more extreme Protestants, who were beginning to be called Puritans, had never turned against the Queen herself, whom they saw as their deliverer from Catholic persecution. The continuing fear of a Catholic succession would alone have held disloyalty in check. But radical Protestant aspirations, combined with what was seen as defence of the historic privileges of Parliament, became importunate in the reign of Charles I (1625–49). It was the breakdown of relations, the formation of two opposed sides in Parliament, and the ensuing civil war that provided Clarendon, who had been intimately involved, with the subject of his history.

Clarendon's history provided the bedrock for all subsequent accounts of the English revolution. *The History of the Rebellion and Civil Wars in England* was begun in the thick of the events described, in the 1640s, with the encouragement and assistance of King Charles, and clearly with the advantage of many eyewitness accounts. Clarendon, whom until his ennoblement after the Restoration we should think of as Edward Hyde, was highly advantageously placed, first as a leading member of the Long Parliament and later as a member of the King's Privy Council and one of his chief advisers. The book was completed, as many ancient histories had been, by the author as an elder statesman in exile, having fallen from power as Charles II's Chancellor in 1667. He died in France in 1674, but the *History* was not published until the beginning of the eighteenth century, when it became an immense success and probably the only work of history whose publication financed the erection of a great building, the Clarendon Building in Oxford.

Clarendon's history both is and is not a work in the classical mould of historiography; it is certainly not in the later Enlightenment one. Some of it was originally written in the form of an autobiography, and it retains some of the informality of a memoir, though it aspires to be comprehensive and to treat of events that Clarendon knew of only from a distance as well as those to which he was privy. It is undeniably from the latter, however, that the history chiefly derives its striking vitality. His manner is noticeably more relaxed and less stately than, say, Hume's in his history of the period published half a century later. Hume, for example, half apologizes for retailing from Clarendon some absurd behaviour of James I as 'though minute . . . not undeserving of a place in history' (p. 195). Clarendon himself clearly felt no need for justification. His work is, of course, focused on public events, as an attempt to understand a catastrophe. It fastens on the characters and behaviour of the public men the author had known – including the King – diagnosing the weaknesses, misjudgements, ambitions and anxieties which had led to the catastrophe, in the classical and humanist manner. Clarendon frequently weighs up alternatives and discusses how things had been allowed to go wrong, and is free with personal reminiscence. Though he sometimes uses the first person and sometimes 'Hyde', his references to himself, though they do not strike the reader as vain or obsessively self-justificatory, have none of the chilly austerity that Thucydides, for example, preserves towards his own role in events.

Clarendon's history is naturally and unashamedly partisan: he writes to judge as well as to recount. But his was the partisanship of a moderate who above all sought reconciliation, first in Parliament and later during the war. He had friends – and enemies – on both sides, and he is measured, not passionate, in his judgements. It was the King who had suggested the project to him, and it was intended as a vindication of most, though not all, of Charles's actions. Clarendon quotes and comments on many of the documents produced by the two sides in the early 1640s, some of which he had drafted for the King: this is, frankly, more than the general reader requires. Clarendon's view of events is naturally to some extent circumscribed after the outbreak of the war. He knows the royalist side better than the parliamentarian, and the campaigns in the south, from his residence in Oxford, better than those in the north. He is also, of course, conditioned by his own cast of mind, which strikes the reader as honourable, shrewd, conciliatory where possible, but also, as one would expect in an early-seventeenth-century parliamentarian, legalistic. He had originally been himself a leader among the parliamentary opposition, but his early associates, notably Pym and Hampden, came to take up positions he regarded as untenably extreme. He did not so much change sides as retain his original principles while events moved on around him, and as the parliamentary leadership became more radical and innovatory this inevitably propelled him into becoming spokesman for the King; it is possible that, after the disasters of the later 1640s, he wrote the history, with hindsight, as more of a royalist than he had been even after he entered the King's service. He was prejudiced against the Scots, disliking their Presbyterian obsessions and their treatment of both Charles I and his son when they were in their power. After having originally taken the parliamentary view of the need to curb the royal prerogative and recognized the parliamentary radicals' fears for their own safety and their need to ensure it, Clarendon came to regard the hard core of the parliamentarians – 'the violent party', led by Pym – as having a long-term plan to subvert the existing constitution.

His general view of events was far from that of Hume later, though neither sympathized with Puritanism or arbitrary rule. Clarendon's was the outlook of a political tactician who saw problems, in so far as he did not view them legalistically, as a matter of getting the right men in the right jobs, and who attributed very wide consequences to the King's frequent failure to do so and to the misguided advice he too often received and acted on in consequence, as well as the harm done by the excluded who were made unnecessarily disaffected. A prime case of the latter was, according to Clarendon, the treatment of the Earl of Essex, who, having been dismissed from the Privy Council, remained in London when the King moved his court to Oxford (1642) and became general of the parliamentary armies. He could, in Clarendon's view, have been won over, with incalculable consequences. If he had been retained in office 'he would never have been prevailed with to have taken command of that army which was afterwards raised against the King's . . . And there can be little doubt in any man who knew well the nature and temper of that time, that it had been utterly impossible for the two Houses of Parliament to have raised an army then if the Earl of Essex had not consented to be general of that army' (V.33). Clarendon may have been over-optimistic, but he had the invaluable advantage over later historians like Hume, writing consciously from a wider perspective, of remembering a time when nothing seemed inevitable.

Clarendon's history, following the unfolding of events, falls in fact though not formally into three sections: the approach to war, the war itself, and the years of exile after the royalist defeat. Initially he was in the thick of the parliamentary debates, though increasingly alienated from the radicals, participating in negotiations with the Court and later within the Privy Council, and taking a leading part in the war of words, of declarations, remonstrances and rebuttals. After the final rupture and the outbreak of war, he was in the royal capital of Oxford, as a member of the Council and adviser to the King. He was influential, but necessarily a spectator of the war itself, though a well-informed one. His accounts of the military operations are free from convention or attempts at the picturesque. They are down to earth, with an awareness, obviously derived from participants, of the misunderstandings and of plans gone awry in the fog of war. Above all, he dwells on the importance of logistics and the problem of discipline, on pay and supply, and on ordnance, weapons and ammunition and the value of capturing them. He meticulously notes and sometimes laments the deaths in action of prominent nobles and gentry. This was a classical and chivalric convention, but in a war in which recruitment and discipline depended so much on personal and local status and support it was also a highly practical matter. It was, as Clarendon notes, not so in the parliamentary army: 'The officers of the enemy's side were never talked of, being for the most part of no better families than their common soldiers' (VIII.160).

Clarendon was eager throughout the war for any possibility of reconciliation. One moment in particular beckoned; it was delusive, but for a short while it gave Clarendon great personal prominence and the role to which he was suited – conducting a war of words, once again face to face and with the possibility of backstairs negotiation and the cultivation of personal relations with opponents. This was the Uxbridge Conference, held with a view to drawing up possible articles of peace, in February 1645. Clarendon was one of the King's commissioners there, and he describes the events of the next three weeks with great particularity, over thirty-five pages (VIII.215–50). Though he does the arguments full justice, his account of the negotiations also evokes a solid world, of carefully arranged chairs and meeting rooms, and men from both sides huddled around the fire on cold nights reviving old companionships. According to Clarendon, the parliamentary commissioners were made wary by the presence of their allies the Scots, which made them fearful to be seen alone with the royalists, 'their old friends whom they loved better than their new'. The three main subjects of contention, to each of which was allotted a certain number of days, were religion, the control of the militia, and the settlement of the Irish rebellion. In discussing the religious issues – essentially the demand for the adoption of a Presbyterian form of church government – the royal commissioners exploited the divisions among their opponents and the ambiguities in key terms. The Scottish Earl of Lauderdale, being put up to explain, made a hash of it, and the royalists demanded a clarification in writing, which 'put the Scots' commissioners in great passion; for all the English sat still without speaking a word, as if they were not concerned. Various divines on each side were brought in to argue the points.'

Days were thus consumed fruitlessly, and Clarendon's hostility to the Scots is apparent. One example of relaxed conversation out of the session is introduced by Clarendon as 'a pleasant accident'.

The commissioners of both sides, either before their sitting or after their rising, entertaining themselves together by the fire-side, as they sometimes did, it being extremely cold, in general and casual discourses, one of the King's commissioners asking one of the other, with whom he had familiarity, in a low voice, why there was not any mention of the Lord's Prayer, the Creed, or the Ten Commandments [in Parliament's religious proposals], (as indeed there is not), the Earl of Pembroke, overhearing the discourse, answered aloud, and with his usual passion, that he and many others were very sorry that they had been left out; that the putting them in had taken up many hours' debate in the House of Commons, and that at last the leaving them out had been carried by eight or nine voices ... Which made many smile, to hear that the Lord's Prayer, the Creed and the Ten Commandments had been put to the question, and rejected ... (VIII.232)

The other two topics were as intractable, control of the militia touching the parliamentarians' fears for their own safety after a treaty, and the King's failure to suppress the Irish rebellion being as much an embarrassment to his side as Presbyterianism to the English parliamentarians. Privately, relations warmed, and Clarendon was able to note the cracks appearing between the parliamentary peers, in particular, and the more radical members of the Commons and the army. But he says he placed no hopes in the former, for the earls of Pembroke and Salisbury feared the latter more than they hated them, and, though they would rather have seen the radicals destroyed than the King, 'they had rather the King and his posterity should be destroyed than that Wilton should be taken from the one of them or Hatfield [their estates] from the other; the preservation of both of which from any danger they both believed to be the highest point of prudence and politic circumspection' (VIII.245). The conference collapsed without outcome. It had sat regularly, Clarendon tells, till one or two in the morning, apart from the preparing of papers, 'so that if the treaty had continued longer it is very probable many of the commissioners would have fallen sick for want of sleep'.

From 1645 onward Clarendon was condemned by the parliamentary victory to a wandering life in the entourage of the Prince of Wales, in which his chief endeavour was to prevent the latter from compromising himself in the eyes of English opinion by association with the Catholic and Francophile inclinations of his mother, the Queen. Chiefly, throughout the years of Charles II's exile, Clarendon says he counselled doing nothing but wait and endure, which was surely the correct tactic. It is not surprising that he saw the Restoration in 1660 as an act of Providence. Meanwhile, Clarendon's account, from a distance, of the indignities to which Charles I was subjected, though second-hand, has a pathos which clearly derived from the personal attachment Clarendon had formed to him. There is the description of his physical appearance, for example, which Hume took from him: grey, with his hair uncut and his clothes old, 'so that his aspect and appearance was very different from what it had used to be', though he was unexpectedly cheerful (XI.157). Clarendon refuses to dwell on the King's last hours and his execution, on the grounds that they are both too distressing and too well known.

The main interlude in his account of the years of exile is the familiar story of Charles II's escape after the battle of Worcester. Second-hand but clearly from the best possible source – the King himself – it is highly circumstantial, taking twenty-two pages of text (XII.84–106). Clarendon takes an understandable pleasure in the 'concurrence of good nature, charity, and generosity, in persons of the meanest and lowest extraction and condition' who assisted the King, not knowing him but knowing they could get a reward for revealing the fugitive. He also mentions the King's recounting 'many particulars of the barbarous treatment' he had received in Scotland, where he had been subjected to sermons and obliged to sign the Presbyterian Covenant.

Inevitably, in general the years of exile and even the period of the Civil War do not have quite the day-to-day dramatic interest of the early years in the Long Parliament, when Clarendon, as a leading parliamentarian and later adviser to the King, was striving to avert the breach which led to war, and it is to these that one wants to turn in conclusion to take the measure of the quality and interest of the *History*. Clarendon's accounts of the sessions and the private conversations are extraordinarily vivid simply because of the way he situates his narrative, among the often tired, anxious, bewildered Members of Parliament, meeting sometimes heatedly in overcrowded, noisy, candlelit rooms. In the debate in 1641 on the proposed abolition of episcopacy it was so late every day before the House was resumed, (the Speaker commonly leaving the chair about nine of the clock, and never resuming it till four in the afternoon), that it was very thin; they only who prosecuted the bill with impatience remaining in the House, and others who abhorred it, growing weary of so tiresome an attendance, left the House at dinner-time, and afterwards followed their pleasures: so that the Lord Falkland was wont to say that they who hated bishops hated them worse than the devil, and that they who loved them did not love them so well as their dinner. (III.241)

The public hubbub is interspersed with private confidences, informal attempts at persuasion, and the judgements of men's qualities and interests – the everyday currency of parliamentary life in a period of extraordinary tension and significance. In recording debates, Clarendon usually summarizes, with injections of verbatim quotation of what was presumably particularly memorable. Some of Clarendon's reports of private conversations passed into political folklore and have been quoted by generations of historians. At the time of the impeachment of the Earl of Strafford, the King's formidable lieutenant in Ireland,

Mr Hyde going to a place called Pickadilly, (which was a fair house for entertainment and gaming, and handsome gravel walks with shade, and where were an upper and lower bowling-green, whither very many of the nobility and gentry of the best quality resorted, both for exercise and conversation) he was accosted by the Earl of Bedford, according to whom the King would make no difficulty if Strafford could be guaranteed his life. (I.161)

The obstacle was the Earl of Essex, to whom Bedford takes Hyde to try to persuade him to be less rigid. Essex is immovable, fearing that Strafford, pardoned, might yet be a danger to them all. 'He shook his head, and avowed "Stone-dead hath no fellow"' (I.164).

A particularly bitter battle was the debate on the Grand Remonstrance, the iteration of parliamentary grievances whose passage in November 1641 Clarendon saw as a decisive blow to prospects of conciliation:

The debate being entered on about nine of the clock in the morning, it continued all that day; and candles being called for when it grew dark (neither side being very desirous to adjourn it until the next day; though it was evident very many withdrew themselves out of pure faintness, and disability to attend the conclusion), the debate continued till after it was twelve of the clock, with much passion.

The Remonstrance was carried by just nine votes. As they at last emerged from the House, Oliver Cromwell, '(who at that time was little taken notice of)', whispered in the ear of Lord Falkland 'that if the Remonstrance had been rejected he would have sold all he had the next morning, and never have seen England more'. So near, sighs Clarendon, 'was the poor kingdom at that time to its deliverance!' (IV.52).

With the final rupture, with some Members, including Hyde, following the King to what was to be his wartime capital in Oxford, the question of the allegiances of the members of the Privy Council also became an important issue. This gives Clarendon the chance for a number of character studies, in which he has a conscious virtuosity. His prose style is sometimes prolix and syntactically involved, especially when deploying an argument. It is the manner of an orator rather than a writer – not in the sense of being rhetorically ornate or impassioned, but in obviously having been written with the assumption that punctuation is a matter for the voice, sometimes injected with a telltale 'so I say that' in the midst of a long sequence of clauses, to be followed by yet more. But the portraits of public men, measured and judicious though they often are, are also sometimes tartly economical and epigrammatic in a fashion that recalls Tacitus and is almost certainly meant to. Tacitus is the ancient historian most frequently quoted, through Clarendon also cites Livy, Plutarch and Thucydides. Such depictions, not only in the time-honoured fashion as obituaries, are scattered through the *History*.

Among the most memorable is that of the Earl of Arundel, made general of the army designed to coerce the Scots. He 'was thought to be made choice of only for his negative qualities: he did not love the Scots; he did not love the Puritans; which good qualities were alloyed by another negative; he did not love nobody else' (II.25). The disreputable Colonel (later Lord) Goring was so good at dissimulation 'that men were not ordinarily ashamed, or out of countenance, with being deceived but twice by him' (VII.69). Of General Monck, the main author of the Restoration, Clarendon writes that 'it is glory enough to his memory, that he was instrumental in bringing those mighty things to pass, which he had neither wisdom to foresee, nor courage to attempt, nor understanding to contrive' (XVI.115). Sir Arthur Aston, the governor of Oxford, preferred to the post by the Queen, 'had the fortune to be very much esteemed where he was not known, and very much detested where he was' (VIII.121). In the middle of a longish appraisal of the Earl of Northumberland we have, 'If he had thought the King as much above him as he thought himself above other considerable men, he would have been a good subject' (VI.398).

Other portraits need to be taken at nearer full length, like the characterization of the Earl of Warwick, commander of the fleet for Parliament:

He was a man of pleasant and companionable wit and conversation, of an universal jollity, and such licence in his words and actions that a man of less virtue could not be found out: so that a man might reasonably have believed that a man so qualified would not have been able to have contributed so much to the overthrow of a nation and kingdom. But with all these faults he had great authority and credit with that people who in the beginning of the troubles, did all the mischieve; and by opening his doors and making his house the rendezvous of all the silenced ministers [of religion] in the time when there was authority to silence them, and spending a good part of his estate, of which he was very prodigal, upon them, and by being present with them at their devotions, and making himself merry with them, and at them, which they dispensed with [excused], he became the head of that party, and got the style of *a godly man*. (VI.404)

The largest character study is the obituary for Clarendon's friend Lord Falkland, a casualty of the war (1643), who was

of that inimitable sweetness and delight in conversation, of so flowing and obliging a humanity and goodness to mankind, and of that primitive sim-plicity and integrity of life, that if there were no other brand upon their odious and accursed civil war than that single loss, it must be the most infamous and execrable to all posterity. (VII.217)

More interesting because more equivocal is Clarendon's estimate of the parliamentary leader John Hampden, killed in the same battle (Chalgrove):

He was of that rare affability and temper in debate, and of that seeming humility of judgement, as if he brought no opinions with him, but a desire of information and instruction; yet he had so subtle a way of interrogating, and under the notion of doubts insinuating his objections, that he left his opinions with those from whom he pretended to learn and receive them. (VII.83)

Clarendon came to attribute to him deep designs of subversion.

Clarendon had a clear sense of the ways in which men's differing qualities made them valuable in different ways. The Earl of Pembroke, for example, 'had a choleric office [Lord Chamberlain], which entitled him to the exercise of some rudenesses, and the good order of the Court had some dependence upon his incivilities' (VII.399). It was a mistake, as the impatient and impolitic Prince Rupert was apt to do, to estimate a body like the Privy Council from the infirmities of its individual members – 'the heaviness of this man, the levity of that, the weakness and simplicity of a third' – for 'all great enterprises and designs that are to be executed have many parts, even in the projection, fit for the survey and disquisition of several faculties and abilities, and equally for the decision of sharper and more phlegmatic understandings' (VII.279–81).

In the fashion that was to become virtually universal until the nineteenth century, Clarendon saw Cromwell as a deep-designing hypocrite, moved always by the lust for power; but even his portrait is not wholly unfavourable. He was 'not a man of blood', and had some virtues. He was also a man of immense ability and power of will, who made all Europe fear him; 'he will be looked upon by posterity as a brave bad man' (XV.147–56). It was, for Clarendon, important to discriminate, lest, contemplating the wreck of the King's fortunes, one be led 'to believe that a universal corruption of the hearts of the whole nation had brought forth these lamentable effects; which proceeded only from the folly and the frowardness, from the weakness and the wilfulness, the pride and the passion, of particular persons' (IX.1). Clarendon had none of the sophisticated general concepts of historical analysis that we find in Hume and Robertson a century later. For him it was axiomatic that, under Providence, the rebellion was made by individual men, not all of them even wicked. He is worth listening to, because he knew them.

Philosophic History

Hume: Enthusiasm and Regicide

Crucial to the emergence of the Enlightenment genre of the history of customs, manners and opinion was what was coming to be seen as an indisputable fact of European history: 'the progress of society'. The growth of commerce and the end of the 'feudal anarchy', the 'revival of learning and the surpassing of the ancients' in the discovery of the New World and the printing press and the improvements in the art of war (something that Guicciardini had been one of the first to note) all contributed to this perception. To this came to be added a conception of the improvement of 'manners' over the previous two centuries, from the rough, pedantic, fiercely intolerant religious zeal and polemics of the time of the Reformation to the eighteenth-century cultivation of a polite, tolerant sociability as the mark of a refined society which was mild, humane and rational.

The ghost at the feast of reason and self-congratulation, in England at least, was the seventeenth-century revolution, the brief but unforgotten reign of the sectaries under the general characterization of 'enthusiasm', and the menace of an egalitarian republicanism. It had apparently been exorcized, but events from the late eighteenth century onward could sometimes give it the appearance of a precedent as well as a warning. Revolution, in relation to progress, came to play something like the role earlier played by luxury and enervation in the classical and civic humanist paradigm: that of a nemesis. 'The great cause of revolutions', Macaulay told the House of Commons in the debates before the first Reform Act in 1832, 'is this, that while nations move onwards, constitutions stand still.' Marx was to say much the same, though from a revolutionary stance, and Hume would say something similar (below, p. 335) of the government of Charles I. So salient was the revolutionary experience to become, and the fear and hope of it, that we have to attend to how historians rose to the challenge this represented to their comprehension and their art.

David Hume is now famous as a philosopher; as a historian he is scarcely known. In the eighteenth and nineteenth centuries it was the reverse. Then he was primarily the author of a monumental, authoritative, though much contested six-volume *History of England* (1754–62). Hume was one of the key figures of the Scottish Enlightenment, and his history is a characteristic product of it, applying to a long tract of political, constitutional and social history some of its most basic ideas: the association of fundamental changes in manners and opinion with the decline of feudalism and the growth of commerce, and a consideration of the influence of religion on social and political life. William Robertson, his contemporary, applied these to the safer ground of sixteenth-century Europe, though his location of John Knox and the Scottish Reformers in a rude age whose characteristics they shared was not without polemical point. But Hume, in taking up the seventeenth century in England as his initial challenge (it was a peculiarity of his history that it was written and published backwards in terms of historical chronology), was confronting some of the most contentious issues in modern English political life. The political labels 'Whig' and 'Tory' derived from the two great factions of the seventeenth century, and even the more sophisticated modern labels 'Court' and 'Country' paralleled to a significant extent the seventeenth-century divisions. Hume's history of the seventeenth-century revolution, the first part of his English history, was published in 1754. In deference to James VI of Scotland's accession to the English throne in 1601 as James I, it was entitled *The History of Great Britain, Containing the Reigns of James I and Charles I*. For three-quarters of a century it came to dominate the field, though it was one of many histories of the English revolution, published from all points on the political spectrum, during that period. G. O. Trevelyan's life of Macaulay shows the latter clearly gratified as well as amused to find Hume's *History* in a bookseller's window, a century after its publication, labelled 'valuable as an introduction to Macaulay'.

Hume's offences to contemporaries' pieties were several, but the chief was his refusal to accept the Whig notion of an enduring 'ancient constitution' subverted by the Stuarts. To him, English constitutional precedents, by the early seventeenth century, were chaotically contradictory, reflecting the shifting balance between Crown and nobility over the preceding centuries: the constitution was 'unintelligible' (p. 111). The early Stuarts could find precedents for most if not all of what they did, and the Tudors had ruled much more absolutely while avoiding theoretical claims. Essentially it was the parliamentary leaders in the 1640s who became the innovators, and there was for Hume in principle nothing wrong with that: the country needed a 'regular system of liberty', which eventually became established. But, though Hume was prepared to welcome the outcome, he offended the more radical Whigs by his obvious distaste rather than admiration for most of the leading parliamentarians, who were unpolished and fanatical. Hume's terms for seventeenth-century English Puritanism and Scottish Presbyterianism were uncompromising. In them 'the genius of fanaticism displayed itself in its full extent', and their inflamed imaginations poured themselves out 'in wild, unpremeditated addresses to the Divinity' (p. 72). Abuse of the seventeenth-century sectaries was common enough in eighteenth-century Britain, but Hume's own notorious religious scepticism, which had prevented him from obtaining, like Robertson, an Edinburgh or Glasgow academic chair, was offensive to many. With so much weighted against it, the dominance exerted by Hume's *History* and its publishing success – it made him rich – are striking.

With some exceptions we shall come to, it is not picturesque: its power is intellectual, in the quality of the reflection and the cogency of the narrative. For, despite the disquisitions with which it is interspersed – Adam Smith, a traditionalist in such matters, objected to the obstruction of the linear narrative flow – it is not an Enlightenment sociological essay but a detailed and full-bodied history, classical in its sense of decorum and annalistic in its arrangement. The convention of invented speeches was falling into disrepute, and Hume prefers to summarize, often representing the opinions of many rather than an individual. Otherwise, however, despite the disquisitions – the longest of which, on changes in society, was in subsequent editions relegated to an appendix – Hume's history is recognizably within a classical tradition of dealing with public affairs and public men. Of course the eighteenth-century genres of the essay on customs and the history of civil society form part of the intellectual inspiration.

One of the most controversial features of Hume's *History* seems at first sight at odds with the sociological concerns of the Enlightenment and Hume's habitually detached and ironic authorial stance. It is the extent of the sympathy accorded to the victims, history's prominent losers – above all, of course, Charles I. There is in fact a conscious exploitation of the pathetic, the 'sentimental' (a technical, rather than a pejorative, term), in the description of the King's captivity, trial and execution.

It is confessed that the King's behaviour, during this last period of his life, does great honour to his memory; and that in all appearances before his judges, he never forgot his part, either as a prince or as a man. Firm and intrepid, he maintained, in each reply, the utmost perspicuity and justness, both of thought and expression: Mild and equable, he rose into no passion at that unusual authority which was assumed over him. His soul, without effort or affectation, seemed only to remain in the situation familiar to it, and to look down with contempt on all the efforts of human malice and iniquity. (p. 678)

The cultivation of sentiment in eighteenth-century historical writing was taken up both by Hume and by his contemporary Robertson, notably in their treatments of the execution of Mary, Queen of Scots. (On this, see Phillips, *Society and Sentiment*.) The pathos of Hume's account of Charles's end was often seen as a proof of Hume's 'Toryism'. Hume was not a Tory or a Jacobite, but he did sit loosely to traditional Whig pieties, and in his essays he revealed a position not common in eighteenth-century Britain. He had lived in France, and he set out a sharp distinction, based not only on the study of the ancient republics but also on the position of a subject of the absolute French monarchy, between public and private liberty. The antique republics had not understood private liberty at all, but, given an ordered monarchy, ruling through the law, it was not incompatible with the absence of public liberty. The life and interests of the individual could be as secure as under a representative system. Indeed,

Hume, in Britain, feared the prospect of anarchy, as a result of unrestrained factionalism, more than absolute monarchy; he described the latter as the 'easiest death, the true euthanasia of the British Constitution'; he was predictably alarmed by the riots on behalf of the radical John Wilkes at the beginning of the reign of George III.

But the issue with 'sentimental' history is not a matter of party labels or liberty or absolutism. One of the objects of Hume's *History* was to abate the violent spirit of faction by the play of an enlightened reason over the contentious recent past. Sentimentalism, in that context, was not partisan but eirenic. Sentiment as an item in the historian's repertoire developed in relation to manifestations of the later-eighteenth-century exploration of sensibility generally, including an increasing value attached to immediacy of representation and empathy in historical narrative. (On this see Phillips's perceptive discussion in *Society and Sentiment*.) Such exercises in empathy and concrete immediacy in historiography have more usually been placed in the nineteenth century (where they sometimes gave a pretext for denigrating the eighteenth for lacking them). Their earlier appearance was related not only to the cult of sensibility, but to attempts to encourage a wider readership for history, notably among women, of which Hume was certainly aware. Pathetic effects are not incongruous with the enlightened detachment to which Hume also aspires, but are actually in a sense part of it. It is *because* Charles is to be seen not as a would-be despot seeking to subvert an established and inherited constitution but as a victim of historical changes, in manners, opinion and the balance of power and property, which he cannot understand or adjust to, that it is appropriate for the enlightened historian, who can understand them, to 'shed a generous tear' for him.

This, indeed, though here turned to purposes of pathos, is the central message of Hume's early Stuart history. Charles could not be expected to have the long perspective, requiring hindsight and the appropriate conceptual equipment, of the philosophic historian. He was not, Hume says, 'endowed with that masterly genius, which might enable him to perceive, in their infancy, the changes that arose in national manners, and know how to accommodate his conduct to them' (p. 381). He was a man lost between two worlds and two roles: 'Had he been born an absolute prince, his humanity and good sense had rendered his reign happy and his memory precious: had the limitations on prerogative been, in his time, quite fixed and ascertained, his integrity had made him regard, as sacred, the boundaries of the constitution' (p. 684). His fatal flaw, humanly venial but politically disastrous, was a failure to read the signs of the times.

What those signs were is set out by Hume in a number of disquisitions, including a whole chapter (VI), subsequently made into an appendix, which strongly anticipates the famous Chapter III on 'social' history in Macaulay's *History*, which aroused criticism from the fastidious for the triumphalism of its insistent contrasts of 'then' and 'now'. Hume's chapter also uses this device, though without the fanfare for modernity. It is not perfunctory, and, exceptionally, it incorporates some statistics. But the central contention is twofold: Hume, like Robertson, sees a new spirit of liberty and independence of thought developing from the sixteenth century especially in association with the rise of commerce (he is explicit about why the greater towns favoured the parliamentary side). And like Harrington and the 'Country Party' polemicists of the earlier eighteenth century, particularly Bolingbroke, he sees power passing from the Lords to the Commons as feudalism ends and landed property is diffused:

The first rise of commerce and the arts had contributed, in preceding reigns, to scatter those immense fortunes of the barons, which rendered them so formidable to both king and people. The farther progress of these advantages began, during this reign, to ruin the small proprietors of land, and, by both events, the gentry, or that rank which composed the house of commons, enlarged their power and authority. The early improvements in luxury were seized by the greater nobles, whose fortunes, placing them above frugality or even calculation, were soon dissipated in expensive pleasures.

The Commons was discovering its power, assisted by the unwisdom of the first two Stuart monarchs in making a theoretical issue of their prerogatives. For Hume, all authority rested ultimately not on right but on opinion, which it was therefore essential to manage. The chief support of established authority was habit and tradition. It was fatal to encourage a disputatious inclination on the part of subjects by theoretical assertions, in religious or political matters.

The fiscal situation, too, favoured Parliament. The Crown was still expected to live on its traditional revenues, though expenses were increasing. Parliament was unable to grasp this, but was very ready to try to take advantage of the King's financial difficulties to exact concessions. Charles's government was driven to resort either to the revival of archaic sources of revenue or to the exploitation of new ones, both of which were bitterly resented. In one respect James and Charles were simply unfortunate, though they unwisely fanned the flames rather than seeking to dampen them. The spirit of religious fanaticism, stemming from the Reformation, had reached a high point. Hume drew on a concept which he had worked out in a well-known essay ('Of Superstition and Enthusiasm'). His name for it – not original, but turned from a pejorative term into a theoretical category – was 'Enthusiasm'. Enthusiasm could arise at any time, being essentially random (rather like Max Weber's 'charisma'), defying all calculations of prudence and considerations of individual interests: 'The fanatical spirit, let loose, confounded all regards to ease, safety, interest, and dissolved every moral and civil obligation' (p. 502). For Hume the opposite of Enthusiasm in the dynamics of religious belief was Superstition. Superstition was irrational also, but arose from the impulse to propitiate and to curry favour. It was therefore servile, and a support of religious and civil establishments; its historical embodiment was Catholicism. But Enthusiasm, filled with antinomian intimations of unique, individual possession by the Spirit, was bold, aggressive, zealous and destructive; it was Puritanism which, with its remembrances of the terrible fanaticism of the seventeenth-century sectaries, could still bring a shiver of anxiety to the Age of Reason. It was encouraging to stress the historical distance between seventeenth-century fanaticism and what Hume called 'the mildness and humanity of modern manners' (p. 98), but the historical examples were still admonitory. James I, according to Hume, was not wrong to see fanaticism as a threat to civil as well as religious authority, but was misguided in challenging it directly.

Hume's own accounts frequently resort to irony – for example on the zeal of the Scots for transplanting abroad their system of church government: 'Never did refined Athens so exult in diffusing the sciences and liberal arts over a savage world ... as the Scotch now rejoiced, in communicating their barbarous zeal and theological fervour, to the neighbouring nations' (p. 449). Hume's distaste was not reduced by his recognition that, in a manner to which the eighteenth century was becoming accustomed, Enthusiasm's historical function was something other than its intrinsic nature. Without the pernicious 'epidemical frenzy' (p. 446), the defence of parliamentary freedoms could not have been sustained and the eventual 'regular system of liberty' (p. 283) would have been aborted. The more 'natural' outcome of the decline of the power of the feudal baronage, seen on the Continent as the rise of monarchical absolutism, would have been consummated. In the circumstances of the time, only a pious fanaticism, regardless of consequences, could have braced men to the necessary hazards and sacrifices to resist this. Behind 'that singular and happy government, which at present we enjoy' (p. 204) lay a dark and fierce irrationality. In the case of the Scots, Hume is particularly explicit on the moral disjunction between the cause and the outcome: 'The Scotch nation were first seized with that frenzy of reformation, which was so pernicious during the time, and which has since proved so salutary in the consequences' (p. 145). Historical causation is another thing than moral quality, and the connection between virtue and liberty is heavily qualified. It was a lesson which, applied by Hume to the Reformation and the political crisis of the seventeenth century, was, as we shall see, applied by his younger contemporary Gibbon to the history of Christianity as such and to the long-term relations of Barbarism and Civilization.

Hume's distaste for 'Enthusiasm' was common in his century, and he expressed it with particular force. In the next century it was to become more muted, as the religious zealotry of the seventeenth century receded further into the past, and as a religious revival brought it greater respect. But Hume's other main preoccupation in relation to the English revolution, the long-term movement of society, was to remain one of the major themes of the history which was to be hailed as the great successor to and replacement for it, Macaulay's *History of England*.

Robertson: 'The State of Society' and the Idea of Europe

'The state of society' was to be a key conception for the most important historical writing of the eighteenth century. There were other innovations too. Some of these are well exemplified by *The History of the Reign of the Emperor Charles V* (1769) by William Robertson (1721–93), which has a claim to be regarded as the first modern work of history. Of course the criteria of modernity are multiple; others would point to different examples, but the claim is defensible.

Modernity is in fact an idea relevant to Robertson's book, in a double sense: the book is about it – about, that is, the emergence of 'modern' Europe in the sixteenth century – and it could not have been written but for other kinds of modernity. In Robertson's view, modernity was a secular cosmopolitanism, both cultural and political (in the latter sense expressed as the idea of 'the balance of power'), which in the sixteenth century was making Europe modern and also making it, for the same reasons, an entity whose history could be written. But Robertson's book is also cosmopolitan – that is, European – not only in its viewpoint but in its genesis and its intention. He had made his name with a successful *History of Scotland*, ten years earlier. *Charles V* was a deliberate bid for wider, in fact for European-wide, attention in the literary market; Robertson arranged for its translation into French as soon as it was published.

It is difficult to think of a precedent for Robertson's book. Hitherto historians had been drawn chiefly to write the histories of their own nations or cities, which needs no special explanation, or to narratives of events in which they had been personally involved or of which they could at least claim some special knowledge and interest. Sarpi's history of the Council of Trent might be claimed as an exception, but he was nevertheless investigating the most significant recent episode in the history of the Church to whose clergy he belonged. Hume's *History of England*, which Robertson considered emulating, before he thought better of it, is not really an exception to this, despite Hume's Scottish perspective. But Robertson had nothing at all to draw him to write of Charles V's empire – nothing, that is, except its centrality to early modern Europe, and the intrinsic interest and importance of the latter as a historical period (which is how Robertson saw it). Robertson's book in fact ranges considerably wider than even the extensive territories of Charles's empire, to encompass the whole history of Europe, and it was the possibility of doing this that made him choose his focal point.

This free range of choice of subject was new, and made possible only by the deluge from the printing presses over the previous two hundred years, including the printing of historical documents. Robertson maintained a network of foreign correspondents in writing his books, notably in Spain, and he lists them in the preface to his subsequent *History of America* (1777), for which he adopted the highly modern expedient of a questionnaire. Even for the *History of Scotland* he lists his main debts in his preface, as well as identifying important sources in appendices, as a modern scholar would characteristically do. Travel was not yet normally part of a historian's working practice: Gibbon, for example, never returned to Rome after his first, fateful, visit. Robertson never travelled on the Continent, but libraries, the book trade and helpful correspondents made it possible for him to write a detailed history of Charles V's empire from Edinburgh, where he was a minister of the Church of Scotland and for thirty years principal of Edinburgh University. There was nothing superficial about his way of writing history: he was a scholar as well as a literary historian.

But it was possible to write for the market, and Robertson did, receiving for *Charles V* a sum from the publisher which awed his contemporaries. He had a patron, Lord Bute, George III's Scottish prime minister, who procured for him the revival of the office of historiographer royal for Scotland, but his clerical living was also important. Though he presided over an academic institution, he was not of course a 'professional' historian in the modern sense of teaching history for a living. History was still not, never had been, and would not for another century be part of the academic curriculum, though there were a small number of endowed professorships. It was easy in the Scottish system to lecture on historical subjects from chairs of rhetoric and belles-lettres, moral philosophy, and law, as Adam Smith and John Millar did, though Robertson did not do so. But published history could pay well. The Earl of Clarendon's *History of the Rebellion* had made unprecedented amounts; Hume's *History of England* had brought him the rewards he had vainly sought from philosophy. The move from dependence on a patron to the independence achieved by production for the market was a theme in eighteenth-century Scottish thought; it was also being achieved in literary men's lives. Robertson was a tolerant, self-consciously modern Scottish cleric – one of the self-dubbed 'Moderates' – and a modern literary man as well as an improving university administrator.

In using the word 'modern' so freely, I am, of course, not travestying but at least semantically simplifying. The eighteenth century was more copious in its terminology: 'polished', 'polite', 'refined'; 'civil', 'civility' and 'civilized' (quite common) and even 'our enlightened age' (Gibbon). We get 'Enlightenment' only toward the end of the century and in German, and 'civilization' (first available in French) also in the second half of the century. But if our own utility word 'modernity' was not in use, the concept certainly was, with its antitheses: 'that rude age', 'illiterate ages', 'superstitious ages', 'barbarism' and 'the feudal anarchy'. The contrast focused Robertson's attention, and it is impossible to explain what he was trying to do in *Charles V*, and even in much of the *History of Scotland*, without invoking it. The antitheses were contrasts of, in another key term, 'manners', which included customs and conventions, values and characteristic conduct – in French, *mœurs*. The relation between an idea of modernity expressed in these terms and an idea of Europe is reciprocal. The history of Europe – and more widely of mankind – could be categorized in terms of manners, changing over time. Modernity could also be characterized in terms of what Robertson in *America*, in a startlingly prophetic phrase, calls the 'mode of subsistence': as the supersession of 'the feudal system' by commerce, which is the hallmark of modernity, and by the associated softening and refinement of manners compared with the military spirit of feudalism. In politics – and this is what above all focuses attention in *Charles V* – feudalism is replaced by 'one great system' governing the relations of the European states, which is 'the balance of power'.

The eighteenth-century sense that the state of society and manners passed through successive stages gave rise over the course of the century to a characteristic genre: schematic abridgement of human history into 'stages', with speculative accounts of the reasons for the transitions. In some cases, if the taxonomic element prevailed over the sequential, as in Montesquieu's *Spirit of the Laws* (1748), the result was more a set of sociological categories, which was neither detailed narrative nor necessarily overtly historical scholarship, though evidence from different parts of the world and different historical eras was cited. History as a sequence of stages, of states of society or of the human mind, was in a sense the 'enlightened' successor to the long-lived Christian universal history, derived from the Bible, Augustine, Orosius and the historical sequence of the Four Empires. The most obvious examples of such hostile rivalry between Christian and Enlightenment universal history were Voltaire's *Essay on Customs (Mœurs)* (1756) and, at the end of the century, Condorcet's anticlerical *Sketch for an Essay on the Progress of the Human Mind* (1794). In France we have also Rousseau's *Discourse on the Origins of Inequality* (1755). Scotland was a notable contributor, with some of David Hume's *Essays*, Adam Ferguson's *The History of Civil Society* (1767), Adam Smith's *Lectures on Jurisprudence*, John Millar's *Origin of the Distinction of Ranks* (1771), Lord Kames's *Sketches of the History of Man* (1774) and James Dunbar's *Essays on the History of Mankind in Rude and Cultivated Ages* (1780). Robertson contributed to the genre with parts of his *History of America*, on the manners and beliefs of the indigenous peoples, and also, in a more limited and strictly European fashion, with the 'View of the Progress of Society in Europe from the Subversion of the Roman Empire to the Beginning of the Sixteenth Century' which he prefixed to *Charles V*.

The motives for the creation of these schematic overviews were to some extent diverse. The most obvious was a general desire to make history 'philosophic'; that is, to uncover its underlying causes and make it a basis for useful generalizations. Montesquieu's enterprise was partly conditioned by what has been called a 'feudal reaction' against the absolutism of Louis XIV in France. By identifying 'despotism' (exemplified particularly by the Ottoman state) as a category distinct from monarchy, and based on the principle of fear, he left the way open to a characterization of monarchy as embedded in the rule of law and checked and supported by a vigorous aristocracy actuated by the principle of honour. Voltaire's and Condorcet's works were attacks on priestcraft and superstition. For the Scots the focus was on the forms assumed by civil society and manners, as in Montesquieu, and the forms of property-holding, as in Harrington. In Smith's *Lectures on Jurisprudence*, in particular, we get a clear delineation of the so-called 'four stages' of society: hunting-and-gathering savagery; pastoral nomadism, with the beginnings of property rights; agriculture (which in Europe after the barbarian invasions was held as property by the institution of the *feud*); and, the latest stage, commerce.

The Scottish focus on civil society, rather than, as was still to some extent true of Montesquieu, on forms of political constitution, was understandable. After the Act of Union (1707) Scotland was no longer a polity, and Edinburgh no longer a political capital. On the other hand the growth of Scotland's prosperity and the concomitant refinement of manners were very obvious. The concept of a polite and progressive civil society offered another form of self-assessment and of possible emulation. The half-jocular but competitive conversations between Johnson and Boswell on the relative merits of English and Scottish society are good informal examples of this.

It was also relevant, however, that within Scotland there were vast differences in characteristic forms of society, not only in the urban–rural contrasts which all Europeans knew, but geographically. North of the Highland line was, so to speak, Indian territory, which during the '45 rebellion had terrifyingly erupted into the civilized streets of Edinburgh. Highland clan society was assimilated by Robertson into his grim picture of Scottish feudalism as an additional source of strength and independence for the feudal warlords, enhancing their ungovernability. Clan society does not seem in general in the eighteenth century to have been carefully distinguished as a category, as it was to be in the nineteenth, when Marxists, in particular, adopted the term 'gentile society' (from the Latin *gens*) as a stage distinct from and prior to feudalism. (Hume came nearer to recognizing this than Robertson, distinguishing sharply between the Scottish version, which, with primogeniture, reinforced feudalism, and the Irish one, with equal division of land among siblings, which was more barbarous.) Similarly, where anthropologists in the later nineteenth century found kinship systems to be the organizing principle of primitive societies, eighteenth-century commentators like Robertson tended to regard such societies as wholly sexually promiscuous, and so as mere hordes. Without property, why would they need to trace descent or identify kin?

On the other hand the perception of the ways in which feudalism was superseded had become much more sophisticated, compared for example with Harrington – particularly in Adam Smith. This marked a characteristic and important shift in the approach to historical causality more generally. The notion of a sequence of stages or forms of society (rather than polities) and of manners had implications for the understanding of the transitions from one to another. Despite the seventeenth-century English enthusiasm for customary law and the idea of an immemorial (and unchanging) constitution, laws and con-stitutions generally sounded like the kinds of thing that would, and certainly could, be deliberately enacted. Manners, however, seemed unlikely to be legislated into or out of existence. Their progress could be artificially retarded, but it seemed likely that when they changed for the better they did so gradually and, to use a favourite word of Gibbon's, also employed by Robertson, 'insensibly'. The mythic reputations of the great lawgivers – Lycurgus, Solon, Numa – at last began to be dismissed. As Adam Ferguson significantly wrote, 'Nations stumble upon establishments which are indeed the result of human action, but not the execution of any human design.' In *The Wealth of Nations* (III.iii and iv) Smith gave his classic account of the gradual erosion of feudalism not by legislation but simply by human nature presented with the opportunities of the market. Given the increasing availability of goods as a result of the productivity of the towns and of commerce, the great feudal lords are drawn to expend their agricultural surplus on these rather than converting it into mili-tary and political power by keeping armed retainers and by imposing military obligations on their tenants; instead these obligations are increasingly commuted for money rents.

Robertson in his *Scotland* gave an account of the ending of feud-alism in France and England largely along Harringtonian lines: it was the result of the deliberate policy of Louis XI of France, implemented by cunning manipulation, and of deliberate legislative action by the English Henry VII, and his son's dissolution of the monasteries, which diffused the ownership of property. The failure of Scotland to emerge from the feudal era was a failure, for various reasons, of the Scottish kings. But in his 'Progress of Society' essay Robertson proposes a more elaborate set of reasons, including the exposure of the European aristocracy to the refinements of Constantinople and the East in the Crusades, and the rise of the commercial city republics of Italy as a rival social and political model to the dominance of the feudal lords. His belief in the benign effects of the Crusades, born though they were in fanaticism and superstition, was an example of another sophistication in the notion of historical causality: the idea of 'unintended consequences', of which Smith's chapters in Part III of *The Wealth of Nations* provide a particularly vivid example. Vices could have desirable consequences; virtue was no guarantee of them. Robertson makes the point explicit in the case of Henry VIII's extravagance, vanity and wilfulness, which had the Dissolution and the English Reformation as its consequences. It was a mismatch of intention and outcome whose natural treatment in historical writing was as irony; Gibbon was to take profuse advantage of it.

Robertson's two introductory-survey chapters in his *Scotland*, devoted to the enduring pernicious power of the Scottish feudal nobility and the weakness of the monarchy, made in a sense a more restricted and bleaker counterpart to the optimistic, European, version he provided ten years later in the 'Progress of Society' preamble to *Charles V*. But whether entrenched or overcome, feudalism, intellectually speaking, would not go away. Scholarship continued to be assiduous in its attention to it. Only two years before Robertson's *Scotland*, in which feudalism played such a leading part, Sir John Dalrymple, the Scottish antiquary to whom Robertson acknowledged debts in his preface, had published *An Essay towards a General History of Feudal Property in Great Britain*. In his highly negative view of the historical role of the Scottish feudal nobility, Robertson set his face against the 'ancient constitutional' tradition fostered by Buchanan in the sixteenth century, in which the nobility were the guardians of liberty. For Robertson, liberty was modern not ancient, while about the ancient history of Scotland before the Romans nothing at all could be known. The introductory survey completed, the narrative part of Robertson's *Scotland* begins with the reign of Mary, Queen of Scots, and the book ends with the accession of her son James VI to the throne of England on the death of Elizabeth in 1603. From then on, as king of England as well as Scotland, James disposed of force and resources which dwarfed those of the Scottish nobility; the history of Scotland as a modern, i.e. post-feudal, society could begin. Like Hume in an English context, Robertson was not an ancient-constitutionalist but a modern Whig. Feudalism had meant anarchy.

It was in *Charles V*, dealing with a period he had chosen for this purpose, that Robertson was able to narrate the consequences of the decline of the feudal nobility on a European scale. Because of this decline, and because of the consequent concentration of power in the major European monarchies, the European states system was created; Robertson's debt to Guicciardini is very obvious. The history of Europe as a whole could be treated in narrative terms, and not merely in a survey or as the histories of individual states. One is reminded of Polybius on the consequences for historical writing of the emergence of Roman power as a unifying theme, but in Robertson the unification was not that of a European-wide empire, which would have been a disaster for mankind. (Robertson, like Polybius, invokes Providence – but not to explain the rise of empire but to give thanks for its failure.) What made Europe an entity, for Robertson, was the balance of power. The unity of Europe, in this paradoxical way, strikes one as rather similar to Smith's account of the creation of the market: each individual (seller, purchaser, statesman) seeks only his own profit/security, but the outcome is an order. Robertson enthusiastically calls it 'one great family' and 'that grand system' (*Charles V*, XI). Gibbon would later compare it to 'one great republic' (*Decline and Fall*, 'General Observations').

Robertson, of course, does not just generalize, but densely narrates the incessant shifts in relative power, the recalculations of advantage by kings and the German princes, the constant reshuffling of alliances, as well as the occasional irruptions of overconfidence (usually from Charles), and of vanity in pursuit of honour rather than interest (Francis I). Resentment and the desire for revenge also impair the operation of the sober estimates of interest and the policies they prescribe. The latter constitute the distinctive quality of modern statecraft, so that Francis's chivalric notions of honour represent a kind of cultural lag.

The greatest intrusion, however, because it involves zeal and intran-sigence, is the distinctively modern one of the Reformation, which Robertson, in a standard move, associates with the new 'spirit of inquiry' and which wrecks Charles's chances of consolidating still-feudal Germany into a unified modern state. Robertson's treatment of the Reformation is notably political: the corruptions of the Church are condemned, but theological issues are marginalized. But if the Reformation is in a sense an aspect of modernity, it is also, as in the *History of Scotland*, carefully culturally distanced from Robertson's own time. Luther and Knox, both performing a necessary task and fitted for it even by their defects on the scale of civility (another example of private vices, public benefits), are also figures firmly located in the past; they belong to a ruder, fiercer, more intransigent age than the present. In this they have some of the same traits as the Scottish nobles who butchered the royal secretary and favourite David Rizzio in the presence of their terrified, pregnant Queen, and who 'fill us with horror at the manners . . . of that age' (*Scotland*, IV). But 'in passing judgement on the characters of men we ought to try them by the principles and maxims of their own age, not those of another. For although virtue and vice are at all times the same, manners and customs vary continually' (*Scotland*, VIII). There is as yet for Robertson no established periodizing terminology, for example be-tween 'Early Modern' and 'Enlightenment', but the way he holds the former period at arm's length is of more than academic significance. It has been pointed out that by his historical contextualizing of the Reformers, the ancestors of the rigid eighteenth-century Calvinist opponents of Robertson's kind of tolerant modern Presbyterianism, he was tacitly depriving them of their claim to be uniquely and auth-entically scriptural in all their characteristics. The concept of at least two periods since the revival of learning is already present. Even academically this was important. Part of the experience of reading history is constituted by such cultural distancing, just as much as its converse, the sense that what lies on the other side of the gulf can be made intelligible by historical imagination and scholarship. Robertson is as sensitive to such issues as any writer in the eighteenth century, and his commitment to studying a period as close as the sixteenth century makes this particularly evident.

The contrasting 'politeness' of the eighteenth century is established not only by assertion but also by the deployment of what his age was beginning to term 'sensibility' – imaginative sympathy or 'feeling' indulged even to lachrymosity – and also by the polished, calm equability of the prose which enforces Robertson's interpretations and opinions. The former is chiefly in evidence in his treatment of Mary, Queen of Scots, who, morally, femininely, frail and politically misguided, is made pitiable in her misfortunes by her conjectured feelings, as in the scene of her enforced abdication: 'Mary, when she subscribed these deeds, was bathed in tears; and while she gave away with her own hands, the sceptre which she had swayed so long, she felt a pang of grief and indignation, one of the severest, perhaps, which can sway the human heart' (*Scotland*, V). Implacable Buchanan, who knew her, merely says that she 'reluctantly agreed to name guardians for her son, and that procurators were sent to arrange that the king should be crowned at Stirling'.

For the moral and aesthetic effect of Robertson's prose one has to take an example, more or less at random. It is said that when Robertson read through one of his own letters he did so beating time, as though hearing a piece of music. It is quite credible. Consider this, from *Charles V*:

Even Melancthon, whose merit of every kind entitled him to the first place among the Protestant divines, being now deprived of the manly counsels of Luther, which were wont to inspire him with fortitude and to preserve him steady amidst the storms and dangers that threatened the church, was seduced into unwarrantable concessions by the timidity of his temper, his fond desire of peace, and his excessive complaisance towards persons of high rank. (X)

Even such a small change as inverting 'timidity of his temper' and 'fond desire' would impair the calculated euphony of Robertson's sentence, but much more damaging – like the omission of a bar in a sonata – would be the semantically relatively harmless excision of 'excessive', 'of every kind', 'manly' or 'unwarrantable'. Robertson's syntax would be rendered insistent and staccato instead of calmly controlled and seemingly inevitable – more like Guicciardini, in fact. Reading Robertson is smooth, easy and reassuring; Guicciardini is abrupt, disturbing and, as a literary experience, a rugged and challenging one. Gibbon spoke no more than the truth when he paid tribute in his *Memoir* to 'the perfect composition, the nervous language, the well-timed periods of Dr Robertson'.

One of Robertson's Edinburgh pupils was Walter Scott. To say this is not particularly to claim that Scott's view of history was influenced more by Robertson than by the historical ideas of the Scottish Enlightenment generally, though it is true that it was Robertson who most focused on Scottish history. But the point is a more general one, about what could and could not be thought and articulated at a given historical moment. Scott learned to be intensely self-conscious about this from the Scottish Enlightenment's understanding of national changes in ideas and manners. Distance in time was also distance in prevailing ideals and modes of conduct. Scott's novel *Waverley* (1814), the first of the series that came to bear its name, set in the 1745 Jacobite Rebellion, originally bore the subtitle ''tis Fifty Years since', amended to ''tis Sixty Years since' in 1805 to retain accuracy. As the novel's eponymous hero travels north, from England to Scotland and from Lowlands to Highlands, he also travels backwards in time, to a partially inadvertent participation in the rebellion. The English manor house in which he is reared is, as Scott makes clear, itself an anachronism: Cavalier, High Tory, Jacobite in sympathies. The uncle who brings him up is obsessed with family tradition and genealogy. When Waverley joins the army, his uncle regrets that it is no longer the fashion for him to take with him a retinue of followers from the estate. His tutor is a non-juring clergyman (i.e. one who has refused to take the oath of allegiance to the Hanoverian sovereign), who writes unreadable High Church Jacobite tracts. His aunt is obsessed with the visit to the house by Charles II seeking shelter after the battle of Worcester. The house is a seventeenth-century time capsule with earlier feudal residues.

In the Scottish Lowlands, Waverley lodges with an even earlier version of the past. The Baron of Bradwardine seems to belong roughly to the fourteenth and fifteenth centuries. He is learned in feudal terms and in heraldry, and deeply attached to the symbols of feudalism. He has no thoughts of a warlord kind of semi-independence, but is loyal (to the Stuarts) even to subservience, being a pedantic antiquary who sets much store by his family's hereditary office, attached to his tenure, of removing the sovereign's boots after a battle, which he supports with copious quotation in barbarous Latin. But the genuine feudal article as a contemporary military reality is the Highland chieftain Fergus Mac-Ivor, whom Waverley meets next. He is a clan leader and warlord who engages in the rebellion not so much out of loyalty as out of self-interest, aspiring to become a great man at a restored Jacobite English court and prepared to use his clansmen's loyalty to himself to achieve this by augmenting Prince Charles Edward's army. But he is a divided figure, and knows it. In acting the part of chief at a clan gathering that Waverley attends, complete with a Gaelic bard, he remains detached, half-apologizing to Waverley for its barbarism. The clan world, it is hinted, is in a sense older than feudalism; Scott makes several Homeric parallels. The contrast with Bradwardine, who is mocked by Fergus as a pedant, reinforces this. But Fergus is also a polished modern gentleman, brought up at the French court. Scott, sensitive as always to period, characterizes him as possible only at that particular point: 'Had Fergus Mac-Ivor lived Sixty Years sooner than he did, he would, in all probability, have lacked the polished manner and knowledge of the world which he now possessed; and had he lived Sixty Years later, his ambition and love of rule would have lacked the fuel which his situation now afforded.' His anachronisms are calculated and manipulative: he maintains the lavish hospitality of a clan chief and crowds his estate with a largely redundant tenantry as a recruiting ground – all in pursuit of a peerage from a restored Stuart dynasty.

Fergus is half-modern, or inwardly almost wholly so; but modernity has two other main faces in the novel. One is Waverley's father, who has reconciled himself to the Hanoverians and become a parliamentary follower of Sir Robert Walpole – a byword for corruption – for the rewards of place and profit. Abandoning the family principles, he seems freed from all principle; in the novel he is only an offstage presence. But modernity has a more honourable face: a military one. Waverley's English prisoner, Colonel Talbot, though able, in the eighteenth-century phrase, to 'make an interest' to procure Waverley's pardon, is wholly devoted to the service of his country. His sense of duty and clear-eyed (Whig) perception of the nation's best interests are contrasted with the unthinking loyalty of the humbler High-landers and with Fergus's self-interested independence, half military, half political. Robertson, who approved of professional armies, would surely have approved of Talbot, as he would have recognized the characterization of Mac-Ivor.

But the general point here is that Scott's own delineation of his characters and his sense of the significance of their spiritually diverse historical locations could hardly have been presented in that way a century earlier. More than a century of historical awareness and reflection lay behind Scott's ability to see them as he did. Scott was thoroughly self-knowing about this. He was an antiquary who made fun of antiquaries; a modern Tory with a fundamentally Whig view of British history, who knew imaginatively what it was to be a Jacobite; a Romantic who knew how to domesticate his Romanticism, knowing that the point about the Sublime, as in Burke's famous essay, was that it was to be enjoyed from a distance. History, offering as it did, in modern representations of it, a gallery of manners or, as Scott's contemporary Sir James Mackintosh put it, a museum of mankind, now afforded a variety of vicarious experiences and even partial identifi-cations which contemporary life could not match. Scott's own house, Abbotsford, was made into such a museum. Fergus's passionately Jacobite sister, with whom Waverley falls temporarily in love, draws an ironic picture of Waverley's future of domestic happiness and lettered indolence; he is not made, as she is, for the cruelty and heroism of a civil war: 'And he will refit the old library in the most exquisite Gothic taste, and garnish its shelves with the most valuable volumes; – and he will draw plans and landscapes, and write verses, and rear temples and dig grottoes ... – and he will be a happy man.' This was at least a partial ironic self-portrait by Scott, with history trans-muted into an epicurean, imaginative antiquarianism. The Victorians loved this trait in him, but remained oblivious that its enabling con-dition was the Scottish Enlightenment's conception of the history of manners.

Gibbon: Rome, Barbarism and Civilization

Gibbon fascinated scholars in the later twentieth century as he did not, in Britain at least, in the nineteenth, and the interest shows no sign of abating. The bicentenary of Gibbon's death in 1794 was impressively celebrated; the festivities, suitably inaugurated by a superb new edition of *The Decline and Fall of the Roman Empire*, by David Womersley (1994), included a conference at Magdalen College, Oxford, so memorably denounced by Gibbon for its neglect of him as an undergraduate. One of Gibbon's predictions in his *Memoir* of his life is clearly falsified: the University of Oxford 'will as cheerfully renounce me for a son as I am willing to disclaim her for a mother'. Our modern understanding of the rich archaeology of his mind has been enhanced not only by studies of him but by copious work on the Enlightenment, on the Machiavellian–humanist tradition, on seventeenth- and eighteenth-century scholarship and antiquarianism, and on the Scottish Enlightenment in particular, to which his debt is at various points apparent and which to the nineteenth century was not even a concept, much less an object of study. Arnaldo Momigliano, in his classic account of the division of seventeenth- and eighteenth-century historical writing into elegant but unscholarly narratives and miscellaneous antiquarian learning, made Gibbon a kind of synthesis, the climax and resolution of the story, as a historian who was also a scholar and a scholar who was an unsurpassed narrator.

Gibbon himself was aware of the situation that Momigliano analysed, and confronted it in his first published essay, originally in French, entitled an *Essay on the Study of Literature* (1761). This was a defence of literature in the wide sense – humane learning, including history – against the contempt often and fashionably expressed in the eighteenth century for mere erudition. In the wake of Descartes's method of philosophical doubt, all facts about the past seemed dubious; the more antiquaries sought to ascertain such facts, the more disconnected and even trivial many of their findings seemed to be and the more uncouth, pedantic and otiose antiquarian learning appeared when judged by the 'philosophic' standards of clarity, system and utility. In his preliminary discourse to the French *Encyclopédie* the mathematician d'Alembert relegated history to the faculty of mere memory. Mathematics, not humanist erudition, was the esteemed paradigm; the ancients had been decisively surpassed, and there was little or nothing more to be learned from them.

Against this Gibbon, already conscious of a vocation as a historian, protested. He himself did not mind teasing the antiquarian 'mere compiler' with charges of pedantry and obsessive, wasted effort, as the footnotes to *The Decline and Fall of the Roman Empire* later made clear, but in his essay he invoked the possibility of a synthesis of the old and new models of intellectual achievement in the 'philosophic historian' – someone who would be learned in the literature of antiquity, devoted to factual accuracy, but also capable of seeing in history a tissue of events connected by deeper causes than those most apparent, and able to present them coherently and perspicuously. Montesquieu was one model: learned but also intellectually probing and systematic. Among the ancients Gibbon above all invoked Tacitus, 'who employs the force of rhetoric only to display the connection between the links which form the chain of historical events, and to instruct the reader by sensible and profound reflections' (*Study of Literature*).

Gibbon did not himself work with manuscript sources, though he was indebted to and appreciative of those who did, particularly the French Benedictine scholars of the Congregation of St-Maur, who, from the later seventeenth century, had produced massive and deeply learned critical editions of the works of the Fathers of the Church – extensively used by Gibbon – and documents of early medieval history. But though Gibbon did not work in archives he was a natural scholar, to whom erudition was a pleasure and not merely an adjunct to literary composition. In his *Memoir* he wrote gleefully of his acquisition for twenty pounds of the twenty volumes of the *Mémoires* of the French Academy of Inscriptions, 'nor would it have been easy, by any other expenditure, to have produced so large and lasting a fund of rational amusement.' The work of the Academy was a testimony to the antiquarian passion devoted, particularly, to the study of ancient artefacts – coins, medals, funerary inscriptions and the like: the kind of material on which historians of the ancient world still heavily rely. The study of it was one way in which Gibbon was later able to go beyond his ancient literary sources, including the historians whom the humanists had been content to recover, imitate and follow. Superficially regarded, Gibbon might seem only a late example of them, with his own narrative depending in the first instance, as among the classical historians themselves, on following and sometimes criticizing or seeking to reconcile the work of earlier historians. But thanks to the scholarship of his own day and of the previous century (much of it denigrated as antiquarian), his own amazingly wide erudition, and his sharply critical approach to his sources, far exceeding the rather reluctant occasional criticisms by ancient historians of the accounts of their predecessors, Gibbon massively transcended them.

It is difficult now to recognize how innovative was Gibbon's choice of his life's work. It was not the practice to write histories of the ancient world (though Adam Ferguson had published a history of the Roman republic), because the ancient historians were thought unsurpassable, both through merit and through superior access. Instead one wrote commentaries – at which Gibbon, as exercises, tried out his apprentice hand on Sallust and Livy – or imitated them on other periods. Half a century later, in the early nineteenth century in England, the topicality of democracy as a contentious political issue gave rise to rival histories of Greece by William Mitford and George Grote. But in its time Gibbon's work was unique, and not only in its scale. To attempt it was undoubtedly a bold step, which Gibbon came to take only gradually. It is noticeable that even when committed to it he chose to begin with the period half a century after Tacitus' work, in the middle of the second century AD. He uses, and sometimes expresses gratitude to, or dissatisfaction with, Dio and Ammianus as well as a number of lesser or epitomized historians, but he had avoided any direct challenge to the author he regarded as the greatest of the ancient historians. Later, of course, as he emerged into the Christian, medieval western and Byzantine era – his history ends only in the fifteenth century, with the fall of Constantinople to the Turks – he was into another world, for the authorities for which he had often as much contempt as regard. But to go there was not originally his intention, for Gibbon's history far outgrew its origins.

Though it is well known, and for that matter somewhat imaginative, it is impossible not to quote Gibbon's account in the *Memoir* of the moment of its conception, though it took many years to bring it to birth: 'It was at Rome, on the fifteenth of October, 1764, as I sat musing amidst the ruins of the Capitol, while the barefooted fryars were singing Vespers in the temple of Jupiter, that the idea of writing the decline and fall of the City first started to my mind.' Two points need to be made at once. One is that the original idea was to write the history of the city – a more antiquarian kind of enterprise – not the empire; it is to the ruins of the city that Gibbon returns only at the end of the vast work which came to range so far beyond it. The history expanded to include Russia, Persia, Mongolia and China, as well as to the limits of the empire in North Africa, Britain and the Near East. It includes the Christian theological controversies before and after the conversion of Constantine, the history of Byzantium to 1453, and the earlier history of its Turkish conquerors; before this Gibbon gives us the rise of Islam and the Crusades. The other point is that the mood of exaltation, clearly evident in his letters at the time, on this, his only, visit to Rome, was aroused in Gibbon chiefly by reminiscences of the *republic*: 'Each memorable spot where Romulus stood, or Tully [Cicero] spoke, or Caesar fell, was at once present to my eye.' Gibbon did not lament the fall of the empire, though he deplored some of its aspects: the lamentation was, though only occasionally explicitly, for an earlier catastrophe – the supersession of the republic. Gibbon was as hostile to the idea of universal empire as Robertson, and as enthusiastic about the modern balance of power: empire drained vitality, which was promoted by independence and rivalry. Rome, for Gibbon, at the outset of his history was already on a gradient of decline, even before Christianity and barbarism began their work. In the first chapter we hear again, as it were, the chanting of the friars: the Campagna, Rome's hinterland, was 'the theatre of her infant victories [an echo of Livy]. On that celebrated ground the first consuls deserved triumphs; their successors adorned villas, and *their* posterity have erected convents.'

Meditation on, and in, the ruins of former greatness was, in the wake of the Romans themselves, an eighteenth-century English classical taste, and one to which Gibbon was always susceptible. Nor was the elegiac note offered only to the Romans of the classical age: it could be sounded even in a context with which Gibbon had no sympathy. The great church of St Sophia in Constantinople, after it has been, for the Byzantine Greeks, polluted by the introduction of the Latin rite, stands deserted 'and a vast and gloomy silence prevailed in that venerable dome, which had so often smoked with a cloud of incense, blazed with innumerable lights, and resounded with the voice of prayer and thanksgiving' (*Decline and Fall*, LXVIII).

After three introductory survey chapters, and with frequent excursions to the provinces, almost all of Gibbon's first volume (of six), before its conclusion with two notorious chapters on early Christianity (XV, XVI), is focused on Rome itself and the failure to solve the problem of peaceful imperial succession, bedevilled by the indiscipline and venality of the standing army and especially the Praetorian Guard, which at one point puts the empire up for auction. In these dozen chapters Gibbon is very close to the moral world and understanding of historical dynamics of Sallust, Livy and Tacitus. It was a cliché of the nineteenth century that eighteenth-century historians had no ability to empathize with past times or recognize their distinctive moral characters. This is nonsense. But what is true is that, in speaking of Rome before the conversion of Constantine, Gibbon's work exists in an easy community of values with the historians of the late republic and with Tacitus, and this is sometimes a handicap in approaching the Christian Church (we remember Tacitus' contempt) and Byzantium. It matters much less in his dealings with the barbarian invaders (where the Tacitus of the *Germania* was actually a sympathetic guide), which are not coloured by republican nostalgia and by Gibbon's regretful respect for the purely politic endorsement by the educated of a generally graceful and tolerant civic polytheism.

It is not surprising that in his presentation of Rome's decline in the third, fourth and fifth centuries we often hear echoes or explicit endorsements of the Machiavellian diagnosis of the nemesis of conquest in the form of corruption followed by loss of liberty – a diagnosis itself grounded in ancient Roman moralizing and satire. It had also been adopted by one of Gibbon's early models, Montesquieu, in his *Considerations on the Causes of the Greatness and Decadence of the Romans* (1734). Elements of it, focusing on the threat to freedom represented by professional standing armies and the dangers of corruption, became embedded in the English rhetoric of political opposition to the executive from the early eighteenth century. Gibbon summarizes it in the appendix to his third volume (Ch. XXXVIII), which at one time looked like being the conclusion to the whole work (with the conversion of Clovis to Catholicism as the groundwork of Charlemagne's 'new' western empire), and which he entitled 'General Observations on the Fall of the Roman Empire in the West':

The decline of Rome was the natural and inevitable effect of immoderate greatness. Prosperity ripened the principle of decay; the causes of destruction multiplied with the extent of conquest ... The victorious legions, who in distant wars acquired the vices of strangers and mercenaries, first oppressed the freedom of the republic, and afterwards violated the majesty of the Purple. The emperors, anxious for their personal safety and the public peace, were reduced to the base expedient of corrupting the discipline which rendered them alike formidable to their sovereign and to the enemy ...

We should beware of taking the 'General Observations' as a short cut to Gibbon's thinking. In fact he offers a number of causes of decline, though still within the neoclassical, civic-humanist frame of reference. In Chapter II he tells us that it was the long peace and uniform government of the Romans that undermined spirit and energy; in Chapter VII it is the mingling of the Romans with the servile provincials and in Chapter XXVII, inevitably, luxury and effeminacy. He also sees the transfer of its seat to Constantinople as marking the empire's definitive orientalization, epitomized as effeminacy and servility, for which he has a Catonic contempt going back, ironically, to the ancient Greeks – the court ritual of the emperors' 'slaves' (there is a reminiscence here of Montesquieu's model of despotism ruling by fear and identified with the Orient) replacing the senatorial dignity which had been at least outwardly observed in Rome itself. All this, apart from the reference in Chapter II to the 'long peace and the uniform government of the Romans, [which] introduced a slow and secret poison into the vitals of the empire', would have seemed common sense to the Romans themselves: that peace presented dangers was a thought which went back at least to Sallust; but the danger of 'uniform government' signals modern ideas of a mixed constitution, national governments and the balance of power.

Gibbon also gave, as Montesquieu in the *Considerations* did not, a role in decline to Christianity; the ancient pagans too, when they became aware of it, had blamed Christianity, though on account of its impiety towards the gods. For Gibbon, theological controversies – on which he had made himself expert – promoted civil strife, while Christian ethics, and particularly monastic asceticism, detracted from the martial virtues. Although it does not stand alone, the humanist formula of decay left deep marks on Gibbon's history and outlook: the fatal sequence of virtue, conquest, luxury, corruption, loss of freedom, and ultimate surrender to hardy barbarian conquerors is taken by Gibbon as something like a universal law, for the barbarian conquerors themselves are, inevitably, launched into the same sequence. It was something the Roman historians had at least hinted at, as in Livy's account of the devastating effect on Hannibal's victorious troops of the enervating luxury of Capua. In Gibbon, Goths, Vandals, Arabs, even the Mongol conquerors of China, succumb to the same civilized virus: 'Alaric [the Goth conqueror of the city of Rome] would have blushed at the sight of his unworthy successor, sustaining on his head a diadem of pearls, incumbered with a flowing robe of gold and silver embroidery, and reclining on a litter or car of ivory, drawn by two white mules' (LI). Power and even civilization itself seem locked into a self-defeating cycle.

After the fractiousness and venality of the professional soldiery – Gibbon's account often reads like a sequel to Tacitus' *Histories*, including the use of irony – the next major theme announced in *The Decline and Fall*, in Chapters XV and XVI but recurring thereafter as a continuous and highly influential presence in both East and West, is Christianity. Gibbon, though he deprecated the fiercer attacks on religion by the French *philosophes* – he calls Voltaire a fanatic – approached it, of course, with the rational and humane distaste of his age for blind superstition and 'enthusiastic' zeal, which Hume had distinguished as the two poles between which the religious mentality oscillated. Much of the eighteenth century's hostility to religious fanaticism derived from a sense of gratitude that the era of religious wars, persecutions and massacres which had characterized the two previous centuries seemed effectively over, if perhaps only dormant. Gibbon's 'our enlightened age' is, among other things, a sigh of relief, and at the outbreak of the French Revolution he immediately saw, in the

French 'patriotic' zealots, the swarms of monks whose fanaticism he had so often castigated in *The Decline and Fall*.

His principal weapon against religion was, notoriously, irony. This takes a number of forms. Sometimes we have a phrase which, depending on the preconceptions of the reader, can be read either devoutly or sceptically, as in St Augustine's 'progress from reason to faith', or a sentence like 'The laws of nature were frequently suspended for the benefit of the church.' There were precedents for this in a scholarly work of the previous century that Gibbon admired, Pierre Bayle's *Philosophical Dictionary*, but Gibbon's examples are much more polished and economical. Much of the mischief, too, is in the diction, especially the employment of an urbane, even prim, eighteenth-century vocabulary for the passionate and often eccentric zeal of early Christian asceticism and belief: 'prudent', 'singular', 'experience'. Origen, the Church Father who was alleged to have embraced chastity to the point of self-castration, had 'judged it the most prudent to disarm the tempter'. St Simeon Stylites, living on top of a pillar as a gesture of withdrawal, had achieved fame 'by the singular invention of an aerial pennance'. Again, 'In the primitive church, the influence of truth was very powerfully strengthened by an opinion which, however it may deserve respect for its usefulness and antiquity, has not been found agreeable to experience. It was universally believed, that the end of the world, and the kingdom of Heaven, were at hand' (XV, XXXVII, XV). It was not empathy, though it was magnificent.

There was nothing perfunctory, however, about Gibbon's treatment of Christian theology and practice or the Christological controversies of the Fathers and the great church councils of the age of Constantine. He is as magisterial, precise and detailed about these as he is about Byzantine court politics or the conquests, manners and new kingdoms of the barbarian invaders. For these last he had some contemporary monographs, chiefly French, such as the history of the Huns by des Guignes – with, of course, the late antique and medieval historians, Jordanes, Priscus, Paul the Deacon and Gregory of Tours. The garrulous charm and weak or non-existent concept of high politics of Gregory were met by Gibbon with stern Ciceronian disapproval: 'in a prolix work ... he has omitted almost everything that posterity desires to learn. I have tediously acquired, by a painful perusal, the right of pronouncing this unfavourable sentence' (XXXVIII).

Conceptually, however, Gibbon was indebted above all to the 'histories of civil society' produced in the Scottish Enlightenment, for his characterization of what he calls (XXVI) the 'Manners of the Pastoral Nations'. Gibbon has derived from these a general concept of the way of life and accompanying manners of pastoral nomadism exemplified by the Huns, Arabs and Mongols and, a little doubtfully, the Germans. Gibbon shows these peoples' peculiar aptitude for war and conquest. His marshalling of the barbarian nations as they successively sweep over the Roman world may recall to us Herodotus' introduction in successive ethnographic and geographical digressions of the nations conquered by the Persian Great King, which are then mustered by him (and Herodotus) for the invasion of Greece. Gibbon clearly enjoys and takes pride in his historian's role of impresario of the nations: 'I shall lead the Arabs to the conquest of Syria, Egypt, and Africa, the provinces of the Roman empire; nor can I check their victorious career till they have overthrown the monarchies of Persia and Spain' (XLVIII). But his own characterizations of barbarian manners offer much more than the lists of barbarian customs and beliefs given by ancient historians. Through the organizing concept of economic 'stages', with their appropriate manners, unfolded in the history of civil society, he makes these traits intelligible as related aspects of a whole way of life. But he remains a historian, not just a sociological categorist, tracing the impact of the barbarians on the settled peoples and the interactions between them, and attending to their special characteristics, such as the formation of the creed of 'Mahomet'.

Gibbon's relations with leading members of the Scottish Enlightenment, as well as his intellectual debts, are worth attending to for a moment, for the influence was also literary and personal. As a pendant to his famous musing on the steps of the temple of Jupiter we may add another, much less well-known, quotation, for together they represent the two intellectual poles, neoclassical moralizing and modern sociological sophistication, between which his work stands. On 8 April 1776 David Hume wrote to the printer William Strachan saying that he was much taken with the new work by Mr Gibbon which Strachan's firm had published, adding that 'Dr Smith's is another excellent work that has come from your press this year.' To have published in the same year the first two volumes of *The Decline and Fall* and Smith's *Wealth of Nations* was indeed a publishing double-first deserving congratulation. The conjunction was apt, for aspects of Gibbon's work are as much an offshoot of the Scottish Enlightenment as Smith's work is its most famous literary monument. Gibbon was on cordial terms of intellectual comradeship with Smith, Ferguson, Robertson and Hume; with the last two, the great historians, even of discipleship. In recounting proudly in his *Memoir* the successful reception of his first two volumes, it was to them that Gibbon gave pride of place: 'The candour of Dr Robertson embraced his disciple; a letter from Mr Hume overpaid the labour of ten years.' Contemplating their achievements as historians had at one time filled him, as he said, 'with a mixed sensation of delight and despair', and this was, as he makes clear, mainly a matter of their mastery of narrative. In them he found what he had looked to in the *Essay on the Study of Literature*: elegance, fluency and lucidity combined with learning devoid of pedantry or ungainliness. His own prose is manifestly related to, say, that of Robertson in *Charles V*, which we have seen that he admired, but more mannered, pointed and memorable. Antithesis is a favourite device, and the syntax is often artfully balanced or cumulative, as when a triad of assertions forms a cumulative series, rounded off with a climax or the false climax of bathos. We have already seen several examples of this. An amusing inversion of bathos is his well-known description of the Roman conquest of Britain, where three ignominious adjectives are concluded with a genuine climax: 'After a war of about forty years, undertaken by the most stupid, maintained by the most dissolute, and terminated by the most timid of all the emperors, the far greater part of the island submitted to the Roman yoke' (I).

Another notable feature of Gibbon's writing which has become famous or notorious is the footnotes, which do far more than just identify sources. Robertson and Hume had used footnotes as a way of bringing erudition to the support of the text without cluttering it with documents. Gibbon made them into an idiosyncratic art form, a commentary in which he gives rein to a relaxed, garrulous intimacy which acts in counterpoint with the tautly controlled formality of the text. They evoke the community of historians, scholars and anti-quaries, ancient and modern, in a kind of camaraderie of admiration, scorn and sometimes smut. It is best just to quote a few random examples: 'See an excellent dissertation on the origin and migrations of nations in the Mémoires de l'Académie des Inscriptions ... it is seldom that the antiquarian and the philosopher are so happily blended' (IX). On the eternal damnation of the pagans: 'The Jansenists who have so diligently studied the works of the Fathers, maintain this sentiment with distinguished zeal; and the learned M. de Tillemont never dismisses a virtuous emperor without pronouncing his dam-nation' (XV). 'The modern Greeks [he means historians] ... have displayed the love, rather than the talent, of fiction' (XXXII). 'I have somewhere heard or read of the confession of a Benedictine abbot: "My vow of poverty has given me a hundred crowns a year; my vow of obedience has raised me to the rank of a sovereign prince." I forget the consequences of his vow of chastity' (XXXVII). On the execution of a heretical bishop: 'The bishopric is now worth 20,000 ducats a year ... and is therefore much less likely to produce the author of a new heresy' (XXVII).

Irony is, of course, a distancing device, as when Gibbon contrasts Roman imperial decadence with the virtues of the republic, or holds up with tweezers for enlightened contemplation the eccentricities of Christian ascetics. It can also be turned inward, with an effect of equivocation. This is a frequent feature of Augustan English writing generally, as well as common in Gibbon, as when a pair of contrast-ing motives is assigned as the cause of an action: 'the credulity or prudence', 'the avarice or humanity' and so on. Equivocation can also become unease and paradox. The sequence of virtue, conquest, luxury, corruption is a frequent generator of such paradoxes. Perhaps virtue and even civilization are self-doomed. The unease as well as the posi-tive weight attached to the word 'civilized' appears in the first para-graph of the history. The opening is proud: 'In the second century of the Christian Æra, the empire of Rome comprehended the fairest part of the earth, and the most civilized portion of mankind.' But what does it mean to be civilized? Three sentences later we find that 'Their peaceful inhabitants enjoyed and abused the advantages of wealth and luxury.' Perhaps to enjoy *was* to abuse. Gibbon's irony feeds not only off the paradox of conquest turning apparently inexorably into servitude – the Roman and civic-humanist paradox – but also off the rather different paradoxes generated by the history of civil society, particularly its concept of 'unintended consequences', which could be benign as well as disastrous but all the more morally equivocal for leaving ill-conduct unpunished or even rewarded. The extreme form of this paradox, which in its formulation was almost universally condemned as well as borrowed, occurred in Bernard de Mandeville's satire *The Fable of the Bees* (1714), whose message was summarized as 'private vices, public benefits'. It was a thought highly familiar to Gibbon, and was even used by him to subvert the language of republican virtue: 'The historian Sallust, who usefully practised the vices which he has so eloquently censured . . .' (XXXI, n. 105). In his presentation of Christianity Gibbon inverts the paradox and bends it to his ironic purpose. The Christian virtues such as piety and zeal must be acknowledged to be virtues, yet their consequences often seem highly regrettable: private virtues, public detriment.

Gibbon, of course, finds this unsurprising, but the double-edged character of civilization was disturbing. He finds hope in the 'modern' thought, announced by Montesquieu and fostered by Hume, that it is only luxury procured by conquest that is enervating, but that the 'opulence' – a neutral word – obtained by industry is innocuous, since it requires a sustained output of energy and discipline.

The Decline and Fall in fact has in a sense two conclusions, one of which at least hints at optimism. The most obvious one is the fall of Byzantium to the Turks and the extinction of the last embers of the Roman empire, by the last of the barbarian invasions. But is it the last? Gibbon in his 'General Observations' had invoked the notion of the revival of European civilization at the Renaissance. The other climax, in Chapter LXX, is the return, as promised, to the city of Rome, where we see the republican revival and the symbolic inauguration of the Renaissance by the coronation of Petrarch as poet laureate. It is a false dawn, however. Republicanism is crushed; the Renaissance itself was timidly imitative rather than a new beginning. Really to infuse his narrative with optimism Gibbon would have had to take it beyond the fifteenth century, to the eighteenth. Schematically and only in a survey, this is what he has done in the 'General Observations'. If it had stood, as originally intended, at the end of the entire work the optimistic trajectory would have been clear, for Gibbon's view of the Europe of his own day, until the outbreak of the French Revolution, is one of undiluted approval. The arts of life have been improved. The fatal uniformity of the Roman empire and the passivity it encouraged have been replaced by a beneficial fragmentation into a diversity of nation states and the energy generated by their rivalry. Under the auspices of the balance of power, Europe can be regarded as 'one great republic' (a significant word): tense, energetic, diverse, but also a partnership in the arts of peace. Civilization has not merely survived the fall of the Roman empire which had for so long been its chief home, but has improved itself. At the end of *The Decline and Fall* as we have it, something like this thought is at least obliquely alluded to. The ruins of the city, left by the decline and fall of the empire, which Gibbon referred to as 'the greatest, perhaps, and most awful scene, in the history of mankind', are now 'devoutly visited by a new race of pilgrims from the remote, and once savage, countries of the North' (LXXI). The pilgrims are civilized or they would not be devout, and their savage past is far behind them. Rome's fall can be contemplated as from a balcony, as an eighteenth-century connoisseur of the Sublime might enjoy its terrors from a secure distance. Gibbon's history is such a balcony, and is therefore part of the victory of civilization in surviving the fall of Rome.

It is useless to look, in Britain at least, for Gibbon's immediate successors. There are none. In France and the United States (below, pp. 429–31, 452) matters were different. The great Anglophile nineteenth-century French historian François Guizot annotated and translated Gibbon's work. In America, Gibbon was revered by the outstanding historians Prescott, Parkman and Henry Adams. But in England there was on the whole neglect and hostility. This is symptomatic of something wider. It is a fairly safe rule that any general Victorian pronouncement on the historical sense or the historiography of the eighteenth century will be dismissive, ignorant and distorting. The mentality of that century which, more than any other, has established the categories of the modern understanding of the history of Europe is habitually characterized in nineteenth-century England as 'unhistorical'. The reasons for this nonsense would make a good subject for the history of ideas. One has the impression that, having been so categorized, the eighteenth-century historians were little read. Denigrating clichés were passed unexamined from pen to pen, even among serious scholars. Leslie Stephen's pioneering *History of English Thought in the Eighteenth Century* (1876) was notably deficient in appreciation of the period's historical writing. One can still hear echoes of this denigration; it is time they died away.

Partly it seems to derive from taking as representative of the eighteenth century the expressions of hostility to history that Gibbon tried to answer in his *Essay*. Partly it seems to derive from an unsubtle reading, as in the case of some ancient historians, of affirmations of the existence of a common human nature, ignoring the fact that these were often followed by reminders of the very different forms this nature could assume under different historical circumstances. One relevant consideration is surely the cultural fault line created by the French Revolution, which made some eighteenth-century pronouncements seem complacent and which retrospectively, in England, tainted the whole French Enlightenment. (The Scottish Enlightenment, as a concept, was of course established only in the later twentieth century.) Voltaire, rather than Montesquieu, though criticized by Robertson and Gibbon as unscholarly and superficial, was taken as epitomizing the age. In the nineteenth century, too, the categories of 'race' and 'nation' were reified and taken with extreme seriousness as bearers of precise and indelible qualities; eighteenth-century cosmopolitanism such as one finds in Hume and Gibbon could be regarded as more evidence of superficiality, whereas we would be inclined to see a sensible scepticism. Against Gibbon, too, as a notorious scoffer and sneerer, stood Christian earnestness. So, for that matter, did agnostic earnestness. The Victorians, as Nietzsche noted, expected critics of Christianity to go about their business with a proper solemnity. It was axiomatic for most that the Catholic Church was wrong. That it might also be funny was a thought not entertained. The literary appreciation of Gibbon in Britain had to wait for Lytton Strachey and Winston Churchill (an odd couple), both of whom admired and in different ways imitated him in the early twentieth century. In the world of scholarship Gibbon's revenge has been comprehensive, and he is now securely installed in the historians' pantheon. This is caught by the phrase used of himself and his colleagues by the outstanding contemporary historian of 'Late Antiquity' – a concept we largely owe to him – Peter Brown: 'In Gibbon's Shade'.

22

Revolutions: England and France

Macaulay: The Glorious Revolution

Interest in England's seventeenth-century constitutional crisis, which had been central to English historiography in the eighteenth century, remained so in the nineteenth. It is true that the later period saw an awakened appreciation of the medieval in cultural contexts, and that the Saxons, partly owing to the sponsorship of Sir Walter Scott, enjoyed a renewed popularity. Towards the end of the century, too, imperialist enthusiasm prompted something of a cult of the age of Elizabeth. But the conflicts of Cavaliers and Roundheads continued to provide political reference points, and inspired a popular iconography. Foreign historians were also drawn to them. Two of the greatest nineteenth-century historians, François Guizot and Leopold von Ranke, wrote on the English Civil War period. In England, two of the leading proponents of a new professionalization in the study of history, Samuel Gardiner and Sir Charles Firth, devoted themselves to setting the seventeenth-century record straight and correcting the errors of their unprofessional predecessors. By far the most popular of these historical accounts, from the mid-century onward, when the *History of England from the Accession of James II* was published (1848–61), was by a Whig Member of Parliament and minister and retired Anglo-Indian official, Thomas Babington (Lord) Macaulay (1800–59).

Macaulay's *History*, which ends with the death of William III in 1702, is centred on the 'second' seventeenth-century revolution, the 'Glorious Revolution' of 1688, by which the Catholic and allegedly tyrannical James II had been overthrown and the crown conferred on

William of Orange and his wife, James's daughter Mary. In the early nineteenth century three Whig politicians, including a subsequent prime minister, had written histories of this Revolution: Charles James Fox, Lord John Russell and Sir James Mackintosh (who bequeathed Macaulay a valuable collection of documents, particularly strong in the pamphlet literature of the period). It was not a surprising interest. Parliamentary reform became the Whig policy in Opposition, leading to the Reform Act of 1832; the constitution to be reformed was that established by the Revolution in 1688 and its confirming legislation, which some regarded as definitive for all time. The Revolution had to be resituated in the Whig canon. It had to be a matter of separating the spirit from the letter. The best way of respecting the achievement of the men of 1688, according to reformers, was not to enshrine their work in constitutional marble, but to do as they had done and make the constitutional adjustments necessary to meet new circumstances. The necessary resituating was the task that Macaulay, drawing on the work of the Whig constitutional historian Henry Hallam, carried through to extraordinary popular acclaim, for where Hallam was dry Macaulay was vivid, dramatic, eloquent and exhilarating.

Two contemporary events helped to shape Macaulay's *History*. One was the 1832 Reform Act. In supporting it, Macaulay, as a Whig parliamentary spokesman, scored a spectacular oratorical success. Macaulay's speeches on the Reform Bill still resound on the page. They have an irresistible brio, and they are informed throughout by a sense of history. Macaulay compares the crisis of his times to that confronting Charles I and the Long Parliament, and his diagnosis is essentially the same as Hume's:

[Charles] would govern, I do not say ill, I do not say tyrannically; I only say this: he would govern the men of the seventeenth century as if they had been the men of the sixteenth century; and therefore it was, that all his talents and all his virtues did not save him from unpopularity, from civil war, from a prison, from a bar, from a scaffold. These things are written for our instruction. Another great intellectual revolution has taken place; our lot has been cast on a time analogous, in many respects, to the time which immediately preceded the meeting of the Long Parliament. There is a change in society. There must be a corresponding change in the government.

The progress of society had created a large, newly prosperous and politically self-conscious class which must be admitted to the franchise and included in the political nation by constitutional change, or revolution would follow, as it had in seventeenth-century England, as it had in France. Macaulay's political convictions were suffused by history and by political reminiscence. He had a strong feeling for the great parliamentary occasions, and they always recalled for him those of the past. He saw contemporary political events as though they were already historical: writing to his sister, he compared being present at the crucial vote on the Reform Bill to seeing Caesar stabbed in the Forum or Cromwell taking the mace from the table of the House of Commons when he expelled the Members and inaugurated his personal rule.

The second, recent, event by which Macaulay's mind and political ideas were decisively shaped was the French Revolution of 1848. The publication of his *History* had been immediately preceded by the wave of revolutions which spread all over Europe in 1848, and he alluded to them as a dire warning, but also as a contrast to the English 'Glorious Revolution' of 1688, which formed the centrepiece of his *History*. England had remained tranquil when, as he wrote in his preface, 'the proudest capitals of Western Europe have streamed with civil blood.' Macaulay had no doubt that it was the 'preservative' Revolution of 1688 and the timely and peaceful passage of the Reform Act of 1832 which had saved England from the revolutions experienced on the Continent, above all in France. The connection in Macaulay's mind between 1688 and 1832, 'between the Revolution which brought the crown into harmony with the Parliament, and the Revolution which brought the Parliament into harmony with the nation', would have been clearer had his *History* run its planned course up to 1832, instead of finishing, because of its author's death, at the beginning of the eighteenth century. As it is, we have some inkling of what the eighteenth-century volumes might have been like in the published collections of his essays, including those on eighteenth-century statesmen.

Reconciliation is a recurring theme of the *History* itself. Its hero is William of Orange, the Deliverer, who, James having fled, presides over the restoration of order and liberty. But the nation, though corrupted by the reigns of the last two Stuart kings, is also an accomplice in its own deliverance, not only through the lords who risk their necks in summoning William, but in the stiffening of constitutional and Protestant resolve in the later stages of James's reign. There is, in Macaulay's account, a rallying in defence of law and liberty and in resistance to James's arbitrariness which foreshadows the moment of (temporary) near-unity in the Revolution itself, when, the King having fled and the Prince of Orange not yet having taken control, Whigs and Tories momentarily sink their differences in defence of law and order and in an impressive show of unity by the respectable part of the nation.

It is natural to take the essay Macaulay wrote on 'History' in 1828 as his definitive statement on the historian's task. This can be misleading as a guide to his achievement. It is sometimes taken as a call for 'social history' (a promise fulfilled only in one chapter (III) of the *History*), as well as for historians to take lessons from the techniques developed in the novel, and especially by Scott. History should discard some of its dignity and descend into the common haunts of men, the exchange and the coffee house. How steep a descent this indicated is open to question: one can go a good deal lower and wider than either of these. Macaulay may have thought he was fulfilling his prescription by his frequent attempts, like Hume's, to summarize the state of public opinion. He certainly succeeded in imparting to historical narrative an unprecedented vividness and dramatic and emotional intensity, for which he saw Scott as a model, but he was not a 'social historian'. His *History* remained chiefly focused on royal policies, parliamentary debates and state trials, and the appraisal of the intentions and qualities of public men.

Macaulay himself was born, not indeed into the Whig aristocracy where he found his early patrons, but into the comfortable middle class, and also in an atmosphere of great public causes. His father, Zachary, was a leading member of the Anti-Slavery League. At Cambridge in the early 1820s Macaulay shone as a debater, shedding the family Toryism and evangelical Christianity. He became an advanced Whig and reformer, but never a Radical. After winning a reputation as a reviewer and essayist and after his success in Parliament, he went in the 1830s to a lucrative post in India, from which he returned with an independent income. He later returned to Parliament and became a minister, but the last part of his life was really devoted to his *History*.

He can, in fact, be seen as in many ways the last great neoclassical historian, writing history after a successful public career. His own culture was above all classical, broadened by a love of eighteenth-century novels and drama, as well as by his reading of Burke, whom he revered, and Scott. Where he was exceptional was not in being a social historian, which he certainly was not, but in the emotional range and depth, the almost pictorial vividness and concreteness, and the dramatic intensity of his historical writing. None of this was exactly new – it was foreshadowed in Robertson and Hume – but in no other historian was it so copiously and even extravagantly displayed. His own model historians were Tacitus and Thucydides, but he had an enduring distaste for Plutarch, on whom he wrote an early essay, and for the tradition of heroic – Macaulay would say posturing – classical republicanism which looked back to him, in late seventeenth-century England and above all in the French Revolution. He was not unmitigatedly hostile to the latter, thinking it productive of good in the long run, but he detested its strain of Plutarchian demogoguery.

Though the Scottish Enlightenment did much to shape his view of the progress of society, he was a modern English Whig who (unlike Hume) cherished the pieties of his political tradition with an eloquence unique except in the work of Burke. In the essay on Plutarch, noting the political rootlessness of his French admirers, he wrote that 'Senate has not to our ears a sound so venerable as Parliament. We respect the Great Charter more than the laws of Solon. The Capitol and the Forum impress us with less awe than our own Westminster Hall and Westminster Abbey, the place where the great men of twenty generations have contended, the place where they sleep together.' Macaulay's frequent invocations of earlier English history are eirenic more than partisan. A typical example (in Chapter V of the *History*) is the reference to the chapel in the Tower of London where the remains of the Duke of Monmouth were interred after his unsuccessful rebellion and his execution in 1685, which Macaulay has described in detail:

The head and body were placed in a coffin covered in black velvet, and were laid privately under the communion table of St Peter's Chapel in the Tower. Within four years the pavement of the Chancel was again disturbed, and hard by the remains of Monmouth were laid the remains of [Judge] Jeffreys. In truth there is no sadder spot on the earth than that little cemetery. Death is there associated not, as in Westminster Abbey and St Paul's, with genius and virtue, with public veneration and with imperishable renown; not, as in our humbler churches and churchyards, with everything that is most endearing in social and domestic charities; but with whatever is darkest in human nature and in human destiny, with the savage triumph of implacable enemies, with the inconstancy, the ingratitude, the cowardice of friends, with all the miseries of fallen greatness and of blighted fame.

Examples follow of the disgraced and inglorious dead.

This was a melancholy set piece, but Macaulay was a high-spirited man who responded to glitter, energy and bustle, without qualms. One example occurs in James's reign with the King's attempt to overawe the capital with a military camp at Hounslow. Civil society is too much for his coercive intentions:

The Londoners saw this great force assembled in their neighbourhood with a terror which familiarity soon diminished. A visit to Hounslow became their favourite amusement on holidays. The camp presented the appearance of a vast fair. Mingled with the musketeers and dragoons, a multitude of fine gentlemen and ladies from Soho Square, sharpers and painted women from Whitefriars, invalids in sedans, monks in hoods and gowns, lacqueys in rich liveries, pedlars, orange girls, mischievous apprentices and gaping clowns, was constantly passing and repassing through the lower lines of tents. From some pavilions were heard the noises of drunken revelry, from others the curses of gamblers. In truth the place was merely a gay suburb of the capital. (VI)

It is a Hogarthian scene, or, if we look for a mid-Victorian parallel, one like Frith's *Derby Day*, full of animation, variety and small vignettes. But there is a significance too, though Macaulay's conscious awareness of it is perhaps not certain. It is a kind of parody of a familiar topos from the stern classical republican tradition: the army suborned and corrupted by the luxury of the capital (above, p. 139).

But Macaulay, though perhaps not used to hailing painted women as agents of the unintended benefit of constitutional liberty, approved of luxury, the fruit of peaceful industry and commerce. The army is not so much corrupted as reabsorbed by the civil society which James had hoped to use it to coerce, assimilated to the nation socially if not yet constitutionally.

The pictorial quality of Macaulay's narratives could also be given a more domestic or melodramatic tone, evoking pity and intimacy. There is, for example, his account of the flight of James's queen from Whitehall by river. James entrusts her and her baby to two French gentlemen:

Lauzun gave his hand to Mary; Saint Victor wrapped up in his warm cloak the ill-fated heir of so many kings. The party stole down the back stairs and embarked in an open skiff. It was a miserable voyage. The night was bleak; the rain fell; the wind roared; the waves were rough; at length the boat reached Lambeth; and the fugitives landed near an inn, where a coach and horses were waiting. Some time elapsed before the horses could be harnessed. Mary, afraid that her face might be known, would not enter the house. She remained with her child, cowering for shelter from the storm under the tower of Lambeth Church, and distracted by terror whenever the ostler approached her with his lanthorn. (IX)

It is a perfect Victorian genre scene of 'Beauty in Distress', shaped by the heritage of eighteenth-century 'sentimentalism': the wild night, the open boat and the heaving dark river; the young woman with her child, cowering for shelter beneath the dark tower of the church, shrinking from the ostler's lantern, the source of light in the picture.

The two rebellions – the abortive one by Monmouth and the successful invasion by William three years later – provide, of course, other pictorial and dramatic opportunities. For Macaulay the crushing of the Monmouth rebellion was the end of the ranting, fanatical aspects of radical Whiggism, republicanism and Puritanism, as well as a tragedy for the Protestant peasantry of the West Country who supported it. Its worst aspect was epitomized in the old intriguer Robert Ferguson, who drafted Monmouth's justificatory declaration. Macaulay's character study is as vehement as his often were:

Violent, malignant, regardless of truth, insensible to shame, insatiable of notoriety, delighting in intrigue, in tumult, in mischief for its own sake, he toiled during many years in the darkest mines of faction. He lived among libellers and false witnesses. He was the keeper of a secret purse from which agents too vile to be acknowledged received hire, and the director of a secret press whence pamphlets, bearing no name, were daily issued. (V)

In 1688 Ferguson attempts to join William's expedition, but is cold-shouldered. Macaulay uses him to make the contrast between William's enterprise and Monmouth's earlier one: 'He had been a great man in the knot of ignorant and hotheaded outlaws who had urged the feeble Monmouth to destruction: but there was no place for a lowminded agitator, half maniac and half knave, among the grave statesmen and generals who partook the cares of the resolute and sagacious William' (IX).

Monmouth's rebellion had been an amateur affair. It was part of Macaulay's distaste for classical republicanism and its revival from the Renaissance onward that he despised its cult of the citizen army as anachronistic in an age of commerce and specialization. He sometimes refers to the armed West Country peasantry as 'clowns'; they were no match for James's professional army. As a follower of the Scottish Enlightenment and a Victorian patriot, Macaulay could be enthusiastic about professional armies – in the right cause and properly subjected to civilian authority. Robertson would have agreed (above, p. 351). Macaulay uses the parade of William's troops through Exeter, the first city to fall to him, further to underline the contrast with Monmouth's pathetic rabble. In its stressed exoticism William's army recalls – and is quite probably meant to – the multi-ethnic composition of Xerxes' great host as reviewed by Herodotus (above, p. 15). Potentially barbaric and terrible, it is made benign, as well as effective, by discipline and by William's firm, controlling hand.

From the West Gate to the Cathedral Close, the pressing and the shouting on each side was such as reminded Londoners of the crowds on the Lord Mayor's day. The houses were gaily decorated. Doors, windows, balconies, and roofs were thronged with gazers . . . the people of Devonshire, altogether unused to the splendour of well ordered camps, were overwhelmed with delight and awe. Descriptions of the martial pageant were circulated all over the kingdom. They contained much that was well fitted to gratify the vulgar appetite for the marvellous. For the Dutch army, composed of men who had been born in various climates, and had served under various standards, presented an aspect at once grotesque, gorgeous, and terrible to islanders who had, in general, a very indistinct notion of foreign countries. First rode Macclesfield at the head of two hundred gentlemen, mostly of English blood, glittering in helmets and cuirasses, and mounted on Flemish warhorses. Each was attended by a negro brought from the sugar plantations on the coast of Guinea. The citizens of Exeter, who had never seen so many specimens of the African race, gazed with wonder on those black faces set off by embroidered turbans and white feathers. Then, with drawn broadswords, came a squadron of Swedish horsemen in black armour and fur cloaks. They were regarded with a strange interest; for it was rumoured that they were natives of a land where the ocean was frozen and where the night lasted through half the year, and that they had themselves slain the huge bears whose skins they wore. (IX)

The last great scene of 1688 is provided by the debates on a constitutional settlement in the Convention Parliament, at which James was declared to have abdicated and, after much wrangling, the crown was offered to William and Mary jointly (X). Oratory is one of the great themes of Macaulay's history, though it is presented in summarized form, not ostensibly verbatim. He has a reverential sense for the great parliamentary occasion, and, as we have seen in his description of the passing of the Reform Act (above, p. 369), gives it additional solemnity by historical reminiscence and prospect. In describing the Convention Parliament he makes space to record the presence of William Sacheverell, 'an orator whose great parliamentary abilities were, many years later, a favourite theme of old men who lived to see the conflicts of Walpole and Pulteney'. House folklore is an aspect of enduring institutions, and it was especially cherished by Macaulay, who in this case was himself a member of the club.

The debates in the Convention Parliament are, of course, given full measure. Macaulay stresses how little they had to do with political philosophy, how much with English law and its stretching to an unprecedented situation: 'If it were a legal maxim that the throne could never be vacant, it was also a legal maxim that a living man could have no heir. James was still living. How then could the Princess of Orange be his heir?' And so on. In 1828, in an essay on Hallam, Macaulay had deplored the petty-mindedness of the parliamentarians of 1688. Now, two French revolutions later, he endorsed their pragmatism. The declaration which gave the throne to William and Mary was illogical and contrary to fact, but it worked, and the settlement it created endured. By a benign fiction that no revolution had taken place, the work of the revolution, once done, continued to be ballasted by precedent. The account of the manner of the Parliament's deliberation is not just description for description's sake, as the subsequent words make clear. It is a lesson and an endorsement:

As our revolution was a vindication of ancient rights, so it was conducted with strict attention to ancient formalities. In almost every word and act may be discerned a profound reverence for the past. The Estates of the Realm deliberated in the old halls and according to the old rules . . . The sergeant with his mace brought up the messengers of the Lords to the table of the Commons; and the three obeisances were duly made. The conference was held with all the antique ceremonial. On the one side of the table, in the Painted Chamber, the managers of the Lords sate covered and robed in ermine and gold. The managers of the Commons stood bareheaded on the other side. The speeches presented an almost ludicrous contrast to the revolutionary oratory of every other country. Both the English parties agreed in treating with solemn respect the ancient constitutional traditions of the state. The only question was, in what sense those traditions were to be understood . . . When at length the dispute had been accommodated, the new sovereigns were proclaimed with the old pageantry . . . To us who have lived in the year 1848 it may seem almost an abuse of terms to call a proceeding, conducted . . . with such minute attention to prescriptive etiquette, by the terrible name of revolution. And yet this revolution, of all revolutions the least violent, has been of all revolutions the most beneficent . . .

One of Macaulay's contemporaries, Thomas Carlyle, had a puritanical contempt for all ceremonious shams and pretences, as well as a considerable contempt for Parliament. It is not surprising that he chose to become a historian of the French Revolution, which to him was the vengeance of history on outworn forms pretending still to be realities. His sensibility and Macaulay's, respectively puritanical and

Burkean Whig, represent two facets of the early nineteenth-century mind confronting history.

Carlyle's French Revolution: *History with a Hundred Tongues*

Thomas Carlyle was born in 1795, the year that signalled the end of the French Revolution, though not, of course, of its effects: the Parisian rising against the new, moderate and corrupt government of the Directory was put down by the cannon commanded by 'Artillery Officer Buonaparte', as Carlyle calls him. It is the last episode in Carlyle's book on the Revolution, published over forty years later. To reach that point in the book leaves the assiduous reader with something of the same emotional exhaustion as must have been felt by the survivors of the Revolution, with all the ideals and most of the leading actors in the six years since 1789 dishonourably buried: 'The Notabilities of France disappear, one after one, like lights in a Theatre, which you are snuffing out' (Volume III, Book VI.III). Carlyle inimitably recognizes the shared fatigue: 'O Reader! Courage. I see land!'

Carlyle was born into a poor, Bible-reading, Calvinist family in south-west Scotland. He received a good education, both classical and scientific, at the University of Edinburgh: geology, chemistry and astronomy provided him with a stock of metaphors. Losing his Christianity while retaining a good deal of his Calvinism, he was unable to make a career as a minister of the Kirk, and had to establish himself as a man of letters, which led to his migration to London. He first displayed his highly individual literary idiom – biblical, Germanic, burlesque and hectoring – in his personal philosophical statement in *Sartor Resartus* (1833–4). *The French Revolution* (1837) was his great bid for literary recognition, and it succeeded. It was, among other things, like all his works in some way or other, an admonition. The Revolution was for him the advent of Democracy (always capitalized), terrible and sublime, in the modern world. It was a demonstration of divine justice, passed on a corrupt aristocracy which believed in nothing.

The Revolution had naturally encouraged apocalyptic speculation.

Carlyle was not, of course, a literal believer in the Christian Apocalypse, though he was a close friend of the millenarian preacher Edward
Irving, but the imagery of apocalypse as conflagration and destruction
always came readily to him, as we see in the extraordinary concluding
page of the book (see above, p. 187) and in the account of the taking
of the Bastille. The book was written in the early years of the liberal
'July Monarchy' in France, which was brought into being by a second
revolution in 1830. In Britain there had been fears of revolution
(not altogether extravagant) not only in the 1790s but in the period
following the Napoleonic Wars and at the time of the campaign for
the Reform Bill in the early 1830s. The decade in which Carlyle's
history was written, the 1830s, saw the growth of Chartism, which
aroused much apprehension and on which Carlyle wrote a long essay
in 1839.

Carlyle responded to the French Revolution with a mixture of awe
and complicity and grim enthusiasm, combined with horror and pity.
He never really adjusted to the more tranquil period of the 1850s and
'60s, which he viewed, with a kind of baffled impatience, as stag-
nation. The French Revolution, though he was condescending to its
sentimentalities and appalled by its atrocities, appealed to his Old
Testament and Calvinist sensibilities, as a divine scourging. Carlyle's
ambivalence comes out most clearly in his treatment of what he
calls 'Sansculottism' – fuelled by hunger and desperation, capable of
heroism and atrocious cruelty. Carlyle at his most abstract – and he
is rarely abstract for long – presented the Revolution as the clash of
such personified abstractions: 'Sansculottism', 'Patriotism', 'Respectability', 'Philosophism', 'Clubbism'. But his rhetoric is often highly
concrete, and these abstractions are sometimes given physical characteristics reminiscent of allegory; those of 'Sansculottism' (sometimes
also personified as the poverty-stricken Parisian suburb of 'Saint-
Antoine') are almost tangible: 'many-headed, fire-breathing'. The
Paris mob is sometimes 'sooty Saint-Antoine', just as the courtiers are
'the Œil-de-Bœuf' (a salon of assembly in the palace of Versailles). In
reintroducing characters – in a useful mnemonic but also a deliberate
evocation of epic convention, for Carlyle saw the Revolution as epic
– he tags them with a repeated adjective or phrase in Homeric fashion:
'Usher Maillard, Méry of the Thousand Orders' (said to have been

written by him in the Hôtel de Ville on the day of the fall of the
Bastille), 'Old-Dragoon Drouet'. Marshal de Broglie, whom the court
relies on vainly for a royalist military coup, is 'Mars', while the court
usher, the Marquis de Brézé, is 'Mercury' (he carries messages), and
several times the source of excellent but also symbolic comedy. It is
he who carries to the National Assembly the King's command to
disperse, which the Assembly defies with the Tennis Court oath. De
Brézé, who also acts as a kind of doorkeeper, and stands for the
Ancien Régime and etiquette, by which he lives, is trying to shut the
door on world history (I.V.II). Brézé has his symbolic moment, but
some of the most frequent, memorable and ominous reappearances
are those of Jean-Paul Marat – to Carlyle 'horseleech' or 'sooty' Marat
– who croaks his messages of hatred and at whose entrance, Carlyle
says, the lamps in the room turn blue.

Marat, squalid and malevolent, is something like the evil genius of
the Revolution, responsible for the massacres in the prisons in Sep-
tember 1792, but in embodying the hatreds and fanaticism of his
Sanculottic followers, he has for Carlyle a kind of authenticity and
power which the 'Anglomaniac' National Assembly and later the
'respectable' republican faction of the Girondins do not. The great
men of the Revolution, Mirabeau and Danton, have this quality of
authenticity or, in Carlyle's word, 'Reality', and even Marat, without
any finer qualities, has it. Carlyle respected fanaticism. 'Reality', wherever found, is a kind of divine emanation, while frivolity and shams
and theories are mere historical debris, to be shovelled away by men
who are in earnest. He has no sympathy with middle-class, respectable
constitutionalism – monarchist or republican – equating it with pedantry and legalism. The crowd scenes in the Revolution, which wind up
his rhetoric to an extraordinary pitch of intensity and almost delirium,
are for him sublime because spontaneous, whereas the commemoration of the fall of the Bastille on 14 July 1790, by an immense
national festival and by oath-swearing on an 'altar of the fatherland',
is sentimental play-acting because prearranged. Mobs, however, *are*
authentic:

Your mob is a genuine outburst of Nature; issuing from, or communicating
with, the deepest deep of Nature. When so much goes grinning and grimacing

as a lifeless Formality, and under the stiff buckram no heart can be felt beating, here once more, if nowhere else, is a Sincerity and Reality. Shudder at it; or even shriek over it, if thou must; nevertheless consider it. Such a Complex of human Forces and Individualities hurled forth, in their transcendental mood, to act and react, on circumstances and on one another; to work out what it is in them to work. The thing they will do is known to no man; least of all to themselves. It is the inflammablest immeasurable Fire-work, generating, consuming itself. With what phases, to what extent, with what result it will burn off, Philosophy and Perspicacity conjecture in vain. (I.VII.IV)

The French revolutionary mob is a portent, and the Revolution itself is still active in the world, 'the crowning Phenomenon of our Modern Time' and a lesson to Carlyle's contemporaries. Feudal aristocracy is everywhere being replaced by a moneybag aristocracy, but 'That there be no second Sansculottism in our Earth for a thousand years, let us understand well what the first was; and let Rich and Poor of us go and do *otherwise*' (III.VII.VI). The French Revolution is both the epic of Democracy and an admonition.

It must be apparent by now that Carlyle is no ordinary historian. John Stuart Mill called him a poet, though it is worth remembering that Lord Acton, not a man to underrate the historian's responsibilities, paid tribute to Carlyle's book as 'the volumes that delivered our fathers from thraldom to Burke'. The book is slow to start, and the reader has to use the early books, dealing with the *Ancien Régime*, to get used to Carlyle's peculiar authorial manners and his experiments with diction and syntax, the frequent vocatives addressed to both the reader and the historical characters, and the occasional use of Gallicisms to convey the flavour of a translation (e.g. 'there to consider himself'). A decadent society on the verge of extinction is depicted through a kind of collage of symbolic vignettes, held together by a rumbling, Calvinistic authorial sermon. There is an occasional welcome touch of grotesque humour or bathos. The colourful dresses at a kind of *fête champêtre* to watch a balloon ascent (the chapter is significantly entitled 'Windbags') are like banks of flowers, so, by a piece of surreal logic, the coaches in which their wearers sit are flowerpots:

Manifold, bright-tinted, glittering with gold; all through the Bois de Boulogne, in longdrawn variegated rows; – like longdrawn living flower-borders, tulips, dahlias, lilies of the valley; all in their moving flower-pots (of new-gilt carriages): pleasure of the eye, and pride of life! So rolls and dances the Procession: steady, of firm assurance, as if it rolled on adamant and the foundations of the world; not on mere heraldic parchment, – under which smoulders a lake of fire. Dance on, ye foolish ones; ye sought not wisdom, neither have ye found it. Ye and your fathers have sown the wind, ye shall reap the whirlwind. Was it not from of old written: *The wages of sin is death*? (I.II.VI)

The narrative really picks up with the summoning of the Estates General to deal with the public bankruptcy (which Carlyle views with grim complacency), leading to the election of a National Assembly in which the nation's hopes become invested, and are, of course, doomed to disappointment. Carlyle, as a narrator of extraordinary idiosyncratic power, needs events, the more rapid and momentous the better, to give the reader his best.

One has to accept Carlyle as a historian, if at all, for what he is; it is no use expecting what he did not attempt to be: a lucid purveyor of linear narrative and careful analyses of cause and effect. These things can be found in the midst of Carlyle's accounts, but his stranger effects were entirely deliberate, made largely out of epic precedent, an Old Testament style of vision, a fierce pulpit manner, and an idiosyncratic cosmic view: a metaphysics made concrete through symbolism. The effect on narrative is a rapid cutting from individuals, often humble and seen only momentarily, and highly particular situations, rendered in full concrete circumstantiality, to cosmic and world-historical perspectives, with many intermediary points between.

Carlyle had meditated much on the writing of history, producing two essays on the subject, and to more penetrating effect than in Macaulay's parallel reflections. Carlyle's view and its effects on his chosen rhetorical strategies are summarized in two notable quotations: 'History is the essence of innumerable biographies' and 'Narrative is *linear*, Action is *solid*.' The former warns us to expect no restrictions imposed by 'the dignity of history'; the latter not to expect straightforward chains of cause-and-effect explanation and accounts of the pursuit of considered, purposive politics. Everything in history is multiply determined; the actors scarcely see beyond their feet, and in every moment an immensity of different events is occurring, any of which may be significant. Our observations have to be successive though the things done were often simultaneous, and 'shape after shape bodies itself forth from innumerable elements.' Narrative, therefore, though it strive against its own linear nature, must try, as it were, to move sideways as well as forwards.

Carlyle's devices for bringing this about are essentially two: the selection of certain events, characters and actions as symbolic of larger realities, and extraordinarily innovative experiments in what may be called multi-voiced narrative, where the authorial voice, so often peremptory, intrusive and bullying, sometimes seems temporarily suspended in favour of a cacophony of other voices, of which he is the impresario, making a babble of catchphrases out of quotations from the newspapers, pamphlets, placards and memoirs he has consulted. This imagined babble in the midst of the revolutionary crowd, where Carlyle aims to place the reader – always, of course, in the present tense – is, to use his own term, combustible. A particular word or incident can ignite it into action and almost randomly determine its direction: to the Bastille, to Versailles, to the palace of the Tuileries, and hence to some of the central events of the Revolution. The combustibility is made up of hunger and hatred, suspicion and rumour. Suspicion, for example, of a royalist military coup, which leads to the storming of the Bastille. On 12 July

the streets are all placarded with an enormous-sized *De par le Roi*, 'inviting peaceable citizens to remain within doors', to feel no alarm, to gather in no crowd. Why so? What mean these 'placards of enormous size'? Above all, what means this clatter of military; dragoons, hussars, rattling in from all points of the compass towards the Place Louis Quinze . . .

Have the destroyers descended on us then? From the Bridge of Sèvres to utmost Vincennes, from Saint-Denis to the Champs-de-Mars, we are begirt! Alarm, of the rogue unknown, is in every heart . . . Are these troops verily come out 'against Brigands'? Where are the Brigands? What mystery is in the wind? – Hark! a human voice repeating articulately the Job's-news: *Necker*,

People's Minister, Saviour of France, is dismissed. Impossible; incredible! Treasonous to the public peace! . . . (I.V.IV)

Carlyle gives a similar preamble/explanation for the march to Versailles, involving the market women of Paris, which in the following October brings the royal family as virtual prisoners back to Paris and inaugurates the next act of the Revolution. There are rumours of a disloyal banquet held at Versailles to celebrate the arrival of a new regiment, where the nation has been insulted and its new tricolour cockade trampled underfoot:

Yes, here with us is famine; but yonder at Versailles is food; enough and to spare! . . . bloody-minded Aristocrats, heated with excess of high living, trample on the National Cockade. Can the atrocity be true? Nay, look: green uniforms faced with red; black cockades, – the colour of Night! Are we to have military onfall; and death also by starvation? . . .

In one of the Guardhouses of the Quartier Saint-Eustache, 'a young woman' seizes a drum, – for how shall National Guards give fire on women, on a young woman? The young woman seizes the drum; sets forth beating it, 'uttering cries relative to the dearth of grains'. Descend, O mothers; descend ye Judiths, to food and revenge! – All women gather and go; crowds storm all stairs, force out all women: the female Insurrectionary Force, according to Camille [Desmoulins] resembles the English Naval one; there is a universal 'Press of women'. Robust Dames of the Halle, slim Mantua-makers, assiduous, risen with the dawn; ancient Virginity tripping to matins; the Housemaid, with early broom; all must go. Rouse ye, O women; the laggard men will not act; they say, we ourselves may act!

And so, like snowbreak from the mountains, for every staircase is a melted brook, it storms . . . (I.VII.III–IV)

The idiom here, of course, is that of epic, but the narrative technique is also an interpretation, right or wrong.

Interpretations of the French Revolution began almost as early as the Revolution itself. Conspiracy was the initially preferred explanation, attributed first to manipulation, using his vast wealth, by the radical head of the younger branch of the royal house, Philippe, duc d'Orléans, who later adopted the name Philippe Egalité and voted for the death of Louis XVI. In the later 1790s the French Catholic exiles, notably the Abbé Barruel, produced a rival conspiratorial version which attributed the Revolution to the Freemasons. In Britain, explanations in terms of 'deeper' causes, particularly economic, soon replaced these early versions, but the conspiratorial view had life in it, at least at the popular level, for a long time. An example is Dickens's *A Tale of Two Cities* (1859), which is sometimes cited as a case of Carlyle's influence. This may be true of the crowd scenes, but in their interpretations of the Revolution the two authors diverged widely. Dickens dwells on an entirely imaginary network of plotters, organized as a secret society, with mysterious signs and passwords for mutual recognition; this reflects conditions in Europe in the mid nineteenth century, particularly in Italy and France, but has nothing to do with either the actual French Revolution or Carlyle. Carlyle presents the French as stumbling from phase to phase of the Revolution, without clear intention, driven by events, by suspicion and fear, as well as by idealism and fanaticism, and arriving where no one had intended or foreseen. Carlyle's originality consisted most of all in the ways he dramatizes this view and enacts it before the reader's eyes – and ears, for one imagines Carlyle's narrator, as he invites one to do, as a heard voice.

The kind of voice it was can be sharply appreciated by the contrast with Macaulay, whose own mode of address was often oratorical. Take, for example, Macaulay's account of what he sees as the moment when the Revolution of 1688 might have descended into anarchy, with William not crowned, the army disbanded, James in flight, and the anti-Popish mob in full cry:

It was a terrible moment. The king was gone. The prince had not yet arrived. No regency had been appointed. The great seal, essential to the administration of ordinary justice, had disappeared. It was soon known that Feversham had, on receipt of the royal order, instantly disbanded his forces. What respect for law or property was likely to be found among soldiers, armed and congregated, emancipated from the restraints of discipline, and destitute of the necessaries of life? On the other hand, the populace of London had, during some weeks, shown a strong disposition to turbulence and rapine. The urgency of the crisis united for a short time all who had any interest in the peace of society. (*History*, X)

It is a situation report from the historian, but the manner, in diction and the measured ordering of the sentences, is also the parliamentary manner. By converting the verbs to the present tense, and inserting 'Mr Speaker' or 'My Lords' at intervals, it is easy to imagine it as delivered by a minister to Parliament (not then sitting). 'My Lords, the king is gone. The prince is not yet arrived. The Great Seal has disappeared. We understand that Lord Feversham, on receipt of an order from His Majesty, has . . .' etc. The voice, whosoever's it is, is in control, and so, the reader infers, is the institution for which it stands. There is nothing like Carlyle's tormented, fractured syntax, just as there is no voice with this kind of authority in Carlyle's *French Revolution*. In England we understand from Macaulay that Rationality and Respectability, however much under stress, are ultimately in control and will win. In Carlyle there is no such reassurance on behalf of either.

Both Macaulay and Carlyle stood at the apex of a long movement, from the eighteenth century, before austere professionalism spoiled the game, to render history for the reader in its full sensuous and emotional immediacy and circumstantiality. But their perspectives are different. The emotions in which Macaulay mainly involves the reader are parliamentary ones, or at least could have been expressed in Parliament – and none the worse for that. Carlyle said that the great element missing from our attempted entry into the past is Fear; he set himself to re-enact it, and succeeded extraordinarily well. His syntax is designed to embody a distracted groping for certainties in a fog of rumour and of events at best only half-understood, in moods of acute anxiety, rage and sometimes dangerous exaltation.

Carlyle's effects to this end were not to be exceeded until the twentieth century and in a different medium. To read Carlyle now is to be reminded of Sergei Eisenstein's cinematic technique in the handling of crowd scenes in another revolution, with the camera panning in and out from the most highly individualized close-up moments to the widest perspectives. Very Eisensteinian, as it were, is not only the intimacy Carlyle achieves but also the sudden shifts of perspective, so that we see the crowd as though from a camera high above, as a river to which each doorway and staircase is a tributary. Another such sudden shift, this time to a cosmic perspective, is achieved by a focusing, very cinematic in anticipation, on an indifferent non-human witness. As the siege rages, 'the great Bastille clock ticks (inaudible) in its Inner Court there, at its ease, hour after hour; as if nothing special, for it or the world, were passing' (I.V.VI). It is part of the infinity of simultaneous events in history, which are also events in infinite space and time. On the evening the Bastille is taken the July sun falls 'on reapers amid peaceful woody fields; on old women spinning in cottages; on ships far out in the silent main; on Balls at the Orangerie of Versailles, where high-rouged Dames of the Palace are even now dancing with double-jacketed Hussar-Officers' (I.V.VII). World history itself is dwarfed by the omnipresence and persistence of the repetitions of daily life and the enduring natural world. The peasant in Breughel's picture who ploughs his field while a distant Icarus falls from the sky is a very Carlylean emblem. At the height of the Terror in Paris twenty-three theatres play nightly and sixty assembly rooms for dancing are open: 'In startling transitions, in colours all intensated, the sublime, the ludicrous, the horrible succeed one another; or rather, in crowding tumult, accompany one another.' The historian, he says, would be glad of a hundred tongues. Lacking them, he must snatch for the reader 'this or the other significant glimpse of things, in the fittest sequence we can' (III.V.I).

In contrast to Macaulay, Carlyle sometimes excuses himself from attending the tedious sessions of the National Convention, making its irrelevant constitution. He visits it, for preference, only in the moments when parliamentary decorum breaks down and the Convention becomes itself a kind of mob – as when the women from Paris, wet, bedraggled, famished and angry, break into its orderly session in Versailles and the President has to order in food for them from neighbouring cookshops, which Carlyle greets, after many allusions, with a genuine Homeric quotation: 'nor did any soul lack a fair share of victual': loaves, wine and 'great store of sausages' (I.VII.VIII). Sausages do not generally appear in national assemblies, nor in history. For Carlyle the Insurrection of Women was both burlesque and sublime. The confrontation of the desire for a constitution with the desire for sausages was an encapsulation of much that the Revolution was about. Always the mundane, the quotidian and the domestic reassert themselves, and Carlyle is as complicit with them as he is roused to celebration of the world-historical moment. Even then, in the epic of Democracy, the heroes are of course ordinary men: 'On then, all Frenchmen that have hearts in their bodies. Roar with all your throats of cartilage and metal, ye Sons of Liberty; stir spasmodically whatever of utmost faculty is in you, soul, body or spirit; for it is the hour! Smite, thou Louis Tournay, cartwright of the Marais, old-soldier of the Regiment Dauphiné; smite at that Outer Drawbridge chain...' (I.V.VI). The main inspiration, it is clear, is Homer; the rhapsodic attempt to render the multitudinous, and the vast energy of the mass, hint for the modern reader also at Walt Whitman.

Carlyle's use of bathos is not only funny but humanizes his narrative, which is not, of course, always at full stretch. When the Goddess of Reason, having been worshipped on the altar, returns home, 'ungoddessed', to her husband, what do we imagine they talk about that evening over supper? It is a question one can imagine no other historian asking, then or perhaps since, and for it one can forgive him much pulpit rhetoric – and has to. History, we are vividly reminded, is the essence of innumerable biographies. Bathos occurs too in the account of the defence of the frontiers by the revolutionary armies, which was for Carlyle another epic of the Revolution. The threat of the invasion by the reactionary powers rouses him to the same helter-skelter mimetic narrative as the storming of the Bastille or the march to Versailles, the rapid concatenation of names and nouns matching the urgency of the hour:

Does not the Coalition, like a fire-tide, pour in; Prussia through the opened North-East; Austria, England through the North-West? ... On Toulon Arsenal there flies a flag, – nay, not even the Fleur-de-lys of a Louis Pretender; there flies that accursed St. George's Cross of the English and Admiral Hood ... Beleaguer it, bombard it, ye Commissioners Barras, Fréron, Robespierre Junior; thou General Cartaux, General Dugommier; above all, thou remarkable Artillery-Major, Napoleon Buonaparte! (III.IV.V)

But there is pathos as well as comic bathos in the expostulation of the municipality of Verdun, known for its patisserie, at finding itself reluctantly implicated in world history and expected to be heroic: 'Resist him [the Duke of Brunswick] to the death? Every day of retardation precious? How, O General Beaurepaire (asks the amazed

Municipality) shall we resist him? . . . Retardation, Patriotism is good; but so likewise is peaceable baking of pastry and sleeping in whole skin' (III.I.III). Verdun, ironically in view of its later status as an icon of resistance, capitulates tamely.

Carlyle, to the modern reader, is a paradox, an extraordinary compound of the archaic, or, worse, the deeply unfashionable, and elements we think of as distinctly modern. Swift and Rabelais before him suggest parallels, as does Whitman after. Carlyle's classmates nicknamed him 'the Dean' in recognition of a Swiftian quality. Relations to earlier historiography are harder to see, though Carlyle greatly admired Schiller and came towards the end of a long period of erosion of the idea of the dignity of history. Carlyle has much time for the sublime, none for dignity. It is not surprising that the classical republican historians make no figure in his work, despite the French revolutionaries' devotion to them. The chief borrowing is, rather surprisingly, from Florence: Carlyle a number of times employs the *carroccio* (above, p. 281) as an image of a symbolic rallying point. For the rest, no humanist he, or *philosophe*, but an Old Testament-nurtured Puritan, at home with the mundane and the transcendental. Humorous, hectoring and at times almost frenzied, he found one guide to his monumental task in Homer's epic realism, and for the rest he went his own way. At his best – and he has more than one kind of best – his history and his prose have enormous imaginative energy, whose degenerations into bombast are the price the reader pays.

Michelet and Taine: The People and the Mob

In France itself, the serious study of the French Revolution began in the 1820s and has never ceased. Interpretation of the Revolution was central to current political attitudes and conflicts throughout the nineteenth century and beyond. The political factions which fought, politically, polemically and sometimes violently, for their different versions of France found the Revolution an inescapable point of reference. The principle of hereditary monarchy continued to be upheld by those spoken of as Legitimists or Ultras (i.e. ultra-royalist) and prevailed during the Restoration of the Bourbon monarchy from 1814 to 1830. The liberal, junior, Orléans branch of the family ascended the throne in 1830 after the July Revolution of that year in the person of King Louis-Philippe, whose father had voted for the execution of his cousin Louis XVI. After the Revolution of 1848, this 'July Monarchy', which was supported by moderate liberal and generally Anglophile constitutionalists like the historian François Guizot (below, p. 405), who became minister of education and later leader of the government, was replaced by the Second Republic, in which class conflict soon produced a second, abortive, insurrection of the Parisian working class, whose leader, Louis Blanc, was himself a historian of the first French Revolution. As Karl Marx ironically noted, the overthrow of the Republic by Louis Napoleon, nephew of the Emperor, in 1851 recapitulated the supplanting of the first Republic by Napoleon. The Second Empire lasted until 1871, ending in military defeat by Prussia, followed by the violent suppression of the Paris Commune, whose methods had aroused vivid recollections of the revolutionary Terror of 1793–4. The Third Republic, liberal, anticlerical but mainly antisocialist, was led by another historian of the Revolution, Adolphe Thiers.

French nineteenth-century history often seemed engaged in recapitulating the different phases of the first Revolution: a partly revived *Ancien Régime*, a liberal–constitutionalist phase echoed in the July Monarchy, the establishment of a Republic, a revolutionary Terror focused on Paris, with Bonaparte always waiting in the wings. The historiography of the Revolution could thus hardly be other than heavily politically charged. All political factions could find historical correlatives for their political allegiances and fears in the events of 1789–97. The continued strife over the status and role, particularly in education, of the Catholic Church, which had been one of the early targets of the Revolution, would alone have kept the divisions which had opened up then in the forefront of politics. Anticlericalism was an article of faith for most republicans.

The political prominence of the past ensured also the prominence of historians. Guizot was an eminent liberal historian, though he did not write on the Revolution. Thiers published one of the earliest histories of the Revolution, in the 1820s, before going on to hold high office under the July Monarchy, when he became Guizot's rival. He was eventually elected as the first president of the Third Republic, established in 1871. Another historian of the first Revolution, the poet Alphonse de Lamartine, was one of the leaders of the Second Republic. Louis Blanc's substantial history of the Revolution has already been mentioned. Under the Third Republic, France's leading socialist, Jean Jaurès, produced a *Socialist History of the French Revolution*.

It was not uncommon in the nineteenth century for politicians to write history: as we have seen, in Britain, early in the century such prominent politicians as Charles James Fox, Sir James Mackintosh, Macaulay and a future prime minister, Lord John Russell, all wrote histories of the English revolution of 1688. In no case, however, was immediate political influence attributed to their histories. By the early nineteenth century, though there were nuances of interpretation, the 1688 Revolution had become in England a symbol of consensus. In the case of France, endorsement or denunciation of the leading actors of the Revolution – Mirabeau, the Girondins, Danton, Robespierre, the Commune of Paris and, for that matter, Bonaparte – immediately established one's contemporary political identity. The word 'Jacobin' itself fell out of contemporary political usage, presumably for lack of overt claimants, though the Jacobins were not without admirers, but the Revolution still provided symbols of allegiance and a political vocabulary, including 'Left' and 'Right', referring to the seating of the factions in the Chamber.

By general consensus the outstanding history of France of the first half, perhaps of the whole, of the nineteenth century is that of Jules Michelet, which eventually grew to twenty-three volumes (1833–67). Into it, out of chronological sequence, was interpolated his two-volume *History of the French Revolution* (1847–53). Though he did not take up a political career, Michelet's political commitment was unmistakable. His lectures at the Collège de France were suspended on the orders of Guizot, his patron and predecessor, now minister; this was a double irony, for Guizot's own lectures from the same chair had earlier been suspended by government order during the Restoration. Under the Second Empire Michelet lost his chair permanently, and the position in the National Archives that Guizot had procured for him, and retired into exile in Brittany, where he continued to work in local archives as well as writing his history and some other, highly idiosyncratic, works.

Before he came to the French Revolution he was known and admired for the medieval volumes of his *History of France*. All Michelet's work was deeply personal and emotional, but one early intellectual influence is noteworthy. In 1827 he translated the *New Science* (1725) of the early-eighteenth-century Neapolitan thinker Giambattista Vico. The extent of Vico's influence on the thought of late-eighteenth-century Germans, most notably Herder, with whom he has a lot in common, and who also impressed Michelet, has never been easy to trace, but Vico's influence on Michelet is clear. To Vico, culture was a collective product of whole peoples. Mythology, in particular, gave a key to the mentalities of 'the first peoples, who were everywhere naturally poets' (*New Science*, 352). Through it we can trace 'a history of the ideas, the customs and the deeds of mankind' (368), because they were 'the manner of thinking of entire peoples' (816). These, lacking the ability to form abstract concepts, expressed their ideas through personifications (209). Lacking the faculty of abstraction, they apprehended and felt particular perceptions all the more vividly, which explains their sublimely poetic mentality (819). In this way Vico establishes what were later to become almost a set of commonplaces, which were certainly subscribed to by Michelet, namely a set of antitheses not only between earlier and later times but between the popular and the educated mentality, in which the former is poetic and sensuous, the latter metaphysical and abstract. The populist Romanticism current in France in the 1830s and '40s, in which Michelet was immersed, was highly sympathetic to such ideas, but in his own case the influence of Vico was direct. *The History of France*, with its emphasis on the life, experiences, thoughts and sentiments of the French people, reads at times like a massive embodiment of Vico's ideas. Michelet's manners as a writer were, as we shall see, declamatory and exclamatory in the Romantic fashion, carried, as in Carlyle, to idiosyncratic extremes, in a way that is now highly unfashionable. But the ways in which his attention as a historian is focused, and his passion for imaginative re-creation – he called writing history 'resurrection' – find an echo in the interests of modern French historians.

In one respect Michelet's injunction to himself to bring about 'resurrection', and his interest in the popular mind, overrode other personal predilections. He was heir to the anticlericalism of the French Enlightenment and the Revolution, but the medieval volumes of his history were admired by the Catholic Right. His treatment of Joan of Arc – whom he regarded as incarnating the self-consciousness of France as a nation – was particularly acclaimed. Michelet's history was thickly textured as well as dramatic; he worked assiduously in the National Archives, to which his post there gave him easy access. He has been called 'the Victor Hugo of history'; Hippolyte Taine compared him with the painter Delacroix. His identification with France and its people was so close that he regarded the *History* as his spiritual autobiography: 'It is through personal sorrows that the historian feels and reproduces the sorrows of nations.' He rejoiced that in his vocation 'God has given me in History the means of participating in everything.'

It was his republican anticlericalism, however, particularly his hostility to the continuing influence of the Jesuits in French education, which turned him, prematurely in terms of his overall scheme for the *History*, to the French Revolution. He had also been exploring what he saw as his roots and resurrecting his own early life in a short monograph called *The People* (1846). In the dedicatory preface, to his friend Edgar Quinet, yet another historian of the Revolution, he celebrated his artisan origins. His father was an unsuccessful printer, exactly from the stratum from which the revolutionary crowds were chiefly recruited. Michelet had worked for him for a while, before the educational ladder created by the Revolution opened wider prospects to him. The paper wars of the Revolution were good for the business, but the Napoleonic censorship had been bad. Before writing on the recent and contemporary life of the People (we need to retain the upper case), Michelet had, as he explained, gone among them, talked, asked questions, and listened. But he also says he found his chief material in the reminiscences of his youth:

To know the life of the people, their toils and sufferings, I had but to interrogate my memory. For I too, my friend, have worked with my hands. The true name of modern man, that of *workman*, I am entitled to it in more than one sense. Before I made books, I *composed* them literally. I arranged letters before I grasped ideas; and I am not ignorant of the dismalness of the workshop, and the wearisomeness of long hours.

In turning in 1847 to the Revolution, Michelet in his own view was entering into the People's greatest historical achievement. The People was the collective hero; for him, as for Carlyle, the Revolution was the epic of Democracy; individual political leaders were secondary and sometimes highly culpable, but the People as such could do no wrong: in the Revolution's 'benevolent period the whole people were the actors; in the period of cruelty only a few individuals'. In the first crisis of the Revolution, among the populace 'each one felt greatness in his breast from hour to hour'.

There are considerable similarities between Michelet and Carlyle, which make the differences instructive. They worked entirely independently, but were subject to some of the same cultural influences, and possessed some similarities of temperament. Both conceived of the task of the historian as being to re-create and re-enact, and both threw their authorial personalities into the action, apostrophizing and exhorting, in moods often of exaltation, almost of frenzy. Michelet said, 'I struggled physically with the clergy and the Terror.' Carlyle complained loudly of the nervous cost of writing history: for a believer in silent toil he could be vigorously plaintive. In speaking of the actions of the crowd, the French language offered Michelet the convenience of an impersonal pronoun. He often spoke of it as '*on*', thus avoiding both 'I' and 'they'; Carlyle sometimes used 'we'. Michelet, in speaking of himself as narrator, asserts his own presence: 'I was at the foot of the Bastille. I was raising on its tower the immortal flag.' Both authors were conscious of straining against the limitations of language. Carlyle, as we have seen, wished the historian had a hundred tongues, while Michelet yearned for 'a new language, the language of a serious, loving Rabelais'. They were, predictably, drawn to the same metaphors. Both spoke with abhorrence of the 'mechanical', which stood for the abstract and soulless. Both invoked volcanoes, and spoke of the making of the new revolutionary world as 'fermentation'. Michelet calls on both images in his description of Danton – whom both he and Carlyle admired with qualifications – and of Danton's club, the

Cordeliers, the rival to the Jacobin Club. We have to see the Cordeliers, Michelet says, 'bubbling and fermenting together in their night sessions in the base of their Etna'. Danton, his face ravaged by the pox, is hideous but sublime: 'This almost eyeless face seems a volcano without a crater – volcano of mud and fire, within whose closed forge one hears the conflicts of nature.' Mud and fire were also Carlyle's two most frequently invoked elements. Without precise recollection, and allowing for translation, the most expert reader could be deceived about which author was responsible for the above quotation.

Both, again, were susceptible to the apocalyptic, but here the differences begin to surface. Michelet's visions are sweeter; there may be a trace of his reading of the medieval mystical philosopher of history Joachim of Flores (above, p. 186), for whom the third age of the world was to be one of freedom, love and harmony. Carlyle's apocalypses were made of sterner, Hebraic stuff: scouring, retributive conflagrations. Carlyle's sensibility was Protestant and Judaic, while Michelet was touched by Indian mysticism. He would never have spoken of God, as Carlyle did, as 'the almighty Taskmaster'. Nature, for Michelet, came to acquire a pantheistic hue. Although, under the influence of German metaphysics, Carlyle was also fond of speaking of the interconnectedness of all things, he, like Karl Marx, conceived of physical nature as something for man to struggle with and wrest his subsistence from.

We have space for only two specific comparisons of Carlyle's and Michelet's respective treatments of key episodes of the Revolution. The first episode is the loyalist banquet at Versailles to welcome a new, royalist, regiment's officers, rumours of which fed revolutionary indignation and fears of counter-revolution in Paris, leading to the march, led by the market women, to Versailles to bring the royal family back to the capital. Carlyle's treatment is uncharacteristically bluff, almost amused. Young men get drunk, brag, say and do foolish things:

Suppose champagne flowing; with pot-valorous speech, with instrumental music, empty feathered heads growing ever the noisier, in their own emptiness, in each other's noise! Her Majesty, who looks unusually sad to-night (His Majesty sitting dulled with the day's hunting), is told that the sight of it would cheer her. Behold! She enters there, issuing from her State-rooms, like the Moon from clouds, this fairest, unhappy Queen of Hearts ... Could featherheaded young ensigns do other than, by white Bourbon Cockades, handed them from fair fingers; by waving of swords, drawn to pledge the Queen's health; by trampling of National Cockades; by scaling the Boxes, whence intrusive murmurs may come; by vociferation, tripudiation [dancing in triumph], sound, fury and distraction, within doors and without, – testify what tempest-tost state of vacuity they are in? Till champagne and tripudiation do their work; and all lie silent, horizontal; passively slumbering. (I.VII.II)

Carlyle's comment is untypically indulgent: 'It was so natural, yet so unwise.'

Michelet takes the episode with deadly seriousness and a sense of outrage. The whole event, in his narration, is hectic, irrational and almost diabolic, as well as operatic. The officers are not only drunk but dazzled and disoriented when the King and Queen enter the royal theatre, 'where the boxes, lined with looking-glasses, reflect a blaze of light in every direction'. The officers tear off their revolutionary red-white-and-blue cockades, the new national emblem, and trample them underfoot. Michelet was always sensitive to symbolism, and employs it himself: in the *History of France* the English, in destroying Joan the Maid, 'thought they were deflowering France' (X). In Versailles

The music continued, ever more impassioned and ardent; it played the Marche des Hulans, and sounded the charge. They all leaped to their feet, looking around for the enemy to appear; for want of adversaries they scaled the boxes, rushed out into the *Cour de Marbre* ... The frenzy of that moral orgy seemed to infect the whole court. (II.vii)

The differences appear most sharply, however, in Michelet's treatment of the first 'Festival of the Federation', on the anniversary of the fall of the Bastille, 14 July 1790. Carlyle's version is above all ironic: the professions of universal goodwill are shortly to give way to massacre and the guillotine. But, in any case, humankind cannot sustain very much fraternity. Though he acknowledges that the Federation movement began spontaneously in the provinces and aroused popular enthusiasm all over France, he treats it as a kind of contagious intoxication and the greatest of the festivals, on the Champs de Mars in Paris, as manifestly artificial and stage-managed, which of course it was. To Carlyle its gospel was merely sentimental: he had, as we have seen, a Presbyterian sourness towards ritual, though he could be indulgent to spontaneous violence (as in the Scottish Reformation). But for Michelet the Federation is the high point of his history and in French national consciousness, pointing the way to a better future. He said that writing about it marked one of the great moments of his life. His description has an ominous element: at the sacramental moment, the swearing of the oath of fraternity, the surly demeanour of the royal family strikes a jarring note. But irony is almost absent, though he goes on to mourn over the contrasting future. The moment of the Federation was 'the holy epoch in which the entire nation marched under one fraternal banner'. He compares the marches to Paris by the participants from all over France to the Crusades: 'What Jerusalem attracts thus a whole nation? ... the Jerusalem of hearts, the holy unity of Fraternity, the great living city made of men ...'; its name is *patrie*. At the oath-swearing in the Champs de Mars

The plain is suddenly shaken by the report of forty pieces of cannon. At that clap of thunder, all rise and stretch forth their hands to heaven ... O King! O People! pause ... Heaven is listening and the sun is breaking expressly through the cloud ... Attend to your oaths! Oh! how heartily the people swear! How credulous they still are! ... But why does the King not grant them the happiness of seeing him swear at the altar? Why does he swear under cover, in the shade, and half-concealed from the people? ... For God's sake, sire, raise your hand so that all may see it. (III.xii)

Hippolyte Taine, a quarter of a century later, offered his own version of the Federation oath, and the Revolution itself, in his *History of the French Revolution*, which formed the second part of a longer work, *The Origins of Contemporary France* (1875–95). His account of the Revolution is in almost every respect the opposite of Michelet's. The contrast between the two invites being treated as archetypal. Lord Acton coupled them as two works reading which formed an epoch in the reader's life: 'No man feels the grandeur of the Revolution until he reads Michelet, or the horror of it without reading Taine.' George Rudé, the chief modern analyst of the composition of the revolutionary crowd, spoke of historians, when referring to the crowd, as following the traditions established respectively by Michelet and Taine, and speaking of it accordingly as 'the people' or 'the mob'. Rudé is highly critical of Taine's use of documents to characterize the make-up of the crowd, but it is a kind of tribute that Rudé expounds his own version, three-quarters of a century later, mainly in the form of an argument with Taine. Taine's research had been thorough, if insufficiently critical of documents which supported his case, and his rhetoric has an enduring power to shock and alarm. Where Michelet saw the essence of the Revolution, the role of the People, as benign, fraternal and inspiring, and blamed for its horrors only those who rejected the fraternal embrace, for Taine the Revolution was from the outset a pathological social phenomenon. The people, in the form of the mob, released from normal restraints, was irrational, uncontrolled and highly dangerous. He wrote in the shadow of the Paris Commune of 1871, which had revived memories of the excesses – and for some the heroism – of the first Revolution, and it shows.

Taine saw the revolutionary leaders as similarly out of control, intoxicated by general ideas which inspired an overconfidence exacerbated by political inexperience. Virtually the only point in common in the attitudes of Michelet and Taine was that neither was at all disposed to idealize, as some had done, the Anglophile constitutionalist leadership, above all that of Mirabeau, in the first stage of the Revolution. But their reasons for this rejection were characteristically different. Michelet, a strongly Anglophobe republican, had no sympathy with constitutional monarchy and the *juste milieu*, while Taine denied that the Revolution had at any time been anything but recklessly utopian. In particular, Taine argued, from the moment, in July 1789, when the Assembly used the people as its shock troops and accepted the popular distribution of arms, the Revolution was set on a predetermined course.

Taine was himself a liberal constitutionalist, naturally drawn to the July Monarchy, which ended when he was twenty – the year he entered the Ecole Normale Superière. He envied England's constitutional stability and responsible and experienced governing class, and read

Macaulay's political essays as a source of political wisdom. He played no part in the Revolution of 1848, in which students were prominent, and wrapped himself self-consciously in the mantle of 'science', far removed from political strife, as his vocation. He was a liberal for all that, believing strongly in freedom of thought and speech. Falling under suspicion by the clergy, who were influential in education in the Second Republic, he was forced into a kind of exile in the provinces for a while, despite his academic brilliance. He established his reputation, however, by his writings in the 1860s, on culture, art and psychology, and for several decades, from the '60s to the '80s, he became the dominant figure in French intellectual life.

Taine stood, above all, for a scientific approach – by which he often meant a psychological one – to questions of art, literature and (a particular interest) national character. In biology he was a follower of Lamarck among others, believing in the inheritance of acquired characteristics, and his slogan *'race, milieu, moment'* – intended to provide a frame for the explanation of all cultural phenomena and collective psychologies – can be rendered roughly as 'inheritance, circumstances and epoch'. He believed that each cultural milieu and era had its master idea or disposition, which determined all its manifestations: thus the French mentality of the eighteenth century, which for him provided the motor of the Revolution, was characterized by an overriding confidence. This confidence was, for Taine, exemplified above all by Rousseau, and resulted in the application of simple abstract ideas of universal rationality – the *esprit classique* expressed during the Revolution by the idea of popular sovereignty and embodied in the Declaration of the Rights of Man.

But until the 1870s, while Taine conducted himself with intellectual hauteur towards government and people alike, his interests were above all in psychology. What was intended as his masterwork, the result of years of study which included attendance at dissections and observation of the insane, was *On Intelligence* (1870). This set out a conception of the mind which attempted, rather tentatively, to combine the philosophy of mind with neurology. In it the idea of the stable ego was dispensed with. Insanity was nearer the surface of the human mind than optimists would think; Taine's psychology had a distinctly pathological turn.

Taine explicitly regarded his work on culture and national character, and later on French history, as applied psychology, so it is important to grasp the outlines of his distinctive view. Taine regarded the
Revolution as marking the onset of a disease from which France was
still suffering; in a letter, he once compared it to the long-term effects
of syphilis. With his psychological theory established, with the Third
Republic inaugurated, and impelled by an appalled response to the
Commune, Taine set out in *The Origins of Contemporary France*, and
in particular in the volumes on the Revolution, to trace its pathology.

Taine's psychological theory was a modification of that tradition in
the philosophy of mind which is sometimes spoken of as empiricist,
or, perhaps more helpfully, as sensationalist. Our knowledge of the
world originates in sensations, which the mind combines as images.
These remain in the mind after the original sensory input which caused
them has ceased. They are therefore in a sense illusions, and in a state
of sanity are known to be so. Taine calls them 'true hallucinations'.
But since the mind harbours only its own images, the line between
those which continue to convey useful information, and are confirmed
by current sensations, and those which are simply, as it were, free-
floating is a disturbingly indistinct one. Images jostle for attention in
the mind – Taine uses an explicitly Darwinian analogy. Sometimes,
prompted by some trigger of memory or emotion, particularly in states
of reverie or high excitement, those which are no longer confirmed by
sensation as real are activated and take over.

The surrender to unreality is of two opposed kinds (this line of
thought was developed more fully by Taine's friend and follower
Théodule Ribot). On the one side lies a jumble of images, none of
them fixed or connected; this is mental confusion, advancing to instability and eventually delirium. On the other side lies the possibility
that one, perhaps quite inappropriate, image becomes fixed, supplants
all the others, and becomes incorrigible. This is the *idée fixe*, and the
state it produces is obsession or monomania. (There is an obvious
analogy with the contrast between anarchy and despotism.) The mental poise which can correct and control the hallucinatory images and
walk the tightrope between delirium and obsession is precarious; loss
of grip on reality – insanity – is always ready to pounce. Taine regarded
the French Revolution as a collective insanity; the distinction between

the two types largely corresponds to the crowd and the leaders. He said privately that since 1789 France had been either infantile or mad.

Taine's account of the Revolution may have been decisively shaped by theory – or, if one prefers, prejudice – but it was also the product of extensive research, and is heavily documented, if not always critically. France in the 1790s is in the grip of an *idée fixe*: the idea of the sovereignty of the people, expressed in Rousseau's *Social Contract* and in the Declaration of the Rights of Man (*FR* I.IV.iii, VI.I.i). This idea is fanatically promulgated by some, who employ it to manipulate and coerce others, who have to defer to it on pain of exile or even death. The revolutionary leaders are intoxicated by their idea; the revolutionary mob, which has no critical powers, is similarly intoxicated by the contagion of mutual excitement which its numbers generate, and driven by need, fear and hatred (I.IV.v). (Taine's work was the forerunner of later studies in crowd psychology and behaviour, particularly of the classic *The Crowd* (1895) by Gustave Le Bon, in which Taine's ideas are applied and amplified.) Elements of the mob, Taine insists, are also bribed.

The ostensible political sovereign, the Assembly and later the National Convention, is in fact at the mercy of the mob and of the political clubs like the Jacobins from which the revolutionary leaders promulgate their demands. The Assembly itself is virtually a mob (Le Bon says this too), in a constant state of hubbub and rowdy confusion, easily distracted, conducting its debates by means of slogans, which seek the applause of the galleries of spectators. These, since they represent the sovereign people, are incorrigible. They add to the din, intimidate those who dare utter unpopular opinions, and are in fact participants rather than onlookers (II.I.i). In the circumstances it is not surprising that the Assembly is given to sudden fits of ill-considered enthusiasm, resulting in hasty and confused legislation. Over-excitement becomes a kind of drug; the Assembly is not a conference for business but 'a patriotic opera' (II.I.i). France's men of experience, the *intendants* (governors) of the provinces, the members of the local *parlements*, the ecclesiastical rulers of great dioceses, are in the main excluded (III.II.iii). The hubris begotten on inexperience by a-priori ideas is unchecked. Suspicion also thrives, and denunciation is encouraged. (Taine always speaks as though all supposed counter-revolutionary plots were fantasies.) The 'bad counsellors' of the Assembly are fear and theory. Abstract ideas and conceit among the leaders, the urge to tumult and bloodshed among the people, feed off each other. Government makes way for 'an intermittent despotism, for factions blindly impelled by enthusiasm, credulity, misery and fear' (I.II.vi). Henceforth, beyond the King, beyond the Assembly,

appears the real monarch, the people – that is to say the mob of a hundred, a thousand, a hundred thousand beings gathered together haphazard, on an impulse, on an alarm, suddenly and irresistibly made legislators, judges and executioners . . . who, with its mother, howling and misshapen Liberty, sits at the threshold of the Revolution like Milton's two spectres at the gates of hell. (I.II.viii)

Michelet, as we have seen, had a strong sympathy with what we may call the folkish elements of the early Revolution: the dancing, singing, street theatre and carnival. Taine, predictably, regards these as ominous as well as orgiastic and pathological. The oath of the Federation in Paris in July 1790 and the outbursts of federative enthusiasm all over France which preceded it are regarded by Taine as mass delusions: 'Never was such an effort made to intoxicate the senses and strain the nerves beyond their powers of endurance . . . The difference between magniloquence and sincerity, between the false and the true, between show and substance is no longer distinguishable.' A whole nation is losing its grip on reality in a kind of delirium which is taken for fraternity. But there is also manipulation, even if it does not recognize itself for what it is. Children, as young as nine years old, declaim patriotic orations: 'it occurs to no one that they are puppets', with words put into their mouths. But people remain as they were: they avoid paying their debts, they lay their hands on public property if they get the chance – 'everywhere there is philanthropy in words and symmetry in the laws; everywhere there is violence in acts and disorder in all things' (III.I.i). Taine does not draw the parallel, but the reader of Thucydides can hardly fail to be reminded of the anarchy and political fanaticism in Corcyra, where words lost or reversed their meanings, just as, elsewhere, Taine's account of the Terror reminds us of Tacitus' description of the omnipresent, suspicious eye of the despot and of the miseries of the Roman proscriptions (above, pp. 84, 121). Where Michelet saw in 1790 a nation in the process of formation, Taine sees a society in a state of disintegration.

Taine does not often narrate events. Rather, he takes soundings of the state of French society, of the agents and the sufferers, across the social and institutional spectrum: in the Assembly and the Convention; in the psychology of the leaders, and in the political clubs which provide their power bases; in the Parisian mob and in the Paris Commune and sections; in the revolutionary tribunals and their victims; and in the provinces – including the representatives, the feared *representants en mission*, sent from Paris with despotic powers to enforce the government's will and often their own. Rather than narration – though there are many interpolated anecdotes – Taine offers a steady accumulation of evidence, from documents, from observers, from the quoted remarks of leading political agents, and from memoirs. He is not writing a narrative but compiling an indictment, which he does with as much weight and skill as vehemence.

The time and energy required by 'active citizenship' tends to bring forward, according to Taine, the worst elements in the population – those with plenty of both to spare and the impulse to agitate and dominate. They control the politics of the small-scale units, the sections: 'Politics became a profession.' The capital was more feverish than the provinces, the towns than the villages; Taine uses the simile of an abscess. The incoherence of the legislation produced by the Assembly, with no possibility of judicial review, plays into the hands of local leaders, who interpret it, and implement it or not, as they please (II.III.iv). The political club becomes 'the champion, judge, interpreter and administrator of the rights of man' (II.III.v).

Book IV gives us Taine's analysis of the psychology and tactics of the Jacobins, which is essentially an elaboration of what he has set out already as the revolutionary mentality. He sometimes draws the analogy with the Puritans. The revolutionary is characteristically an antinomian, convinced of his righteousness, out of touch with reality. He sees himself as the authorized executor of the common will. 'Marching along in the procession formed for him by this imaginary crowd, sustained by millions of metaphysical wills created by himself in his own image, he has their unanimous assent, and, like a chorus of triumphant shouts, he will fill the outer world with the inward echo of his own voice.' He is therefore a pathological case: 'Something which is not himself, a monstrous parasite, a foreign and disproportionate conception, lives within him' (IV.I.iii). The link to the argument of *On Intelligence* is particularly apparent here.

In the next three books, Taine goes on to consider at length how the Jacobins' power is established and exercised. Book VIII is devoted to 'the Governed': to the nobles, clergy, bourgeoisie and populace, and how they respectively fared during the Revolution. His history ends with the advent of Bonaparte. The Jacobin dictatorship could not last because it lacked the essential characteristic of a political society, mutual respect, particularly between governors and governed, and therefore was unable to establish mutual trust and confidence. In French civilian society by 1797 'there is not one among the three thousand legislators who have sat in the sovereign assemblies that can count on the deference and loyalty of a hundred Frenchmen.' In the army, however – 'military France' – it is otherwise (IX.I.x). Taine has largely ignored the wars on the frontiers: he speaks always of the revolutionary leadership as autonomous, driven on, deterministically, by its own vanity and obsession, ignoring the pressures to which the leaders were subjected. His indictment is immensely powerful, but it has the weaknesses of a deterministic demonstration.

Now, however, the frontiers, and the army which has seized and expanded them, become relevant. It is not just a matter of discipline. In the army have grown up mutual dependence, respect and sympathy. Hence the army is a society, and with its consent its commander can wield power, while 'civil France' will welcome him as its liberator and restorer. The outcome is a despotism. The Revolution had left itself no alternative to the omnipotence of the state – towards which it had tended, though incoherently, from the outset. What was left from revolutionary chaos was the omnipresence of government as a result of 'the absence of local and private initiative, the suspension of voluntary free associations, the gradual dispersion of small, spontaneous groupings, the preventative interdiction of prolonged hereditary works, the extinction of sentiments by which the individual lives beyond himself in the past or in the future' (IX.I.x). From this passage alone one could tell that Taine was an admirer of Burke and of

Tocqueville. His metaphor for the state of France is a barracks: clean, well-built, symmetrical and 'better adapted to the discipline of the average and lower elements of human nature . . . In this philosophical barracks we have lived for eighty years.'

Taine's work was predictably subjected to heavy criticism for its apparent mono-causal determinism, its simplifications, its indulgence towards dubious sources which suited his case. One of the most prolonged attacks was the book entitled *Taine, Historian of the French Revolution*, published in 1907 by Alphonse Aulard, who in 1886 had taken up the chair of the history of the French Revolution newly founded at the Sorbonne by the municipal council of Paris. Aulard, in announcing his credentials, identified himself as 'a respectful and grateful son of the Revolution which has emancipated humanity and science'. To understand the Revolution, he declared, one must love it. His attitudes were not far from Michelet's, though his manner was much more sober – 'dull' is an adjective it has incurred. Like Michelet he regarded the people as the hero of the Revolution, though he insisted that the conduct of the revolutionary leaders should be judged in the light of their circumstances and the reasonable fears these engendered. He also seemed to go some way to justifying the Terror by arguing that it was necessary for survival and to preserve the gains of the Revolution; this was an argument which others, later, would apply to Stalin.

This is hindsight, but appreciation of Taine is likely to be enhanced by an awareness of the grimmer features of twentieth-century history. Admittedly Taine exaggerates. His work is far from, and does not aspire to, what was becoming an ideal of disinterested history (but so is that of all the other historians of the Revolution in the period). However, when one has allowed for exaggeration, for Taine's mon-ocular vision and his own obsessions with Rousseau and the effects of the *esprit classique*, his indictment remains formidable, as well as a rhetorical tour de force, a powerful psycho-drama. His easy accept-ance of some dubious sources does not invalidate others. In the 1870s he described the emergence of the characteristics which, in the twentieth century, came to be spoken of as 'totalitarian'.

History as the Story of Freedom: Constitutional Liberty and Individual Autonomy

Stubbs's Constitutional History: *From Township to Parliament*

'We have no thread through the enormous intricacy and complexity of modern politics, except the idea of progress towards more perfect and assured freedom,' Lord Acton, newly appointed as Regius professor of history, told his Cambridge-undergraduate lecture audience in 1895. He could have added 'history' to 'politics' and many nineteenth-century historians in various European countries would have agreed with him. François Guizot (1787–1874), for example, France's greatest nineteenth-century constitutional historian, had taken this as the theme of his lectures at the Sorbonne in the 1820s (published as *The History of Civilization in Europe*, English translation 1846). Other civilizations, he argued, had been theocratic, despotic, democratic or regulated by caste, but in Europe no one principle had ever dominated all the others. Europe's dynamism derived from liberty and the diversity which had preserved it – a consequence of the multiplicity of influences which had shaped European civilization: Roman, Christian and barbarian.

The importance of Rome and the heritage of civic republicanism which in the ancient world had stood for liberty was a debatable issue. It was common, above all in Britain, to draw a line under the ancient city state, as essentially archaic and hence, in the modern world, an inappropriate model, whose dangers had been revealed by the enthusiasm felt for it at the time of the French Revolution. It was from the German invaders of the Roman empire, bringing with them the Tacitean freedom of the German woods, that modern European liberty essentially descended (above, p. 308). Guizot, in insisting on recognition of the Romanized character of Gaul, especially in the south, from which he himself came, was more moderate. He stressed in his *History of Civilization in France* (1829–32) that the municipal institutions of Roman Gaul had survived into the early Middle Ages, coalescing with the government of the urban Christian communities under their bishops, who were magistrates as well as pastors. But Guizot was obliged to admit that no direct continuity could be established between them and the city communes of the later Middle Ages; a French bourgeoisie was the product of the recovery of commercial life and the growth of the professions.

In any case, the semi-independence of the late-medieval towns had been crushed by the centralizing absolutism of Richelieu and Louis XIV. Much the same had occurred among the late-medieval city states of northern Italy, which, as Guicciardini had described, had succumbed, apart from Venice, to their own internal divisions and the military power of France and the Empire. The classic historical account of this for the nineteenth century was provided by the Swiss historian Charles de Sismondi, whose *History of the Italian Republics* began to appear in 1807. Sismondi, a liberal, described the life of the free Italian communes with enthusiasm, but his story was one of failure, which he explained, in traditional humanist and indeed Roman republican fashion, chiefly by failures of character and public virtue. It seemed that the autonomous city republic, as a political form, had proved a blind alley.

But England, at least, seemed to prove that the liberty of the German woods had proved enduring, and that its future lay with a liberal, parliamentary constitutionalism and limited monarchy. For the French, however, there was a difficulty. Not only was monarchy in France a deeply divisive issue since the first French Revolution, but just as, above all for the British, the republican model had been discredited by that Revolution, so, in France, the notion of the Teutonic inheritance was tainted by its association with aristocratic domination. French aristocratic writers, from the late seventeenth century, had claimed descent for the French nobility from the Teutonic conquerors of Gaul, the Franks. The point was to rebut the claims of monarchical absolutism: it was an axiom, from Tacitus, that German kings were elected and their powers limited; we have seen this argument in Hotman in the sixteenth century (above, p. 312). It also followed, however, that the common people of France – the so-called Third Estate (i.e. neither noble nor clerical) – being the descendants of the Gauls, were a conquered people. There was, understandably, something like a plebeian reaction, most influentially, at the time of the Revolution, in the Abbé Sièyes's pamphlet *What is the Third Estate?* (1789). If the nobility were essentially German invaders, then they were aliens whose titles derived from an act of violent usurpation. It was time for the descendants of the Gauls to recover their sovereign rights as a nation, of which the nobility formed no part.

No such divisiveness clouded the English understanding of the Teutonic invasion and settlement of post-Roman Britain as essentially free and even democratic. In the works of John Mitchell Kemble (*The Saxons in England*, 1849), Edward Freeman (*The History of the Norman Conquest*, 1867–79) and William Stubbs (*The Constitutional History of England in its Origin and Development*, 1873–8), England's Teutonic settlement was celebrated as the origin of the national tradition of liberty. It was above all Stubbs who stamped his authority for several generations on the constitutional history of medieval England and gave it a central place in the newly established history faculties in the universities, which from the 1860s onward permitted students to take examinations and to graduate in history (below, p. 455). For Stubbs, though not for Freeman, the heritage of Rome stood not for civilization but for tyranny, and it was gratifying to him that in England there was so little evidence of it. England's Teutonic invaders were settlers and pioneers. They had not, as in Gaul, established themselves as a landed aristocracy – as later did the Normans – served by an underclass of native Romano-British; these had been, it was confidently asserted, exterminated or driven to the margins in the Welsh mountains, not interbred with or enslaved.

For a while, on this basis, there were close relations between English and German historians. Kemble had been a pupil of the great German folklorist, linguist and legal antiquarian Jacob Grimm. As the French legal historians had done in the sixteenth century, from the late eighteenth century onward German scholars led Europe in the scholarly exploration of the legal customary roots of ancient Greek, Roman and Teutonic societies, notably with the work of Barthold Niebuhr on early Rome (above, p. 116), of Karl von Savigny, who was also a Roman legal historian, and of Grimm, whose work was in the field of early German language, myth and customs. German scholarship in this period was inspired and infused by a populist conception of the uniqueness and creativity of each primordial *Volk*, expounded above all by Johann Gottfried Herder (1744–1803); the possible connection between his ideas and those of Vico (above, p. 391) is unclear. The spirit of the *Volk* manifested itself in all aspects of life: language, myth and customary law and institutions. It was an understandable enthusiasm among a people increasingly conscious of national identity but without a nation state to stand as the protagonist of its history.

Most relevant of those investigations here is the attempted reconstruction by German scholars of early Teutonic customs, and particularly those of the supposed primitive nucleus of ancient Teutonic society, the village or *Mark* community. English scholars followed them in this from the mid-century, though in Stubbs's case with reservations – not enough, according to his later admirers and critics. There were distinguished German experts on English constitutional history, to whom Stubbs paid tribute. Each country seemed to have something to offer the other. It was in Germany, particularly in Schleswig, that some customary evidence survived that might give a clue to the institutional ideas and practices carried with them by the Saxons. But in England the Teutonic traditions could, it seemed, show what Germany could not: an unbroken lineage from Germanic institutions to a fully developed national parliamentary constitution.

Stubbs (1825–1901) began his scholarly career as an editor of medieval manuscripts. Reaching behind these to make out the practices and conceptions they referred to and embodied became the bedrock of his work and his reputation, leading to his election in 1866 to the Oxford chair of medieval history. Through them one could register the tremors of slow-moving social and institutional changes which characteristically no legislation had brought into being but which were registered, for those who could detect them, in technical terms and procedural forms, in administrative, fiscal and judicial devices, in the growth and waning of privileges and exactions, in the augmentation and dwinding of functions. In Anglo-Saxon England,

Stubbs wrote, 'there are no constitutional revolutions, no violent reversals of legislation: custom is far more potent than law, and custom is modified infinitesimally every day. An alteration of law is often a mere registration of custom, when men have recognised its altered character. The names of offices and assemblies are permanent, while their character has imperceptibly undergone essential change' (*CH*, 69). A simple example of such changes is the mutation of the functions of royal officials such as the steward and the chamberlain: originally servants in the king's household, they become first great officers of state and then dwindle into mere honorific court titles.

Ever since the work of the legal historians of the sixteenth and seventeenth centuries, the possibility had existed of a kind of history that was impersonal, undramatic and technical, concerned with long-term changes rather than deliberately implemented policies. So far it had been chiefly exhibited in antiquarian monographs devoted to particular, often narrowly specific, institutions. The Enlightenment concept of 'unintended consequences' had fostered that possibility from another angle: of tracing large-scale, unplanned social changes, which Gibbon called 'insensible revolutions', but generally in the form of essays rather than monographs, as in Adam Smith's brilliant few pages in Book III of *The Wealth of Nations* on the rise and decline of feudalism. Now the new constitutional history, in Stubbs's hands, partly prompted by the German idea of culture and custom as the productions of the anonymous *Volk*, brought the two approaches together. Stubbs's *History* was minutely investigative and scholarly but large-scale, with the notion (again stemming from the sixteenth century) of an inheritance of Teutonic liberty as its guiding theme. Stubbs brought the antiquarian, investigative tradition to a new level of dense scholarly rigour, and synthesized its results in a three-volume survey, ending in the fifteenth century, of English medieval history as the story of the preservation and growth of constitutional liberty, beginning in the smallest units of local self-government and culminating in a national parliament.

Stubbs was both self-conscious and confident about the kind of history which could do this. He knew it involved sacrificing the dramatic episodes and clash of personalities, the celebration of heroic deeds – in short the sympathetic identification with the figures of the past and the inspiration of noble characters – which probably drew most readers to history. He said so in his preface:

The History of Institutions affords little of the romantic interest, or of the picturesque groupings which constitute the charm of History in general, and holds out small temptation to the mind that requires to be tempted to the study of Truth. But it has a deep value and an abiding interest to those who have the courage to work upon it. It presents, in every branch, a regularly developed series of causes and consequences, and abounds in examples of that continuity of life, the realisation of which is necessary to give the reader a personal hold on the past and a right judgement of the present. For the roots of the present lie deep in the past, and nothing in the past is dead to the man who would learn how the present comes to be what it is . . . Constitutional History has a point of view, an insight, and a language of its own; it reads the exploits and characters of men by a different light from that shed by the false glare of arms, and interprets positions and facts in words that are voiceless to those who have only listened to the trumpet of fame.

Though kings and barons play their parts, the principal agents of Stubbs's history are multiple, obscure and even anonymous. They build up the fabric of English institutions over time, by countless imperceptible actions, as Stubbs's contemporary Charles Darwin saw coral reefs created by 'myriads of tiny architects'. The protagonist of Stubbs's *Constitutional History* is the English people itself, obscurely operating and slowly transforming, in small spontaneous innovations and adaptations, the institutions by which it lived. Reading Stubbs often seems like witnessing the scholarly illustration and historical elaboration of the thought of Edmund Burke: such slow, accumulative growth and constant adaptation was a sign of life. Continuity in the history of English institutions was not merely the guardian of English liberty: it *was* English liberty, in constant, spontaneous action. And, because it was spontaneous, anomalies abounded; method and substance were ultimately the same: 'Complexity is a sign of growth; simplicity of detail signifies historically the extinction of earlier framework. That which springs up, as our whole system has done, on the principle of adapting present means to present ends, may be complex and inconvenient and empiric, but it is natural, spontaneous, and a crucial test of substantial freedom' (*Lectures on Early English History*, p. 326).

In Stubbs's account of English medieval history the old perceived tension and dialectic between civilization and progress and the survival of liberty was still alive. The threat to liberty was the necessary framework of law and order imposed by a powerful monarchy. 'In general,' Stubbs wrote in his *Lectures on Early English History* (published in 1906) 'the chances are greatly in favour of tyranny, resulting from the destruction of the old bases; England alone has a history in which ancient freedom made its way through, and utilized all that is good in feudalism, widening from precedent to precedent into perfect political liberty' (p. 265). The greatest threat to inherited English liberties had been the Norman Conquest. The survival of the basic Teutonic institutions on to which strong monarchy and feudal conceptions had been imposed by the Conquest had been a close-run thing. They had survived, according to Stubbs, in the smallest and most obscure forms of local self-government, the village moot and the jury:

In the preservation of the old forms, – the compurgation [exoneration by sworn oath] of the accused, the responsibility for the wergild [compensation], the representation of the township in the court of the hundred, and that of the hundred in the court of the shire; the choice of witnesses; the delegation to chosen committees of the common judicial rights of the suitors of the folkmoot; the need of witnesses for the transfer of chattels, and the evidence of the hundred and shire as to criminals and the duty of enforcing their production and punishment, and the countless diversity of customs in which the several communities went to work to fulfil the general injunction of the law – in those remained the seeds of future liberties . . . They were the humble discipline by which a downtrodden people were schooled to act together in small things until the time came when they could act together for greater ones. (*CH*, 80)

It was in these minuscule ways that the original Teutonic liberties had survived. Stubbs did not accept the full *Mark* theory, as it was called, of an original village co-proprietorship of land. Some late-nineteenth-century polemicists saw in the co-proprietorship theory a justification for modern socialism and a demonstration that private property represented a usurpation of communal rights. Stubbs, a Tory in politics and eventually a bishop (of Oxford), was not one of them. For him it was on the free holding of land, known as allodialism, that the original Teutonic liberty had rested. Celtic peoples might have held land communally, as a group of kin – there was evidence to that effect – but the Teutonic evidence pointed to the individual freeholder, a member of the self-regulating village community in which each freeman had a voice: 'In the allodial system is the germ of all the institutions of freedom' (*EEH*, 204). The history of English freedom, however, partly on account of the Norman Conquest, was not a simple, triumphant advance but a kind of pilgrim's progress, beset by many threats and vicissitudes until the trumpets could sound for the transformation into national parliamentary sovereignty. The lineage which linked the Teutonic freeholder to the modern voter and juryman was allegedly unbroken but was admitted to have been at times almost subterranean, invisible except to the eye of minute scholarship.

The English nineteenth-century vaunting of that heritage could seem more than a little smug. Acton – cosmopolitan and a Catholic – saw in it a regrettable parochialism and neglect of universal principle. Even the best institutions were valuable only as they provided security for a higher interest: the liberty of the individual and the use he made of it. For Acton there was a more important kind of history: intellectual, moral and religious. As he told the audience for his inaugural lecture as Regius professor of history in Cambridge in 1895, 'A speech of Antigone, a simple sentence of Socrates, a few lines that were inscribed on an Indian rock before the Second Punic War, the footsteps of a silent yet prophetic people who dwelt by the Dead Sea and perished in the fall of Jerusalem, come nearer to our lives than the ancestral wisdom of barbarians who fed their swine on the Hercynian acorns.' The lofty dismissal of barbarian swineherds is accentuated by the use of the classical name for the German forest. A general 'History of Freedom' was the cherished project that was to have been the climax of Acton's scholarly life, but it was never written, and he left only fragmentary clues to its nature. It is clear that freedom as a moral principle, and its ultimate recognition as such, would have been the core of the story. By contrast, for Acton the English tradition was over-concerned with property rights and, latterly, with race. The Revolution of 1688 had been a half-hearted muddle, prompted by self-interest. It was only in the demand of the Puritan Independents in the 1650s that the English tradition reached the level of general principle, and only in America that it became fully self-conscious and came to understand, as it were, its higher self, in the formulation of the concept of universal human rights.

Guizot had distinguished two kinds of history of freedom, the institutional and the intellectual: 'I do not propose to study with you the history of the interior of the human soul; it is the history of ... the visible and social world that I shall occupy myself with.' Acton's Cambridge lectures made similar gestures. As tradition and the syllabus suggested, they followed a predictable course of mainly political history: Philip II, the Thirty Years War, Louis XIV, before culminating in the American Revolution. (There was another series devoted wholly to the French Revolution.) But Acton gave plenty of indications that the interior of the soul was his true if postponed business: religion was for him virtually the same as the history of freedom, since both were concerned ultimately with conscience. He also gestured more than once to 'the movement of ideas, which are not the effect but the cause of public events'. The 'History of Freedom', we can conjecture, would have been a wide-ranging history of ideas, with the development of free institutions as secondary to the development of full, self-conscious awareness of freedom and its moral responsibilities as the self-realization of humanity. But, possibly because of its fragmentary indications, Acton's kind of history of ideas seems alarmingly spasmodic – a series of underexplained epiphanies. The spirit seemed to blow where it listed among a historically motley collection of Catholic theologians, Puritan zealots and American squires. Acton was not shy of naming the day and the hour when revelation descended. Thus it was in America, as he said in a later Cambridge lecture, that the law of nature, which he sometimes called 'the higher law', became incarnate: 'On that evening of 16th December 1773 it became for the first time the reigning force in history.'

It was the religious struggles of the Reformation which had – unwillingly, since the leading Reformers were not tolerant men – begotten religious liberty and the idea of freedom of conscience. But Acton's musings on the history of human self-consciousness also found a place for the Renaissance, though it had played no part in the inculcation of respect for political and human rights. In Acton's characterization of the Renaissance in his Cambridge lectures there seem to be traces of the outstanding nineteenth-century treatment of it, and indeed of the culture of any epoch, the Swiss Jacob Burckhardt's *The Civilization of the Renaissance in Italy* (1860). Acton spoke of this, in a review of a book on the Borgias, as 'the most penetrating and subtle treatise on the history of civilization that exists in literature'. In his lectures he referred to 'the finished individual of the Renaissance, ready for emergencies, equal to every fortune, relying on nothing inherited, but on his own resource . . . little recking rights of others, little caring for the sanctity of life'. This is a portrait recognizable to any reader of Burckhardt, and it forms another, in some respects lurid, chapter in the nineteenth century's preoccupation with the history of freedom.

Modernity's First-born Son: Burckhardt's Renaissance Man

Burckhardt's book forms part of, yet also stands at an angle to, the nineteenth-century conception of the history of freedom. There is enough emotional complicity in Burckhardt's work to prevent us from regarding it as an ironic critique of that conception, but it takes it into wild and alarming moral territory. It would be wrong to think of contemporary ideas of modernity as simply congratulatory: many were highly critical, focusing, as the century wore on, on philistinism and conformity, against which Burckhardt reacted. There were other kinds of criticism dwelling on atomization and selfishness. Burckhardt's work broke new ground, however, in its way of presenting the origins of modernity and the newly emancipated European in Renaissance Italy, who was seen as fiercely amoral, but fascinating and capable of greatness. Out of the Machiavellian concept of *virtù* (energy and prowess) and traits from European Romanticism, Burckhardt compounded an enduring archetype – as his younger colleague at the University of Basle, Friedrich Nietzsche, with help from the idea of the Dionysiac, was to create a new image of the ancient Greek. Both authors are exhilarating to read. Burckhardt's man of the Renaissance is the liberal hero without his surrounding decorum of principles: 'the spirit of freedom' becomes antinomian, self-justifying and freed from all restraint.

Burckhardt's work is of enduring interest both in its method, which is highly original, and in the coherence and vividness of its interpretation, which, though recognizable as at best an exaggeration, lodges abidingly in the mind. Burckhardt spoke of 'a' civilization, not just of civilization as such, though one which was a moment in a longer development, a civilization 'which is the mother of our own'. In Burckhardt, narrative has virtually disappeared, though illustrative anecdote abounds and is, in fact, a major part of the method: it is as though we are given the stories told by Gregory of Tours in a clearly envisaged, tenaciously realized conception of contemporary morals and mores. One precedent (though Burckhardt's task was wider and his evidence less tangible and therefore more difficult to handle) was the attempts made, since the art historian Johann Winckelmann's studies of the Greeks a century earlier, to regard the character of an artistic or architectural style as the product of a whole people, and to discern from this their inner character and aspirations. Ruskin, for example, immediately before Burckhardt, in *The Seven Lamps of Architecture* (1849) and *The Stones of Venice* (1851–3), had obsessively moralized (and in the case of the Renaissance immoralized) the formal characteristics of architecture. Art and life were inseparable, and art revealed the soul of a society, in its elevation or baseness. Burckhardt himself was highly visually sensitive: he lectured on art history at Basle, wrote a guide to Italian art (the *Cicerone*), and left art out of the *Renaissance* only because he intended to treat it separately elsewhere.

In Germany the idea of art as the expression of spirit is associated particularly with Hegel, as it is later in France with Taine. Burckhardt shied away from the teleological meaning Hegel gave to his conception of the World Spirit whose moments form the moral and intellectual history of mankind, but there seems no doubt it helped him to see a unity in the particular moment of civilization represented by the Italian Renaissance. Rather than just categorizing this moment, he set out copiously to illustrate and in the process to explain it. The *Renaissance in Italy* lives above all, apart from its anecdotes, in its adjectives. The origins of art history had lain in connoisseurship. Burckhardt was a connoisseur of the manifestations of the human personality, historically and geographically located. This, too, was a German preoccupation: since the time of Goethe and Schiller the aesthetics of personality was a matter of acute moral and cultural interest, and the categories borrowed from the appraisal of art were a major aspect of it.

The concept of the Renaissance as a period had been significantly elaborated since its self-consciousness about its achievements had expressed itself in the claim to be a rebirth of art and letters. This had sometimes explicitly consigned the preceding thousand years to the status of a barbarian interval or hiatus, a 'middle' age. The late-seventeenth-century German scholar Christoph Keller (Cellarius) has been credited with being the first systematically to employ the familiar tripartite periodic division, Ancient, Medieval, Modern. But the concept of modernity itself increasingly needed differentiation, as the age of the humanists receded into the past. We have seen in Guicciardini a registration of the achievements – printing, the discovery of the New World, and modern artillery – which surpassed those of the ancients, and therefore made the notion of revival inadequate. In Hume and Robertson we have seen how the age of the Reformation too, uncouth and fanatical, was distanced from the current enlightened and polite one. But established periodic nomenclature was still somewhat meagre. Earlier, Voltaire in his *The Age of Louis XIV* (1751) had enlarged his concept of the age beyond that of the reign, by including cultural as well as political achievements and by extending the scope of the age both laterally and chronologically, so that the cultural achievements became those of seventeenth-century Europe: Galileo, Bacon, Locke and Newton as well as Descartes and the great French literary figures of the *Grand Siècle*. But his method here remained essentially that of a catalogue or inventory of achievements. Arguably the seventeenth century still lacks a satisfactory period label; Carl J. Friedrich, in the middle of the twentieth century, understandably borrowed from art history and chose *The Age of the Baroque* (1952) for his general study of European history and culture. It was, however, in the 1830s that the term 'the Renaissance' was first employed in the modern comprehensive and periodic sense – by Michelet, when he gave it to a volume of his *History of France*. 'Early Modern' is a twentieth-century coinage.

Acton was right to recognize Burckhardt's subtlety: his is a book which insinuates its themes and the thinking behind them. At first one can feel overwhelmed by the sequence of anecdotes, from chronicles, biographies and memoirs. But, as one reads on, the outlines come into focus and a coherent picture, explanatory but never merely reductionist, emerges.

The first part is entitled 'The State as a Work of Art', a concept which obviously owes something to Machiavelli, though Burckhardt has plenty of other evidence. The key figure, it transpires, is that of the *condottiere*. Burckhardt, while recognizing the cruelty and treachery that were essential elements in the mercenary captains' trade, and their ruthless ambition to found dynasties of their own, treats them more respectfully than does Machiavelli, to whom they are sometimes risible. In Burckhardt the *condottiere* typically displays a Machiavellian *virtù*, but divorced from civic patriotism: boldness and resolution coexist with cool calculation and a ruthless determination to let no person, principle or loyalty stand in the way of the path to greatness. The *condottiere* is a military entrepreneur and political adventurer, acting entirely for himself and relying only on his own skill, adroitness and foresight for his survival and success. The network of class, chivalric code (including loyalty) and social hierarchy based on birth, which surrounds the warrior nobles of northern Europe, means nothing to him. He is, literally, the freest of freelances, of no state, with no fixed social position, pitting his wits, courage and determination against fortune for high stakes: wealth, a dukedom, a principality even. Even when he becomes a ruler his power remains personal not dynastic, and essentially without legitimacy; only awe, splendour, popularity or fear can sustain it, and it is always insecure.

Burckhardt makes this role, and the type of personality which embraces and can sustain it, into the conceptual core of his book, because the other skills and roles he sees as characteristic of the Italian Renaissance are in a sense civil versions of the military adventurer, and those who possess and enact them are the bearers of Renaissance civilization: artists and architects, humanist scholars and men of letters. They too are the entrepreneurs of their own talents and personalities. Footloose, they typically move from patron to patron, in search of advancement or as the result of quarrels. Like Michelangelo, they sometimes proudly assert their own worth even to the most highly placed, like the Pope. Like the *condottieri* and petty rulers, they benefit from the multiplicity of autonomous states that the unresolved conflict for domination of Italy between the papacy and the empire has allowed to grow up; the frontier is always helpfully near, beyond which another patron, with luck, will be accommodating. They too, in Burckhardt's picture, are typically without the supports and the constraints of traditional institutions – of guilds or universities – or are only very loosely attached to them. Their habitat is courts and cities, where the golden prizes are won – and as suddenly lost. They and the rulers are linked by mutual need: they for rewards and status, the despots for the legitimation conferred by the talents and skills of artists and humanists. The parvenu rulers needed to be surrounded by splendour; to be impressively represented at foreign courts and on public occasions, like the reception of ambassadors by elegant Latinists; to be celebrated, eulogized and elegized, and lauded as munificent patrons.

The hazards encountered by a soldier of fortune are self-evident, but Burckhardt takes pains to stress that they applied in a remarkable degree to what might otherwise seem to be in all probability the quiet lives of scholars and craftsmen:

For an ambitious youth, the fame and the brilliant position of the humanists were a perilous temptation . . . He was thus led to plunge into a life of excitement and vicissitude, in which exhausting studies, tutorships, secretaryships, professorships, offices in princely households, mortal enmities and perils, luxury and beggary, boundless admiration and boundless contempt, followed confusedly one upon the other. (Part III)

The humanist characteristically has no fixed home; Burckhardt draws a parallel with the Greek Sophists, 'but the scholar of the Renaissance was forced to combine great learning with the power of resisting the influence of ever-changing pursuits and situations.' An inordinate pride was a necessity for survival: the humanists are 'the most striking examples and victims of an unbridled subjectivity'. Burckhardt uses an early-sixteenth-century work, Piero Valeriano's *On the Infelicity of the Scholar*. The lives Valeriano describes are indeed lurid. We are introduced, Burckhardt says, to men who

in times of trouble lose, first their incomes, and then their places . . . to unsociable misers, who carry about their money sewn into their clothes, and die mad when they are robbed of it; to others, who accept well-paid offices, and then sicken with a melancholy longing for their lost freedom. We read how some died young of a plague or fever, and how the writings which had cost them so much toil were burnt with their bed and clothes; how others lived in terror of the murderous threats of their colleagues; how one was slain by a covetous servant, and another caught by highwaymen on a journey, and left to pine in a dungeon . . . (Part III)

Valeriano obviously had a ready ear for academic grumbles, but the picture, as a picture, has an extraordinary power. This was freedom, but it was a picaresque freedom of extreme hazard and an unrelenting demand for self-reliance. It was also compatible with extraordinary achievement, and even a spur to it.

Burckhardt makes much of the erosion of class barriers in the Italian towns, of the free intercourse between nobles, scholars, artists and rulers. Birth allegedly counts for little, ability for almost everything. To speak in modern terms of a 'career open to talents' seems almost a mockery, implying regular hierarchies to ascend. The world conjured up by Burckhardt is one in which one stakes one's will and talents on the turn of fortune's wheel. At times Burckhardt's man of the Renaissance seems a kind of victim of modernity: he is the first to experience, in a radically unrestrained and unprotected form, the spiritual ordeal of the modern condition, alone and with only his own resources to sustain him – 'The Italian of the Renaissance had to bear the first mighty surging of a new age' (Part VI).

The first three parts of the work, dominated as they are by the *condottiere* as their archetypal image, are the most exhilarating in their brio and excitement. Part II, 'The Development of the Individual', treating of the intense self-awareness and the interest, in biography and portraiture, in the qualities of the individual personality, is central. Burckhardt's contrast of the medieval condition in this respect and that of the Renaissance has inevitably drawn criticism for exaggeration:

In the Middle Ages both sides of human consciousness – that which was turned within as that which was turned without – lay dreaming or half awake beneath a common veil. The veil was woven of faith, illusion, and childish prepossession, through which the world and history were seen clad in strange hues. Man was conscious of himself only as a member of a race, people, party, family, or corporation – only through some general category. In Italy this veil first melted into air; an *objective* treatment and consideration of the state and of all the things of this world became possible. The *subjective* side at the same time asserted itself with corresponding emphasis; man became a spiritual *individual*, and recognized himself as such.

The third part, 'The Revival of Antiquity', though it contains the colourful account of the humanists' lives quoted above, is naturally a little more predictable. Then 'The Discovery of the World and of Man' picks up the theme of objectivity, which is presented as another characteristic of the Renaissance individual, forced into the need for cool calculation and into an understanding of the world as it is and not as it might or should be. But the clear-sighted contemplation of the external world is also a source of delight to him.

Though Burckhardt's book stresses the pagan amorality of the Renaissance and hardly recognizes the quality of Renaissance piety, the final part, 'Morality and Religion', shows awareness of the difficulties in striking the moral balance sheet of a whole society. Presenting the Italian Renaissance as an example of refined sensuality and cruelty, addicted to the elegantly macabre, especially in the pursuit of revenge, was no novelty. It rested on the Borgias' reputation for poisoning people; on Machiavelli and the English Jacobean revenge tragedies, habitually set in Italy; on recollections of stories from Dante – all these fostered this reputation, which was added to by the eighteenth-century Gothic novel, again often with an Italian setting, and by the poetry of Byron and Browning. In Germany, the *Sturm und Drang* movement in literature sometimes went to Italy for scenes of violence and horror, while the German love affair with Italy epitomized in Goethe's *Italian Journey* dwelt on the country's pagan seductiveness. Burckhardt, coming after all this, still managed to create an indelible impression, and, though he sometimes emphasizes distinctly Italian traits, it is above all the Renaissance as modern, as *proto*-modernity, that takes his attention. The Renaissance Italian was 'the firstborn among the sons of modern Europe'.

Acton qualifies his praise of Burckhardt's book by saying that 'its merit lies in the originality with which the author uses common books, rather than in actively new investigations.' This was a piece of characteristic Actonian condescension: the author would be none the worse for a more protracted spell in the archives. That is more than doubtful, but there was a truth here, though condescension is not called for. Despite the range of Burckhardt's references, and though he does not particularly signal the fact, it is possible to see in his general conception of the Renaissance personality and its circumstances, and therefore in his original treatment of it, a synthesis of a handful of notable works and characters which dominate the book: Vasari's *Lives of the Artists* (skill, technique, pride); Benvenuto Cellini's *Autobiography* (a picaresque, amoral life, led by a master artist, sustained by a self-confidence amounting to impudence); Aretino (the pen as a weapon of self-assertion, cruelty and revenge); Machiavelli, of course; Francesco Sforza, the most successful of all the *condottieri*, who made himself duke of Milan; Petrarch, the pioneer of an intense self-awareness as well as a passion for antiquity; Castiglione's *The Courtier*, most celebrated of pattern books for the 'all-round man', in any case a preoccupation of recent German, neo-Hellenic moral and philosophical cultural concerns. To say this is not to detract from Burckhardt's originality, but rather to admire the way he wove these themes together into a plausible and arresting synthesis which, however much qualified, has remained a challenge and point of reference for historians of the Renaissance, enshrined in a still very readable book.

It is hard, in fact, to imagine that Burckhardt will ever altogether lack readers, at least so long as a Nietszchean version of the liberated hero continues to fascinate. In general the nineteenth-century histories of freedom have themselves passed into history. G. M. Trevelyan's Italian Risorgimento trilogy (1907–11), focused on Garibaldi, was perhaps the last substantial work of history to be conceived as a liberal-democratic as well as nationalist epic. Trevelyan himself, who was Macaulay's great-nephew and fought a long campaign against the new professionalism's scorn for picturesque narrative, spoke in his preface to *Garibaldi's Defence of the Roman Republic* (1907) of the 'chord of poetry and romance' in Garibaldi's life, but wondered 'whether his memory will now appeal to the English of a generation . . . said to be at once more sophisticated and less idealistic than the

Victorian'. He was too pessimistic at the time, but surely right in the long run. In general, the new intellectual climate of the last years of the nineteenth century, gripped by fears of socialism supported by mass electorates, often prompted glum reassessments of democracy and dampened enthusiasm for tracing the origins of parliamentary institutions. So too did the cult of 'science' and 'objectivity' in history, associated with the rise of a historical profession. Charles Petit-Dutaillis, in the preface to his 1908 *Supplement* to Stubbs, spoke condescendingly of Stubbs's intellectual genesis in the liberal patriotic German scholarship from which he derived his 'optimistic and patriotic conception of English history'. Nowadays, he went on, 'when so many illusions have been dissipated, when parliamentary institutions set up by almost every civilized nation have more openly revealed as they developed their inevitable littleness and when the formation of nationalities has turned Europe into an armed camp, history is written with less enthusiasm.' He was right that nationalism, so long associated with Romantic, liberal versions of history, was now finding its watchword in *Realpolitik*, the new term for 'reason of state', the pursuit of success by any means, and often of domination rather than merely independence. The implications of the 'new' nationalism for historiography will mainly concern us in a later chapter (Chapter 25). But first there is a new world to discover.

24

A New World:
American Experiences

The Halls of Montezuma: Díaz, Prescott and the
Conquest of New Spain

The making of the United States of America could be seen as a story of freedom in the widest possible geographical frame. To the first historian of the United States, George Bancroft (1800–1891), American freedom was a democratic extension of the freedom born in the German forests. Others, notably Frederick Jackson Turner (1861–1932), saw it in more self-contained terms, as shaped by the land itself, by the open frontier which had ceased to exist only in his own lifetime. The Tudor Puritan conception of the English as an elect nation, brought by the seventeenth-century settlers of New England, also became woven into North American self-consciousness.

But the history of America can also be told as a story of dispossession, subjugation and enslavement, beginning with the earliest European penetration of the continent, the Spanish conquest of Mexico. The first historians of the New World were Spanish, and they told the story of the conquest, naturally, as an epic achievement, coloured by the conception of a crusade. When the New England settlers of Plymouth Plantation struggled, in the 1620s, for bare survival, under the eye of their God, it was already a hundred years since Cortés and the Spanish conquistadores had overthrown the Aztec empire of Montezuma and founded 'New Spain' on its ruins. It was over fifty years since the Spaniards had begun to erect the vast baroque cathedral of Mexico City on the site of the great Aztec temple in which human sacrifices had been conducted on an almost industrial scale. The story of the conquest, which took only two years (1519–21), is one of the most extraordinary that history records. Xenophon's 'Persian Expedition', which shares some of the characteristics of that of Cortés, led to no new foundation. The expeditions of Alexander were on an even greater scale, but considered just as a story they do not have quite the dramatic cohesion of the Spanish one, as Alexander and his army, after their conquest of the 'barbarian' empire, move on eastward.

The Spanish historians who had been drawn to chronicle their countrymen's epic adventure and its aftermath can, to most English readers, be mainly only names. One exception is Fra Bartolomé de las Casas, whose championing of the cause of the conquered Indians (as they will be called here) has recommended him to posterity. Another is one of Cortés's companions on his march from the coast to the Aztec capital and in the hard fighting before the city was taken, Bernal Díaz. His account, written in old age, is a vivid and vigorous narrative, free of conventional tropes and rhetorical flourishes, from the landing of approximately four hundred Spanish soldiers, with sixteen horses and ten brass guns, on the coast of Yucatan, to the bloody siege, destruction and capture of Tenochtitlán (Mexico City) which marked the completion of the Spanish victory. Its merits as an eyewitness account and as a narrative have earned it a modern English translation (as *The Conquest of New Spain*).

The other classic narrative in English is *The Conquest of Mexico* (1843) by William Hickling Prescott (1796–1859). Prescott, like all the notable American historians who wrote in the mid nineteenth century, was a Harvard-educated New Englander. His considerable body of work – a triumph over near-blindness – began with a history of Spain (1838) under the monarchs who presided over its unification in the late fifteenth and early sixteenth centuries and were the patrons of Columbus, Ferdinand and Isabella. Later he added a pendant to his *Mexico*, *The Conquest of Peru* (1847), and an unfinished history of Philip II of Spain. For *The Conquest of Mexico* he used Díaz's account extensively, referring to him in his now published *Notebooks* as 'my staple authority', though condescending to his humble literary merits and to the 'homely texture' of his style (*Mexico*, V, endnote). Díaz claims no more for himself. Prescott was a considerable scholar, who had worked in the Spanish archives. He was therefore less dependent on Díaz than Robertson had been for the conquest section of his *History of America* three-quarters of a century earlier. Prescott published a preface of acknowledgements, and provided substantial footnotes to a variety of sources.

Both Díaz and Prescott can still be read enjoyably, and their merits are contrasting and complementary. Their story begins essentially with the appointment of Cortés, an adventurer with a somewhat wild past, recounted by Prescott, to command an expedition sponsored by the governor of Cuba, Velasquez, to explore the Yucatan peninsula. This had been discovered by the Spaniards two years earlier, in 1517; Díaz had accompanied them, and recounts their experiences. The governor soon regretted Cortés's appointment and tried to detain him, but Cortés slipped away. Velasquez subsequently sent a larger force after him, but Cortés, with masterly tactics, first defeated and then recruited it. The story of the expedition is that of a military campaign in which Cortés both fights and wins over the satellite peoples of the Aztec empire, through whose territories the army passes. He is able to exploit both their restlessness under the rule of the Aztec emperor Montezuma and the awe produced by the Spaniards: bearded men in armour with firearms, a few riding horses, all wholly outside the Indians' experience. Cortés poses as their deliverer; Díaz does not comment on the duplicity involved in this, but Prescott is explicit:

Alas! they could not read the future, or they would have found no cause to rejoice in this harbinger of a revolution more tremendous than any predicted by their bards and prophets . . . The light of civilization would be poured on their land; but it would be the light of a consuming fire, before which their barbaric glory, their institutions, their very existence as a nation, would wither and become extinct! Their doom was sealed when the white man had set his foot on their soil. (II. vii).

The Spaniards were aided throughout, and not least by its influence on the mind of the emperor Montezuma, by the Mexicans' myth that their god Quezalcoatl had prophesied the arrival to rule them of a race of white-skinned demigods.

The strange terrain through which the Spaniards marched and their progressively deeper acquaintance with Mexican civilization make this one of the most fascinating of campaign narratives. The Spaniards

wondered at the Mexicans' technological skills and distinctive crafts-
manship in gold and silver, cotton and feathers, and at the extensive,
well-planned cities and stone architecture, but were horrified by the
frequent evidence of highly ritualized and copious human sacrifice.
The culminating revelation was the city of Tenochtitlán, standing in
a lake and intersected by canals running at right angles and crossed
by causeways. Its huge population (by European standards), the vast
marketplace, the great pyramidal towers for sacrifices facing each
other down long avenues, and the palace of Montezuma, with its
gardens, menagerie and elaborate court ritual, were like nothing previously seen in the new world discovered by Columbus almost three
decades earlier. It is understandable that, as Bernal Díaz tells us, the
Spanish soldiers felt as though they were living in the fantastic stories
of romance, which were the staple popular tales of the early sixteenth
century.

Díaz – who was, as he admits, 'no scholar' – sometimes confesses
to a sense of inadequacy in expressing his and his companions' reactions. He mentions their wonder, but knows that he cannot adequately
convey it, though he tries. But his pedestrian honesty may seem an
advantage to the modern reader, as it did to Prescott, preserving him
from ready-made conventional metaphors and stylized diction. He
refers, certainly, to chivalric romances, and aptly compares the siege
and destruction of the great city to the fall of Jerusalem. He also
mentions that Cortés, in his addresses to his troops, compared their
feats with those of the Romans (*New Spain*, pp. 405, 131). But his
history in general is immune to literary self-consciousness. He tells his
reader, in the modern phrase, how it was. Prescott, who called him
an 'untutored child of nature', also paid tribute to the qualities of his
narrative. Prescott compares it to photography, or rather daguerro-
type, which must be one of the earliest instances of such a literary
comparison: 'He introduces us into the heart of the camp, we huddle
around the bivouac with the soldiers, loiter with them on their weari-
some marches, listen to their stories, their murmurs of discontent, their
plans of conquest, their hopes, their triumphs, their disappointments'
(*Mexico*, V, endnote).

This is no more than just. Díaz not only tells us his extraordinary
story well (though readers are indebted to the modern translator

who has excised the digressions and repetitions); he humanizes the conquistadores, occasionally referring to them by name, or saying 'I forget his name', and casually individualizes them. Cortés himself is an inspiring leader but tricky; Fra Olmedo, the humane priest with the expedition, sometimes exercises a wise restraint on the soldiers' iconoclastic zeal. But there are also humbler figures: the very ugly musketeer whom Cortés says the Mexicans will take for one of their idols (p. 117); the Spaniard found on the coast of Yucatan who has 'gone native' and refuses to return to his own people, of whom Díaz speaks without censure (p. 60); the incompetent astrologer (pp. 297, 301), who leads Díaz into an uncharacteristically and surely unconsciously Homeric touch: 'His astrology did not help him, for he too died there with his horse.' Then there is the soldier, 'a decent man, though difficult to understand', who, posted guard over the captive Aztec emperor, shouts, 'To hell with this dog! . . . I'm sick to death of always guarding him!' (pp. 253–4). There is Montezuma himself, of course, who is respectfully and sympathetically described, and among ordinary Mexicans there are, particularly memorably, the fat *cacique* and his ugly niece (Mexican women are often described by Díaz as beautiful, and he takes one himself), whom Cortés has to receive as a gift 'with a show of pleasure' (p. 125). It is noteworthy that resulting children of mixed race who were born to the leaders, including Cortés's own, became recruited, as recorded by Prescott, into the Spanish aristocracy.

Díaz can strike the reader as both callous and humane. He gives the impression of a tolerant man who took human beings of all kinds as he found them, who pities Montezuma, and who is appalled, as all the Spaniards were, by human sacrifices to the Mexican 'idols'. It is a mark of the munificence and dignity of Montezuma, conveyed by Díaz, that the reader as well as the Emperor is shocked when Cortés has him put in chains. When he is killed – Díaz says accidentally, during an insurrection of the people against the foreigners – the Spaniards mourn apparently unaffectedly: 'Cortés and all of us captains and soldiers wept for him, and there was no one among us that knew him and had dealings with him who did not mourn him as if he were our father, which was not surprising, since he was so good' (p. 294). On the other hand Díaz is entirely unrepentant, and rebuts the subsequent condemnation by Las Casas, over the massacre perpetrated on a large number of Indians suspected, perhaps correctly, by the Spaniards of treachery. Díaz's argument is twofold: the conquest was justified – a crusade in fact – and the massacre was essential to the army's survival, without which there would have been no conquest. Prescott consistently insists that this should be judged by the standards and ideas of the sixteenth century, not those of the nineteenth, while admitting that a more selective and restrained reprisal would probably have sufficed (*Mexico*, III.vii).

Though he inevitably offended the descendants of both peoples, Prescott himself strikes the reader as commendably judicious. He is no Puritan. He had learned on his travels in southern Europe to respect Catholicism. This saves him from the insistent and aggressive provincialism (despite an education partly in Germany and a diplomatic career) which disfigures the work of another Harvard historian on the sixteenth century, John Lothrop Motley's *The Rise and Fall of the Dutch Republic* (1855). In Prescott's gentlemanly tolerance there is a distinct flavour of the eighteenth-century Enlightenment, without its iconoclastic zeal: he uses the significant word 'philosophical' freely. His own stance towards the conquest is equally far from Christian triumphalism, reflex Protestant anti-Catholicism, nineteenth-century racial arrogance, and the modern principled opposition to imperialism. To those who would find it a fault that his work is not written with a fierce partisanship on behalf of any of these he had his own answer, though he addressed it only to himself, in his *Notebooks*: 'Never call hard names; it is unhistorical, unphilosophical, ungentlemanlike.' The three adjectives, turned into their positive form, do well in characterizing Prescott. He views the conquest both as an extraordinary achievement and adventure – he applies the words 'epic' and 'romance' to it – and as the doom of a culture and a people, though he is anxious not to overrate the Mexican achievement on the scale of civilizations.

Prescott is not averse to judgement: the age of a rigorous cult of 'objectivity', meaning not judgement but abstention from it, had not yet dawned in historiography. As we have seen, he sees the standards of the sixteenth century as relevant to appraising the conduct of sixteenth-century men. Nor, on the other hand, is he blinded by the horrors of human sacrifice to either the beliefs which prompted it or the fact that hundreds of thousands of Montezuma's subjects led apparently peaceful, confidently traditional lives which the Spanish conquest would utterly sweep away, and which had been greatly preferable to the future, for themselves and their descendants, as involuntary Catholics and subjects of Charles V and Philip II. The brave Mexican allies of Cortés in his campaign against the Aztec empire are pathetic dupes, unknowingly collaborating in the destruction of their relative autonomy and their culture.

Prescott's tolerant even-handedness is bound up with what has proved perhaps a still more controversial quality, much admired in the nineteenth century but sometimes harshly denigrated in the twentieth: the self-conscious, and it is not inappropriate to say 'Augustan', literariness of his writing – precisely the quality from which Díaz's account was wholly free. It is clear from Prescott's notes to himself that the manner mattered to him as much as the substance, and that, though he was naturally drawn to the conquest as a subject by his work on earlier Spanish history, it also attracted him as a theme with high epic and picturesque possibilities. Comparing it with Washington Irving's life of Columbus, he spoke of his own project as 'the most poetic subject ever offered to the pen of the historian'. He had no axes to grind, but he had been inspired to become a historian by Gibbon's autobiography, and there are many Gibbonian echoes in his prose. We also find him brooding on Livy's manner of narrating Hannibal's crossing of the Alps, and this too seems to have echoes in The Conquest of Mexico. He reminds himself of the need to diversify the military history with

the description of the grand and picturesque scenery through which the Spaniards march; faithful descriptions of the various architectural remains, of the vegetable products, the mountains, the towns, etc, contrasted, moreover, with their present condition, affording an agreeable and instructive variety, and giving life and colouring to the picture; the description of Montezuma's palace, court ceremonies, way of life, his garden, collections of natural history, etc; the city of Mexico, its buildings, markets, manners of the people, etc . . .

The modern reader, knowing Prescott's history was produced almost halfway through the nineteenth century, is quite likely to register something old-fashioned, 'eighteenth-century', in Prescott's writing (e.g. 'agreeable and instructive'). There are some signs that he was aware of this, particularly in relation to his great eighteenth-century predecessor in recounting the conquest (though much more briefly), William Robertson. 'Beware of Robertson,' he admonished himself in his journal. 'Never glance at him till after subject moulded in my mind and thrown into language – I must not get my manner from him.' The admonition was perhaps not wholly successful. Prescott was born in the eighteenth century, and in the early decades of the nineteenth American literature was still highly derivative from English (and Scottish) eighteenth-century models. Twentieth-century commentators have objected strongly to this in Prescott. Quite why it should trouble us, however, that an author writing a century and a half ago should sometimes sound like one writing over two centuries ago seems unclear; perhaps it seems un-American.

Prescott makes very Gibbonian use of 'or', both to point an antithesis and to insert a doubt or qualification: 'The religion, or to speak correctly the superstition, of Montezuma . . .' (*Mexico*, II.vi). Italics too are used as Gibbon characteristically does to insinuate doubt: 'Six thousand victims *are said* to have been annually offered up in their sanguinary shrines' (II.vi). There is a Gibbonian loftiness in his comment on interpretations of Mexican religion. Originally it was seen by the Spaniards as devil-worship, but

before a century had elapsed the descendants of the same Spaniards discerned in the mysteries of the Aztec religion the features, obscured and defaced indeed, of the Jewish and Christian revelations. Such were the opposite conclusions of the unlettered soldier and of the scholar. A philosopher, untouched by superstition, might well doubt which of the two was the more extraordinary. (IV.iii)

This was 'the philosophic historian' still at work: the raised eyebrow in the last word descends directly from the eighteenth century. Elsewhere Prescott seems to play variations on a famous antithesis in Gibbon ('To resist was fatal, and it was impossible to fly' – *Decline and Fall*, III): Cortés's army seems trapped so that 'To fight and to fly seemed equally difficult' (*Mexico*, III.vi).

The Augustan stateliness of Prescott's prose makes it an apt instrument for registering the grandeur of the Aztec capital and the refinement, luxury and ceremonial which surrounds Montezuma. Prescott does not miss, of course, the opportunity to draw the oriental analogies, including the standard reference to 'effeminacy':

[Fishponds] afforded a retreat on their margins to various tribes of waterfowl, whose habits were so carefully consulted that some of these ponds were of salt water, as that which they most loved to frequent. A tessellated pavement of marble enclosed the ample basins, which were overhung by light and fanciful pavilions, that admitted the perfumed breezes of the gardens, and offered a grateful shelter to the monarch and his mistresses in the sultry heats of summer . . .

The place is now a tangled wilderness of wild shrubs, where the myrtle mingles its dark, glossy leaves with the red berries and delicate foliage of the pepper-tree. Surely there is no spot better suited to awaken meditation on the past; none where the traveller, as he sits under those stately cypresses gray with the moss of ages, can so fitly ponder on the sad destinies of the Indian races and the monarch who once held his courtly revels under the shadow of their branches. (IV.i)

To the Aztecs, of course, it was the Spaniards who were wondrous, and Prescott catches well the awe and astonishment the latter inspire, as when they build sailing ships for the siege of Tenochtitlán and these are seen for the first time gliding across the lake which surrounds the city: 'It was a novel spectacle to the simple natives; and they gazed with wonder on the gallant ships, which, fluttering like sea-birds on their snowy pinions, bounded lightly over the waters . . .' (VI.iv).

Where the eighteenth-century flavour of Prescott's tropes and diction does become undeniably tiresome is when he has to use them to describe battle and bloodshed, where the weight of past conventions lies heavily on the narrative. Predictably, Díaz is good precisely at this – detailed, realistic and soldierly. He is particularly good at conveying the exhaustion produced by prolonged combat, as well as the terror beforehand. In other respects, of course, Prescott's range includes effects which are not within Díaz's reach or aspiration.

Historical perspective, as we have seen, is one of these effects, and with it a fuller sense of the pathos of the Mexicans' situation, which Díaz registers only when, under his own eyes, it affects an individual and a monarch, Montezuma. Sensitivity, too, to the sublime and picturesque qualities of the landscape which forms the setting is, as we have also seen, a quality deliberately cultivated by Prescott, but it also marks changes in European sensibility in the three hundred years between Díaz and himself. Prescott was working within aesthetic categories of the sublime and the picturesque developed over the previous century. Díaz responds to gardens and flowers, to ease and abundance, and in this he is not only a soldier, with an eye to comfort, but a man of his time. A sublime landscape is characteristically an uncomfortable and even dangerous one, and its appreciation, which began in the ancient world, is essentially hyper-civilized. In a way Díaz does not, Prescott revels in the landscapes progressively revealed to Cortés's men: the characteristic vegetation, or lack of it, of the diverse microclimates created by differences of altitude, and precipices which give glimpses of the profuse vegetation of the valley floors. (Prescott drew on the recent work of the geologist and geographer Alexander von Humboldt for some of his descriptions of landscape.) The army's march led it across the arid remains of volcanic activity:

Working their way across this scene of desolation, the path often led them along the borders of precipices, down whose sheer depths of two or three thousand feet the shrinking eye might behold another climate, and see all the glowing vegetation of the tropics, choking up the bottom of the ravines. (III. i)

Then, of course, there were the distant vistas – above all, that which gave the conquistadores their first sight of the Aztec capital. Their approach to it has Díaz expressing a sense of his inadequacy and reaching for an analogy with the popular romance of *Amadis de Gaul*: it was 'like an enchanted vision from the tale of Amadis. Indeed, some of our soldiers asked whether it was not all a dream . . . It was all so wonderful that I do not know how to describe this first glimpse of things never heard of, seen or dreamed of before' (*New Spain*, p. 214). For Prescott the wonder begins with the distant prospect of

the fair city of Mexico, with her white towers and pyramidal temples, reposing, as it were, on the bosom of the waters, – the far-famed 'Venice of the Aztecs'. High over all rose the royal hill of Chapoltepec, the residence of the

Mexican monarchs, crowned with the same grove of gigantic cypresses which at this day fling their broad shadows over the land. In the distance beyond the blue waters of the lake, and nearly screened by intervening foliage, was seen a shining speck, the rival capital of Tezcuco, and, still further on, the dark belt of porphyry, girdling the valley around . . . (III.viii)

Prescott is prolific with such effects, and, as he intended, they give his history some of its character and appeal. Another landscape, the North American wilderness, knowledge of which in the seventeenth and eighteenth centuries was virtually bounded by the Mississippi river, was to be the chosen scene of the histories written by the second great nineteenth-century American historian.

Outposts in the Wilderness: Parkman's History of the Great West

The land itself, which he often called simply 'the forest', was the central inspiration of Prescott's younger New England contemporary Francis Parkman. It was more dominant than in Prescott, because in the great northern wastes there was no unexpected indigenous civilization to focus the historian's and the reader's attention. Instead there were the forest-dwellers, both indigenous and European or half-European: hunters and trappers – in the French phrase (and most of the latter were French), *coureurs de bois*. Parkman was fascinated both by them and above all, as he made clear, from his earliest years by the forest itself; this included its Indian inhabitants and the French Catholic missionaries and traders who first explored it along its river systems, from the St Lawrence and the Great Lakes to the Gulf of Mexico. Parkman recognized that the English-descended pioneer farmers in western Pennsylvania, New York and Virginia, as settlers, had more durability and represented the land's future. But Parkman was a Romantic, not a propagandist for Anglo-Saxon virtues, and he was frankly less interested in them. He knew that they spelt destruction to the forest and to the Indians' way of life, as surely as Cortés and his men did to the ancient civilization of Mexico, and his feelings about them were at best fatalistic, never enthusiastic.

Parkman's intense love affair with the American forest began early. On vacations from school in New England and as an undergraduate at Harvard, where he read the ancient historians, he spent as much time as possible in the backwoods of New Hampshire and Maine. His first, very distinguished, publication was a first-person account of his extended and physically demanding visit to the far west, *The California and Oregon Trail* (1849), usually known as *The Oregon Trail* (the reference to California was a topical touch in the year of the gold rush). It is one of the outstanding travel books of the century, alongside C. M. Doughty's *Travels in Arabia Deserta* (1888), with which it bears some analogies. Parkman, despite the lifelong ill health which dogged him – like Prescott, he had among other afflictions severe eye trouble – lived for some weeks with the Indians, who still preserved their traditional way of life.

He makes clear in his historical works that he was often drawing on this experience, though the Indians he describes there were not the mounted buffalo-hunters of the prairies he had seen at first hand but the forest-dwellers in the area of the Great Lakes and the Ohio and Mississippi valleys. In *The Oregon Trail* one learns a good deal about Parkman himself and his attitudes: his view of life as a struggle (before Darwinism, though one sometimes sees its influence later); his attraction to the picturesque though also squalid life of the Indians and their characteristics, combined with a determination not to idealize them; his own stoicism and admiration for bravery and self-reliance in others; his complete conviction of Indian untrustworthiness and lack of fixity of purpose.

Parkman's *oeuvre* began back to front. His first historical work, *The Conspiracy of Pontiac* (1851), treated the Indian rising against the British, after the latter's final victory over their French rivals in North America, in the 1760s. After an introductory section on the Indian way of life and the characters of the various tribes, *Pontiac* (named after the exceptionally able Ottawa chief who led the rising) goes on to consider the two European powers which had confronted each other in North America for two centuries, and their relations with the Indians: good in the case of the French, who in the west were missionaries, trappers and traders and interbred freely with the Indians; bad in the case of the British settlers and the British government, which, after the defeat of the French, was tactless and arrogant – the immediate cause of the rising of the confederation of Indian tribes organized by Pontiac.

The three chapters in which Parkman surveys Anglo–French–Indian relations over the previous century are an initial statement of the interests which led to his subsequent seven volumes on the French and English (chiefly the former) in North America, from the sixteenth century to the final resolution of their conflict in the mid eighteenth century. These volumes, apart from *Pontiac* and the final volume, appeared in chronological order up to 1892, shortly before Parkman's death. In between he published two novels and a book on roses, on which he was an expert. The nature of his historical *oeuvre* is adequately conveyed by the separate titles: *Pioneers of France in the New World* (1865), *The Jesuits in North America* (1867), *La Salle and the Discovery of the Great West* (1869), *The Old Regime in Canada* (1874), *Count Frontenac and New France under Louis XIV* (1877), *Montcalm and Wolfe* (1884), and *A Half-Century of Conflict, 1700–1750* (1892). The predominance of France in Parkman's interests is clear. For him the romance of American history, in so far as it did not dwell in the forest itself and its Indian inhabitants, pursuing their immemorial and doomed way of life, belonged to the French: to the *coureurs de bois*, who sometimes became virtually Indians themselves, and to the heroic Jesuit missionaries, who established isolated outposts in the remotest wilderness, of which they were among the earliest European explorers and in which they often found the martyrdom they sought, and whose work proved in the long term as fragile as the traditional ways of the Indians. But Parkman does not neglect the struggle between the European powers, which he dwells on particularly from the perspective of the French governors of Quebec.

Perhaps the most interesting, as he was the most ambitious, of the explorers, Cavelier La Salle (1643–87), was not a priest but initially a trader. He was a French bourgeois who was the first to travel from the Great Lakes down the Mississippi to the Gulf of Mexico, and who dreamed of creating a vast French empire in the west, linked by the river and with its southern port on the Gulf, thus challenging both Britain and Spain. He is one of Parkman's heroes, along with the aristocratic – and autocratic – French governors, Champlain at the end of the sixteenth century and Frontenac in the late seventeenth, who established a chain of outposts along the Great Lakes, and the two great soldiers, Montcalm and Wolfe. One is tempted to add Pontiac, for, though he by no means draws Parkman's unqualified approval, Parkman admires Pontiac's fortitude and statesmanlike qualities and understands the desperation that drives him to revolt. The capture of Quebec by the British and the capitulation to them of the whole of New France was, for the Indians, Parkman says, 'wholly disastrous'.

His comments on the British and German settlers, ploddingly extending the borders of cultivation in western Pennsylvania, New York and Virginia, are respectful of their spirit of independence, in which they far surpass the docile French peasants of Quebec province under their feudal overlords, and of their dogged perseverance, in which they contrast with the footloose *coureurs de bois*. But they have no romance: 'In every quality of efficiency and strength, the Canadian fell miserably below his rival; but in all that pleases the eye and interests the imagination he far surpassed him' (*Pontiac*, I.iii). Among the British there is no great vision like Champlain's, no imperial dreams for the continent like La Salle's. It is they and their kind, and not settlers, who stir Parkman's imagination, as in the climactic moment when, canoeing down the Mississippi, La Salle and his companions sense the approach not only of spring but of a warmer, southern climate and, still more, after over a thousand miles of dangerous travelling and harsh privations they (like Xenophon's men) feel the proximity of the sea:

With every stage of their adventurous progress, the mystery of this vast New World was more and more unveiled. More and more they entered the realms of spring. The hazy sunlight, the warm and drowsy air, the tender foliage, the opening flowers, betokened the reviving life of Nature. For several days more they followed the writhings of the great river, on its tortuous course through the wastes of swamp and canebreak, till on the thirteenth of March [1682] they found themselves wrapped in a thick fog. Neither shore was visible; but they heard on the right the booming of an Indian drum and the shrill outcries of the war-dance.

After meeting for the first time Indians who live in houses of baked mud and have a temple in which they worship the Sun with human sacrifices, they know that they are nearing their journey's end.

As he drifted down the turbid current, between the low and marshy shores, the brackish water changed to brine, and the breeze grew fresh with the salt breath of the sea. Then the broad bosom of the great Gulf opened on his sight, tossing its restless billows, limitless, voiceless, lonely as when born of chaos, without a sail, without a sign of life.

La Salle plants a column bearing the arms of France, and a cross, and proclaims the sovereignty of Louis XIV. Parkman's comment intimates the evanescence of the dream:

On that day, the realm of France received on parchment a stupendous accession. The fertile plains of Texas; the vast basin of the Mississippi, from its frozen northern springs to the sultry borders of the Gulf; from the woody ridges of the Alleghenies to the bare peaks of the Rocky Mountains – a region of savannahs and forests, suncracked deserts, and grassy prairies, watered by a thousand rivers, ranged by a thousand warlike tribes, passed beneath the sceptre of the Sultan of Versailles; and all by virtue of a feeble human voice, inaudible at half a mile. (*La Salle*, XX)

Even within its narrower boundaries, the state of Louisiana was not to remain in the long run French; the Mississippi would not become, as La Salle called it, after the great French statesman, the river Colbert.

Parkman clearly enjoys these references to the ancient world of Europe, to which La Salle returns to outfit an expedition to the Gulf by sea, which, missing the mouths of the Mississippi, perishes miserably on the inhospitable shore, where La Salle himself is murdered by mutineers. The frequent reminders of the strange conjunction of the western wilderness and the intrigues and formalities of the French court appealed to Parkman's imagination. 'Many a gallant gentleman, many a nobleman of France, trod the black mould and oozy mosses of the forest with feet that had pressed the carpets of Versailles' (*Pontiac*, I.ii). He worked in archives in England and France as well as North America. Books like his had to be constructed very largely from primary sources: letters, memoirs, dispatches. He was himself a kind of pioneer, and he recognized the analogy. His estimation of the French, while it recognizes the incongruous conjunctions of old and new, emphasizes not only the rigidity of the social structure they carry with them to Quebec but also their flexibility in their relations with Indians, which goes right up to the governor. Count Frontenac (1620–98) lorded it among the Indians like a paternal and affable *grand seigneur*, and 'plumed and painted like an Indian chief, danced the war-dance and yelled the war-song at the camp fires of his delighted allies' (*Pontiac*, I.iii). Among the English, William Penn enjoyed exceptionally good relations with the Indians, but it is difficult to imagine him in a similar situation. The Jesuit missionaries even more strikingly straddled the two worlds:

We see them among the frozen forests of Acadia, struggling on snow-shoes, with some wandering Algonquin horde, or crouching in the crowded hunting-lodge, half stifled in the smoky den, and battling with troops of famished dogs for the morsel of sustenance. Again we see the black-robed priest wading among the white rapids of the Ottawa, toiling with his savage comrades to drag the canoe against the headlong water. Again, radiant in the vestments of his priestly office, he administers the sacramental bread to kneeling crowds of plumed and painted proselytes in the black forests of the Hurons ... (*Pontiac*, I.ii)

But the Quebec heartlands of New France had 'no principle of increase', while in the forest 'the savages did not become French, but the French became savages.' Meanwhile, further south, the British settlements were slowly but steadily chipping away at the wilderness, where 'forests crashing to the axe, dark spires of smoke ascending from autumnal fires, were heralds of the advancing host.' In the valley of the St Lawrence and along the coast of the Atlantic, 'Feudalism stood arrayed against Democracy, Popery against Protestantism, the sword against the ploughshare' (*Pontiac*, I.ii). But the British settlers, by the mid eighteenth century, were still only beginning to pass the barrier of the Alleghenies, so that the campaigns of the British army in the west against the French and the Indians were fought out just beyond the borders of Pennsylvania and west Virginia. After the British victory it was the settlers there who, apart from the tiny garrisons in the remote outposts taken over from the French, bore the brunt of the Indian uprising instigated by Pontiac, and suffered its horrors.

The most complex situation was in Pennsylvania, and Parkman brings to it a kind of grim humour and not unlimited sympathy. The frontiersmen, goaded by the fate of their families and friends, turned their anger and hatred against the domesticated Indian Christian converts living peacefully in the state. When these were taken into custody in Philadelphia for their own protection, the hard, undisciplined men of the frontier caused a riot and tried to storm the jail. The protectors of the Indians were the Quakers. They figure less well, in Parkman's account, however, as sentimentalists who are sceptical about the atrocity stories from the frontier, and as pacifists who are recalcitrant in organizing a defence force against the rising. The exasperated frontiersmen were largely of Protestant Ulster stock, and their militant invocations of the Bible, calling for the punishment of evil-doers, are starkly at odds with the rival Quaker reading of the holy book. Parkman adopts the detached posture of 'a student of human nature' (Prescott would have said 'a philosophic mind') and deplores both 'the enormities of white barbarism', which sometimes outdo those of the Indians, and the absurdity, as he sees it, of pacifism (which sometimes became compromised) in the face of Indian war parties (*Pontiac*, II.viii).

But Parkman's story of the rising to which he affixed the name of Pontiac (who remains a largely shadowy though impressive figure) is mainly the story of the small forts scattered along the Great Lakes which are immediately put under siege. All but that of Detroit, which, supplied across the lake, holds out for over a year, are overwhelmed and their garrisons are butchered or made prisoners; some of the prisoners later escape or are released, and it is from their accounts that Parkman gets much of his information, though the story of unconquered Detroit is naturally largest and fullest. Parkman brings his distinctive descriptive gift to bear on the situation of these small, isolated groups of beleaguered soldiers (mostly Scottish), utterly cut off from civilization, as well as on the ordeal suffered by the soldiers who became prisoners. The escapee faced loneliness, terror, hunger and bewilderment, and Parkman clearly used his own experience to evoke his plight, surrounded by 'the thousand pitfalls and impediments of the forest', made more formidable in darkness:

At length, he can hear the gurgle of a neighbouring brook, and turning towards it, he wades along its pebbly channel, fearing lest the soft mould and rotten wood of the forest might retain traces enough to direct the bloodhound instinct of his pursuers. With the dawn of a misty and cloudy morning, he is still pushing on his way, when his attention is caught by the spectral figure of an ancient birch-tree, which, with its white bark hanging about it, seems woefully familiar to his eye. Among the neighbouring bushes, a blue smoke curls faintly upward, and, to his horror and amazement, he recognizes the very fire from which he had fled a few hours before.

Parkman continues reconstructing the typical experiences of the novice in the forest, with death and torture close behind him until by chance he reaches some frontier post or 'perishes in despair, a meagre banquet for the wolves' (*Pontiac*, II.v).

To the Indian, of course, the forest is home and sustenance. 'He will not learn the arts of civilization, and he and his forest must perish together. The stern, unchanging features of his mind excite our admiration from their very immutability' (*Pontiac*, I.i). Some of Parkman's references to the Indians' character and appearance will grate on post-colonial susceptibilities (he is fond of 'snake-eyed', for example), but by the standards of his time his attitudes are complex. He would have said that they matched the inconsistencies of the Indian character, which have to be classed 'with the other enigmas of the fathomless human heart'. He admires the Indians' 'haughty independence', dignity and fortitude. The Indian is not always centre stage, but it seems that for Parkman he is the cynosure: 'to depict him is the aim of the ensuing history' (*Pontiac*, I.i).

One cannot take the measure of Parkman's attitude to the Indian apart from his attitude to civilization, and both seem equivocal, even tragic. All life is a mixture of good and evil; beauty and the picturesque are often at odds with utility; he speaks, in a significant phrase, of the cotton snake's 'loathsome beauty'. His cultural roots lie not in previous historiography but in the literature of European and American Romanticism: in Byron and Scott, who frequently provide the epigraphs for chapters in *The Oregon Trail*, and in Fenimore Cooper, though he also consulted the scholarly authority on the Indians, Henry Schoolcraft. Equally powerful, however, is what one feels inclined to call a prospective Darwinism. It is a matter of sensibility as well as opinion. There is a vignette in *The Oregon Trail* (i.e. ten years before the publication of *The Origin of Species*) which bears this out:

I went and lay down by the side of a deep, clear pool, formed by the water of the spring. A shoal of little fishes of about a pin's length were playing in it, sporting together, as it seemed, very amicably; but on closer observation I saw that they were engaged in a cannibal warfare among themselves. Now and then a small one would fall a victim, and immediately disappear down the maw of his voracious conqueror. Every moment, however, the tyrant of the pool, a monster about three inches long, . . . would slowly issue forth with quivering fins and tail from under the shelving bank . . . 'Soft-hearted philanthropists', thought I, 'may sigh long for their peaceful millennium; for from minnows up to men, life is an incessant battle.' (XIX)

It is no surprise to find that Parkman had no sympathy with the Boston anti-slavery abolitionists and was notably hostile to the campaign for women's suffrage. His attitudes seem to have a good deal in common with those of the Mississippian Basil Ransom in Henry James's *The Bostonians*. The regrets, whose expression generally Parkman stoically repressed, found vent in irony. Describing a volcanic outcrop along the Mississippi once adorned with an Indian painting of what a Jesuit eyewitness described as a 'monster', Parkman adds a footnote: 'In 1867, when I passed this place, a part of the rock had crumbled away, and instead of Marquette's monster, it bore a huge advertisement of "Plantation Bitters"' (*La Salle*, V). Elsewhere, commenting on the regrettable aesthetic effects of geological erosion in the vicinity of Minneapolis, he speaks of 'other changes equally disastrous, in an artistic point of view' in the form of the city of Minneapolis, 'which, in 1867, counted ten thousand inhabitants, two national banks, and an opera house', while the rival city on the opposite shore 'boasted a gigantic water-cure and a State university' and so was no longer picturesque (*La Salle*, XVIII). Civilization and geological change are equally irresistible. The former, so often seen in the eighteenth century as a precious and even fragile inheritance, is now, it seems, to be seen as a kind of juggernaut, whose course is marked by banality and whose message is adapt or die.

But, though a stoic, Parkman is anything but a bleak writer. Some austerely fastidious twentieth-century commentators found him an excessively exuberant one. In fact he is a sensitive literary artist, a master of evocative, sensuous prose. He was naturally shaped by his period, as were Macaulay and Michelet, who also transgress later and more thin-blooded notions of literary restraint. The American wilderness had already been lauded and celebrated. In Parkman's histories it is omnipresent and central, and it provides, more than anything else, the powerful imaginative dynamics of his work.

Henry Adams: From Republic to Nation

American historical writing follows a familiar course: from history as a highly literary form of composition, written by amateur men of letters, to increasing professionalism and a commitment to objectivity sometimes spoken of as 'scientific'. From Prescott's work in the 1840s to that of Henry Adams in the 1890s marks the distance travelled in this direction. There is also another difference. Prescott wrote on the history of a continent as yet unsettled by Europeans, Parkman of one where the English colonies had not yet coalesced into a political union, while Adams was to write on the early history of the new republic.

History written in English about the experience of the New World had begun at the time of the earliest English settlement in the seventeenth century. William Bradford, the first historian of the New England colony, was also a leader of the colonists when they made their landing on Cape Cod in 1620. They were a group of separatist English Puritans who had left their country to live as a godly congregation, worshipping God only in the manner they believed he had prescribed, and uncontaminated by the corruptions of the world. America was incidental, a last resort: initially they had transplanted themselves as a body to Leiden, in Holland, but though free there from religious persecution they found it hard to sustain themselves and to keep their young people, in particular, from being drawn into the wider, ungodly, world. After their eventual landfall in North America, Bradford became their governor – though not, of course, as the name would later imply, appointed by the Crown. Unlearned but not uneducated, he was clearly a man of talent, and one of his talents was as a historian.

The understandable self-consciousness of a community situated by its own collective will, as his was, naturally inspired a desire to record its fortunes and, above all, the mercies of God towards it despite its frailties. Bradford's *History of Plymouth Plantation, 1620–1647* was consulted in manuscript by later historians, but was not actually published until 1912. The journal of John Winthrop, first governor of the settlement in Massachusetts Bay, also long remained in manuscript, but was published as *The History of New England from 1630 to 1649* at the end of the eighteenth century. Captain John Smith wrote accounts of the older colony in Jamestown, Virginia: his concern was to advertise the attractions of American colonization.

But the *History of Plymouth Plantation* is unmistakably history – or one might prefer to call it chronicle, for Bradford's work has, of necessity, some of the characteristics of medieval monastic chronicles, in its localism and its enforced concentration on the strictly bounded community, given a universal dimension by an overarching piety. Peter Gay has called it 'an authentic masterpiece'. After an account of the landing and the desolation which awaited the settlers, Bradford's book becomes the well-written annals of the affairs of the colony. Bradford is eloquent about the difficulties, whose starkness emphasizes the goodness of God's providence in preserving his saints: 'Being thus passed the vast ocean . . . they had no friends to welcome them, nor inns to entertain or refresh their weatherbeaten bodys, no houses or much less townes to repaire to, to seek for succoure . . . Besides, what could they see but a hideous and desolate wilderness, full of wild beasts and wild men.' Bradford wants the children of the settlers to know 'what difficulties their fathers wrestled'.

The settlement was to be that of a covenanted people: 'By these presents solemnly and mutually in the presence of God, and one of another, [we] covenant and combine ourselves, together into a civil body politic.' But these were not 'Americans' but Englishmen, whose self-consciousness was that of a godly 'gathered people'. When Winthrop drew an image that was to become famous, this was the conception he was invoking: 'For we must consider that we shall be as a city upon a hill. The eyes of all people are upon us.' They were, that is, to be exemplary, but as a community of God's saints, voluntarily set apart, not yet primarily as inhabitants of a new land.

Perry Miller showed more than half a century ago, in his pioneering study *The New England Mind*, that it took several generations for that self-consciousness to become distinctively American. With inevitable disillusionments came also the adoption of a repeated historical dynamic, drawn from the Old Testament, and applied to the colony's history, in what Miller calls the 'jeremiads'. The people were constantly slipping from grace and as constantly visited with divine wrath. This was the pattern which, in some contrast to Bradford's matter-of-fact providentialism, informed the general history of New England produced by the most prominent Calvinist minister of the day, Cotton Mather, in 1702.

The best history of the political crises of the 1760s and '70s is generally agreed to be the *History of the Colony and Province of Massachusetts Bay*, written by the state's loyalist governor Thomas Hutchinson, who completed his account, like many a public man turned historian before him, in exile, in Britain. It is a reminder that the War of Independence had some of the characteristics of a civil war. The most prominent of the historical celebrators of the Independence period was to be the Unitarian minister and teacher (later president) at Harvard Jared Sparks (1789–1866). He produced a twelve-volume Life of George Washington, which was essentially an edition of Washington's letters. Sparks held at Harvard, from 1839, the first chair of history in the United States. His work was necessarily rather in the field of the accumulation of documents and in the inspiration and patronage of historical writing generally than as a historian himself. Parkman, who was a pupil, dedicated *Pontiac* to him.

The first historian of the United States, George Bancroft (1800–1891) was a protégé of Sparks. He was not a man of means like Prescott and Parkman, and his career included a spell teaching history at Harvard, after study in Germany, in Göttingen and Berlin, where he took a doctorate. He also, like Motley, became American minister in London, and later (1867–74) in Berlin. He had had a directly political career as Secretary to the Navy. His history eventually reached twelve volumes, published between 1834 and 1882, and was massively popular. He was a Jeffersonian Democrat, and his history was an uncritical celebration of America as the land of liberty and democracy. His dictum that 'the organization of society must more and more conform to the principle of freedom' places him firmly among the liberal historians we considered in the last chapter. He was, however, also an enthusiastic democrat, which by no means all his European counterparts were: for him it was true that the voice of the people was the voice of God. Bancroft's somewhat naive, parochial and uncritical approach to American history, while it may have ensured his nineteenth-century popularity, brought an inevitable reaction, and his history, though not ill-written, does not have the literary eminence to raise it above the shifting currents of historiographical and ideological fashion. Twelve volumes – American nineteenth-century historians were nothing if not copious – are also rather a lot even for sympathizers. His history is undeniably a monument, but seems likely for the foreseeable future to remain a largely unvisited one.

Henry Adams's detailed study, originally in nine volumes, of the third and fourth presidencies, *The History of the United States of America during the Administrations of Jefferson and Madison* (1889–91), is a very different matter, and is still highly regarded. Adams is a historians' historian. This is said neither in compliment nor in denigration, but simply as a statement of fact. He himself, commenting with characteristic irony on the small number of copies he had sold, remarked that history was made an aristocratic pursuit by the paucity of its material rewards. In fact Adams himself was the nearest America could get to a hereditary aristocrat: the Bostonian great-grandson of America's second president and the grandson of another. Adams's stance or pose of fastidious disillusionment, presented in his autobiographical *The Education of Henry Adams*, confirmed his patrician image. He conformed to type in that his career included Harvard (taught and later teaching), German universities, and a spell at the London embassy, that magnet for American historians, when his father was ambassador.

As a historian, Adams began as a medievalist, first collaborating on a book on Anglo-Saxon law and institutions. His choosing the 1800s for his American magnum opus has sometimes been thought to require explanation, but the suggestion that it was because the period contrasted badly with the presidency of his great-grandfather John Adams (1797–1801) has been strongly disputed. He had become expert in the period by editing the papers of a statesman he much admired, Albert Gallatin, who was Secretary of the Treasury under Jefferson and Madison and had played a part in negotiating the Treaty of Ghent (1814), which ended the war with Britain, and which forms a kind of climax to Adams's history. Adams's narration, as he explores the major episodes during the two presidencies, especially the purchase of Louisiana from the French and the onset of the war with Britain, is dense, intricate and long for its scope. In the main narrative part of the text he deals principally with the traditional subjects for history: legislation and the strife of parties, diplomacy and war. Like Prescott and Parkman, he worked in archives in Europe as well as the United States; his themes obliged him to estimate the motives and manoeuvres of Talleyrand, Napoleon and the British prime minister Spencer Perceval, as well as those of the American presidents and other politicians. He deals as expertly with the proceedings and dissensions in the British House of Commons as with those of Congress. The tone of his history is predominantly dispassionate – he is nothing like Bancroft – but undeniably patriotic: he sets up an antithesis between American energy and, increasingly, willingness to innovate and European conservatism and rigidity, personified in a simile of the British Life Guardsman in boots and cuirass, while the American is like a prizefighter stripped for the ring.

To the non-professional reader, however, the most attractive part of Adams's work is not the narrative, which frequently offers the experience of navigating an impressive but daunting complexity, but the long prologue, followed by a shorter epilogue of the same character, in which Adams surveys the state of American civilization in 1800 and which can still be read with profit and pleasure. It provides an analogy with Macaulay's famous chapter on the state of England in the reign of Charles II, and the comparison is to Adams's advantage. His survey is all the better for being without the declamatory triumphalism in which Macaulay incongruously clothed his essay in social history. It also sometimes recalls, not altogether accidentally, Taine's formula for cultural explanation: 'race, milieu, moment' – in Adams's case, inheritance, land, and the current historical challenge and opportunity. Adams shared Taine's desire to see history as a deterministic science of social and cultural development. The concluding section of the prologue, on 'American Ideals', and the conclusion of the epilogue (which attempts to measure developments between 1800 and 1817), entitled 'American Character', clearly represent for Adams the crown and a large part of the point of the whole exercise: once characterized, ideals and character represent what is to be explained by the survey and the history. This admittedly difficult attempt is not wholly successful, but the prologue as a whole – which is divided into a superb section on 'Physical and Economical Conditions', one on 'Popular Characteristics', and three on the 'Mind', respectively, of New England, the South and 'the Middle States' – is, however, a tour de force. Geography initially dominates the reader's impressions, as according to Adams it still not only shaped but interposed massive barriers to the progress of American civilization and national unity. He sees the land not, like Parkman, romantically, except in so far as there is a kind of romance in mastering it, but as presenting formidable obstacles, of which he gives many examples, to intercommunication within the recently founded republic.

Adams emphasizes the primitiveness and parochialism of much of American life. Drawing on his knowledge of medieval Europe, he compares the situation of the settlers in the western states (as they then were) with those of the Angles and Jutes of early England, while 'Even in New England the ordinary farmhouse was hardly so well-built, so spacious or so warm as that of a well-to-do contemporary of Charlemagne.' If to Parkman civilization sometimes presents itself as a kind of steamroller or juggernaut, to Adams it seems in 1800 more like a cart jolting over rough ground, with its wheels often sticking in the mud. The United States, politically unified, was a raw society whose scattered elements made its disparate character more evident than its unity. Even in the long-settled east the delays, hazards and hardships of travel between the major cities were formidable and the average journey times discouraging: the regular fast mail route from Maine to Georgia habitually took twenty days. The 'hero' of this part of Adams's book, and even, symbolically, of the book as a whole, was the steamship designed by Robert Fulton, which had its maiden voyage in 1807. It brought the promise of easy and regular travel for passengers and freight through the great waterways, the rivers and lakes, of America. Thus it carried unification and the efficient exploitation of the continent's resources on its decks. Adams could not resist a triumphant jeer: compared with this 'the medieval barbarisms of Napoleon and Spencer Perceval signified little more than the doings of Achilles and Agamemnon.'

The only relative failures in these admirable surveys, at once detailed and central to the imaginative economy of Adams's book and the contrasts it draws, are the finale of the prologue and the corresponding one on 'American Character' at the very end. As an essayist attempting to grasp this tantalizing but elusive phenomenon, Adams is decisively inferior to contemporaries like Walter Bagehot and Taine (in his *Notes on England*, 1862). It seems surprising that he nowhere mentions Tocqueville's *Democracy in America* (1835 and 1840). In an attempt to preserve a stance of objectivity, Adams for much of the time hides behind the positive and negative opinions of others, which he juxtaposes but hardly manages to compose into a satisfying picture. From him we get scattered judgements rather than anything like a synthesis or a novel and coherent interpretation.

In considering such a long and in many ways highly impressive achievement as Adams's history it may seem perverse and unfair to dwell on a particular weakness. This is in a sense true, but there is evidence that these sections, relatively short as they are, far from being peripheral are for Adams the most important of all. They are the testing ground (as the manoeuvrings of politicians to which he devoted so much more space could not be) for a scientific historical explanation of social development, to which he aspired but which he spoke of rather than practised. Adams's enthusiasm for this possibility, and for the concept of 'science' generally, appears to have had a number of sources: Darwinism, of course, but also, it often seems, Herbert Spencer and Taine, as well as the attempts at a science of history presented by Auguste Comte and by H. T. Buckle. It results sometimes in portentous and not particularly lucid pronouncements not characteristic of him as a historian. He wrote to a friend, 'History is simply social development along the line of least resistance'; the 'line of least resistance' is part of Herbert Spencer's general formulation of the idea of evolution, not Darwin's. In his *History*, Adams wrote that the great men of an age helped 'more or less unconsciously to reach the new level that society was about to seek'. For Adams there was a conceptual connection between 'scientific history' and the activities of 'the average man' which made American history a particularly promising field. Despite his lack of enthusiasm for democracy as a political form, he wrote to Parkman that 'the people' was the only subject for history; its 'fixed and necessary development was to be revealed by psychology, physiology and history' (this, in a different order, seems to be Taine's *'race, milieu, moment'* again).

Adams provided a fuller statement in the epilogue to his history: 'Should history ever become a true science it must expect to establish its laws not from the complicated story of rival European nationalities, but from the economical evolution of a great democracy.' North America provided the best prospect 'for the spread of a society so large, uniform and isolated to answer the purposes of science'. There the scientific historian would be able to study 'a single homogeneous society . . . under conditions of undisturbed growth'. Apart from registering that it is not much of a historical science that backs away from 'the complicated story of rival European nationalities' (which makes up a good deal of its modern subject matter), we can recognize here a recurrent nineteenth-century inclination to establish a particular nationality as a norm – Max Weber's later concept of an 'ideal type' would be useful here – whose history would constitute the central line of historical development, from which deviations could be identified. We find this in Guizot's *Civilization in Europe* and in Buckle's *History of Civilization in England* (1857–61), presented, in Buckle's case, specifically as a basis for scientific historical explanation; Buckle drew an analogy with the statistical mean. Adams was now proposing the United States, because it showed 'the steady growth of a vast population without the social distinctions that confused other nations'. ('Confused' seems rich.) The outcome was to be 'to define national character', but it cannot be said that Adams got very far with this. This is not to say that his interpretations were particularly ill-judged, but that they are ill-matched with the proclaimed, wider, scientific purpose.

The rhetoric of 'science' was becoming a historical commonplace from the 1880s onward. Not all historians went beyond a defining notion of 'objectivity' to embrace that of 'laws', as Adams clearly wished to do; Acton did not. But Adams's commitment to objectivity was becoming a convention. The historian, he said, 'should study his own history in the same spirit and by the same methods with which he studied the formation of a crystal'; he means, presumably, by the close and objective examination of documents, as practised by many of his contemporaries and juniors. Actually, though Adams generally adopted a dispassionate, analytic stance, and wrote a prose that was restrained and even austere compared with Prescott's or Parkman's, his *History* is some way from the neutrality of crystallography, and we may be grateful for it. Adams has a vision of the new United States, its difficulties and potentialities, as Parkman has one of the American forest. The Louisiana Purchase and the war with Britain are not merely the salient events in the two presidencies he has undertaken to recount: they represent the future of the United States on the continent and a vital stage in its unification as a nation.

The Louisiana Purchase, the negotiation of which Adams presents as a tense drama with amusing aspects, finally settled the question whether Spain, France or the United States would dominate the continent in the territories beyond the Mississippi. The war with Britain – not so much the war itself as the willingness to accept war rather than knuckle under to British demands to stop and search American ships and confiscate cargoes – he sees as the first great test of American nationhood. The countermeasures against Britain, which severely but selectively damaged American commerce, with New England the chief loser, placed the Union under great strain. (Adams, of course, was writing after the much more severe test of the Civil War.) The negotiations with Britain were long and tortuous, and Adams approaches them from both sides. America's resistance and the war were for him the demonstration that the nation existed and that the Union could act in defence of its national honour and its vital interests; anything less would have been shameful and would have shown that the republic still fell short of nationhood. In his characterization of American attitudes in the approach to war, Adams's own neutrality drew the line at those who put sectional commercial interest before patriotism. He clearly took much pleasure in such successes as the war brought, particularly in naval actions, and was scathing about the conduct of military ones. For him the war was the culmination of the process of feeling not Englishmen in America, not members of a group of associated states, but Americans. Patriotism, not naive or blatant, a sense of continental destiny, and a strong feeling for the integrity of the Union are the guiding undercurrents of Adams's *History*.

Adams's attraction to the notion of 'scientific history', as we have seen, was an aspiration only, and one he shared with numerous others. Adams was born to be a mandarin, or rather Brahmin, but the world was changing, and his role with it. By the end of his teaching career at Harvard he was behaving like a 'professional' historian. He was training, to use the fashionable phrase – 'baking' he more colourfully called it – future historians (see below, p. 455). The number of history teachers in American universities was growing rapidly; the *American Historical Review* began publication in 1895. Adams was president of the American Historical Association in 1893 when Frederick Jackson Turner pointed out that the open frontier was now closed and asserted its central importance in the shaping of American society. Harvard was losing its near-monopoly; Johns Hopkins was another nursery of the new professionalism. Turner himself grew up in Wisconsin, and his famous 'frontier thesis' was a socio-economic challenge to the Anglocentric notion that American democracy had been shaped by its Germanic and English heritage. Another step in the same general direction was Charles A. Beard's heretical *An Economic Interpretation of the American Constitution* (1913), which saw the move to independence as a struggle against British mercantilist economic policy, and the Founding Fathers as essentially concerned to secure private property against 'levelling' tendencies. From the 1880s it was – as one of the marks of the emergence of a historical profession – an age of 'theses'. One of the most notable was A. T. Mahan's *The Influence of Sea Power on History, 1660–1783* (1889), which, unusually for a work of history, was to exercise, inadvertently, a baleful influence on European power politics by fostering Kaiser Wilhelm II's determination to build Germany a navy to challenge Britain's.

The lifetimes of Prescott, Parkman and Adams span a century and a quarter (Prescott was born in 1796; Adams died in 1918). The sequence of their works has allowed us to consider in turn the conquest of Mexico by America's first European colonists, the Spaniards; then the virgin land of North America, its indigenous inhabitants and its earliest European, i.e. French, explorers; and finally the emergence – slow, partial and at times painful – of an American national consciousness, which Adams saw as still being created in the early nineteenth century. But there is another sequence, a cultural one, affecting the ways in which history was written. Prescott's work, closest to the eighteenth century, is aptly described as 'neo-Gibbonian' (Adams also greatly admired Gibbon, but influence is indiscernible); Parkman's belongs unmistakably with the literature of Romanticism, with Wordsworth, Scott, Byron and Lermontov, and in America with Fenimore Cooper and Thoreau. Adams, the only university teacher of the three, is, in his pronouncements about history and in his later career, part of the rapid professionalization of history, in Europe as well as America, towards the end of the nineteenth century. It is this that we now have to consider more generally, as the chief influence on the writing of history from then on.

25

A Professional Consensus:
The German Influence

Professionalization

The multi-volumed, collaborative *Cambridge Modern History* began publication in 1902. The prospectus, by its first editor, Lord Acton, has become famous for its commitment to objectivity and impersonality in historical writing: 'Contributors will understand that . . . our Waterloo must satisfy French and English, German and Dutch alike; that nobody can tell, without examining the list of authors, where the Bishop of Oxford [Stubbs] laid down his pen, and whether Fairbairn or Gasquet [a Catholic cardinal], Liebermann or Harrison took it up.' Readers here may enjoy an unintended ironical reminiscence of the anonymity and serial contributions of the medieval chroniclers, but to contemporaries this represented the acme of modernity in the writing of history and the ethics of the historical profession. (Acton, incidentally, was in the narrow sense no professional, but an aristocrat of private means, who taught in a university only at the end of his life.) Even more eloquent than the prospectus was the enterprise itself, a multi-authored compendium of international scholarship, testifying to a belief in the collaborative and cumulative character, appropriate to a science, which history had come to assume. In that sense the series was a product of several decades of growing European (and also now American) self-consciousness about the requirements of rigour and objectivity in the scholarly practice of history. The moment seemed ripe for such a project, and Acton its ideal editor. He was qualified by his cosmopolitanism as well as by the acknowledged range and profundity of his erudition and his frequently proclaimed emphasis on the critical treatment of sources as the defining characteristic of a historian.

The development of a historical profession in the most advanced countries in the later nineteenth and early twentieth centuries was part of a more general process of professionalization and specialization as middle-class education expanded, which of course also created increased opportunities for teaching careers. Specialism was an obvious and, though sometimes deplored, inevitable response to the rapid growth of knowledge, which itself was both a cause and a consequence of the research ideal. In the natural sciences it had in some cases an obvious utility, which other learned professions came to envy and claim a share in, as well as sometimes loftily to repudiate. History was an ancient intellectual practice, but not one, until the early nineteenth century – Göttingen was the forerunner – with a firm university teaching base, apart from a scattering of endowed professorships. It benefited, though it had sometimes to fight for its independence, from close association with the more ancient academic disciplines of classical scholarship and law, and was thus well placed, compared with modern literature, sociology or anthropology, to become a major player in the expanding academic world. The old tradition of 'pragmatic history', as proclaimed by Polybius (above, p. 74), could be refurbished to support the idea that history was useful in the education of statesmen and civil servants. It might also be able to foster patriotism, a national consciousness and consensus, opposing ultra-radical and socialistic tendencies.

The character of the most advanced and industrialized states at the end of the nineteenth century was, with local variations, increasingly bureaucratic, and the organization of education, and even research, was part of this. Earlier in the nineteenth century it had been a patriotic act for governments to sponsor the serial printing and publication of medieval manuscripts of national importance (there was some commercial, private printing as well, such as the Camden Society edition of Jocelin's chronicle used by Carlyle). The acknowledged and sometimes envied precursor was the *Monumenta Germaniae Historica*, which began publication in 1821, sponsored by the Prussian statesman Karl von Stein. Guizot, when he became a minister in the 1830s, was able to foster a similar enterprise in France. Such series became in a sense schools of research and (not always without difficulty) establishers of common scholarly standards. Stubbs acquired his scholarly training for himself by working as an editor of documents for the equivalent English enterprise, the so-called Rolls series.

The growth and prestige of history as a teaching and research profession was most advanced in Germany. The organization of historical faculties as miniature bureaucratic hierarchies was longest resisted in Oxford and Cambridge, particularly the former, where the older notion of the individual academic freehold, analogous to the clerical living, to which many Fellows of colleges succeeded, long retained a hold. Tensions ensued between professors who wished to organize 'their' faculties, as on the Continent, and Fellows of the quasi-independent colleges. These tensions also tended to coincide, though not absolutely, with those between research and pedagogical models of the historical profession. On the Continent and increasingly in the USA and in the new English provincial universities, relations between professors and research students, i.e. the next generation of historians, tended to be closer and to be central to the self-image and practice of the profession, retaining an element of clientage in an otherwise bureaucratic structure.

Though there were also ancillary professionals such as archivists, the core of professionalization was the growth of paid posts in universities, combining teaching and research. More or less autonomous historical faculties grew up (in Oxford and Cambridge, as independent faculties, from the early 1870s) – sometimes, particularly initially, in association with other disciplines – with provision of training for research. In England, written examinations as a requirement for graduation, with classified lists of candidates, gave control over the content of the syllabus to those who set them. The existence of such university history schools both nurtured and in a sense presupposed a professional consensus about standards of research (as the qualification for appointments) and about its presentation, with the maintenance of sobriety – some said dullness – and a neutrality of tone becoming de rigueur. The results of research would characteristically be presented, at least initially, in the specialized academic journals recently founded for that purpose, whose editors were in a position to enforce such standards. Germany was again the precursor: the *Historische Zeitschrift* began in 1859, and an earlier publication, the *Historisches Taschenbuch* ran from 1830 to 1892. The *Revue*

Historique was founded in 1876 – French historiography was heavily influenced by the example of Germany after 1870. The *English Historical Review* began in 1886, and the American Historical Association was inaugurated in 1884. The *American Historical Review* followed in 1895.

Consensus not only on how history should be written but on what history was about was not just a product of enthusiasm: for the aspiring professional it was enforceable. In the later nineteenth and early twentieth centuries history meant above all political history, including, notably, in modern history, a focus on the relations of states in the European inter-state system. It also included constitutional and legal origins and, with increasing prestige, economic history. The only German historian to whom Acton gave as much prominence as to Leopold von Ranke in his article on 'German Schools of History' for the first number of the *English Historical Review* was the economic historian Wilhelm Roscher; one of the handful of university lecturers in history appointed in Cambridge in the same decade to teach for the recently (1872) independent History Tripos (School) was the economic historian William Cunningham. Social and cultural history, despite the example of Burckhardt, were decidedly poor relations. To most historians these priorities no doubt seemed self-evident, as it also seemed that history, in acquiring professional recognition and organization, had found its identity. The long history of historical writing and inquiry from Herodotus onward had reached its terminus: Clio was unveiled and holding a chair, probably in Germany.

The rhetoric for expressing this in the period was, of course, that of 'science': history, properly practised, was an objective and cumulative form of knowledge, the accumulation of results of the industry of many dedicated professionals. More would, of course, be learned, but modern historical practice was, it was sometimes claimed, itself the result of a 'Copernican revolution', in the diffusion of obligatory standards for the critical examination of sources. It was reasonable to expect no subsequent revolutions: one cannot be more scientific than science. History was too innocent of overarching theory, other than the generalized exhortation to critical rigour, for the results of research to produce seismic theoretical consequences such as those beginning to be felt in physics from Clerk Maxwell to Einstein. How had this consensus on how to study history and, more problematically, what history was itself about become established? It was not, after all, much like the recent developments we considered in Chapter 22 above, with their dramatic narratives and increasing focus on 'the people' as a historical protagonist. To begin to answer this we have to turn to Germany.

German Historicism: Ranke, God and Machiavelli

From the early years of the nineteenth century onward German scholarship, and particularly historical scholarship, enjoyed immense prestige. Its organization and productions were envied and to some extent imitated in France, Britain and the United States. Associated with that prestige was the reputation of Leopold von Ranke, widely regarded as the doyen of the German historical profession on account of his longevity (1795–1886), his strategic situation as professor of history in Berlin, the distinction of his pupils, and the sheer impressiveness and volume of his historical works (sixty, in the collected edition). His life almost spanned the century, and at its end his pupils, though some deviated up to a point from his interests and precepts, dominated the German historical profession.

German historiography had been shaped from the medieval period onward by the fact that, like Italy, Germany was seen as a nation but not, despite the German base of the Holy Roman Empire, a state: in comparison with Italy, however, the power of the Emperor and the princes was greater than that of the 'free cities'. Germany as a whole had never been subjected to Roman rule, so for both these reasons ancient Roman civic republicanism could not have the same resonances as in Italy. Tacitus' account of the Germanic tribes and their villages became the ancient sourcebook for German history. The results are understandable: on the one hand an imperial perspective, that of Christendom or universal history, and on the other a focus on the local, including but also other than the city – the principality, or else the basic institutions of local rural society in which were thought to reside the residues of the freedom described by Tacitus.

Then, in the mid nineteenth century, came a watershed, corresponding to the crisis in German liberalism after it became apparent from the failure of the all-German parliament in Frankfurt in 1848 that the unification of Germany, desired with increasing ardour, could be accomplished only by Prussian or Austrian power. First the idea and then, after 1871, the fact of a German nation state became mesmerizing. Local particularism was less cherished or was even denigrated; the universalism of the eighteenth century and the Enlightenment and the notion of an overarching natural law, binding even on sovereign states, were thrust aside. A new Machiavellianism, *Realpolitik* – the term coined in 1851 originally to express the idea of unification only by power, but coming to legitimate the pursuit of national goals by any means – became current. In the work of the so-called 'Prussian School', which included Ranke's pupils Heinrich von Sybel and Heinrich von Treitschke, German history came to be seen teleologically (as English liberals saw the history of their Parliament), with the Prussian ruling dynasty, the Hohenzollern, as the predestined instrument of unification. (Though his standards of scholarship were much patchier, one should probably annex Carlyle to the canon of the Prussian School; Goebbels read his life of Frederick the Great to the Führer, as an aid to morale, in the Chancellery bunker in Berlin in 1945.) Acton spoke of the Prussian School as 'that garrison of distinguished historians that prepared the Prussian supremacy together with their own, and now [1886] hold Berlin like a fortress'. But not all Ranke's pupils travelled this route. They also included the medieval constitutional historians of an older persuasion Georg Waitz, Rudolf von Gneist and Reinhold Pauli, while Burckhardt too was a pupil, though a deviant one.

In the nineteenth century, after the Napoleonic invasion of 1806, in which the Prussian state had crumbled, and then in the so-called 'national awakening' of 1813 and the renewal of the war against Napoleon, the conception of the state moved centre stage, though without displacing that of the nation. *Völkisch* scholars (see above, p. 408) had initially regarded it with aversion, as a lifeless machine clamped down on the spontaneous creativity of the *Volk*. The eighteenth-century German courts were French-oriented in their culture, and the model 'Enlightened' states were despotic and highly rationalized. It is not surprising that the first analysts of bureaucracy were German. Even the state's admirers focused on its mechanical artifice and efficiency. But as, after the 1813–14 'war of liberation', the concept of the nation became increasingly politicized, the 'Idea of the State' was gathered into the thought world of Romanticism; the State as conceived by Fichte and Hegel – as the embodiment of ethical life, a spiritual agent – became, in the metaphysical technical term derived from Herder, not just a machine but a historical 'Individuality', the complement of Herder's concept of the Nation, also a unique Individuality. The two concepts achieved a kind of fusion in the idea of the nation state.

Participation in the nation state did not entail democracy, or anything like it, but an intensification of the consciousness of belonging to a higher spiritual entity, and identification with it. The State represented the individual's highest self. Hence the State was not a mere instrumentality but a spiritual reality, a self-realizing Idea, which, in the European states system, contended with other states, other Individualities, in its quest for survival and self-fulfilment, and was energized and schooled by these encounters. There is an echo here of the Roman and Machiavellian notion of the vitalizing effects of conflict and the dangers of tranquillity (above, pp. 87, 286). For Hegel, in the last part of his *Philosophy of Right* (1821) (324, 325), it was crucial that the State, in war, could call on the citizen to sacrifice his life. War was no longer, as in the eighteenth century, an affair merely for mercenaries. The State's right to the individual's life was, according to Hegel, the definitive demonstration that the State was not just an instrument for his protection (the contract theory), or for the production of welfare (Enlightened Despotism), but a higher spiritual entity than the individual. The requirement of his life was not tyranny but self-sacrifice, submission to one's own higher will and participation in the life of a higher entity.

German liberal intellectuals in the first half of the nineteenth century became increasingly irked by the political fragmentation of Germany into a multiplicity of states and were impatient for unification. Treitschke even at one point contemplated a Prussian invasion of the princely states to unify Germany by force. The conception of the nation state, striving to fulfil itself, as the supreme modern historical Idea became central to the nationalists' conception of modern European history; many German liberals had adopted the label 'National Liberal', a significant addition to the noun. European history was the encounter and interaction of self-moving, autonomous spiritual Individualities. Germany, it was argued (not by Ranke), could not become a full player until the nation was politically embodied in a single state, whose need for fulfilment overrode both the interests of individual citizens and the dictates of a law of nations grounded in natural law.

From the mid nineteenth century onward, in the work of Ranke and his pupils, there was a renewed fascination with the idea, formulated in sixteenth-century Italy and echoed ever since, of the interaction of European states as an unstable balance of powers; this was seen as the keynote of modern European history. Much of Ranke's work was devoted to examining this, from the sixteenth century onward, beginning, in the early modern period, with his *History of the Popes* (1834–7). States as Individualities in history were to Ranke thoughts in the mind of God, whose presence was continuously sensed. God's thoughts dwelt much in 'the Great Powers' (the title of an essay by Ranke). Ranke was not a philosopher, and affirmed the superiority of history to philosophy. We do not find the metaphysics which clearly in some sense suffuses his writing laid out systematically: 'the plans of the divine government' to which he refers (*History of the Popes*) are implicit, not spelled out in detail, and are glimpsed by the historian, not abstractly summarized as in Hegel's philosophy of history. Nevertheless, they are sometimes unignorable, as in the guiding idea of the existence of unique historical Individualities. It was the faith in these points of access to the divine mind which underwrote the labour Ranke devoted to reconstructing, on a scrupulously investigated documentary basis, what to him were the central themes of European history. It was the historian, and he alone, who could discern the hand of God in unique historical configurations of events and forces. This is the core of what is sometimes called 'Historicism' (*Historismus*). Ranke repudiated Hegelian teleology, which embodied the idea of successive stages towards an eventual consummation in history, which philosophy could grasp. He did not dissent, however, from Hegel's rationale for the power relations between states; certainly he did not deprecate war.

The link between the commitment to exhaustive, exact scholarship and the underlying metaphysics was the notion that the historian's business is not with abstractions but with the unique spiritual entities, the Individualities concentrated as states, which are his protagonists and with the dense texture of their relations with each other. The understanding of history could not be teleological, as in Hegel, because every age, as a famous Rankean aphorism put it, was equally 'immediate to God' and therefore required not to be placed in a sequence (though the idea of 'universal history', to which he devoted his last years, was always a brooding presence in Ranke's work), but detailed, objective investigation. This repudiation of historical teleology brings Ranke closer to modern ideas than some of his contemporaries; his confidence in the possibility of objectivity, of seeing, in another famous aphorism, 'wie es eigentlich gewesen' ('how it really happened'), which was then common, does not.

Ranke's *oeuvre* was vast (most of it is untranslated into English), and it is hard to summarize a modern consensus on him because it is not clear that one exists. Almost everything seems contested: his almost exclusive devotion to political and, above all, 'diplomatic' history; the extent of his influence; the importance to him of metaphysical or mystical notions; even the quality of his narrative, which was much praised for its Olympian detachment. Acton called it 'colourless', and probably meant this as a compliment. He wrote that 'Ranke is the representative of the age which instituted the modern study of history. He taught it to be critical, to be colourless and to be new. We meet him at every step, and he has done more for us than any other man.' But it can hardly be complimentary when, in his review (1867) of Ranke's work on English history, Acton says that 'scenes which Macaulay had made as vivid as anything in epic poetry, are described with elaborate dullness', or speaks of his later works as 'tame and frigid'.

The extent of Ranke's overriding preoccupation with the affairs of states is the most serious of the disagreements about him, because it affects the general argument being made here. It is not advisable to be dogmatic about sixty volumes: it can only be said, impressionistically, that it was so – counter-arguments seem to run the risk of making much of sightings of occasional swallows. Acton also said that Ranke had produced more excellent works of history than anyone else, but no single masterpiece. This is perhaps an assured route to esteem and influence among one's contemporaries; it is less recommendable if one wants to captivate readers a century and a half later. For most such readers, especially English and American ones, it seems most realistic to try to understand Ranke as an influence, a model and a portent rather than a still-living author. To do so is perhaps, in any case, an implication of the idea of a historical profession and its cumulative body of knowledge.

Not Quite a Copernican Revolution

In his Cambridge inaugural lecture, which we have already visited, Acton introduced his hearers to the new era, for which Ranke archetypally stood: 'The accession of the critic in place of the indefatigable compiler, of the artist in coloured narrative, the skilled limner of character, the persuasive advocate of good, or other, causes, amounts to a change of dynasty, in the historic realm. For the critic is one who, when he lights on an interesting statement, begins by suspecting it.' The new dynasty was the historical professionals, with their defining craft, the critical examination of sources, and Ranke (Acton had attended his lectures in Berlin) was its doyen.

The inaugural lecture was a rhetorical occasion calling for piety and exhortation rather than dissent. Nine years earlier, in his article in the new *English Historical Review* on 'German Schools of History', Acton's view of Ranke had been more qualified. Now he simplified and therefore somewhat exaggerated the novelty of the historiographical revolution in critical scholarship he attributed to the nineteenth century. He recognized that its principles had been well understood earlier; he was on safer ground in claiming that it was a novelty to apply them in writing narratives of modern history, which also depended on the opening of state archives, but this was a qualification easily forgotten. It was also important to apply them comprehensively and to seek out manuscript sources systematically, not sporadically, which he accused even the younger Ranke of doing. To consult *all* the relevant sources is good advice, but it is hardly a Copernican revolution. That primary sources are to be preferred to secondary, and that misrepresentation, ignorance and even forgery are all always possibilities; that secondary sources are therefore to be rigorously tested for possible motives to distortion and for access to the truth – these were, as he admitted, not a mystery but more like common sense.

The distinction between primary and secondary sources is recognized as a crucial one for historians. Essentially it is that between a document by which something was done, like an order, a commission, a charter or a contract, and a commentary or narrative. In the first, truth and falsehood are not the issue (apart from forgery), though good faith and intention may be, and meaning certainly is. As Acton said, 'The chronicle is a mixture of memory, imagination and design. The charter is reality itself.' Another primary source is documents in which agents attempt to influence events, which therefore form part of what the historian investigates; the question whether the agent told the truth is probably secondary to questions of intention and efficacy. In secondary sources – typically narratives and commentaries – the reverse is the case. The most obvious and vital question is whether they are true. There is also, of course, in assessing them, a relevant distinction between eyewitness testimony and hearsay. There is an analogy between the practice of the critical historian and the passion of the fifteenth-century humanists for recovering the purest, least contaminated version of a classical text: the suspicion with which a historian like Ranke regarded chroniclers and previous historians parallels the humanists' scorn for the medieval commentators.

The distinction between primary and secondary is a flexible one, however. The same document may be both, as a commentary may be written as a political act. A document that is secondary in one kind of inquiry may be primary in another. Ranke apparently liked to form an impression of the personality of the source of a document, as part of an assessment of its trustworthiness. The biases of the chronicler stood as a kind of screen between the historian and the truth. But in Germany, in particular, in the study of the early periods it had been fully acknowledged that myth might be treated as forming a part of their history. This had inspired some highly influential scholarship and speculation, including, for example, one of the seminal works of the nineteenth century, David Friedrich Strauss's *Life of Jesus*, in which the Gospels are dismissed as history but reinstated as evidence for the first-century Jewish mind. But in searching for the truth of mainly modern history it seems not to have occurred to Ranke (though Acton was aware of it in principle) that the lenses through which the chroniclers looked at the world were themselves material for history, part of the times in which they wrote, and in that sense potentially primary sources. This reflects the primacy assumed in the Rankean world by high politics – chroniclers were small beer, useful or unreliable servants – and of the assumption that facts and events were what history was essentially made of. Chroniclers were recorders of these, not part of history themselves. We find the same attitude in so distinguished a medievalist as V. H. Galbraith, writing in the 1950s on medieval English chroniclers as irritating colleagues. Any historian now old will probably have met this attitude – or shares it.

Much of Ranke's influence seems to have been personal, through the systematic way he trained his pupils in his famous Berlin seminar in the practice of the critical use of sources, with discussions of documentary examples. In this, as Acton knew, he had been anticipated by classical philologists, who also taught in this way. An American student recalling his days in Berlin at this time wrote an enthusiastic reminiscence of his seminar experience: 'There the student appears, fortified by books and documents borrowed from the university library, and prepared with his brief of points and citations, like a lawyer about to plead a case in the court room . . . Authorities are discussed, parallel sources are cited; old opinions are exploded, standard histories are riddled by criticism.' In this enthusiasm for a system now familiar – even if it does not always generate such breathless excitement – one can hear the doors of a new pedagogical experience opening. Henry Adams, who, like most notable nineteenth- and early-twentieth-century American historians, had trained in Germany, introduced such a seminar at Harvard in 1871 (there was another at Johns Hopkins) and supervised several of the earliest Harvard PhDs in the early 1870s, half a century before such seminars began to be introduced in England.

Much distinguished history was produced, of course, by Ranke and his pupils. In the process, the kind of history on which they chiefly focused became virtually definitive of modern history. The professional imperative to test particular kinds of source for their truth

to events, joined with the contemporary political interests and pressures we considered earlier, promoted a focus on the uncovering
and dissection of state papers, some only recently available, as the
historian's central task. Other kinds of history, apart from constitutional, which had its own firm base among medievalists, were marginalized, though in any case the emphasis on political history and
foreign affairs was a continuation of the long-standing ancient and
humanist conception of what was proper to the dignity of history.
There was also in the nineteenth century a reciprocal relation between
the assumed role of the historian in ferreting out secrets and a history
concerned with the intentions of statesmen: the closet politics of the
sixteenth century and the *Ancien Régime*; the pursuit of covert diplomacy (the adjective is almost redundant). On all these Ranke wrote
extensively. The more covert the policies, the greater the challenge to
the professional historian to uncover them by investigating archives.
The first book of documents on which Ranke worked closely was a
collection of Venetian ambassadors' reports from the sixteenth to the
eighteenth century, which seem to have become something of a fetish
and a paradigm for him; even contemporaries sometimes complained
that his history was excessively princely.

There were costs, as Peter Burke points out, claiming that Ranke
took history away again from the broadened 'civil history' of the
eighteenth century, and returned it to the more restricted subject
matter of humanist history. Burke also draws attention to the breadth
of the interests of the Göttingen school of the later eighteenth century,
'cut off in their prime by the historical revolution associated with
Ranke', though he admits that Ranke's own interests were more
eclectic than he is sometimes given credit for.

The point can be given further amplification. There is a marked
contrast with the 'sentimental' and dramatic treatments of events
cultivated in the eighteenth century, as well as with Carlyle's and
Michelet's demotic kind of history of the French Revolution. It was
noted earlier (Chapter 21) that writing history for the market included
writing for women. The emergent profession, however, was independent of the market, and was masculine in its ethos and largely in its
composition; the smell of pipe smoke still clung to it in the 1950s.
Its prejudices were to be long-lasting and restrictive, narrowing the

illumination the study of the past could bring to a culture. In general, overly triumphant versions of the nineteenth-century 'revolution' in historical studies were an aspect of, and helped to feed, what we have already noticed: the century's apparent ignorance of the scholarly innovations of the sixteenth and seventeenth centuries and its systematic denigration of eighteenth-century historiography. The notion of a nineteenth-century 'Copernican revolution' reinforced an enduringly distorted version of the history of historiography, slanted towards the nineteenth century and Germany, which the present book has attempted to correct. The professional consensus of which this notion formed an important, and restrictive, part was to be a tough and lasting one, persisting well into the twentieth century. The methods of examining documents, of course, remain the same now as then, and as they were earlier still.

The rhetoric of 'objectivity' and 'science' did eventually become muted or abandoned in the twentieth century, with greater awareness of the complexity of the issues the terms raised and some awareness of their costs in the writing of history. The hierarchy of esteem for various kinds of history, however, proved more tenacious, with political history and international affairs sharing some of their prestige only with institutional history, chiefly medieval. Social and cultural history stood somewhat on the margins. Intellectual history, if it existed, was probably someone else's business. German Idealist metaphysics and English pragmatism ironically concurred in the primacy, in the modern period, of political history. The English took the centrality of Parliament – and earlier of their kings – for granted because it had occupied that position in English life for so long. The Germans exalted the state because, as the nation state, it had arrived for them so recently. (This occurred in an age when, in historical scholarship, France and the United States, whose intellectual traditions were different, became something like clients of the Germans.) How the professional consensus around the primacy of political history and the dedication to a 'scientific' ideal of objectivity began to disintegrate we have to consider in the next chapter.

26

The Twentieth Century

Professionalism and the Critique of 'Whig History'.
History as a Science and History as an Art

In this final chapter I have attempted a necessarily brief account
of the main innovative developments in twentieth-century historical
writing, of which there are many, and have tried to show what is
interesting or valuable about them. There is an obvious danger, which
I have consciously resisted, of any more comprehensive attempt growing disproportionately to the rest of the book, if only because so much
more history was written during the twentieth century than in any
previous one, and a general survey of even the most impressive historical writing the century produced could issue only in a kind of opinion-
ated bibliography. A list of important and original twentieth-century
historians who are not mentioned here would therefore be a very
long and distinguished one. It would include almost all – even the
most original – who contributed to genres which were established and
familiar by the later nineteenth century, including the study of high
politics and constitutional, diplomatic and military history. The attention given in this chapter to social and economic history, however,
which assumed much importance in the middle and later twentieth
century, is not meant to imply that there were no notable earlier
examples, as there were for cultural history, which has also risen
greatly in prominence in the twentieth century. Precedents, as noted
in earlier chapters, have included, for example, the sixteenth-century
French advocates of 'perfect' (total or comprehensive) history; the
Enlightenment interest in the 'History of Civil Society' or civilization,
and the flourishing study in Germany, particularly in Göttingen at the

end of the eighteenth century, of 'universal history'; Vico's pioneering ideas about cultural history, and later the influential thought of Herder and the work of Michelet. To a greater extent therefore even than in earlier chapters, I can make no claim to completeness, but I am consoled by the thought that readers will probably be more familiar with twentieth-century historical writing than with that of previous eras.

It is important to recognize at the outset that what is intended in a distinction between new or relatively new and more traditional types of history is not a contrast in quality. Not all innovative work is good, and far from all the work in well-established genres is routine. If in (roughly) the last third of the century in particular a hundred historiographical flowers bloomed, some very soon also wilted. I have therefore tried in this chapter only to consider examples of novelty which were influential or representative, as well as some I find particularly impressive. I absolutely do not conceive it as my business to tell my fellow historians how to do their own, or to offer rebukes or prizes, issue prescriptions and make predictions, any of which would have given the book at the end a polemical character alien to its purposes. Meanwhile the older genres continue, sometimes in novel guises, and we should be grateful for it, though I have no space here to express proper appreciation of them.

In surveying the history of historical writing in the twentieth century it is tempting to try to relate the various forms it most typically assumed in the various European countries and in the United States to those countries' recent historical experiences. Any suggestions along these lines are bound to be subject to qualification, but it does seem possible to make out some broad outlines. As we shall see, the notably innovatory kinds of history produced in France have involved moves away from the focus on the nation state towards everyday life, as well as downwards to the regions and villages and outward to the history of the world. This seems to reflect the decline of France, earlier than that of Britain or Germany, as a great power, and disillusionment with the notoriously centralizing tendencies of the French state inherited from Richelieu, Louis XIV and the Revolution. Historians in the United States have naturally been drawn to study the creation of their nation and its testing in the ordeal of civil war, and have had to confront the steps by which it became the world's superpower; this has meant calling on the resources of traditional genres of political history, including the history of foreign policy, in which the United States has enjoyed an exceptional freedom of choice. The sense has been that America represents the world's future, so that to write of America is to engage with the history of the world.

In Germany, attention to the steps to the nation state, which riveted the attention of nineteenth-century historians, has necessarily been succeeded by attempts to understand its two great catastophes in the twentieth century, in 1914 and 1933, providing explanations in the long or the short term, again drawing predominantly on the well-established genres of political, diplomatic, military and to some extent national cultural history. Though it and the largely institutional reasons for it form too large a subject to be dealt with here, account has to be taken too of the fact that much internationally influential thinking about the major social and cultural transformations of Europe from the early modern period has been conducted in Germany under the label of sociology rather than history. It is enough to mention the names of Max Weber, Werner Sombart, Georg Simmel, Theodor Adorno, Norbert Elias and Jürgen Habermas.

Britain has been receptive, since the 1970s, to developments elsewhere, notably in France. It has also been remarkable for the range of its attention to the histories of other countries. An interest in Germany and Russia in this period may be taken for granted, as may attention to Asia and Africa, of which Britain once ruled so much. No historical imperative seems to have dictated that English historians should have become leading authorities, even in those countries themselves, on the histories of Spain, Italy, Poland and Sweden, but such has been the case. One of the outstanding English historians of his generation, Richard Cobb, who devoted his life to the history of France in the revolutionary period, earned from *Le Monde* the accolade of 'l'étonnant Cobb'.

In the early twentieth century what I called the professional consensus was essentially unshaken, but it was becoming critical of what in Chapter 23 was spoken of as the liberal conception of history as the story of a continuous growth of freedom. The new professional temper was cooler, and we saw an example of this earlier in the prefatory remarks of Charles Petit-Dutaillis to his *Supplement to Stubbs' Constitutional History* in 1908 (above, p. 422). This conveniently marks the difference in period between Stubbs's work, with its enthusiasm for the freedom of the German woods and the continuities of parliamentary history in England, and that of its revision and supplementation over a generation later. Secularization was one aspect of the transition. Stubbs was devout. Frederic William Maitland, the outstanding and sharply sceptical legal and institutional English historian of the early twentieth century, was not. Stubbs, a cleric who passed easily from an Oxford chair to the bishopric of Oxford in 1884, had declared in his inaugural lecture in 1866 that the study of history was essentially religious; even then this had raised a few eyebrows. Not all histories of liberty were overtly confident of finding in it the presence of divine providence, as Stubbs's was. But that God had willed the English constitution or the freedom of the United States was a thought by no means alien to the mid nineteenth century.

It is true that militant secularism had tended in France to drive a wedge between religion and liberty – though not for Guizot – while in Germany in the age of Ranke the God who presided over history had characteristically more statist concerns, and endorsed *Realpolitik*. But in the later nineteenth century liberalism as a political creed was entering choppier waters. Universal suffrage and the prospect it raised of 'socialism' – a loose term at the time, meaning any kind of collectivism or welfare legislation – were widely perceived as threatening. Economic protection in the service of nationalism, which made a motive for imperial acquisitiveness, eroded the central liberal orthodoxy of Free Trade. These were powerful challenges to liberal optimism, to which the First World War administered an even graver shock.

Liberal historical triumphalism was essentially a narrative; professional zeal for exactitude, exhaustiveness and causal explanation naturally tended to tilt the balance from narrative to analysis. The tension between the two was to become particularly evident in both Britain and France from the later 1920s, though it was already apparent in the eighteenth century, with explanations presented in disquisitions or digressions. As we have seen (above, p. 333), Hume made use of these, to Adam Smith's disapproval. The professional historians of the middle years of the twentieth century became notably drawn to technical explication and the search for long-term causes in ways which naturally diverted attention to an important extent from narrating the events themselves. This tendency came to full fruition with an increasing input from sociology, anthropology and Marxism (which inevitably stressed 'underlying' changes which were the business of economic as well as social historians). The narrative of events seemed superficial by comparison. The French called it *histoire événementielle*, contrasting it with the *longue durée* of structural change; Marxists saw it as tracing only changes at the level of the political 'superstructure', compared to those of the 'real' economic forces and the formation of classes. The new watchword, in both cases, was 'structure'. In 1929 Lewis Namier, in his *The Structure of Politics at the Accession of George III*, struck a powerfully influential blow at key aspects of the liberal grand narrative of freedom – particularly at the idea of the historical continuity of the two great English political parties, Whigs (the defenders of freedom) and Tories, and at the notion that later-eighteenth-century English politics had been dominated by a Whig defence of constitutional principles against a monarch, George III, bent on restoring royal power.

Lewis Namier – the names were a drastic Anglicization – was a Polish immigrant and a Jew. He arrived in England in 1908, young enough to spend student years at the London School of Economics and Balliol College, Oxford. He was to devote himself to the politics of eighteenth-century England – almost, it seems, as a kind of solace for the ideological illusions of nineteenth-century liberalism and Europe's chaotic twentieth-century politics, finding relief in an adoptive English patriotism and a period of history which he chose to see as devoid of ideological pressures. By the time Namier left it, party principle had virtually been swept out of eighteenth-century English politics altogether, leaving only the motives and manoeuvrings of perennial political man in an ideological vacuum. Namier was said to have emptied the ideas out of history. In doing so, with immense erudition in his chosen field, he also emptied history out of it – i.e. much of what was historically specific.

Namier's devotion to the narrowest of time bands may have been exaggerated by his failure, like that of virtually all historians, to carry out all his projects, but it seems highly unlikely that these would have failed to embody his enduring detestations, his scholarly inclination towards miniaturism, and his contempt for evocative narrative and for the history of ideas. It was an axiom with him that the real considerations at work were to be found in the private correspondence of ministers and Members of Parliament – relatively unlikely repositories for inspiring declarations of shared principles. That the movement of events was essentially dictated by individual motives and calculations and that political ideas were merely rhetorical froth was thus more or less circularly guaranteed by the particular choice of sources. Public utterances were prima facie discredited because they were public. Namier is an extreme case of the tendency for the devotion above all to manuscript sources to predetermine what was to count as real history.

Namier's characteristic method – *The Oxford English Dictionary* gave its imprimatur to the verb 'Namierize' in 1976 – was the close examination, exhaustively carried out, of the lives and political connections of individual Members of Parliament – what is known also, when more generally applied, as 'prosopography', which was notably used by Sir Ronald Syme in 1939 for the study of the later Roman republic and by A. H. M. Jones for that of the empire. Namier's initiative resulted in the collectively produced *History of Parliament* (actually of the House of Commons), undertaken by a group of historians, including Namier himself, with government sponsorship. 'Namierizing' was what 'The History of Parliament' apparently *meant*: nothing like Stubbs's liberty 'widening from precedent to precedent' (above, p. 411) here. Namier's influence on the profession in England – but virtually only in England – was very powerful and formidably narrowing. George III was rehabilitated, however, and the concept of the continuity of parties, which G. M. Trevelyan had declared only in 1926 to be 'a great fact in English history', was left very battered, though the concept of party itself, in the eighteenth century, proved not beyond rehabilitation in the hands of younger scholars.

A parallel attack on the tradition of liberal history to Namier's was Herbert Butterfield's essay – it was no more than that – *The Whig Interpretation of History*, published in 1931. The two historians were entirely independent of each other, and Butterfield's relations with Namier were always to be tense and sometimes antagonistic, so the fact that they should have pointed coincidentally in the same direction seems all the more significant. Butterfield's essay was an attack on liberal triumphalism in history, for which he chose rather unfortunately to use the parochial English name 'Whig'. He identified it as anachronistic and unhistorical or even anti-historical. Whig history, in Butterfield's definition – there was virtually no illustration – purveyed a conception of progress as the central theme of English history, dividing historical agents into canonized forefathers and mere obstacles, depriving the latter of any real benefit of historical understanding of their intentions and predicaments, and travestying even the 'winners' by tacitly crediting them with a kind of obscure foreknowledge of later ideas, needs and practices. These anticipations were their significance for history. In these ways, the past, which had once been its own 'present', with its own interests, concerns and urgencies, was sacrificed to modern concerns and turned into a bland and benign anticipation of the present. Believers in Providence like Stubbs, we may add in retrospect, were really on firmer ground than their successors in presuming a long-term significance to history of which historical figures were the agents. It is quite proper and in a sense not anachronistic to attribute historical foresight to Providence, if not to men. Butterfield actually had his own, not altogether explicit, conception of Providence in history, but Providence manifested itself, it seemed, chiefly in a capacity for irony: for playing games with unintended consequences and confounding mere men's anticipations and progressive notions.

As his use of 'Whig' indicates, Butterfield's polemic was focused essentially on the deficiencies of a partisan version of English history, but the logic of his argument, as has subsequently come to be widely recognized, is capable of and in a sense requires much wider application. It has become common among historians to speak of 'whig history' – the use of the lower case is a useful indicator of the wider sense – for any subjection of history to what is essentially a teleological view of the historical process. It is a description which will often be employed in this chapter. In this sense, because history has supposedly an anticipated terminus from which it derives its moral and political point, Marxist history is characteristically whig. So were the older, simpler, versions of the history of science. The advance of science could be seen as a series of victories over pre-scientific thinking, and only the views of the genuine and hence progressive scientists (or even only those parts of their views which were authentically scientific, for some were regrettably eclectic) were of much interest. This was an intelligible stance in a modern scientist, but in a historian it was a kind of self-contradiction. It was magnificent, but it was not history.

Butterfield's own later trajectory was to be more erratic and in some ways elusive than one might have supposed. During the Second World War he published an essay (*The Englishman and His History*) in which the Whig (not 'whig') interpretation, while still being held at a distance as history, was said to have had desirable political consequences: 'Whatever it may have done to our history, it has had a wonderful effect on our politics.' This essay can be regarded as a *pièce d'occasion*, an effort of patriotism under stress, but Butterfield also recognizes an enduring emotional pull: 'In every Englishman there is hidden something of a whig that seems to tug at the heart-strings.' Butterfield was also to be one of Namier's strongest critics, denouncing the extrusion of principle from eighteenth-century politics, and of narrative and the broad sweep from historical writing. It can be argued that his own work pointed to no satisfactory reconciliation of historical writing with what he called 'technical history', which needed to have room made for it but which ought not to be allowed to take over. An unease, however, was evident.

This is not surprising. A story is inherently whiggish, and the longer its timescale the more marked this will be, requiring an artificial protagonist enduring beyond the span of individual lives and therefore, generally, of individual purposes. A story is selective, looking forward to its later episodes or its eventual outcome for its criteria of relevance. A sense of its artifice has drawn authors of modernist fiction to disrupt or play with narrative expectations in order to draw attention to this. In the present book I have consciously resisted the narrative urge to impose a unitary story. To succumb to this would be to turn the book into a teleology (see Introduction). Here the warning in Butterfield's early essay, slight and in some ways unsatisfactory as it is, still casts its long shadow. The impulse to write history has nourished much effective narrative, and narrative – above all in Homer – was one of the sources of history as a genre. It would be a strange paradox if narrative and history turned out to be incompatible. But the example of Homer may teach us not to take the paradox too tragically. The *Iliad* has a climax, the fall of Troy, but it has many perspectives, and it would be a drastically impoverished reading of Homer's epic that saw as its 'point' an explanation of Troy's fall. The concept of a story is in essence a simple one, but that does not make all narrators either simple-minded or single-minded. Narrative can be capacious as well as directional. What is the 'point' of *War and Peace* or Thucydides?

The tension noted though not resolved by Butterfield between setting out the results of technical scholarship and literary narrative presentation was a long-standing one in England. Its recognition had provoked controversy, and was to continue to do so. We can see it in the determination of the founders of the *English Historical Review* in 1886 to make their journal the preserve of 'scientific' history and to keep out the men of letters. In Oxford and Cambridge in the last decades of the nineteenth century the creation of the undergraduate syllabuses and examinations had divided the new history faculties roughly between the proponents of a broad historical education (mostly the college tutors) and the advocates of 'training in research' (mostly the professors). In Oxford, the inaugural lecture in 1904 of the new Regius professor, Charles Firth, who had made his criticisms locally specific, produced an indignant collective response from the tutors, who thought he had impugned their scholarship. In Cambridge in 1903 the inaugural lecture of J. B. Bury, entitled 'History as a Science', had a similar tenor but remained at the level of generalities; it contained the by then usual hymn of praise to German scholarship, and was made controversial by Bury's rejection of 'literary' history and his notorious conclusion that history is 'simply a science, no less and no more'. A rejoinder was published immediately by Macaulay's great-nephew G. M. Trevelyan, who repeated it with alterations in 1913 in his *Clio: A Muse*. There Trevelyan, as well as effectively attacking the analogy with physical science, made a plea for the educative function of history, and associated this with the effectiveness of its literary presentation. Lamenting the fact that 'Two generations back, history was part of our national literature', but it had now become 'merely the mutual conversation of scholars', he declared that 'the art of history remains always the art of narrative.' He himself was to achieve an enormous popular success with his *English Social History* (1944).

In the next generation the leading proponent of Trevelyan's prescription for history as part of the national culture was his Cambridge pupil J. H. Plumb. Though Plumb, as a historian of the eighteenth century, had to show that he had mastered the 'Namierizing' techniques for parliamentary history in vogue from the 1930s to the 1950s, his emotional allegiance was given to Trevelyan, and in his retrospective, semi-autobiographical reflections *The Making of an Historian* (1988) it was natural for him to take Namier and Trevelyan as the two representative figures of rival traditions of scholarly introversion on the one hand and humane literature with responsibility to a public wider than the merely professional on the other. One might object that 'traditions' is over-rigid. Though it may be difficult to combine the historian's dual responsibilities in a single work, many historians – including Plumb – have combined them in their careers. The contemporary representative, for Plumb, of a dedication to narrowly technical scholarship more or less chose himself: his Cambridge rival the Tudor historian Geoffrey Elton. That is, Elton at least partially acted up to the role assigned to him, even if it was to some extent an exaggeration. Elton did at times reach out to a wider readership, at least in schools, but his own views of the historian's responsibilities, as combatively expressed as Plumb's, were significantly different (cf. *The Practice of History* (1967)). Elton had made his name as an administrative historian, with *The Tudor Revolution in Government* (1953). To him – it is tempting to say in the Rankean tradition – the training of research students was also a vital part of his role. He could speak of the Public Record Office as of a garden of delights.

Elton, like Namier, was an immigrant – in his case from Germany – and was similarly Anglophile, though much better assimilated. He was crustily resistant to foreign fads like Freudianism (unlike Namier), Marxism and sociology: the historian had to keep at arm's length not only literary fudging but also theory. Yet, looking at a career so dedicated to the study of bureaucracy as the engine room of the Tudor monarchy, it is hard not to see a German predilection for the state rather than the English shibboleth of Parliament. It was in Germany that, in the late eighteenth century, bureaucracy was first distinguished as a category, while the concepts for analysing its tendencies and effectiveness were given classic form at the beginning of the twentieth century by Max Weber. Elton, however, referred to Weber only in connection with his *The Protestant Ethic and the Spirit of Capitalism* – and with characteristic trenchancy: 'historical nonsense'.

Plumb too, though drawn when young to Marxism, had no use for theory. He had wanted originally to write novels, like his friend and early patron C. P. Snow. His conversation had some of the qualities of Balzac's *Comédie humaine* and of Thackeray's and Rowlandson's versions of Regency England. It was appropriate that, as he tells us, he should have begun his writing career as a historian (with *England in the Eighteenth Century*, 1950) in a Brighton hotel. He delighted in the wider reputation his writing brought him, and encouraged his pupils to be adventurous. In a time and place whose preferred tone inclined to be dry 'grey' was Plumb's word – he had a liking for grandeur and excess, undercut by a sense of the comic and grotesque. Individual tuition from him was, as he intended, intimidating, exhilarating and never dull.

Coincidence or not, it is remarkable how prominent a part Plumb's pupils and younger colleagues at Christ's College, Cambridge, have played in bringing history before a wide public in the last couple of decades. One example was Roy Porter, prolific historian of medicine and madness, chiefly in the eighteenth century. David Cannadine, in addition to tracing elegantly the stratagems of the British aristocracy and monarchy in the modern world, is the author of a study of Trevelyan (*G. M. Trevelyan: A Life in History*, 1992), whose view that history should be written so as to form part of the national culture he has polemically restated. The widest audiences have, of course, been reached by television, as in Niall Ferguson's programmes subsequently published as *Empire: How Britain Made the Modern World* (2003) and Simon Schama's engagingly written and presented outline *History of Britain* (published in three volumes, 2000–2003). The success of Schama's series, in particular, surely owes something to the contrast its sweeping overview presents to the teaching of history in schools as a set of disconnected 'projects'. These seem to reflect a priority of 'method' over comprehensive understanding, and an imitation at an early age of a feature of the historical profession: specialization. Trevelyan at his most pessimistic can hardly have expected Bury to triumph even among schoolchildren.

'Structures': Cultural History and the Annales School

Namier had an interest not only in the working out of individual psychological drives and dispositions, which is evident in his studies of eighteenth-century politics, but also, almost inevitably in a Central European Jew of his generation, in Freudian psychology, which is not. In France, however, debts to psychology and claims for the help it might offer the historian were more overt, particularly in the work of Lucien Febvre (1878–1956). Febvre was, with the medievalist Marc Bloch, one of the two founders in 1929 (the same year as Namier's *Structure of Politics*) of the journal which became known simply as the *Annales*; its full original title was *Annales d'histoire économique et sociale*, and it gave its name to a whole school of French historians, the most influential such school in twentieth-century historiography. 'The *Annales* school' is now an indispensable piece of historians' shorthand, though it covers a number of complexities.

Before coming to Febvre, however, and his contribution to cultural history in particular, we have to consider the work of the most notable cultural historian to publish in the years after the First World War, working essentially in the German tradition of cultural history, the eminent Dutch historian Johan Huizinga. Huizinga, whose importance was recognized by Febvre, is known chiefly by his classic *The Waning of the Middle Ages*, first published in 1919. He too was interested in psychology; he had studied under the famous German psychologist Wilhelm Wundt. Huizinga had a conception of culture as a kind of inventive game that human beings play, involving the masks worn by different ages, by which they presented and recognized themselves, and established their sense of identity. 'Representations', the term employed in the sociology and anthropology of Emile Durkheim, later became the fashionable term for the conceptual images through which people structured their sense of the world and of their society, and the self-images and beliefs they shared as part of a common cultural stock. These were clearly historically variable, and therefore invited treatment by historians, though they were just as unamenable as social and economic structures to traditional narrative treatment. The achievement of Burckhardt, who was the most obvious precursor to Huizinga's work, in *The Civilization* [actually 'Kultur'] *of the Renaissance in Italy*, had been of an essentially non-narrative kind. Huizinga's work, which stood to the later Middle Ages as Burckhardt's to the Renaissance, and was clearly intended to, now bears some archaic features, not least the title and the periodic resort to organic metaphors. But it has retained an enduring popularity. It has clear claims to be regarded as the outstanding work of cultural history in the first half of the twentieth century, and a notable predecessor of much that was to come.

Huizinga was a highly self-conscious historian, who in some of his essays, published as *Men and Ideas* (1960), set out to characterize cultural history, which he says must concentrate on 'deeper general themes' ('The Task of Cultural History', 1926). Culture exists only as a 'configuration', so that only 'when the scholar has to determine the pattern of life, art and thought taken all together can there be a question of cultural history'. Elsewhere he speaks of the objects of cultural history as 'the forms and functions of civilization . . . as they consolidate into cultural figures, motifs, themes, symbols, concepts, ideals, styles and sentiments'; 'form and function' was a phrase current in the study of animal and plant morphology.

Huizinga is clearly touched (as was to become a feature of avant-garde historiography) by influences from contemporary psychology, sociology and anthropology, as well as from biology. He mentions as relevant, for example, the German sociologist Max Scheler, and the French anthropologist Marcel Mauss, a disciple of Durkheim. It is not surprising therefore to find him adumbrating what were to become aspirations for the *Annales* school, or to find his work recognized by Febvre, who was to call for 'a history of the emotions'. Huizinga spoke of the possibility of a 'history of vanity', and claimed that the seven deadly sins were seven chapters in the history of culture waiting for treatment. He also exhibits a marked anti-whiggism in Butterfield's more generalized sense. By making someone a precursor 'one lifts him out of the framework of his own time, and in doing so one distorts history' ('Historical Ideals of Life'). He praises Burckhardt as being the first to view the Renaissance apart from the concern with enlightenment and progress, and to see it not just as a prelude but as *sui generis*.

In *The Waning of the Middle Ages*, Huizinga attempts to trace the configurations mainly of the courtly culture of the Burgundian lands in the later medieval period, focusing on the attitudes, often embodied in ceremonial and artistic aspects of life, to birth, love, marriage, death and knighthood. He is particularly interested in the rituals and symbols expressive of ideal forms of life, religious and chivalric. Like Burckhardt, he is visually sensitive, and aware of art as a source for uncovering ideas when its meanings are decoded. His book is highly sensuous in its evocations of town life at all levels, including everyday experiences and special fetes, like those associated with royal entries, marriages and tournaments. He regards thinking in images and personifications as particularly characteristic of his period, developed and systematized to the point of decadence. In such thinking, natural objects are never merely themselves and seen as such (their perception is the subject of a whole chapter in Burckhardt), but are always the bearers of specific meanings, often multiple, within an overall symbolic code which is generally understood. The world is structured as a hierarchy of such symbolic meanings, in which colours, plants and flowers, animals, minerals, planets, biblical stories and the ordering of society all play parts and constantly evoke each other and the moral qualities with which they are associated. Resemblances, of any kind, constitute symbolic connections; it is a world not so much of causality as of correspondences, which relate objects in this way rather than, as a later world of thought would relate them, taxonomically and causally.

Huizinga recognizes that this is a kind of game, though a serious one, because for him man is a game-playing animal; one of his other works is entitled *Homo Ludens*. But for those who participate in it – which in some degree Huizinga thinks is everyone, since the distinction between high and popular culture is not as marked as it became later – it constitutes their world and conditions their responses to it.

Huizinga lays particular stress on a pervasive mood of melancholy, which contrasts with the sense of renewal associated with the Renaissance. It is an autumnal world, and 'long after nobility and feudalism had ceased to be the really essential factors in the state and in society, they continued to impress the mind as dominant forms of life'. To understand an age, one has to understand not only the forces transforming it but its illusions.

Huizinga, though he wrote in Dutch, belonged to a German tradition of cultural historiography, *Kulturgeschichte*. As a result of the diaspora created by Nazism, a strand of that tradition was to be relocated to London with the library of the art historian and mythographer Aby Warburg, which formed the nucleus of the later Warburg Institute. This was particularly associated with iconography as a tool of both art history and the history of ideas, and with the later Middle Ages and the Renaissance. The affinities here with Huizinga are obvious, but, as was mentioned earlier, there were also points of overlap between him and Febvre in France and hence with the *Annales* school, though the emphasis of *Annales* became more emphatically social. Febvre's chief collaborator, Marc Bloch (1886–1944), was a medievalist, whose interest in the history of mentalities led him to produce a classic and eventually highly influential study of the healing powers attributed to the medieval kings, as an aspect of their sacred character (1924, translated into English as *The Royal Touch*, 1973). Despite the *Annales*' proclaimed interest in economic history, the influences of psychology and anthropology were strong. Both Febvre and Bloch had been taught at the Ecole Normale Supérieure by the anthropologist Lucien Lévy-Bruhl, author of *The Savage Mind* (1922). Behind him in the Ecole tradition lay Durkheim, and beyond him his own teacher, its director and a distinguished historian of ideas and institutions, Numa Denis Fustel de Coulanges, author of a classic study of the rituals he claimed constituted the ancient household, which eventually became subsumed in the city (*The Ancient City*, 1864).

Febvre's 1938 *Annales* article 'History and Psychology', which begins with a reference to Huizinga, goes on to proclaim the need to reconstitute the whole physical, intellectual and moral universe of each successive generation; not surprisingly, Michelet was another revered predecessor. In a later article entitled 'Sensibility and History'

(1941) Febvre spoke as Huizinga had done of the need to recover the emotional life of the past. Febvre thus became associated with an aspect of the *Annales*' interests which came to be known as the study of historical 'mentalities' (*mentalités*) – the ways, in particular societies at particular times, of structuring and representing views of the world and human life. The emphasis was on unconscious assumptions rather than articulated theories, expressed in current symbols, metaphors and categorical distinctions ritually expressed. The similarity to the way in which Durkheimian anthropology had developed in the early twentieth century, particularly from Durkheim's last work, *The Elementary Forms of the Religious Life* (1917), was very apparent. There, identifying religion as an essentially public, social phenomenon, so that assertions of belief are to be seen only as the provision of subsequent rationales for established practices, Durkheim had gone on to speak of societies as recognizing, and therefore in a sense constituting, themselves though public rituals enacting 'collective representations', through which, to use the term he had coined earlier, a 'collective consciousness' (*conscience collective*) was constructed. Durkheim's study was based empirically on descriptions of totemism among the Aborigines of Australia, but it was conceptually a short step to an interest in the mentalities and culture of the medieval and early modern European peasantry.

The *Annales* approach was essentially anthropological. The study of 'mentalities' as a way of doing cultural history came to incur drawbacks associated both with anthropology in the mid twentieth century and with the earlier, often organic, metaphors and models employed by cultural historians. Holistic, historical conceptions of culture stretched back to the early nineteenth century and beyond, with the German term *Zeitgeist*, the spirit of the age, as one of the earliest signals of their presence. Other terms, apart from the Marxist 'ideology', which came to the fore in the twentieth century, were the sociologist Karl Mannheim's *Weltanschauung*, world view, drawn from astronomy, and Michel Foucault's *epistème*. The trouble with treating cultures as integrated wholes was that it seemed to imply a view of them as totally integrated: static, and impermeable to change. Both anthropologists and cultural historians came eventually to recognize the need to complicate things (though Marxists, with the *force majeure* of materialist explanation, operating at the economic level, to account for change, felt the impulse less). But it took time. Febvre, for example, famously declared in his major substantive work *The Problem of Unbelief in the Sixteenth Century: The Religion of Rabelais* (1942, trans. 1983) that atheism in the sixteenth century was impossible, which seems to have been simply untrue (he contradicted it elsewhere). 'Popular culture', too, came to seem harder to circumscribe than the phrase itself gave warning of. The problems which global conceptions of thought-worlds had in explaining change were also indirectly acknowledged as intractable by Michel Foucault in *L'archéologie du savoir* (1969, translated as *The Archeology of Knowledge*, 1972), where he waved a dismissive hand at them and announced he was doing not intellectual history but the archaeology of knowledge: archaeologists, apparently, did not need to bother about such things. The dismissal of narrative, or what narrative existed to deal with, namely change, left a perceptible unfilled space when narrative was superseded by the analysis of structures and mentalities.

The next generation of scholars associated with the *Annales* was dominated by the figure of Fernand Braudel (1902–85). With him the *Annales* returned more to its roots in social and economic history, and also developed an interest in counting things – sometimes, it seemed, more or less anything. Braudel's own great classic study of the Mediterranean area in the sixteenth century is rooted in geography (more prominent in French education than elsewhere) and economics, though it also transcends them (*The Mediterranean and the Mediterranean World in the Age of Philip II* (1949, 2nd edn trans. 1972)). It came to be enlarged to two volumes, the first of which is an enormous panoramic study of the interaction of the physical and 'human' geography of the Mediterranean area over what Braudel calls *la longue durée*, brought to life chiefly through the use of sixteenth-century archives, which makes Braudel's work one of the great historical studies produced in the twentieth century. It is an imaginative and scholarly achievement of the first order; it was intially an afterthought to the sixteenth-century political history of the second volume, but Braudel came to see it as an essential preamble.

The last part of the first volume is fairly orthodox (though impressively thorough) economic history, with an emphasis on currency, prices, demography and transport. The first part is an immense survey of life on the Mediterranean seaboard and its hinterlands in the sixteenth century, as structured by distances, natural resources, and their opportunities and imperatives; by the configurations of land and sea and islands, the varieties of terrain and peoples, and the latter's interactions. Braudel considers the shaping influences of mountains, with their unyielding, rocky soils and their seasonal semi-nomadism between uplands and lowlands; the plains, often marshy and malarial as well as cultivatable; peninsulas, islands and harbours; cities and villages and the trade between them, large- and small-scale. Then he turns to the river systems, the trade routes mainly northward, to Rouen, to Hamburg and Danzig, and to the Black Sea and Russia.

Despite its diversity, Braudel insists, the Mediterranean area is also a unity, the sea criss-crossed by trading ships, from headland to headland and island to island. The floating population of sailors was mixed and polyglot; sailors transferred readily from one service to another, so a single crew might include almost every people around the Mediterranean, from Spain to Greece. In *la longue durée*, regular patterns, the almost unchanging repetitions conditioned by topography and habitat, are constantly being re-enacted in different places, like 'the eternal war between peasant and shepherd'. Local economies expand and contract, cities rise and sink, but the needs they supplied remain, to be more amply satisfied elsewhere. It is an unforgiving world that Braudel depicts, with no idealization, but with a human sympathy that seems perceptible, though unuttered, through the detail of the archives. The reader is left with a powerful sense of the harshness and hazards of life: toil, epidemics (especially in the cities), the chances of trade, pirate raids and kidnappings for enslavement (just as in the ancient world), near-starvation at times on the subsistence afforded by poor, stony soil – 'The clearing of stones from the fields of Minorca in the plain behind Mahon was not completed until the eighteenth century.' The islands generally were 'lands of hunger', dependent on imports and impoverished by monoculture for export. Sometimes they were besieged, while the mountains of their interiors were 'the no-man's land of the Mediterranean, the refuge of the poor, bandits and outlaws'.

In the generation after Braudel, from the 1970s onward, the influences from the *Annales* group became wider and more diffuse, and began to acquire outliers in Britain and the United States. Area studies, much more modest in scale than Braudel's – essentially a way of doing French local history with a geographical preamble – were produced under his influence. As mentioned earlier, the *Annales* school became known for embracing quantitative methods. It was inevitable that computers should have an impact on historical studies. In the United States, and Britain too, quantification became a recognized historical technique; the term ironically coined was 'cliometrics'. It became controversial in the States when applied to the question of the economic balance sheet of slavery; its practitioners seemed to be displaying the same insensitivity as 'One that would peep and botanize / Upon his mother's grave' (Wordsworth) – or someone else's.

In Britain it was historical demography that responded most to the quantitative impulse, epitomized in the work of the Cambridge Group for the History of Population and Social Structure. Its godfather, Peter Laslett, presented its early results in popular form in his *The World We Have Lost* (1965). Drawing on parish registers, Laslett's perhaps most startling conclusion, in refutation of received ideas, was that the nuclear family was as much the norm in pre-modern as in modern England. New families typically set up new households; people waited to marry until they could do so; widows moved out. The received picture of the pre-modern 'traditional extended family', with three generations and some collaterals under the same roof, was apparently a myth.

In France, developments from the 1970s onward took up where Febvre had left off; in the Braudel years the study of mentalities and popular culture was somewhat in abeyance, and Braudel himself devoted no attention to the notion of a distinctive Mediterranean culture centred on honour, shame, chastity and vendetta. From the 1970s, studies in ancient, medieval and modern history began to be produced addressing the history of the emotions and the senses, and conceptions of and attitudes to the universals of life and death, whose historical dimensions were increasingly explored. Philippe Ariès, pioneer of the history of childhood, declared that childhood was not a concept until the seventeenth century. Dying, sex, the body, cleanliness and dirt, and even smells, have been given historical treatment.

In a way, some of this harks back to the ethnographic digressions in ancient historiography, from Herodotus onward, but it is transformed, as folklore was converted into 'popular culture', by the historical and anthropological turn given to it. Perennial features of life and death could be historicized because all were perceived and conceptualized through 'representations' which were historically variable, as was much else. As Huizinga had claimed, for example, the spaces assigned to public and private life varied from one society to another: in the Middle Ages the public sphere was much larger, the private virtually non-existent. Before the Second World War the German sociologist Norbert Elias identified the history of 'the public sphere' in ways which have been influential since.

But before pursuing some of these themes to the end of the century we have first to halt at the mid twentieth century, and even to some extent to reach back behind it, to take account of one of the most powerful influences on historiography in that period: Marxism. In particular, attempts were made, beginning in the 1920s and culminating in the 1950s, to fasten Marxist explanatory categories on to the two great revolutions, the English Civil War – henceforth 'the English Revolution' – and the French Revolution.

Marxism: The Last Grand Narrative?

Marxism achieved a substantial embodiment in history only in the middle years of the twentieth century. Marx's own reputation when he died in 1883 was as an economic writer who had predicted the collapse of capitalism through successively more severe crises of underconsumption. In America, just before and after the First World War, it had looked for a while as though some historians, in turning towards social history, might also be on the verge of adopting a Marxist explanatory scheme for it, in the so-called 'New History' of James Harvey Robinson and Charles Beard. But American Marxist history, like the American proletariat and the American socialist party, did not materialize. The Marxist historian of ancient Greece Moses

Finley established himself in Britain from the 1950s. In Europe, however, the Russian Revolution, the 1929 crash and the Depression, which seemed as though it might be the capitalist collapse Marx had predicted, all helped to foster a Marxist view of contemporary history and, as a corollary, of the past. The rise of fascism, moreover, seemed in the 1930s to promise to bring nearer the final, perhaps military, confrontation of Communism and capitalism, after burying 'bourgeois liberalism'.

It was from the late 1930s onward, in particular, that attention focused on the English Civil War and the French Revolution as test cases for the Marxist conception of history in what became, in the twentieth century, the party line. If these conformed to the Marxist category of 'bourgeois revolutions', sweeping up the debris of feudalism and paving the way for the advent of capitalism as the necessary preliminary to its own eventual collapse, there was all the more reason to expect that collapse and thus the final victory of the proletariat, already apparently presaged by the Bolshevik Revolution.

In England, the Marxist interpretation had roots, not yet systematically Marxist, earlier in the century and even in the later nineteenth. The turn, begun then, to economic history as the shaper of social change had a leftward slant from early on – through not by any means among all economic historians. This bias was understandable, because the origins of economic history in the later nineteenth century lay to a large extent in the impulse to turn from pure economic theory to measuring the social implications of the operation of its laws, and the social costs of industrial capitalism. Such an impulse significantly prompted the activities of the late-nineteenth-century German Verein für Sozialwissenschaft (Social Science Association) and the work in economic history of the German so-called 'socialists of the [academic] chair', Wilhelm Roscher and Gustav Schmoller. Religion, as well as ethics, was in some cases a component; in England, the writings of John Ruskin are also often to be found among the intellectual antecedents. In this tradition was Arnold Toynbee, uncle of the author of the grandiose philosophy of history which made a stir in the 1940s and '50s. The elder Toynbee was credited with coining the phrase 'the Industrial Revolution', in lectures delivered in Oxford in the 1880s. He introduced his lectures by saying that political economy had been too much divorced from history; it was not hard to decode this. Toynbee was followed, in the next generation, by R. H. Tawney (1880–1962), who fired one of the opening shots in what was to become a scholarly battle over the causes of the English Civil War, in an article ('The Rise of the Gentry, 1588–1640') in *Economic History Review* (1941).

Tawney was at that point the author of two main publications, united by an ethical socialism and a deep detestation of capitalism. He was an Anglican Christian, and what is still perhaps his best-known work, *Religion and the Rise of Capitalism* (1926), was first delivered in the series of Gifford theological lectures at Glasgow University. The title acknowledged the influence of Max Weber's *The Protestant Ethic and the Spirit of Capitalism* (1904–5), from which it derived its central thesis, but in Tawney's hands this thesis became something notably different. Weber's book was a study in the aptitude of a particular religious psychology, that of sixteenth-century Calvinism, to foster the spirit of capitalist enterprise and a frugal self-discipline which encouraged reinvestment and the maximizing of profits. Weber approved of these, and thought the German bourgeoisie of his day had too little of them. His approach was coolly analytic, and his own ideological drive was nationalistic. Tawney, with a formidable capacity for Christian indignation, and no liking at all for entrepreneurial virtues, turned the Weberian thesis into a study of the relaxation, in the course of the English Reformation, of traditional clerical attempts to moderate economic competition.

Tawney's other major work, *The Agrarian Problem of the Sixteenth Century* (1912), took up, as a matter for analytic economic history, the sixteenth-century protests against the enclosure of land and the conversion of arable to pasture, with consequences in dispossession and unemployment. This was the starting point of Tawney's interest in agrarian history, on which his 'Gentry' article drew. The article revived the seventeenth-century thesis of Harrington (above, p. 318) which attributed the overthrow of the monarchy to the eclipse of the feudal baronage, pursued as a policy by Henry VII, and the economic rise of the gentry, accelerated by the dissolution of the monasteries and the dispersal of their lands. Politically the gentry were dominant in the House of Commons. Tawney attempted to demonstrate their rise economically. The Second World War then intervened, but the debate, which assumed an exceptional acrimony, was afterwards taken up in *Economic History Review*, by Lawrence Stone (1948), supporting Tawney's thesis, and by Hugh Trevor-Roper (1950), attacking it. The controversy ended with Tawney's thesis no nearer being established and with no firmer grounds for asserting either an economic decline of the aristocracy or a relative rise of the gentry.

Tawney was an English socialist, not a Communist. He was too old to embrace the intellectual Communism current in the 1930s. Very much a product of that enthusiasm was the other historian who in the 1940s focused on the supposed socio-economic origins of the English Civil War, Christopher Hill, whose Marxist credentials were prominently displayed in his first book, *The English Revolution* (1940). The war was boldly declared to have been a bourgeois revolution of the classic Marxist type. Hill, who later became Master of Balliol, the college which was also that of Toynbee and Tawney, had been, not unusually for the period, a student Communist before the war, and, more unusually, had gone to Soviet Russia for a year to sit at the feet of Soviet historians of the English seventeenth century. *The English Revolution* was the outcome. Hill, who left the Communist Party after the invasion of Hungary in 1956, subsequently modified but never abandoned its central thesis. 'The English Revolution' was the work of an entreprenurial bourgeois class, which included gentry. Its main effect was to break through restraints on the further development of capitalism.

A generation later the main consensus of historians of the period had turned decisively against this interpretation. Some aristocrats, as well as some gentry, had behaved entrepreneurially, but there was no discernible correlation of this, or of more traditional economic attitudes, with political inclinations. Even the political allegiances of the leading citizens of the towns provided no simple picture of bourgeois class consciousness. In the work of the more extreme 'revisionists', as they are called, even the Civil War itself seems to be dissolved into a series of conflicts between local elites, unleashed by the collapse of authority at the centre, where it was divided by religion.

Ever since the early nineteenth century, English radicalism, at least with the (very gradual) softening of the grievances of Dissenters against the Established Church, has tended to fasten on two features of English history. The first, as in Tawney's *Agrarian Problem*, was the dispossession of the rural poor from their rights in the land, reaching a peak with the Enclosure movement of the eighteenth century. The second was the social consequences of industrialization from the late eighteenth to the mid nineteenth century. These preoccupations became combined, from the 1820s to the 1840s, in the debate called 'The Condition of England' question, to which Macaulay and Carlyle notably contributed on opposite sides. Later historiography tended to echo the terms of this debate, particularly in Toynbee's and Tawney's socialist treatment of English economic and social history, promoted by the writings of the great Victorian social critics and prophets, Carlyle, Ruskin and William Morris.

A late product of their tradition was E. P. (Edward) Thompson, whose first major work was a massive study of William Morris. His highly influential *The Making of the English Working Class* (1963) had noticeably Marxist features but sat loosely to Marxist notions of the historically correct, and particularly to economic determinism. Thompson's chosen period was from the English radicalism of the time of the French Revolution to the Chartism of the 1840s, but his book was much more than a study of the thought and activities of English radicals. It dealt also with rural discontent and resistance to mechanization in agriculture; with the experiences of the increasingly unemployed handicraft workers and various other categories of workers; and with ethical ideas and traditions of organization in working-class communities. Its guiding thread, however, was the notion of the coalescence and increasing self-articulation of the labouring poor in a national working-class consciousness. Marx himself had devoted much of the latter part of his life to the cause of educating the English workers in their class interest and promoting their organization in trade unions. But Marxists, both theoreticians and historians, had devoted little attention to *how* class consciousness was actually formed: it tended to be assumed to follow almost automatically from the concentration of workers by the system of factory production; they became unified and disciplined in collective action by bargaining over wages and conditions, and perhaps helped to articulate their interests and historical role by middle-class adepts in

Marxist theory. Thompson's account went deeper, and emphasized the pre-existence of ideas of justice and rights, as well as the multiple forms of working-class association. He accepted the importance of the changing 'objective' conditions of existence, but repudiated economic determinism.

In so far, however, as it is a study in the formation of the sense of identity of a class (which therefore, presumably, is then poised to become a historical agent, though we are not really taken that far), Thompson's, like all Marxist histories, can hardly avoid being a kind of whig story, a sort of *Pilgrim's Progress*, in which the protagonist, the working class, encounters various obstacles, which Thompson identifies, on its historical path to self-realization. The faith in the English constitution is one, which helps to foster political radicalism but also initially misdirects it. Methodism taught methods of self-organization, but its political quietism was pernicious and its emphasis on personal salvation a deviation. The promises of the ideology of the employers, of increased prosperity for all from entrepreneurship and industrial production, were seductively delusive. Thompson's indictments are formidable and at times are expressed, as he surely knew, with something of the vehemence of the radical early-nineteenth-century journalist William Cobbett: the unholy trinity of 'magistrates, mill-owners and Methodists' is almost pastiche Cobbett. It is easy to think of the various snares threatening the working class's recognition of itself in allegorical capital letters. Accosted by 'Introspective Guilt', 'Odious Subservience' and 'Emotional Onanism', Bunyan's Christian would have needed to think quickly. As in an inverted temperance tract, the educated Radical Francis Place is led into bad company by his inability to drink in taverns, leading to his consorting instead with 'Utilitarian and Malthusian doctrines'. The reader can only shake his head over a good man gone wrong. The metaphors, too, for states of emerging but still unachieved class consciousness are significant, suggesting malign enchantment: it is 'transfixed' by the ideas of Tom Paine, which included respect for the profits of entrepreneurship, and 'enmeshed' in constitutional argument.

The Marxist interpretation of the French Revolution may be said to have begun in the 1920s, in the work of Albert Mathiez, though he was not a Marxist but a pupil of Aulard, whom we have noted (above, p. 404) as a critic of Taine. It was continued by Albert Soboul, and, at a higher level of scholarship and sophistication, by Georges Lefebvre, in the mid-century. It was Lefebvre who declared that 'the Revolution is only the crown of a long economic and social evolution which has made the bourgeoisie the masters of the world.' Soboul explained the Revolution in bluntly Marxist terms, as the outcome of 'a contradiction between the relations of production and the character of the productive forces'; in other words, the contradictions at the level of the substructure were grinding out as usual their consequences for the arrangements of the political superstructure. At that level 'the commercial bourgeoisie ... guided, with a sure awareness of its interests, the Revolution to its objective.'

The first really effective shots against this were fired by an English historian of France, Alfred Cobban, particularly in his *The Social Interpretation of the French Revolution* (1964). He noted there that the demolition of the Marxist appropriation of 'the English Revolution' had already begun. It had 'blown up the supposed bourgeois revolution, leaving aristocracy and gentry, royal officials, lawyers, merchants, people, rising and falling classes, feudal and bourgeois society, labourers and peasants, scattered in fragments about monographs and textbooks'. The society of the French *Ancien Régime* had been no less complex and intractable; no single formula availed to express an individual's social position, or the 'class' represented by an aggregate of such individuals. It was a society of multiple roles and various ways of estimating status: social, economic and legal criteria intersected in ways which defied simple class categorization. For Cobban, as for the English Civil War revisionists, the Revolution was essentially political and exemplified no single underlying determinism. It was also, to a significant degree, a revolt *against* modernity.

The leading French critic of the Marxist interpretation, François Furet, particularly in his *Interpreting the French Revolution* (1978, trans. 1981), argued to similar effect but with more attention to the motives and mindset of its proponents. He pointed out that the French Revolution had remained part of politics, rather than being recognized as history, where he made a plea for it finally to be relocated. Having shaped French political life for a century and a half, 'The French

Revolution is over.' Instead of remaining an object of commemoration, it needed to be emancipated for open-minded historical inquiry. Noting that in the nineteenth century the Revolution was already thought of as a stage destined to be superseded, rather than as an achieved political event, Furet argued that its interpretation was bound to remain politicized so long as the Revolution was taken as presaging the proletarian revolution to come. The first act of that proletarian revolution had been identified as the Bolshevik Revolution of 1917, leading Mathiez to make a connection between the Jacobins and the Bolsheviks.

The hero of Furet's argument, in a sense, is Alexis de Tocqueville (1805–59), who, in *The Ancien Régime and the Revolution* (1850), had established an administrative continuity between the centralizing drive of the monarchy from the seventeenth century onwards and that which also characterized the Revolution. According to Furet, we have to go behind the consciousness of the revolutionaries to see the work of the Revolution as the progressive seizure of power from the institutions of civil society and from local communities by the centralizing state. The Revolution was certainly an important event (Cobban once asked, 'Was there a French Revolution?'), but it was a political and ideological one, centralizing power and diffusing and sanctifying a democratic ethos. The Marxist interpretation, however, embraces a number of categorical confusions in describing it, conflating monarchy and aristocracy, aristocracy and feudalism, bourgeoisie and capitalism. The attitudes of the bourgeoisie to entrepreneurialism were complex, and the aristocracy was by no means devoid of entrepreneurial interests.

It is the nature of historical revision to have no end: revisions of revisions are no doubt taking place even now. That is the norm for the historical profession. It does seem likely, however, that strictly Marxist interpretations of the two revolutions – interpretations whose collapse, incidentally, was prior to that of Soviet Communism – have become past episodes. A simple class terminology no longer sings its siren song to historians, and it is hard to imagine that an aspirant future Hill or Soboul, if there is one, could again see glad, confident morning while hailing the rising bourgeoisie.

Anthropology and History: Languages and Paradigms

In 1963 Keith Thomas published a striking article in the leftist journal of social history *Past and Present* (founded 1952). Entitled 'History and Anthropology', it was a protest against historical specialization by subject matter, contrasting this with the way in which anthropologists studied small-scale societies in their totality. He also pointed to substantive overlaps between the matters to which anthropologists characteristically gave attention in the preliterate societies they studied, such as witchcraft, the blood feud, myths and genealogies, and some of the phenomena of preliterate European societies studied by historians. The plausibility of Thomas's case, in pointing to anthropology as a possible source of guiding practice for historians, really depended, apart from the French example, on the revolution which had taken place in British anthropology since the 1920s, partly under the influence of Durkheimian ideas, away from evolutionism and towards the conceptual understanding of small, self-contained exotic societies through the key terms of structure and function.

Sir James Frazer, the most famous of all British anthropologists at the beginning of the century, had seen the possibilities in combining the study of exotic or 'primitive' societies with that of pre-modern European folk beliefs and practices, then habitually described as 'folklore'. But he and his peers had worked under the aegis of a prevailing evolutionary perspective, which relegated folkloric superstitions, magical beliefs and the recurring rituals of rural societies to the category of 'survivals', fragments of earlier stages in human society, left stranded in the wake of evolutionary progress. From the conception of them as survivals nothing could really be made except antiquarian recording, and confirmation that European societies had once, as evolutionism dictated, been savage. The adoption of 'function' as a central explanatory concept offered an alternative, first in the study of non-European societies, but also in the study of the European past. The attention of anthropologists themselves remained for the most part fastened on the former, though the Oxford anthropologist E. E. Evans Pritchard, exceptionally, wrote an essay on 'Anthropology and History' (reprinted in his *Essays in Social Anthropology*, 1962).

The concept of function had the same capacity to transform folklore, and the study of the thought-worlds of pre-modern, mainly rural, European societies, as it had done in anthropology. As Thomas saw, by asking what thoughts hitherto conceptualized as survivals meant to those who thought them, and what these people's ritual and other practices did for them, it could be possible to see how these phenomena fitted into people's lives and conceptions of the world, opening up the study of pre-modern societies in a new way, alongside what Thomas described as specialization by subject – the familiar studies of political, constitutional and ecclesiastical history and the analysis of socio-economic structures and conditions. Folklore could be repositioned as the study of popular culture and mentalities, in the fashion advocated earlier in France.

It is perhaps significant that the most obvious counterpart in the United States to Thomas's article, later reinforced by his own classic study *Religion and the Decline of Magic* (1971), was entitled *Sociology and History: Methods* (1968), edited by a historian and a sociologist, Richard Hofstadter and Martin Seymour Lipset. Albeit looking in slightly different directions, it was a similar kind of call for history to be opened up to the influences of the social sciences. Sociology was becoming of interest to British historians too, but its position in the United States was more assured. The American tradition in anthropology focused on the distinctive traits of particular cultural circles (from the German *Kulturkreise*), or on individual psychological development, as in the Samoan work of Margaret Mead, rather than on the dynamics of small-scale societies. Hofstadter, in his preface to *Sociology and History*, mentions, as themes to draw to the attention of historians, occupational structure, social stratification, quantitative methods (he cites opinion polls), 'religious styles', immigration, and 'the social role of ideologies'. As is clear from this list, the freedom of the German woods being unfashionable, the Middle Ages was no longer expected to be part of the American story, which now began with Puritanism. In America, Max Weber was a much more potent external influence than Durkheim, and Weber is emphatically a Protestant individualist in his social thinking, while Durkheim's lies in the neo-Catholic tradition dominant in French sociological thought, with its interest in the social functions of religion and ritual, ever since Comte and Fustel de Coulanges in the mid nineteenth century.

In Europe, where Marc Bloch was the obvious pioneer, medieval and early modern historians from the 1970s onward became increasingly attentive to what they had always known but were now seeing new ways of approaching: that the world they studied was peopled with spirits and demons and exorcisms, and was infused with ideas of the sacred, with initiation rituals, purifications, miracles, cults and sacraments as points of access between the seen and unseen worlds. 'Superstition' was a term from the Enlightenment, 'faith' one from Christianity; a phrase like 'system of belief' relativized and historicized both, and was implicitly comparative. The eminent historian of Late Antiquity (a category he has led us to see as a necessary one) Peter Brown, in his studies of early Christianity, has employed to telling effect an essentially anthropological conception of the sacred – in considering, for example, the Eastern Christian cult of the holy man, qualified for his role by ascetic practices and armed with powers of exorcism (*Society and the Holy in Late Antiquity*, 1982). Christianity in the fourth and fifth centuries had, like some modern historians, been much preoccupied with attitudes to the body.

It may seem a long step from the study of mentalities, largely through images, ritual practices, symbols and assumptions, to the intellectual history created by highly literate elites. It too, however, has been influenced since the 1960s and '70s by a turn, if not to anthropology, then to the shared web of language. The 'history of ideas', at the highest level of abstraction, found a home initially, between the wars, chiefly in the United States. The *Journal of the History of Ideas* (1941) was established under the influence of A. O. Lovejoy, whose remarkable work *The Great Chain of Being* (1936) put forward the notion that there was a limited stock of what he called 'unit ideas' (he drew an analogy with the supposedly finite number of fictional plots), which could be seen working themselves out in history. 'The Great Chain of Being' was one of these; it proved difficult to find others. The 'Great Chain' was the conception of a hierarchy of forms of being, from the most spiritual to the most material; ramifications of the idea, Lovejoy showed, spread out through philosophy, theology, science and literature from the Greeks to the eighteenth century. Lovejoy's book was a notable tour de force, but it did not provide the pattern for subsequent work that he had clearly hoped for. One thing this prescription for the 'history of ideas' tended to generate was histories of a *word*, for example 'Gothic', which certainly ramified into different intellectual fields, but was not quite what had been envisaged.

From a historical point of view, Lovejoy's work was at least an improvement on focusing simply on the ideas of great thinkers, treated in isolation but arranged in chronological sequence. This conception of the history of ideas, if it can be called a conception, was thoroughly superseded between the late 1950s and the late 1970s, most notably by two scholars trained as historians, John Pocock and Quentin Skinner. The dominant genre here, chiefly for institutional reasons – it is hard to see others – was, and to a significant extent remains, the history of political thought. Courses in this subject were and are to be found in the syllabuses of history and politics departments; courses in intellectual history as such, at least as a practice that dares to speak its name, were generally not. (Whether we speak of intellectual history or the history of ideas here is of little importance.) The logic, however, in studying, say, Rousseau's *Social Contract* but not his *Emile*, or Locke on Civil Government but never Adam Smith on Moral Sentiments, is elusive. Pocock's chief scholarly contributions in these years were *The Ancient Constitution and the Feudal Law* (1957) and *The Machiavellian Moment* (1975), and Skinner's *The Foundations of Modern Political Thought* (1978), all of which have been drawn on in this present book. Skinner also produced a number of sparkling polemical articles in the 1960s, attacking ahistorical and 'whig' treatments of the canon of political thinkers (reprinted in *Visions of Politics*, vol. 1).

Pocock's early methodological reflections testified to a kind of 'linguistic turn'. To see the web of intellectual life as one of socially transmitted meanings (which does not mean the reduction of its study to social history) has become common ground in intellectual history. Pocock spoke of the rival 'languages' in which political and social debates were constructed. In his preface to his edition of Harrington's works he distinguished three such relevant languages in seventeenth-century England: the language of the common-law tradition, that of

Puritan millenarianism, and that of republican virtue and corruption. Compared with others exhibiting the linguistic turn – Foucault, for example, who seems to regard language as a kind of prison – Pocock sees such languages both as multiple, and hence malleable, and as enabling. Skinner has emphasized the necessity of interpreting texts, mostly from the Renaissance (including the pictorial) and the seventeenth century, by setting 'vocabularies' in the web of contemporary meanings on which they drew and without which they would have been unintelligible to their age. Though it is not usually done, it might seem appropriate even to speak of the 'mentalities' of the learned, provided it is understood that the analysis of them is not psychological.

Recollections of the intellectual influences at work in this scholarly revolution vary among the participants. They were not so much precepts or models as converging indicators, more or less prominent for each individual, of a relevant intellectual climate in the 1950s and '60s. My own would include Michael Oakeshott's metaphor for intellectual life as 'conversation', and the Wittgensteinian slogans, perhaps not very well understood, 'A language is a form of life' and 'The limits of my language are the limits of my world.' Others might cite R. G. Collingwood's historicizing of philosophy and J. L. Austin's concept of 'performative utterances', language as doing, which was effectively used by Skinner. It was also important that Duncan Forbes (my own Cambridge undergraduate supervisor in 1956) was then virtually single-handedly creating and expounding the conception, now indispensable, of an eighteenth-century 'Scottish Enlightenment'; I remember another Cambridge historian referring to it as 'something Scottish, I believe'. Pocock then spoke, at least in the exposition of his ideas on 'languages', of Thomas Kuhn's use of the notion of 'paradigms' in the history of science (T. Kuhn, *The Structure of Scientific Revolutions*, 1962).

Kuhn's thesis was a bold extrapolation from the familiar concept of a Copernican revolution. A paradigm in Kuhn's sense establishes a particular way of explaining phenomena which is mandatory for a given scientific or philosophical community. It is wider than a theory: it specifies the criteria a successful theory must meet. Evolution, often spoken of as a theory, would be for Kuhn an example of a paradigm, since it establishes a whole mode of explanation, initially in opposition to creationism or the 'argument from design', which was the previous one. From a paradigm, subordinate theories and explanations can be generated. To explain the structure of the eye by reference to its functions could be compatible with either the paradigm of design or that of evolution by natural selection. But a paradigm can also accommodate debates, which generate research. Rival theories, for example, of which line of hominids culminates in *Homo sapiens* would both have to accept the evolutionary paradigm.

Paradigms are historical phenomena. A 'paradigm shift', according to Kuhn, occurs when the whole explanatory thrust is changed or reversed: creationism (usually) speaks of the world as adapted to man; Darwinian evolution by natural selection speaks of man as fitted for survival in the world. The classic case of such a shift, literally a transposition, replaced the earth by the sun at the centre of its system in the Copernican revolution. Paradigm shifts occur when the accumulation of anomalies generated by the accepted paradigm requires so much 'explaining away' that the simplicity achievable by a canvassed new paradigm becomes more attractive. Why, Darwin asked himself, did the beaks of Galapagos finches differ slightly from island to island? Why did God do that? (Most of these examples are not Kuhn's.) A paradigm, as an established consensus, is socially as well as intellectually sustained, and is enforced especially on apprentices, who thereafter acquire a vested interest in it. Hence a scientific community, which is the tribunal which determines what counts as an explanation, is essentially conservative, but subject to occasional drastic upheavals. The history of science is only in part a history of accumulation: it is also periodically revolutionary.

Kuhn's book had the effect of such an upheaval on a view of the history of science as the progressive accumulation of truth through the use of scientific method. Predictably, his thesis has been challenged, particularly for its apparent relativism in making historically variable paradigms determine what counts as explanation. But, whatever flaws it may have, its importance here is that it identified science as a human and collaborative practice, and characterized a mature scientific community partly in terms of the exercise of power. In doing so it opened up the possibility of a different kind of history of science, with more of a role for historians. A good deal of work, for example, has been done on the formation of an evolutionary consensus, and its varieties, in mid-nineteenth-century Britain; a paradigm shift can have resemblances to a political revolution.

Simultaneously but independently, emanating from the tradition of iconography and cultural history embodied in the Warburg tradition (above, p. 481), the work of the Renaissance scholar Frances Yates, in particular, rejected scientific whiggism in another fashion. Whiggish history of science had not only characteristically divided its cast into enlightened pioneers and their opponents. It had also used later and hence anachronistic criteria to discriminate what was interesting, even within the thinking of the pioneers of science, discarding the religious, astrological and alchemical rubbish with which it had sometimes been encumbered as of no concern to the history of *science*. Given a particular definition of the phrase this was consistent, but it is not what historians mean by history. Frances Yates, beginning with her *Giordano Bruno and the Hermetic Tradition* (1964), shifted the focus of attention from identifying and appraising the portents of modernity to the total thought-world of her protagonists, much of it subsequently set aside as of only antiquarian interest. ('Antiquarian' used pejoratively, by historical whigs or non-historians, means 'historical'. Historians of political thought have sometimes been accused by political philosophers or political scientists of being antiquarian, meaning that they are historians.) Yates's work was in a sense the high-intellectual equivalent of taking the witchcraft beliefs and practices of a peasant society seriously, as a historical phenomenon.

Suppressed Identities and Global Perspectives: World History and Micro-History

Thompson's *Making of the English Working Class* is a Janus-faced work, looking backward to its Marxist origins and also forward to the historiography of the last quarter of the twentieth century. Thompson's 'Working Class' was still incipiently the revolutionary proletariat. But the formation of working-class consciousness, as Thompson richly describes it, is also the formation of what a more neutral sociological language would call a subculture, to which the historian needs to attend for its own sake. Thompson's famous statement of his intention, in his preface, identified his book as a precursor of new historical attitudes in the 1970s and '80s, while the concept of working-class consciousness traced its origin back to Marxist orthodoxy: 'I am seeking to rescue the poor stockinger, the Luddite cropper, the "obsolete" hand-loom weaver, the "utopian" artisan, and even the deluded follower of Joanna Southcott [a millenarian prophet], from the enormous condescension of posterity.' This chimed resonantly with the mood of the 1970s and after. Reconstructing the thought-world of the inarticulate or illiterate and semi-literate (though some of Thompson's radical cast were very articulate and literate indeed) came to seem a worthy task for the historian. Prospectively fashionable, too, was the way Thompson explained his title: '*Making*, because it is a study in an active process, which owes as much to agency as to conditioning.'

We find the same verb, and the same reasons for it, in one of the most notable American works of the 1970s, Eugene Genovese's *Roll, Jordan, Roll: The World the Slaves Made* (1974). 'Made' here has perhaps an even more striking active force than Thompson's 'Making'. Using letters extensively, and attempting to do justice to the variety of ways in which slavery was experienced, Genovese traced the culture the slaves created for themselves, under the most adverse of circumstances, out of the Bible, contact with white society, and African influences, as something new and unique, not merely traditional or imitative. Genovese's is a highly impressive book, which made an important general point. The notion of collective identities being culturally forged, as an autonomous creation, gripped imaginations in the latter part of the twentieth century. It meant seeing as agents and makers groups which had hitherto tended to figure in historical accounts only as sufferers of their grim fates or, for the administrative or governmental mind (reflected in some historians), as problems and even nuisances.

We can illustrate this by a contrast. It dates from the later nineteenth century, but the way of thinking it enunciates remained powerful, even orthodox, for another three-quarters of a century. The prefatory note to the first number of the *English Historical Review*, in 1886, anonymous but actually by James Bryce, announced, more or less redundantly at the time one might have thought, that 'States and nations will be the chief part of its [the *Review*'s] subject.' The reasons Bryce gives are rather more interesting than the declaration itself, and they are relevant here. Rejecting as too vague the view that history meant providing 'a picture of the whole past', he defined it as 'the record of human action', adding that 'the acts of nations, and of the individuals who have played a great part in the affairs of nations, have usually been more important than the acts of private citizens.' The use of 'important', rather than the weaker 'worth attending to', makes the claim tautological.

Bryce's argument was echoed seventy-five years later, in the course of an argument against Butterfield's *Whig Interpretation*, in E. H. Carr's influential *What is History?* (1961). Carr's perspective was emphatically whiggish: 'History properly so-called can be written only by those who feel and accept a sense of direction in history itself' ('history itself' seems to be the phrase in serious need of analysis here). Carr went on, 'History is, by and large, a record of what people did, not of what they failed to do; to this extent it is inevitably a success story' (or an inevitable success story?). One recognizes the echo, if diminished a little, of Bryce's 'played a great part'. Under cover of making a general point about history, Bryce and Carr are issuing a prescription about what kind of history is worth doing – indeed, what counts as history. All historians choose what history interests them, but the choice need not be universalized and made mandatory; a confident consensus was speaking here.

In fact the arguments are fragile throughout. The antithesis that Bryce refers to, 'a picture of the whole past', is vague only because of the level of generality at which it is presented, which makes it seem absurd as a prescription. To reformulate it less generally, as a claim that *any* aspect of the past *may* be made the subject of historical inquiry, makes it neither vague nor absurd. It is worth reflecting for a moment on what Bryce may have been thinking of, and repudiating for the *EHR*. It seems most likely to have been the publications of the local antiquarian and archaeological societies which were the provincial and established rivals of the new national journal of constitutional and political history. The contrast was not only between old and new, political and domestic, but between metropolitan and local.

Local history was in a sense the predecessor of what we have soon to turn to, the modern genre of 'micro-history', and therefore needs a moment's attention.

What we might have thought, and what Bryce probably thought, as others certainly did, was wrong with antiquarian and archaeological publications was not that they were vague but that they were all too specific, though miscellaneously so. John Richard Green, another of the *EHR*'s founders, spoke loftily of such societies' archaeological interests as 'ecclesiastical architecture slightly tempered by an enthusiasm for Roman camps and old helmets', and referred to their memberships as 'country parsons and old maids'. Antiquarian publications typically dealt in inventories of facts about costume, buildings, weapons and other artefacts, aspects of domestic life and locally notable families, local traditions, and random cullings from local archives. They were certainly eclectic, and in that sense took 'the whole past' as their province. They were clearly not products of disciplined specialization, and were therefore in Bryce's sense 'vague'. One can convey their flavour best through a series of titles, which are sufficiently self-explanatory and even disarmingly frank. Here are some from the first volume (1875) of the *Transactions of the Royal Historical Society*. Despite its grand name and London base, the Society, founded in 1868, had been born in the world of antiquarian printing societies, and at this stage still bore its marks. The articles were predominantly if variously local: 'The Personal Expenses of Charles II in the City of Worcester'; 'The Mounds at Dunblane and the Roman station at Alauna'; 'Tudor Prices in Kent, chiefly in 1577'. Clearly men with access to and perhaps the care of a particular local archive bore a heavy responsibility for a list of this kind. The archive was consulted because it was there – though it has to be said that in the 1950s articles in the *Economic History Review* (founded in 1929) were not invariably excitingly related to wider historical issues either.

By the mid twentieth century, however, as Keith Thomas saw, history other than 'the affairs of nations' had the chance to reconcile comprehensiveness and coherence. Anthropologists had learned how to do so. There were indeed critics of the static worlds offered by British anthropology, and there were charges of triviality and references to anthropological monographs on particular societies as 'stamp collecting', but in the 1960s and '70s small no longer meant trivial. Thomas had chosen his moment well. To the emerging historical sensibility, cultures and the collective identities they helped to constitute were 'made' by their participants, mainly anonymously, in sustaining a particular collective way of life. Virtually all adults were in that sense agents, and even successful ones, active participants in social relations, mediated by participation in a language: passing on memories and precepts between generations; receiving, reshaping and transmitting, often confusedly, ideas about the world and human life. We are reminded of Carlyle's 'History is the essence of innumerable biographies' – a thought which underlies the modern genre of 'oral history'. Oral historians record individual memories while their possessors, who would be unlikely to write them down, are still able to transmit them through the spoken word. It is a kind of revival of one of the oldest of historians' practices, the interrogation of eyewitnesses; largely superseded in the intervening period by the profusion of written documentation, it has been resuscitated by the invention of the tape recorder.

Modern conceptions of culture and its value are recognizably related to those of Vico, Herder and Michelet, which were marginalized in the age of Ranke and *Realpolitik*. The impulse is sometimes similar to Herder's desire to awaken in the Germans a sense of their then undervalued identity, through a cultivated awareness of the anonymous creation and transmission to the present of a common national culture. Though this might seem at odds with the modern concern with subcultures, it in fact also made room for focusing on the traditional ways of life of local communities. This left a significant trace in historiography, as we have seen (above, p. 408), through the once fashionable conception of the Teutonic village community of co-proprietors as the supposed bedrock of all Teutonic (including English and Scandinavian) society. This anticipates modern interest in the small-scale, but the latter is no longer necessarily thought of as germinative. All the same, *Volk*, though virtually a proscribed word, is still an influential concept, though we squeamishly prefer 'people's history'.

The later twentieth-century revival of cultural history, of which some of the interests of the *Annales* school were precursors, came to coincide and typically coalesce with the awakening of an articulated self-consciousness or awareness of identity among groups which thought of themselves as hitherto suppressed, ignored or marginalized. These were often not Herder's 'nations', though some could be thought of as such, for example in 'post-colonial' contexts; much less were they Bryce's. But the nineteenth-century conception of nationality could sometimes embrace something less comprehensive than 'German culture'. Augustin Thierry, author of *The History of the Conquest of England by the Normans* (1825), which embraced the cause of the subjugated Saxons, had a particular interest in suppressed 'nationalities' – Bretons, Aquitaineans, Provençals – which many contemporaries might have refused to recognize as such (and the French state certainly did). Thierry's ideas, rooted in the populist strain in European Romanticism, can also seem prophetic, now that the sense of identity is not monopolized by the nation state. Awareness of a multiplicity of possible historical protagonists has become much more acute, common and assertive.

To take an example near home, the United Kingdom seems a more problematic historical creation than it did in the heyday of Whiggism. (See Linda Colley – another Plumb pupil – *Britons: Forging the Nation, 1707–1837*, 1992.) Ethnic minorities find voices; so do populations once colonized and incorporated into someone's imperial dream. Emancipated from this dream, the creation of identity, and winning assent to it, can be a matter of political and even literal life or death. (A West African student of mine once said, 'What my country needs is a lot more whig history'; I thought this profound as well as witty, recalling the later Butterfield's distinction between the historical demerits and the political advantages of whiggism.) For of course the characteristics of whig history can be not rejected but simply relocated, endowed with a different protagonist; manifest destiny is a game any people can play. So, from the 1970s onward, there has been a proliferation of identities recognized and invested in by historians: the history of formerly suppressed nationalities, women's history, black history, working-class history, ethnic history, peasant history, as well as the history of minority sexual inclinations, of bandits, of rebels and of unfashionable religious sects. Collectively, much of this has come to be known, not always accurately, as 'history from below'. The partial displacement of the nation state as the essential protagonist of history has encouraged not only an interest in categories which cut across it, like those of ethnicity and gender, but also moves outward and downward, to the history of the world in one direction and to that of small communities such as the workshop and, more often, the village or parish.

World history, which is still more an aspiration than an established body of historical writing, has many precedents. The older term, going back to Polybius, was 'universal history' and medieval chronicles characteristically began with universal history before narrowing to often very local concerns. 'Universal', of course, has to be understood relatively. Polybius made his focus the rise of Rome to domination of the Mediterranean and its hinterlands; even in his day it would have been recognized that this excluded the Persian empire. Medieval universal history, derived from Orosius, Jerome and Isidore of Seville, arose from attempts to blend Judaeo-Christian biblical history with the history of the Graeco-Roman world (above, p. 189). New versions appeared in the twelfth century and beyond. Germany and Italy, lacking the focus of a nation state, were particularly receptive to schematized and apocalyptic versions of universal history, including prophecy, as in the strongly Augustinian work of Otto of Freising (1114–58), who was a member of the imperial family, and the writings of the Franciscan mystic Joachim of Flores (above, p. 186). Joachim had an enduring influence on later apocalyptic ideas.

The best-known universal history of the Renaissance period, at least in England, Sir Walter Raleigh's *History of the World* (1614), was emphatically biblical. The eighteenth-century Enlightenment, as we saw above (Chapter 21), produced what were in effect though not in name universal histories that were emphatically and even polemically secular. Voltaire's *Essay on Customs*, which exalted the Egyptians as against the Jews, was written *against* the *Universal History* (1681) of the Catholic Bishop Bossuet. The new concept of civilization provided a kind of key, and the history of mankind was presented, highly schematically and conjecturally, in two kinds of story: the history of the human mind, in which the overcoming of superstition was crucial, and the history of the socio-economic stages of civil society. The writings of Marx and Engels, in their historical dimension, can be seen as a continuation of the 'civil society' tradition, in which the economic organization of civil society was seen as determining the political order and ideas of each of its stages.

Germany continued to be receptive to the idea of universal history. In the later eighteenth century it was a major theme in the flourishing historical school based in Göttingen. Although this was supplanted in the nineteenth century, as described in the previous chapter, by the school of Ranke, with its major focus on the political and diplomatic history of early modern Europe, Ranke himself, in old age, reverted to the earlier interest in universal history by producing a seventeen-volume world history (1880–86).

By the more stringent standards of the later twentieth century, in the age of post-colonialism, all these forays into the universal were not nearly universal enough and were vitiated by an essentially European perspective. The same could be alleged, in different degrees, of the best-known world histories produced in the earlier twentieth century, between the wars: Oswald Spengler's *The Decline of the West* (1918–22), H. G. Wells's popular *Outline of History* (1920), infused with the idea of evolutionary progress, and, most massively, Arnold J. Toynbee's ten-volume *A Study of History* (1934–54). Toynbee's reputation, always controversial, became greatly dimmed, and his particular preoccupation with the history of religion has had no perceptible long-term influence, but originally he blazed a trail. One of the most highly regarded modern world historians, the American scholar William McNeill, began his career as Toynbee's collaborator; the chief torch-bearer for world history among English historians, Geoffrey Barraclough, succeeded to Toynbee's chair at the Royal Institute of International Affairs (Chatham House) in London in 1956. More recent notable English contributions have been J. M. Roberts's *History of the World* (1995) and in 2004, engaging with the modern period of 'global history' – a phrase becoming increasingly fashionable – C. A. Bayly's *The Birth of the Modern World 1780–1914*.

One stimulus to a global perspective has been Marxism, in which, from the outset, capitalism has been seen as an international force and the motor of modern world history. Marx and Engels wrote in the *Communist Manifesto* (1848) that 'the bourgeoisie has through its exploitation of the world market given a cosmopolitan character to production and consumption in every country ... In place of the old local and national seclusion and self-sufficiency, we have intercourse in every direction, universal inter-dependence of nations.' A modern historian who has applied this thought over a series of four volumes covering the period from the French Revolution to the late twentieth century – a series which has become more and more a history of the world and not just of Europe as capitalism's birthplace – is Eric Hobsbawm. The last of the series, *The Age of Extremes: The Short Twentieth Century, 1914–1991* (1994), is essentially a recent history of the world. Hobsbawm's Marxism has been comprehensively shorn of any lingering utopianism. One can sense, however, a wry pleasure in his observation that the collapse of the Soviet system exemplifies a Marxist truth: 'Rarely has there been a clearer example of Marx's forces of production coming into conflict with the social, institutional and ideological superstructure which had transformed backward agrarian economies into advanced industrial ones, up to the point where they turn from forces into fetters of production' (p. 497).

Britain has not, however, been particularly academically hospitable to world history compared with the United States, where it has found a more assured place in university curricula. But the most famous later-twentieth-century historian to be drawn towards world history has been Braudel. After his study of the sixteenth-century Mediterranean world he went on to produce works of even greater scope: in 1963 a *History of Civilizations* (in the English translation), and then a three-volume study of material civilization and capitalism from the fifteenth to the eighteenth century. Braudel's geographical and economic interests and his interdisciplinary inclinations naturally pointed towards the perspective of world history. Characteristically, he was anxious to create a basis for empirical historical research on it, though in this respect his legacy in France has not been as vigorous as he must have hoped.

The connection of world history with social-science concepts and themes is not accidental. In its evolutionary days, in the later nineteenth century, sociology was often, as in Herbert Spencer, a highly abstract and schematized history of the social development of mankind, while the more empirically substantial and historically rooted work of Max Weber also pointed outward to non-European societies, most notably China, which could be drawn on for the application of such characteristically Weberian concepts as 'bureaucracy', 'traditional authority' and 'charisma'.

World or global history necessarily raises questions of definition. These are helpfully discussed in *Writing World History 1800–2000* (eds. B. Stuchtey and E. Fuchs), published under the auspices of the German Historical Institute in London in 2003, which also provides an introduction to past and recent work. World history, being essentially comparative and concerned with, in Braudel's phrase, *la longue durée*, needs large-scale organizing categories which are not distinctively national or specific to a narrowly defined period, and it is therefore likely that it will share these with other disciplines. Histories of societies recently emerging from alien rule, written from their own perspective rather than that of their former rulers, may make contributions to it, but in themselves they are candidates for the long-established genre of national histories, including, sometimes, references to emancipation from alien oppression or domination. Stubbs's *Constitutional History*, in which the Normans are the colonial power, is describable in these terms, as is Thierry's *Conquest of England* and a good deal of German history. But in dealing with wider themes and aiming at comprehensiveness, projected world histories necessarily focus on themes which are also of interest in other disciplines: cultural contact and exchange, economic take-off and the world economy, colonization and decolonization, slavery, migrations, urbanization, industrialization and other experiences loosely grouped as modernization. Archaeology, anthropology, geography, sociology and economics are all relevant.

Turning from the global to the village or other small community at a particular place and time brings us to micro-history. Its affinities are with anthropology, from which it has derived ideas about the life of small-scale societies, but also with the novel and with biography – though the biography of the obscure and even inarticulate. The three examples presented here can form not a conclusion or climax, but a suitable kind of coda to this book; they are respectively Italian, French and English. They are research-driven rather than theory-driven: that is to say they originate from a particular archive or text and a historian with the imagination to see its potentialities.

Characteristically, micro-history takes a small area, a narrow time band, perhaps a protagonist, though one with varying degrees of dominance, and a small community. It illuminates something more general than itself, but it is not necessarily to be thought of exactly as 'evidence' of a given type, a brick to be added to an edifice of generalization built on the accumulation of cases, though in principle it could eventually be used in this way. Sometimes its subject is a single central event, or a sequence of them, understanding whose meaning requires painstaking scholarship, and perhaps some resort to available generalizations from elsewhere; sometimes its events are more diffuse, though focused in a certain way. In other words there may be unity of character and plot or something looser – an area, a particular time, a pattern of behaviour and of beliefs. There is typically a single main archival source, with Inquisition, court and parochial records prominent.

A popular and well-known early example was Emmanuel Le Roy Ladurie's *Montaillou* (1975), a study in the mentality of peasants in a village in Languedoc in the early fourteenth century, filtered through the records of the interrogations conducted by the Inquisition investigating the Cathar heresy, locally rife. It grew in a sense out of the *Annales* genre of area studies: an earlier, more general, work of Ladurie's was *The Peasants of Languedoc* (1966). A later work, also in the *Annales* tradition, has been *Carnival* (trans. 1980). Natalie Zemon Davis's *The Return of Martin Guerre* (1983), a vignette of French rural life in the seventeenth century, focused on marital relations, has been made into a film. *The Great Cat Massacre* (1984), by Robert Darnton, a distinguished American historian of eighteenth-century France, was derived, he tells us, from a class in Princeton taught jointly with the anthropologist Clifford Geertz: the title essay interprets a bizarre act of hostility by the employees of a Parisian printer in the 1730s.

Carlo Ginzburg's *The Cheese and the Worms: The Cosmos of a Sixteenth-Century Miller* (1976) is, like *Montaillou*, based on Inquisition records. Ginzburg's protagonist is an autodidact miller known as Menocchio; he was born in northern Italy in 1533, and was burnt as a heretic, after being given, as was customary, a second chance by the church authorities, in 1599. He was denounced, not altogether surprisingly, by the parish priest, with whom he argued and whose authority he therefore challenged. He paid the penalty of an apparently irrepressible impulse to argue and to share his idiosyncratic ideas on religion with his uncomprehending fellow villagers. It was this inveterate disposition, exercised without associates and apparently for no other reason than his own satisfaction and because he could not help it, that eventually wore out the Inquisition's patience. He was sentenced, imprisoned, and in due course released, but his candour survived the ordeal and he was eventually burnt. There was nothing half-hearted about his heretical opinions, though they were peculiar to himself and associated with no sect. He was a solid man, apparently popular, who had begotten eleven children and been mayor of his village, but, though his views are fascinating when dissected by his historian, one begins to feel he was a man to avoid in a taverna.

His opinions were very unorthodox indeed. His conception of the world as a cheese inhabited by worms – a miller would be familiar with worms, which would appear to him to be self-generating – was only the beginning. The worms were angels, and God was created at the same time as they were. Moreover, and the Inquisition thought inconsistently, 'Everything we see is God, and we are gods.' Jesus was an ordinary man – the Virgin Birth was dismissed on common-sense grounds – and lower than the Holy Spirit, which was in all men, including infidels. The Scriptures were partly true and partly not, and clerical ordination was worthless. Almost Menocchio's only stock opinion seems to have been his disapproval of the gap between rich clerics and the poor. Ginzburg is very aware of the possibility of distortion of Menocchio's views, both as recorded by his scandalized but frequently baffled interrogators and as coming from a man whose life might depend on his answers. In general, however, Menocchio's honesty seems to have been as marked as his garrulity. What he thought, he said, and what he said was very odd indeed. It was not, however, entirely evolved out of his own mind.

For Menocchio was literate, and an avid reader of the books that randomly came his way; he and his opinions were made possible only by literacy and books. The case of Menocchio is explored by Ginzburg to show the inadequacy of studying the history of literacy simply through titles and statistics of book production. We have to try to understand *how* books were read and what was made of that reading, by someone like Menocchio. Inferring ingeniously from Menocchio's garbled answers to his inquisitors, and drawing on his own erudition in the literary culture of the Renaissance, Ginzburg uncovers the archaeology of Menocchio's remarkable opinions and makes some sense of them.

It is clear that Menocchio was far from merely reproducing opinions he had read. He had read little, and he fastened with all the greater intensity on what he had haphazardly found, and reshaped it in terms of his own mental and social world. This was what produced the opinions which so startled and alarmed the court which tried him. He read actively, supplying his own emphases and interpretations. He read as an autodidact reads, ignoring much, fastening on what appealed to him and elaborating it. He was certainly no fanatic: it was reading and indiscretion, not religious zeal, that was his undoing. Menocchio had learned a kind of religious relativism and a general tolerance from reading accounts of other religions and beliefs, which he found in the travels of Sir John Mandeville. He even excavated heresy from Boccaccio. His authors would not have been so indiscreet as he was. It was all too much.

In Ginzburg's hands the case of Menocchio rebukes too simple an understanding of the idea of popular culture and also too simple a conception of literacy and the dissemination of books, and their implications. Menocchio died horribly partly because he was a man at the interface of two worlds, literate but uneducated.

Bryce had made room for one additional category as worthy of the *EHR*: those who, like Luther, had changed the world's opinions. Menocchio, a heretic but not a heresiarch, had hardly done that, though his opinions are what make him interesting. Yet few if any readers would deny that Ginzburg's study of him is history 'properly so called', as Carr would say, and a distinguished example of it. This gives a measure of an intellectual distance travelled, not only since the 1880s but since the 1960s. For it is not clear that Menocchio 'did' anything but read and talk too much for his own good, but that is surely not the point.

Another case: Alain Corbin, in *The Village of Cannibals: Rage and Murder in France, 1870* (1990), investigates the public torture and murder by a number of assailants of a young aristocrat in a village in the Dordogne during the dying days of the Bonapartist Second Empire. Corbin's work lies recognizably in the tradition of the *Annales*; he is also known as the author of a history of smells (1982, trans. as *The Foul and the Fragrant: Odour and the French Social Imagination*). *The Village of Cannibals* is a study in rumour, class hatred and political attitudes. To the outsider they seem confused, but Corbin makes them intelligible. The murder was the immediate outcome of acute, misdirected collective anxiety seeking an outlet. French defeats on the frontiers by the Prussians were made ominous by recollections of earlier Prussian invasions, in 1793 and 1815, the first threatening counter-revolution, the second instrumental in restoring the Bourbon monarchy. Counter-revolution, to the peasants, meant the possible revival of feudal obligations. Therefore aristocrat = Prussian, and the unfortunate young man – who was personally popular and not a harsh landlord or politically active – was described as a Prussian by his murderers and tormentors. He was also, falsely, and one would have thought inconsistently, alleged to have called out 'Long live the Republic.' Hostility to republicans seems to have dated from unpopular taxation during the Second Republic twenty years earlier.

The Bonapartist murderers were not his immediate neighbours, who seem to have looked on or, in the case of the mayor, protested half-heartedly. They were gathered from the surrounding area for a village fair, and did not know him personally. In the afternoon, for several hours, they pounded him to death, almost ritually, each taking a share, with agricultural implements, as though threshing, and then burnt his body – an act which was referred to as like roasting a pig. There was no literal cannibalism: that was a term of horror adopted in wider, shocked comment on the deed, which appalled the general public, irrespective of political inclinations.

Corbin turns this into an illustration of changing attitudes to violence and mutilation of the body. To the peasants who perpetrated the deed, used to killing animals, what they did seemed natural as well as politically virtuous. They did it openly, as a patriotic act, and expected to be congratulated and rewarded. But there had been, fairly recently Corbin claims, a marked change in attitudes to the body and to pain. The ringleaders, who were subsequently tried and executed, were caught in a cultural time-lag between two historical types of sensibility. Corbin tells his story dramatically, and through it he reveals much in the politics and sentiments of the time and place that would otherwise be baffling.

Finally an English case: a remote Exmoor parish in the south-west of England in the age of the Reformation, described in Eamon Duffy's *The Voices of Morebath* (2001). Morebath was in a conservative part of the country, but the parish seems to have been made unusual chiefly by the particularly full and vividly presented parish accounts, kept by the priest, Sir Christopher Trychay. ('Sir' was the normal prefix for the ordinary secular clergy.) Sir Christopher's incumbency spanned the whole course of the Reformation, from the solidly Catholic earlier years of Henry VIII, in 1520, to 1574 in the reign of Elizabeth. He was therefore parish priest not only when the first shocks were felt from Henry's breach with Rome, but through the vigorously reforming years of Edward VI's reign and the Catholic revival under Mary, and a further if rather milder re-Protestantizing of worship after the accession of Elizabeth. Duffy obviously likes Sir Christopher, and treats sympathetically his clearly reluctant bending to each wave of reforming zeal: loyal in his heart to the Catholic old regime, his strongest commitment was to the parish. Duffy does not milk the situation for pathos, but the poignancy of Sir Christopher's situation must be apparent to every reader, while, despite the author's restraint, even keenly Protestant ones may end by loathing the zealously reforming Dean of Exeter, the proximate source of enforced innovation, representative of the distant and fearsome Privy Council. Dean Heynes, in offending the conservative chapter of Exeter Cathedral by his contempt for tradition, may remind more than one reader of Trollope's Mr Slope, though without his hypocrisy.

Duffy uses the priest's accounts, which he quotes at length and 'translates', to reconstruct the rich and complex life of the parish centred on the church and its worship in the pre-Reformation period. It was focused largely on the cults of the various saints in the parish church, which were the responsibility of different groups of villagers, represented in rotation by various 'wardens'. Because of the wardens' duty to report on their financial stewardship to the parish, their reports figure largely in the priest's account books. It is clear that Sir Christopher wrote up all the reports on the wardens' behalf. Rotation meant that wardenships fell to poor men and minors, so that this was probably very necessary, and he seems to have presented the reports by reading them aloud. The entries have the characteristics of the spoken word, and the priest clearly used the public meetings at which they were read to encourage devotion and to conciliate in cases of dispute. It all presents a picture of very wide social involvement by the parishioners, and also the value attached to consensus as well as accountability. As Duffy says, 'The accounts are saturated with a rhetoric of collective identity and shared responsibility.'

The cults of the church's particular saints were central to all this, and their extinction, on the orders of distant authority, had a devastating effect on the social interactions of the parishioners: involvement perceptibly declined and narrowed as a result. Responsibility for the money used for the adornment and upkeep of the saints' images and tabernacles, and their lights, having been assigned to specific groups, the funds so established were called 'stores' and were designated by the saint's name. The roles of the young men and young women, corporately organized and with their own wardens (with heads of households sometimes acting for them), are particularly striking. There was the Young Men's store and the Maidens' store. The Young Men were also responsible for the management of the 'Church Ales', periodic festivities at which they were expected to make a profit from sales. This profit was an important resource, and the banning of Church Ales by Puritan zeal was financially grievous. Otherwise the parish's collective wealth was in its sheep, assigned to sustaining the various stores for the upkeep of their sainted patrons, so that one could speak of 'Our Lady's sheep', 'St Antony's sheep', 'St Sidwell's sheep' (St Sidwell – female – was the only Exeter saint).

The destruction of much of this is the English Reformation in miniature, and it tilted the balance from the community to the individual. Duffy shows, from an obscure and half-obliterated entry, misread previously, that five young men were equipped by the parish to join the 1549 West Country rebellion against the religious changes and several may have died. Duffy is a leading authority on the English Reformation; his other well-known work is a general study, *The Stripping of the Altars: Traditional Religion in England c.1400–c.1580* (1992). His study of Morebath could not have been made so illuminating without that general erudition, but it is also a remarkable tour de force to have reconstructed so much of the parish's life, and the personality of Sir Christopher Trychay, from a single, apparently unpromising, source. It required exceptional imagination and sensitivity, as well as erudition, to bring the latter to life.

There is some similarity, of course, to the medieval monastic chroniclers' recording of the lives of their communities, with special attention to benefactions, which needed to be remembered in prayers and kept accounted for. There is even a parallel with what was described above, in the Prologue, as one of the earliest impulses to historical recording and narrative: the ruler's gifts to the god, housed in the temple. It is fascinating, with Duffy's guidance, to see lists turning into narratives in a similar fashion, and the occasions are the same: recording and accounting for offerings to the god, or in this case Christ and the saints. The narratives are brief, but rhetorically vastly different from just the recitation of lists. They explain how the gifts came to be made, and paid for, and what is done with them: 'Item as for the 6/8d for Roger Budd's grave with other bequests . . . it is assured that Agnes Budd will be here shortly and pay it [wylbe here schortly and pay hyt].' The past comes to life in a sentence, and more fully in

Item we received by the death of Agnes at Hayne [a surname] a gown and a ring at price of 12.s, in the which money Nicholas at Hayne is contented to send to London by William Hurley, when he goeth thither next, and to buy us a banner of silk and so to bring it into this church ['this' indicates where the account was presented]: and if the banner do not cost the full 12.s he saith ye shall have that is left when the banner cometh in to this church.

The Morebath accounts were first edited, with some errors, by a Devonshire antiquarian, in 1904. We should be grateful that they were preserved, and have to applaud the interest that prompted the task of editing. But if there is continuity here there is also a large intellectual distance. Questions of individual talent and imagination apart, the earlier period alone would surely have prevented the first editor from producing anything at all like *The Voices of Morebath*. But why? Duffy does not speculate, nor was he obliged to. It is not a responsibility of busy historians to make life easy for the historian of their craft, a marginal figure at best. But perhaps methodological reticence, not shared by Alain Corbin, who has a French attitude to methodological matters, is itself significant. There are no general references to conflict resolution in small-scale societies, or to the social functions of ritual – which, in general terms, a Catholic can assume anyway. But in seeing no need for these, Duffy, apart from personal inclination, is (especially if one compares this with Thomas's justified urgency in 1963) perhaps registering by omission a greatly widened imaginative consensus among historians about what it is possible for them to do.

This book can have no conclusion: the study and writing of history is still going on. Technological innovations may already be pointing to a new era. From the 1970s onwards, microfilm gave historians access at a distance to manuscripts as well as published works. The internet now opens even greater possibilities for research, whose boundaries and implications we cannot yet see. For the moment, the greatest technological innovation in the writing of history remains the printing press, which immediately guaranteed the survival of works which might in the past have been lost. But we should remember, as we noted in chapter 21, how gradually the full implications of the printing press were absorbed, enabling for example Robertson, in the eighteenth century (with some help from Spain), to write an erudite history of the reign of the emperor Charles V without leaving Edinburgh. It is probably safe to say that the internet will result in *more* history being written, if only because it reduces research time; we may not know whether that history will be different or better for some while.

In the presentation of history, the chief new medium is obviously television. Access to film archives is an important aspect, but has been a mixed blessing, concentrating attention on the twentieth century and on what news agencies, film makers and government propaganda thought worth recording. Television programmes, apart from this, are often like extensions, to a vast audience, of the old formula of the lantern-slide lecture: a presenter or commentator supported by images. They can be well done, as some of the examples mentioned earlier in this chapter, or badly, of which there is now a plethora. But genuinely new possibilities are also being explored, as with great distinction in the remarkable series made by Ken Burns on the American Civil War. Restrained but informative commentary, sensitive editing, haunting photographs and music and readings from letters and diaries made this a deeply moving production, matching the scale of the events it recounted in a way no printed book could do. Considered as the presentation of an epic theme on a grand scale this has claims to be the outstanding work of history of the twenty-first century so far.

So there is no conclusion, only extensions of existing possibilities, and only the ending of a book. I hope it will be attributed more to modesty than to self-importance if I finish on a purely personal note. I have had two purposes. First, to convey the particular qualities of the histories discussed, and particularly what makes them readable with pleasure by non-specialists. In doing so I have also tried to convey the authors' intentions in writing them. Second, I have tried, as in this chapter for the most part, to trace and if possible to explain major shifts in the ways in which attention to the past was directed and applied. But I have always been conscious of what historians share. The notion that they formed a kind of community was registered as long ago as by Polybius, in his belief, probably correct, that if he died before he completed his history another historian would carry the subject on (above, p. 70). Medieval chroniclers were intrinsically collaborative, though sequentially. It hardly needs stressing that there is now a professional community – or perhaps it would be more realistic to say a set of overlapping ones – and, though not always recognized, past historiography is part of it. Historians are, after all, interested in the past. One can never tell when or how the work of a dead historian will suddenly seem relevant, or evoke fellow feeling or annoyance, as with a colleague. We have the advantage of hindsight, but historians have learned to be wary of overexploiting this. One has usually only to utter the dreaded word 'whig' to induce a sudden modesty; one of the advantages of hindsight is to have learned not to abuse it.

I have, as I say, always been aware here of writing about a practice which stretches back two and a half thousand years, and of its practitioners as a kind of community of the dead and the living. To all of them the past mattered: it was worth investigating and recording and keeping alive for future generations. It is with the same respect and interest, and often with admiration, that I have written about them. To some I have done scant justice; to innumerable others, some of whom I am guiltily aware of, I have been able to do none at all.

Select Bibliography

Most translations from Greek, Latin, French and Spanish are those of editions of the texts published by Penguin Books. I have very occasionally provided an alternative version of the translation of a particular quotation. I am also indebted to the very helpful introductions to these editions. The place of publication of these is in all cases London.

The citations to the texts of ancient historians are to books and the numbered subsections into which they are conventionally divided, not to pages. Reference can therefore be made to any edition. This applies also to the section numbers given for Vico, Hegel and Stubbs. Dates given in this bibliography are of the editions used, not of first publication, which are normally provided in the main text. The list of secondary works does not claim to be comprehensive: I have selected the works I have found particularly useful, and I hope their authors will accept this general acknowledgement of my indebtedness to them. Occasionally I have cited a modern author in my own text, where I was conscious of following a particular interpretation especially closely and wished to acknowledge the fact.

GENERAL

Boyd, K. (ed.), *Encyclopaedia of Historians and Historical Writing* (2 vols., London, 1999)

Cameron, J., et al. (eds.), *The Blackwell Dictionary of Historians* (Oxford, 1988)

Woolf, D. R. (ed.), *A Global Encyclopaedia of Historical Writing* (New York and London, 1998)

Kelly, D. R., *Faces of History: Historical Writing from Herodotus to Herder* (New Haven and London, 1988)

Momigliano, A., *Essays in Ancient and Modern Historiography* (Oxford, 1977)

Hay, D., *Annalists and Historians: Western Historiography from the VIIIth to the XVIIIth Century* (London, 1977) is more limited in scope but useful.

Thompson, J. W., *A History of Historical Writing* (2 vols., New York, 1942) is still useful for reference.

Two classics which I have often disagreed with but which are still a source of inspiration are E. Auerbach, *Mimesis: The Representation of Reality in Western Literature*, trans. W. R. Trask (Princeton, 1953), and R. G. Collingwood, *The Idea of History* (Oxford, 1946).

PROLOGUE

Butterfield, H., *The Origins of History* (London, 1981)

Gardiner, A., *Egypt and the Pharaohs* (Oxford, 1961)

Gurney, O. R., *The Hittites* (rev. edn, London, 1990)

Staggs, H. W. F., *The Babylonians* (2nd edn, London, 1998)

GREECE
Texts

Herodotus, *The Histories*, trans. A. de Sélincourt, rev. with intro. and notes J. Marincola (Penguin, 2003)

Thucydides, *History of the Peloponnesian War*, trans. R. Warner, intro. and notes M. I. Finley (Penguin, 1972)

Xenophon, *The Persian Expedition*, trans. R. Warner, intro. and notes G. Cawkwell (Penguin, 1972)

Arrian, *The Campaigns of Alexander*, trans. A. de Sélincourt, intro. and notes J. R. Hamilton (Penguin, 1971)

Quintus Curtius Rufus, *The History of Alexander*, trans. J. Yardley, intro. and notes W. Heckel (Penguin, 1984)

Secondary

Fornara, C. W., *The Nature of History in Ancient Greece and Rome* (Berkeley and London, 1983)

Marincola, J., *Authority and Tradition in Ancient Historiography* (Cambridge, 1997)

Moxon, I. S., et al. (eds.), *Past Perspectives: Studies in Greek and Roman Historical Writing* (Cambridge, 1986)

Murray, O., *Early Greece* (London and Cambridge, Mass., 1993)

Usher, S., *The Historians of Greece and Rome* (Bristol, 1985)

Bengtson, H., et al., *The Greeks and the Persians: From the Sixth to the Fourth Century* (London, 1968)

Pearson, L., *Early Ionian Historians* (Oxford, 1939)

Fornara, C. W., *Herodotus: An Interpretative Essay* (Oxford, 1971)

Gould, J., *Herodotus* (London, 1989)

Thomas, R., *Herodotus in Context: Ethnography, Science and the Art of Persuasion* (Cambridge, 2000)

Adcock, F., *Thucydides and his History* (Cambridge, 1963)

Connor, W. R., *Thucydides* (Princeton, 1984)

Hornblower, S., *Thucydides* (London, 1987)

For Xenophon, Arrian and Curtius Rufus consult the introductions to the Penguin editions.

ROME

Texts

Polybius, *The Rise of the Roman Empire*, trans. I. Scott-Kilvert, selected and intro. F. Walbank (Penguin, 1979)

Sallust, *The Jugurthine War. The Conspiracy of Catiline*, trans. and intro. S. A. Handford (Penguin, 1963)

Livy, *The History of Rome from its Foundation*:

(I–V) *The Early History of Rome*, trans. A. de Sélincourt, intro. R. M. Ogilvie (Penguin, 1971)

(VI–X) *Rome and Italy*, trans. B. Radice, intro. R. M. Ogilvie (Penguin, 1982)

(XXI–XXX) *The War with Hannibal*, trans. A. de Sélincourt, ed. with intro. B. Radice (Penguin, 1965)

(XXXI–XLV) *Rome and the Mediterranean*, trans. H. Bettenson, intro. A. H. McDonald (Penguin, 1976)

Plutarch, *Makers of Rome*, trans. and intro. I. Scott-Kilvert (Penguin, 1985)

Appian, *The Civil Wars*, trans. and intro. J. Carter (Penguin, 1996)

Cassius Dio, *The Roman History: The Reign of Augustus*, trans. I. Scott-Kilvert, intro. J. Carter (Penguin, 1987)

Tacitus, *The Annals of Imperial Rome*, trans. and intro. M. Grant (Penguin, 1959)

—— *The Histories*, trans. and intro. K. Wellesley (Penguin, 1975)

—— *The Agricola and the Germania*, trans. and intro. H. Mattingly (Penguin, 1970)

Suetonius, *The Twelve Caesars*, trans. R. Graves, ed. and intro. J. B. Rives (Penguin, 2007)

Josephus, *The Jewish War*, trans. G. A. Williamson, ed. and intro. E. M. Smallwood (Penguin, 1981)

Ammianus Marcellinus, *The Later Roman Empire AD 354–378*, selected and trans. W. Hamilton, intro. and notes A. Wallace-Hadrill (Penguin 1976)

Secondary

Dorey, T. A. (ed.), *Latin Historians* (London, 1966)

Grieve, E. S., *The Image of Rome* (Princeton, 1969)

Wiseman, T. P., *Historiography and Imagination: Eight Essays on Roman Culture* (Exeter, 1994)

Also, Fornara, *The Nature of History*, Marincola, *Authority and Tradition*, and Usher, *The Historians of Greece and Rome*, all cited above.

Walbank, F., *Polybius* (Berkeley and London, 1972)

Earl, D. C., *The Political Thought of Sallust* (Cambridge, 1961)

Luce, T. J., *Livy: The Composition of his History* (Princeton, 1977)

Walsh, P. G., *Livy: His Historical Aims and Methods* (Cambridge, 1961)

Barrow, R. H., *Plutarch and his Times* (London, 1967)

Jones, C. P., *Plutarch and Rome* (Oxford, 1971)

Millar, F., *A Study of Cassius Dio* (Oxford, 1964)

Dorey, T. A. (ed.), *Tacitus* (London, 1969)

Martin, R., *Tacitus* (London, 1981)

Woodman, A. J., and Luce, T. J. (eds.), *Tacitus and the Tacitean Tradition* (Princeton, 1993)

Wallace-Hadrill, A., *Suetonius: The Scholar and his Caesars* (London, 1983)

Barnes, T. D., *Ammianus Marcellinus and the Representation of Historical Reality* (Ithaca, NY, 1998)

CHRISTENDOM AND THE BARBARIANS

Texts

Eusebius, *The History of the Church*, trans. G. A. Williamson, rev. edn and intro. A. Louth (Penguin, 1989)

Gregory of Tours, *The History of the Franks*, trans. and intro. L. Thorpe (Penguin, 1974)

The Fourth Book of the Chronicle of Fredegar with its Continuations, trans. J. M. Wallace-Hadrill (London, 1960)

Munz, A., *From Roman to Merovingian Gaul: A Reader* (Peterborough, Ont., 1999)

Secondary

Brown, P., *The Rise of Western Christendom: Triumph and Diversity* AD 200–1000 (Oxford, 1996)

——*The Cult of the Saints: Its Rise and Function in Western Christianity* (London, 1988)

Chadwick, H., *The Early Church* (London, 1960)

Dahmus, J., *Seven Medieval Historians* (Chicago, 1982)

Markus, R. A., *Saeculum: History and Society in the Theology of St Augustine* (Cambridge, 1970)

Smalley, B., *The Study of the Bible in the Early Middle Ages* (London, 1974)

For figural interpretation of the Bible the classic source is E. Auerbach, *Scenes from the Drama of European Literature* (Gloucester, 1973).

Barnes, A. T. D., *Constantine and Eusebius* (London, 1981)

Wallace-Hadrill, D. S., *Eusebius of Caesarea* (London, 1960)

Young, F., *From Nicaea to Chalcedon* (London, 1983)

Wallace-Hadrill, J. M., *The Barbarian West 400–1000* (London, 1967)

——*The Long-Haired Kings* (London, 1962)

Wormald, P., et al. (eds.), *Ideal and Reality in Frankish and Anglo-Saxon Society* (Oxford, 1983)

BEDE AND ANGLO-SAXON ENGLAND
Texts

Alexander, Michael, (Trans. and ed.), *The First Poems in English* (Penguin, 2008)

Bede, *A History of the English Church and People*, trans. and intro. L. Shirley-Price, rev. edn R. E. Latham (Penguin, 1968)

English Historical Documents, vol. 1: *c.500–1042*, ed. D. Whitelock (London, 1968)

The Anglo-Saxon Chronicle, ed. D. C. Douglas and D. Whitelock (Norwich, 1961)

Secondary Works

Campbell, J., *Essays in Anglo-Saxon History* (London, 1986)

Bonner, G. (ed.), *Famulus Christi: Essays in Commemoration of the Thirteenth Centenary of the Venerable Bede* (London, 1976)

Mayr-Harting, H., *The Coming of Christianity to Anglo-Saxon England* (3rd edn, London, 1991)

BRITISH HISTORY
Texts

Gildas, *The Ruin of Britain and other Works*, ed. and trans. M. Winterbottom (London, 1978)

Nennius, *History of the Britons*, ed. J. A. Giles in *Six Old English Chronicles* (London, 1848)

Secondary Works

Hanning, R. W., *The Vision of History in Early Britain: From Gildas to Geoffrey of Monmouth* (London, 1966)

Leckie, R. W., Jr, *The Passage of Dominion: Geoffrey of Monmouth and the Periodization of Insular History in the Twelfth Century* (Toronto, Buffalo and London, 1981)

MEDIEVAL ENGLAND
Texts

English Historical Documents, vol. 2: *1042–1189*, ed. D. C. Douglas and
  G. W. Greenaway (London, 1953)
The Chronicle of Jocelin of Brakelonde, trans. H. F. Butler (London, 1949)
The Ecclesiastical History of Ordericus Vitalis (IV.vii–viii), ed. and trans.
  M. Chibnall (Oxford, 1975)
Chronicles of Matthew Paris, ed. and trans. A. Vaughan (Gloucester, 1984);
  quotations from *Deeds of the Abbots* are from this edition.
The Illustrated Chronicles of Matthew Paris, ed. and trans. A. Vaughan
  (Stroud, 1993); quotations from the *Greater Chronicle* are from this
  edition.
William of Malmesbury, *The Kings of England*, trans. J. A. Giles (London,
  1847)
——*Historia Novella: The Contemporary History*, ed. E. King, trans. K. R.
  Potter (Oxford, 1998)
Geoffrey of Monmouth, *The History of the Kings of Britain*, trans. and intro.
  L. Thorpe (Penguin, 1966)

Secondary Works

Hay, *Annalists and Historians*, cited above, is useful here.
Galbraith, V. H., *Kings and Chroniclers: Essays in English Medieval History*
  (London, 1982)
Gransden, A., *Historical Writing in England, c.550–1307* (London, 1974)

CRUSADER AND CHIVALRIC HISTORY
Texts

Joinville and Villehardouin, *Chronicles of the Crusades*, trans. and intro.
  M. R. B. Shaw (Penguin, 1963)
The Alexiad of Anna Comnena, trans. E. R. A. Sewtor (Penguin, 1969)
Jean Froissart, *Chronicles*, selected, trans. and ed. G. Brereton (Penguin,
  1968)

Secondary Works

Barber, R., *The Knight and Chivalry* (London, 1970)

Keen, M., *Chivalry* (New Haven and London, 1984)

Riley-Smith, L. and J., *The Crusades: Ideas and Reality 1095–1292* (London, 1981)

CIVIC CHRONICLE AND HUMANIST HISTORY: THE RENAISSANCE

Texts

Villani, Giovanni, *Florentine Chronicle: Selections*, ed. P. H. Wicksteed (London, 1906)

Machiavelli, Niccolò, *The Florentine History*, trans. N. H. Thomson (2 vols., London, 1906)

Guicciardini, F., *History of Italy*, trans. S. Alexander (New York and London, 1972)

Secondary Works

Baron, H., *In Search of Florentine Civic Humanism* (Princeton, 1988)

Fryde, E. B., *Humanism and Renaissance Historiography* (London, 1983)

Grafton, A., and Blair, A., *The Transmission of Culture in Early Modern Europe* (Philadelphia, 1990)

Green, L., *Chronicle into History: An Essay on the Interpretation of History in Florentine Fourteenth-Century Chronicles* (Cambridge, 1972)

Gilbert, F., *Machiavelli and Guicciardini: Politics and History in Sixteenth-Century Florence* (Princeton, 1965)

Phillips, M., *Francesco Guicciardini: The Historian's Craft* (Toronto, 1977). I am greatly indebted to this book in the section on Guicciardini.

——*Marco Parenti: A Life in Medici Florence* (London, 1989). This is an original study of civic life and intellectual history based on the papers of a fifteenth-century Florentine citizen.

Reynolds, L. D., and Wilson, N. G., *Scribes and Scholars: A Guide to the Transmission of Greek and Latin Literature* (Oxford, 1974). Also useful for the classical inheritance in the Middle Ages.

Skinner, Q., *The Foundations of Modern Political Thought* (2 vols., Cambridge, 1978), vol. 1

——*Machiavelli* (Oxford, 1981)
——*Visions of Politics* (3 vols., Cambridge, 2002), vol. 2

THE SIXTEENTH AND SEVENTEENTH CENTURIES
Texts

Bacon, Francis, *The History of the Reign of King Henry VII* (Cambridge, 1998)

Buchanan, George, *The Tyrannous Reign of Mary Stewart* (Edinburgh, 1958)

The Political Works of James Harrington, ed. J. Pocock (Cambridge, 1977)

Hotman, F., *Franco-Gallia* in *Constitutionalism and Resistance in the Sixteenth Century*, ed. J. Franklin (New York, 1969)

Clarendon, Lord (Edward Hyde), *The History of the Rebellion and Civil Wars in England* (6 vols., Oxford, 1961)

Secondary Works

Douglas, D. C., *English Scholars 1660–1730* (London, 1951)

Ford, F. L., *Robe and Sword: The Regrouping of the French Aristocracy after Louis XIV* (Cambridge, Mass., 1962). Discusses the continuation of ancient constitutionalist arguments into the eighteenth century.

Grafton, A., *The Footnote: A Curious History* (London, 1997)

Hale, J. R., *The Evolution of British Historiography from Bacon to Namier* (London, 1967)

Haller, W., *Foxe's Book of Martyrs and the Elect Nation* (London, 1963)

Huppert, G., *The Idea of Perfect History: Historical Erudition and Historical Philosophy in Renaissance France* (Urbana, Ill., 1970)

Kelley, D. R., *Foundations of Modern Historical Scholarship in Language, Law and History in the French Renaissance* (New York and London, 1970)

Kendrick, T. D., *British Antiquity* (London, 1970)

Levy, F. J., *Tudor Historical Thought* (San Marino, Cal., 1967)

McKisack, M., *Medieval History in the Tudor Age* (Oxford, 1961)

Phillipson, N., and Skinner, Q. (eds.), *Political Discourse in Early Modern Britain* (Cambridge, 1993)

Piggott, S., *Ruins in a Landscape* (Edinburgh, 1976)

Pocock, J. G. A., *The Ancient Constitution and the Feudal Law: A Study in English Historical Thought in the Seventeenth Century* (Cambridge, 1957)

——*Politics, Language and Time: Essays in Political Thought and History* (Cambridge, 1971)

Ranum, O., (ed.), *National Consciousness, History and Political Culture in Early Modern Europe* (Baltimore, 1975)

Skinner, Q., *The Foundations of Modern Political Thought* (2 vols., Cambridge, 1978), vol. 2

—— *Visions of Politics* (3 vols., Cambridge, 2002), vol. 3

Smith Fussner, F., *The Historical Revolution: English Historical Writing and Thought, 1580–1640* (London, 1962)

Wootton, D., *Paolo Sarpi: Between Renaissance and Enlightenment* (Cambridge, 1983)

Worden, B., *Roundhead Reputations: The English Civil Wars and the Passions of Posterity* (London, 2002). Indispensable for an understanding of the place of the Civil War period in English historical memory and scholarship.

Wormald, B. M. G., *Clarendon: Politics, Historiography and Religion 1640–1660* (Cambridge, 1951)

THE EIGHTEENTH CENTURY: THE ENLIGHTENMENT

Texts

Hume, David, *The History of Great Britain: The Reigns of James I and Charles I*, ed. D. Forbes (London, 1970)

The Works of William Robertson (10 vols., London, 1821)

Gibbon, Edward, *The History of the Decline and Fall of the Roman Empire*, ed. D. Womersley (3 vols., Penguin, 1994)

Bolingbroke, *Historical Writings*, ed. I. Kramnick (Chicago, 1972)

Lehmann, W. C., *John Millar of Glasgow* (Cambridge, 1960) incorporates Millar's *Origin of the Distinction of Ranks* (3rd edn, 1871)

Voltaire, *The Age of Louis XIV and Other Selected Writings*, ed. and abridged J. H. Brumfitt (London, 1966)

Secondary Works

Hont, I., and Ignatieff, M. (eds.), *Wealth and Virtue: The Shaping of Political Economy in the Scottish Enlightenment* (Cambridge, 1983)

Kidd, C., *Subverting Scotland's Past: Scottish Whig Historians and the Creation of an Anglo-British Identity* (Cambridge, 1993)

Kramnick, I., *Bolingbroke and his Circle: The Politics of Nostalgia in the Age of Walpole* (Cambridge, Mass., 1968)

Meek, R. L., *Social Science and the Ignoble Savage* (Cambridge, 1971)

Momigliano, A., *Studies in Historiography* (London, 1966). The classic study of Gibbon's relation to the erudite tradition. For an aspect of the latter, see D. Knowles, *Great Historical Enterprises* (London, 1963) on Benedictine historical scholarship.

O'Brien, K., *Narratives of Enlightenment* (Cambridge, 1977)

Phillips, M., *Society and Sentiment: Genres of Historical Writing in Britain, 1740–1820* (Princeton, 2000). I owe much to this pathbreaking book and to conversations with its author.

Pocock, J. G. A., *The Machiavellian Moment: Florentine Political Thought and the Atlantic Republican Tradition* (Princeton, 1975)

Forbes, D., *Hume's Philosophical Politics* (Cambridge, 1975)

Phillipson, N., *Hume* (London, 1989)

Brown, S. J. (ed.), *William Robertson and the Experience of Empire* (Cambridge, 1997)

Burrow, J. W., *Gibbon* (Oxford, 1985)

McKitterick, R., and Quinault, R. (eds.), *Edward Gibbon and Empire* (Cambridge, 1997)

Pocock, J. G. A., *Barbarism and Religion* (Cambridge, 1999–); four volumes of this monumental study of Gibbon and his intellectual context have so far appeared.

Womersley, D. (ed.), *Edward Gibbon: Bicentenary Essays* (Oxford, 1997)

REVOLUTIONS

Texts

Macaulay, T. B., *The History of England from the Accession of James II* (2 vols., London, 1903)

Carlyle, Thomas, *The French Revolution* (London, 1902)

Michelet, Jules, *History of the French Revolution*, abridged ed. G. Wright, trans. C. Cocks (Chicago and London, 1967)

Michelet's dedicatory epistle to *The People* is translated in F. Stern, *The Varieties of History from Voltaire to the Present* (Cleveland, 1956)

The New Science of Giambattista Vico, trans. T. G. Bergin and M. H. Fisch (Ithaca, NY, and London, 1968) is considered here in connection with Michelet.

Taine, Hippolyte, *The French Revolution*, trans. J. Durand (3 vols., Indianapolis, 2002)

Secondary Works

Burrow, J. W., *A Liberal Descent: Victorian Historians and the English Past* (Cambridge, 1981). Part I elaborates some of the points made on Macaulay in the present book.

Clive, J., *Macaulay: The Shaping of the Historian* (New York, 1973)

Rosenberg, J. D., *Carlyle and the Burden of History* (Oxford, 1985)

Mitzman, A., *Michelet, Historian: Rebirth and Romanticism in Nineteenth-Century France* (New Haven, 1990). Useful on Michelet's biography, though the insistent Freudianism may put off some readers.

Weinstein, L., *Hippolyte Taine* (New York, 1972) is a useful introduction to Taine's thought generally.

THE HISTORY OF FREEDOM

Texts

Guizot, F., *History of Civilization in Europe*, trans. W. Hazlitt, ed. L. Siedentop (London, 1997). The discussion of the context in the editor's introduction is more fully developed in Siedentop's *Tocqueville* (Oxford, 1994), ch. 2.

Stubbs, William, *The Constitutional History of England in its Origin and Development* (3 vols., Oxford, 1873–8). For a vulgarized version see Edward Freeman, *The Growth of the English Constitution from the Earliest Times* (London, 1872).

Selected Writings of Lord Acton, ed. Rufus J. Fears (3 vols., Indianapolis, 1985)

Burckhardt, Jacob, *The Civilization of the Renaissance in Italy*, trans. S. G. C. Middlemore (London, 1951)

Secondary Works

Burrow, J. W., *A Liberal Descent* (see above) Parts II and III for Stubbs and Freeman

McClelland, C. E., *The German Historians in England* (Cambridge, 1971)

G. P. Gooch, *History and Historians in the Nineteenth Century* (2nd edn, London, 1962) and J. W. Thompson, *A History of Historical Writing* (cited above) are still useful for reference.

AMERICA

Texts

Díaz, Bernal, *The Conquest of New Spain*, trans. J. M. Cohen (Penguin, 1963)

Prescott, William H., *History of the Conquest of Mexico* (rev. edn, London, 1887)

The Literary Remains of William Hickling Prescott (Norman, Okla., 1961)

Parkman, Francis, *La Salle and the Discovery of the Great West* (Bristol, 1962)

—— *The Conspiracy of Pontiac and the Indian War after the Conquest of Caroda* (2 vols., London, 1899)

Bradford, William, *History of Plymouth Plantation, 1620–1647*, ed. S. E. Morison (New York, 1966)

Adams, Henry, *The History of the United States of America during the Administrations of Jefferson and Madison*, abridged edn E. Samuels (Chicago, 1967)

Secondary Works

Gay, P., *A Loss of Mastery: Puritan Historians of Colonial America* (Berkeley and Los Angeles, 1966)

Kraus, M., *A History of American History* (New York, 1937)

Levin, D., *History as Romantic Art: Bancroft, Prescott, Motley and Parkman* (Stanford, Cal., 1954)

Miller, P., *The New England Mind* (2 vols., Boston, 1953)

Vitzthum, R. C., *The American Compromise: Theme and Method in the Histories of Bancroft, Parkman and Adams* (Norman, Okla., 1974)

Gale, R. L., *Francis Parkman* (New York, 1973)

Bishop, F., *Henry Adams* (Boston, 1979)

Wills, G., *Henry Adams and the Making of America* (Boston and New York, 2005)

PROFESSIONALIZATION

Heyck, T. W., *The Transformation of Intellectual Life in Britain* (London, 1982)

Kenyon, J. P., *The History Men: The Historical Profession in England since the Renaissance* (London, 1983)

Levine, P., *The Amateur and the Professional: Antiquarians, Historians and Archaeologists in Victorian England 1838–1886* (Cambridge, 1986)

Novik, P., *That Noble Dream: The 'Objectivity' Question and the American Historical Profession* (Cambridge, 1988)

Ringer, F., *The Decline of the German Mandarins: The German Academic Community 1890–1933* (Cambridge, Mass., 1969)

Rothblatt, S., *The Revolution of the Dons: Cambridge and Society in Victorian England* (Cambridge, 1981)

——*Tradition and Change in English Liberal Education: An Essay in History and Culture* (London, 1976)

Slee, P. R. H., *Learning and a Liberal Education: The Study of Modern History in the Universities of Oxford, Cambridge and Manchester, 1800–1914* (Manchester, 1986)

Soffer, R., *Discipline and Power: The University, History and the Making of an English Elite 1870–1930* (Stanford, Cal., 1994)

GERMANY

Ranum, O. (ed.), *National Consciousness, History and Political Culture in Early Modern Europe* (Baltimore, 1975), ch. by L. Krieger

Reill, P. H., *The German Enlightenment and the Rise of Historicism* (Berkeley, 1975)

Barnard, F. M., *Herder's Social and Political Thought: From Enlightenment to Nationalism* (Oxford, 1965)

Butterfield, H., *Man on his Past: The Study of the History of Historical Scholarship* (Cambridge, 1969). On German historical scholarship before Ranke, the Göttingen school.

Gooch, *History and Historians in the Nineteenth Century*, cited above, is useful on the 'Prussian School'.

Grafton, *The Footnote* (cited above) gives a brilliant account of Ranke's methods in a perspective provided by Renaissance and eighteenth-century scholarship.

Iggers, G., *The German Conception of History: The National Trend of Historical Thought from Herder to the Present* (Middletown, Conn., 1968)

Iggers, G., and Powell, J. M. (eds.), *Leopold von Ranke and the Shaping of the Historical Discipline* (Syracuse, NY, 1990)

Krieger, L., *Ranke: The Meaning of History* (Chicago, 1977)

Laue, H. von, *Leopold Ranke: The Formative Years* (Princeton, 1950)

Meinecke, F., *Cosmopolitanism and the National State*, trans. R. B. Kimber (Princeton, 1970)

——*Historism: The Rise of a New Historical Outlook*, trans. J. E. Anderson (London 1972). ('Historism' has not become current; 'historicism' is the now usual translation of the German *Historismus*.) Meinecke was both a commentator on and a participant in German historicism.

Stuchtey, B., and Wende, P. (eds.), *British and German Historiography 1750–1950* (Oxford, 2000)

THE TWENTIETH CENTURY

I have treated the citations of key texts in this chapter as self-explanatory. I have, however, given at the end the publication details of the three last works to be discussed in some detail.

The Critique of 'Whig History': History as a Science and an Art

Bentley, M., *Modernising England's Past: English Historiography in the Age of Modernism 1870–1970* (Cambridge, 2005). Balances the elements of persistence and of innovation. Particularly good on Butterfield and Namier.

——*Modern Historiography: An Introduction* (London, 1999)

——(ed.), *Companion to Historiography* (London, 1997)

Cannadine, D., *G. M. Trevelyan: A Life in History* (London, 1992)

Collini, S., *English Pasts: Essays in History and Culture* (Oxford, 1999). Also relevant in the 'Marxism' section, below, for Tawney.

Colley, L., *Namier* (London, 1989)

Elton, G. R., *Modern Historians of Britain 1485–1945: A Critical Bibliography 1945–1969* (London, 1970)

Lamont, W. (ed.), *Historical Controversies and Histories* (London, 1998)

Huizinga and the *Annales* School

Texts

Huizinga, J., *The Waning of the Middle Ages*, trans. F. Hopman (Penguin, 1955)
——*Men and Ideas: History, the Middle Ages, the Renaissance*, essays trans. James S. Holmes and Hans van Marle (London, 1960)
A *New Kind of History from the Writings of Febvre*, ed. P. Burke, trans. K. Folca (London, 1973)

Secondary Works

Burke, P., *The French Historical Revolution: The Annales School 1929–1989* (London, 1990)
——*Varieties of Cultural History* (Ithaca, NY, 1997). Relevant also in the 'Cultural History' section below.

Marxism

Coleman, D. C., *History and the Economic Past: The Rise and Decline of Economic History in Britain* (London, 1987)
Hofstadter, R., *The Progressive Historians: Turner, Beard, Parrington* (New York, 1968)
Kaye, H. J., *The British Marxist Historians* (Cambridge, 1984)
Eley, G., and Hunt, W. (eds.), *Revising the English Revolution: Reflections and Elaboration on the Work of Christopher Hill* (London, 1988)
Furet, F., *Interpreting the French Revolution*, trans. E. Foerster (Cambridge, 1981)
Lucas, C. (ed.), *Rewriting the French Revolution* (Oxford, 1991)

Cultural History, 'History from Below' and World History

Bryce's anonymous 'Prefatory Note' to the first *English Historical Review* is reprinted in F. Stern, *The Varieties of History*, cited above.
Burke, P. (ed.), *New Perspectives in English Historical Writing* (2 vols., Cambridge, 2001)

——(ed.), *History and Social Theory* (Cambridge, 1992)

Stuchtey, B., and Fuchs, E. (eds.), *Writing World History 1800–2000* (Oxford University Press, 2003, for German Historical Institute, London)

Micro-History

Texts

Ginzburg, C., *The Cheese and the Worms: The Cosmos of a Sixteenth-Century Miller*, trans. J. and A. Tedeschi (London, 1980)

Corbin, A., *The Village of Cannibals: Rage and Murder in France, 1870*, trans. A. Goldhammer (Cambridge, 1992)

Duffy, E., *The Voices of Morebath: Reformation and Rebellion in an English Village* (New Haven and London, 2001)

Index

PENGUIN HISTORY

THE CLASSICAL WORLD
ROBIN LANE FOX

The classical civilizations of Greece and Rome dominated the world some forty lifetimes before our own, and they continue to intrigue, inspire and enlighten us. From Greece in the eighth century BC to Rome at the time of Julius Caesar and Augustus in the first century BC, their art and architecture, drama and epics, philosophy and politics have been the foundation of much of what we value today. Their heroes, from Achilles to Alexander, are still powerfully evoked in our modern culture, films and writing.

The Classical World brilliantly describes the vast sweep of history in which these two great civilizations ruled – from the epic poems of Homer and the beginning of literacy through the foundation of Athenian democracy and the turbulent empire-building of Alexander the Great to the establishment of the Roman Republic, the rise of Christianity, and the challenges this new faith faced in the Roman imperial age.

For those who are new to this enthralling subject and for the many who continue to share his fascination with classical Greece and Rome, Robin Lane Fox's account is a wonderfully exciting historical tour of two of the greatest empires the world has ever seen.

Praise for Robin Lane Fox

Pagans and Christians

'Brilliant…it is readable and rereadable, even gripping' *Spectator*

'This open-hearted and learned book is one that any scholar of the ancient world and of early Christianity would be proud to have written… Lane Fox has opened his pages to let in an entirely new world' *The New York Review of Books*

'Here is richness indeed… a magisterial analysis' *The Times*

PENGUIN HISTORY

THE LAST THOUSAND DAYS OF THE BRITISH EMPIRE
PETER CLARKE

'Brilliant … Clarke tells [the story] with such wit, verve and scholarly insight that one seems to encounter a brave new world' Piers Brendon, *Sunday Telegraph*

In 1945 Britain was victorious. Its future – and that of its empire – seemed assured. Yet in less than two years after what Churchill termed its 'finest hour', a bankrupt nation found itself the ghost of its once-great self, forced to give up control over the 'jewel in the crown' of India and the prized territory of Palestine. How did this rapid change of fortunes come about? Peter Clarke's brilliant book examines how Britain was dealt a losing hand after winning the war, how it found itself overshadowed by America, and how the sun finally set on the British Empire.

'A bold and thought-provoking work, as well as a hugely enjoyable read' *Independent*

'Compelling … rich in detail, entertaining in manner, sympathetic and often witty,' Allan Massie, *Daily Telegraph*

'Clarke writes compellingly and with great wit' Simon Heffer, *Literary Review*

'Understated humour and pithy, accurate judgements' Felipe Fernández-Armesto, *The Times Literary Supplement*

---

www.penguin.com

He just wanted a decent book to read ...

Not too much to ask, is it? It was in 1935 when Allen Lane, Managing Director of Bodley Head Publishers, stood on a platform at Exeter railway station looking for something good to read on his journey back to London. His choice was limited to popular magazines and poor-quality paperbacks – the same choice faced every day by the vast majority of readers, few of whom could afford hardbacks. Lane's disappointment and subsequent anger at the range of books generally available led him to found a company – and change the world.

'We believed in the existence in this country of a vast reading public for intelligent books at a low price, and staked everything on it'
Sir Allen Lane, 1902–1970, founder of Penguin Books

The quality paperback had arrived – and not just in bookshops. Lane was adamant that his Penguins should appear in chain stores and tobacconists, and should cost no more than a packet of cigarettes.

Reading habits (and cigarette prices) have changed since 1935, but Penguin still believes in publishing the best books for everybody to enjoy. We still believe that good design costs no more than bad design, and we still believe that quality books published passionately and responsibly make the world a better place.

So wherever you see the little bird – whether it's on a piece of prize-winning literary fiction or a celebrity autobiography, political tour de force or historical masterpiece, a serial-killer thriller, reference book, world classic or a piece of pure escapism – you can bet that it represents the very best that the genre has to offer.

Whatever you like to read – trust Penguin.

To my sister, Candice, the only person in the world who might know my characters better than I do.

CHAPTER 0

EVAN

THE WORLD'S A SPIRAL OF red and gray. Monochrome trees reach toward a sky that's green before it burns crimson. My uniform is red too; it was tan this morning. Probably shouldn't bleed on it so much.

My head hits the ground. Pain flash-bombs through me, and dark spots cloud my eyes. Niobe-va. Blood pumps from my shoulder. My teeth chatter...so cold.

From a distance, explosives wail; the ground quakes.

A heartbeat later, my body stops shivering. Everything goes black.

Warm breath touches my ear. *Come to me.*

Cool energy flows into my limbs. Color seeps into the darkness, brightening it until the world reappears, fuzzy and dim. Have to get up. I push onto my knees. Bile burns my throat, and I spit up salt and copper.

Come to me.

Crawling. The ground becomes more rock than dirt and slants downward into a cave. I flop on my face. Can't

feel my arms.... I can't feel.... A plummeting sensation rips through my gut. I'm falling? Can't tell...can't see....

Come to me.

Need stirs deep inside. On my knees again. The tunnel opens into a wide cavern. A shallow pool stretches out in front of me. Green light glows from its depth.

Come to me.

I slide into the tepid water. My knees scrape against the black floor of the pool. The green light radiates from an emerald. My hand closes over its smooth facets. Peace floods me. *Shh*, it whispers. *Go to sleep.* Water kisses my chin, cheeks, covers my eyes. My hand uncurls, and the stone slips through my fingers.

ChildofMagicChildofMagicChildofMagic.

Darkness closes in.

1

LAWRENCE

JEREMY GIVENS SAT RIGHT NEXT to me, wearing his best shit-eater, and said, 'Dude, ain't no way you can ride that Big Wheel down that slide!'

'Ain't no way' never met Lawrence Ladreth. Hell, this Big Wheel never met me either, and here we are about to be the viral video of the week.

"Lawrie! Lawrie! Lawrie!"

A big grin nearly splits my face open. I love when people get fired up. A crowd from my high school, mostly juniors like me, gathers around the swimming pool. Jeremy stands by the ladder of the slide, shaking his head, and I smirk.

"Hold this." I toss the pink and purple Barbie Big Wheel at him.

"You don't have to do this," Jeremy says.

Pshaw! Of course I do. Jeremy said 'ain't no way' to me. That's a dare, and besides, "Seems like fun." I climb the damp rungs of the twisty slide, loving the squeaky sound of contact between my skin and the slick metal.

When I reach the top, I stand up straight, pump both fists in the air, and toss my head back, "Aaoooooooooo!"

The night's humid and the sticky air sizzles with energy. The bass from the hip-hop music playing in the house drives my heartbeat. My senses are dancing. Everything's alive. I look around at the people staring up at me, cat-calling and sipping sodas, in jean shorts and bathing suits. Through the windows, I see other kids from school dancing in the living room.

The porch lights illuminate the backyard and the lights in the pool make the water shimmer like Blue-Raspberry Kool-aid on ice. I breathe in deep, inhaling the scents of chlorine and watermelon hookah in the air. Plastic scrapes the backs of my heels and I turn my head to see Jeremy below, shoving the Big Wheel at me. Stooping to grab it, I say, "Use my phone to record this. Yours sucks."

"Whatever. Just don't kill yourself."

I laugh and stand up, holding the Big Wheel over my head. In a booming voice, I yell, "Citizens of my backyard!"

"Whoop! Whoop!" holler my loyal subjects.

"I am assuming the position."

Cackling, I set the Big Wheel down on the slide. Adrenaline pumps through my veins faster than the driving beat of the music. Don't know what it is about doing stuff that can get me killed, maimed or grounded until Jesus comes down and says, 'Whazuuuuuuuuuuup?,' but nothing spells good time like scaring the shizz out of myself. I squeeze my butt into the purple seat and blow my crazy curly hair out of my eyes.

"Count it down!" I yell, and my fans cheer me on.

"Three...two...."

I stick my legs out over the pink pedals and push off the walls of the slide with my hands. "Aoooooooooooo!" Wind rips around me. Cool water from the slide splashes my bare chest. I whip around one curve. The Big Wheel teeters to the right, so I shift my weight to the left. The wheels screech as they bounce to the end of the track. I grip the handle bars as the Big Wheel flips, whooping at the rush from going head-over-heels into the blue-raspberry pool of....

Green. The water in the pool glows green.

I hit head first.

The water is warm and shallow. My knees scrape the smooth pool floor. My head bobs. I'm floating. There's something under me. A fluorescent emerald? I reach out to touch it and my fingers close over its slick facets. A strange, crawling feeling inches its way into my gut, followed by a need to do something so strong I want to scream.

A voice comes from nowhere. *Child of Magic.*

What the.... I try to move, to break the surface of the water, but something's holding me down. The Big Wheel? I can't see it. It's gone. The bottom of the pool is supposed to be white, but right now it's black.

What the hell? Oh God. I finally did it. I killed myself. I'm dead! I feel myself floating upward. The emerald slips from my fingers and, as it drifts away, it becomes handle bars. Barbie's Big Wheel. The little bike sinks as I rise. I hear muffled shouts and driving bass.

The water shines blue-raspberry again, and through my burning, blurry eyes I see something else in the water—a person beneath me, body slack with hair billow-

ing over the face. A flash of green light sets the body on fire before it sinks to wherever Barbie has gone, and that voice whispers, *Come to me.*

A heavy feeling sets deep in my chest, like someone close to me is dying. I try to stretch out my hand, maybe I can grab the guy; maybe I can swim to him. My lungs ache and burn. I try to breathe, and inhale a lungful of water.

Blue-raspberry and bright green become red, then gray, then black.

CHAPTER 2

LYLE

I KNOW ALL ABOUT THE magical power of a kiss. That sway is pure pleasure. People who claim it's 'love' are useless idealists. No one thinks, 'Oh, I love you so much' while they're making out. They don't think at all, not really. They just feel. And the feelings, the flood of dopamine that erupts inside and makes people see so-called 'sparks,' is Pixy Stix on steroids for a telempath, like me. The only time telempathy isn't hell is when I'm in the backseat of a car with someone. Then, I don't mind being bombarded with another person's thoughts and emotions. Pleasure-feedback is sweet and right after, there's complete mental silence. Mental silence equals pure telempathic bliss.

I want that kind of quiet now, but no such luck.

"So, it's just gonna be me and the girls all day tomorrow," Heather says, as her mind sings: *Paul Davis's yummy mouth all over mine all day.*

I smile at her. "It's okay. I understand." And I do.

Paul's yummy mouth tomorrow, Lyle's hot mouth

tonight. Through her mind's eye, I see her glorified perception of me standing in front of her: tall, dark and man-pretty, like an actor oiled up to play an Arab prince in a TV movie. I smirk; guess I kinda look like that. But hell, where's my camel?

Heather misinterprets my smile and grins at me. She brushes her lips against mine, but when I feel her tongue try to push itself into my mouth, I step back, wiping my lips. "I'll call you."

She blinks at me, hurt flashing in her blue eyes and flickering through her aura, but the pain shifts to anger so fast I almost don't feel the emotion from her. Heather's eyes are bright and her pretty lips twist into a snarl. "Forget you! You're so stuck-up!"

The cheerleader storms to the back door and rips it open. Muted hip-hop music becomes more defined during the seconds it takes for her to flip me off and slam the door closed again. Love how she slammed the door to *my* house in my face.

Goodbye. She's a great kisser, but after a week her thoughts drove me crazy. All she cares about is being popular and keeping her frenemies jealous. She's shallow, but not a horrible person compared to a lot of other people I know. Human beings in general are selfish, two-faced and hopeless—only good for kissing. Sometimes, I think the only people I can care about are family. They don't lie about loving me.

My flip-flops clack across the hardwood deck as I move to the railing and squint across the backyard to the driveway. My stupid little brother drags something through the open garage door onto the paved drive. I sigh, feeling frenzied mania pouring off Lawrie in waves

as he runs into the backyard with his prize. Adrenaline junkie.

Backtracking toward the deck furniture, I head for the blue, cloth hammock and fall back on it, grinning when the fabric groans and stretches to support my weight. Tucking my arms behind my head, I stare up at the dark sky looking for the Big Dipper.

I can just about draw the sky from memory. I should've brought my sketchpad out. An image of the unfinished portrait of Heather dances around in my head and I scowl.

"Lawrie! Lawrie! Lawrie!" people chant.

Thoughts from Lawrie's annoying friends drift through me.

This fool's crazy.

Best party ever.

I tighten the thought-barrier around my mind, humming a stupid nursery rhyme under my breath. Chants and songs are great distractions to block outside thoughts; keeps me sane in crowds. Uncle Jonas taught me the trick when I was ten. He'd said: 'Hey Ly, this is how you keep your head.' Thirty-four years as a psychic had taught Uncle Jonas plenty of coping mechanisms. Though, none of Uncle J's sixty-six methods had kept him from swallowing a bottle of Valium and drowning in his own vomit last year.

"Aoooooooooooo!"

I sit up, putting my elbows on my knees and leaning forward, to see Lawrie standing at the top of the pool slide holding Nikki's Big Wheel over his head. A plastic bottle of strawberry soda sits on the ground next to my hammock, and I grab it, twisting the cap off. Heather

left it behind—finders keepers. Pressing the bottle to my lips, I take a deep swig of warm berry goodness as Lawrence somehow sits down on the baby bike.

I swish the soda over my tongue, rolling my eyes at the sound of a loud splash followed by cheering, then choke. The soda burns my throat as an explosion of pain rips through my left shoulder. My body jerks backward, and soda sloshes onto my white T-shirt, turning it red.

War breaks out before my eyes. Screaming and shrieks of charging explosives fill the air, along with the smell of charring flesh. Light blasts from short guns with single barrels. High velocity blood-spatters paint the purple ground red; the double suns in the green sky burn crimson. Double suns?

Where am I? Where—whose head am I lost in?

Oh God. It's happening again.

Panic wracks me.

Agony. It's blinding. I can't see anything but red and gray. My whole body goes cold and numb, dying. There's green light, and I'm wet. Underwater. A hand, smaller than mine, reaches out and closes around something—some kind of jewelry, a stone.

ChildofMagicChildofMagicChildofMagic.

There's a face—a teenage guy with bronze skin, the same color as mine, and dark blond hair. Clear green eyes laugh in a face so familiar it hurts, because I know and don't know who this guy is.

A voice. A feeling that I need to do something.

I gasp as I'm yanked from the water, from the weird world. The spiraling sensation in my stomach makes me want to throw up. My back hits fabric that groans beneath me, and I look up at the night sky. Midnight blue,

not green.

My body is damp like I've been swimming, drowning in strawberry soda, but I'm back. Back in my own head, back in the yard, but something's wrong. Flashes of fear strike my mind and there's yelling. I bolt up.

A crowd's around the pool, Lawrie's crowd, thinking: *Oh God, he's not coming up! He's dead!*

I vault the deck railing. Hitting the grass running, I shove people out of the way as my heart pounds. I see Lawrie's shadowy figure at the base of the pool. He's not moving. Terror punches me in the chest as I dive into the pool. I swim to Lawrie, grabbing him under the arms and pulling him up. My head breaks the surface of the water and I gasp for air, shifting to bring Lawrie's head above water too. I paddle to the side of the pool where Jeremy Givens kneels with his hands out.

I pass my brother to Jeremy, not letting go until I feel Jeremy tugging Lawrie out of my arms, and boost myself out. Panting, I crawl to where Jeremy's pressing his ear to Lawrie's rib cage. He's not breathing? I knock Jeremy out of the way. My brother's still as a corpse. I lean over Lawrie, touching his face and tilting his head back. God, please let me remember how to do CPR.

Don't die, don't die, don't—

Lawrie jerks forward, water spewing out of his mouth as his eyes fly open. I sit back on my hands, insides reeling in relief, as my brother rolls onto his side, coughing up pool water.

Then, irritation sets in. I smack Lawrie over the head as he sits up, wheezing and shivering. "Idi—" I start to say.

Lawrie's wet hands grip my biceps and squeeze, his

green eyes urgent. "Ly, Ly, there's a guy in the pool! I tried to get him but he sank. All the way to the bottom."

He stops, hacking up more water. I pat his back and look in the water. "There's nobody else in there. Hey! Did somebody else jump in?"

The crowd of people around us gets bigger, but nobody's doing anything, just staring and whispering. Useless morons.

"I can call an ambulance," Jeremy says.

I bite my lip and look my brother over. His skin's usually darker than mine, but right now he's pale, green eyes shadowed. "Are you okay?" I ask. "Does your head hurt? Did you hit it?"

"Ly, look again. There's a guy in the pool! The water turned green and he was there...." Lawrie trails off, eyes boring into mine and I feel a knock-knock in my head. I sense it's Lawrie, the aura feels like him, bold and reckless, but it's also acidic with terror—which is weird because Lawrence is never afraid.

/What?/ I hate mind-to-mind contact. It feels like brain-rape; it's too raw. I can't keep the other person's feelings out or mine in. My brother's emotions are so strong they have a taste—salty raspberries.

You gotta read my mind. Somebody's dyin'. Somebody named....

My insides reel again. Licking my lips, I taste bitter chlorine. *Child of Magic* echoes through Lawrie's head. What happened to me happened to Lawrie too. Was it some sort of vision? I've never had a vision before, but it's not a stretch to believe I could have one. But Lawrie's not psychic at all, though; how could he have had a vision?

My stomach churns. Over the sounds of the crowd talking, Lawrie's heavy breathing and muted hip-hop music, I hear the phrase: *Child of Magic.*

I CAN'T BELIEVE MY LUCK: Mom and Dad out of town for the next two weeks, little sister is at Grandma's for the summer, house party raising my rep into the stratosphere, and Keelie Sheppard alone with me. I feel the fast rhythm of the music downstairs through the soles of my bare feet as the balcony pulses and I can't keep my body from moving to the beat. The night is hot and loud and all mine.

"Whatcha' smiling about, Dev?" Keelie's voice is raspy like a rocker girl's after a concert; it's crazy hot. I really shouldn't be talking to her right now, because she just broke up with one of my football teammates. But she looks good in white short-shorts and a clingy white top. Every time she reaches for something the top rides up, showing me her MVP abs.

What the hell? Shane's already talking to another girl. He can't get mad about this.

Keelie's standing near the thick balcony railing, peering down at the swimming pool, and I close in be-

hind her, wrapping my arms around her waist. A fire starts in my belly as I pull her against my chest. I set my chin on top of her head, her springy black curls soft on my skin. She reminds me of a Hershey's Kiss and suddenly that's all I wanna do, kiss.

I stroke her stomach under her shirt and wait. If she smacks me or pulls back, I'll leave her alone. She laughs and I feel the vibration of her laughter echo through my chest and chin. I push her head gently to one side and kiss her neck, letting my hand wander up, feeling the spandex fabric of her bikini top. She swats my hand with a chuckle and moves away.

I take a step back, watching her.

Keelie leans forward on the railing, putting her elbows on it. "Oh my gawd! Lawrie's going down the slide on a Big Wheel!"

The hell?

It's like having cold water poured down my pants. I stomp to the railing, glaring down into the yard. Lawrie is on the pool slide with Nikki's baby bike. "Stupid."

Mom and Dad told me to look after my brothers while they're gone. The rules are:

1. No parties
2. No overnight guests
3. No drugs, alcohol, or porn
4. No trips to the ER.

Breaking the first rule is a given. Along with that comes some of the other forbidden stuff, but a trip to the ER means a call to the parents, and no car keys for the start of senior year.

It's not fair. Lyle should get in trouble too. We're twins, but I always get stuck with the most crap because

Lyle is sensitive. That's just another word for weird. No one knows about the psychic thing but family, and it's staying that way—a family secret. People can't think my twin brother is crazy, because if he is, what does that make me?

I grit my teeth. "Sorry Keels, gotta kill my little brother. I'll be back later."

"I'm here now," Keelie says. She turns around, dark eyes scanning my body, and I grin. I'm proud of my build. I run every morning and lift weights at night. I slide a hand through my spiky brown hair and look down at Lawrie plopping his stupid ass down on that Big Wheel. Whatever.

Keelie's soft hand rubs my bare abs and my skin tingles where her fingers touch my flesh. I bring my head down to kiss her forehead, then her nose, then her lips, feeling them slowly parting....

The air is sucked out of my body. My lungs convulse, empty. I choke out a wheeze, stumbling back into a wooden lounge chair that vanishes beneath me as I splash into a pool of green. The balcony, the party, Keelie...they're all gone, replaced by a bright, green light at the bottom of a pool.

ChildofMagicChildofMagicChildofMagic.

The light comes from a small rock and I see a hand reaching for it. As soon as the fingers close over the stone, a feeling of longing hits me so hard I want to cry. The stone slips away, vanishing, the shadowy figure of a limp body wavering in its previous place.

My chest burns; I need to breathe. I inhale, water filling my lungs.

"Devon!" Small hands are on my biceps, shaking

me.

I'm lying on something soft; the night air is warm. I gasp in and out, sitting up, eyes flying open. The balcony. I'm on the balcony, sitting on a lounger with Keelie straddling me, her face inches from mine. Her hands clutch my arms. "You passed out or something and you were choking like you couldn't breathe!"

There's shouting below.

My body's shaking.

Something's happening. Something's wrong.

"Do you have asthma? Do you need medicine?"

I shake my head, staring at Keelie's worried face. What the hell just happened? What was that? It was like a vision, but I don't have visions; that's Lyle's weird thing. I'm not weird. I can't be weird. I don't want to be weird.

A scream from downstairs. "Oh God, he's dead!"

Who's dead? I try to get up, but Keelie's on my legs. The phrase 'Child of Magic' echoes in my head. No, no, this isn't me! I don't hear voices! I'm normal.

I'm normal.

"Devon!" Keelie shrieks and her weight's gone from my legs. She's sprawled on her backside on the wooden floor, giving me bug eyes like something big and hairy is on my shoulder ready to bite.

Still shaking, I look down at my hands, and groan. In my grip are two severed lounger arms, their wooden ends ragged where they've been torn off the chair...by me. I guess I must have grabbed onto them. Laughter bubbles in my gut, furious laughter because it's not funny. I lost control of it.

I lost control of it in front of somebody. This has never happened before. No one's seen it but me.

"Keelie."

"How did you do that? I know you're totally ripped, but you just broke them off. You didn't even strain!"

"Don't tell anybody," I growl.

"You're like friggin' Superman!"

Superman, the alien.

Looking down into Keelie's wide eyes and seeing her fear and amazement, I want to be sick. I jerk to the left, leaning over the side of the chair, and puke. I ignore Keelie's "Gross!" as I stare at the clear puddle I've made. Nothing but water, like I drank an ocean…or a pool.

What's happening to me?

"You okay, Superman?" Keelie's hand is on my shoulder, but I keep my eyes on the water, and tune into the sounds of pandemonium below.

"What's going on down there?" I choke. "Go look?"

Her feet shuffle away and I straighten up, wiping my mouth on my forearm. I drop the arms of the chair on the ground. Mom's gonna kill me.

"Oh my gawd, I think somebody drowned in your pool! I think it's Lawrie!"

I'm on my feet, racing to the railing. I peer down at the crowd near the pool and my little brother sprawled on the grass with Lyle over him. Fear cracks ribs in my chest.

I spring up onto the railing and jump, not afraid of hitting the ground or of people seeing me do it.

I'm not normal.

Over blaring hip-hop music, oblivious laughter from inside the house and murmuring from the crowd around the pool, *Child of Magic* thunders in my head.

CHAPTER 4
LAWRENCE

IT'S FUNNY HOW PEOPLE CLEAR out when they think the police are on the way. Most of the time I think Devon is an idiot, but even I gotta admit sending out that group text— NGHBRS CALLD POPO!—was genius. I've never seen the football team move that fast.

The party's over in like two minutes. I'm sprawled out on the den floor, face down, eating carpet and feeling like shizz. My sinuses are clogged to hell, my ears are ringing, my lungs burn when I breathe, and my stomach's full of pool water. I swish when I move, so I try not to.

My brothers walk around me; I can tell who's who just by their footsteps. Devon stomps around like a bear, while Lyle's more light-footed. The only reason I hear Lyle is 'cause he's wearing flip-flops. Trash bags rustle and glass clinks.

"Is this friggin' gum in the carpet?" Devon's voice gets high when he's pissed.

"Forget the gum and help me get these pictures

back up." Lyle's voice is lower and calmer.

Devon and Lyle have the same voice, but I can always tell them apart. Devon's got a sharp way of talking, like everything's life or death, while Lyle's more chill: let it all blow up, I'll drink to that. Only Lyle would drink to the world blowing up around his ears. I don't think he'd miss any of us all that much.

I snuffle and grunt as pain stabs me behind the eyes. Ouch. I bring a hand up to squeeze the bridge of my nose. Stomach juices roil and I swallow hard as pressure builds in my chest. It's like someone put a balloon in my aorta and pumped it full of helium. Lyle would probably say I feel anxious. Maybe. I don't have much experience with anxiety. I don't worry about much of anything, except maybe being bored.

I'm not bored now. I keep thinking about being underwater and seeing that guy floating under me, fingers outstretched.

"You still okay, Lawrie?"

I keep my head down as Lyle comes to stand next to me. I feel air shifting around on my bare skin. A hand plants itself on the small of my back

"Maybe you need to go to the ER anyway."

"M'fine," I grumble. The people at Memorial Hermann have a standing bet on how many times I'll come through the ER this year. I have a crush on the receptionist whose bet is ten, so I gotta keep my number at that.

Lyle digs his fist into my spine and I yowl, rolling onto my side and facing him. He's sitting with his long legs stretched out as he glares down at me.

"I swear, if you kill yourself, I'm gonna make sure 'stupid' is tattooed on your ass for the angels to see," he

growls.

"Pshaw! You don't believe in angels." Grinning makes my jawbone crack.

Lyle raises a brow, then sighs, blowing straight brown hair out of his eyes. "I don't believe in a lot of things, but I believe that guy you saw in the pool is real."

Is? Not was? "You don't think he's dead? Why not?" I really want to sit up, but I think my head'll implode. My 'gotta do something at all times' hormones rev up. "Was it a vision of the future? You get visions of the future now? Awesome sauce! And hey, I got it too! Maybe I'm getting psychic abilities!"

Oh hell yeah. I think I deserve a little telempathy. It's not fair Lyle gets powers while I get nothing. Even if he says they're not worth the pain.

"Dumbass. If you had any kinda psychic gifts, you'd have known it a long time ago," Lyle says, looking down his nose in that way only he can do. It's like he's dissecting me bit by bit to see which cells are infected with stupid.

"Okay, then," I say. "If I'm not psychic and didn't get a vision, you tell me what happened."

Lyle scratches his head. "I don't think what we saw was a vision." He stares off into space. "It was too personal."

"Personal how?" I ask. "I don't know anybody that swims in glowing green water."

"Lawrie, you saw that guy's face. We know him. I felt connected. Like you can make me hear you when you need something, he made me hear him." Lyle sounds dazed. He's still staring off into space, like he's in another world. He does that when he's really thinking about

something.

'Gotta do something at all times' calms down and that weird anxiety creeps up on me. "But only family can do that, Ly."

"I know." Lyle takes a deep breath. "I think..." he trails off, eyes going to the white French doors separating the den from the foyer. Devon stands there with his arms folded over his chest.

"It'd be nice if I could get some help cleaning this place up," Devon says, looking straight at Lyle and pretending I'm not here. Dev's been ignoring me since he diagnosed me with Indestructible Bastard Syndrome fifteen minutes ago.

"Yeah, yeah." Lyle gets to his feet. "I got the upstairs." He shoots a look at me that says 'Later' and trudges after Devon.

'Later.' But I 'gotta do something' at all times, so I grit my teeth and get up. I need to do some research and the good computer is in my lair. Mom converted a spare room into a project space for me when an IQ test told her I was the next Einstein. I took it when I was eight, but Mom started having second thoughts about me being Einstein II after the 'Green Twinkie' incident of 2016. Come on, I was ten and bored, a dangerous combination. Not that sixteen and bored is any less volatile. Anyway, she continued to reserve the spare room for me, just in case.

I make my way through the den, smirking at the SPILL SHIT ON THIS AND DIE signs taped to the leather furniture. Devon was a poet in his former life; I feel it in my bones. I stagger into the empty foyer, heading for the spiral staircase that sits smack in the middle

of the room.

A tuning fork vibrates in my ears as I make my way up the stairs; the dull hum makes my head ache. The air conditioning kicks on and a blast of cold air hits me like a wet blanket. Devon had put the thermostat on arctic and proclaimed that only girls keep the temp above seventy. Douche bag. I'd turn the A/C off, but my brother's six foot two, and about two-hundred pounds of muscle. I got about six more inches to grow and a lot more bulk to gain, before I can stand up to that.

I reach the top of the stairs and shuffle through a second den into a hallway, crushing a couple of empty soda cans on the way. I walk past my bedroom and stop in front of the padlocked door to my lair. I dig the key out of the back pocket of my swim trunks.

The crunchy smell of dirty laundry, Ranch Doritos and hot glue greets me at the door: Welcome home! Two steps over the threshold, the landing-strip lights at my feet flicker on and my ceiling clock moos at me. Kicking the door shut, I salute the Chick-fil-A cows on the star-stickered ceiling. My feet make suction sounds against the wood floor as I move to the center of room, and sink into a monster-sized black saucer chair dubbed Old Faithful because it's the only seat in the room I haven't broken.

After a minute of not moving, the floor lights dim and the stars on the ceiling glow a faint green. I close my eyes and picture myself underwater, the body drifting away from me, and try to recall the guy's face. Lyle was wrong. I hadn't seen it.

"Endymion," I say, stifling a yawn that makes my jawbone crack again. "Pull up SeCaetaAG.net."

My PC hums to life and a baritone voice with a British accent says, "Hello Master."

I open my eyes. The wall in front of me is all hardware. My PC, with its forty-six inch screen, perches on a black desk attached to a fully loaded entertainment center. A large flat-screen TV, four gaming stations, two D-recorders, a monster external modem, and a gutted laptop blink at me as my PC's black screen shifts to show a background image of me and my ripstik, airborne on a skating ramp. After a second, the background dissolves and the website I want appears. The home screen flashes SeCaetaAG.net: Humans Enter at Your Own Risk.

Galeo SeCaeta's got a flair for dramatics worse than my aunt Becky at family reunions.

"Endymion, search site database for psychic messages."

Michael Jackson's *Thriller* blares from Endymion's speakers and a blue and white Skype box pops up.

"Whozit?" I ask.

"Galeo SeCaeta," Endymion says.

I snort and look up at my cow clock. It's 1:23 AM in Houston, Texas, meaning it is 2:23 AM in Washington DC where Galeo lives. "Endymion, accept call. Turn on webcam."

The small blue and white message box expands, turning into a video-chat window. SeCaeta Galeo Ami-Irideus is wearing a gauntlet-sleeved gold dress with silver stripes and a matching beret. I know he's gotta be standing back so the webcam can get a full shot of his clothes.

"What the hell are you wearing, man?" I ask.

"This is ceremonial attire worn in appreciation for the homecoming of a respected family member. My fa-

ther has returned and we had a celebration today." Galeo moves closer to the camera and now I can only see his head and shoulders. "But I do not think the garb flatters my complexion. What do you think?"

I laugh. I have no idea what would look good on a purple alien with purple eyes and black hair, but after today I know what doesn't. "I think you look like a granny, dude. That thing looks like a friggin' muumuu."

Galeo frowns and I bet he's looking up what a muumuu is. For a guy who's only been here a year, he's picking up English and American slang fast. He's still missing some contemporary vocabulary, but he's passable. I mean, if I'd never seen him in all his purple glory, he'd fool me into thinking he's an Earthborn kid around my age. And shizz, it's not like he's got six eyes and antennae. Aside from looking dyed by grape juice, he's got human features.

"Ah, a dress for fat, old ladies. Yes, I do believe I see the resemblance. Fortunately for me, all of my immediate family members are planning to remain onsite for the next six months. I will not have to wear this delightful little number again anytime soon."

"You guys are staying longer on Earth? Thought you'd be trading out," I say, running a hand through my hair. My fingers get caught in curly tangles.

"No, my father has chosen to remain the Inyan Ambassador for Earth. And he's requested to stay stationed in DC, because our other option is Moscow and Father hates the food. Perhaps, one day, we will finally meet in person."

"Yeah man," I say. A meeting is past due. I've been Skyping this guy for six months since I found his website

and started following his posts. He's an encyclopedia of what passes for cool with off-planet kids, plus he's got some gold nuggets about psychics and magic and other stuff that's not so common Earth-side.

"We will figure something out to get you here for a holiday," Galeo says.

"Don't wear the muumuu." I laugh as Galeo pantomimes: cross my heart, hope to die, stick a needle in my eye. "Who the hell'd you learn that from?"

"YouTube." Galeo removes his beret and scratches his head. He's got three fingers and a thumb on each hand. He said once upon a time Cyriae like him had five fingers like me, but evolution happened and bye-bye pinkies. His hypothesis is that it'll probably happen to humans too, but I disagree.

"So, what brings you to my site so late?" Galeo asks.

"Ah, just some research," I say. Galeo doesn't really know all that much about my life. He knows my name's Lawrence. I've got two big brothers, a baby half-sister, a corporate lawyer mom and a businessman stepdad.

"Hm. Well, I can be of service then. What topic?"

"I was reading up about psychic messages, and I found an interesting case. So, in the article, the message received seemed more like a vision, but it was an obvious cry for help," I say. "And the person sending it was busy drowning, so he didn't say all that much."

"Mm. Persons in extreme situations can send out strong signals. They may not even be aware of it, and any psychic nearby might pick up on it," Galeo says.

"What if a non-psychic receives it?" I ask. "Is that strange?" I shift around on Old Faithful and sniffle. Gah,

the pressure in my sinuses increases like someone's pushing bricks against my face.

"Not if the non-psychic is related to the person sending the message," Galeo says. A meow sounds from off-screen and Galeo looks to his left. "No, Shegal." He switches from English to Cyr, and moves off-camera. There's hissing and shuffling.

A minute later, Galeo reappears in a black Save the Music T-shirt. "I apologize for the interruption. My sister's cat is now in its cage. Bothersome beast. Now, let me ask you, why are you so interested in psychic studies? All of your research on my site centers around psychic phenomena, and the questions you propose are most curious."

I smirk at Galeo as his eyes light up. It's funny how they actually glow when he thinks he's onto something. It's like a Christmas light tour when we play online Battleship. "Why are my questions most curious, Gale?" After one too many cracks from him about my nickname being girly, I just had to give him one.

"Because only a psychic would ask them, Lawrie," Galeo says. "Now, it is more than likely you do other research on much better sites than mine about psychic phenomena and have run across these questions. But something tells me you ask from direct observation."

Touché, Galeo. Of all my friends, he's the only one who can keep up with me intellect-wise. Sometimes, I wanna tell him everything to see what he'll make of it. But if it ever got out that I did, let's just say I have a preference to be cremated; please scatter my ashes on Taylor Swift. She's like thirty, but she's still hot.

"So, are you ever going to tell me who the psychic

in your family is?" Galeo leans back, a small 'don't be pissed' smile on his lips. "I will not tell anyone. I know what else you have been searching for, and I may have an answer for you if you are honest with me now."

Some people get all nervous when contemplating opening the family vault of secrets to outsiders, but I'm kind of a sociopath in that regard. I gotta literally be on fire—or underwater—to experience what normal people feel in situations that should be nerve-wracking.

"What else am I searching for?" I ask.

"A person," Galeo says, kneading his fingers together and placing his chin atop them. "But you are not doing Google Earth searches, are you? I know you hijacked my computer last night."

I sit up straight. I thought I'd covered my cyber-prints.

Galeo smiles. "I know you did not get far beyond the security parameters. But all you need to do is ask for my assistance and I will gladly access the SilAl-neb to help find your birth father. That is who you are looking for, alias Derrick Ladreth."

Hot damn. I don't have to open the family vault, Galeo already stole the silver. Adrenaline kicks in. I'm crossing into forbidden territory. All most people know about Derrick Ladreth is that he's a useless nobody who'd disappeared when I was three.

I know that Derrick Ladreth was legally married to my mom. They have four kids: my brothers and me. When Derrick decided he couldn't stay, he took one of my brothers with him. The guy didn't say where he was going or if he would be back—simply vanished. But real people don't just disappear, not completely, and not with

a kid. There's always a record somewhere. I've cracked national and international databases looking for this guy and found a lot of nothing.

Conclusion: Derrick Ladreth doesn't exist. Not on Earth anyway.

"Lawrie? Are you all right?" Galeo's voice is concerned.

I shake my head. Guess I'd been staring off into nothingness. Ly's not the only one who spaces out when he's really thinking. "Yeah, yeah, fine. Derrick Ladreth, huh?"

"I can find out the name of any Visitors to Earth who assumed that particular alias around the time you were born. I will have to use my father's computer, but it can be done." Galeo goes quiet, eyes still flaming purple marbles in their sockets. His smile is strange.

"You're not gonna tell anybody—" I start.

"I told you I would not," he snaps. His smile fades as I sit back in Old Faithful.

My head's such a snot balloon I can't force myself to figure out what he's getting all grouchy about. He knows mixed kids have targets on their backs. If you can pass for completely human, you're better off.

"Have you seen the latest YouTube Underground craze?" Galeo asks, his voice flat, eyes still bright. "Let me send you the link."

Galeo sends me videos of flash mobs in malls and people singing their orders at McDonald's. I have a folder just for those videos. I look at them when I'm bored, but from the look in Galeo's eyes and the tone of his voice, I know I gotta watch this one now.

"Endymion, open link."

A new window pops open, covering the video chat, and a YouTube Underground video posted by B@d@$$B@by06 loads up. A brick alleyway slowly comes into focus. A group of guys in jean jackets and baseball caps are standing around drinking beer.

A mixture of voices speak:

"Yeah, brother. We're takin' out the trash today."

"Here he comes!"

A tall, skinny guy in jeans, a gray T-shirt and a skull cap approaches the group. He looks right at the camera and his face changes from indifferent to 'Oh shit.'

"Get his ass!"

The camera angle shifts and the lens is shuttered by denim and different colored flannel shirts. Sneakers scuffle across concrete and the sick sound of fists connecting with flesh accompanies a series of grunts. The guy sounds muffled, like there's something in his mouth.

"Alien trash!"

"Nah, nah! This piece 'uh cow patty here ain't just a damn vader. This patty is one 'uh them vulatties. Your momma sleepin' with one 'uh them red Martians? Your momma a vore, huh, boy?"

I lean forward. Fury burns me up and I grip my knees, hard. If I had the power, I'd jump through the computer screen and start kicking some racist ass.

Whoever's recording the video straightens up, pointing the camera at a blue sky freckled with clouds. It's a pretty day for a beat down. The angle lowers, catching the tops of maple trees and buildings, then a brick wall and a green dumpster. Then it's shoved in the poor guy's face.

His nose is bleeding from both nostrils, one of his

eyes is swollen shut; his lips are bloated and gushing blood. The skull cap he'd been wearing is gone; two small white nubs sit side-by-side in the center of his forehead. His ears are Tolkien-elf pointy and they glitter with piercings. Aside from the horns and ears, he looks like a regular human kid, pasty and geeky, but he probably is a vulatto: half human, half Visitor.

There's a glint of silver and a knife comes into focus. The kid's crying, tears and snot mix with the blood on his face as he struggles. Someone holds him from behind as the blade touches one of his ears.

"We're gonna help you out, vulatto, 'cause you one ugly sonuva bitch. You wanna fit in here, you gotta look normal. Them ears ain't normal."

"Neither's them horns!"

The kid screams, "I never did nothing to you!"

"Endymion, stop playback." My mind races; fireworks explode behind my eyes. I see red and purple when I blink. 'Gotta do something' is in overdrive like I grabbed a fork and stuck it in a light socket. I'm frying. I wanna fight something, anything to run off this energy because it's making me sick. My heart's going faster than a techno-pop song; I feel my pulse in my throat.

"Endymion, scroll to the comment section and enlarge." The screen scrolls and the video comments move up onto the screen.

Stop the Hate! South Carolina Allegiance Team.

Posted: This Morning   Views: 77,961
👍 21,065   👎 9,042

LuvNotWar2360
Praying for Jordan Gri'Olak

👍 341   👎 98

MrMister67
this iz n charleston? i ddnt no vulatties wuz there 2. itz a invasion LOL

👍 286   👎 45

GuruDude@ss2
GO HOME VADERS AND TAKE YOUR VU-
I ATTIES WIT U. PRAYING THESE GUYS
DONT GO 2 JAIL 4 PROTECIN HUMANITY.

👍 243   👎 190

BlazeTCoolCat8$
I'm tired of reading comments from prejudiced assholes like you, Guru. You're afraid
of what you don't understand and it makes
human beings as a species and race look
bad!

In reply to GuruDude@ss2

👍 206   👎 79

GALE0SA
You tell him BlazeTCoolCat8$. I find all of
the derogatory comments made about the
beating and mutilation of this young man recorded and posted upon this site, for entertainment purposes, disgusting. I hope all of
you out there who judge Visitors so harshly
do not believe that the same judgment is not
being passed upon you for actions such as
these. Keep this up and Earth will never be
an accepted planet in any planetary allegiance and valuable resources and opportunities for advancement and enlightenment
will be lost to you.

👍 124   👎 13

GuruDude@ss2
F U GALE0SA AND BLAZETCOOLCAT8$.
BET UR BOTH NO GOOD VADERS OR
WORS VULATTIES. NOBDY CARES ABT
SPACE ALINE GARBAGE. ET PHONE HOME
THEN GET THE F*** OFF EARTH AND TAKE
YO HALF-TRASH WIT YA.

👍 59   👎 24

"Endymion, close YouTube."

The window goes away and I'm staring at Galeo.

He's watching me, chin resting on kneaded fingers. "You could help people like Jordan Gri'Olak, Lawrie. You could be a strong leader of a tolerance movement. Masses listen to people like you. You are very charismatic."

I scowl at him. "No, masses spit on people like me"—if we come out of the closet, that is. I swallow, thinking about that poor guy all bloodied up. I would have done something if I were there.

"Adversity like that does not stop someone like you," Galeo says. "You are fearless." His eyes burn even brighter. "Your mother is running for a public office this year, correct?"

I nod. "Yeah, district judge." District judges gotta have impeccable public images. Mom's got the perfect pedigree for politics; the family on her side can be traced back to the forefathers. Dirt runs off her like rain, until the muckrakers look too close at my brothers and me. A blind man can tell we aren't All-American good ol' boys. Two pale white people don't pop out a bunch of bronze babies who look kin to Aladdin, so everyone knows our real dad's from somewhere else. Though, I doubt they suspect he's a Visitor.

"Ah," Galeo hums. "I see."

He sounds disappointed, but resigned. His dad's a politician; he knows the deal. Gotta keep up that public face no matter what. Big Wheels on slides aren't front page news the way sleeping with aliens is. But that's

only if Derrick Ladreth really is/was a Visitor.

"You said if I answered your question about my psychic research, you'd find Derrick for me." I slump down in Old Faithful, massaging my temples.

Galeo blinks at me, and smirks. The incandescent light in his eyes goes out and he sits back. "Yes. If you tell me why you are so curious about psychic phenomena, I will find your father for you."

He says 'find your father' how a guy says, 'Sure I'll lend you five bucks.' Like it's the easiest thing in the world, like it's not something I've been failing at for years.

"One of my big brothers is the psychic." I close my eyes, and green water splashes behind my lids. Slim fingers stretch toward me, another Jordan Gri'Olak I can't help. An emerald slips through those outstretched fingers, glinting as it drifts away. I open my eyes, locking my gaze onto Galeo's.

"My brother got the message from the drowning guy." I cough. "But I nearly drowned tonight because I got it too. I felt like someone close to me was dying. You said drowning guy's probably related to us, and my brother thinks so too. He also suspects the guy isn't dead yet. Do you suppose he was trying to send a nine-one-one call?"

"Can you describe anything else about the experience?" Galeo asks.

"Well..." I say with a juicy sniffle. I hope I don't get sick from this. Summer colds suck. "When the message hit me, it was like I was the guy. He was drowning, I was drowning. The water looked green, but I'm pretty sure the light was coming from a glowing rock. There was

this voice too. It kept saying: 'Child of Magic'."

Galeo's eyes are high beams again. "Child of Magic? Huh."

I frown at him, then snatch a random T-shirt up off the floor behind Old Faithful and blow my nose in it. The shirt, funky with B.O. and grease stained, is beyond saving. "So, what do you think?"

Galeo hums Bon Jovi as my brain click-whirs and my nose runs.

I think—

"I think," Galeo says, breaking my train of thought, "that I should find Derrick Ladreth sooner rather than later, because you have indeed received a long distance distress call. And there is no telling how many cousins you have out there who might be as reckless as you are."

He winks and I snort.

"Thanks." Anxiety balloons in my chest again. Something's very wrong and time's not on my side. "Gale, do you think other people saw the vision, people closer to the drowning guy?"

Galeo's eyes dim, but he smiles. "I am sure the memo went to others, and someone else is helping your caller as we speak. However, I will still do what I can to find your father and extended family and check their statuses to make sure everything is fine."

I struggle to pop the anxiety balloon. It stretches and flattens, but it's still got air in it. I make myself smile. "Thanks, Gale." The balloon deflates completely as I look at my friend. I don't know what I did to make this guy like me, but I'm glad.

"No prob, Bob," Galeo says with a cheesy salute.

I press a hand over my eyes, stifling a weak laugh.

"Where the hell'd you learn that?"

"*Sesame Street.*"

"Galeo, do yourself a favor and don't tell anyone else about that."

CHAPTER 5

LYLE

OTHER PEOPLE'S DREAMS SMELL LIKE oranges. I don't know why. Maybe it's some kind of psychic fail-safe. When I smell citrus, I know I'm not in my own head. Uncle Jonas said dream-walking is the telepathic equivalent to sleepwalking. It doesn't happen too often, but when I go to sleep, sometimes my mind wanders and I wake up in different heads as far as Canada. I don't stay there long; the figments are lost as soon as I roll over or scratch my nose.

I stand in a white-washed tunnel. I press my face against a blank wall, forehead rubbing against the warm, smooth surface. A scorching wind blows in through the wall, drying out my skin and making it feel stretched across my face. The wall becomes transparent, and I'm looking through a picture window into someone else's nightmare.

The sky is green, double red suns glare down at a bloody battlefield. Men are firing guns with bullets that explode, showering metallic glitter that melts the skin

off the poor saps beneath the clouds. Bombs shriek through the sky, arcing back to strike the purple soil, creating mushroom clouds of debris and body parts. Thick blood spatters into the air. Men and women writhe on the ground, screaming and clutching wounds that leak blood, guts, urine, and bile.

My stomach shudders and I swallow spit that tastes like tangerines. I touch the window with my palms and gasp as the clear shield between the war zone and me shatters into tiny fragments of rock candy. I stagger forward onto the uneven terrain. My bare feet crunch across the hot, rocky dirt, grit working its way between my toes. The atmosphere is hazy with dust and smoke. The sharp scent of boiling orange juice wafts under my nose on a hot breeze.

I recognize this battlefield. It's from the guy's message. A woman collapses, her head inches from my foot. Her neck is twisted at an unnatural angle and her eyes stare blankly at me.

I was here a few hours ago. A man roars as acid glitter eats the skin off his face.

A hand closes on my shoulder from behind and I yelp, whirling around and falling on my ass. I pass right through the lady with the broken neck. She's a ghost, a shade. She vanishes, as do all the other bloody, convulsing soldiers on the ground. The bombs stop exploding and the acid glitter dissolves as I stare up at the person I'd last seen face-down in a pool of glowing water.

Drowning Guy's a pretty boy type with dirty blond hair in an armpit-length braid over the shoulder of a tan shirt with pockets at the biceps. His pants are tan too and loaded with pockets at the knees, ankles, and hips. Hints

of silver, from the compartments of a thick utility belt, gleam in the sunlight. Drowning Guy, DG, grins at me, and extends a slim-fingered hand.

"Well, you're a new development," he says.

When I don't take his hand, he grabs my arm and yanks me to my feet with surprising strength. DG looks about fourteen years old. He's a head shorter than me, and skinny, but he's got the stance of a fighter: feet shoulder width apart, arms loose at his sides but looking ready to grab or block a hit. His posture reminds me of Devon. Devon's always ready to fight somebody with fists or insults. The word missiles are usually aimed at me, the distorted reflection he can't stand.

"Can you talk?" DG asks. His voice has a chime-like quality to it, and his phrases are accented with a Scandinavian-sounding lilt.

I frown. "Say something else," I demand. For some reason, I don't think he's speaking English.

"I don't usually have dreams about men in their un-derwear," DG says, and his grin widens as I glance down at my Houston Rockets boxers.

He laughs, the cackle setting my teeth on edge. He sounds like the friggin' Joker on helium. "Maybe I'm developing new preferences," he says.

I narrow my eyes. When I concentrate on his speech, I hear another language over a bad English dub. But when I let go and focus on him instead of the sentence, I understand him just fine.

"So, who's coming to save me?" DG asks.

Huh? Save him? "Oh, I...."

His smile fades and his eyes narrow. "You are an underdressed emissary come to tell me extraction is un-

derway, right?" He bounces on the balls of his feet. "Or I'm already extracted and I'm in a coma. You're a psy-ops agent sent into my head to wake me up?"

Damn. This guy thinks I'm a professional here to help him. His eyes go glassy for a second and I see fear in them. Hell, I *feel* the fear in him, and that flips my SNAFU switch. This guy's in trouble somewhere and he's stuck with me.

"Uh, I'm not—I'm not any of those things, but you—you sent me a message. Earlier, when I was awake, I saw you drowning—felt you drowning." My lungs constrict and I crack my knuckles to give my hands something to do.

I've been in plenty dreams, I've even talked to the sleepers, but never like this. No one's ever needed me to do anything, and no one's ever been dying. I guess it'd be decent of me to contact someone for him or something, but....

"I don't even know where you are," I say. In a place with two suns, local nine-one-one probably isn't an option. "Can you tell me who I can call for you and how?" This guy's a Visitor, no, an alien on another planet. An alien with a familiar face who can broadcast directly into my head like only Devon and Lawrie can.

The prickling sense of déjà vu ripples through me, and a tip-of-the-tongue sensation brings DG's name so close to the surface of my mind I almost say it. I know it.

"You're not Remasian," DG says, deadpan. "And you're not speaking Common Tongue at all." He takes a step toward to me, invading my personal space.

I want to jump back so I can breathe. I hate when people crowd me. It's harder to block out surface

thoughts. I keep twelve inches of space between me and anyone who's not family or a girl I'm messing around with.

DG won't let me back away from him. He stalks forward with each step I take back. His eyes glint and his jaw is set like my mom's when she's determined to win. "I bet you don't even know who I am, do you?" he asks. "You." He reaches out and snags my shoulders, holding me in place.

This guy's strong as Thor! I go rigid as DG leans forward and runs his friggin' nose over my chest, neck and shoulders like he's part canine.

"You smell like something I used to know." His nose twitches like a rabbit's as he studies me. When his grip eases up, I break out of it, shoving him away from me.

"What the hell, man!" Okay dream, you need to end before this guy sniffs my crotch too. Screw helping him.

"Where are you from?" DG's still looking me up and down.

"What does it matter? Look, dreams don't last forever. If you want me to try to do something, before you—I don't know—die...."

In a blur of motion, DG whips a small silver dagger with a jeweled hilt from one of his bicep pockets and begins cleaning his short nails with it. His expression is dangerous. "I asked you a question," he says.

I hold both of my hands up, fingers splayed. My heart beats fast. I need to take control. This is DG's dream, but I can alter it if I need to. I've changed my clothes and made black horses appear in dreams before. I visualize steel. I want a wall between DG and me. I close

my eyes, seeing steel beams stacking themselves. I push the beams outward, sending them from my mind into the dream space, and wait for the tugging nausea that comes with the mental strain of tampering with someone's head. But I feel fine.

I open my eyes and balk. There's no wall. Why is there no wall? Tiny tremors race through my body as I continue standing on an empty battlefield with no protection between DG and me. He hasn't moved any closer, but he's changed his stance. He's got his arms folded over his chest. The dagger's gone and irritation pulses from every fiber of his being, trickling into me and making me sweat. I lick a salty droplet off my upper lip.

"Don't strain yourself, Dream-walker," DG says. "In my head, I'm the boss." His voice is hard as the steel I'd failed to create. He sighs. "Look, I don't have my coordinates, but my emergency code is—"

Blood dribbles down his chin. He gurgles, spitting up more blood. He rubs his mouth with his right hand, and it comes away bright red. I feel panic explode inside him like a punch to my own stomach.

"Oh gods." His voice sounds syrupy and congested. He doubles over, and a thin string of blood yo-yo's from his lips. Violent choking noises become the soundtrack over an otherwise silent battlefield. DG staggers to his knees, clutching his left shoulder, and I gape as blood seeps through the spaces between his fingers.

Horror grabs me and won't let go. My minor tremors turn to full-blown shakes. Pain echoes from DG's body into mine. Something sharp tears a hole through my left shoulder, severing tendons and splintering bone. I expect to feel hot blood running down my arm and tor-

so, but I only feel beads of sweat rolling down my face and back.

ChildofMagicChildofMagicChildofMagic.

The voice seems to come from everywhere and nowhere.

The wind blows so hard I barely stay on my feet. I spin around, and see tall gray trees with V-shaped leaves surrounding the battle area. They weren't here before. The warzone isn't a plowed field on a plain; it's a clearing. The trees sway in the wind, bending so that they're bowing backward and marking a path through tall blades of purple grass. A deep feeling of need squeezes my guts together in a vice grip better than DG's. I gasp as my legs start moving on their own. I'm walking toward the path.

No! No! I try to plant my feet, but they won't stop. I'm not in control; psychics always have to be in control. If they're not—if I'm not, I lose my mind.

"D-don't leave. H-help..." a broken voice calls.

Something snaps like a tether line stretched too far inside me. I stumble a few steps before I can stop walking and stand, feet together, fists clenched. My heart practically vibrates it's going so fast, and my lungs burn from too much air. I've been breathing in but not out. Fear prickles under my skin. I feel scrubbed raw.

"D-don't go. Please. I don't want to die," the broken voice calls again. Hitching breaths and hoarse sobs make me turn around. DG is curled on his right side, in fetal position. Blood saturates the dirt around him, red and purple mix together making black.

I take slow steps to reach him, kneeling down and grimacing at the warm, sticky feeling of blood on my bare knees. Resting a hand on his back, I peer into his

face. His eyes are squeezed shut, feathery lashes fluttering like he's in REM sleep. He could be waking up from his dream, meaning I'll be waking up soon as well. I should be relived, but I'm not.

"Hey." I shake him and his eyes open, but they're dazed, pupils dilated. "What were you telling me about an emergency code? I need to know now. I think you're waking up."

His mouth opens.

ChildofMagicChildofMagicChildofMagic.

Need floods me again. I have to move, to follow the path. I hold onto DG to keep myself in place. "Tell me what you want!" I yell at him.

"Need to go. Help me up." His voice is stronger.

My hands hover over a huge blood stain on his uniform. There's no new blood. In the blink of an eye, his uniform's clean again and he looks like he did when he first appeared to me.

He sits up, right hand going to his left shoulder and squeezing it. "It stopped." His eyes are fully alert. They lock onto mine. "I have to go that way." He nods toward the bending trees. "And so do you, I think."

My guts squeeze together again. "Yeah," I mutter.

I stand up with a grunt, grimacing at the bloody clots of dirt stuck to my legs. I offer a hand to DG out of reflex before remembering I'd wanted to put a wall between us a few minutes ago. Now that he's not bleeding out, I don't feel so sympathetic. He grabs my hand before I can snatch it back, and pulls himself up. He's silent on his feet as he pushes past me, heading toward the bowing trees.

I find myself jogging after DG to keep up. He's fast.

The copse of trees gets thicker and taller as we travel deeper into the woods. The double suns are blocked by purple leaves wide and long as kamikaze kites. The scent of oranges mixes with a subtle hint of mint. Waist high purple grass hides the rocky dirty beneath it. I let my fingers trail on either side of me and a zing of pain makes me hiss. I bring my hands back, and suck my right index finger where a blade of grass cut the tip. The copper taste of blood fills my mouth, and my stomach churns.

I shouldn't be able to taste that in a dream. This is wrong.

Wake up. Wake up.

"It's here." DG's voice sounds miles away. His tone is wondrous.

I look forward. The trees thin up ahead and there's a mountain face with an open cave. Images dart through my mind. I see DG, blood-spattered and dying, crawling into a cave and sinking into the floor. I scrub my eyes with the heels of my hands and open them again to see DG, whole and healthy, staring at me like a curious cat.

"Dream-walkers don't usually stay so long," he says slowly. "They bring or take messages, and then go. You're talented, but even so, how are you holding onto me still?"

Long curls spring around his face from where they've escaped his braid, which evokes an image of Lawrie's wild, curly hair flying all over the place as he shakes his head.

"I don't know. I'm only this strongly connected to relatives," I say, taking in his face again. Déjà vu dances at the back of my head but, before I can try to bring it up front, need hits, doubling me over.

Something's calling.

DG gasps and clutches his left shoulder. No blood comes away on his fingers, but he grits his teeth as if he's in pain. He starts toward the cave, and I have to follow. My legs are moving again, and I can't stop them.

DG walks just in front of me, I follow so closely I step on his heels a few times. He doesn't say anything as the cave floor begins to tilt downward, taking us underground. He walks with his head down, watching the ground. His bare neck is exposed and I frown at a tribal tattoo that starts at the base of his skull and vanishes beneath the collar of his shirt. I want to freehand the shapes on art paper and block them in with a charcoal pencil.

"How far does your tattoo go?" I ask.

"My tattoo?" DG asks, sounding confused.

"On your neck."

"That's not a tattoo," DG says with a frown in his voice. "Don't you know anything? You...must be human. That's the smell!" He spins around to face me, walking backward. "I haven't been around humans in a long time. Are you from Earth, do you live there?"

I nod slowly, pondering his questions. When was the last time he'd been around humans? A few years ago, it was revealed that Visitors have been on Earth a hell of a lot longer than 2017, when the first embassies were built. Turns out there had even been some diplomatic trips to certain planets made by foreign ambassadors in the late 90s. Wonder what that'd be like, to leave this place and, as far I know, never come back: no family, no ties to people who make you feel guilty for not playing well with others.

"I used to live on Earth. I was really little. I don't

recall a lot of it, but I remember that all of you smell like salty dirt. I love that smell. It's so mortal and natural. Too many people alter themselves to live longer and it just stinks them up. They smell like metals and artificial ingredients."

DG talks like he's singing. His voice is awesome to listen to. I have a feeling lots of people sit around to hear this guy talk.

I almost forget where I am, until the tunnel opens into a cavern with a high ceiling. The walls shimmer with black stones. I run my hand along one, feeling the smoothness of it. From the corner of my eye, I see a soft, green glow. I turn my head from the walls, and look to the center of the cavern where a small pool sits.

DG stands at the edge of it, peering down. I pull my hand from the wall and take small steps toward him. When I get to DG's side, I follow his gaze and jump back.

A body floats, face down. Dark blond curls billow and blood taints the water pink.

"Oh, God!" I yell, snapping my head from the body to DG. "That's you! But you're not dead…right?" I have never spoken to a dead person. I am not a medium.

DG's eyes are huge in his face. He enters the pool. The water's little more than knee-deep and two steps put DG at the body's side. Carefully, he kneels and turns the body over. I cover my mouth and stare.

"You're dead," I choke. This guy, who can be scary and fantastic at the same time, is dead. A deep feeling of remorse burrows in my chest. But why do I care so much?

"I'm not dead." DG holds a hand over the corpse's

face, his eyes look far away and I feel concentration rippling through his aura. "I'm...."

He blinks and lets go of the body, then leans forward and fishes for something under the water. I breathe twice before DG pulls up a closed fist. He opens his palm and I wheeze, staring at the emerald and feeling....

A call...to do something...I don't know what, but it's ripping me apart inside.

"Put it down, put it down!" I shout.

DG seems mesmerized, though. He stares at the emerald. "It's keeping me alive. It doesn't want me to die, but...it doesn't have the power to do it forever."

He looks at me. "You said I called you?" His words pick up speed and intensity as he squeezes the gem. "I did call you, because...when I touched this thing it told me to! We're connected. Do you feel it?"

The only thing I feel right now is sick. I've never puked in a dream before, but—I bend over and gag hard, hurling liquid that feels and tastes like microwaved orange soda. My throat burns, and my eyes water. Dream-puking is as miserable as the real thing.

A hand makes rough circles on my back. My stomach stops clenching and I spit tart pulp onto the ground. Wiping my mouth, I straighten up and look at DG beside me, dripping. The emerald's gone, and the pool's still glowing. The body floats on its back, face pale and slack.

"My name is Lauduethe. You have to contact the Silver Allegiance of Planets and tell them I'm alive and on Onkurus, about an hour's trip by foot from the last battlefield. Tell them to look for a cave."

"Wha...?" I know I asked for this information before, but what do I do with it? Silver Allegiance...Onku-

rus...Lauduethe?

"I don't have much time."

Panic sets my skin on fire. I know he doesn't have much time. I can feel him—the body in the water. Lauduethe is right, the body's not dead, it's breathing, its heart is beating, but each beat, each breath, is carefully measured, rationed.

I can't handle this. It's way too much. I'm ready to bust out of my skin and howl.

"Why did you call me? It's gonna take me forever to figure out how to contact a Silver Allegiance!" The guy's gonna die, and, unless I do something, it's on me.

The thought of failing is a sucking wound in my chest. Why do I care so much? "Please, call someone else," I say.

"I don't know if I can," he whispers.

I stare at Lauduethe. He's way too close again. He's in the personal space I only give to family and future conquests, but my skin's not crawling with feelings of invasion. Somewhere between the battlefield and this cave, something happened. Lauduethe can invade my space all he wants, because I feel it, a bond, a connection—the one I felt when he first contacted me.

He's looking at me, his eyes seeming to drink me in. Something's changed in them, maybe it's been different for a while now and I hadn't noticed. Does he know me? Because I know him. My stomach flutters. "You're...."

ChildofMagicChildofMagicChildofMagic.

We both jerk as the voice comes again, loud and booming off the cavern walls. The glow from the pool lights the room, but it's dimming. Lauduethe pats my back and points down into the pool. I don't want to look

at his body again, but I'm compelled to follow his finger with my eyes.

I blink. There's an image in the water. It's a table with people sitting around it. Lauduethe inches forward and I move with him. He sits on his knees, looking down. I mirror his motions.

"What is this?" he whispers.

I peer at ten people seated around a table. Four of them are young guys. One looks up, cocking his head as if he hears something.

I gasp. He has my face. I dip my fingers in the warm water, trying to touch the image.

"No, don't!" Lauduethe shouts.

He grabs my shoulders, but something stronger catches my wrist and pulls me into the pool.

CHAPTER

6
DEVON

THE NEIGHBORHOOD'S QUIET AT SIX in the morning. The only people out are joggers and folks walking their dogs. I nod to them as they pass by panting and sweating, earbuds secure. I love early morning people; they don't talk much. We all have a purpose: workout. We got no time for keeping up appearances. Mrs. Garner, a lady who's always in pumps and nylons at the damn grocery store, runs in a ratty old sweat suit. Mr. Taylor, three-piece Armani man, runs in biker shorts and a tank. I love being alone and not having to slow down to keep pace with teammates.

I'm miles from my house, running through the suburban maze known as the Better Side of Town. Houston's so big there's no telling how many suburbs are out there claiming to be H-Town's 'Best Part.' One day, the Greater Houston Area is gonna take up half the state. Every five minutes some new little town gets annexed. Just last month, the city reigned in another million dollar neighborhood—though a lot of people protested because

it's full of aliens.

I still remember the insanity when aliens first started buying houses in the area. All the humans moved out, saying the Visitors were bringing down the property value. But, you know, one thing I can say about Visitors is that they keep stuff clean. Since the regulars moved out, that whole place friggin' sparkles. I like running by it every now and again.

My sneakers pound the pavement, pat, pat, pat. I love that sound more than listening to my iPlay. The sports watch on my wrist tells me I've gone ten miles in forty-nine minutes. My skin's dry and I'm not breathing hard; my heart beats slow and steady.

The sun's not up until seven, so the sky's dark and streetlights are still on. A few cars are in the street, and the red glow from their taillights wash over my tan skin. The woman staring at me through a bay window makes me wonder what I look like bathed in red light.

I slow my pace, waving at the woman as she stands behind open blinds, curtains drawn, holding a mug and watching. A little smirk crosses her lips and pride flushes through me. I know that smirk. I grin and make a show of rolling my T-shirt up over my abs and fanning myself with it. I pass her window, but I know that cougar's probably ogling my ass. A lot of PTA moms do.

I run through the subdivision's gate. The entry is a stone playhouse made to look like a miniature version of the houses in the neighborhood. It's about six feet tall. I look around—no cars, no people—and leap onto the roof of the thing, breathing in deep. Mornings around here smell like pinecones and flowers from the manicured trees and gardens winding around the brick fences

that surround various subdivisions. The gardens stop an inch before the sign announcing the city limits, and wild grass and weeds take over.

I jump off the roof. My feet hit the grass with a thump and I run towards the edge of the city. I jog into the parking lot of a shopping strip with a grocery store, pawn shop, Chinese restaurant, and a Mom and Pop donut place. The lights are on inside Silva's Donuts. Through the glass door and big windows, I see Monica sitting on a stool behind the counter, head tilted up, probably watching the TV mounted on the far wall.

The store's empty aside from Monica, and the only vehicle in the lot is her Kawasaki. I'm completely into college chicks with motorcycles; too bad she treats me like jailbait. I'm seventeen, the age of consent woman, come on. The gravel of the parking lot is crispy under my shoes as I sprint toward Silva's. A bell over the door rings as I let myself into the store and a waft of hot sugar and roasting coffee beans makes my stomach growl.

Monica barely glances at me, but gives me the "hello" nod. Silva's isn't fancy, but it's clean. The walls are Peep yellow and the tables are small and round with white tablecloths. A glass case up front displays donuts, kolaches, and cheese danishes. I make my way to the bar and hop up on a stool.

Planting my elbows on the bar's surface, I grin at Monica. "Hey."

"Hn." She slips off her stool and goes to the donut display, pulling out two sausage and cheese kolaches and dropping them on a paper plate in front of me. After a beat, a bottle of chocolate milk appears too. "There's your breakfast, Champ. How far did you run today?"

I glance at the pedometer. "Fifteen miles."

"You're slacking," Monica says. Her voice is kinda deep for a girl's, but it's nice. Not as sexy as Keelie's, but still hot. "How'd your party go?"

I bite into a kolache. "It was okay," I mumble, mouth full.

"Must not have gone well if that's all you got to say," Monica says, passing me a napkin.

She sits back down on her stool and I stare at her. She's in a tight T-shirt that makes her boobs pop and low-rise jeans that fit her like a second skin. She's probably got on cowboy boots too. Monica doesn't care how hot it is; she's always got on jeans and boots, always ready to ride.

I set the napkin on the counter and lick sticky cheese off my lips, thinking about what I want to say to Monica about the party. Hmm. So, it's like this, Monica. The party was going great until I had a seizure and ripped apart a chair. Oh, and I can't leave out the part where Lawrie almost drowned.

I grind my teeth. I almost killed that idiot when he wasn't dead. I thought for sure when I got down there and saw him stretched out on the ground that he was a goner. But then he sat up and clung to Lyle, and the both of them looked at me like I was as useless as the rest of the losers standing around watching. And from that spazz look in Lyle's eyes, I know he and Lawrie were probably doing that mind-to-mind telepathy crap.

I didn't ask Lyle about it because I was afraid I'd hit him, but if he used his powers to send me that vision, I would have—God, I don't know. We aren't close like we used to be when we were kids, but he's still my twin.

"Devon? Devon?" Monica waves her hand in my face.

"Huh?" I blink and stare at her.

She's got great eyes, so brown they look black with thick lashes around them. She doesn't wear all that makeup high school girls do and she keeps her black hair long and straight with red streaks dyed under the bottom.

"Your party?" Monica presses. She pulls the top off my chocolate milk and takes a swig.

"Oh, had to break it up. Somebody called the police," I say, reaching out to take my chocolate milk back. I make sure I brush her wrist before snatching the bottle. I chug milk, then wipe my mouth with the back of my hand.

"You're lying," Monica says and takes my milk back when I set it on the table. "Your mouth does this thing when you lie. It kinda twitches at the corner, like you're trying not to smirk."

"What?" I scowl. "You're making that up!"

"No, I'm not." Monica grins. Her fingers head for my mouth and I freeze as a strawberry jelly scented index finger traces the right corner of my mouth. "Here. You twitch."

I'm ready to suck that finger, but she'd probably throw the rest of the chocolate milk in my face. God, does she want me or not? I swear she's flirting with me.

"You're such a baby," she says with a laugh and pulls her hand away.

"All right. So, I'm lying. I broke up my own party because my little bro's an idiot and I wasn't in the mood to deal with too many people afterward." I touch the tip of my tongue to where her finger had been. Tastes like

strawberries.

"Let me guess, you're talking about the nutcase," Monica says, shaking her head. "You know, there's medication he can take for that."

"My parents made him go to a behavioral therapist. Something she said must've really pissed Dad off, because he told her where to stick it."

"Mm...spouses telling people where to stick it isn't good for the public image," Monica says. "I've seen your mom's campaign posters up in some front lawns. She's hot. She's got my vote."

I snort. I'm used to people saying my mom's hot. All my teammates call her a MILF. Nasty.

"I hope she loses." I don't want any extra attention, especially not after last night.

Uneasiness seeps into my flesh. From the corners of my eyes, I see the green glow from that rock and I almost feel the warm water on my skin as I sink into a pool. I shake my head and reach for the milk at the same time Monica does. My clumsy hand hits the bottle and she catches it before it spills.

"Whoa, careful," Monica says and tilts her head. "You look sick."

"M'fine," I mumble. "How are summer classes?"

"You wanna talk about school?" Monica drinks more milk and starts eating what's left of my kolaches, eyes still on my face. I like when girls look at me, but Monica's doing a laser beam thing. In a minute, I'm gonna get a complete psychoanalysis. "Well, if you must know, I didn't go to class yesterday," Monica says. She finishes off the kolache and bends over to open a cabinet under the counter. Her T-shirt rides up and I get a good

view of the panda tattoo on the small of her back. After a minute, she comes up with a Mac Notebook. "Move your food."

I push the plate away and she puts her laptop down.

"So, I skipped class to go to a Stop the Hate Texas meeting. You seen this? Happened yesterday." Monica clicks a few buttons and YouTube Underground loads up.

I sit back and watch a bunch of assholes beat the snot out of an alien kid. Poor guy doesn't stand a chance. Some of the jerks hold him while the others punch him. Then one pulls out a knife.

"Jesus." I close the laptop.

Anger and fear pulse in my chest. I can't stand watching helpless people get picked on. Nobody tried to help the kid, and he didn't even try to fight. But at the same time, what if he did try to fight? What if he had some kind of power? All he'd do is make people freak out because he'd prove aliens are dangerous to humans. Things would get worse. I mean, that guy...he could be me, or Lyle. If word got out we have power, it'd be awful.

Toilet paper in the yard, broken windows, threats, might even get chased out of our neighborhood into the annex all the aliens live in. School would be a nightmare. We had one Visitor kid come to our junior high once. She got locked in the janitor's closet on her first day, had her clothes stolen out of the girls' locker room the next. She transferred on the third day.

"You know, Stop the Hate meets at seven tonight at the Student Center on campus," Monica says. "You wanna come with me? It's cool. We just talk about ways we

can make things better, get people to see Visitors are all right. It's been almost five years since they set up embassies. And twenty to thirty years ago, before people knew what was going on, we had folks settling and mixing. Who knows who's mixed with what now, right?"

Monica's looking at me with those laser beams again and my flesh twitches. I want to meet her outside of her job at a place where talking to me isn't just good customer service. And hell, she wants to take me to one of her college things like I'm adult enough to hang out with her and her crowd. I'm in, right? Wrong.

I can't go to a meeting about Visitor and vulatto rights. U of H is a big commuter school. I know too many people who go there.

"Well, you wanna come with me to the meeting or not?" Monica taps the counter with her short nails. She's got on red polish with black tips.

"Uh." What do I say? I can't tell her something lame, but she must see the need to lie on my face, because her laser beams shut off and her expression closes up.

She picks up her laptop and narrows her eyes at me. "Really, Devon? You're one of those guys? I knew you were shallow, but I thought you were growing up. Guess that's what I get for taking a high school kid seriously."

Taking me seriously? She.... "What?"

Monica leans forward, putting her face in my space. I can almost taste the chocolate milk on her breath. "I talk to you because you're different, Devon," she says. "I pay attention to people. I want to know more people like me. We have similar backgrounds. Your parents do well for themselves. But way back when, before they got

all high and mighty, one of them had themselves a little fun with a Visiting stranger and here we are. Our parents tell us 'be good and hide it,' but I'm too old for that now. Not with the world like this."

My eyes are wide, drinking in this beautiful woman who's telling me, "Are you a...?"

"Vulatto?" Monica sneers, not pulling away from me. "Would it matter?"

I swallow. She's perfect. There's nothing inhuman about her, but there's nothing inhuman about the way I look either. "And you think I'm one too? Why?"

"I've seen you at your peak. Normal kids don't run twenty miles in an hour. You don't pay attention when you're really into what you're doing."

I gape. If she's been watching me and noticed that...I think I'm gonna puke right here on the floor. I swallow a few times.

"Relax," she says, finally sitting back and I can breathe again. "You live in the right place to go unnoticed. People in this part of town have their heads stuck so far up their own asses they don't see anything."

She touches my wrist, putting her fingers against my throbbing pulse. "Your heart's gonna explode. What are you so scared of?"

"I don't know if I'm a vulatto," I blurt out and want to clamp my hand over my mouth. Why the hell did I say that to her?

"How do you not know if you're half alien?" Monica quirks a brow at me.

"I'm missing a parent," I say, "and I'm not gonna assume he's anything weird until—"

"Weird? Is that what you call it?" Monica asks.

"Listen, my parents were both born here, but my mom's dad, he wasn't. Grandpa's from one of those planets where everybody can make themselves look human, so it was easy for him to hide. But he got tired of hiding and left. I only just now started talking to him. My mom didn't want me to. He's a cool guy, Dev, not weird at all. I wanna go out and meet him. He says he'll pay."

I feel like I swallowed a load of wet bath towels. My stomach's full of damp polyester. If I burp, fluff'll come out. I sit like a stuffed penguin, waddling from side to side on my stool, staring at Monica Trevino, a vulatto.

"You want people to throw trash at you and call you names?" I ask.

"I'm ready to be who I am," Monica says. "I don't care who knows it. Dev, Stop the Hate is awesome. There are more people like us in it, Earthborns, and there are a few Visitors, and regular humans. We just talk. And God, Dev, you need to hear Visitors talk about their lives off Earth."

I look over my shoulder. The shop bell hasn't rung, so I know nobody's here besides us, but still. You can't talk about this kinda stuff in public. When I look back at Monica, she's watching me and tapping her fingers again.

"You're not ready," she finally says. Disappointment flickers in her gaze.

Dammit, how did I let this go bad? Why does this have to be the reason she's interested in me?

I open my mouth. "I can't. I'm not even sure, and I...."

I just want to be normal. Normal's easy and safe. Not being normal gets you hurt. Why put yourself out

there when you don't have to? Images of Lyle come into my head. Him answering my questions before I asked them. Him breaking dishes without touching them, because I pissed him off when I told him I didn't want to hear any more about his psychic junk. Lyle and Lawrie, last night, doing that mind-to-mind crap.

They can embrace that alien stuff, not me.

"Maybe some other time." I slide off the bar stool.

My muscles itch to move again. I think I'll take the long way home.

"Yeah, sure," Monica says.

I know she's watching me walk to the door; I feel those lasers.

"Hey, Dev?"

I turn.

"You have a good heart. You're gonna be somebody one day, I know you are. You just gotta break that high school mentality you got going on. The adult world is a lot different, and man, you got people who'll help you if you come out."

Come out? Admitting you're a vulatto is like coming out of the closet? Well, people live their whole lives in the closet and they're fine, happy, because life is cake. I like cake.

"Yeah. Sure," I echo her earlier tone. "See ya around."

I push through the glass door and sprint through the parking lot. I can't get away from Monica fast enough. I should stick to high school girls.

But I really like her.

The wet laundry feeling in my belly is heavy, but it doesn't slow me up much. I glance at my watch, six

minutes a mile. That's okay for a high school athlete, I guess. None of my teammates can do it, but none of them are really into running like I am. I pass the stone house entrance sign to my subdivision.

I'll run to the park and maybe double back—

Ow.

A stitch in my side takes a bite out of me, and I stumble to a stop. I grip my right flank and bend over. Panting and rubbing out the cramp, my mind twists. I see Lyle's face, hear his voice. It's saying....

/Oh God./

Panic stabs me in the chest, but I'm not the one who's afraid.

/Oh God./

Lyle?

I think about my brother, hard. I picture his face, his last words to me, the last time we shared a room when we were ten. Back when we were close, all I had to do was think about him and he'd pop into my head and ask, /What's up?/

It's not happening that way now.

Lyle?

I could be too far away. Maybe I need to be closer to the house, assuming he's still at home. He was asleep when I left, and Lyle never gets up before noon in the summer. I straighten up, trying to block out Lyle's terror as I force my legs to run. I'm going home.

And if Lyle isn't in trouble, I'm gonna kill him.

THE SENSOR ON THE BACK door chimes as I let my-self into the house. I kick the door shut with my sneaker and plow through the kitchen to the back stairwell. Tak-ing the stairs in three's, I reach the top in seconds, and crash through Lyle's bedroom door. The room is dark, blinds drawn, and the only sound comes from the air conditioning vent overhead.

"Ly?" I rub my hand over the wall by the door, flip-ping the light switch.

"Lyle!" I stalk to the bed, hopping over a pair of discarded jeans. Anxiety runs up my spine and makes me shudder. Lyle is the lightest sleeper I know. I leap onto the bed, rocking it with my weight. Lyle's body bounces, but he doesn't stir. Gripping his clammy, bare shoulder, I shake him. "Lyle! Wake up!"

I flip him over onto his back and almost fall off the bed. His eyes are open and blank, like a dead person's. But he isn't dead. I'd know it. I rip the sheets off his tor-so and press my ear to his chest. His breathing is shallow.

"Lyle?" I sit up, staring down at him.

He might be having some kinda psychic fit. What am I supposed to do again? Uncle Jonas told me once, but I'm spazzing. Grabbing Lyle's shoulders, I pull him up and his head flops onto my right shoulder. "Dude, come on!"

Knock, knock, Lyle. You can hear me. I know you can.

He gasps, a big sucking sound, like he's been un-derwater for hours and finally coming up for air. I nearly jump out of my skin. I tilt him back and yelp as his head rocks backward and his eyes roll around in their sockets

before closing. "Dammit." Nine-one-one?

Easing him back down on the bed, I pat myself for my cell phone, then frown. Where the hell's Lawrie? He's gotta hear me yelling, but then again, Lawrie sleeps like the dead. Damn. I lean over Lyle and peel one of his eyelids open. That green eye, the same color as mine, stares through me, into my soul, and I feel the same tug I get in my gut when a rollercoaster reaches the top of the hill and starts to drop.

Black…green…black…green, I'm falling head over feet through another world until I hit warm water with a soft splash and sink beneath the surface.

Hands grip my arms tight and I open my eyes to see Lyle staring back at me.

/Aw shit/ he thinks.

And I can't agree more.

7
LYLE

'AW SHIT' DOESN'T BEGIN TO cover this, but it's all that comes to mind. I'm not creative with words. I hang on to Devon as a force sucks us down a watery tunnel. For some reason, I don't need to breathe. I can't feel my lungs expanding. Don't even know if I have a pulse.

A blast of hot air blows my hair around my face and someone gasps—no, not someone, me. Air whooshes into my lungs. I open my eyes, and stare at Devon kneeling in front of me, his eyes wild. Pain radiates from my kneecaps, and I glance down to see my knees planted on cold, white stone.

"Lyle, what is this? Where are we?" Devon's voice is a fragment of its usual annoyingness.

His eyes drag away from mine and roam. His skin gets grayer by the second. I rub my face and glance around.

Everything's made of ash white stone: the floors, the columns, the walls. Against the walls are unlit torches leading up to what looks like an altar. Sunlight shines

in through a circular hole in the ceiling, giving the holy table a halo. Behind it, there's a corridor. Voices carry.

"It's like some ancient temple." Devon talks fast. "Why are we in an ancient temple? What the hell did you do?"

"What did I do?" I ask. Why does everything have to be my fault? "What did you do? I was falling into this mess alone—" Wait, no I wasn't. I look up, and see nothing but the stone ceiling. What happened to Lauduethe?

Dull pain gnaws my chest. If he's not here, I don't know how to get back to him. And I still don't know how to wake up.

"You were in my head," Devon says, running both hands through his hair. "I was trying to shake you awake and wham. What is this?"

"A dream." I watch my brother carefully. His nerves writhe beneath the surface of my skin. Devon freaks out when he's in over his head. I usually want to strangle him during these episodes, but this time a little freaking out is justified.

"You have dreams about water and temples." Devon chuckles, nerves bobbing apples in a barrel. "Most guys dream about Playboy's Legacy Mansion. You dream about church. Feelin' guilty about something?"

An image of a girl we met last summer flickers through his mind. He'd liked her, she'd preferred me, and I'd learned about the psychic relief kissing brings. He'd been touchy for weeks after, but it wasn't like he and the girl ever had a thing.

"Are you serious?" I ask. "Get over it."

I flinch at the hurt rippling through Devon. He looks at me like he doesn't know me, but whose fault is that?

He's the one who cut me off, not the other way around. If he'd bothered to ask, I would have told him that girl only wanted a hook-up. Devon isn't a hook-up kinda guy; he likes relationships. I'd saved him from that. I scowl at him and he looks away.

"I'm over it," he grunts. He stands and takes a deep breath. "Smells like we're in the mountains. Did you make this place up or is it someplace you read about? I know you've never been here." He faces the altar. "And there are people down that hall. Who are they?"

His defense's up. There's a curtain over his thoughts and a plug on his emotions. Uncle Jonas taught Devon how to do that when we were little, but he didn't start using it until high school. I squash down old feelings of betrayal, remembering how lonely freshman year had been without him. He was the only friend I had.

"I don't know," I say. "There's...." He hates when I talk about my power, but tough shit. "We're in someone else's dream. I was just with that person before I fell into this, a second stage of the dream maybe. We—the guy and I—were looking at a pool of water when I got pulled in."

Devon turns to meet my eyes. "In someone else's dream? How did you get in someone else's dream? Isn't it dangerous? Can't you get lost?"

He looks worried and, to be honest, I'm not being fair. We don't talk anymore, but he does care. I can't feel it through his plugs and curtains, but deep down, I know my brother. He's the good guy I'll never be. He cares about people in general.

"I know how to get out of dreams," I say. Not this one, but others no problem. Devon looks me up and

down. The twitch at the corner of his mouth tells me he doesn't believe me.

"So, what now?" he asks. "Do I pinch you? Do we have to complete some task? Give me something to work with." He uses his captain of the football team voice, and I smirk. He resorts to that when he's talking out of his butt crack.

I want to find Lauduethe. I can't even feel him anymore. What I do feel is the need from before. It burns the base of my ribcage. The voices from the corridor get louder and a chord plays beneath them: *Come to me.*

Devon goes rigid. "Do you hear that? Something's saying 'Come to me.' You hear it, right? I'm not crazy?" The captain of the football team is gone. Dev's pitch goes haywire. "Ly, something's...happening...to me."

I push off the ground, standing. My brother's back is to me, his hands clenched at his sides, his shoulders ramrod straight. The plug on his emotions wears thin. Agitation leaks through. He's terrified about something, but it's buried too deep beneath the surface of his feelings for me to reach it.

"Hey." I reach out to squeeze his shoulder, but pull back. I'm not one for comforting people. I touch them and all their baggage unloads on me. But this is Dev and even without physical contact, his pain, like the deep-seated ache of an abscessed tooth, rolls through me and I'm scared. I'm lost in a dying person's dream, being called by some strange power to do something I don't know how, and the only scary thing right now is Devon having a complete melt down.

Devon's Adam's apple shudders as he swallows and his jaw tightens. He wants to say something, I know it,

but instead he shrugs, breaking contact. The plug corks
all of his feelings back in the bottle and a second curtain
falls around the tattered first. He clears his throat and
stalks to the altar. "Come on. Something's telling me I
need to go this way."

And he assumes I'll follow, because he doesn't look
back to make sure I am. To spite him, I should stay right
here, but that chord....

Come to me.

It's not just going to stop if I don't listen. My legs
move on their own again. I take long strides, catching up
to Devon and walking at his side. At first glance, someone might look at us and think they're seeing a mirror
image of the same person, but second glances usually
clear up that mistake. Devon's got an air around him,
one that really can't be questioned when he's in the right
mood. People do what he says. Me? If I care to talk, they
might listen to me just because they know I'm his brother, but there's no air around me that says anything.

The altar is small with tiny carvings of flowers
glazed with red paint.

"It's blood," Devon says softly. "Don't you smell
it?"

I shoot him a glare. My fingers hover over the flowers. I almost touch them. "I don't smell anything," but
orange juice.

"It's fresh. I bet it's wet," Devon says. "Someone
must have cut their hand, or something, and dripped it
on here. There's not enough blood to be, you know, a
sacrifice or anything."

He means there's not enough blood here for it to
seem like there'd been a sacrifice. There might be anoth-

er altar at the end of the corridor where the voices are. Maybe they're holding a ceremony for the big sacrifice and Devon and I are about to crash it.

I try to plant my feet on the floor, but my legs start walking again, past the altar and into the hall. Devon's beside me. Torches, thick sticks of short wood wrapped in cloth, burn blue and yellow, lighting the path. The white expanse of stone beneath my feet is cracked by purple roots. The voices are louder, and warm air hits me in the face in a concentrated shot. I step over the threshold into a large, open room. The burbling comes from water coursing through large flowers carved into alabaster walls. Little golden troughs collect the water before it reaches the floor.

The ceiling is open, and a yellow sun is high in the sky, lighting the entire room. A round, stone table stands in the center of everything and six people dressed like cosplayers at a Renaissance convention sit around it. They seem to be in groups. Two guys and a girl are in combat gear, all leather sheaths and metal breastplates. Bronze swords lay across the table in front of them. The other three people, women—green-skinned women—sit on the other side of the table, wearing long white dresses like sacrificial virgins.

"Okay, we saw," Devon says, voice rusty. "Can you wake up now?"

"Move it, Jain!" A voice grunts behind me and a hand plants itself on my lower back, shoving me forward.

Devon and I whirl around in unison and I choke. Lawrie, dressed like a cheap imitation of Robin Hood, smirks at me with a hand on his hip. His curly hair is

short, almost cropped to his head. Lawrie has never worn his hair that short, and his face...there's a scar beneath one of his eyes, and his aura is....

"You're not Lawrence," I say. "Who are you?"

"Honestly, Jain, you're such a worrier. There's nothing to be afraid of!" the guy who looks like my little brother crows, patting my shoulder as his gaze moves to Devon. "Hah, you lose the bet, Padain. I told you Jain would bite his nails until we leave, no matter what we find in here."

Padain? Jain?

Crazy laughter echoes through the corridor, and the Lawrence-poser rolls his eyes with a grin. Lauduethe steps out of the hallway, wearing a get-up similar to Lawrence-poser's.

"What the hell is going on, Lauduethe?" I stalk past the poser to grip Lauduethe's collar. He blinks at me and takes hold of my wrists, squeezing the bones until I gasp and let go of his shirt.

"Calm down, Jain," Lauduethe says. "Honestly. If you want to wait outside, go right ahead. I thought you would have calmed him by now, Padain."

I turn to Devon. He's staring at Lauduethe in shock. "Lyle, what is this?"

"I don't know, but that one's not Lawrence, and this guy's the one having the dream. He—"

Devon looks at me, face pale. "This guy?" His voice is soft, but incredulous. "What did you call him?"

"He told me his name's Lauduethe," I say. Lauduethe and the poser are frowning, looking beyond Devon and me like we're not here anymore. "He's on some other planet—"

"This is his dream?" Devon asks.

I growl, but nod, and Devon grabs Lauduethe's arm. "His name isn't Lauduethe!" Devon's giving me an 'are-you-really-this-stupid?' look that pisses me off.

Lauduethe blinks and shifts his attention to Devon, a question in his eyes.

"He's our brother," Devon says.

And I could slap myself. That's what's been on the edge of my thoughts all this time. It's been thirteen years, but I should have recognized him. Hell, I did recognize him. I was just too overloaded to put it all together.

Lauduethe, or maybe I should call him Evan, grins and laughs. "Yes, Padain, I am your brother!" He says it like the joke's on us. You big dummies, of course I'm your brother! Haha!

I want to shove Devon out of the way, shake Evan and ask, 'Where's our father? Why don't you call him for help?' Unless he's dead. Was he in the battle with the acid glitter?

I feel like I'm on a freeway, my thoughts are colorful Nascars speeding past me honking horns and blowing exhaust in my face. My big brother, Evan Ladreth, missing for years without a word, is suddenly right here in front of me and so alien. Damn. Just…damn, what the hell do I say to him? What do I feel?

Evan knocks Devon's hand off his arm and pushes him aside. "Stop being rude. We are in the presence of royalty!"

Evan strides in the direction of the table. The poser follows, tugging the long braid hanging down Evan's back. The people around the table gaze up at them. The looks from the warriors aren't friendly.

Before I meet his eyes, I feel Devon staring at me.

"Explain this dream, now," Devon says. "Is it symbolic? Why are you dreaming about Evan? And why is he...bigger? He was five when we saw him last, now he's like...I don't know, fourteen?"

"Maybe he just looks young. He's gotta be eighteen. I'm sure this is in real time," I say, my voice is light. Dizziness makes my head spin and something pulls at me. My legs cramp and the muscles twitch.

Devon's breathing is heavy and he's suddenly very close to me. "Lyle, I want to go sit at the table, I think. Why do I feel like I have to? Why won't you tell me what's going on!"

Curtains and plugs are gone. Devon's fear is fresh and disorienting as it tries to drown me.

"I don't know!" I say. "I don't know anything about this dream. I've never been in one like it."

My legs are moving, taking me to the table. The people around it don't even look at me as I take a seat next to Evan. I hear stone dragging across stone and, in my periphery, I see Devon sitting next to me.

All of the other people around the table, Evan and the poser included, look official and serious, in their war costumes and Renaissance garb. I'm still in my boxers and Devon's in shorts and a tank. He's even got his iPlay strapped to his bicep. Next time, I'm going to sleep with some damn pants on, and maybe a pencil. A crazy urge to draw these people creeps into the back of my mind.

The air becomes thick and hard to breathe. It has the cloying floral scent of old lady perfume. My throat burns and my eyes and nose run. I hear wind howling before I feel it stir. I struggle to keep my eyes open as

air particles become visible. They swirl, turning into a funnel of white mist fanning out a few feet from the table. The funnel falls straight, becoming a doorway that swings open, revealing a rectangle of pure darkness for a split second before a person steps through.

"Holy shit, she's got four boobs," Devon says.

My body is frozen. If it wasn't, I'd have punched Devon for that. A ten-foot-tall silver woman, white hair crackling with electricity, with black holes for eyes, steps through what looks like a rip in the space-time continuum—and that's what stands out to him? Evan lets out a low whistle and utters something under his breath. Soft chuckles pass between him and the idiot posing as Lawrie.

The woman steps up onto the table and stands in the middle of it, turning slowly to look down at everyone. She shakes her head and crackling hair covers her naked body like a robe. Power radiates from this woman, a strength that gives me chills. Her eyes speak. Her full lips draw me in. Who or what is this thing?

"You are a god!" one of the green ladies shouts. "I thought you had all abandoned us!" She sounds excited.

A god? Really? If I were at home, the spell would have broken. God and gods, all religion and mythology sound the same stupid to me. But sitting at a table with this giant woman screaming at me with no sound makes me question myself.

Boisterous laughter erupts from one of the warrior people. "The gods are long gone, Maiden Moira. This is a siren monster. I've cut the heads off many! Though she is the largest I've seen. Ah!"

The laughing warrior clutches his ears and blood

drips from his nostrils. His eyes roll in his head for a few horrible seconds and the table is dead silent. The giant woman continues to emit hot energy until the man screams, "Forgive me!"

The woman's lips curve into an ugly smile. Her teeth are long and jagged, and her voice is claws on a chalkboard. Like Evan earlier, if I don't concentrate I can understand what everyone around the table is saying, but when this woman speaks it feels as if the translation is being branded onto my brain.

"Be honored, for I have chosen you."

My brows shoot up. Who the hell says things like that?

"I have not spoken to underlings in nearly two rebirth cycles. I have created and destroyed many worlds in my time away from this one. And, as far as I can see, no other god has improved this place in my absence."

Underlings?

"My name is Order, and I have returned to this world to deal with my son. He spoils the fine work accomplished by the Others and I tire of the talk."

'What's it got to do with me?' I want to say, but my tongue is a brick in my mouth.

"And how does the matter concern us, Lady Order?" another green lady asks, sounding like a teacher's pet. Her eyes glisten as she looks at the monster goddess.

"I need to leave this temple. However, my true form outside of this place would obliterate you all. My son's true form is the same. Our essence can be implanted into bodies and objects. I am afraid my son has spread himself rather thin in doing so, and he

has infected much. He must be destroyed."

I blink. Destroyed? She wants to kill her own kid? My insides are trembling knots.

"Is he evil?" Evan's voice is calm and I'm able to tear my eyes off Order to look at him. He's got his hands under his chin, and his eyes are clear and curious.

"Evil is a concept created by underlings, but I will agree that my son is not what he was when I left him. His influence has led to much war and death."

Order's black eyes fix on Evan and the knots inside me get tighter. She's watching him like a lion about to grab a zebra by the neck.

"You would have us blame your son's influence for the Sector Wars we're fighting now?" Evan asks. "You're claiming our enemies are possessed...by your son, a god?"

Order gives that hideous smile again. "You may blame me as well for abandoning him here. Allow me to correct my error."

"By letting you possess us?" one of the warriors, the woman, asks, her voice strident and carrying. "That is what you are asking, because you cannot physically leave here. If you are a god, why do you even need to ask? Why not just take us?"

Order does not look away from Evan. I don't feel good. This whole thing is wrong. I don't know what the hell is going on, but Devon and I need to get out. All of these people need to get out. A scent wafts under my nose, peppermint over rotting vegetables.

Alarm bells scream in my head and fear clogs my arteries. The smell of oranges is gone, has probably been gone for a while. This has never happened before. Did I

wake up? No, because I'm still here...but....

THIS

"I am not the god who created you, so I must explain myself and ask permission."

IS NOT

"But even so, a mere touch of my essence would burn your tissue. You are poor vessels."

A DREAM

"I offer, instead, tokens infused with my essence and gifts of power. So that you can complete the task I have honored you with."

I try to get up. I can't. I try to scream. I can't. I try to look at Devon. I can't do anything but sit and stare at the center of the table where Order's smiling and look-ing more and more like a big cat ready for dinner. She's gonna eat us whole.

"Honored us?" The lady warrior sounds angry. Her stern face is set in a scowl. "You've honored us with cleaning up after your child? We are already engaged in the Sector Wars. The victory my brothers and I shall declare will be for our own allegiance. I, for one, care not for religion, but on Zare the only god we pray to is Krevai, and you are not him. I do not trust that you have our best interests in mind, Lady Order, and I will not turn our battles into a holy war for you."

I wait to feel Order's hot power strike at the lady warrior. I wait to see blood dribbling from her nose and ears, but nothing happens. Instead, Order makes a sound. God! I can't even cover my ears, because the sound's in my head. It's knives on glass. Order's laughing.

Then she stops. **"I can give you what you most desire, Majesty Yarhin—power to defeat all your ene-**

mies and to prove a queen can be more powerful than a king."

The lady warrior, Majesty Yarhin, frowns, sitting back and looking thoughtful.

"And you, fair Maidens—the green ladies raise their chins with a bit more interest—I can give you the power to maintain your society as it is."

Evan's voice seems loud. "And what would you give us?"

Order takes a moment to turn to him. Her black hole eyes seem to savor him.

"To you, Corin Peredil, I would give the gift of Magic."

Child of Magic.

But why did she call Evan Corin? Why am I Jain and Devon Padain? The guy who looks like Lawrie, who is he? Who are these people? Where am I? Sweat trickles into my eyes and cold fingers touch my knuckles. Devon.

/Devon, can you hear me?/

Hot power burns my ears and makes blood pulse at my temples.

Order steps off the table and my chair glides across the floor, shooting backward into the wall. My teeth clip my tongue and I taste blood. I pant and struggle to turn my head. Everyone's chair has been thrown back from the table. Order touches the table with both hands and the stone shatters, heavy granite hitting the floor with quaking thuds.

The debris shudders...and changes.

I'm on my feet, something drawing me forward. I feel Devon's warmth at my side. Everyone but us leans over the broken table. I stand beside Lawrence-poser and

look down. On the ground lay weapons: a humongous sword, a smaller sword, and a dagger set made of the shiniest metal I've ever seen. The warriors each kneel down and take the weapons, no questions asked; their faces blank.

An assortment of thick silver bracelets lay in front of the gowned ladies. I'm no jewelry appraiser, but I don't think that's the kind of silver they sell in the mall. It looks solid and heavy. Each lady takes a bracelet and the metal bands slither onto their wrists, coiling like nesting vipers.

I blink at the ground. Nothing's left but broken rock. But Evan/Corin squats down, hand stretching toward one of the fragments and the rock begins to glow, ragged edges crumbling away as it becomes a palm-sized emerald—the emerald in the pool.

Lawrence-poser is next, reaching for a stone. It hums as it glimmers, facets turning white diamond clear and refracting light. I see Devon's fingers creeping toward a rock, and it shivers before glittering red. I can't keep my hand from shooting out to grab the last rock. It's cool and smooth in my palm. The weight is perfect; my fingers curl around it and I want to bring it to my chest.

It's mine, a part of me, something I need and want.

I gaze down at the blue gemstone in my fist and tickling warmth spreads through my palm into my fingertips, up my arm and vibrates throughout my body. It's in my blood now. Power stirs deep inside, speaking to me: *This is what I can give you. This is what you want.*

Order is looking at us. **"Will you accept my gifts?"**

Longing and need are so strong in me it hurts. I think I'm bleeding inside. There's a knife in my gut that

only stops turning when I look at the sapphire.

The stone resonates, making me shiver. It knows my name, it knows who I am. I can't be without this gift.

"Yes," I croak. "Yes!" And the pain stops.

Other voices fill the room. "Yes!"

"By taking my gifts you will be able to sense Kahine's presence. You will discover new abilities. You are now my eyes, ears—"

And mind. She now has your mind. You must listen to me, says an unknown voice.

I can move on my own. I swing around, looking for the person talking to me. Everyone in the room is staring at Order, but there's someone else here. Lips touch my ear, and I turn again. Evan/Corin is beside me—a different Evan/Corin. He's taller, older.

Do not let her keep your mind. When the time comes, you must think for yourself.

/When the time comes for what? Wait, did I agree to something?/ My mind reels. Order asked a question and I answered, but what did I say? What did she really ask? I just wanted the pain to go away.

The world spins.

You've agreed to finish a war. I don't have the power to show you what really happened. Wake up. Save your brother. The Stone of Magic will keep him alive, but not forever.

/I don't understand! Who are you?/

I am Corin Peredil. You were Jain Peredil. The others were Padain and Aman. Together, we were the first Four of Rema. And now, you and your brothers will be the last Four.

/What...?/

I'll call again.

The cool pad of his index finger touches my forehead and the twang of citrus assaults me, before I slam into a wall of blackness. My body flips head over feet. Everything's out of control.

Then I eat carpet with a weight on my back and something that feels a lot like an elbow poking into my spleen.

8

DEVON

I SIT ON TOP OF Lyle's desk leafing through one of his medium-sized sketchbooks, while he digs around in a hall closet just outside the door. The drawings are amazing: landscapes and people. A twinge of jealousy makes me grit my teeth. I can't even draw stick people and my twin's an artist, though he won't admit it.

I set the sketchbook aside and look up as Lyle enters the room, holding a brown, leather photo album. He drops it on the desk beside my thigh and dust mushrooms from it. The leather yawns as Lyle flips the cover open to reveal an old family portrait that I haven't seen since—hell, I don't know. I just know I've seen it.

It was never on a wall or in a frame. I think Mom didn't like looking at it. Six people are in the picture. Lyle and me, we look about four, dressed in jeans and polo shirts and sitting flat on our butts with mean looks on our faces. I can't really tell who's who. Damn, we used to be identical. There's Mom, with long hair, looking like Barbie's bitchy twin sister. Lawrie's in her lap.

His hair's a messy mop of curls and he's grinning like he did something. Next to Mom is a man Lawrie's gonna look like in a few years: dark bronze skin, loose curly hair, green eyes.

I trace his image with my index finger. I don't really remember his voice, but I get flashes of smiles and being tossed into the air and riding on high shoulders. I wonder if he was/is strong like me, or if he's smart like Lawrie, or both.

"Ly, do you—"

"No doubt about it, it was him." Lyle's voice is soft.

I stop focusing on Derrick Ladreth's face and take in the blond kid sitting on his knee. My big brother, Evan Timothy Ladreth, smiles like an angel but he'd been a mean little shit. I remember broken toys and dirt in my peanut butter.

My mind shifts to the memory of a teenager with blond hair in a braid to his waist wearing a Renaissance Fair get-up. The quadruple-breasted nightmare goddess had called him Cor-in. Corin, Padain, Jain...and I don't know what Lawrence had been called.

"So, you think Evan's on some planet where they dress up like Robin Hood and—" I stop as Lyle frowns at me. Something else is on his mind. I see it in his eyes.

"I've always known it, you know? That our real dad was a Visitor. I mean, how else does a guy just disappear like that? And how Mom acts sometimes...?" Lyle runs a hand through his hair as he rambles. "But wow. This..." he waves his hand at the photo album.

My chest feels tight. "Lyle, I don't want to—"

"I need you to listen to me," Lyle says, closing the photo album. "I don't want you to interrupt or say you

don't want to talk about it, because you don't get that
option. Not after what just happened."

I'm trying to be calm. But that freaky dream had
been so real that if I'd stabbed myself in it, I bet I'd have
woken up bleeding. I shut my eyes, feeling the ghost of
that ruby in my hand. A deep pang in my gut throbs. I bet
the gem's worth millions, but I wouldn't sell it for anything. I'm not one for jewelry. I don't do rings or chains,
and I only wear a watch when I run, but if I had that ruby
right now, I'd keep it on me somewhere. It was mine.

It *is* mine.

I shake my head, pressing my hand to my aching
forehead. What's happening to me?

Lyle shoves me over a few inches then sits beside
me on the desk. His hand jerks, like he wants to put it
on my shoulder, but he pulls back. I want to tell him it's
fine. I won't bite him. But it's been years since we were
easy with each other like that.

"Last night, during the party, when Lawrie was in
the pool, he saw that emerald from the dream, and he
saw Evan drowning."

Images swirl in front of me: glowing water, a
body, an emerald—the same one Goddess Multi-tits had
made—along with the ruby I'd held. Panic works me
over, my palms are wet.

"The hell? That was Evan in the pool? He looked
dead!"

Lyle blinks at me, his eyes distant, giving me the
mind-reading look. Rage floods me.

"Get out of my head!" I shout.

"You got the message," Lyle whispers. "He called
all of us—you, Lawrie and me."

I push off of the desk, needing to put space between Lyle and me, needing to...ugh! I backhand the desk chair and watch it shatter under my open hand, fragments splintering and flying in crazy directions.

Lyle yelps and the wood spiraling toward him pauses in mid-air as he stares at me. "What the hell, Devon?"

I can't get a good breath. Lost control again. I back away as he jumps off the desk. The slivers of wood in the air fall to the ground as he advances on me.

"Get away from me," I say. That's two times in less than twenty-four hours that I've gone Hulk. And what the freak is up with wood stopping in mid-air?

"I know you work out, I know you bench press a lot, but that chair practically exploded when you hit it. And your hand..." Lyle trails off.

I stop moving back and raise my right hand to peer at it. The skin's ripped and I can see the meat underneath it. Blood dribbles down my wrist, but I don't feel it. We both watch as the skin begins to knit. In a few hours, there won't even be a scar. If the injury had happened on the football field, I'd wear a bandage for weeks just for show. I've done it a few times.

Lyle laughs, it's a dry sound. He shakes his head and tilts it back toward the ceiling. "You're a real bastard."

My stomach churns as horror sets in. No one's supposed to know.

"You treat me like I have some kinda disease," Lyle says. "'Don't be weird around me. You should be normal, like me.'"

Lyle and me have the same voice, but our personalities make the timbre different. No one ever gets us

mixed up that way, except when we're mocking each other.

"You." Lyle stops to chuckle. "Get ready; I'm gonna use a big word. You are a hypocrite. Let me spell that for you, d-o-u-c-h-e."

"Keep it to yourself, okay! Nobody else has to—"

"Screw you." Lyle grabs the photo album and storms out of the room.

"Come back here!" I growl and start to chase after him, but stop myself.

Breathe.

I can handle this; I just need to think of everything as: problem, solution. Problem: drowning brother, solution: talk to Lyle. Problem: I'm out of control. Solution: ....

One problem at a time.

I leave Lyle's room, sneakers crunching over the broken wood littering the carpet. From downstairs, I hear a door alarm chirp. It doesn't take me long to reach the stairs or the living room. Through the open patio doors, I see Lyle walking across the backyard. Lawrie squats by the side of the pool with Nikki's Big Wheel in front of him.

Idiot.

I get to the deck just as Lyle reaches a sopping wet Lawrie. Lyle shoves the family album in Lawrie's face.

"Gah!" Lawrie turns and sits on his knees, glaring up at Lyle. "I don't want this thing!" Lyle snatches it back and opens it to the family portrait.

"I told you we knew his face!" Lyle points at Evan in the picture and Lawrie squints.

"Dude, I never saw his face! You said I did." Law-

rie sniffles and wipes his nose with his palm.

I move to stand beside Lyle as he sighs and tells Lawrie about the freaky experience we'd just shared. Lawrie's eyes widen and cross at certain places in the story, but he doesn't interrupt Lyle. Instead, he sits, looking thoughtful, and is quiet for a moment after Lyle finishes. I frown at him, wondering if he's buying any of it. I know I wouldn't if I hadn't been there. It sounds like a pipe dream.

"Okay," Lawrie drawls. "So, our big brother needs us to get the message to somebody who can actually help him." He nods to himself, thoughtful look still intact. "And you really seem to believe it." He nods again, chewing his lower lip and looking at his knees, probably thinking hard. When he looks up, he smiles. "All right, I'll go with you on this. I mean, last night was crazy, right? So, the explanation's gotta be crazier, and I don't have anything better. Geez...Evan, huh? Should have guessed that one." His laugh sounds kinda forced. "This just gets better and better."

He ruffles his curls and his expression turns analytical. "You sure that glowing rock-thing actually wants him to live? You would think it'd find someone a lot closer to him to call for help."

And that's that. I marvel at how easily my little brother can just throw himself into a pit of crazy without asking too many questions.

"I think we might be the only ones it can call," Lyle says. He closes the family album. "Come on, Lawrie. You're the brain. What can we do?"

Lawrie runs his fingers through his hair, pulling wet curls off his face and holding them out of his eyes.

"Galeo," he says suddenly. "My friend's supposed to be calling me back with some information about..." he trails off. "Well, anyway, I'll call him instead. His dad's an important guy. Maybe he can help."

"Ga-lay-oh?" I sound it out. What kinda name is that? It sounds like, "You have a Visitor friend?" How the hell did he get a Visitor friend?

"Yeah," Lawrie says, sounding off-hand as he stands up. "Well, this thing's a lost cause." He kicks the Big Wheel back into the pool and smirks at the splash. Then he strolls toward the patio doors whistling Spiderman's theme song.

Wish I could be like that.

Lyle follows Lawrie and I grunt, trailing them into the house.

Lawrie runs up the stairs and leads us to his lair, jiggling and dripping as he pulls keys from the back pocket of his swim trunks.

"You're getting water everywhere," I snap.

"I'll wipe it up later." Lawrie unlocks the door, letting us in.

Lights on the floor come to life and something moos from the ceiling.

"Did something die in here?" I ask, pulling my shirt up over my nose as the stink of the room hits me.

Lyle goes to a window and pulls the blinds while Lawrie heads for his computer.

"Endymion, call Galeo."

"Yes, Master," a British dude says in a deep voice. I spin around, looking for where it came from.

A large LCD monitor flickers on and a picture of a purple guy wearing Mickey Mouse ears dances on the

screen. He's friggin' purple.

A message box pops up: BRB

"Damn," Lawrie says and falls backward into a big saucer chair that shudders under him. "Endymion, call Galeo's cell phone."

A phone number with a long distance area code zips across the screen. Darth Vader's theme blasts from the computer's six speakers.

"Hello, you have reached...."

"Endymion, end call," Lawrie says. "Uh, Endymion, send text message to Galeo's cell phone. Message: Call back right now. End message."

Lawrie's loud sneeze makes me jump.

"Warn somebody next time," I say and toss a towel lying on top of a sawed open radio at him.

"Mmhm." A few juicy honks make me frown at him.

"You sick?" I ask.

"Mmph." He throws the towel back at me.

I jump out of the way, letting the snot rag hit the floor. "You nasty little freak!"

Lyle moves to stand next to Lawrie's chair. "What do you tell your friend about us?" he asks, and Lawrie hesitates a beat too long.

Fear and anger make me faster than usual. I'm across the room and gripping the wooden rim of Lawrie's chair in less than a second. I tower over him, snarling. "You talk about us to strangers?"

He wouldn't. He's not that crazy.

Lawrie sighs, looking up at me through tangled bangs. He doesn't seem guilty, scared or even worried. "Gale's running a search on Derrick Ladreth, trying to

find him for me. He's got access I don't. I also told him about the message. He wants to help."

"And what does he get out of it?" I ask. "Who all else have you been talking to about us before this?" I shake the chair and Lawrie rocks to the left, almost falling.

"Look, relax!" Lawrie snaps. "You were fine with me coming up here to call Galeo about your crack dream. What does it matter if he already knows some stuff beforehand?"

"Get off him!" Lyle shoves me, and I let go of the chair and push him back. As my attention shifts to Lawrie again, there's a hard crash. Adrenaline races through my body; I look over. Lyle's staggering away from a Lyle-sized dent in the wall, looking blitzed.

"Oh no." My voice is so low I barely hear it.

I don't move, but Lawrie does. He flies off his saucer chair and stops in front of Lyle.

"Ly, you all right, man?" Lawrie asks.

Lyle's rubbing the back of his head and wincing. Lawrie takes his elbow, pulling him closer.

"Holy shiggity! Your head's bleeding!"

My teeth chatter hard and my fingertips tingle. The sun shines through opened blinds, and a dusty ray of light makes the patch of blood in Lyle's brown hair gleam like my ruby.

"Oh God." I feel sick.

"What the hell is wrong with you?" Lawrie glares at me.

"Shut up." Kolache and chocolate milk race each other up my throat. I can't look at Lyle. I don't want to see him looking at me.

"I'm outta here," before I throw up and make the room smell worse than it already does.

"No way! You just put a friggin' dent in my wall! How did you—"

"Just let him go," Lyle says, sounding rough. "We don't need him."

I put my eyes on the door to avoid Lyle's gaze, but I doubt it matters. Lyle's probably not even looking at me. He's good at shutting people down, his girlfriends, kids at school. He puts on this total asshole front, and I swear it makes girls fall all over him. Makes me wonder why I waste my time being nice.

I head for the door.

The opening riffs of *Thriller* boom from Lawrie's computer speakers.

"About time, man," Lawrie's saying, as I leave the room. "Give me a sec, though. Got some blood to deal with."

I shut the door and glance at my hand. The pink scar from the chair is still there. What is it with me and chairs lately? At least the one I broke last night on the balcony is fixable. One problem at a time. Problem: broken chair. Solution: fix it.

I can handle this one.

CHAPTER 9

LYLE

I SIT IN LAWRIE'S CRUSTY old chair with my head in my hands as he talks to his friend Galeo. The cut on the back of my scalp burns from the peroxide and Liquid Band-Aid Lawrie rubbed into it a few minutes earlier. I want to be pissed at Devon, but the look on his face when he'd left kinda scared me. I'm just glad he didn't put his curtain back up, so I can sense he's not doing something emo to himself.

Shuffling footsteps come toward me. "I want you to meet my brother," Lawrie says, over his shoulder. "He's got some more information about that message for you."

I sigh and raise my head, looking toward the web-cam pointed in my direction. On the large monitor, a Visitor peers at me. The end of an electric toothbrush perches between his lips as he brushes his teeth with his mouth shut.

"This is Galeo. Galeo, this is my brother, Lyle. He's the psychic one." Lawrie whirls around and lets out an

epic sneeze. "Ow…shizz! I'll be back, you two make nice."

Lawrie has his hand over his nose and mouth as he jogs out of the room.

Am I supposed to talk now? I'm not too big on starting conversations, especially with strangers, and I've never talked to a Visitor before. Doubt it's much different from talking to a human, but I don't know.

"Hi." I would nod my head, but it hurts.

Galeo pulls the electric toothbrush out of his mouth and swallows. "It is a pleasure to meet you. You and Lawrence do look somewhat alike. Do you also enjoy jumping off roofs and skiing on asphalt?"

"No." And from the look on Galeo's face, I probably didn't have to answer that question. It's odd how he looks so normal, despite being purple with purple eyes and wearing a 'Burn Smurf Village' T-shirt. His facial features are human.

"So," Galeo says, "what other information can you share about your message? And do you have anything that might help me better locate your father? So far, I have not been able to find records on any Visitor registered under the alias of Derrick Ladreth."

Derrick Ladreth. I close my eyes and picture the smiling man in the family portrait. I just don't remember him, and Evan is even blurrier. I don't have many clear memories of anything that happened before I was five.

"Well, for one, I know our father's real last name, I think. It's Lauduethe. He's got my brother, Evan, with him. Evan's the one who sent the message. I don't know if he actually uses the name Evan, though."

"Lauduethe? Evan Lauduethe?" The strange note in

the Visitor's voice makes me open my eyes.

"You know him?" I ask.

Galeo blinks at me. "No, not exactly, but I know of him. Who does not? Evan Lauduethe has one of the most known faces in Greater Allegiance Space." Galeo scoots closer to his webcam; his head becomes a blimp on screen. "Are you certain the name is Lauduethe?"

My stomach flutters. My brother's popular? Well, he's not ugly, so I guess I can see it. "Who is he, I mean, for him to be so renown?" Maybe he's a star soldier. But he's only eighteen; he can't have been a soldier long enough to be famous for it.

Galeo moves back from the camera and sits down in a black, rolling chair. "Evan Lauduethe is the leader of Rema."

"Leader of what?" I ask.

"Ah...." Galeo clicks his teeth and his eyes dart to one side before focusing on the camera again. "You probably would not have ever heard of Rema. It is a planet in a Sector very far from this one."

"Sector is your term for galaxy, right?" I never pay much attention to space-talk. It doesn't interest me, but Galeo said Rema is a planet. My brother is the leader of a planet. How did that happen?

Galeo frowns. "No, think of Sectors as imaginary dividing lines, like the ones that define your countries within continents. Sometimes, the lines are neat and a Sector is completely comprised of a single galaxy, but some are larger than that and some are smaller."

Huh. Wouldn't have figured that, but there are a lot of things I wouldn't have guessed today. "So, Evan is... in charge...of this faraway planet?"

And just what does our father do, if Evan's the leader? If he's even alive. My stomach's being put through the wringer. I don't know Derrick Lauduethe, or whatever his real name might be, so I don't think I'd feel like I would if Mom or Dad died, but it wouldn't make me happy.

"Not so much," Galeo says, sounding thoughtful. "Leaders of Rema are like...hmm...the Queen of England. They're ceremonial when it comes to politics. Rema is run by a council whose members have been serving since Original Creation. Well, perhaps they are not that ancient. The leaders are expected to head the military in battle, but they never choose their battles."

Why would anyone willingly choose a fight? "Well, Evan's in combat now, and he's down and he needs help. How do I get a message to the Silver Allegiance? That's who he said to contact, but if you know someone else who can help..." I trail off at the incredulous look on Galeo's face.

"Contact the Silver Allegiance? You cannot just contact the Silver Allegiance. That's like saying 'call the United Nations'."

"He tried to give me his emergency code, but we got distracted and then—"

"His emergency code?" Galeo's voice is high. He clears his throat. "But he did not, correct? If you had gotten that code, then perhaps...."

Fear. Dammit, I screwed up.

"Did you at least get his location?" Galeo asks.

"Yeah, he's on a planet called Onkurus. He's an hour's walk from the last battlefield, in a cave," I say. I got that much.

"Onkurus? A battle on Onkurus?" Galeo frowns, spins in his chair, and scoots off camera. I hear shuffling and a hissing cat.

I don't bother looking over my shoulder at the sound of footsteps and sniffling coming up behind me.

"You tell him much?" Lawrie stands next to me with a wad of toilet paper in his hand. "Shove over," he says, and I have no choice but to move or end up with one of Lawrie's butt cheeks on my thigh.

"Where'd he go?" Lawrie tilts his head at the screen, then at me.

"I told him our brother's name and he knew it." I frown at Lawrie. He has dark circles under his eyes. "If you're contagious, get away from me."

"You never get sick. Chill," Lawrie says and drops the wad of toilet paper on the floor.

I roll my eyes, but it's true. I don't get sick—no colds, no chicken pox, nothing. Neither does Devon.

"What are you doing, Gale?" Lawrie peers at the computer monitor. Galeo's still gone, but there's some serious rustling going on off-screen.

A minute passes before Galeo reappears. He's holding something that looks a lot like an iPad and his frickin' eyes glow like a cat's. He touches the screen of his iPad-thing and then turns it to face us. A 3D image of my oldest brother in a dirty tan uniform, shaking hands with a tall lady, projects from the screen.

"Is this is who you saw?" Galeo asks.

I nod. "His hair's longer than that now, but that's him."

Galeo hums. "Well." He sets the tablet down and scratches his nose. "Tell me what happened to you

again."

"Why? You know enough." I don't think I've ever been this frustrated.

Galeo huffs. "So I can figure out what it really means. What you say is impossible. Onkurus is a neutral planet. It is located in a Cold Zone, a border between Silver Allegiance annexes and Nazflit Coalition territory. It is illegal to war there."

I blink. None of that makes sense to me. "Why does it have to mean anything different than what I saw and heard? There was no symbolism. Everything I saw was a recollection, my brother's memory..." and someone else's. Maybe Corin Peredil's.

Galeo stares at me. Even Lawrie is quiet. I glance over at Lawrie. He's staring off into space, his aura buzzing.

"Because," Galeo says slowly, "if your brother is truly on Onkurus and was in a battle, then he was committing war crimes. Due to his elevated position, his punishment will be severe."

My blood runs cold. "His punishment? But he's...."

"Punishments for war crimes committed by leaders are usually highly publicized executions," Galeo says, his eyes practically neon. "So, you must understand my hesitation. If I bring this to my father's attention, and he chooses to believe me and give a report, your brother might be rescued only to be court-martialed."

I grip my knees. "But he's a kid. It's obvious he was acting under someone else's orders. He can't get in trouble for that!"

Galeo sighs. "Leaders may not make any true decisions about going to war, but leaders will take blame for

anything that goes awry."

"That's shullbit," Lawrie says. His left knee jiggles as his aura continues to buzz. "Why would anyone sign up to deal with that kinda crap?" Buzz-uz-uz-uz.... "How are leaders chosen on Rema? I bet it's not an election process. Is it an inherited job, is our dad somebody special?"

Galeo strokes his chin. "Devrik Lauduethe is an ambassador, like my father. Or rather, Devrik *was* an ambassador. He is known for being a bit of a ladies' man and is rumored to have caused some trouble on his last assignment..." a smile cuts Galeo's features "...which would have been more than twenty Earth years ago!"

I look between Galeo and Lawrie, both of them are grinning like nut jobs. "What?" I ask. Galeo said something funny? I don't get it.

"Ly." Lawrie slings an arm over my shoulder. "It's the big question we, well maybe just me, want an answer to: Who is Derrick Ladreth and what happened?"

"Oh." It doesn't sum up the mix of emotions inside me, but it's all I got.

"Devrik's last assignment as a Remasian ambassador is documented as being in this Sector before he went on unofficial leave," Galeo says. "The official planet specified is Amphora—Venus, but there is no evidence that he remained on Venus for the duration of his sojourn. These files simply tell me that he did not leave this vicinity for several years. Your birthdays fall within that time frame. Then, Devrik lost his title for reasons unrecorded, and he was recalled. He returned to Rema with a Marked Child."

Lawrie blows his nose on his wad of toilet paper. In

a thick voice, he asks, "What's a Marked Child?"

Galeo gazes at me. "In the message you received, did you notice any markings on Leader Lauduethe's skin?"

"A tattoo." As I say it, an image of the tribal tattoo starting at the base of Evan's skull and trailing down into his shirt collar wavers behind my eyes. If I had paper, I'd draw it.

"Rema selects its leaders based on an antiquated practice that dates back to the Prophetic Cycles."

"Prophetic Cycles?" Lawrie asks.

"The period when everyone believed in gods and prophecies." Galeo waves a dismissive hand. "Only a few places still worship gods and such now. Rema has no real religion, but the people do still follow one Prophetic ritual, the Rite of Leadership. Every ten to twenty Remasian revolutions, a child of Remasian descent is born with a brand on its back, straight up and down the spine."

My fingers are like screwdrivers in my kneecaps.

"There is only one at any given time, and that child is usually born close to when the current leader is near the end of his or her prime," Galeo says. "It is Old Magic."

My head spins as I see myself at a stone table surrounded by cosplayers and a monster goddess giving out gifts. I'm light-headed; my fingers and knees ache.

"Ly, hey, breathe." Hands shake me.

Lawrie's voice is smooth, calming and real; something I can latch onto. I suck in two deep breaths and let my head fall back on the cushion of Lawrie's nasty chair. The ceiling is covered with stars, the constellations ar-

ranged perfectly one moment before they seem to shift, creating different patterns.

"He's spazzing out," Lawrie says. "Maybe we need to—"

I unclench one hand and reach out to swat Lawrie's arms. "I'm fine."

"You look like crap," Lawrie says. "You need water?"

Water? If I swallow anything, I'll puke. "Does the story of that Rite of Leadership have anything to do with a goddess named Order?"

"Yes." Galeo's voice is uneasy. "But how do you know about that?"

The cold tip of an imaginary knife taps the skin of my left shoulder, before plunging deep inside. I gasp and clutch my shoulder, my fingers searching for breaks in the bone, but nothing's there. My arm is fine.

"Shizz, Lyle!" Grains of salty fear flake from Lawrie. "What's the matter?"

"Nothing." I lean forward, rubbing my shoulder. "Evan has a shoulder wound that looked like someone punched a hole straight through it."

Lawrie makes a hissing noise, hand brushing his own shoulder.

"You sense Leader Lauduethe's pain?" Galeo asks.

I nod, wishing I couldn't feel it. "In Evan's dream— well, in his head," my shoulder throbs in time with my pulse, "there's an emerald. Evan thinks it's keeping him alive." My shoulder screams and I clench my teeth, holding back a sympathy yelp.

"Are you—" Lawrie starts, but I shake my head.

Galeo is silent.

"Then the scene changed." I'm still hesitant to re-count what happened, but hell, it's too late now. "Every-one called me and my brother Devon Jain and Padain. Evan was Corin and Lawrie was—"

"Aman?" Galeo asks. "The Peredil brothers. The Four of Rema."

The Four. "So, they were real people." I don't think I ever doubted their existence. It's just occurring to me that I should have, but I know—I just do—that I'd spo-ken to a real person last night.

Galeo rocks in his chair. "They were great leaders, until they went mad."

"They went crazy?" Corin hadn't seemed crazy.

"They had more power than they had any right to and they claimed to have received gifts from the God-dess Order, gemstones that amplified their natural abili-ties. Aman was an elemental who could move mountains with a glance. Padain could shatter bones with a pinch."

I stare at the dent in the wall Devon made.

"Jain was a psychic rivaled by none." Galeo's eyes gleam. "There seem to be some interesting parallels be-tween you and the Four. Corin was a magic-user who could do the unthinkable, and Leader Lauduethe's magi-cal prowess is unnerving."

'Child of Magic' echoes through my head.

"Padain and Jain were twins." Galeo smirks in Lawrie's direction. "And if I believed any of this...." He gives a strangled laugh, the kind of giggle that says: I'm trying not to freak out. "If I did, I would say the walking enigma named Lawrence Ladreth has been solved."

My brother's head snaps toward the computer screen.

"What are you talking about?" Lawrie asks.

"Well, elementals take a long time to mature, and they have certain distinct personality traits."

"Like?" Lawrie frowns.

"The inability to sit still, for one. They are constantly charged by the world around them. If that energy is not properly exercised, they may engage in destructive behavior, such as consuming large garbage bags full of pop-rocks and washing them down with a gallon of Mountain Dew to see if they will explode."

Lawrie holds up a hand. "Hey, I'm still intact."

"Precisely."

Lawrie fidgets; his nerve endings are sizzling firecrackers. His head's gonna start spinning on his neck soon. The phantom in my shoulder aches, but the throbbing weakens with each beat.

"The other people in the story: the ladies and the warriors?" I ask.

"They are still around. The Maidens are old as Creation and could be the same ones from the story, actually. None but their own people have seen them in cycles. Monarchs of Zare come from dynasties. There have been many."

"But in the story, there were three of them in charge at the same time. Are there three now?" I let my shoulder go. The pain's gone.

"No," Galeo says, then bites his lip. "Well, not officially, but the youngest prince comes of age soon. There are always three thrones, a precedent set by the Champions of Order."

"It sounds like a lot of governments are based on a mythology you don't believe in," I say.

"Your country's foundation is built upon a god not all of your people believe in," Galeo says, his voice soft and without bite.

Every time I close my eyes, Corin Peredil's grave face is behind my lids. "Let's pretend you believe the mythology is real, and that I was contacted by—" Oh God, this is gonna sound stupid— "Corin Peredil. I saw him and his brothers picking up gemstones, and one of them looked a lot like the one Evan found."

And the others are out there somewhere. A sharp pang of want grips me. My gemstone is waiting for me.

My gemstone? Great, now I sound like something out of 'The Lord of the Rings.'

Galeo tucks his arms behind his head and leans back in his chair. "Okay, so I am pretending I believe in Order myths." His tone is light, but his face is undecided. "So, that would mean Order's Burden is real."

"What's that?" Lawrie asks.

Galeo sighs and sits up. "Order's Burden was a method by which primitive people rationalized evil. They blamed it all on Order's Son, in Common Tongue he is called Pandemonium. He possesses people and makes them commit horrendous crimes. He causes war, intolerance, and basically everything we do not want to take credit for. We all want to say—"

"The devil made me do it," I finish.

Galeo nods. "Planets within the Nazflit Coalition and Su Allegiance are in direct conflict with planets in the Silver and Gold Allegiances, and are often identified as evil. I am sure the feelings are mutual. Anyway— aside from primitive planets, such as Earth, and planets in established Cold Zones—Nazflit, Su, Silver and Gold

reign over this dimension."

"This dimension?" Lawrie's elbow grazes my side.

"There are other worlds, Lawrie," Galeo says, sounding patient, as if dealing with my brother is second nature to him. "Nazflit, Su, Silver and Gold are the Big Four, and so far, everything is balanced. However, Order's Burden claims that the planets within Nazflit and Su are tainted by Pandemonium and must be destroyed or conquered in the name of Order. And, of course, the planets from which Order's Champions hail are all within the Silver and Gold Allegiances. You can see why planets like Rema and Zare are very willing to follow Rites dating back to Order. Order's Burden gives them great importance."

"So, the Burden basically sets off a war of the worlds," Lawrie says.

"It would be the end of virtual peace," Galeo agrees. "We would fall back into war time practices with limitations on freedoms and rights to travel between planets and Sectors. It would mean the end of embassies. We would go back to the days of conquering. Earth would be taken into an allegiance willingly or by force."

Lawrie frowns. "And to keep it from happening? I mean, maybe we're the only ones who know about the Stone. We don't have to say anything—"

I grip Lawrie's thin shoulders. "We were contacted because our brother needs help."

"And Gale can just tell his dad Evan's hurt, and his dad will do what he can to get a message to somebody who can help Evan out. That's that. Leave out the weird stuff," Lawrie says, his tone self-assured, but I hear his big brain whirring and clicking.

He takes a shuddering breath in the silence that follows his stupid comment. "It won't work that way, will it?"

"No," Galeo says. "To explain this to my father, I will have to reveal your identities and why you believe this distress call was able to reach you from so far away. If he believes Leader Lauduethe did indeed send you a psychic missive for help, and that he is on Onkurus, violating Silver Allegiance law, the only thing that will save your brother is proof of Order's Burden. His crimes may be excused if justified by divine guidance."

"But it wasn't—"

"That is how the Remasian Council will portray it. It would be his only defense aside from the Council itself taking responsibility for the crime, which it will not. If Leader Lauduethe is found innocent, Order's Burden will be reinstated as religion instead of myth, and the Silver and Gold Allegiances will bring all of its pieces together to start a war with Su and Nazflit."

"All of its pieces?" I swallow hard.

"The Maidens, the Zare monarchs, and the Four of Rema. The Rite of Leadership on Rema is supposed to be Order's Mandate. Her magic chooses the planet's leaders until it is time for Her Four to return." Galeo's eyes turn a dull, dead purple.

"Corin said we're the Four now," I say.

So, that's what he'd meant. I'd volunteered myself to finish a war; a war started hundreds of years ago, by touching a rock.

One I don't even have.

10
LAWRENCE

"SO, WHAT DO YOU WANT me to do?" Galeo asks, and I stare at him.

Duh. We gotta get my brother out of that pond. Evan, my brother. Last time I saw him was over the rim of a sippy cup. I don't even know how I feel about him, not really. Don't know him to miss him, but still he's my brother. That means something.

"Can you talk to your dad for us?" Lyle's voice is rough and his eyes are hollow.

Fizzy anxiety prickles under my skin.

Galeo hesitates. "Yes."

I sigh in relief. Had I really thought Galeo would say 'no?'

"Thank you," Lyle says. "Uh, do we owe you anything?"

"I do not think I am the one who is going to need anything extra once I tell him," Galeo says. "Lawrie raised a valid point earlier. Perhaps you are the only ones who have received the messages. If no one else knows

about this situation, then perhaps we can just let it go."

A tidal wave of locusts rolls in my guts. I almost double over. What is this feeling? When I said maybe no one else had gotten the distress calls, I was getting at the fact that we could change it up to leave out the prophecy garbage, not that we could ignore it.

"No way, man!" I jump up and snatch a shirt off the floor to wipe my nose with. "We're not leaving our brother to die."

Galeo looks tense. "I am scared, Lawrence. I wish you had someone else who could help you." He looks down.

He's scared? The tidal wave's still rolling. Am I scared too?

"I'm sorry, Gale. I really am. But you're the only first step we have. You gotta do this man. I think I'm..." scared. "Please?"

I feel Lyle's eyes on me.

Galeo clears his throat and lifts his head. I don't know what to make of the look on his face. It's sad and lost.

"I have not known you for even a fraction of the time I have known my other friends," he says, "and I would not do this for any of them. What is it about you that makes me want to do something that could change everything I know?"

Galeo sounds resigned. He's gonna do it, but I'm still trying to wrap my head around what this is gonna mean for him. He's not saving his brother, he's saving mine and, in doing so, things might go to hell for him, for me, for the planet...planets. Shizz. I saw the message, I believe Lyle, but that prophetic stuff about

war and gods? My bull-o-meter is sensitive. It should be screaming right now, but it's not.

I swallow hard and blow my nose in the shirt. My ears pop. I close my eyes for a split second and then open them. Galeo's eyes are incandescent again.

"My father should be awake by now. I will contact you when I have more information." His hand stretches toward the screen, covering the camera's view. The connection breaks.

"Call has ended," Endymion says.

"Thanks man," I murmur, even though Galeo can't hear me anymore. It's just Lyle and me, and he's being real quiet. I shoot a look at him and find him watching me. I can't read his expression, which doesn't mean much. Lyle's good at controlling his face.

"So, that's your friend Galeo," Lyle says after a moment. "You never talk about him."

I shrug. "Sure I do." I just never mention him by name or say he's a Visitor. Everyone thinks he's just another Skype buddy of mine. I should tell people he's a good friend.

Lyle nods and goes back to being quiet. I don't know how he can go so completely still. It'd drive me crazy.

After a minute of nothing, my brother clears his throat. "Think we should call Mom?" he asks, looking at his hands.

Mom? In my mind, I hear squealing brakes and then see a truck smash into a brick wall. Calling her is not a good idea at all. Mom is unstoppable, a Terminator-1000, the liquid metal one you can't kill. If she gets involved, well, that'd be it for us. She'd take over and

we'd probably never hear another thing about Evan or Derrick or Rema.

My heart pounds and blood roars in my ears. Would it be so bad for her to take over? The confusing feelings that come with what's going on now will go away. It won't be my problem anymore. But with those feelings comes something wild and exciting. Maybe I don't want it, maybe I do, and not knowing is insane.

"No, Ly! We can't tell Mom, not yet!" I pace around Old Faithful. "We should learn more; see what Gale can do for us. Then we can, you know, maybe, tell her."

"She's gonna find out," Lyle says. "If Galeo's father believes me, and starts something, this thing is probably gonna blow up. She'll be pissed if she finds out about this from someone else." He squeezes the bridge of his nose between his thumb and forefinger. "She might even know something or have something we can use."

True. If Derrick left a way to contact him, she'd probably have it. But the fact that she hasn't contacted him—hell, maybe she has and isn't telling—means she wants to leave us out of it.

"She should know about Evan," Lyle says. "It's wrong not to tell her. She'd want to know."

Lyle. I get him and I don't. For the most part, he's a voice of reason, but his conscience is fifty-fifty. When he watches the news and sees horrible stuff, he asks, 'Wonder if they deserved it?' I'm thrown for a loop trying to link that detached brother to this one.

I touch his shoulder. "I still say we wait."

After a moment, he sighs and gets out of my chair. His eyes are shuttered and his face is cool. "I'm leaving. I gotta get out of here or my head's gonna blow. Uh...."

He looks at me, floundering.

"I'll call you if, you know, anything happens," I say.

"Thanks." He leaves the room, shutting the door behind him.

I need a shower. I trudge out of my lair, triple-locking it, and go to my room. Clothes are everywhere, on the floor, on the furniture. My old ripstiks and skateboards are nailed to the walls. BMX and Motocross posters are wallpaper with black Sharpie squiggles over them—I like to write thoughts and ideas down and I don't always have paper.

I enter the small bathroom attached to my room and turn on the shower, letting the water get hot. I stare at my sorry reflections in the mirrors over the sink and on the medicine cabinet beside it. I look like holy hell. Steam fogs the glass and I strip down and jump in the shower. Hot water and steam make it easier to breathe through my nose.

I step back on the shower plug, flipping the switch that closes the drain. Water collects around my feet after a minute and I frown. Lyle said the pool Evan's in is shallow enough to stand in, maybe as deep as a standard-size bathtub. I shudder, thinking about blacking out in the pool last night. That was only for like a second or so. What's it like for Evan? Does he feel himself drowning? I don't know what I'd do if I was in a situation where I couldn't save myself. Waiting to die. I turn the water off.

Stepping out of the shower, cold air hits me and makes me sneeze. Sniffling, I shoot another look at myself in the mirrors and frown. Inching closer, I rub my palms over both surfaces to smear away the fog. I twist to get a good look at the back of my neck. I run my hand

along the ridges and push my hair out of the way.

Black dots, like little moles, make a straight line from the nape of my neck up into my hair line. It doesn't make a design; the dots aren't connected. It's a rash, but the skin in the affected area isn't raised and doesn't itch.

This wasn't here yesterday. I pull the towel off my waist and use it to rub at the black spots. Huh. They don't come off; no smudges on the towel. What is it? It's not the weirdest thing in the world, but still.

A muffled ringtone sounds from the depths of the laundry pile on my bed and I trudge out of the bathroom. Tossing jeans and a bag of pretzels off the comforter, I find my phone laying on top of a *Popular Mechanics* magazine, and pick it up. Two missed calls from Jeremy Givens.

He's probably checking up on me. The guy's been my best friend since we were eight. Says he'll be the best man at my funeral. I hit the Miss Piggy icon I chose for Jeremy and roll my eyes at his lame ring-back tone.

"Dude, what the hell?" Jeremy picks up after a minute of Get Lucky. "Where you been? I called you twice."

"Shower." Don't know if that's good enough. I didn't check the time stamp on his other call, just the last one. "S'up?" I grab some clothes off the floor and struggle into them.

"Just making sure you weren't dead, man. I kinda thought you were last night." His voice is gravelly.

Another chill runs through me and I shudder. "Uh... sorry?" Am I really apologizing for not drowning?

"Yeah, whatever," Jeremy says.

I hear a pinging sound from some game in the background. "I'm bored. You wanna hang out?"

I glance at the digital clock on my nightstand: 10:53 AM.

Is it right to think about having fun with so much hanging over me? I'll go to Hell or something for even considering it, right? But Dev's doing his emo-thing, Lyle's going out, so why should I stick around the house? I got Skype on my phone. Galeo can reach me anywhere. Energy courses through me, my arms and legs tingle, and 'gotta do something' overrides guilt.

"Yeah, I'm all for hanging out. Whatcha' wanna do?" I put the phone on speaker as I dig a pair of socks out from under my bed.

"Boardwalk? Janelle Rodriguez and her friends are goin'. Saw the tweet a minute ago," Jeremy says, sounding smooth. The guy has the biggest crush on Janelle.

"Yeah, yeah, that's cool. I'm driving or you?" I hop on one foot as I get on my sneakers.

"I'm driving. I wanna live to talk to Janelle," Jeremy says. "Hurry up. I'm only waiting like ten minutes before I leave."

"That hurts, man."

I tuck the phone in my pocket and grab my wallet, keys and a random rubber band off a doorknob. I make a low ponytail, and let it flop onto my neck. Hopefully, it'll keep that black patch of skin covered so no one will think I have pox or something.

I jog through the den. A stream of cussing drifts across the room from the open door to the balcony. Devon's out there, crouched by a patio chair. He's got a glue gun in his hand and an expression better suited for a Rottweiler on his face.

Yeah, don't think I'll bother him with a 'be back

later.'

I slide down the banister to the first floor and stop off in the kitchen to grab a can of Mountain Dew before going out the back door and locking it after me. The backyard doesn't look like it's seen a party in years. Devon and Lyle cleaned it up so good last night, *CSI* wouldn't find a clue. The pool shimmers a bright blue, but somewhere under that sheen is a message.

I frown and walk closer to the pool, but stop at the blare of a car's horn and metalcore music.

"Douche bag, that was not ten minutes," I mutter.

I jump the waist-high wooden fence separating the backyard from the driveway and head to the curb where Jeremy waits in his silver RAV4. I get in the passenger side. After plunking my Mountain Dew in a cup holder, I punch his shoulder. "Yo."

Jeremy shifts the car into drive. "You look like shit."

I don't know how he can see that. He's got his Jay-Z thing going on, wearing big, dark sunglasses that cover half his face.

"You okay, man?" he asks.

"Yeah," I say. "So, Janelle, huh? What friends is she with? Reagan?"

Reagan's hot. Never talked to her before, and never is a concept I like to conquer.

"Yeah."

Jeremy speeds up once we hit the highway. I slump back in the seat and stare out the window at trees and fenced in pastures full of cows. Wonder what streets are like on Rema. Do they even have streets?

My phone buzzes in my pocket. It's only a text, but

my hand shakes when I dig the phone out. Staring at the face, I see the text is from Mom, not Galeo.

If you're not awake already, get up.
♥ Mom

Hah.

"Who's that?" Jeremy asks.

"My mom."

"Oh?" He sounds interested. A smile creeps onto his face. "She find out about last night?"

"Nah," I say, frowning. "Why?"

"Your hands are shaking."

Well, damn. I set the phone on my knee and make fists on my thighs. I hate this situation and love it at the same time. I don't know what's gonna happen next and waiting makes me wanna—

I toss my head back and howl, not caring about Jeremy being there.

"Just drive man," I say. "You're gonna hook up with Janelle today."

"You got issues," he says after a beat.

"Like you wouldn't believe," I mutter. My cell phone bounces in my lap and I force my eyes off it and look out the window again. Wonder what color the sky is on Rema.

11

DEVON

I GLARE AT THE LOUNGE chair from last night. Me and hot glue are good friends, but even friends let each other down. The arms I broke off and glued back on sit crooked, one wrong touch and they'll fall off. I'll probably be better off buying some new chairs and hoping Mom won't notice the difference.

Sweat trickles into my eyes. It's not noon yet, and it's already sweltering. I hear tapping on the sliding door and I look over.

Lyle leans in the doorway, fingers on the glass. "I'm leaving. You okay here?"

Am I okay? "I threw you into a wall." I look at my hands. "Are you okay?" He doesn't look dizzy, and the blood's all gone. Maybe I didn't hurt him so bad. But I still hurt him.

"Yeah," Lyle says, then shrugs. "A headache, but it'll go away."

Silence. Well, silence from us. Cars whizz down the street, dogs bark, and the brats playing in the pool next

door shriek. I know Lyle's staring at me, waiting. What the hell? What's he want? Does he think I'm gonna spill my guts to him or something, like I owe him?

I glance at the lopsided chair again. "I need to buy new chairs."

"You broke this one?" Lyle asks. "Like you broke the chair in my room?"

I take a deep breath and crack the knuckles on my right hand.

"How long, Dev? When did you find out you had a...a power? Was it that summer, before high school, when you told me you didn't want anything to do with my weirdness?" Lyle sounds calm, careful. The wood creaks beneath him as he steps onto the balcony.

I crack the knuckles on my left hand. "Maybe a few weeks before that." What does it matter now, if he knows when it happened?

"Why didn't you just tell me about it?"

I see him in my peripheral vision. He leans against the balcony railing, not looking at me. "I don't get it," he presses. "Why condemn me and keep this to yourself? Is being different really that bad?"

I snort. "Ever watch the news?"

"Ever see me on the news?" Lyle asks. "Telling me and telling the world is different. What did you think would happen? You think I would want to start some kinda vulatto movement because we have powers?"

"No," I snap. Lyle start a movement? Lyle doing anything to willingly involve himself with a group of people? "That's not it."

"Then what?" he asks.

I feel like I'm under attack. With all the messed

up shit going on, why are people focusing on me? "It doesn't matter," I say. "Wh-what did Lawrie's friend say about, well, you know?"

Lyle sighs. "Nothing good, but we won't know much else until he calls back."

My stomach twists. "What do you mean nothing good? He can do something about Evan, right?"

Lyle shrugs. "I don't want to talk about it. Gabby's waiting for me to pick her up." He pushes off the railing and out of my line of sight.

"Gabby? Volleyball Gabby?" Wait, a memory hits me: Cheerleader Heather, leaving the house after I ended the party, giving Lyle the stink-eye. "Um, Heather dump you?"

Lyle chuckles. "I dumped her."

"And now you're with Gabby? Dude, were you already with Gabby?" I turn around to stare at him. He's got his asshole front up again, and looking at him now, I'm not sure if it's a facade anymore.

Lyle rolls his eyes at me. "No, I'm not a cheater."

"Then why..." all the girls? All the time. There's nothing wrong with dating a lot, but Lyle's something else. The guys on my teams would beat him up if he wasn't my brother. I don't get it, though. With his psychic stuff, shouldn't being with so many people bother him?

"It doesn't matter." Lyle mimics my voice.

I growl. "Stop it."

"Fine. Later." Wood creaks, his steps going farther away from me.

My stomach keeps twisting with either guilt or fear. I don't know which one, but I don't like it. "Wait." The

footsteps keep moving. "Ly, come on!"

I spin around to see him halfway through the door. "Look, I didn't tell you because I wanted to pretend it wasn't happening. I couldn't do that with you knowing everything all the time."

There. I said it. I was, am, a wussy.

"And that made it okay to treat me like shit?" Lyle asks, leaning in the doorframe, face void of expression. He does that a lot, makes himself a statue. It's kinda creepy.

"I never treated you like shit!" I didn't and I don't. "I just told you I didn't want to hear about your psi-junk. If you stopped talking about it, and stopped doing that stuff, and got on teams, and made friends, and tried, then—"

Lyle blows a raspberry. "Later." He walks away.

I failed today, utterly and completely. Failed with Monica, failed with Lyle, failed with— "Hey!" I chase Lyle into the den and grab his arm to stop him.

"What?" He snatches his arm back. His eyes are fiery, but the rest of his face is cold.

"You can't just leave! I need to know what Lawrie's friend is doing for, you know." I mumble the last part because of the look he's giving me. It's like he's watching something pathetic. Anger sizzles under my skin.

"Well, if you hadn't stomped out like a chick on the rag, maybe you'd know more," Lyle says, words clipped.

"Frickin' A!" I fold my arms over my torso and grip my biceps tight to keep from myself from shaking the hell out of Lyle. "What can I do to apologize, I mean. I... there's too much to deal with, man."

This morning, I could deny I was a Visitor's kid.

I could say: I'm not sure where my real dad's from. I have freaky strength, but maybe I got mutated by the hormones in whole milk. And yeah, I'd know all that was bull, but it'd still be a possibility.

Now it's not, and on top of that, "I haven't thought about Evan in a long time, Ly. I wonder about our real dad, a lot, especially when I think about what I can do. But Evan, almost never, and now I have to, even though there's probably nothing I can do for him. Did you ever think about him much before this?"

The fire in Lyle's eyes dies and his shoulders slump. "Not really. It's not like I totally forgot about him or anything, I just...he's not here. And for that short time I was with him, I didn't get a chance to feel him out."

That's right. The first part of Lyle's dream had just been him and Evan. "And he didn't say anything about himself? You don't think he recognized you at all?"

Lyle shrugs. "He was more worried about figuring out what was going on and getting the hell out of there. Who knows how long it's been for him, right? I mean, we're assuming he got hurt last night when we all felt it, but maybe it happened before that. Maybe we're getting delayed messages. I don't know. And as for him knowing who I was, I don't think he did. He didn't...."

"What?" I ask.

Lyle looks thoughtful.

"Nothing," he says after a beat, then smirks. "Are we having a heart-to-heart sisterly moment? You wanna hug?"

"Don't be a jerk," I growl as his smirk widens. Something I don't like glitters in his eyes. My brother isn't supposed to give me that look. That's an expression

reserved for strangers you want to go away.

"Just being me, Dev. But you wouldn't know that," Lyle says.

If there is a Jesus or a God, please stop me from ripping my brother's head off. "Let it go!" I shout. Desperation tastes like laundry detergent, the powder kind that leaves grit behind. I don't know what my face looks like but it must be pretty damn funny, because Lyle laughs at me.

"Your voice gets so high," he says, still laughing.

"Shut the hell up!" And this time I hear it too. Dammit.

Lyle wipes his eyes. "Oh God." He sniffles and shakes his head, before meeting my eyes again. He seems lighter, friendlier. "You're really serious, aren't you? You really think you're a loser." He chuckles.

"Asshole." I glare at him as he shrugs and starts down the stairs.

Do I let it end like this? It doesn't feel right. We're all scattering. I saw Lawrie leave a little while ago, and now Lyle's taking off. We should stick together to ride this out.

"I'll call you if Lawrie hears from his friend," Lyle says over his shoulder.

It's something, but not enough.

"What kind of news are we waiting for?" I ask. "Rescue news?"

"Don't know, honestly." Lyle pauses midway on the steps. "So much is going on, my head's spinning." He comes back up and sits on the top step. His back's to me, but he's closer.

"Okay." I keep my voice calm, wanting him to go

on.

Lyle puts his hands on his knees and leans his head forward. I frown at a strange mole pattern starting at the top of his neck. The hell? Lyle's never had moles. I cross the chasm between us and plop down next to him to ogle his neck.

His head whips around and he jerks away from me, eyes wide.

"What the—" he starts.

"There's something on your neck." I palm his head and push it down so I can get a better look. His arms flail, one smacks me good on the side of the face.

A trail of tiny black dots leads from base of Lyle's hairline down into his T-shirt collar. I touch it and it doesn't smear. The skin feels flat, smooth. I let him up, and he shoves me in the chest, glaring.

"There're spots on your neck, man," I say.

Lyle scowls at me and rubs his neck. "I don't feel anything."

"They aren't bumps. It's like someone got a Sharpie and drew on you," I say.

Lyle blinks a few times and gets up. He doesn't look back at me, doesn't gesture, but I follow him anyway. He goes into a guest bathroom and stands in front of the mirror, trying to look at the back of his neck.

I snort.

"Turn around, let me see yours," Lyle says. He watches me in the mirror.

"Let you see my what?"

"Your neck, dumbass!" Lyle reaches out and grabs me, whirling me around. I grunt, but don't fight him. He rubs the nape of my neck, hard. "What the hell is this

crap?"

"It's on me?" I can't help but try to gawk at my neck in the mirror too.

Lyle looks like he's swallowed something nasty. I frown. "Dude, are you okay?"

"No," he says. He scrubs his face with his hands. "It's not like his," he mutters.

"Not like whose?" I ask, kneading the skin at the nape of my neck.

"Evan's! He's got this tattoo-looking mark on his neck that goes all the way down his back."

"And you're bringing that up because you—we—have spots on necks?" I'm lost.

"Yes!" Lyle pulls his hands off his face and pushes past me out of the bathroom. I go after him.

"So...?"

"So what?" Lyle snaps.

"Where are you goin'?" I feel like I'm chasing him as he stalks toward the staircase.

"You know, ginseng is great for memory problems. I'm picking up Gabby." He doesn't stop or look back at me as he takes the stairs.

I follow as far as the top step, before letting him go. When the alarm chirps and the back door slams, I know I'm alone.

I go back out onto the balcony. The lounge chair mocks me. One good kick sends a lopsided arm flying over the railing. I don't look to see where it went, but I don't hear it land, so it must have ended up in the grass somewhere. To make both sides match, I snatch the other arm off the chair and throw it. Hope it doesn't hit anyone, or break a window, 'cause that bad boy's gone. It

hurtles fast and far until it disappears.

News at 11: flaming projectile from space proves to be a severed arm from a fancy balcony chair purchased at...hell. I don't even know where the furniture came from, and don't care. I'll grab some look-alike chairs from wherever. I just want out of the house, like everyone else.

I tug my cell phone out of my back pocket and snap a couple of pics of the unbroken lounge chair. Maybe I should take a page from Lyle and call a girl to go with me. Keelie might want to. She still seemed to like me when she'd left last night. I breathe out, thinking about Monica. Would she go if I swung by in my truck and asked her to come with me after her shift ends?

I see her disappointed eyes and hear the tone in her voice when she'd said, 'You're not ready.'

I'm not ready, don't want to be ready, but I get the feeling it's not gonna be my choice to make. The back of my neck tingles and a shudder runs through me. I don't think anything's gonna be my choice for much longer.

My cell phone vibrates and I glance at the screen.

Message from Keelie.

Well, here's a choice I'll make.

I text her back.

Wanna go 4 a ride?

12
LAWRENCE

THE BOARDWALK RIDES SUCK. THERE should be laws against roller coasters that can't hit seventy-five miles per hour. Jumping off the roof's a lot more fun.

"You look so bored," Janelle purrs. She's trying to glue herself to me. Every step I take, she's right there. She's pressed herself against me in every line we've stood in, rode next to me on the rides, and even tried to get me to eat half her ice cream cone from Marble Slab. She's real cute and all, but Jeremy likes her.

I throw a glance over at Jeremy. It's afternoon and the sun's pretty high in the sky. Everyone's sweating, but Jeremy's a walking icicle. The Boardwalk has its own signature scent of salty ocean, waffle cones and cake, but over it all is the stink of Jeremy being pissed.

I give Janelle a grimace and walk closer to Reagan and Monique who are steady texting, each other, I bet. Legs for days, Ballerina Reagan, shoots me a wary look and Killer Lips Monique keeps her eyes on her phone.

Damn. I don't like Janelle because Jeremy likes her,

and Reagan and Monique probably aren't gonna talk to me because Janelle very possibly told them: Hands off, he's mine!

I pick up the pace, outstripping the girls and Jeremy. The Boardwalk is crowded. Cobblestone-paved walkways between the shops and restaurants are covered with families pushing strollers and chasing after brats. Sprinklers erupt from the ground in the center of the two-story, outdoor shopping plaza and kids in bathing suits scream and splash in the recycled water. I head for the Midway Games plaza, passing by booths and games like tossing ping-pong balls in milk bottles.

"Lawrie! Can you win me something?" Janelle jogs up and tries to link her arm through mine. I keep my arms close to my sides, but this girl tugs with all her mini-might 'til she gets her little arm through the crack she makes.

Okay. Enough is enough. "Janelle, look...."

"...cheated, ya alien freak! I'm not giving you shit!"

I halt in my tracks and turn. A crowd gathers around a strength testing game. I squint to see a stringy little guy with spiky green hair and jaundice, holding a large mallet over a wide peg connected to a tall strength-o-meter. The bell at the top of the meter rings and flashes: Hum-Dinger! Stringy Guy's strong, but the guy in the muscle-tee running the booth looks pissed.

"I played by the rules," Stringy Guy yells. His voice is surprisingly deep. "Hit the peg, win a prize." He lets the mallet clatter onto the mat. "Give me the prize."

"The rules aren't written for aliens!" Muscle Tee shouts. "Get lost!"

"I'm not an alien! I was born in Atlanta!"

"Yeah, but where were your parents born, huh?" Muscle Tee throws right back. "This game is for humans. You can't cheat with your alien powers."

"I don't have alien powers. I just look like this, okay? Now, come on. Give me the prize, so I can give it to my girlfriend and go home!"

"Yeah, that sounds good! Go home!" somebody from the crowd shouts.

I push through the crowd, ignoring people cussing at me for stepping on their feet. I need to be in front, right where it's happening. My heart's pounding, adrenaline's pumping. I 'gotta do something' right now or I'll bust. Maybe it's because Stringy's so little and skinny, or maybe it's because Muscle Tee's discriminating. I couldn't do anything for that YouTube kid, probably can't do anything for my bro, but Stringy's right here, right now.

"Lawrie!" A tight grip clamps around my elbow and I'm yanked backward until I crash into Jeremy and rebound. "What are you doing?" Jeremy grunts.

"Don't know," I mutter, snatching my arm back.

I have to jump up and down to see. The crowd pushes forward and the people in front of me get taller. I barely make out Stringy and Muscle Tee now that so many people are between us.

"I said get lost!" Muscle Tee yells. I don't hear a reply from Stringy, but I see the top of his head. It looks like he's moving away.

"Give him the prize, jackass! He won it!" A man's voice yells from somewhere in the crowd.

"Vulattie-lover!" Someone else yells.

So many people talk and yell at once, it makes my

head swim—or maybe that's just my sinuses. My head is full of helium; I feel myself floating forward. I shove people, guys, girls, I don't care. I want to get to the front.

Jeremy's following real close behind me, shouting. "Lawrie! Are you crazy? Lawrie!"

Smack!—the first sound of a fist slamming into flesh. Grunts, screams and insults fly as the crowd turns into an angry mosh pit. People with kids grab their rugrats and run. Bodies crash into me, making me stumble. I'm wading in an ocean of arms, legs and sharp elbows, not getting anywhere. Shizz. I could really use an alien power right now. If Lyle were here, he could do something. Hell, Dev could probably kick everyone's ass.

Screw this. A roar builds inside me, starting from my gut and rumbling in my chest. "Aarrrgh!" I lower my head, stick out an arm, and charge forward, football style. I knock a few more people out of my way, before I slam into somebody a lot bigger than me and stagger a few steps backward. The bigger guy grabs me and throws me into the person behind me. That person shoves me forward and I swing at the guy who threw me in the first place.

"Get outta here, kid!" A tall man, probably college-aged, wearing a Houston Texans jersey snarls at me. A big dude rams into college-aged man from behind and gets a fist in the mouth.

Someone grabs me under the arms and starts dragging and I use both elbows to catch them in the chest.

"Dammit, Lawrie! Let's go!" Jeremy again. He's like a bloodhound.

"You go!" I push him off and fight my way through the crowd. People are on the ground getting trampled,

and I see Stringy. He's down and getting stomped on by Muscle Tee and two other guys. There's a girl standing on the counter of the strength booth, screaming and crying as she watches.

"Aaaaaargh!" I throw myself on Muscle Tee.

He's a lot bigger than me, but I manage to knock him off balance and we both go down, me on top, punching his head. Rage sets me on fire. I see YouTube Guy and my brother down and out with no one to help them and I can't stand it. I hate it.

"You little freak!" Muscle Tee shoves me off with one hand and I fall on my back and roll out of the way of his stomping sneakers, jumping to my feet.

A guy throws a swing at me and I dodge, but end up catching a hit from someone else. Pain erupts from the right side of my jaw, but it doesn't stop me. 'Gotta do something' pulsates at maximum speed, and the balloon in my chest from last night comes back, but this one is filled with baking soda and vinegar. It shudders as it stretches. My head's pounding, my heart's jack-hammering. It's hard to breathe.

I fall on my knees. I know the ground's hard, but it feels soft, inviting, like plopping down on Old Faithful. I shake like a diabetic on a sugar crash. The sensation of a billion fire ants on Red Bull races under my skin. I wanna rip it off.

"Whassamatter, kid? Thought you could kick my ass?" A foot digs into the middle of my spine. I catch myself on my hands, and heat from the ground shoots through my palms like an atomic pulse, filling me to bursting point. White noise rises to a fever pitch and blocks all other sound as the shakes turn into slow, stom-

ach-churning spasms. One-one thousand, shudder, two-one thousand, shake, three-one thousand.... The balloon explodes, and the vinegar, baking soda, Red Bull ants, and white lightning that tastes and feels like 'gotta do something' on crack gush into the ground.

The cobblestone beneath my hands splits fault-line style, the ragged fissure spreading as the ground quakes.

I hear Muscle Tee shout, "Whoaa! Earthquake?!"

Over the sounds of people fighting and crying, there are shouts of surprise and "What the hell?"

Police bullhorns fill the air. I don't know what they're saying. I don't know what anyone's saying anymore. I only see mouths moving. Muscle Tee and the guys with him run away. People scatter as rent-a-cops in black T-shirts flood the area.

I need to get out of here, but my body deflates. The earth calms as I lie down. The ground's cool and better than any bed I've ever slept on. The Boardwalk is nothing but a wade pool of shapes and colors drifting around me. A rectangle splashes toward me. Is it talking? I don't know.

Where's Stringy Guy?

Did I help him?

The pool turns black.

And I feel nothing.

13
LAWRENCE

"...HELL, REGGIE, IF HE DID all that, we shoulda left him. He's dangerous!" squawks a woman's voice. "We don't need any of that being associated with us!"

"Dammit, Laney, it already is! Bet those fools back there think I did it!" a deep voice says. It sounds like Stringy.

"And now we done kidnapped this kid!" the woman continues to screech. "We need to dump 'im off somewhere. He's got a phone on him. And look at this! Rich boy's got 'uh wallet full 'uh cash. We should charge him for the ride."

Both voices lower to grumbles as I keep still. Awareness creeps back in, feeding me sensory input piece by piece. Sound: the purr of a car engine, soft country music, tires on a rough road. Smell: watermelon bubblegum, old leather, and sand. Touch: my arms rub against cracked leather, a band's across my chest cutting into my neck, probably a seatbelt.

I count the seconds between breaths.

"Kid, you awake?" the woman asks.

Something isn't right. My head throbs and flashes of the Boardwalk fight flicker behind my eyes: Jeremy pulling me back, shouting; Muscle Tee standing over me, laughing; pressure cooking inside me; my insides exploding; the ground cracking.

My eyes snap open and I jerk forward, spitting up hot, salty copper. Blood dribbles onto my ripped jeans, and I pant, fixating on the tiny red spatters on my thighs.

"Holy—Reg, this kid's puking blood!"

"We're almost there!"

My head thuds against the window as the car veers to the right. I look up from the blood, staring at the pale, skinny lady sharing the backseat with me the lady who'd been on the counter screaming when Stringy was getting beat up. She's got a ring in her lip and a stud in her right nostril.

Her words sound angry, but her face is full of fear. She's afraid of me?

"H-hi," I try words. I sound like a chain smoker. "Where are we going?"

Exhaustion rolls in and grays out the woman's complexion for a second before I see in full color again. My body's hot and cold. Shivering sets in. The woman brings her bare knees to her chest. She's not wearing a seatbelt or shoes, and she's got funky feet with second toes longer than her big toes.

God, I hate feet.

"What are ya?" she asks, voice low.

I blink.

She scoots away from me, pushing herself against the opposite door. "You a Visitor, mixed, what?"

"Laney, leave the kid alone!" Stringy snaps.

"Reggie," Laney whines, but stops, glaring at me instead.

I turn my head forward, staring at the back of the driver's seat and the spiky blond hair poking above it. "Reggie," I try. "You get that prize?"

Laughter rolls from Stringy Reggie. "Naw, but it was a cheap piece of shit anyway."

The corners of my mouth ache as they stretch into a grin. "Sucks, man."

"Yeah." A beat goes by. "Hey, what you did back there—those guys were gettin' crazy. So, thanks. Uh, I don't know if you were there with somebody or not, but the rent-a-cops was cuffin' everybody and the real cops came, so I just...."

Took me with you? I can go with that.

"We're just goin' to my place, offa' forty-five and Telephone," Reggie continues.

Not too far from home.

"Your phone's been going off. You can call whoever it is to come get you, if you don't wanna hang around and rest or something. I think you used all your earth juice, man."

Earth juice?

"When I felt that blaze comin' outta you, I almost pissed myself. What's somebody like you doin' here?" Reggie asks. The car makes another sharp turn, and I bring myself to look through the windows.

Roach motels, Mexican meat markets, uneven streets and sidewalks; mismatched wood fences partially hide brick one-stories with jungles for lawns. The car slows and makes another turn, going down a residential

block lined with similar homes. We pull into the driveway of a brown house with burglar bars on the windows. The rusty garage door screeches open and the car crawls into the junky space.

My eyes slide closed when the car cuts off and doors open. Mildew-scented air hits me from all angles as the door on my side opens. My fingers fumble with the seatbelt buckle. Metal clicks under my thumbs, and I rest against the seat, totally spent.

"You with me, kid?" Reggie asks; his pizza breath makes me gag. I double over, horking up blood and chocolate chip Eggo Waffles. It's hard to breathe between heaves.

"Shit." A hand pats my back. My muscles turn to liquid and I slump sideways.

"Whoa!" Hands steady me. "Hold on, man. I gotcha."

I'm flying. My feet aren't on the ground, and I'm moving fast. My body tingles, nerves sizzling. Something soft's under me now.

"Eew, Reg! Don't put him on the couch! He'll get puke all over my blanket! Quentin's gonna catch a case!" Laney shouts.

"He'll be outta here before Quent gets back. He just needs to rest up. Can you...?"

"Nah, Reg, this is your problem. I didn't even wanna go to the Boardwalk in the first place, and I ain't tell you to bring that!"

"Fine!"

Doors slam.

Hands roll me onto my side. "If you need to puke again, there's a bucket. Hey, man, you with me?" Reg

asks.

Am I with him? Don't know. Something's wrong. Something's broken.

"Hey, don't pass out! Dude, don't pass...."

FUZZY FACES HOVER OVER ME. It's like a scene from an alien abduction movie. Hope it's not at the dissection part. I mean, I don't care if they cut me open, but I kinda wanna watch. The smell of spaghetti sauce ruins the mood when coupled with the AC/DC Iron Man theme song. I'm rolled up like a burrito in something soft and warm.

"Hey, you're awake!"

"Mmm." Best I can do. My head pounds as my stomach twists. I shut my eyes and open them again to one blurry face slowly sharpening into focus. Reggie's looking down at me, his yellowy skin and black eyes remind me of a banana.

"You passed out, man," Reggie says. "You didn't seem to be breathin' your last, so I let you sleep. But, uh, your phone rang again. You probably need to call someone and let them know you're okay."

"Mmm." My body's useless.

"Easy, kid, easy." Hands help me sit up, but as I rise, so does my stomach. I gag hard and taste blood at the back of my throat. My insides clench and cramp.

"Dammit," Reggie says. My body lowers. "Guess you ain't ready for that yet. Jesus. My roommate's gonna

be home soon, and you were supposed to be on your way outta here before that."

I gurgle and swallow, then clear my throat. "Your roomy not a friendly guy?"

Reggie breaks into a grin, showing straight white teeth, before letting out a deep laugh. "He's mean, but him and me go way back. He's got something to do tonight and some people coming over. Don't think he's gonna appreciate you here."

Right. I wouldn't appreciate somebody who barfed on my stuff either. "Kay," I croak. "I'll be gone."

Just need to figure out how to get up. I feel like a dead battery. What the hell happened?

A couple of pillows are shoved under my head and Reggie boosts me up again, slowly, until I'm halfway sitting. I'm in a den. There's a recliner and some end tables. An old LCD TV with a built-in DVD player sits on a coffee table covered with soda cans, nail polish and a box of saltines. A University of Houston Cougars flag is tacked to the wall.

"Here." The metal rim of a soda can is pushed against my mouth and I take a sip. Sprite oozes over my tongue and cuts through the salty taste of blood. The sugar hits my system like a mini-jumpstart, and the pounding in my head eases up a bit.

"Thanks."

"Yeah, don't mention it." Reggie tips the can again so I can take another sip. "You need to drink it all, man. And then you gotta eat. You're on empty. What made you go and burn yourself out like that?"

Soda sears my throat as I swallow wrong and cough.

"Careful." My burrito shell turns out to be a fluffy

blanket covered in Care Bears. Reggie uses a corner of it to wipe my face.

"You shook up the ground real good back there. The three o'clock news is saying it was an earthquake." Reggie frowns at me. "You didn't know you could do that?"

I lick Sprite off my lips.

"Whoa," Reggie murmurs, eyes widening. He doesn't have eyebrows. How funky.

"So, uh, you're half, right?" Reggie asks. "What's your kin, man? I'm part Jarq."

I hesitate before answering. "Rema, my dad's from there."

Reggie stares at me so long I squirm. What'd I say?

"Uh, didn't know Remasians came to these parts, man." He gives me another sip of soda. "Didn't think Remasians had boss powers like that either." He sits back, frowning some more.

I belch. "Course they do." My brothers are awesome.

Reggie shrugs. "Yeah, guess they do, 'cause you definitely got them, dude. That was badass, but you gotta regulate that or you'll kill yourself."

"Kill myself how?" My abdomen trembles as I struggle to sit up.

Reggie scratches his head, black eyes seeming to add me up like an equation. "Your dad ain't around, is he? You don't know shit. Damn, man. So yeah, you threw your own energy into the ground and got it to start quakin' and instead of pullin' back, you probably left yourself open, and the ground started sucking more energy outta you."

My hands shake as I recall flashes of cobblestone ground cracking under me, and feel pressure exploding out of my body and pouring into the rocks. "I friggin' owned that." I have power. I used it. It was amazing.

Reggie snorts and gives me a crooked grin. "You're a weird kid."

"Name's Lawrie." Fatigue ragdolls me and I slump back on the pillows, eyes sliding half closed as I stare at the dingy, popcorn ceiling. Sugar crash?

"Hey, what are you doin?"

Hands slap my face, but they don't stop the lights from going out.

"WHO DA HELL IS THIS?" a gruff voice with a Hispanic accent asks.

"Shh. It's fine," Reggie says. "He's like us. He saved my ass in Kemah today, and needed somewhere to crash for a minute. He won't be a problem."

"Like hell he won't. Look, Reg, the plan changed."

The voices fade.

I keep my eyes closed. Think the TV's still on; a laugh track plays. Lemon-lime scented barf greets my nostrils and I wanna barf again. This is an all-time low, sleeping in my own puke. Could be worse, could be naked.

"Dammit, Quent! You done lost it, man! I ain't gettin' involved in shit like that." Reggie sounds pissed.

"You need to, bro! This ain't gonna stop 'cause of

people joinin' Make Friends with Aliens groups. You saw that video about that Jordan guy. There's eight more like it now, goin' viral. And now the Boardwalk!"

"I ain't down with hurting people," Reggie says.

"Whatever. I don't need you with me. You should get outta here for a while and take Laney."

"Yeah," Reggie says, sounding relieved. "But you shouldn't be in this either. Your parents would—"

"My parents can kiss my ass. They get on my nerves actin' like nothin's goin' on. My dad loses his damn job for no reason and they don't think it's 'cause he's vulatto. My dad's been here all his life. But they treat him like he just jumped offa space ship!"

"Calm down, man. It's been rough. Things'll—"

"They takin' away my scholarship. Saying I don't meet some damn requirements they just made up. I got one more semester 'til I graduate and they pull this shit?"

"Quent, just let the group meet up like we usually do. We'll figure somethin' out to help."

"Just get lost, Reg." Quent sounds defeated.

The laugh track from the TV plays again.

"Fine. Let me get this guy up, and we'll go," Reggie says.

A beat, then, "Nah, leave him where he is," Quent says, voice cool.

"Huh?" Reggie sounds confused.

"You said he makes earthquakes," Quent says. "We can use him tonight."

My breathing picks up as my heart thumps against my ribcage.

"He's a kid!" Reggie's voice is hard.

"He's a vulatto with a good power. We don't got

many of those. And besides, you said he helped you. Maybe he'll wanna help me."

Two sets of footsteps come toward me, and I close my eyes.

A heavy hand lands on my shoulder and shakes hard. "Wake up."

My eyes open. Hope I look dazed and confused, because inside neurons are firing messages that read: Oh, hell yeah! I get off on Danger Kool-Aid. It's like I'm flying and it's hard to keep my mouth muscles from twitching into a smile. I hate the idea of hurting people, my stomach churns at the thought, but the adrenaline I get from knowing I gotta get myself out of this? I've died and gone to a heaven full of Mountain Dew and Lamborghinis.

"My friend Reg says you got some awesome skills, man."

I turn my head and bite back a groan as the room spins. A lanky man comes into focus. He squats in front of me. Dude's real skinny with bad acne and liquid black eyes that show no white. He's got slits for nostrils and ears that stick out like stop signs on a school bus. This guy couldn't pass for human in the dark.

"Yeah?" I croak and try to clear my throat. I choke on the dryness, coughing until I taste blood.

"Quent, he's bad off," Reggie says. He kneels next to Quent.

"He won't be once I feed him." Quent smiles at me with rounded teeth. "I know how to take care of you, if you'll take care of me later."

"Dammit, Quent!" Reggie says. He shoves Quent and then gasps as Quent grabs him in a headlock. Reggie

convulses, eyes rolling in his sockets as he goes limp.

"Sorry Reg," Quent whispers, letting Reggie slump to the ground.

My eyes are wide as I pant. The hell? Did he just....
"Did you kill him?"

"Naw," Quent says. He looks at me, mouth a straight line. "Reg is my boy, but he got no heart. He don't stand up when he should. I wanna talk to you. Find out where you are in all this."

"All what?" I ask. Reggie's body lays on the cheese colored carpet. His chest doesn't look like it's moving.

"Vulatto Movements. You know how we get treated. You seen the hate crimes. You helped Reg 'cause you didn't like what was goin' on. You make it a habit to get involved in stuff like that?"

I blink. Reggie twitches, and guilt twinges through me as some of my excitement dies because Quent isn't a murderer. I put my full attention on Quent, not liking the way his black eyes shine like unmarked eight-balls. "N-not really."

Quent sneers, his eyes rolling over me. "You a pulatto," he spits, his face twisting up like he's eating something nasty. "I hate you passing pendejos. You look human enough. Good-lookin' too." His tone drips with... envy?

"If you could, you'd pass too," I say.

Pain explodes through my temple as Quent backhands me. "Watch your mouth, brat. I ain't no chicken shit that wants to go around pretending I'm not what I am. And I wanna give you a chance to show you ain't one either."

I wanna cut my head off it hurts so bad. "How?"

My stomach rocks and I choke back a gag.

Quent sets a white, plastic bucket on my stomach. "Tonight, me and my squad are gonna do a demonstration. We gonna march to the U of H Welcome Center and bust it up. Welcome my ass...then we gonna march to the Student Union. We're gonna raise hell 'til we get dragged out. 'Til we get on the news and somebody lets us talk."

"That's the plan?" Crap. My mouth and my brain don't always get along.

Another backhand. I retch and taste bile and blood. I can't roll over. Quent grabs my shoulders and jerks me into a sitting position, forcing my head over the bucket. I cough up what's left in me.

"Yeah, that's the plan, ojete, and I want you in. You can do a lotta damage."

I spit and choke for a few minutes. My throat is raw meat. "Do I— " Spit. "Have a...." I cough, swallow and try to breathe at the same time, and the world goes black for a second. I come to with Quent holding me up. The bucket's gone.

"If you want me to take care of you, you gotta help me out," Quent says, his cheeseburger breath millimeters from my face. "You in a bad way. Reg said you didn't know what you was doin'. I can help you, but if you don't work with me, I'll throw you outta here. And you ain't gonna last on this block."

"I don't know how to use my power," I choke out.

"You'll learn," Quent growls.

"Gimme my phone. You can throw me out, and...."

"Naw. You don't get no phone. You don't get nothing. And bro, ain't nobody gonna do nothing for you out

there. You see, on this block, they gonna know you came from this house, and they gonna know what you are. They'll watch ya die, kid."

That tidal wave of locusts comes back, flooding my veins and filling my gut. Quent's black eyes gleam in the low light. This guy is crazy.

14

DEVON

FURNITURE SHOPPING IS MY NEW favorite thing. Never knew patio chairs were sexy 'til Keelie showed me her Catwoman pose on top of one. She's wearing a T-shirt dress that I can see her green bra through, and running from me as I chase her. The store is set up like a mansion full of rooms loaded with fancy spreads. I run around a kiddy bedroom with bunk beds and chairs shaped like walruses into a den room full of shells and sand dollars.

Damn. I duck behind a recliner as a sales guy storms by looking pissed. Wonder if he got complaints about Keelie and me from the handful of customers here today. His fat ass hustles out of the den, and I spring up and run into a Roman-styled living room. In a large mirror mounted on the wall between two columns, I see a flash of white and gold—Keelie's dress and sandals. A grin splits my face as excitement makes me hot. I don't move as she comes out from behind a white couch and creeps up behind me. Her reflection smiles at mine before she

leaps onto my back, wrapping her arms around my neck and her legs around my waist.

I give her a ride through a dining room full of long-horns and cowhide and into a master bedroom draped in black and silver silk. Walking to the king-sized bed, I un-hook her arms from my neck and dump her backward on the bed, then fall onto it myself. She rolls into my side, putting her head on my shoulder. Her curly hair tickles my nose, smells like Cocoa Puffs.

I roll over, letting her head slide off my shoulder, so that I'm facing her.

She smirks. "Are we playing house?"

"If you want," I say.

She pushes her lips against mine and I open my mouth to let her in. All the anger, tension and confusion from earlier today melt away as we kiss and I move my hands down Keelie's back. I laugh when her hands tuck themselves into my back pockets and squeeze.

She pulls her hands free and pushes me onto my back, straddling my thighs and grinning like she won something. "I don't know, Dev. I think you gotta prove you wanna play."

"Yeah, how?" My hands grip her hips.

"I wanna see you fly, Superman," she purrs.

I push her off and sit up. One of her long legs lies across my lap.

"Don't talk about that," I say.

She sighs. "What are you so mad about? It's all good."

"No, it's not," I grunt. Panic slams me hard. "You didn't tell anybody what happened last night, did you?"

Keelie shrugs. "We all think it's cool."

We? "Who the hell did you tell?" I clench my hands into fists to keep myself from grabbing her wrists.

"Don't worry about it," Keelie says. "Just some girls from the team. They all wanna know how good you are at making out, and I had to tell them why I didn't finish finding out."

No, no, no.

"I told you not to tell!"

"It's no big deal, Dev," Keelie says, giving me a WTF look. "It's not like you're a vader or anything. A lot of athletes do 'roids to be better. Nobody's gonna say anything." She nudges me in the ribs with an elbow, like we're sharing a secret.

What? Does she do drugs?

"It's kinda cool," she says, "knowing you're not so perfect. It's sexy, Dev. Really." Relief makes me light-headed. But is it better for her to think I'm a druggie than what I really am? Her tone implies that it is, but images of Monica, sitting in the doughnut shop, looking at me like I'm a loser, flit through my mind. She's ready to be who she is. She's proud.

Why can't I be proud?

Keelie starts kissing me again and I respond, pulse speeding up.

I could ask Keelie to be my girlfriend. We'd look great together. Probably get voted Most Popular Couple or something, but Monica's still here. She's frowning at me, disappointed.

"What's wrong?" Keelie's mouth hovers inches from mine.

"Nothing," I whisper.

She studies me a moment before pulling away from

me completely. "You're not like your brother."

I blink. "Which brother?

"Lyle. He just wants to, you know, all the time." She shrugs.

"We're not alike," I snap. Then scowl. "You dated Lyle?"

She smiles. "Not really."

"What does that—"

She presses a finger against my lips. "Oh!" She reaches into her bra and extracts my phone. How the hell did it get in there? I pat my empty back pockets, and remember her hands had been there. Thief.

"Your phone's been vibrating for the past two minutes," she says, dropping it on my chest. She flops down, lying on her back, and folding her arms over her breasts.

I unlock my screensaver and check my messages— five missed calls, all from Lawrie's friend Jeremy. A bolt of irritation shoots through me. Jeremy only calls when Lawrie's done something especially stupid. I sit up and press the button to call Jeremy back.

"Be back," I grumble and shuffle into a room with an aquarium theme.

Jeremy answers on the third ring. "I can't find Lawrie!" he blurts. "I lost him!"

"Slow down. What?" I pace around the bedroom, picking up a stuffed turtle and throwing it into a waterless fish tank full of colored pebbles.

"We went to Kemah," Jeremy says. "There was a fight, Lawrie jumped in, and all hell broke loose, man."

I feel a pinch in my finger and there's a cracking noise. I glare at the new fissure in my black phone case. Great. "The police come?"

"Yeah, man. First, it was just rent-a-cops cuffing people, but then the real cops got there. After that earthquake, it was a mess. I tried to find him."

Dumbass. If he's in jail...but then again, if Lawrie was in jail I'd know, because Mom would be blowing up my phone about it. I stop and frown. "Did you say 'earthquake'?"

"Yeah. The place was rocking like LA. Then Lawrie just disappeared. I keep calling, but he's not picking up. And he's got that stupid hack on his phone to keep your mom from tracking it, so I can't trace it either." Jeremy's a pretty chill guy, but he sounds freaked.

"Nobody can. Dammit," I say. "Thanks for calling me. You call Lyle?"

"Uh," Jeremy drawls. "Don't have his number. I, um, don't think he likes me."

"Don't take it personal. He doesn't like anybody," I say. "Don't worry. We'll find Lawrie."

"Yeah," Jeremy says, sounding a little calmer. "Call me when you do, so I can come over and kick his ass."

"It's a plan," I say and hang up. Stupid little brother. I'm not worried. Lawrie always turns up all right. I try Lyle's number next. He doesn't pick up the first or second time, but third's the charm.

"Yeah?" Lyle slurs like he's high. What the hell's up with that?

"Ly?" I ask.

"Nah, not Lyle. Wrong number." But he doesn't hang up.

I roll my eyes. "You hear from Lawrie?"

He chuckles, then drawls, "Nooooo. That all you want?"

Good God. "Are you high?"

An outright laugh. "I'm on a date. What do you want?"

Okay, Lyle's obviously out of his mind, but I still need him. "Lawrie's missing and not answering his phone."

"Want me to do anything?" Lyle asks, tone disinterested.

"Yeah. Meet me. I'm on my way home." That's where Lawrie's likely to turn up, if he's okay.

There's silence on Lyle's end.

"Lyle?"

"Yeah, I'll be there." He sighs between words and hangs up.

I stare at the phone. What was that? Did Volleyball Gabby give him something to smoke? I've heard things about some of the girls on the volleyball team. I don't want him driving if he's high. Dammit. I only have to call twice for him to answer this time.

"What?"

"Where are you?" I ask.

"Huh?" He laughs.

"If you're high, I'm coming to get you," I say with a growl.

Lyle snorts. "I'm not high, and I'm leaving in a few minutes." He disconnects.

I scowl, then dial Lawrie's number, letting it ring until it rolls to voice mail.

Dammit.

I go back to the red and gold bedroom where Keelie's sitting on the bed, yoga style, texting. "Hey," I say.

She glances up. "Something wrong?" Her eyes go

back to her phone.

"Yeah. Gotta cut this short. You want me to take you home, or drop you off somewhere?" I shrug and meet her eyes when she looks up again.

"You can take me home," she says after a second. "I don't think we were gonna go anywhere anyway."

I don't have a response to that. She's pretty and normal, but...I'm not interested in her. And she wouldn't be interested in me if she knew what I am, and maybe I'm okay with that.

In my head, Monica smiles and gives me chocolate milk.

Keelie scoots off the bed and strolls past me, still texting, and I follow.

"There was an earthquake today," Keelie says as we walk to the store's entrance. I never did find those patio chair replacements.

"Yeah, I heard." We leave the store and the sun beats down on me as I scan the parking lot for my truck.

"Weird, huh?" she murmurs. "Glad we didn't go to Kemah."

"Yeah." I spot my truck and stride toward it with Keelie at my side.

"Some vulatto guy was getting beat up by some other guys and a riot broke out," Keelie says and I cuss.

Why can't people just leave other people alone? Fear slams me. Some vulatto guy could mean Lawrie, but no one would know he was a vulatto unless he opened his big mouth.

"Somebody saw your brother leaving with the guy, the vulatto." Keelie's voice sounds guarded. "Looked like he was being carried."

"Lawrie or the guy?"

"Don't know, that's all the tweet says," Keelie says.

We reach my truck and I look at her. She wears a strange frown.

"Are we leaving because of that?" she asks.

I thump the side of my truck with a fist. "I guess. You know more than me, it seems. Whose tweets you following?"

"My friend's, but she's just re-tweeting stuff. People were taking pictures and saying the vulatties got a gang together to trash the Boardwalk with that earthquake." Her eyes narrow. "Saying Lawrie's with them."

"What?"

"They don't know Lawrie's name. Keep calling him the dark-haired kid." Keelie puts a hand on my shoulder and stares into my eyes. "Lawrie wouldn't hang with a bunch of vulatties, right?"

Autopilot kicks in. "Course not."

"Huh." She takes her hand off my shoulder and walks around to the passenger side and I don't bother to come around and open the door for her. I unlock the truck and get in, ready to get back on the road and rid of her.

My thoughts race as I pull out of the parking lot and merge onto the feeder. What the hell did you do, little brother?

Keelie plays with my radio and she continues texting, glancing at me intermittently.

I drop her off in front of her house. She holds the passenger door open for a second. "Hope your brother's okay."

I nod. "Thanks."

"See you around." She shuts the door and walks to the porch, not looking back.

That went well.

Turning off the radio, I drive home in silence, insides folding like origami as I think about Lawrie maybe being carried off by a stranger after getting in a fight. If he's not answering his phone, he either lost it, or he's unconscious somewhere. Unconscious, just unconscious, not dead.

I come home to an empty house and sit at the kitchen table, waiting and watching the wall clock. I pull out my phone and speed dial Lawrie again and again. Voice mail.

Dammit, little bro. Pick up and say you're fine. Say you're stranded. Say you've been stripped butt-naked and robbed. Hell, say anything.

An engine purrs in the driveway. I look out the kitchen window. Lyle's black Jetta inches its way to the garage. I swear if he's messing around with drugs, I'm gonna kill him.

I tap out the beat to a pop song and make it halfway through the chorus before keys rattle in the back door. Lyle enters, movements totally coordinated, but his eyes are bright, and I get up and storm over to him, grabbing him by the collar. His pupils are pinpoint.

My fist flies at his chest. An explosion of pain. My fingers crack against an invisible wall between my hand and Lyle's body.

He gives me a lazy smile. "I was ready for you that time."

I cuss and shake out my throbbing hand. Think I broke my middle finger. Broken bones suck. I gotta wait

a while for them to knit. "What the hell'd you do?"

"Stopped your fist," Lyle says. "So, tell me what's going on. I wasn't paying attention earlier. Lawrie's missing?" He sounds unconcerned, looks it too. He strolls over to the fridge and roots around.

"What did you smoke?" I ask.

"Nothing," Lyle says. He turns around, holding a Coke. "Just had a good time." That lazy grin of his is freaking me out. I've never seen him this laid back.

"Lawrie's not answering his phone." I tell Lyle what Keelie said.

Lyle tilts his head. "Hm. I called him too. Went to voice mail." He moves to the table and sits down.

"Some jerk-off's tweeting about the whole thing," I say. "Hold on, I'll follow Keelie and see if I can pick up the tweets she was getting."

Lyle sips his Coke, looking down his nose at me.

"What?" I shout. I stare at my swelling middle finger. The pain's died down, but I'm not ready to throw another punch at Lyle.

"I can find Lawrie," Lyle says.

I frown, then want to punch myself. "Your psi-junk. Think you can?"

Lyle shrugs. "I'm always clearer after...." The lazy grin comes back. "I think I have a good chance."

"Why didn't you try before?" I ask.

The grin vanishes. "I don't extend in public. I never know what might happen."

"What could happen?"

"I could lose myself and black out." He guzzles his Coke. "Even if it's just you, I don't want to be by myself, okay?"

I almost smile at that, feeling a little flattered. "Do your stuff. I'm here," I say, sitting down at the table across from him.

Lyle smirks, pupils still pinpricks. "Okay," he drawls. "Here. I. Go."

"Yah!" I yelp as Lyle's head falls forward. "Ly?"

Silence.

I reach over and take his Coke, and after a few sips, I'm a little calmer. Lyle will find Lawrie and everything will be fine. I'll thump Lawrie good and then I'll—maybe I'll surprise Monica tonight at her Stop the Hate Texas group meeting.

Lyle's head jerks back up. His pinprick pupils dilate.

"You found him? He's OK?" I jump to my feet.

Lyle blinks, his expression queasy. He swallows a few times and licks his lips like he's thirsty.

"Ly?" He's scaring me.

"I don't feel good," Lyle murmurs.

"You don't...wait, you feeling Lawrie? He's hurt?"

"I...yeah," Lyle says, and swallows again before clamping a hand over his mouth and rushing to the sink. He retches a few times, and I grimace before going to him. Yech.

I turn on the faucet to wash away—damn, is this blood? "Holy hell!" I stare at Lyle as he wipes his face with the back of his hand. He still looks sick. "Are you okay?"

"Yeah," he chokes and spits out another mouthful of blood. "I can find him."

My body starts shaking. Lawrie's hurt and Lyle's spitting up blood.

"Maybe you better stop," I say. "I'll do the Twitter thing."

"I can find him." Lyle sighs and rubs his temples. "He was sick this morning, but it was just a cold or something. This is different."

"Is he spitting up blood, like you? Did you talk to him?" My legs are Jell-O.

Lyle leans on the sink's rim. "No, couldn't talk to him. And I don't know about the blood thing. Maybe."

"He scared?" Dumb question. Lawrie's never scared.

Lyle closes his eyes, face chalky. "Can't tell." Another gag brings up a thin string of blood. "Throwing up blood seems to be a popular past time for us." He laughs, sounding punch-drunk.

"What are you talking about?" I grab Lyle by the elbow and pull him back to the table, sitting him down.

"Evan spat up blood," Lyle says. He covers his eyes with one hand and sprawls out in the chair, letting the knuckles of his free hand trail the floor. He chuckles after a minute.

What the hell? Don't freak out. "Did you take something? Do you need your stomach pumped?" Maybe that's why he's puking blood.

"Nothing," he slurs. "Just a good time, s'all. Relax."

I open my mouth, but Lyle speaks before I can. "I'll find Lawrie when he wakes up. Be ready. He's gonna need help."

Lyle's hand falls off his face; looks like he's sleeping it off.

I tap my fingers on the table and grab my phone.

I log into Twitter and search for Keelie's screen name and any hash-tags about Kemah, vulatto, fight and earth-quake.

15
LAWRENCE

SOMETHING ROUGH AND CRUSTY SCRAPES over my mouth and salty nastiness trickles in. I want to open my eyes, but can't. Don't have the energy. The salt water tingles over my tongue as it rolls toward my throat, and chokes me. I can't....

Soft fingers massage my throat above my Adam's apple, helping me swallow.

"It's okay, kiddo. Just relax." The voice is kinda deep, but it's a woman's, I think.

Voices buzz around me, loud and soft, angry and giddy. My head feels like it's in a glass bottle. Everything on the outside is distorted.

"Here's some more." The crusty thing presses against my lips again, it's kinda grainy. A towel maybe? I struggle to swallow, but the simple reflex is as complicated as doing a one-armed pull-up after doing one-hundred before it. The hand rubs my throat again.

I don't know how much time passes with me being useless and this lady doing all the work for me, but

with each swallow, things become clearer. The voices
are scattered. Some sound like they're a few feet from
me, and others sound like they're in another room. Low
rock music plays, and the TV's still going. The smell of
spaghetti mixes with the stale odor of beer, and the tang
of motor oil and lighter fluid.

My head throbs and my body's limp as a noo-
dle, but I force my eyes open. Light attacks me, and I
squeeze my lids shut, before opening them again. A girl
leans over me. She's pretty, with dark hair and eyes. She
looks worried and scared.

"Hey there," she says quietly, and presses a finger
to my lips. "Don't talk. Just—God this is gonna sound
lame—blink two times for 'yes' and three for 'no' if you
can't nod and shake your head."

Move my head? Is she serious? It took all my juice
to open my eyes. The rest of my body's a slab of wet
concrete.

"You look like somebody I know," she says. "Do
you know Devon Ladreth?"

Whoa. Okay, I can do this. I blink twice, quick as
I can.

She smiles. "Is he your brother?"

I blink twice again.

She strokes my hair. "You're...Lawrence?"

I blink twice. What's she to Dev? A girlfriend?
Confusion makes my head swim. She's here with Quent,
meaning she's probably a vulatto and part of his group.
Dev doesn't hang out with her type. Unless he doesn't
know, which is possible because he's stupid about girls.
The last two girls he dated were so hot for Lyle it was
embarrassing, and he never noticed.

"Quent's gone bat shit." She keeps petting my head. I wonder if she knows she's still doing it. She looks past me at something. "He called the group and said he wanted to get together to organize a sit-in on campus. Soon as we came through the door, his punk ass snapped pictures of all of us sitting in the kitchen. Then he dropped his crazy bomb and said we're all accomplices now. If we don't help him, he'll tell the police we were all in on it. Who's gonna believe we weren't? We're a bunch of vulatties. And hey, if some of us say 'piss off' and try to leave anyway, he's got that jerk Zeke watching the door." She sounds bitter. "My parents are gonna...."

She straightens and pulls her hand out of my hair. "What?" she snaps at someone over my head.

"You get him to drink?" Quent.

"Yeah," Devon's lady says, dark eyes glinting.

"Good." All of a sudden, Quent's ugly mug is in my face and I can't do anything about it, but blink. "You drink a few bottles of that stuff, and you'll be feelin' a lot better in no time." He pulls away and glares at Dev's lady. "One bottle for now, Monica. Understand?"

"He needs more than that. He's one of us! Why are you letting him suffer?" Monica, Dev's lady, Monica. Wait, Donut Girl?

"'Cause I need him dependent on me," Quent snarls. "Just like you are, mami. Make me mad and your picture's going up on my special FaceSpace post all about tonight."

Monica mutters under her breath, glaring daggers.

"Do your job," Quent says, "and no one will ever know you were here." He taps her under the chin with his index finger and moves off, yelling at someone else

on the other side of the room. "Yo, careful with that! You wanna burn this place down?"

How many people does Quent have in here, and how many are helping him because they actually want to? Can't some of them fight back? A memory of Reggie slumping to the carpet assaults me. Damn. Maybe they're scared of Quent.

I scan as much of the room as I can, looking for Reggie. A small group of people sit around a junk table in a corner looking sullen. A larger group laughs while passing around a bag of chips.

"How do you feel?" Monica asks, frowning at me.

I sputter and cough, before I can choke out, "Like hell." No point in lying, she'll find out the truth when I pass out again. My body burns hot, and then freezes cold; my teeth chatter.

She presses the back of her hand to my forehead. "You're burning up. Quent says it's because you used too much power at the Boardwalk. That earthquake was really you?"

"Yeah," I say, and cough hard. Pain flares in my chest. "I guess "

"So, you all have powers, you and your brothers, I mean. I know Devon does," she says, smiling a bit.

I blink at her. She knows? "Dev told you?"

"I figured it out," she says wryly. "That brother of yours is kinda careless."

"What about you?" I ask, swallowing and wincing.

She smirks. "I see auras, colors, around people. I can tell the kind of person you are." The smirk fades. "It doesn't always work out so well, but I know Dev's a good guy."

"Yeah," I rasp. "He's all right." And probably wondering where the hell I am. Bet Jeremy's called him by now. My phone. "H-hey, I had a cell phone. I think Reggie took it."

"Reg?" Monica asks. "Reg wasn't here when I got here. Not surprised. Reg isn't into civil rights. He just wants to do his thing and keep his head down."

"Quent knocked him out earlier," I say.

Monica jerks. "Quent hurt Reg?" She runs a hand through her long hair and cusses a mean streak.

Weakness fills my bones with air. "You got a phone?" I ask.

"Quent confiscated it," she growls. "He took all our phones or somebody would have called the police by now."

Why can't Quent be a complete idiot?

Monica grips my hand. "He wants to bring the Student Union down. He doesn't care who's in there. And he thinks you can do it. He's gonna keep you half-dead until he gets you on campus and then he'll give you just enough juice to knock down the building."

A sucking hole opens in my stomach at that. Quent's put a lot of faith into me being able to make another earthquake. What will he do if I can't? And hell, what will happen to me if I can? I'm half-dead now, I might end up all dead later.

"You know," Monica says, voice tight, "I tried to talk your brother into coming here with me tonight. He turned me down. I was kinda pissed at him, but now I'm glad he's not here."

Funny, I wish he was—him and Lyle.

I frown. Thinking Lyle's name makes me feel worse

than I already do, like someone's yanking on a rope attached to my brain.

Lyle.

Tug.

The rope's fraying, fragile, but it's holding, vibrating as it's stretched to its limit.

/Lawrie?/

Lyle's voice is a whisper in my ear.

"Ly." I choke on the syllable. Can't talk to him that way. He won't hear me. *Ly!*

"What's the matter, kid? You need to lie down again?" Monica asks, hand on my shoulder.

"'M'okay," I mumble. *Ly?* Where'd he go? The rope frays more and a plague of black bugs eat their way into my intestines. God, I'm scared again.

/Lawrie...where...you?/

My heart races. *Help! I'm with a crazy guy who wants me to hurt people at U of H. U of H! The Welcome Center._*

If we're cut off, at least he knows where I'll end up.

/...where...you?/

God, did he hear me?_*U of H! Gonna be at Welcome Center, soon! Call—*

The police? No, there are people here who'll get busted with Quent and go down for being in the wrong place with the wrong people. But if it stops people from getting hurt, then there's no choice.

/We...get you. Don't...scared. Don't be scared./

Maybe Devon and Lyle can handle Quent, but there's no telling who else in his cooperative group have fighting powers.

Crazy guy's got people with him who don't wanna

be here. Don't want them to get in trouble.

/...don't.../

Ly?

The rope breaks and an explosion of red ruptures behind my eyes. Monica cusses, grabs a brown dish rag and holds it over my mouth as I hack up blood.

It takes a few minutes to get my breath back. The world has a hazy, surreal quality to it. When Monica speaks, she echoes. "Kiddo? Stay with me!"

I fall slow.

"Quent, give me another bottle, now!" Monica's screaming.

If she's screaming for me, I wanna tell her: Don't be scared.

But I can't, because I'm scared shizz-less as everything goes black.

16
LYLE

"I DON'T CARE WHAT LAWRIE told you! We have to call the police." Devon paces around the kitchen table. "But what do we tell them?"

I keep my head pillowed on my arms as I watch Devon wear out the floor.

"I mean, we can say we got an anonymous tip. But they'll want our phones to trace who called us." Devon rumples his hair. "Then they'll get Jeremy's number and he'll be in this too." He stops moving and sits across from me at the table, eyes dead serious. "You wanna tell them about your psi-junk? I mean, you can prove it and stuff."

I stare at him. My mental shields are rock solid. Dev's emotions are all over the place and I don't want to freak out because he is. One of us has to be cool—though it probably shouldn't be me. I'm the one who connected with Lawrence. His mind's always chaotic, but there's a logic that holds it together. His brain waves come in patterns of wild geometrical shapes with equa-

tions swirling around the joining lines. When I reached out to him, the lines were gone, and the equations fell into a cloudy, black spiral spreading wider with each devoured number. He could just be in the process of passing out, because I did lose him, but something doesn't feel right. He doesn't feel right.

Devon slams his fist on the table. "You just gonna stare at me all day?"

I blink down at his hand on the table. There's no evidence that he'd cut it open earlier. "No, I'm thinking," I say. "Lawrie said no police, because he doesn't want other people to get in trouble. But he's definitely afraid of whoever's got him, so somebody's dangerous."

"If they're dangerous, we need the police. The whole thing sounds like some kind of terrorist deal. Though I can't figure out what the crazy guy wants with Lawrie, unless he knows Lawrie can probably build an H-bomb for him or something."

I hum. With the right materials, my little brother could probably build anything. "I don't think that's the case."

"Why not?" Devon drums the table.

"I don't know, just don't," I snap. I raise my head and frown at the throb of a lingering feedback headache. Making mental connections turns me into a punching bag. Emotions and physical feelings hit harder than thoughts. Linking with sick or hurting people is psychic suicide. I don't do it, but I didn't know Lawrie would be a sick or hurting person.

Fear rides high in my chest, touching the base of my throat. It tastes like black licorice, sickeningly sweet and poisonous. But I play poker with the bad boys; my

voice is composed and my face stays smooth. Devon's on edge; I need him rational, which means he needs me level. And calm is so much easier to fake after a good date.

Even the memory has power. A whirlpool of euphoria spins inside me, drenching fear and trepidation with bliss as Gabby's pleasure rolls through my veins and quiets all random outside thoughts. I'm in control.

I sit up straight, grinning at nothing in particular, and Devon looks at me like I've lost it.

"What are you—" he starts.

"We put in an anonymous tip to the police about possible terrorist activity at U of H. The place will be flooded with cops," I say.

Devon rolls his eyes. "That's your genius plan?"

"We do it from the U of H Student Union," I say. "That puts us in place for Lawrie. Nobody will question us being on campus. We look like students."

"You want to go there?" Devon stares at me. "With the terrorists and the H-bombs?"

"Before the H-bombs," I murmur. "Let's leave now." A little nudge at the base of my skull says this is right. "We'll beat them to the school."

"And then call the police?" Devon frowns at me. What does my face look like? I thought my poker mask was on, but Devon looks worried.

"Yeah, we'll call the police," but maybe not right then. Fingers tap my ribs from the inside when I think about the police. The fingers move toward my spine. I can't explain it, but when this sensation comes, it means whatever I'm thinking about doing is a bad idea. It's stopped me from going to parties that got busted hours

later.

"You think we shouldn't call the police," Devon says slowly. "You got that look you get when the phone rings and you know who it is before you check the ID."

So much for my poker face. I shrug and stand up, stretching. "You driving or me?"

"Ly, this is Lawrie we're talking about," Devon says, his eyes dark. "If you're wrong, then what? I don't like this."

I wish he'd trust me. Years ago, he would have. But I understand. It sounds crazy. "Just...." The feeling's more than a tap now. Claws scratch my brain stem and I squeeze my eyes shut: Stop it. "You have to trust me. Just for a little while, okay? If we call the police, something's gonna go wrong."

"Tell me what," Devon says.

"I don't know." I never know until it happens. "Look, you said you wanted to make things right between us? Go with me on this and maybe we'll get there." Something hot runs under the skin of my neck. "Please."

Devon stands and pushes his chair in, leaning on it a moment, not looking at me. "Remember that time you told me not to climb that tree in Grandma's backyard?"

"Yeah." We were eight.

"That bastard Cody climbed it instead. He just had to prove he was the best," Devon says with a dark chuckle.

The sounds of Cody's scream when the snake in the tree struck him and the snap when he hit the ground and broke his collarbone are still with me.

"Could have been me," Devon says. He goes to the key rack hanging by the door. "I'll drive."

CHAPTER 17

LAWRENCE

HOT KIWI-STRAWBERRY GATORADE OVERLOADED with salt tastes nastier coming back up. Someone's got me, holding me, rubbing my back, wiping my face. I wanna sleep. But when the darkness comes, jolts of electricity crackle through my skin. Quent. He's like an eel. He discharges electric currents through his oily hands. Every time I come to, his nasty face, a big black and brown oval, hovers inches from mine, his breath rank. "Can't let you do that, kid."

"He's throwing up everything!"

Monica's voice hurts my ears.

"Keep givin' it to him! Something's gonna stay in his stomach." Quent doesn't sound so sure. "Yo, don't drive so fast! You tryna' get us pulled over?"

"S-sorry, just, just, yo man, this don't seem like such a good idea no more," a guy stutters. "What if the kid, like, dies or somethin'? What if somebody gets really hurt? I don't wanna go to jail, man."

"You turnin' into a chicken shit on me?"

Gatorade runs over my tongue and I spit it out. No more.

Sharp pain snaps my head to the left and my cheek smacks against something soft and warm, a shoulder maybe? Rapid-fire Spanish floods the vehicle from several different voices. Pain rips over my scalp as a hand grips my hair and jerks me upright. The plastic rim of a bottle rams into my teeth and Gatorade splashes in. Another tug brings my head back, and I choke. I spasm and gasp, hacking up snot and juice, and an elbow presses against my throat, forcing me to swallow.

"Puke again, ojete, I dare you."

I swallow hard as my gag reflex twerks and my stomach lurches. I don't put it past this bastard to slam his hand over my mouth and make me eat it. I shudder so hard my teeth rattle in my skull; hot and cold, black and white, conscious, unconscious—an electric shock. I hang on and a hand rubs my back.

"That's good, kid," Quent whispers. The bottle's pressed to my mouth and juice trickles in. I swallow. My stomach gurgles, but doesn't heave.

"Slow and steady. Go 'head; give him the whole bottle now."

Not unconscious, but not awake, I drift, listening to humming, soft breathing, and the sound of tires on a paved road.

"HEY." HANDS NUDGE ME. "UP ya go."

My eyes flutter open as a warm breeze hits my face. Smells like ozone and burned Chinese food. Vertigo flips me upside down as someone tosses me over their shoulder. My face smacks against rank fabric and bounces against it as we move. I raise my head—shizz, this hurts—to see the gray insides of a parking garage. There are a couple of cars around, but for the most part this place is empty. My cheek rubs against smelly cotton again. Head turned, I see a few people shuffling next to me wearing all black and carrying backpacks. There's a logo on the shirts, looks like the Lone Star flag but there's words too.

We go down a musty, stone stairwell and emerge into a dark lobby. Building must be closed. What time is it?

"Get us in, Shawn," someone hisses. "Hurry it up!"

Moving again, fast. The room is dark until somebody pulls out a flashlight. The beam is small and weak. A few more flashlights flicker on. I gasp as I'm shifted off the guy's shoulders and laid on the floor. I lie on my back, staring at a dim ceiling with low hanging lights. Around me, I hear the rattling of spray cans and aerosol bursts. Spray paint. Vandalism isn't so bad. Maybe they'll punk out and just stick to this.

"You sure you got this, Shawn? I don't want no alarms goin' off," Quent grunts. He's close by.

"Yeah, man. I got this." Guess that's Shawn, a dude with a high voice and a Midwest accent.

"That's it. Use it all. Get the couches!" Quent says.

The stench of gasoline saturates the air. Crap.

"Quent, you didn't say—"

"Shut the hell up. We gonna light this place up and march down to the Student Union with flaming torches. They gonna know we did this!"

Curses fill the room.

"Can the rest of us leave after this? You said we didn't have to show our faces if we helped you get this shit here!"

"Yeah, yeah, you can leave after this. Whatever. We don't need no punks for the next part."

Rough hands grab me under the armpits and hoist me into a sitting position. People spray-paint big loopy words on the walls and furniture, while others pour liquid from canteens on couch cushions tossed onto the floor. U of H banners are covered with graffiti that reads: Stop the Hate.

A clear bottle of blue liquid pushes against my lips. "Drink, kid."

I sip. Each swallow kills my stomach, but I refuse to be sick. Gotta keep it down to get strong enough to get away.

The thought of running makes my chest hurt. There are people in this room that don't want to be. Quent just said they could go, but I don't trust this guy as far as I can throw him. If he can terrify them into coming out here and doing this much, what's to keep him from making them go the rest of the way? But hell, what can I do about it? I can't help myself.

A hand rubs my shoulder. "Good," Quent says in my ear. "How you feel?"

"Better," I rasp.

"Not much longer 'til it's your turn, kid," Quent says. "You gonna show them bastards what we got. They

ain't gonna push us around no more after this! We can take this place over if we all come together like this. Vistors, they just as bad as humans. They don't help us neither. They live in their little neighborhoods and go to their private schools and come to crap like Stop the Hate and preach about how great it is to be an alien. But when it gets tough, they get back in their fancy rides and blast off. We can't do that. We ain't got no spaceships. Ain't got no families on Saturn waiting for us to come live with them. We got here, and here's gotta change."

"Not gonna change by doing this." My head explodes with pain from the slap.

"Shut your ass, baby boy," Quent growls. "You soundin' like them fools back there. They don't know, but they will. When they taste the power I'm 'bout to give 'em, their eyes will open. We'll start recruiting vulattos from everywhere. There'll be more stuff like this going on all over the place!"

"You sound like a barrio version of Bin Laden!" I blurt.

To my surprise, Quent laughs. "You got jokes, hermanito." He pats my back, and yells over his shoulder, "Grab those fake ass flags from over there. Yeah, get them all and light them up."

Metal chair legs rattle. A few people walk over with an assortment of flags. Some are American, and some sport U of H colors. Yellow and orange flames spring up and spread over the couches, rugs and tables. The smell of burning polyester and wood stinks up the place. Smoke stings my eyes.

"Oh crap, oh crap," some dude chants, sounding ready to crap his pants.

The big flags get dipped in the fire, coming away blazing beacons. An alarm blares and grinding noises, like branches stuck in a lawn mower, sound overhead.

"Dammit, Shawn! Thought you said you had this!" Quent yells. Feet pound across the floor. "Shut that thing up!"

"I'm getting outta here!" Oh Crap Guy screams and I see him. He's short and fat with blue skin and eyes that glow like simmering cigarette butts. He runs in my direction, but he's looking past me at something else. A flash of purple light strikes him in the back and he jerks, burning eyes going wide as he clutches his chest and falls down with a thud.

"Gods, Zeke! You crazy bastard!" a woman shrieks, breaking away from the group and running toward the blue guy.

"Stay there, Nisse, unless you wanna die too," a baritone voice growls.

The woman shudders, frozen in place. She covers her face with her hands. Frantic chatter and moans erupt from everyone else.

I stare at the blue guy sprawled face down on the floor. His back's not rising and falling. Quent staggers to the body and turns it over with his foot. He kneels and gapes for a second, looking as sick as I feel. A low string of Spanish comes from him.

A tall, lanky guy runs over, staring down at the body and Quent, then says, "We gotta go." From the Midwest accent, this guy has to be Shawn. "Security and the cops are gonna bust this place before we—"

Shawn yelps as sparks of electricity dance up the legs of his jeans. Quent glares up at him. "He's dead,

Shawn. Chinga!"

A big man with a goatee and snake tattoos up and down his bare arms walks up to Quent and Shawn. "If we're gonna do this, we gotta do it now. You need me to take over?" His baritone voice is condescending.

Bet this guy's crazy, bastard Zeke—crazy, bastard, murderer Zeke.

A heavy block of ice sits in my gut, freezing gastric juices and crushing my intestines. The plague of locusts living in my stomach migrates to my chest, buzzing as my heart pounds. I flop onto my back, staring at a ceiling full of laughing faces.

Is this terror?

Hysterical laughter bursts from a group of voices and feet march across the floor. Heat builds, and sweat beads on my forehead. I hear the fire hissing and crack-ling. Rough hands grab me under the arms and I'm fly-ing, gut smacking over the hard blade of a shoulder, teeth rattling as my chin rebounds off thick back muscles. Then, I'm moving.

A rush of sticky air hits me along with the smell of fast-food and smoke. A mellow beat comes from a distance, and there's the sound of puttering car engines. Voices around me chatter, some frenzied, some freaked, some grieved.

"Everybody's in this now! We gotta stand together," Quent says. He's close again. "Nobody leaves 'cause—"

"You got a death wish if you leave." I feel the rum-ble of the deep baritone through my body as the man talks. Shizz, Murderer Zeke's carrying me.

"You ain't runnin' off tellin' nobody," he growls.

"You can't!" A cry of pain and muffled gasps.

A few of the kids following Zeke start singing something in a language I've never heard before. It's got a rousing melody and feet start stomping to it. There are shouts of surprise.

"Take them out as you see them, Zeke," Quent says. "Ain't no goin' back."

Quent sounds like a suicide bomber.

"Pour the rest of that lighter fluid on the bushes and toss those flags," Quent hisses.

Crazy Zeke shrugs me off his shoulders and sits me down at his feet. Blades of grass poke at my hands as I slump against his legs, the back of my head resting on his kneecaps. Backpacks are unzipped and homemade bombs are dumped on the lawn. I strain to turn my head We're next to a large building with glass doors and large windows. I see people inside eating and watching a big screen TV. A few of them look out the windows, maybe they see us, maybe they are looking past us. Quent's gonna blow them up. He's gonna friggin blow them....

I blink. Two guys, tall and brown-haired, come to the doors. They're staring. Are they looking at me? The doors open and they step onto the concrete walkway.

/Lawrence./

Oh God, Lyle. Tears of relief spring to my eyes. Oh God.

/Don't move./

I want to scream at him not to move, Zeke's a killer, but my voice catches in my throat. I cough on the warning as the first bomb explodes.

CHAPTER 18

DEVON

THE FIRST EXPLOSION SOUNDS LIKE a car back-firing. The force of the blast vibrates under my feet and a window breaks behind me. Several more explosions shatter the rest of the Student Union's front windows and glass entrance doors. I dive off the front walkway into the grass and cover my head with my hands. Students and workers inside the building scream and I hear pounding feet. I don't look back to see if anybody got cut by the glass. I'm focused on Lawrie and the bastard I'm gonna kill for gripping my brother's collar like that.

Lawrie's at the rear of a small group of people in black T-shirts standing on the lawn about fifteen feet from the Student Union's entrance. He's a ragdoll being dragged off to the side by a big dude with tattoos. Rage turns the edges of my tunnel vision red. I throw myself into the crowd, shoving people out of my way; most of them jerk away from me. Something hard crashes into the back of my neck; pain explodes down my spine for a brief second before I'm over it. I pause, mid-stride,

to shoot a look over my shoulder at a guy standing like a dumbass, holding a metal flag pole. I whirl around, palming the pole as Dumbass swings it at me again, and I stare into his terrified blue eyes before flinging him, pole and all, toward the flaming Student Union. He flies about fifteen feet, rebounding off a wall and sprawling on the walkway.

"Oh my Gawd!" a few voices shout.

I whirl back to Big Dude and Lawrie, and growl. Big Dude's put a few more yards of distance between us. He glares at me, teeth bared, and shakes Lawrie with one hand. Then, he stretches his other hand in my direction, palm out. A bright purple flash of light erupts through his fingers, hurtling toward me. I stop short.

Holy hell! What is this guy?

Before I can leap out of the way, the light deflects like it hits some kind of barrier and surges upward into the air. Second and third blasts do the same and Big Dude's backing up, dragging Lawrie with him.

Big Dude shakes my brother, yelling at him. "Do something!"

Anger takes over and I charge at Big Dude, linebacker style. His purple crap can't touch me. A body slams into me from the side, going for a tackle, but it's like a Pomeranian jumping a Great Dane. The guy gets his bony arms around my shoulders and tugs to bring me down, but I'm still running.

"Aaah!" Somebody drops a live wire over my shoulders. Bolts of electricity zap through my pores, frying nerve-endings, as Pomeranian dude digs his bony fingers into my collarbone. I stagger, going down on one knee with Pomeranian draped over my back. What the

hell is going on? I feel my body trying to heal itself, but as fast as the damage is repaired, the constant shocks break the tissue again. Is Pomeranian doing this? I try to shake him off, but he hangs on. My joints lock up like they need oil.

My eyes roll around in my head, and my tunnel vision expands to take in the rest of the scene in slow motion. The group in black T-shirts stand like a geeky choir arranged for a concert in front of the Student Union, burning flags, waving signs, and singing songs. College kids pour out of the building, having to push through the protest group to get away from the flames. They stand on the lawn, crying and bleeding.

My head falls forward and I stare at the ground in front of me. Meters of space span between the two groups. I'm in the middle with Big Dude, Lawrie and the electric Pomeranian. Smoke billows into the air as sprinklers spew water everywhere and alarms blare.

Big Dude lets Lawrie flop onto the ground and kicks him; then Big Dude raises a hand flaring with purple light. "Make the ground quake and get a wall up between us and them, kiddo, or I'm gonna cook your insides!"

Fear and protective rage flood me. I have to do something. The electric current cuts off, and Pomeranian slides off my back like a heavy blanket. I blink, nerve-endings raw, but body mending. Still can't move.

Big Dude brings his flaming hand down, aiming at Lawrie's head.

Can't move. Need to move.

Police sirens fill the air, beautiful and loud. Thank God.

Big Dude gasps and spasms, then falls forward on his face to reveal Lyle standing behind him, panting and looking strained. Lyle kneels by Lawrie, touching little brother's neck, sitting him up, and lifting him over one shoulder.

Lyle's eyes are wide as he runs to me. "Shake it off! We gotta get outta here!"

Why? The police are here now. My head hurts. The heat from the burning building warms one side of my face and I blink. Some people in the protest group are still singing, waving burning flags and shaking signs on sticks, but a lot of them look scared to death. Students, covered in glass and smeared with soot, point and shout at the group...at me. My joints loosen and my head clears. My mouth flaps open as I gaze up at Lyle. Those people think we're with the bad guys? We're an island in an ocean of grass between the black T-shirts and the normal kids.

Police cars jump curbs, driving through the masses, creating a barrier of steel in front of the accusing crowd. Officers pour out with pistols and rifles. Ambulance sirens shriek and blue and red flashing lights wash the area making it a circus show. Purple lights crackle through the air. Big Dude's awake and on his knees, both hands blazing as he shoots his mojo beams at the police. On the ground next to me, Pomeranian lies in a heap; he rolls onto his back, moaning. I struggle to my feet. Good, I can move.

Police radios squall. People scream and run on both sides. Officers duck behind their vehicles. "Drop your weapons! Hands in the air!" several officers yell in staggered unison.

Purple lights flash, striking police cars and setting them on fire. Bullets fly.

Lyle pushes me. "Run, idiot!"

I can't move again. Bullets. The police are shooting—at us.

"No! We're not...." I'm out of control. I'm shaking, my knees are gonna go—an arm wraps itself around my waist and pulls me from behind.

"Devon, come on." Monica? What the hell is she doing here?

My feet stumble backward and then I'm running with a cluster of people, my brothers, Monica, another girl and a guy, a couple of others too, but some of them break away from us after passing a few buildings and a parking lot. With Monica in the lead, we clear sidewalks and lawns and weave through a garden of giant metal artwork. The Student Union is far behind us.

A deep, disembodied voice booms. "Humans gotta learn this is our planet too!"

Purple fireworks explode in the sky and a strong force rocks the ground, knocking me off my feet. I hit the grass face first and roll head over feet a few times, neck and shoulders taking the brunt of everything. I lay half on grass, half on concrete, aching, throbbing, and confused.

Hands yank me, dragging me to my feet. They won't let go. I struggle to keep up as I'm pulled along. The world slowly comes back into focus. The night wails, bursting with sirens and alarms and yelling. The air is heavy and hot. I cough, choking on fumes, and turn my head to look behind me. The Fine Arts Building stands tall and ignorant of what's going on, but in the horizon,

a fire blazes.

"Goddess Aneki," the girl with us whispers.

"Mayra," the guy sobs. "I think she got shot."

A crowd grows in the parking lot of the Fine Arts Building. Lights from cell phones illuminate faces. Voices rise to a fever pitch.

"What happened?"

"Vulatties did it!"

"Oh God! Is anybody dead?"

"Damn, you're banged up!"

"They're with that vulatto group!"

Hands grip and push me. The crowd's swarming, and then nothing. People stumble backward like they're smacking against glass walls. I shake myself, willing my mind to get with it. I can't stay spazzed out. Concentrate. Focus. I turn my head, Monica's next to me, face smudged with dirt and grass stains, hair wild. Two people, a tall, thin girl with spiky purple hair and a guy with dark skin and yellow eyes are next to Monica. Lyle stands slightly in front of us with Lawrie over one shoulder, eyes unfocused, hands quivering.

I recall trying to hit him and breaking my finger against a psychic barrier he'd made. The finger's healed, but a phantom ache echoes through it. I scan the area. The crowd's got maybe twenty people in it right now. Ly's holding them all back?

With the way he's trembling, bet he can't do it much longer. I pat his shoulder, and clear my throat. "My truck'll fit everybody. We parked two streets over. Run."

I pull Lawrie's limp form off Lyle's shoulders, get him over mine in a fireman carry, and take the lead. Lyle keeps good pace a few steps behind me. I hope Monica

and those other two can keep up, because I'm not slowing down. My priorities are my brothers. I was useless
in that fight back there; the least I can do is get them out
of here.

More onlookers flood the scene, some excited,
some horrified, heading toward the chaos. Additional
police cars line the streets, and we have to run between
a few.

"Hey!" gets called more than once in our direction,
but I don't stop.

My truck comes into view and I fumble in my back
pocket for the keys. Closing my fingers around the thick
keychain, I stagger a few steps to my double cab Dodge
and unlock the doors. "Everybody in."

I open the front passenger door for Lyle and ease
Lawrie off my shoulders. My little brother slumps
against me, skin burning through my T-shirt as I hold
him upright. Lyle climbs into the front seat and signals
for me to lift Lawrie in. I almost don't want to let go.
Anger makes me see red again. What did those bastards
do to my brother?

I boost Lawrie into the truck and Lyle pulls Lawrie
in the rest of the way so I can shut the door. Monica,
the purple-haired woman and the yellow-eyed guy are
already in the backseat. I run to the driver's side and hop
in, starting the engine. The street's crowded, maneuvering the area is not easy. Police barricades block certain
routes. I jump the curb and drive through grass medians
and fields until I reach a clear street. A trail of cars follow
behind me like I'm leading a march to freedom.

I-45 North and South are nightmares as rescue vehicles drive the wrong way down ramps, probably going to

U of H. My foot's on the brake, engine vibrating though the rubber soles of my sneakers, as we sit in an iron grid-lock. I roll down the driver's side window, fully letting in the sounds of sirens and honking horns, and airing out the smell of smoke, puke and BO trapped inside the cab. My nerves are on edge, my heart's got a techno-beat, and my palms are sweaty on the wheel.

The radio's off and the car's silent, except for heavy breathing and some sniffles from the back. I turn my head slightly to glance at Lyle. There's barely an inch of space between us. Lawrie's head is across Lyle's knees, and his eyes are closed.

"How is he?" I ask.

There's an unsteadiness to Lyle's voice that worries me. "He's out. Something's wrong with him. I can't fig-ure out what it is."

"He needs electrolytes and lots of salt," Monica says, her head peeping over the seat. "He used too much power today."

"Lawrie doesn't have any power," I snap and she winces. Guilt flashes through me. I don't want to be mean to her, but dammit what was she doing with those people hurting Lawrie?

In a light voice, she says, "He's an elemental, Dev-on. He moved the earth today."

"That wasn't him!" My voice is loud. Lyle flinches and brings a hand to his forehead.

Monica sighs and sinks back into her seat. "What-ever you say, but he still needs salt and electrolytes if you want him to live."

She talks like Lawrie's dying. Lyle's face pales like he thinks so too. My heart's in my throat.

"She thinks she's right," Lyle says after a few seconds. He looks out the window and swallows. "There're some stores a few miles off the freeway. I'll get out and go grab some stuff."

"You're not getting out in that mess!" I yell, gripping the steering wheel and frowning when the metal crunches under my fingers.

"I don't think he can wait until we get out of traffic." Lyle's still looking out the window; then he moves. Lawrie's head flops onto the seat as Lyle gets out of the truck. He rearranges Lawrie's legs and shuts the door behind him. A handle clicks and I glance in the rearview mirror to see the purple-haired girl getting out of the truck too.

I lean the back of my head on the headrest, watching Lyle and the girl climb over a street divider and walk down the hill the freeway's carved into. That's just great. I look down at Lawrie's head and, with a sigh, ease it onto my knee. He's pale with bruises from a couple of hits on his cheeks. I wanna brain the bastard who did that.

"Your brother," Monica says, "Lyle, right? He's amazing."

Jealousy's heavy in my chest. She'd seen Lyle keep that crowd off us. 'Course Lyle would be her hero. She'd had to push me to run when I was too scared to move.

"But you were too," Monica says. "I saw you go right for Zeke. You didn't care that he was shooting at you." Her voice is warm and it makes me feel lighter somehow.

"What were you doing with them?" I ask. I can't help it. I gotta know.

Monica's voice turns bitter. "Remember Stop the Hate Texas?"

"You gotta be kiddin'."

"It wasn't supposed to be like that. We were gonna have a sit-in at the Student Union. We had signs and lunch boxes full of peanut butter sandwiches." Monica gives a flat laugh. "It all went to hell."

"Only takes a few lunatics to do that," the yellow-eyed guy says in an easy voice. "I've never liked Zeke and Shawn. Quent's got a temper and a chip on his shoulder, but I don't think he would have done this without Zeke and Shawn encouraging him."

Monica blows a raspberry. "Bet Zeke wanted to do something like this since he joined, but he's too messed up to organize his own shit."

"Why didn't you run and call the police?" I ask. Did they have a psychic tell them not to? I grit my teeth, but I can't really be mad at Lyle. The police shot at us. Wonder what would have happened had we called them from jump? Would we all be in jail?

"No phones, and between Zeke and Quent...those bastards can hurt you, and Shawn can scramble any machine within thirty feet of him," Monica says. "They promised nobody would get hurt. They said we could leave after the Welcome Center, but I knew they weren't gonna let us go."

She sounds shell-shocked. I feel shell-shocked.

"Why?" I ask. Why would anyone want to do something like that?

Monica sighs. "Because things aren't fair, Dev. People will only be peaceful for so long. Quent said he thinks this is just the beginning of what's to come. We

need change, a major reform, groups with a voice, leaders to meet our demands and maintain order. Stop the Hate is supposed to be that, but...."

Stop the Hate's not strong enough.

My insides twist as I think about what she said. We need leaders. I squeeze my eyes shut as the word resounds through me—leaders.

An uncomfortable silence fills the car. I flip the radio back on to break it up and let my eyes slide closed. A stupid pop song ends as a male DJ comes on.

"HPD doesn't have any official statements at this time, but reports on the scene say that a terrorist group attacked several buildings on the University of Houston campus between six forty-five and seven fifteen this evening. The group is believed to have consisted of several Visitors and vulattos who are members of an off campus organization called Stop the Hate, which is also the name of a national movement for Visitor and vulatto rights."

"Suetha! They're smearing the name!" Yellow Eyes shouts.

"Such a tragedy," a female DJ's voice cuts in. "Several deaths have been confirmed along with multiple injuries. The exact numbers haven't been released. And no surprises to be had, multiple videos of the attack have already gone viral."

"Turn it off," Monica growls.

I hit the knob. The radio goes dead.

"You got a phone on you?" Monica asks. I dig it out of my front pocket and toss it over the seat.

"Password's my name," I say.

"Your screen's cracked," Monica mutters.

Minutes later, I hear the start of a video clip. A

guy's narrating, laughing and sounding excited. "Holy hell, look at that! The whole place is gonna go up—oh damn! It's like Star Wars, 'cept that guy's hands are the freakin' light sabers! Vaders rule!"

Hysteria bubbles in me. I laugh, letting the spasms roll through my aching shoulders. Feels good.

"Suetha, that's me!" Yellow Eyes groans. "They've got me on camera. I think that's you over there, Monica."

I turn cold. They got Big Dude on camera with his light saber hands. I was only a few feet from him; Lyle was right behind him.

No, no, no.

"Not good," Monica mumbles. I hear another video clip start, this one with a girl's frantic narration.

"Oh my Gawd! I know that girl! She's in that vulattie group!"

"They're probably going to release all of our names on the News at Eleven," Yellow Eyes sighs. "My father is going to kick my ass. That is, if he can get to it through the prison bars." Yellow Eyes slumps in the seat. He sounds mad enough to spit, but his face is drawn, sad.

"Jazz is dead," Monica says after a beat. "Just bam, and he fell. I knew he was gonna run. I didn't stop him. I watched."

Yellow Eyes lowers his head. "What do we tell people? How is it going to come out? We want everyone to get along, but look at us. I just keep thinking…maybe if we had all just jumped on Zeke…. Quent can't do anything unless he's touching you."

Monica swallows, looking sick, and shrugs. "Somebody else would have died. I—it wasn't supposed to be like this." Tears stream down her face and she wipes

them away with the heel of her palm. "I think GiGi's dead too. Maybe Zeke. Maybe Quent."

The sound from the video dies.

I breathe it all in: the heat pouring off my unconscious brother into my thigh, the two vulattos in back crying about dead friends, the freeway chaos, U of H burning, the police firefight, being electrocuted by another vulatto. Can I just go back to yesterday, when all I cared about was getting Keelie Sheppard up on the balcony for a make-out session? I want my life before visions and dreams about brothers I don't know, before anyone but me knew I was a freak. I want to jump out of the car and howl at the sky like a crazy man.

In my future, I used to see football and track scholarships, definitely some hot girlfriends and eventually a trophy wife. There was a big house and a couple of kids, a boring job that paid for a sweet ride. Nothing special, nothing strange. I'm not seeing any of that at the moment. Right now, there's only chaos.

If this is who I am, what the hell am I supposed to do with it?

CHAPTER 19

LYLE

THE OFF-BRAND GAS STATION stinks like micro-wave burritos and burned coffee. The guy behind the counter is buff as hell with a Confederate flag tattoo on his pink scalp, and piercings through his brows and lower lip. His dark eyes follow us like a Pit Bull's as we drift through the store.

Wonder what I look like? I glance up at the small old school TV over the cashier's head displaying various camera angles. I see an image of myself in the drink aisle and grimace. I'm dirty, wrinkled and ragged, like a punk fresh out of a fight.

My head feels worse than I look. I think a sadist drilled a crater in my skull, poured in some Rice Krispies and kerosene then struck a match: Snap, Crackle, POW! The barrier between my mind and the outside world is full of gaping holes. I'm gonna fall in.

"Hey."

A small hand touches my shoulder and I jump, then stagger, into the glass door of a soda fridge. Leaning in

for support, I stare at the Visitor girl with purple hair. Nisha—Nicey—don't remember what she said her name is. Her head is full of scenes from a place with orange grass and water for roads; she wishes for her dad's Earth assignment to end so she can go back home.

Snap, crackle, POW.

The holes in my shield get bigger. I don't want to see in her head, but there's no keeping it out.

Snarling thoughts from the cashier punch their way in.

...*better not try ta take nothing. Got my taser this time.*

"Are you okay?" Nisha-Nicey asks, silver eyes piercing and straightforward. "You look terrible."

I nod, gripping the rubber handle on the drink re-frigerator door. I rest my cheek on the cool glass, want-ing to stare off into space, but Nisha-Nicey isn't having it. She plants herself in front of me. She's pretty, heart-shaped face with a button nose and large deep-set silver eyes that match her glittery skin. Need ripples through me. Oh God, I need quiet.

"You're telekinetic?" Nisha-Nicey asks.

"Yeah, some, mostly telempathic," I mumble, my tongue too big for my mouth. My brain's melting, and in a second it'll ooze through my ears. Why am I here again? I'd hiked miles to a gas station for Lawrie, for me. I had to get out of Dev's smothering truck with that guy and girl feeling all black inside. Had to get out of that screaming traffic. Everyone was so angry about be-ing late, about being stuck, about being alive.

"Did you use telempathy to knock Zeke and Quent out?" Nisha-Nicey asks.

Images of the pit-faced guy with big ears who'd been on Devon and the ogre that had had Lawrie by the collar flash through her mind. They'd been easy to take down. All I had to do was funnel some of the psychic feedback I was getting from the crowd into their heads. Two seconds of noise had them on the ground crapping their pants.

"Yeah," I mutter.

"You're going into psychic shock. Your pupils are blown to Hades," Nisha-Nicey says.

"Blown to Hades?" My shoulders shake. Am I giggling?

Her callused hand touches my cheek then peels my lower lid down as she leans in closer. The physical contact, her face so close. I need quiet.

She frowns, confusions tumbles through her, then sudden confirmation.

Snap, Crackle, POW.

"I've been around enough psychics to know your shields are busted," she says. "What do you do to repair them?"

She'd slap me if I told her.

"Just rest." I push off the fridge door and stand back, watching her open a drink fridge and pull out three large bottles of Gatorade. She passes them to me and grabs three more.

"Come on," she calls to me. "I put the rest of the stuff on the front counter already."

That's right. It'd been my job to get the Gatorade. I fumble up to the cashier, meeting his surly stare, and drop the frosty bottles on the counter. He rings up the Gatorade, two boxes of protein bars, a big box of Sal-

tines, four liter-sized canisters of Morton's salt, and a Mr. Goodbar, then scowls at me for payment.

I fish for my wallet, but Nisha-Nicey slams a fifty on the counter with a sneer that eats his Pit Bull glare for breakfast. The cashier grunts and takes the money, giving Nisha-Nicey change before bagging the groceries in plastic sacks and narrowing his eyes at me again.

What'd I do?

"Have a nice evening," the cashier drawls as we leave. "Filthy vore," he mutters just loud enough for me to catch.

Ah. He thinks I'm sleeping with Nisha-Nicey. I wish.

Nisha Nicey slams through the store's painted glass doors, flipping off the surveillance camera on the way, and I stand, dazed, watching her hips. Oh God, this is bad. Scrubbing my hands over my face, I grab all the grocery bags and follow her as she stalks to the sidewalk hugging the dark road back to the freeway.

"I can't wait to get off this wretched planet," she shouts and starts muttering in a guttural language that sounds almost German. "Visitor Rights," she grumbles "Earth is categorized as a Civilized Planet, but that's wrong. This place is primitive!"

Her mood whips back and forth from outrage to just needing to be comforted. "The sweetest person in the world died today for no reason." Her voice trembles.

I keep easy pace beside her. If I concentrate on what she's saying, and walking, I can almost ignore the insanity roaring around my head.

"Hey." Her hand's on my arm. She takes a few of the lighter bags. "How's your head?"

I hum. Don't feel like talking, just wanna walk.

"What you did back there was incredible. I didn't know there were psychics as skilled as you on this planet. Are you Visitor or vulatto?"

"Vulatto."

"Hm." Nisha-Nicey's mental questions hit me like an eighteen wheeler: *What the hell are you mixed with? Who the hell are your parents?*

I stumble. She catches my arm and steadies me, staring hard. "You're too strong to be here—you and your brother that makes earthquakes. Travelers with your type of powers don't settle on Earth. It's not a suitable environment."

"I deal." Do I?

"Who trains you?" she asks.

"Uncle," I murmur.

She's standing way too close. I feel her warmth and smell gasoline on her skin. The holes in my shields are as big as bay windows. Stringing together sentences is getting harder to do. Her arm brushes mine and the contact sends want and need spiraling through me.

"Gods, you're shaking." Her hands are on my wrists, holding me in place. Plastic rustles and weight is removed from my arms. I blink; she's taking the bags and setting them on the sidewalk.

She stands on her toes to look into my eyes. "You're all pupil now."

She looks nervous. Her mind crashes into mine, her thoughts and feelings climbing through the windows. She's scared, she's homesick, she's grieving, she's angry, she's lonely, she wants....

I bring my arms around her and after a beat she rests

her head on my shoulder. /I can make you feel better./
And I can. Telempathic bliss goes both ways. It's
crack for everybody.

Now? she thinks. Surprise and desire murmur
through her.

In her head, I see a guy, tall with dark bronze skin
and clear green eyes. He looks like one of those air-
brushed teen show actors. Is that me? That's how she
sees me?

I kiss her, feeling her frazzled nerves, desperate for
some kind of release, start to relax. She wants this. My
head clears a bit as I scan the area. A strip mall's about a
minute's walk ahead. The rundown storefronts are dark,
but I can get a door open.

I start pulling her toward the strip mall, but she
stops, picking up the groceries. The groceries. Lawrie
needs.... No, I need, now. I pull again once she picks up
all the bags. Thoughts scream at me from everywhere in
English, Spanish, Vietnamese, alien. So many languages
mix together I can't understand a thing, but the emotions
are clear. Happiness, sadness, frustration, disgust, need.

Need. Need. My breath wheezes in and out as we
reach the small parking lot of a grouping of four stores
with dirty glass and cardboard behind the windows. A
homeless man sits in front of an old barbershop with a
rolling suitcase and a lit cigarette. He raises a brow at
me, and asks in a scratchy voice, "Got change, kid? Need
to catch a bus."

Chevron...cigarettes....

/YOU'RE GONNA BUY CIGARETTES! LIAR!/

The man's face screws up and he grips his head in
both hands.

"Oh gods, what are you doing to him? Stop it!" Nisha-Nicey yells. She hits me square in the back with a bag of Gatorade. The physical pain grounds me. The homeless man curls up on the concrete, cigarette rolling across the cracked sidewalk. His chest rises and falls rapidly as he sobs.

I did that.

"I don't want to be with you anymore! I'm going back to the car!"

My head screams as she pulls away from me. No, no, no. I grab her arm. She wanted me before. /You wanted me. Remember?/ I funnel my feelings of want into her.

Her fear tinged thoughts calm, but uncertainty wars inside her. Her eyes are large; she blinks like a drunk confronted with a multiplication problem.

An image of me standing over the homeless man drifts to the forefront of her mind, and I stroke it away because it's not right. That's not the 'me' she wanted. That 'me' makes her unhappy. I want to make her happy, give her happy. I need it.

My head hurts.

...never does anything right! Bast....

...can't find my....

Grief, sadness, anger. I don't know whose feelings they are. They come from everywhere. It hurts.

Confusion passes through the girl in front of me. Confusion, desire and concern.

She reaches up, her hand tickling the skin above my lips. "Your nose is bleeding," she says. "Are you...?"

Salty blood drips onto my lips and I lick it away as I cover her hand. Her thoughts shiver. She wants me.

I kiss her fingers, and then place my other hand on her face, running the pad of my thumb over her soft cheek.

/You wanted me./

Sifting through her thoughts is easy as slicing through room temperature butter. I find the picture of airbrushed-actor me and push it forward, smiling when she sighs and pleasure ripples through her...and me.

Her whole body relaxes. When I tug her to me, she rests her head against my chest. That's good. I turn my head to the door of the old barbershop. A mental nudge from me turns the lock inside the door. There's a soft pop, and I jiggle the handle, opening the door. Musty aftershave and bug spray scented air makes me sneeze as I pull Nisha-Nicey into the store after me. It's dark and I hear the sound of tiny scurrying feet from far corners of the room. Light, do I need light?

Don't need light. The door closes behind us. Plastic bags rustle and hollow boxes clatter to the floor. Thin, muscular arms wrap around my neck and soft lips touch mine.

Need.

Hers and mine.

We sink backward onto the cold, hard floor. Fuzz balls make my back itch, as she nibbles my neck. Desire twists my guts into pretzels and pulls hard.

It hurts.

My head reels as my brain rattles, pieces of it breaking off. Nisha-Nicey gasps as I run my fingers down her flat abdomen. Each swell of bliss from her sends a thrill through my body that teases the knots inside my guts looser. I let go, relaxing my shield and letting myself out so she can feel what her emotions do to me. She moans.

Mom's ringtone chimes from my back pocket, the vibrations tickle. It's kind of nice. Nice.

Nisse, her name is Nisse.

/I'm Lyle./

She doesn't care.

I hear the homeless man sobbing outside.

And I don't care either.

CHAPTER 20
DEVON

I HIT 'END CALL' WITHOUT leaving a message. Lyle's not answering his phone. He's been gone for almost forty-five minutes and traffic's starting to move a little. We're up two exits from where we were when he'd gotten out. I keep one hand on the steering wheel and the other on Lawrie's back, needing to feel it rise and fall. He looks like a wax figure sprawled across the seat.

"Let me try Nisse's number," Monica says, reaching over the seat for my phone.

I let her have it. Hopefully, her friend will answer and tell us where the hell they are. I'm thinking about jumping off the freeway at the next exit and driving Lawrie to a hospital. Bet Lyle would do his psi-thing and tell me doctors are a bad idea, but you know what, screw him. He's not here.

"Uh." Monica shoves my phone back over the seat. "Your mom's calling, Dev."

The words are big hands laden with brass knuckles punching me in the ribs. Mom. I am a dead man walking.

I take the buzzing phone. Crap. Crap. "Hello?"

"Hi." Mom's voice is flat.

Crap. Crap.

"Where are you?" she asks.

"Driving," I say. I wince at my high pitch.

"I called your brothers. No one's answering and I have a question to ask."

I gulp. "Yeah?"

"Did I tell you that you could throw a party while we were away?"

I blink and barely keep a big grin off my face. "Um, no."

Oh, relief feels so good. The party, she's mad about the stupid party. Just yesterday my biggest fear had been that she'd find out about it.

"My house better be spotless, everything better be in its place, and you all better have breakfast waiting when we get back. We'll need to deliberate your punishments on full stomachs." Mom uses the matter-of-fact tone she gives to her clients and colleagues.

"Uh, ye-yes, ma'am," I stammer, trying not to laugh.

She's quiet and I start to sweat. I hate when she does this. She's willing me to say something else and incriminate myself.

"Anything else I should know about?" she asks after a long while.

My chest constricts. Oh God, there's so much she should know about. Evan, Derrick, Lawrie, the news, my power, Lawrie's power. But how do I tell her? I don't know what to say, so I mutter, "No, ma'am."

"You're sure?"

"Yes, ma'am."

"All right then. Tell your brothers to return my calls. No company from here on out." She sounds stern. "I love you, sweetie, and don't forget to pick us up at the airport on Saturday."

"Love you too," I whisper. My phone beeps, the call's gone, but I keep the phone to my ear like she's still there. Mom, the person who always fixes everything, but could she fix this mess?

I pop my phone into a built-in media holder on the dash and ease the truck another inch forward as traffic gives way. Another fifteen minutes has us almost at the Telephone Road exit.

A knock on the passenger side window makes me jump. Lyle stands outside the door with Nisse and several white plastic bags. I unlock the doors and watch them climb in. Lyle puts the white bags on the floor in front, then shifts Lawrie's legs and gets in. Nisse crawls in back; Monica and Yir scoot over for her. She's flushed and scowling and Lyle looks sick to his stomach. Neither one looks at the other, keeping busy in their own respective places.

Damn. Did they have a fight?

Monica frowns at Nisse; then pokes her head over the seat. "Let me up front. I know what to do with that stuff."

Four people up front is a bit of a squeeze, not that I'd mind Monica pressed against me, but it'd just make more sense for Lyle to switch places with her. Lyle scoots closer to the window, but makes no move to jump in back. Out of the corner of my eye, I see Nisse stiffen. WTF?

"I got him for a sec. Just climb over," Lyle speaks softly. Lyle gets Lawrie under the shoulders bringing his head off my knee and pulling him up. Lawrie slumps back onto Lyle's chest. I smirk as Monica's long legs make their way over the seat and she slides in next to me, soft hair tickling my face and arms. She smells like smoked bacon. I love bacon.

Monica takes Lawrie's legs and shifts them across her lap and mine, then she inches closer to Lyle, and leans over to rifle through the plastic sacks on the truck floor. She pulls out a bottle of Gatorade and a big blue canister of salt. I feel my eyes bug out of my head as she chugs a third of the Gatorade then pours an ass-load of salt into the bottle. Pink juice turns white and chunky. She shakes the mess up like a smoothie, and then pats Lawrie's cheeks.

"Can you wake him up a little?" she asks Lyle.

Lyle hums, and closes his eyes for a moment. Then, I hear the most wonderful sound: "Wazz off," Lawrie slurs like a drunk.

I want to pump my fists and shout, 'Yeah!'

Little brother's eyes stay closed and his body's still limp, but he'd spoken.

"Good evening to you too, kiddo," Monica says. I hear the smile in her voice. "I got juice for you."

Lawrie's quiet. Monica puts the Gatorade bottle to his lips and tips some in. She rubs his throat after a few seconds, coaxing him to swallow. She has to repeat the process twice, before Lawrie swallows without prompting. The feed is a slow but steady process.

"Gah, how are you drinking this crap, Lawr?" Lyle asks, his voice still freaky soft.

"He needs it," Monica says, tilting the bottle a bit more. Lawrie's about halfway through it. "Protein will be next."

"God, what did he do?" I ask. "I know you all say he made an earthquake, but why's it..." killing him?

Monica shrugs, but Yir chimes in, spouting some crap about Lawrie making that Kemah earthquake all wrong and letting the ground suck the life out of him.

"What the hell does that mean?" I ask.

Yir sighs. "It means he didn't know what he was doing and almost killed himself."

Now that sounds like Lawrie.

After a beat Yir asks, "What are you guys doing here? People like you don't live on Earth."

"What do you mean people like us?" I growl.

Yir clears his throat. "I mean, people with your level of power. Earth's not a conducive environment."

"Someone else said that," Lyle says, ducking his head.

I look at Nisse in the rearview mirror. Her cheeks are red. She looks out the window and folds her arms over her chest.

I jump as Lawrie chokes. Lyle sits Lawrie up straighter, pounding his back as thick, pink goop dribbles from Lawrie's lips. Little brother's lashes flutter and his eyes open, looking bleary and unfocused.

"Thank God!" I say. "Lawrie, you okay?"

"Mmmmmm." Lawrie blinks, lids droopy.

Monica gives him more Gatorade and he slurps the nasty stuff down like Hawaiian Punch.

We reach our exit, and I jump off I-45. Going down the exit ramp is slow, but once we hit the feeder, it's a

matter of driving through a few parking lots before I find a clear street. I end up having to use every random mental map of the city I know to weave around traffic, but I get us home in forty minutes.

Lawrie's sitting up and drinking the Gatorade on his own by the time I pull my truck into the driveway and park in front of the first garage door.

"You know," Monica says as we get out of the truck, "if you were identified on any of those videos people are posting, staying at your house probably isn't a good idea." She passes me plastic grocery bags.

Damn. I never think about stuff like that. She puts her hands on my shoulders and gives me a smile that makes me feel like less of a loser.

"You did good, Dev, but we can't stay here long." She strokes my hair and turns away from me, looking to Nisse and Yir.

Nisse scowls and Yir seems nervous. Lyle gets out of the truck and helps Lawrie. I give the groceries back to Monica, and Yir takes a few from her; then I go to my brothers.

"Gotcha', bro," I murmur as Lyle gets Lawrie on my back.

Lyle walks in front of us, giving Nisse wide berth as he goes to the backdoor and opens it up. Cool air greets us, and I sigh. I hadn't realized how muggy it'd been outside and how sweaty I am, 'til now. God, I stink; everyone stinks but Monica. I don't think being stinky is physically possible for her, at least not to me.

The lights come on and the clean, stainless steel kitchen comes into focus as we cross the hardwood floor to the living room. I take one look at Mom's spe-

cial white couches, shake my head 'no way' and head straight for Nikki's playroom. It used to be a second den, but when Mom had the old playroom converted into a lab for Lawrie, Nikki needed somewhere to put her army of Barbies. I lead the group into a room with pink and white wallpaper and dump Lawrie onto a pink and white polka-dotted couch.

"No, not Barbie Hell," Lawrie moans, rolling onto his side and shutting his eyes.

I plop down beside him, sinking into the soft cushions of the full-sized couch. A white table used for tea time turns into a medicine table as Monica and Yir drop the grocery bags onto it and push it closer to the couch. They start pulling out the supplies and sorting them out. I sit Lawrie up, and he slumps into my side. Damn, he's burning a hole through my shirt he's so hot, and he reeks worse than any of us.

"You smell like puke, Lawr," I mutter.

"Here." Lyle's voice is behind us.

I roll my head back to see him standing behind Lawrie. He gets Lawrie's arms up over his head and works off little brother's soiled, soggy T-shirt. The fabric clings to him it's so gross. When the shirt's off, Lawrie's arms flop back to his side and he slumps into me again with a happy sounding sigh.

"I'll get some..." Lyle trails off, and I look at him again. He's staring at Lawrie's back and I frown.

"What?" I ask.

"Sit him up and lean him forward," Lyle says in a shaky voice.

Still frowning, I do as he says, easing Lawrie upright and pushing his head toward his knees. As I do, my

eyes grow wide. What the hell is that?

Lyle uses a hand to push Lawrie's hair off his neck and we both stare at a thick black tattoo of weird symbols and shapes making a column of ink down the length of Lawrie's spine. I run my fingers along it. No raised skin, no smear marks.

"Ly?" I gaze up at him.

"It's the mark," Lyle says, "the one I told you I saw on Evan."

Lyle looks ready to bolt, but he doesn't, instead, he turns around and pulls off his own T-shirt. As the fabric rolls up, inches of the same black symbols are exposed on his spine as well. Fear spreads in the pit of my stomach like crunchy peanut butter.

"Is it there?" Lyle asks.

I nod. "Y-yeah."

I hear someone suck in a breath and I turn my head to see both Yir and Monica staring at Lyle's back. Jealousy stirs again as Monica's eyes look appreciative. Yir looks like he's been smacked in the face with a rubber chicken. His eyes are wide and his mouth's slack.

"Why would you get tattoos like those?" Yir asks, sounding confused. "Well, I guess on Earth no one would care."

"About what?" I ask, trying to read his expression. Lyle's better at analyzing faces, but when I shoot him a look and gesture to Yir, Lyle blinks at me.

"That's—the design's called Order's Mark in Common Tongue. I don't know how to explain this to you." Yir rubs his hand over his short black hair. He's a pretty human looking guy, except for those burning yellow eyes.

"You don't have to tell us about Order and prophecy. We know," Lyle says. "Dev, can you...." He nods his head at my shirt, and I yank it over my head and lean forward.

"Well?" I ask, though I feel pretty hopeless. I had the same black spots Lyle had this morning, why not the same full-out tattoo now?

"Yeah, it's there," Lyle says.

I study Lyle. He's so Zen, like random tattoos appear on his back all the time, but he'd freaked earlier. The peanut butter fear in my stomach bubbles and I want to fart it out.

Monica looks lost. She sits, shaking up more salt smoothies and watching us like we're all about to strip naked and dance for her. A burning pang at the thought of her maybe wanting that from me cancels my fear for a bit. I'd dance if she wanted me to.

"Okay," Monica says, "so y'all bribed somebody to make you matching tattoos. Looks like it hurt and cost a fortune, but it's kinda..." her eyes roam my chest and she smirks, "hot."

"They're not tattoos," Lyle murmurs.

He puts his shirt back on. Good, I don't like the way Monica's eyes keep going to him. I don't get it. I'm ripped, Lyle's okay, but I'm the one she should be looking at. I keep my shirt off.

"Did you tell us what you were mixed with?" Yir asks.

Lawrie sits up, rubbing his face and looking an insane combination of wasted and loaded. "Remasian. Our dad."

He grabs another Gatorade salt smoothie with a

shaky hand and struggles to get the top off. I take it from him, twisting off the lid and handing it back.

"Mmph." He slurps the chalky slush and I grimace.

"Remasian?" Yir moves supplies out of his way and sits on the tea table, knees inches from mine, staring across the narrow chasm between us. "Remasians don't have an embassy in this Sector." He looks chicken-whipped again. "Why did you get tattoos of the Mark? Getting inks like those is illegal in some Sectors."

"What's so special about them?" Monica asks. "And who cares where Remasians have an embassy? Maybe their dad was just Visiting."

Yir makes a noise similar to blowing a raspberry, except he does it through his nose. "Whatever. Forget it."

Monica doesn't look like she wants to forget it. She opens her mouth, but Lyle interrupts.

"I ignored a call from Mom," he says out of the blue. "I should call her—"

"Call!" Lawrie jerks, like he's trying to get to his feet, and flops back on the couch with a groan. "My phone. Galeo. What if he called?"

A battering ram crashes into my chest. I feel winded. Holy crap. I completely forgot about that. But hot damn, how many people can I worry about at once? And when one of those people is someone I don't really know, should I really feel that bad about forgetting? Lawrie's first.

"Your phone's probably with ours, which is wherever Quent hid them, remember?" Monica says.

Lawrie massages his temples, then tries to stand up again and fails. "My computer. I can get missed calls off it. Help me up?"

The pitiful plea is aimed at me, and I gaze at Monica. "He done with all this stuff?" I nod at the supplies.

"I don't know," Monica says, frowning at me; then glancing at Yir who looks just as clueless. "Quent was the one who told us what to do." Her eyes move to Lawrie. "To be safe, I think you need to drink the rest of this stuff, and eat the protein bars."

"I can do that upstairs." Lawrie's eyes gleam with excitement—and anxiety?

Lawrie's worried? That's weirder than ketchup on hotdogs.

"Dev, don't you care?" Lawrie asks.

I blink.

"I got you." Lyle comes around and gives Lawrie a hand, letting Lawrie lean on him.

Well, dammit. I grab up the last bottle of Gatorade and a box of protein bars, following my brothers out of the room and up the stairs.

"Hey, wait!" Monica chases after us. There's a second set of footsteps as well. Yir, probably. I blink. Where the hell's Nisse? She hadn't been in the playroom. I take the stairs slow, because Lawrie can only handle one at a time. I walk behind him just in case he falls and Lyle can't catch him.

"Where's Nisse?" I ask.

"In the kitchen," Yir says, sounding apologetic.

What for? Not his fault his friend's moody. Then again, not his friend's fault she got hijacked by crazy people and ended up stuck with us. Hell, guess I could offer to take her somewhere else later, since Monica says we can't stay here.

The thought of home not being safe pisses me off.

We didn't do anything wrong, but it might not look like that on camera. My legs feel watery as I remember police bullets whirring in our direction. I could've been shot; could've died. The police would've called Mom and Dad and said, 'Sorry, we killed your kid. But he was just a no good vulattie. You'll get over it.'

The weak feeling in my legs fades as I grit my teeth and clench my fists. Screw the police. We reach the top of the stairs, and head to Lawrie's lair.

"Crap! The key," Lawrie whines.

Lawrie only whines when he's had it. Through terrorists, salt slushies and being lugged around like a baby, he'd moaned a little but hadn't whined. I sigh, about to nudge Lawrie and Lyle out of the way and force the door open, when it swings inward on its own.

"Huh?" I peer into the room. There's no one inside. "How—"

"Locks that take keys are easy," Lyle says, maneuvering Lawrie through the door.

"So what, you break into houses and cars in your spare time?" I mean, how else would he know he could do that? Who the hell are you, Lyle?

"I've never locked myself out," Lyle says simply. He doesn't snap or sneer, he just doesn't look at me.

"Stop digging around in my head," I growl.

"I don't have to do that to know what you're thinking." Lyle eases Lawrie down in the saucer chair in front of the monster computer.

I don't know what makes me madder, what he says or the laid-back way he says it.

Monica's soft hand touches my shoulder and her body brushes mine as she stands next to me. "What is

this?" She gestures around Lawrie's lair with her hands. "Your brother some kind of hacker?"

With wires, tools and computer guts spilled everywhere, I can see why she thinks that. I shrug. "Yeah, he's some kind of everything." Genius, crazy, slob, annoying, and my responsibility. I march to the saucer chair and shove the Gatorade into Lawrie's chest and drop the box of protein bars in his lap. "Drink, then eat."

Lawrie rolls his eyes, opening the bottle and taking a dutiful sip before talking to his computer. "Endymion, check my voicemail."

The computer clicks and whirs to life, monitors come on and blue lights flash. "Yes, Master."

I laugh when Monica jumps.

"What was that?" Yir asks. He stands by a steel workbench covered with wheels and gears, eyes wide.

"His computer." I shake my head and rest a hand on the back of Lawrie's saucer chair. Lyle stands on the other side of it, arms folded over his chest.

"Twenty-eight messages, sir," Endymion says.

Damn.

"Any from Galeo?" Lawrie asks after taking another swig of juice.

"Six, sir."

"Call Galeo." Lawrie slurps more slush, and then rips open a protein bar.

"How is the computer talking to him like that?" Monica whispers in my ear.

"Don't know," I murmur back. "Don't ask."

A picture of Galeo pops up on screen as Darth Vader's theme plays for a total of ten seconds, and the call's answered. A video chat window takes over the monitor,

and a wide-eyed Galeo wearing a white 'Let Them Eat Cake' T-shirt fills the screen.

"Where have you been?" he demands.

"With friends." Lawrie lets out a light laugh and I snort.

Galeo stares at him and frowns. "You look terrible. Are you all right?"

"Don't know," Lawrie drawls and fear spikes inside me.

I touch his shoulder. "You don't feel better? You want to go to the hospital?" I should have taken him.

"The hospital?" Galeo sounds scared. "What happened to you?" His eyes scan the rest of the room. "To all of you? You look as if you have been through war."

This guy talks like an English teacher. It's annoying.

"You can say that," Lawrie says, saluting Galeo with a half-eaten protein bar. Lawrie smiles, but there's a darkness in his gaze that makes me wanna hurt somebody. Those bastards did that to my brother, and I didn't kill them for it.

"Whatcha' got for us?" Lawrie asks.

I don't miss his shoulders tensing up or Lyle going still.

Galeo's concerned expression shifts to regret. "Nothing good I am afraid."

I bite my lip. The watery feeling in my legs returns.

"I talked to my father about Leader Lauduethe's predicament," Galeo says slowly.

Leader Lauduethe? Who the hell is that?

/Leader Lauduethe is Evan. You missed a lot./

I glare at Lyle, but he's looking at Galeo.

"So, my father researched Leader Lauduethe's whereabouts and, as I suspected, the leader is documented as being on a retreat far from Onkurus. When my father brought the matter to one of his colleagues and council was granted with a Remasian Allegiance Representative, he was told that certain matters are to be kept private and that arrangements have already been made."

I blink, my legs solid again. That doesn't sound so bad.

"What kind of arrangements?" Lyle asks. He looks rattled and Galeo doesn't seem happy.

"What? What's wrong?" I ask.

Galeo clears his throat. "When an official says 'arrangements have been made' in regards to a situation involving illegal acts committed by a political figure, it usually means—"

"They're writing him off," Lyle finishes. "If they don't do anything, no one will know anything happened, right? They can explain away his disappearance with something else." He cracks his knuckles, my nervous habit.

Galeo nods, eyes downcast. "I am sorry."

"So," Lawrie says, "they aren't even gonna consider the prophecy thing or our story about the message? Did your dad even get to tell them about that?"

Galeo sighs. "No one believes the story, Lawrie, not even my father. He only spoke to his friend to appease me. He did not think it would go as far as to reach the Remasian Representative. That much convinced my father that your message about the leader committing war crimes on Onkurus is true."

"He's not committing war crimes!" Lyle snaps.

"He's just...he was...." He runs a hand through his hair.

"Leader Lauduethe was in combat gear when you met with him in his dream, correct?" Galeo asks. "He had weapons?"

Lyle sighs and looks up at the stars on the ceiling.

What the hell is Evan into? Goddesses, rubies, warriors and him face down in a pool swim in my head. War crimes and combat? There was a battle in the vision. Is Evan a bad guy? Should I want to save a bad guy even if he's my brother? I sit on the floor and rest my head against the side of Lawrie's chair. I just wanna go in my room, crank up my music and lift some weights.

"Perhaps," Galeo's voice is light, "you could accept that your brother made a decision to follow orders, and he has fallen due to that decision. It is not your fault, and you have done more than anyone could expect in an attempt to help him."

"Shullbit," Lawrie says. He stands up, knees wobbling, but he doesn't teeter. "Look at this." He turns around slowly, exposing his bare back to Galeo. "It's not a tattoo. It started showing up this morning."

Galeo gasps, eyes running up and down Lawrie's spine. "Suetha," he hisses.

"We've got them too," Lyle says. He pulls his shirt over his head and turns to show Galeo his back. I stay on the floor, staring at my brothers, confusion making my mind spin.

"Suetha." Galeo starts muttering in another language. His eyes are neon lights.

No one says anything for a long time.

The air stirs around me and then the smell of bacon and the soft touch of Monica's hair brushes my arm as

she sits down and crosses her legs in front of her. "Devon, what's going on?"

Hell if I know.

"Can you come here, to DC?" Galeo asks. His voice seems loud. "You have to show my father. If he sees those markings in person and can have them authenticated, he may be convinced. What else could they be but a sign of Order?"

"We've got those emergency bank accounts," Lawrie says, he's back in his chair and looking up at Lyle. "It's enough for airfare."

"Send me your travel plans and I will ensure transportation from the airport once you arrive," Galeo says. His eyes are brighter than ever. He claps once and seems to pulse with nervous energy. "Well, we always knew we would meet in person one day, Lawrie. It seems the time has come."

"Yeah," Lawrie says. "Just wish it was for a different reason. I'll send you what you need after we make the plans. Thanks for everything, man. I'll, uh, see you soon."

Galeo nods. He sits watching us for a moment more, then the video chat ends and a blank screen blinks back at us.

"Okay," Lyle says, his tone cool and together. "Look up some flights that will get us to DC as soon as possible." He glances at his watch. "It's almost nine. There might not be that many we can make tonight."

"Right," Lawrie says. "Endymion, look up all nonstop flights from Houston to Washington DC that leave tonight or early tomorrow morning."

Everything's moving so fast. Lawrie and Lyle talk

to each other like no one else is in the room. Monica puts
her hand on my thigh.

"Dev, are you okay?"

I stare at her. She's sooty, sweaty and so beautiful I
wanna kiss her. It takes everything in me not to grab her
face and pull her to me. Adrenaline's making me crazy.
"I..." I stammer, looking from her to my brothers and
getting fed up.

"Stop!" I shout.

Lyle and Lawrie look down at me.

"What are we doing? What are you doing? Somebody tell me what's going on!" I jump to my feet so that
I tower over Lawrie and stand eye-to-eye with Lyle.

Lyle's eyes are dark, and there's no snark in his
tone or sarcasm in his expression. "We're saving another
brother, and if you're really ready to hear what's going
on, I'll tell you in a little while."

I swallow.

The computer speaks, "The last nonstop flight from
George Bush Intercontinental Airport, on Wednesday,
July the twenty-first, departs at ten forty PM via Delta
Airlines—"

"Endymion, stop. We'd never make it there in
time," Lawrie says. "Endymion, give me the earliest
nonstop morning flight."

"The earliest nonstop flight, on Thursday, July the
twenty-second, departs George Bush Intercontinental
Airport at six twenty AM via American Airlines and arrives at Ronald Reagan Washington National Airport at
ten seventeen AM, sir."

"How's that?" Lawrie asks Lyle. "I mean, I bet
there's some flights we can make tonight that have lay-

overs, but...."

Lyle shakes his head. "We shouldn't hang around too many different airports. Two's enough. Go for the nonstop flight."

"Endymion," Lawrie says, "book three tickets. Use Information File Three from the Emergency Fund folder on Code Black protocol. Set Galeo SeCaeta as the contact person."

Lawrie bites into another protein bar like he didn't just go King Pin a second ago.

"Information File Three and Code Black?" I ask. "What the hell is all that?"

Lawrie smirks at me. "Well, how else are we gonna access those funds for plane tickets without Mom getting an alert?"

"You got plans for that? What are you, mafia?" Nah, something tells me even the mob would be scared to let my brother into their ranks.

"Processing," Endymion says.

There's a tug on my jeans and I sit back down on the floor by Monica who's staring at me. "Dev, I'm freaking out here."

"You're not the only one," I mutter and take her hand. She curls her fingers around mine and I grin like a dope. If one good thing comes out of this....

"Um." Yir's voice sounds from the window. Damn, I forgot about him. Shuffling feet move across the floor, nearing me. "If it's not a hassle, I'd like to go home soon. I don't think I want to be part of what happens next."

Hey, you and me both, Yir. But I'll be damned if I take his hand.

A soft whump on the floor makes me look over to

where Lyle had been standing to find him sitting. He gazes at me, eyes flitting to Monica and lingering on our joined hands.

"So, let me fill you in."

21
LYLE

IT TAKES AN HOUR AND a half to get to the airport and ten minutes to go through security. No one looks at us twice or has any questioning thoughts. We're old enough to be left alone.

We sit in plastic seats by large windows overlooking the runway. The waiting area outside our flight gate is empty aside from us. Flat screen TV's mounted to various walls show CNN and the Cartoon Network. I set my backpack on the floor by my leg and lean my head back against the cold glass of the window, closing my eyes. Numb sleepiness thrums in my veins. I've been up for nearly twenty-four hours straight, but I don't want to sleep.

Devon and Lawrie sit on either side of me. When I mentally reach out to them, Lawrie's thoughts are dull, like a dreamer's, asleep then, but Devon's mind is loud and awake. His thoughts ramble, full of nervous energy and fear. I open my eyes to see one of his knees bouncing. Maybe he wants to talk about stuff, but I....

I close my eyes and shut off sound from the outside world. Silence, perfect silence—a gift I stole. A deep shudder runs through me and nausea turns my stomach inside out. I want to give the quiet back—and I don't. I'm pain free and in perfect control of my power, but, I swallow hard, the look on her face afterward won't go away. The horror in her eyes makes me wanna throw myself on the runway and let a plane take me out.

I don't really recall everything. I remember how good it felt. The high had lasted for a few minutes before it was gone, pressure-washed away by a flood of revulsion. Whatever I'd done to get Nisse's lips on mine wore off. She'd punched me hard in the chest, and I'd sat on my ass and wheezed, drowning in the black feedback she pounded me with while she cussed at me.

Before I could choke out an apology, she'd pinned me on my back and straddled me, attacking my mouth with her lips and tongue and pushing her body against mine. Want rolled off her in hot waves, drawing me to her, but the lulls between the waves were black. It'd hurt like hell. We left the barber shop, side by side, collecting the grocery bags we'd left on the sidewalk and letting them swing between us, not talking.

"Hey," Devon says.

My eyes snap open and I stare at him. "What?"

Devon sighs and his shoulders slump, he looks beaten down. It's a strange expression for him, but he's kinda looked that way since we got Lawrie back. Sure that girl Monica had improved his mood a lot, but a 'loser' mentality echoes off him. He'd sat through my update, listening to the information Galeo had given me, without interrupting and has backed down from every

argument we started to have.

"What you did, you know, back there." He looks at his hands in his lap, and I'm glad because I don't know what my face looks like right now.

Did Nisse tell him? Did Nisse tell Monica and Monica told him?

That black feeling comes over me, and I almost break out in full-body shudders. I think I need to be punished for what I did. I changed Nisse's mind, forced her to remember what I wanted her to.

Imaginary knuckles crash into my gut.

I didn't know I could do that, didn't know I could do any of those things. I hate people, but I don't want to turn them inside out like that.

"At the school. You saved my ass, and Lawrie's," Devon says, still looking down. "I couldn't do shit. You…I just…I want…." His mind spits random words at me as he stutters and an overall feeling of humiliation radiates from him. "I wanna learn. I mean, I need to learn how to use my power. You totally owned yours. How did you do it?"

My stomach hurts I laugh so hard. Don't think Devon expected me to laugh. Surprise, embarrassment and irritation swish around inside him. Wiping tears of mirth from my eyes, I swallow hard and try to catch my breath.

"You know what?" Devon snaps. "Forget it, man! You really are an asshole."

And he means it, but he's more hurt than I am at the realization. Guess he always thought I was better than that. He gave me too much credit.

Nisse's silver glare, dark with passion, burns me when I close my eyes.

Devon grunts beside me. He's an angry tornado of thoughts and emotions. I add an extra coat of armor to my mental shield, blocking him out, and sink deep into myself. Silence pads my senses and the world becomes a blank sheet of paper, ready for a Number 3 pencil to create new life. Sound bleeds away. It's me and the quiet.

Just how I like it.

A COOL BREEZE RUFFLES MY hair and my eyes snap open. I'm surrounded by rocky walls. The sudden sound of trickling water and the smell of wet dirt causes me to stumble backward. What the hell? Déjà vu makes me shudder. The cave. Evan's cave. Am I asleep? No. I don't smell oranges. Fear cuts me with a dull knife as I scan the room for Order, Corin Peredil, or the sapphire. Need replaces fear as images of the sapphire flood my mind. I feel the gem's warmth in my left hand and I curl my fingers to meet the naked flesh of my palm. There's nothing there.

"Hello?" I call.

My voice echoes off the walls as I travel further into the cave. I near the end of the corridor and follow it into the open cavern area with the shallow pool. I stop at the water's edge, bracing myself to see a dead body floating face down, and blink. The emerald's there, but the body's not.

Thwap!

I turn. In a far corner, a person in a blood stained

uniform pulls something out of the stone wall in front of
him. A thick rope of blond hair swings like a pendulum
over his back. My abdominal muscles clench as nerves
take over.

What do I say to him?

Evan spins around, and dim light glints off a dagger
in his left hand as he stares at me. I move closer. He really does look like Mom, and even a bit like Devon and
me, with Lawrie's curls.

"Oh, it's just you," Evan says, twirling the dagger
between his fingers. Light relief echoes off him as he
whips around like a baseball player winding up for a
pitch and hurls his knife full speed at the wall.

Thwap!

The knife buries itself to the hilt in the stone. How
strong is he? A match for Devon, maybe? Evan stalks
to the dagger and yanks it out of the stone as easy as
pulling a toothpick out of a sandwich. The blade leaves
behind a thin hole, like a notch for climbing. I frown at
the vertical line of notches spanning above and below
the new one.

I clear my throat as he readies himself to throw
again. "Were you expecting someone else?"

Thwap!

Okay. "Hey," I start. "Do you, uh, know who I am?"

He yanks the knife out of the rock, then turns and
leans against the wall, smirking at me. "So, you've figured it out."

I narrow my eyes. Something about his posture
bothers me. "Yeah. When did you know?"

"After I sniffed you," he says, running a finger along
the tip of the blade. "I knew we were related, but I didn't

know how until I figured out you were from Earth." He pushes off the wall and comes forward, stopping inches from me.

"Which one are you?" he asks.

I blink at him. "I'm Lyle."

He nods. "One of the twins. You're the only psychic?"

"Yeah."

"Well." He stares at me a moment longer before looking at his knife. "Nice to meet you, again. Didn't think I'd see you after that last time."

A flash of sadness quickly smothered by indifference comes from him, and I gulp down a bowling ball of fried nerves. There's no underlying hope in him. His stance is stubborn but resigned as he goes back to knife-throwing.

"So, I talked to Lawrence and Devon about you, and we got in contact with connections to the Silver Allegiance," I say, my voice low like I'm afraid someone will hear me—like I'm scared he'll hear me. I don't want to tell him the next part.

"Hm," Evan hums, pulling his knife from the wall. No hope. No excitement. No fear. He continues his routine.

I watch him for a moment, nerves twitching. "You know they don't want to help you."

A dry chuckle. "It's been too long. If they were going to extract me, they would have done it already. They're cutting their losses and saving face, aren't they?"

His detachment from what he just said slaps me across the face so hard I lick my lips expecting to taste blood. My brother is standing here as if being left to die

by people who are supposed to care about him doesn't matter. Like he's not terrified. If he were Devon, I'd know without having to reach into his mind that his calm act was bull. If it were Lawrie, hell, he'd be raging and plotting to save himself. But Evan?

Thwap!

"We're doing something, though," I say, and move to stand next to him, invading his personal bubble. The connection from when I'd first realized I knew him is still here. It's the family bond that eats at my core when I'm around relatives. "Look." I pull my T-shirt over my head and put my back to him.

Cold fingers run along the ridges of my spine. "You didn't have this before?" Evan breathes. "How...?"

I slowly turn around to meet his stunned gaze. "You know anything about the Prophetic Cycles?" I ask.

His eyes glitter with dismay and a furious stream of foreign, one syllable words pour out of him. It's bizarre. Everything else he says sounds like perfect English; guess cussing needs no translation. The knife vanishes up his sleeve as he paces like a caged leopard.

"Hey," I call. He grew up with this Prophecy stuff. He's had Order's Mark for a while. Why's he so worked up? If anything, he should have guessed Prophecy when he found that emerald.

"I don't want this!" Evan howls, then curses some more. He whirls and stalks to me, grabbing my shoulders. "Do the others have the Mark?" When I nod, he growls and grips so hard his nails bite into my shoulder blades.

"Ow, man!" I shove him in the chest and he lets go. Green eyes lock onto mine.

"You don't know about Order's Burden, do you?" he asks, his voice a quiet storm.

"I...." We join a war for people I don't know and don't care about. A rockslide of pressure pummels me, almost crushing the wind from my lungs. Galeo had said it. It was heavy then, but now, now that it really might happen? We're getting on a plane to show these Marks to people who know about Prophecy stuff, people who are gonna freak and make calls and change my world.

But is change so bad? Am I happy how I am, where I am? No. But will I be happier somewhere else, joining a cause I don't care about? Doubt it.

Evan growls. "Order's Burden is the endgame. The Four of Rema—who would now be us—are keystones. We decide who wins. But it won't be easy as simply selecting a favorite faction, Good or Evil, and that one wins. It means our actions can be the downfall of either side. Every choice, every screw up, affects the final outcome, but we won't know what that is until it's all over and millions of people are dead...and millions more hate us."

"Good and Evil. What's Good and Evil for you?" I mumble. There are no clear definitions for me.

Evan gives a humorless half smile. "I don't know, and I don't want to know. I just...." The horror is still in his eyes, but beneath the dread there's a tiny flicker of hope. "I don't want to die now. If this means I don't die, then...."

I stare at him, frowning as he seems to look beyond me. Is someone there? I turn and my blood runs ice cold. A shadow looms on the wall of the cavern, tall and ugly. A whisper of need and longing runs through me along

with the dim memory of black fathomless eyes and shark teeth.

"I'll take it. I accept," Evan breathes, and I want to run away. How the hell do I get out of this cave, out of whatever this is? Last time, I think Corin Peredil gave me a push. But he's not here now.

Evan moves like a ninja, his feet quiet over the cave floor as he goes to the pool and kneels. I sound like a galloping horse in comparison. I sit next to him and watch as he dips a hand in the shallow water and waits. The glowing emerald in the center of the pool dims and begins to move, drifting towards Evan's hand.

"What the hell?"

Evan grins, not turning his head to look at me. "Just a little magic. Funny how I can use it in here."

"Funny why?" I ask. "Gal—someone told me you're good with magic. Is it weird for you to be able to do things in this...?"

"Limbo?" Evan laughs. "I don't know. I've never been in limbo before. But," he pulls the emerald out of the water and studies the perfectly cut gem, "in the battle, before all this, I couldn't use any magic at all. My powers were being blocked somehow."

His face and tone turn bitter. "I should have known it was a trap as soon we set foot in that conference room and no one had the twozz to light a candle."

He's in combat gear. He's got weapons. "Did— were you—breaking the law? I mean...." Damn. How do you ask someone if they committed war crimes?

Evan tears his eyes away from the emerald and looks me up and down, before smirking. "Been talking to politicians I see." He chuckles. "Yeah, I broke the law.

Upon request."

My insides clench. Great, my brother's a war criminal.

"Everyone does," Evan says. "It's politics." He sighs. "I don't know how much you know about Cold Zones."

"They're territories not part of any allegiances," I say. "And you're not supposed to do anything military in those areas."

Evan tosses his head back and laughs like a maniac. It makes my skin crawl.

"That's the idea of Cold Zones, yes. But think about this, you've got vast expanses of territory between Sectors that can be used to hide all sorts of operations for the right price. There's no such thing as a dead Cold Zone. So, I went in with my court and a negotiations team, and we were buying property in the Onki Southern Valley. The contracts were done, they just needed my seal, and suddenly, we were under attack."

He pauses, tilting his head as he watches me, then continues. "It turned out Onkurus had already sold itself to another government before we'd even opened the channels of communication. It was a lure, the whole thing, and we walked right into it. I knew something didn't feel right when we left the ship. I wanted to scrub the mission, but I can't override the Council's orders. I took my people in," he clutches the emerald and shuts his eyes, "I don't know if anyone got out. Some of us escaped the building, but a Ruj military unit was waiting outside."

He doesn't have to tell me anymore. I saw the battle.

"And you managed to get away, by yourself?" I ask.

His breathing is slow and shallow. "I wasn't by myself at first. I was with a friend." He shakes his head. "I made him leave me. I could lead the Ruj away. All anyone had to do was follow the blood. I promised I'd find him later. I don't lie, I can't. So, I meant it. I'll find him later." He swallows. "I'm not going to die."

Guilt, loneliness and determination blend into a mix that leaves the nasty aftertaste of leftover spinach in my mouth. This guy feels so strongly about his people, that court and the team he'd led, he'd probably jump off a cliff if he heard none of them made it out alive. He's so lonely that I wish I were the kind of person who spontaneously hugged, but his determination trumps it all. The emotion's quiet at first, a hollow presence, but it spreads, blanketing everything. He wants to win.

Evan stands, tucking the emerald into one of his many pockets, then stretches his arms out on either side of him. A hum of energy dances and crackles. The whole cavern seems to sing. The air smells crisp and sweet.

"What's your next move?" Evan asks me. His arms drop back to his sides and his body practically vibrates with power. Did he do something, to himself, the room?

"Uh." A soft breeze touches my face, one that smells like oranges. "We're going to meet someone. His father's an ambassador who's got connections. We're going to show them the Marks and see what happens."

"You'll need my emergency code."

The smell of citrus is so strong my eyes water.

"It's easy," Evan says. "It's our mother's name for our father."

"What is it?" I ask, my voice is a fragment of itself.

I'm drifting away, waking up. "Hurry!"

"Ricky," Evan says, "short for Devrik. And Derrick."

I JERK FORWARD, HANDS GRIPPING soft leather armrests. My eyes snap open and I stare at the back of a leather chair. The scents of refrigerated air, coffee and jelly donuts ground me. I turn my head to see Devon on the left of me and a small portal window on my right with the shade pulled closed. An airplane.

"You with us now?" Devon asks. He looks tired and grouchy.

"Yeah," I mumble. "Sorry. Did I...?"

Devon snorts. "You were on autopilot for a while. You walked and grunted, and then blacked out once we got on the plane. Don't see how you guys can sleep."

His iPlay sits in his lap. He's playing a video game. I look past him to Lawrie across the aisle from us. He's spread over the two seats, curled on his side, and tucked under a travel blanket.

I frown, checking out our seats: second row, all leather, plenty of leg-room. "First class? How'd we get here?" I ask.

"They had an upgrade option and Lawrie worked his geek magic," Devon says. "The plane's not full. No one asked any questions."

I shrug. My legs are too long for any coach flight to be comfortable. "Cool."

"You okay?" Devon asks after a moment of silence. The whole plane's kinda quiet aside from some snoring.

"I don't know." And I don't know why I shared that with him.

"Do you...?" he bites his lip. "Can we, I don't know, talk?"

He needs to talk. His mind is screaming for someone to unload on, and so is mine. I stare at him. Evan's determination and guilt, Nisse's hate, Order's burden, me and what I'm capable of. God, I need to talk.

/Yeah, yeah, we can talk./

I wait for him. He's gotta accept my way; he's gotta accept me.

God, Ly, just tell me we're not gonna die. I only need to hear it once.

I sigh.

/Evan told me he's not gonna die, so we're not gonna die either, Dev./

His mental laughter is soothing and after a minute, I laugh too. It's stupid though. Evan said he can't lie. When he says he won't die, it's gotta be true. Well, at least to him, it's true. I lie all the time. So what good is it when I say stuff?

Nisse's dark eyes flash and I feel her sharp nails down my back as she hates my guts between hungry kisses.

/I did something terrible./

CHAPTER 22
LAWRENCE

A COMBINATION OF NYQUIL, VICKS, and Tylenol Cold keeps me in a sleepy fog for most of the trip. If someone told me I'd been teleported from Houston to DC, I'd believe it.

We get chauffeured from the airport in a silver Escalade and brought to a gated community with houses made for celebrities. I feel like hired help as we are ushered through side doors and back hallways to a guest parlor where we wait for our 'guides' to get the young master. The parlor is octagon-shaped with silver wallpaper and dark wood floors. The furniture is old fashioned with curly-cued armrests and patterned cloths done in dark colors.

When a door opens, I half expect the virgin Queen Elizabeth in one of her hoop skirts to bob in. Instead, I get Galeo in black jeans and a bright orange t-shirt that reads: What Does the Fox Say?

"Lawrence!" Galeo grins and rushes to me, wrapping me in a big hug that I return. I thump his back and

step away, smiling and looking him up and down. He's about as tall as me with the same slim build. His irises, up close, have dark rings in their centers instead of pupils and his light purple skin is freckled with tiny royal purple flecks that make him appear darker.

I think I need to upgrade my monitors.

"You are shorter than I thought you would be," Galeo says. His voice has a purring quality to it that my speakers never quite conveyed. "But this is wonderful." He hugs me again; then looks past me.

Oh. My bros. I turn around and smirk at my sibs. They stand together, like defective mirror images of each other, watching Galeo and me like we're both aliens doing a mating dance.

"Gale, meet Lyle and Devon, my big brothers."

"It is a pleasure," Galeo says, nodding at them. He blinks and then extends a hand. "Handshakes? I have been working on mine."

"Oh, uh, yeah." Devon shakes his head and moves forward to take Galeo's hand and pump it up and down. "Nice to meet you, man. We appreciate what you're doing."

Lyle shakes Galeo's hand, but doesn't say anything. He looks exhausted. I thought he slept on the plane, but I guess not.

"Follow me. Let us talk in my room. I need to get you ready to meet my father and prepare you for what might happen after that," Galeo says, then clears his throat and offers us a small smile. His nerves show in the way his mouth trembles.

I fall into step beside him as he leads us down a long hallway. The paintings on the walls are of national land-

marks: Mount Rushmore, the Statue of Liberty. Where are the paintings from Galeo's home world? Come to think of it, the only alien things I'd ever seen Galeo with was that ceremonial muumuu and that funky iPad I want for Christmas. Everything else has been American pop culture T-shirts, Michael Jackson and Microsoft. Is it an assimilation thing? Being purple kinda cancels out assimilation, but guess a guy can try.

Galeo says, "You still look awful."

I shrug. "Been better. Lot of crap happened yesterday."

"Do you want to talk about it?" He frowns, looking concerned. "The other things can wait, if you need...."

I shake my head and shudder, the scent of kerosene burns in my nostrils. I do a triple sneeze into the baggy sleeve of my sweatshirt.

Galeo pats my back as I pull a thick wad of toilet paper out of my pocket and blow my nose. We stop at a slightly ajar door and Galeo pushes it open all the way with a suspicious expression on his face. "I closed this. Mifs, Shegal!"

A tiger-striped, fat cat runs through Galeo's legs. I yelp, jumping over it as it streaks away with a necktie in its mouth. Devon curses and Lyle snorts.

"Damnable cat," Galeo grumbles. "I am going to feed it to one of the Dobermans behind the security gates."

"You will do nothing of the sort!" A girl's voice snaps from inside the room.

Galeo balks and storms inside. "Get out of my room, Saphera!"

I enter Galeo's room, smirking at the psychedelic

wallpaper and 80's movie posters, and stop as I come face-to-face with SeCaeta Saphera Umi-Irideus, Galeo's little sister. She's an inch or so shorter than me, but she tilts her head up to make us even. Purple-gray eyes sparkle like fireworks as she gives me a million-watt smile. Straight black hair in a layered cut frames an apple-cheeked face.

"So, you are my kwichin's Earth friend," Saphera says.

I take it back. Galeo doesn't purr, this woman does. Locusts morph into humming birds that send buzzing sensations through my chest.

"Yeah, that's me," I say, stuffing toilet paper back in my pocket. "You're Saphera. Nice to meet you."

Saphera gives a light laugh and goes to sit on Galeo's round, king-sized bed. She's got on a T-shirt thing that comes mid-thigh when she crosses her ankles. Silver bells jingle on her anklets as she flexes her feet. She's wearing rainbow socks with four individual toes. I give her points for covered feet. Toes give me the creeps.

"Stop staring at my sister," Galeo hisses in my ear and I grip his shoulder.

"Dude, why didn't you tell me she's hot?"

Galeo rolls his eyes. "That is disgusting. Out, Saphera! This is important."

"Important enough for you to sneak three humans into the house before the morning meal?" Saphera brings one knee to her chest and plays with an anklet. "I bet it has something to do with why Pim was annoyed with you yesterday. After you came in here to sulk, Pim ended up conferencing for the rest of the evening."

Galeo winces.

I frown. "You got in trouble?"

"Not really," Galeo sighs, then goes to his bed and grabs Saphera's hands. With a rough tug, he pulls her off the bed. "Out!"

Saphera laughs and tosses her head as she walks by Galeo. "I am willing to help you, kwichin. You should not be so quick to put me out."

Galeo growls under his breath and gives the small of her back a little push. "This is not your business, kwighinee."

"Not yet," she says, offering me a grin as she moves to the door.

Lyle and Devon part to let her pass, their heads turning to watch her go. She doesn't smile at them like she smiled at me. This never happens. Girls choose the twins over me. It really must be the end of the world.

"Make yourselves at home," Galeo says, gesturing around at the big Arabian Nights-style pillows heaped in piles on the green shag carpet. His computer sits on a table designed to look like a giant Coke can.

I go to the computer. It loads up quick; windows pop up displaying international newsreels with subtitles in a squiggly language I don't recognize. A smaller window floats at the top of the screen receiving a constant feed of text in the same strange language. Music from several iHeartRadio stations play a blended cacophony of current pop, retro rock, and classical.

Something solid hits the back of my knees and I look down at the desk chair Galeo's pushing into me. "Sit," Galeo says, "before you fall over and—"

"Strip?" I say with a chuckle. "Damn, Gale, didn't know you just wanted a net hook-up."

"I prefer my 'hook-ups' a bit softer with larger endowments in areas you lack," Galeo says.

I peel off my sweatshirt and pull up the T-shirt under it, exposing my back. Galeo's fingers are a little leathery as they trace a few of the symbols on my spine.

"It is a beautiful design," Galeo says. "The language is so ancient I can't make out the words."

"There are words on our backs?" Devon asks. His voice is close. "Look at mine."

Galeo's fingers leave my skin. I rest my head on Galeo's desk.

"The pattern of the designs are the same on you both, but some of the letters are different," Galeo says, sounding awed. "These Marks are unique."

"Aren't they all? Other people have had Marks. Were they all different?" Lyle asks.

"I have only seen the Mark in presentations," Galeo says. "They were all images of Marks from former Remasian leaders long gone. I will admit that I did not pay attention to the lettering."

"Can you pull up those images now?" I ask, raising my head.

Galeo hums and reaches over me, running his finger over his screen. A circle appears and Galeo taps it twice. Images and strange words swirl as the circle expands, becoming a wheel of selections. A few more taps change the screen into a projector.

"Whoa," I breathe as a 3D image of what looks like the Mark on my back hovers a few inches in front of my face.

The chair I'm in rolls backward as Galeo pulls it away from the computer desk. With a wave of his hand,

the image follows me. Lyle and Devon walk around the construct, staring at it and wearing matching expressions of anxiety. Two more images of Marks appear on either side of the first. They all share the same column formation, shaped like multiple vines layered and woven over and through each other with symbols branching off their trunks like flowers.

I squint. "All of these Marks look the same. Ours are different?"

Galeo sighs. "Yes." He bites his lip, looking uneasy and I frown at him.

"You think they won't buy that our Marks are real?" I ask.

"I bet someone has an image of the Mark on Evan's back," Lyle says. He sits on a blue Arabian Night pillow. "It's probably different too. It's only right that it should be. He's—we're—not like those other leaders."

Galeo nods. "It might depend on what your Markings actually say as well."

Galeo and my brothers keep talking, soft background noise against the loud pounding in my ears. I need to lie down. I yank my sweatshirt back over my head and slide off the desk chair onto the floor, crawling to one of the massive pillows. It feels like a bed. All I need is a blanket.

"Lawrie?" Sounds like Devon. "You all right, man?"

"Mmm." I'm a lot of things, but all right probably isn't one of them.

"Ly, come here. Touch his forehead."

A big hand's on my face and I swat it away. Hate being pawed. I sit up slowly, scrubbing my eyes with

the heels of my palms. Dull knives saw at my muscles. Devon, Lyle and Galeo sit around me, staring like I'm gonna melt.

"We have a family physician onsite," Galeo says, "but he's Cyriae. I can get a car and we can take Lawrie to a human doctor." He almost sounds hopeful.

"I don't..." Lyle begins and sighs. "We have to talk to your father first, Galeo."

Lyle's eyes look strange. Galeo tilts his head to one side.

"Your pupils are pinpoint," Galeo says to Lyle. "Are you having a vision?"

"IIcy. Stop i!" Devon waves a hand in Lyle's face until Lyle blinks. "Don't use your psi-junk. Can't you turn it off?"

I brace myself for Lyle to go postal on Devon, but weirdly, he doesn't. He just shakes his head. His eyes are bright, maybe even scared.

Lyle looks at Galeo. "Your dad's getting ready to leave for work. We have to show him now."

Galeo gapes, nods a few times and gets to his feet. "All right then." He holds a hand down to me and I take it, letting him pull me up.

Galeo leads us out of his room and through another hallway decorated with golden mirrors and portraits of dead presidents. I catch glimpses of my sorry self at multiple angles. I look like I crawled out of bed after being dead for two days. In contrast, Devon and Lyle look like pop stars following their entourage. I really hate them sometimes.

Voices drift from ahead. A man with a moderately deep voice speaks in a guttural language. Galeo picks

up the pace, and we step into a den with fur rugs and dead animals mounted on the walls. A burly man with purple skin and thick black hair stands in the middle of the room talking to a floating head in front of him. Holy shiggity, that's awesome.

"Pim?" Galeo calls.

The man turns, a welcoming grin on his lips until he lays eyes on me and my brothers, then the smile dims to polite but impersonal. He looks back to the floating head and says a few more words in that guttural language. The head answers back in the same language and disappears. Had it been a projected image like the ones from Galeo's computer earlier? If so, where's the projection base? Light glints off a round button on the man's lapel.

"Good morning, Galeo," the man says as he comes toward us. "I was not made aware of our guests."

He looks troubled and I don't blame him. If I were paying security to watch my butt, I'd be pretty pissed about people sneaking into my house too.

"Pim, these are my friends," Galeo says, sounding a bit nervous. "I am sorry to interrupt your business, but you do remember our conversation from yesterday?"

The man, Pim, no, Ambassador SeCaeta Irideus Ami-Kaihin gazes at my brothers and me, his dark purple eyes thoughtful and thorough. His stance is proud, his presence huge, but he's not intimidating.

"Welcome to my home," he says. There's a lilt in his accent, but other than that his English seems flawless.

Galeo sighs. "Pim, I am afraid I must ask for your time and kindness again."

"Galeo." SeCaeta's voice has a note of warning. "I do not mind that you have invited your friends. I am not

angry at you for yesterday, but please do not try my patience."

I grimace. 'Gotta do something' pumps fast. I grip the bottom of both my sweatshirt and T-shirt, whip them over my head, and turn my back to SeCaeta. From the corner of my eye, I see Devon and Lyle getting their shirts off as well.

I almost laugh and ask Galeo to put on some music for our routine, but a gasp from the ambassador knocks the humor right out of me. Large, warm hands run along my spine.

"Suetha," SeCaeta breathes. "This is the oath of the Peredils and what look like coordinates." He touches my shoulders, turning me around. Glowing purple eyes bore into my soul. "Where did you receive this marking? Tell me, and you will not be punished."

"Pim," Galeo begins.

"It just appeared, after I—we—got a message from our brother," I say. My scratchy voice breaks on the last word, "Evan Lauduethe. My father is Devrik Lauduethe."

It's hard to hold the ambassador's gaze. His eyes glow so damn bright my eyes water. My body trembles, but I don't know if it's from nerves or chills. Maybe it's both. This guy's gotta believe me, and I can't tell if he does from his facial expression.

The pressure on my shoulders vanishes as the ambassador moves past me to Devon and Lyle, running his hands along their backs as well.

"The coordinates vary," SeCaeta murmurs, "but the Peredil oath is the same as the one on Leader Lauduethe."

"You've seen Evan's Mark?" I ask. I slip my shirts on.

"Yes." SeCaeta removes his hands from Lyle's back, his face a mixture of awe and sadness. He gestures with his hand for us to follow him as he moves through the den into a smaller room with a cherry wood desk, a desktop computer and leather armchairs. He waves us inside, letting us walk past him so he can shut the door behind us.

He leans against the frame for a moment. "Please sit."

My knees wobble as I make my way to an armchair and sit down. The room smells a bit like peppermint and pink bubble gum. There's a tiny, old fashioned gumball machine on a small, round table in a corner. The walls are light blue and loaded with black and white photographs of old drug stores and jukeboxes.

Devon and Lyle choose chairs around me, putting me in the middle. Galeo perches on the arm of my chair, and SeCaeta sits behind his desk. He's solemn as he lays his hands in front of him. My heart does a dance to the jungle-beat in my head.

SeCaeta leans forward and sighs through his nose. "I know who you three are. Yesterday, when my son informed me of your message, I validated your identities. Because I was sure of your relation to Leader Lauduethe, I spoke on your behalf."

The ambassador clears his throat and the glow in his eyes dies out. "I am sorry it was not enough."

"But now?" Lyle asks. His face is smooth as stone, but his pupils are pinpoints again.

SeCaeta frowns, purple eyes starting to gleam

again. "Can you see the future, child?"

"No," Lyle says. "I just feel things."

"And what do you feel?" the ambassador presses, mouth a straight line.

Galeo shifts on his perch and I look up at him. He's watching his dad with bright eyes.

"That this is a delay," Lyle says slowly. "That what you're afraid of is going to happen anyway. I think we started something that can't be stopped."

"Ly," Devon growls, "be careful."

Be careful? I blink and look past Galeo to Devon. His hands grip the armrest of the fancy chair. How much pressure can that wood take before it—

Cre-ee-ack.

The wood in Devon's hands breaks; fabric rips. Devon flushes and lets the curly-cue arms of the chair fall to the floor with two solid thunks. The torn cloth that had coated the severed limbs sag.

"Shi—crap! I'm sorry!" Devon springs to his feet, looking at the chair and chewing his lip. He picks up one arm and groans. "I can buy you a new one." He turns to the ambassador and stops.

I peel my eyes off the amputated chair and look at SeCaeta too. The man's on his feet, staring at Devon like he's Jesus resurrected.

"Suetha!" SeCaeta shouts. He comes around to the chair, peering at the damage then back at Devon. "You were not even trying to do that, were you?"

Devon flushes darker and rubs his neck. "No, I—I have accidents."

"And you," SeCaeta points at Lyle, "have psychic ability."

Lyle shrugs.

SeCaeta's glowing eyes rest on me and I sit up straight struggling to keep my head from falling forward. Galeo's hand touches my back.

"He is an elemental, Pim," Galeo says. "He has all of the symptoms. Well," Galeo pauses and studies me, concern flickering over his features, "not now. But he is usually extremely active."

I cough to clear the gunk out of my throat. "I used my power for the first time yesterday. I made an earthquake. You can look it up online."

"You what?" Galeo blinks at me, the concern's more than a flicker now. He grabs my wrists, the pads of his fingers searching until he finds my pulse.

SeCaeta kneels in front of me, taking my face in his hands. His gaze goes unfocused. Slight pressure pushes against my brain and my body feels invaded, then he lets go. SeCaeta removes his hands, but doesn't rise.

"Is he all right, Pim?" Galeo asks, sounding anxious.

SeCaeta nods. "Your stored energy reserves are fine. You have only depleted your active reserves, which is probably why you feel so badly now."

Lyle lets out a loud breath. His eyes glitter like glass. Locust wings beat in my chest at his expression.

"You're psychic?" Lyle asks.

"I am an empath," SeCaeta says with a nod. "But I do not believe I am anywhere near your level." He grunts as he gets up and moves toward his desk.

Lyle blinks rapidly and looks at the floor, going stiff. Devon sucks in a breath and my head volleys between the both of them. Come on guys. No fair keeping

twin secrets.

"What does this mean, Pim?" Galeo folds his hands in his lap. "Does this mean you will help them?"

SeCaeta looks heavenward. "I do not want what this revelation will cost the allegiances if it is revealed. We are moving toward a more positive era than I have seen in centuries." His eyes snap forward, locking on us.

"I have seen many wars between planets and sectors. In this last century, I have seen calm. I have seen treaties and alliances that have been honored, for the most part. With this," SeCaeta gestures to us, "all of that progress will be destroyed. This will be the start of a holy war, which are the bloodiest."

"But you sense conflict anyway," Lyle says slowly. He traces the fabric on his armchair. "You've been nervous for a while, way before we got here."

SeCaeta looks startled. He watches Lyle then rubs his thick chin. "I cannot even feel you in my mind, child. How you are even able to enter my mental barriers is amazing."

"I'm sorry," Lyle says, wringing his hands. "I'm not trying to read you, but everything you feel is out here for me to latch onto. You have a barrier up?"

"A barrier you are reaching through like water," SeCaeta says, "and you do not even realize it. You could hurt someone and not know it."

Lyle cringes—what's that about?—and says, "I don't have anyone to show me how to do it right. I had an uncle who tried, but he didn't really know what to do with his power either."

I see a brief flash of skinny Uncle Jonas, a man who forgot to eat and got lost wandering his own neighbor-

hood. Lyle had looked up to him. I'd thought he was a nut-job.

Devon, who'd been on the floor trying to pick up the mess he made, gets up and goes to sit on the arm of Lyle's chair. It takes me back to when the twins used to be close. Talking to one of them meant talking to both of them. When had all this twin-y stuff come back?

Dude, pass out for an evening and miss everything.

"So." Devon raises his chin and puts on his 'I'm-the-captain' look. "What needs to be done next? We're not here to talk about war stuff. We want to know what it's gonna take to get someone to pull our brother's unconscious body out of that pool."

Hot damn. Color me impressed. I stare at Devon, drawn to the passion he just spewed. Could I ever do that, be like that, when the mood strikes me?

SeCaeta sits on top of his desk and tilts his head at Devon as his eyes gleam. He doesn't seem mad, just curious, and maybe amused.

"You," SeCaeta says with a laugh in his voice, "just reminded me of Leader Lauduethe. He is not one to mince words either, but you show far more patience."

Devon grunts. "So?"

I grind my teeth. Don't need to be psychic to know this is it. The decision's being made.

SeCaeta gives a slow, cautious smile. "Well, I suppose I will help you. One life opposed to millions is trivial when one considers future possibilities, but that time has not yet come." He winks at Lyle.

Relief courses through me, Devon lets out a "Phew!" and Lyle slumps in his chair seeming dazed. Galeo pats my shoulder.

"However...."

Damn.

"There is something, a word, and if you can supply me with it, I am sure things could be expedited. Did Leader Lauduethe give you a code, an emergency—"

"No, Pim," Galeo says. "I told you before that—"

"Ricky," Lyle says, "his emergency code is Ricky."

Ricky? Like Devrik Ricky? Really? That's kinda... lame.

SeCaeta nods and smiles lightly. "Thank you. Now, I will need you two," he gestures to Devon and Lyle, "to come with me. Your Marks will need to be authenticated. We will also have to take DNA samples. And you," he points at me, "will follow my son to his room where our physician will be summoned to see to you." He sighs and gestures to all of us. "Your Earth parent is not aware of the situation, I assume."

Mom's gonna grill us with green onions and eat us for dinner.

"No, sir," Devon says. "Do you want us to call her?"

"There will be time for that later," SeCaeta says. "Under the United States law, I believe I would need to have her permission to take you into my custody, but the laws of this country will no longer apply to you. No Earth laws will. You do understand that once you agree to come with me, you become subject to Silver Allegiance law? Your world, this world, can no longer protect you."

My little locusts quiver so hard in my chest that my whole body rattles with them. Stop it. This is nothing to freak out about. I mean, we're just renouncing the Earth.

23
DEVON

I LIE FLAT ON MY stomach on a cold metal table, shirt off, as a tall, skinny purple dude in red scrubs smears warm gook on my back. The SeCaeta family's personal physician whistles as he works like a dumb cartoon character.

"This is so exciting!" Dr. Aderyn chirps. He chatters like one of my aunts after too many margaritas—loud and fast. "Who would have thought that someone like Devrik Lauduethe would do something so beneficial to society?"

"Someone like Devrik?" I grouse.

My voice is muffled, my face buried in a large feather pillow. The room is cold, just how I like it, but it's got a sterile hardness to it that makes me nervous. SeCaeta told us the doctor's in-house clinic used to be the mansion's panic rooms before the family moved in. The steel enforced walls are coated with murals showing white grassy plains and orange skies, but when the heavy outer doors shut, it feels like being trapped in a

multi-roomed tomb. The pillow softens things up a bit. I'm glad someone thought of it. Hope they gave Ly one.

A pang of guilt makes me cringe. Lyle's in another room where I can't reach him. I don't like him being so far from me, not now. I totally fail as a brother. I'm probably the biggest asshole ever born.

"Is the gel bothering you, Devon?" Dr. Aderyn asks. His fingers pause.

"No," I croak. Taking a deep breath and pushing Lyle out of mind, I say, "Tell me about Devrik. I don't know the guy and he's supposed to be my dad."

He's not, though. My dad's name is Frank Conway, an average height, pale-skinned guy with hairy knuckles and the ability to eat sixteen Coney Island chili cheese dogs in one sitting.

Dr. Aderyn laughs and goes back to smoothing bubble gum scented gel over the lines of my Mark. His fingertips feel like tiny paint brushes. "Oh-oh-oh, Devrik! He and I are about the same age, and, well, liken him to one of your Kardashians."

I blink. It's so weird when aliens talk about human celebrities. Sci-fi movies usually depict aliens as greater beings and so beyond us it's surreal, but I'm starting to think most of them are just as gossipy and shallow as humans.

"Following the wild exploits and bad behavior of Devrik Lauduethe used to be so popular! He was so free and fun and, as you humans put it, hot."

Hot? WTF?

The doctor gives my butt a light slap. I almost smack him, but he removes his hand.

"All done. I will be back with the probe."

Now he's starting to sound more like a sci-fi movie.

I turn my head on the pillow, staring at the murals. Devrik is an alien Kardashian. I smirk. *Hey, Ly....*

No. I don't want him using his psi-junk anymore today. He can't turn it off, but he doesn't have to push himself. He told me he's still juiced up from Nisse, and I want to keep it that way.

That's so messed up I don't know what to think about it. My stomach aches as I picture Lyle's face. His eyes had been bright like he was gonna cry, but he'd kept his mouth tight. He'd tricked Nisse and he wants to hurt for it.

I crack my knuckles. A growl rumbles in my chest. I wanna smash the hell outta something, don't care what it is. I'd been right there and hadn't been able to help either one of my brothers.

Dr. Aderyn's voice makes me jump. "Hold still. You are going to feel some pressure. I will touch the area with my fingers to let you know where I am going to put the probe each time."

"Just do it," I sigh.

Soft fingers tap the nape of my neck and then cold metal touches the skin. A searing sensation runs along my spine before the metal clamps onto my neck like tiny jaws and starts pulling at my skin in sections. The procedure continues with soft finger taps then sharp metal bites. I grit my teeth and clench my eyes shut.

"Your blood is deceptively human when running basic tests," Dr. Aderyn says as he works. "The structure of your red and white blood cells is similar to a full human's. Of course, that is what made it possible for your parents to be able to produce offspring together in the

first place, but still. It is amazing how compatible Devrik was with your mother. Most hybrids do not have blood that can pass for human under a microscope."

"Why do you say it's surprising? I mean, Devrik looks like me. He didn't—doesn't have extra eyes or three livers." Wait, I don't know about the livers.

The metal probe bites down and I hiss. Dr. Aderyn pats my back gently. "Well, Devrik is a hybrid himself. His mother was a lesser Amphoran princess, but his father, the infamous Kavka Lauduethe, was well-known for being a hybrid of an unusual blend. I would think Devrik would not be a compatible mate for many races."

The doctor lowers his voice. "In fact, years ago, the rumor was that Devrik was sterile. Next thing anybody knows, he disappeared for years and reemerged with Leader Lauduethe."

Soft fingers pat again, then another hard metal bite. Ow—it hurts more the lower it goes.

"Honestly," Aderyn sighs, "with all of Devrik's affairs, if he was fertile, one would think the man should have dozens of illegitimates. There has never been a mention of even one. But on second thought, we are only now finding out about you three, so perhaps there are more."

My face feels hot. "I'm not illegitimate."

Aderyn laughs. "No, you are not and that in itself is also amazing. Devrik Lauduethe married, to one person, for years!"

"Is Devrik like some interstellar player?"

Aderyn snorts with laughter. "I love human phraseology! Yes, Devrik was deliciously scandalous. He has grown quite boring now." Aderyn sighs. "I miss those

days. Opening the Reels and going to the celebrity section to see what Devrik was up to."

I hiss as the probe pierces the skin just above my ass.

"All done," Dr. Aderyn sings. "You were fantastic. Now, I am going to apply a topical analgesic to soothe the skin. You may be sore for a few days."

Aderyn slathers a thick cream on my back. Its bubble gum scent is much stronger than the gel's. The whole room smells like a candy store after two breaths.

"The results are calculating and should be available in a few minutes." Aderyn's hands are deft as he rubs in the medicine and the light burn in my back fades to almost nothing. "Feel better?"

"Yeah," I mumble. "Can I sit up?"

"Maybe give it a few minutes," Aderyn says.

Yeah, well, I hate all this lying down. I push myself up. Ouch. It's like having a sunburn all over my back. The skin feels tight and forcing my muscles to move under it stings like hell. I hunch over, letting my legs dangle over the side of the metal table. The burn dies down as the crap Aderyn rubbed on my back kicks in. Coldness settles over my skin like a blanket of ice and I shudder.

Something soft touches my knees and I look down. My shirt. I glance at Aderyn who grins and lets go of the T-shirt as I take it. I drape it over my chest, afraid to pull it over my head and have it touch my back.

"Oh, here it is." Aderyn says out of the blue. A solid projected image of the Mark floats in front of him, and I frown.

That's me, huh? I've never seen the Mark on my own back. It looks like the ones on Lawrie and Lyle.

Aderyn is still as a statue.

"Doc?"

"Y-yes?" The humor and good cheer is gone from Aderyn's tone and posture. His voice sounds, I don't know, reverent, I guess. Like he's talking to someone important. Wait, he's talking to me.

"It—your Mark." He shakes his head and wrings his hands together. "It is authentic, no falsehoods. And your DNA proves you are indeed the son of Devrik Lauduethe."

"You really thought we were fakes?" I ask. I just don't get why people think we'd lie. We'd have to be pretty twisted, but then again, the world's pretty twisted, so maybe.

"It crossed my mind," Aderyn mumbles, his eyes day-glow blue. What is it with these purple guys and their neon eyes? Bet they can't bluff for shit. That's gotta suck.

"I don't get why." I chance pulling my shirt on. There's only a slight burn as I tug the fabric down. When it rests snug against my skin, it feels good, secure. Something else between the world and me. I glance at Aderyn who fidgets with his collar and sigh. "Can I come with you?"

Ly's waiting in the next room for Aderyn.

"S-sure," Aderyn says, tone still awed.

Is this what I'm looking forward to? Minions, fans, worshippers? Do people treat Evan like this?

I blink, thinking about Evan. I see a guy with long hair wearing a Robin Hood tunic and boots. But no, Lyle said that hadn't been Evan, it was a dude named Corn— no, Cor-in. But he looked a whole lot like Evan does, or

so Lyle says.

"If you are ready, sir," Aderyn says.

Sir?

"I'm ready," I say and slide off the table.

I follow Aderyn into a narrow hall with a door at the end. Aderyn knocks before entering, with me steps behind him. Lyle sits on a metal table just like the one I'd been on.

"Hey," I say, feeling kinda dumb. What else can I say?

Lyle studies me a second, then looks to Aderyn. "My turn?"

Aderyn gives a tight nod. "Please lie down, and remove your shirt."

Lyle complies and looks over at me. "You're staying?"

"Yeah," I say with a shrug. There are no chairs, only Lyle's table, and a counter with silver machines on top of it shaped like cylinders and spheres right out of a geometry class nightmare. Aderyn repeats the same motions he performed on me.

It doesn't seem to take long for the doctor to say, "All done," and apply the gray, topical ointment to Lyle's skin.

"You okay, Ly?" I touch the top of my brother's head and feel him nod.

An image splits the empty air in front of Lyle's table, displaying Lyle's Mark; scattered symbols flicker around it.

"And there you are. Two authenticated Marks of Order," Aderyn says softly. He clears his throat. "I will just send these results to the ambassador. Ah, I am go-

ing to have to step out. There is a viewing screen in the
room. Should I turn on a program for you to watch?"

I blink. "You got ESPN?"

I hate that I sound eager, but I could really go for
some sports right now. Don't care what it is. There's
nothing like letting physical activity take over for thinking too much. The only thing that would be better than
watching a game right now would be working out for a
few hours. Or, I frown down at Lyle, I could talk to my
brother.

"Put the TV on." Lyle's voice is rough.

"Hey, I don't need—"

"Yeah, you do. Your head is loud," Lyle grumbles.
"I want..." he trails off.

Was he gonna say quiet? Worry wracks me.

Lyle sighs loudly. "Dr. Aderyn?"

"Yes?" Aderyn's still there, staring between my
brother and me, an intrigued expression on his face.

"Is there something you can give me to help me
relax?" Lyle asks.

Aderyn studies Lyle intently. "Your pupils are dilated."

"He's psychic," I blurt, "and he's having trouble
with his—"

"Shut up!" Lyle growls, but I don't care.

"His head's been bugging him for a while now. Is
there anything you can do?" I ask, feeling kinda hopeful.
Maybe aliens have medicine for psychics.

"Are you a telepath?" Aderyn asks.

"Telempath," Lyle mutters.

A light smile crosses Aderyn's thin lips. "I imagine
being on a world with so many untrained minds is pain-

ful." He makes a clicking noise with his teeth. "It is a marvel that you are still sane."

Worry turns to fear. I see a flash of pale Uncle Jonas popping pills from a blue bottle he carried everywhere. Aderyn moves to the counter of silver machines and runs his fingers over one shaped like a sphere. The soccer ball-sized machine seems to yawn as a small hatch in its face opens and a shelf about as wide and thin as a receipt rolls out. A clear, pen-shaped cylinder full of shimmering blue liquid sits on the shelf. Aderyn takes it gingerly between two fingers and comes back to the table.

"I am going to inject you," Aderyn says, touching the blunt tip of the cylinder to the side of Lyle's neck. "Take a deep breath; then hold very still." Aderyn places a hand on the other side of Lyle's head, holding it steady. "Breathe."

Lyle sucks in a loud breath, and I pat his back.

Aderyn squeezes the device and the blue liquid shoots into Lyle so quick I almost miss it. Aderyn releases Lyle's head and my brother goes limp, moaning and cursing. He's gotta be okay if he can string together those kinds of sentences.

"There you are," Aderyn purrs. He strokes Lyle's neck at the injection site. "You will feel the effects momentarily."

Aderyn and I are treated to another minute of cursing before Lyle sighs. "Oh...God."

"You okay?" I ask. "You sound..." drunk.

"M'fine." Lyle turns his head to look at me. His pupils are so dilated his eyes seem black. "Ooh, that was nice." His eyes flutter shut.

I stare at Aderyn. "What did you give him?" My

voice comes off hard.

Aderyn frowns at me, wariness seeping into his stance. "A cocktail of neuro-sedatives. It calms the neurons and temporarily lowers the sensitivity of their thresholds, so that unnecessary neurotransmitters are not released. Most psis react to stimuli non-psis do not register, so their neurons fire hundreds of times more often. It makes them sensitive."

Sensitive. The family's word for psychic conditions, but the irritation that grips me whenever I hear that word and Lyle in the same sentence doesn't surface. I gaze down at my brother. He's got a sleepy smile on his face as he breathes easy.

"Ah, so, he'll be all right from now on?" I ask. If Aderyn just cured my brother, I'll shake his hand.

Aderyn purses his lips, eyes thoughtful. "All right? For now, I suppose. He is strongly gifted and trapped on a planet full of deadheads."

"Deadheads?"

"Deadheads are people with no mental barriers, because they do not need them. I imagine most Earth people are deadheads. There are no humans who are natural psychics. Any human who has a talent like that is of mixed descent."

I frown. That means there's more alien in my blood, because psychic runs on Mom's side of the family. But nobody's ever said anything about Visiting relatives on her end. Not that they would.

Aderyn puts away the empty cylinder he'd used on Lyle. "Because this planet does not produce its own psis, the natural population does not have a genetically developed defense against them. On planets where it is normal

to have psis within the populace, the people have natural, unconscious barriers. Psychics will still feel the strain from time to time, especially in large crowds or when someone is in distress, but they will not drown."

My head spins. I hate thinking. "So, what do psychics do on a planet full of deadheads, to cope, that is?"

Aderyn could write Lyle a prescription for the medicine he just gave him. Imaginary fingers grab my gut strings, and tie them in knots. From using people to drugs, there's gotta be something else.

"They leave," Aderyn says. He runs his hand over another machine, this one shaped like a pyramid. An image spirals from its pointy tip, then widens until it's a 3D projection of a soccer game, Brazil versus Germany. "A psi cannot survive and keep his or her sanity on a world of deadheads for long. They will eventually self-destruct in a quest for mental peace."

I swallow hard and the knots in my gut swell so big I feel like a pregnant lady. "But they can get better when they leave the place?"

Aderyn watches me, and then looks at Lyle, understanding in his eyes. "Not all long-term damage can be healed."

"Does he...?" I feel like an ass talking over Lyle's head like this, but his eyes are closed. He's either asleep or doesn't care. "Can you check him for damage?"

What if he's broken?

"Only a psi-healer can perform that analysis," Aderyn says softly. Then, he smiles. "However, when you and your brothers relocate to Rema, you will have a number of extremely talented psi-healers at your disposal who will try to work miracles because of who you are!

I will be right back!" He prances out of the room.

I feel like I've been slapped in the face with a brick. Relocate to Rema. I mean, I knew that, right? I can't claim to be an alien leader, set out to prove it, and then think I can go back to playing football and dating cheerleaders, or Monica. A flash of pain hits me in the chest as images of Monica's face, the feel of her hair on my cheek, her lips on my neck, revolve around my brain.

I don't want this.

I want to be strong. I want to be able to protect the people I care about. I need to be able to control my power. But I don't want my life to change. Why can't we be leaders of Rema here? Don't aliens have Skype? And what the hell can I offer aliens anyway? I'd make a suck-tastic leader. They should shake my hand for saving Evan for them. He can keep doing his job now.

But what kind of job does Evan do? He's out fighting and getting shot and dying. Does he get to make laws and wear fancy clothes and dance with princesses and junk? Do alien paparazzi go through his trash and make up stories about him sleeping with goats—or whatever the alien equivalent of a goat is?

Does he even want to be leader? Lyle had said Evan wasn't happy about the prophecy stuff at all, so no, he probably didn't want to be one of the Four of Rema, the friggin' Four. Sounds like a dumb comic book. The Four. But....

"Hey, Ly?" I ask, glancing at my brother. He's staring at the wall.

"Hm?" Lyle slurs. He sounds completely lit.

"I know Evan doesn't want to be, you know, a special leader, but could you tell if he liked his regular job?"

I ask.

Lyle doesn't look away from the wall. "I don't know. He didn't like being hurt, or drowning. That was all I..." he trails off, licking his lips.

"What?" I look at the wall too. I don't get it. Same mural, same colors, what's so interesting about it?

"It's moving," Lyle murmurs.

Holy hell. "Sounds like the doc gave you some good stuff," I say. I feel sick at the drugged-out grin that crosses Lyle's face.

I sit down on a steel counter, watching the soccer game. Looks like Brazil scored. The crowd's going wild on their side. My butt vibrates and I jump off the counter.

My cell phone.

I pull it out of my back pocket, expecting it to be Mom. I'll answer the phone this time. I'm gonna tell her about this cluster-fuq. The number on the caller ID is unknown. Who's this? "Hello?"

"Devon?" The voice is rough and shaky. My heart thumps.

"Monica?" I frown. "Are you okay?"

"No," she mutters.

There's clattering in the background and a lot of voices.

"Where are you? You need me to come get you or...." Hell. Come get her, how? I feel the plastic edges of my phone giving way and I ease my grip.

"I'm in jail," Monica says in rush, and the air sucks right out of me. "We got arrested: Nisse, Yir and me. Everybody who was there. That asshole Shawn said we were all in on it. And Quent was right. He was right about everything. The police won't listen to us. Witness-

es at the school ID'ed us."

There's a black hole in my chest, vacuuming up my intestines. "Oh God. What can I do?"

She breathes. I listen close, waiting to hear a hitch in her breathing, wanting to know if she's crying. She's not, or if she is, I can't hear it. But she's gotta be scared. I sure as hell am. Monica's in jail for burning down a building. Is that a felony? I think it's a felony. She could go to prison.

"Look, my mom's a lawyer," I say. "I'll call her right now."

"Devon, shut up," she says so matter-of-factly that I do. Her voice lowers to a whisper. "Look, Shawn didn't know your name, but someone on campus did. They've been showing some of those cell phone videos on the news, and somebody called in. When the officers were questioning me, they asked about you. They want to know where you are, Dev. They went to your house already."

I try to breathe and can't. Everything's trapped inside the black hole. Oh God. Oh God. The police were at my house.

"I gotta go," Monica blurts. "Hey, you're my phone call. I only got one, and I called you. Just wanted you to know."

The call ends and I stare at the blinking screen. Call Ended. Call Duration: 2:23.

I was her 'phone call.'

The black hole collapses, and air rushes back in. I choke for a second, and then rub the screen of the phone with my thumb.

The police are looking for us.

I shut my eyes, seeing bullets flying as the police shoot at me like I'm with the crazy guys trying to kill people. I see the crowd pointing at me, like I did something wrong.

I swallow. "Ly?"

"Hmm?"

"I'm calling Mom."

24
LAWRENCE

I LIE ON GALEO'S BED, scowling up at Dr. Aderyn. After he went cray-cray over me looking 'just like Devrik when he was [my] age!' with a teeny-bopper crush glowing in his eyes, I don't trust him.

"Hum." Dr. Aderyn cocks his head to the left; then reaches into the side pocket of his loose pants. He pulls out a clear rod the size of a pen, taps the tip with his finger, and runs it over the length my body. "Your energies are unbalanced."

"We already know that," Galeo says, sounding irritated. "Can you help him?"

Aderyn huffs. "Why are you in such a nasty mood, Ami-Irideus?" The doctor shakes his head and runs the rod over my body again. "He will need a good regimen of vitamins to replace what he has lost and a dose of immunity serum."

Shizz. What the hell did these two do to piss each other off? I swear Galeo looks ready to strangle Aderyn.

"Hey, guys," I grunt. "Knock it off. Just give me

the shot."

Aderyn snorts and gives an amused smirk. "I think I see a resemblance to Leader Lauduethe."

I frown, watching Aderyn as he puts away the rod. "Why do you guys call Evan 'Leader Lauduethe' all the time? It sounds funny, especially when you call Devrik by his name."

"It's a sign of respect," Galeo says. "You do not call Queen Elizabeth simply Elizabeth."

"Thinking about it now," Aderyn drawls, "we will not be able to call Leader Lauduethe by that title for much longer, as there will be three other Leader Lauduethes soon. Whatever will we do?"

"Is that—" I start.

"I have to run back to the clinic for the serum. I will return." Aderyn leaves the room quick as a cat.

Rude.

"What were you trying to ask?" Galeo sits on the bed beside me.

"I just wanted to know if titles, for us, you know, are really that important." It seems stupid. I'm a guy who likes to skateboard in drained pools. Why would anyone call me something special?

Galeo gives a half smile. "Oh, Lawrie." His eyes look sad. "There are so many titles and proper forms of address you are going to have to learn. You will meet so many majesties and imperial highnesses and your graces. Although, I have heard Leader Lauduethe ruins formal addresses every chance he gets just to make people angry."

My head swims. Evan and fancy parties, wazzing people off. He sounds like a funny guy. Thinking

about meeting him gets me excited, but what if I don't like him? I mean, he's not like Devon and Lyle to me. Though he should be, I guess. I might not like Devon and Lyle all the time, but I'll always care about them. It's unconditional.

I want to save Evan because of that unconditional bond too, but I don't know how I'll feel about him once he's real to me. And how will he feel about me? I'm helping to save him, yeah, and my life's doing a three-sixty because of it, but so will his. He wasn't a special leader before this and hell, who knows when was the last time he thought about any of us. He may not want us in his life.

I squeeze my eyes shut. Hurry up with that shot, Doc. I'm going emo here.

Galeo puts a hand on my shoulder. "Listen, Lawrie. We, my father and even I, were so worried about how you and your brothers would change things for us, I never really thought about how things will change for you. There will be fighting, yes, but aside from that there are so many challenges you will face. There will be so many choices you will not get to make for yourself," Galeo says.

Like what I'll be called.

"Some people break under the pressure and become shadows of their former selves just letting others pull their strings," Galeo says. "Pim said a lot of Remasian leaders were like that. They just did what they were told. And sometimes, they did terrible things."

Like Evan committing war crimes.

"I do not want that for you," Galeo says, voice tired. "You are worth more. You should be a leader who gets a

voice. I am afraid Rema will break you."

"Why do you think so much of me?" I ask. Nobody else has ever told me they thought I could do more than figure out new ways to break myself in half. "I mean, besides the fact that I'm smart."

"And modest too," Galeo says with a laugh. He pats my shoulder. "There is something about you, something that shines bright. People will follow you because of that light, and it will give you confidence to do what you feel needs to be done."

I grin at him. "You did tell me I could have minions easy."

"I never used those words," Galeo says, rolling his eyes. "But...." He looks down for a second, before meeting my eyes again. "I believe one day people will bow to you."

Laughter bubbles in my chest at that. People bowing to yours truly? Really? I can't say I don't like the notion, but I can say I don't believe it.

"And what about you?" I ask. "What are you gonna do? You gonna be an ambassador like your dad one day? I mean, I bet you could lead some masses. You're pushy enough."

I chuckle when he shoves my shoulder.

"Pim's position," Galeo says after a beat, "is an inherited one. Ambassadors are not appointed or voted for. When he is ready to retire, he will give his title to either Saphera or me."

"You gotta compete with your sister?" Where is Saphera anyway? Not that I want her to see me looking like the Walking Dead or anything, but I wouldn't mind her coming in to hang out. I wanna figure out if she was

really flirting with me before or if it was just the fever frying my brain.

"Yes," Galeo sighs, "and Saphera wants the position as badly as I do." He looks at the ceiling. "I had hoped I would do multiple things here on Earth. So far, I've only done one. I am the founder of the Stop the Hate movement and I am president of the DC Chapter."

"And you wanted to recruit me." I smirk, seeing Galeo in a new light. He wants to be a politician. "You had an ulterior motive when you first started talking to me. You still do."

Galeo shrugs and I laugh. I wonder if shrugging is something Cyriae actually do, or if it's another human characteristic Galeo picked up.

"Well," Galeo drawls, "it is not as if you did not have ulterior motives as well." He pokes my shoulder. "We are both opportunists. Though, it helps that we like each other."

We're quiet for a few minutes, and I drift off to the sounds of Galeo's New Age tranquility music until Aderyn comes back in with a big ass syringe that he jabs in my left butt cheek. He chatters about Devrik Lauduethe until I'm sick of hearing about the guy, and then leaves after Galeo insists he can monitor me for allergic reactions as well as Aderyn can.

"My hero," I moan and roll onto my side. My butt cheek throbs like it got stomped on by a cleat.

"You are a rather unattractive damsel," Galeo says.

I wink at him, and he sits on the bed again, swinging his legs up on the comforter.

"I do not know how long you and your brothers will stay here with us, but I am glad you are here. I do not

have any friends on this planet. It has been lonely."

Am I a bad person for thinking about Jeremy and my other buddies? Ah shizz, I didn't even call Jeremy to let him know I'm alive. He's gonna kill me, if I ever see him again. An ache that's got nothing to do with being sick starts in my chest.

Damn.

A cautious knock at the door. I turn my head to see Galeo pushing off the bed and going to open it. He steps back as Devon pushes in with Lyle behind him. Lyle.

"Your house is a maze, man," Devon says. "I think the maid got lost. She took us in so many circles."

"She wasn't lost," Lyle says almost dreamily.

I blink. Is it me, or does Ly look wasted?

Galeo follows Devon and Lyle as they come to the bed.

"A maid? You were not escorted by a guardian?" Galeo's frowning. "Were you—"

"Supposed to leave?" Devon turns on Galeo, scowling at him. "Probably not, but you know what? I didn't think we were prisoners on lockdown or anything. We're guests, right?"

"Right, but..." Galeo trails off, licking his lower lip. "It is all right. Please sit. Have you been offered food or drink?"

Devon shakes his head. "Not hungry. Look, something's going on, and I need to get out of here, go home or something." He runs his hand through his hair and starts pacing.

Lyle watches him for a second, and flops back on the bed with me. "Heya, Lawrie." A lazy grin stretches his features.

My lips twitch. Lyle's pupils are blown to hell and he's flushed like he's been running. I don't know who to pay more attention to—Devon who's got something up his ass, or Lyle who's high out of his mind. They're both pretty damn interesting right now.

Lyle starts humming *The Star Spangled Banner*. He's not half bad.

"Monica, Yir and Nisse are all in jail," Devon says as he turns to look at me.

My heart skips a beat. "What?"

Devon scrubs a hand over his face. "The police are looking for us too. They called Mom. I talked to her just now."

"Mom?" Run and scream, or jump and cheer? "Is she coming?"

"Yeah," Devon says. "She and Dad are hopping the next plane. She said 'hang tight,' stay here and be quiet. But Monica's in jail, man. She said the police are treating her and the others like—"

"Vulattos?" Galeo supplies.

Devon glares at him, then sighs and looks away. "Yeah. Like vulattos."

"And what do you think you can do about it?" Galeo asks, not in a condescending way, but Devon glares at him all the same.

"I don't know," Devon shouts. "But I feel like an asshole staying here all safe and hidden, while my girl's—"

"Your girl," Lyle crows, and laughs. "You asked her out?"

"No!" Devon's face turns red. "But I would have! I will! Shut up!" Devon stops, scowling at Lyle. "Forget

it."

Lyle grins and pretends to button his lips shut. Okay, now I've seen my brothers do some weird shizz, but that deserves a prize.

"Dude, what the hell's up with you?" I ask Lyle. And why is Devon acting like it's normal? Devon's usually the first to complain about strange behavior from Lyle or me.

"Dr. Aderyn gave him something to help his head," Devon said. "Hope it wears off. Now."

I shudder, thinking about Aderyn and that needle.

"Will our mom be allowed in?" Devon asks Galeo.

Galeo seems thoughtful. "I do not see why not. You really are not prisoners here. We just—I think my father fears for your safety and would like to know where you are."

Devon nods. "He never suggested we call her, though. He pretty much said say goodbye to Earth and that our mom wouldn't be able to help us. I mean, was he planning on blasting us off into space without giving word to anybody?"

"I doubt those were his plans." Galeo's voice goes cold.

"Hey, guys," I say. "Cool off. Gale's dad is helping us out. He doesn't have to. We asked for this. Remember?"

"I didn't ask for this," Lyle says all sing-songy.

"Oh bull!" Devon snaps. "You were the one who was running around shouting about your stupid dream."

Lyle smirks. "I didn't ask to be an alien, didn't ask to be psychic, and I most definitely didn't ask for a glowing rock and a rocket ride to outer space. I must have

been a douche in my former life." He beams at Galeo. "You ever hear anything about one of the Peredil brothers being a douche?"

"No," Galeo says evenly. He looks to Devon. "You said Aderyn gave him something to make him act this way?"

"Yeah," Devon says, looking guilty enough to bust. "Forget about it though. Should we go to your dad and tell him about our mom coming? And do you think there's anything he can do about Moni—our friends? They got set up. They don't deserve to be in jail."

Galeo frowns. "Pim cannot involve himself in legal matters that have to do with citizens of Earth."

"But they're vulattos and Visitors!" Devon shouts.

"Vulattos are Earthborn and the Visitors in question are probably on visa, making them temporary citizens," Galeo says. "Besides, Pim can really only speak for Cyriae on Earth."

"But he's talking for us."

"You affect Cyriae. You affect everyone. You...are my guests," Galeo says.

"We're your exceptions," Devon grumbles. "Fine then. I'm getting outta here."

"To go where?" I struggle to sit up; my arms tremble under my weight. When'd I get so heavy? Lyle sits up and grabs one of my arms to help me out.

"Yah!" My nose bumps into Lyle's shoulder as he yanks me too hard. He ruffles my hair and laughs. Jerk.

"I need you to do your geeky magic and get me a flight back to Houston," Devon says, face bulldog stubborn.

"What good's that gonna do?" I ask.

"No good! But if Monica's gotta be in jail, then I'll be in jail with her!"

I stare. Hell, we all stare, and then burst out laughing.

"That's the stupidest thing you've ever said!" Lyle wipes his eyes. A bit of the drug haze must have lifted, because he sounds more like himself. "And you've said some stupid shit."

"Shut the hell up!" Devon snaps. "What would you know about loving someone?"

I think I'm gonna be sick. I mean, really? I thought I was emo.

"You think you're in love." Lyle's voice drips with condescension. "Oh please."

"Dude, you're messed up right now, and you're saying crap that's pissing me off. Just shut up." Devon moves to Galeo's desk and sits in the chair.

"Might be messed up, but at least I'm not stupid," Lyle says. "You're not in love."

Devon spins around in Galeo's chair, putting his back to Lyle.

"She's not in love with you either," Lyle continues.

"Shut up!"

"She likes you, though. Thinks a lot of you," Lyle looks thoughtful, "and she thinks you're hot. You didn't go wrong picking her. You've got mutual feelings. But she's like everybody else when it comes down to it— sweet candy shell on the outside, tasty chocolate just beneath the surface, dirt at her core. She's no good."

Devon knocks over the computer chair, launching himself at Lyle. The bed depresses as Devon crashes on top of Lyle and rears his fist back.

Holy shizz. I shut my eyes. Devon's face…he looks ready to kill.

"Stop it!" Galeo yells.

Flesh hits flesh. Lyle yelps and Devon makes this horrible choking sound. A weight lifts off the bed. I open my eyes and gape. Devon hangs in the air, inches above the mattress, legs bicycling. He holds his throat like he's being strangled, his eyes bugging out of his head.

"Sweet Suetha," Galeo breathes. He backs into the wall on the other side of the room, away from the bed… my brothers and me.

I look at Lyle. Blood drips from a split lip. His eyes are unfocused. He breathes like someone in a yoga trance, slow and deep.

"Ly?" My voice shakes.

Devon gurgles, eyes watering.

"Ly." I touch my brother's arm, and he starts, sucking in a breath and shaking his head. He blinks rapidly and there's a thud. I look down to see Devon on the carpet. He rolls onto his side, holding his throat, coughing and gasping.

Holy shizz.

"What happened?" Lyle asks, touching his split lip and grimacing. "What happened?" His eyes go round. "Oh God." He slides off the bed and goes on his knees beside Devon. "Oh my God. I didn't…it just…you…. You looked like you wanted to…."

Lyle doesn't have to finish talking. I know what he wants to say, because I'd seen it too. Devon's temper is hot and he'd been so mad. Just yesterday he'd slammed Lyle into a wall so hard it left a dent. But he hadn't tried to kill him. Lyle—if I hadn't touched him, and he hadn't

snapped out of whatever the hell that was....

Lyle's dangerous. Devon's dangerous. My hands shake as Kemah comes to mind. I'm dangerous. A flash of purple light and a burst of electricity. I see Zeke and Quent, and smell smoke and lighter fluid. A feeling shifts inside, one I don't want to understand, but I do. Maybe leaving Earth isn't just about us being special people, maybe it's just for the better. Look at what we're doing, and dude, we're just getting started. People are scared of vulattos and after knowing what we can do, I get it.

I really get it.

"I'm sorry. I'm so sorry," someone's saying.

I can't tell the twins' voices apart anymore. I don't know who's apologizing, or if they both are. My eyes go to Galeo who hasn't come a step closer to any of us. I open my mouth to say something to him and the door opens.

Ambassador SeCaeta stands in the threshold. He steps in, and two men in black suits with gleaming FBI badges on their breast pockets come in after him.

Words die on my tongue.

"Boys, I need you all to prepare yourselves to leave with these gentlemen," SeCaeta says smoothly. His eyes are dim, but his fingers twitch at his sides. Is he nervous? "I am afraid there is nothing I can do for you right now."

25

LYLE

THOUGHTS AND SPOKEN WORDS ARE colors and shapes. People talk, I see rainbows. People think, I see pink hearts, yellow stars and blue moons. I lick my upper lip. Tastes like copper; stings like crazy. That's real. Devon hit me, twice. The terror was black licorice and lime, sour and disgustingly sweet at the same time, because I enjoyed it a little, but I didn't want to.

I liked watching someone else lose control. Maybe loved it. Don't know. I'm in a room with blank walls. At least I think they're blank. A minute ago, there were purple horseshoes, but they're gone now. Definitely blank. Boring, plain. There are two chairs, a desk, a lamp, a bottle of water, a package of peanut butter sandwich crackers, a call button.

Voices outside. Rainbows peek in through the slats in the door. No windows. Just that door. Maybe Dev and Lawrie are in similar rooms. FBI took us, that's what the badges said, FBI, but I don't know who has us now. They wear business suits with badges on chains, no weapons,

but not the police, not FBI. Do I care?

Hm. Gears in my head grind and fog rolls in. There are horseshoes on the wall again, and green clovers! I like the clovers best. Don't know why. All the marshmallows taste the same, but...guess maybe clovers are lucky. They make the cereal Lucky Charms. There's a point to them. Oh wait, then there's a point to the horseshoes too, I guess. Aren't they lucky? But who the hell wants to carry a horseshoe in their wallet?

Ow. The split in my lip cracks open more as my mouth stretches into a grin. The horseshoes and clovers fade. I hear more words now, see rainbows.

Something about S.A.O.P.

Dummy can't spell "soap."

No, wait. Wait, that's important. S.A.O.P.

And now I hear....

Too foggy to reach out with my mind, too fuzzy to catch thoughts. It's nice. My head's full of cotton candy until I think about Dev. My lip stings. I reach up to run my fingers under my nose, careful not to touch my lip. Dry. No more blood. Somebody gave me a wet towel to clean up. The towel smelled like oranges.

I slide out of the chair and lie on the floor. It's wood. Always thought offices like these had tile. Tile keeps things cold. The wood's freezing. I press my cheek against it. Feels like I'm spinning. I hug the floor so I don't fly off.

I shut my eyes and see, smell, and taste the color orange. It sounds like coke after the can's been shook up and popped open. Fizz. It's wet. I dive into a floor that feels like water in a sink after somebody pulled the plug. Circling the drain, down the pipes, until I stop. My cheek

rests on cold rock. I open my eyes.

Here again.

I sit up, gazing around the temple. The shadow of the stone table we'd sat at is burned into the ground, a black rectangle. Black rectangles. That won't work for cereal. Sounds gloomy and gross. Bet they'd taste like liver and onions. Hearts, stars, and black rectangles. Yuck.

"Hello?" I call. My voice echoes off the walls. Place is dead, empty. It's so quiet I hear my heartbeat. Fast. Why so fast? Am I scared?

A familiar crazy laugh.

Evan steps out from behind a white column and stands in the black rectangle, smirking at me. "You look touched. What did you drip?"

I frown. Okay. That made no sense. Was it supposed to? And where the hell did Evan come from? This place still feels empty.

Evan kneels down in front of me, nose almost touching mine as he stares into my eyes. "You're dripping kanja water? Mifs, brother! Trying to kill yourself?"

"Why do you feel empty?" My tongue is thick. I bite it twice.

Evan leans back, sitting flat and putting his hands behind him. "I'm masking my presence. You should learn how. I knew exactly when you got here and knew right where you were—are. Took no effort at all."

He's empty because he wants to be? Who wants to be empty?

"There's a man here," Evan says, eyes tracking the walls. "He's been here a while. He won't let me see him, but I feel him, smell him, all over." He rubs his arms

through his sleeves. "How's your plan going?"

"Plan?" Cotton candy's rotting my brain.

Evan narrows his eyes and reaches out a hand, index finger poking me in the temple. Warmth pools on the pad of his finger and there's noise like jingle bells, and then a tiny pressure bomb blows the cotton candy out. My ears pop.

"That's better," Evan says with a smirk. "So, what about your plan? Did you talk to anybody yet?"

I'm cold, scared, anxious, disgusted—with me. Evan's here, and he's real; impatient and nervy, ready for action, on edge. I frown. "Thought you were masking your presence or whatever."

"No point in keeping it up. You know I'm here." Evan taps his finger on my temple again. "Well?"

"We spoke to Ambassador SeCaeta. He believes us and says he's going to call in some favors."

"Hm, don't think I've heard of him." Evan hums as his mind spins through a catalog of people he's met. There are a lot of names and faces, but no conclusion. A mental shrug and his brain switches to other topics. "Any status on those favors?"

I crack my knuckles. "A doctor decided our Marks are real and sent word to some Silver Allegiance officials, I guess."

Evan sighs. "So slow. I feel like.... I don't know. This place makes my skin crawl. Something happened here. The residual energy makes me seasick, and there's damn specters hiding in every corner. I catch glimpses of their arms and legs before they disappear."

"Specters?" I ask.

"Dead people, spirits, ghosts." Evan's irritation

burns hot. "I hate specs. And they're all old. So old they don't even know Common Tongue. I can't understand them." He rubs his eyes.

"You believe in ghosts?"

His look skewers me. I shrink back from him, raising my hands in an 'I come in peace' gesture. He cocks his head to the left and studies me like a two-headed grasshopper.

"I thought I sobered you up," he says. "Should I try it again?" He brings his hand to my temple and I jerk back.

"I'm fine." I would smack his hand away, but I don't know how he'd take it. "But...ghosts, really?"

He grabs his braid and throws it over his shoulder. "So, on Earth, you don't have ghosts?"

"No." I shrug with a frown. I don't sense crazy coming off Evan, just exhaustion. Maybe his brain's burning out. "Do you sleep at all in here?"

"I don't know," Evan sighs. There are dark circles under his eyes. "I don't think so. Time passes in here and it doesn't. It feels like cycles, uh, days, since I saw you last, but it probably hasn't been that long. Has it been a long time since we talked?"

I shake my head. "About half a day."

He stares at me, and then nods. "Twenty-four hours in an Earth day, right?"

"You remember Earth stuff or did you just study it on Rema?" I ask. "Can you still speak English?"

He snorts. "I speak many languages. But I don't need Earth language to talk to you now, just like you don't need Common..." he trails off, eyes darting around so fast they seem to roll.

He jumps to his feet. "What do you want?" he shouts at the walls. His voice echoes around the room and thunders down the hall. Twenty Evans holler back, "What are you going to do?" More yell, "What are you going to choose?"

"Gods," Evan mumbles. He pulls two thick handled, long blades from his sleeves and shifts into a fighting stance, eyes bright and alert. "Can you fight?" he hisses at me.

"Uh." I see Devon dangling in the air, clutching his throat, eyes turning red.

"Keep behind me," Evan whispers, "and do whatever I say."

Oh man. I step closer to him, almost stepping on his heels while watching the darkness beyond the columns. Tension radiates off his back like heat.

A shape peels away from the shadow of a column a few feet in front of us and becomes a solid man. He's not tall or big. Long blond hair swings in a braid past his butt, and he smiles, green eyes crinkling as he says, "I told you I would talk to you again."

Corin Peredil.

"Niobe-va." Evan steps back and I gasp as he crunches my big toe and jabs his elbow into my ribcage. "Move back, cratch," he says. And at Corin, "You, stay there!"

I taste Evan's fear, lemons and olive oil. His mind screams: *Why does this guy look like me?*

Corin cackles and moves into the black rectangle. Evan growls deep in his throat and heat pours off him again. It isn't tension.

"Aah!" I yelp, stumbling back and shielding my

face as bursts of orange-red flame engulf Evan's blades. I uncover my eyes and see him snap his right arm back and fling it straight out, fire roaring toward Corin.

"No!" I yell. "He's not a..." bad guy? What do I know?

The wall of fire flying at Corin splits in two and revolves around the old leader before winking out in puffs of white smoke. Another growl and more walls of fire jet at Corin. One after another, they split and burn out.

Corin makes a noise of approval. "You're good!"

"Okay," Evan murmurs and then becomes a blur of motion in Corin's direction. In a whiplash second, he's got Corin on the ground, foot on his windpipe.

My insides twist. Is he gonna kill him? Can he kill him?

"You're a face-stealer?" Evan's voice is low and cold. He twirls a knife, the milky blade gleams as it catches the light. It's not even singed.

Corin gives a half-strangled chuckle and rasps, "I really like you."

Evan's twirling blade catches fire again. "I'm sick of this place. Sick of the walls. Sick of the ghosts. Sick of the voices." He gets louder and angrier with each new sentence. "You—"

Corin's gone. Just like that.

"I'm glad." Corin's voice comes from behind me.

I spin around and yell. "What the hell?"

"Brother, come here," Evan calls to me.

Something in me wants to dive behind Evan, my ninja, fire-bending brother, but something else in me doesn't feel any malice coming from Corin Peredil. Maybe I'm glad he's here.

"Do as I say!" Evan barks.

"Relax, little leader. I'm not here to hurt you," Corin says, his voice so like Evan's I watch Evan's lips to make sure they hadn't moved. "I need to talk to you and I thought you might be more responsive with your brother here."

I blink and turn to Corin. "Him? Last time, you said you wanted to talk to me."

Did something change?

"I knew I wouldn't be successful in approaching him if you weren't—"

Glints of silver, the sound of air being sliced by metal, and a dull, fleshy thwap. My mouth falls slack as I back away from Corin, eyes glued to the knife stuck in his throat.

"You're fantastic, you know." Corin's voice is beautiful, like a song.

I want to hear him sing, but he can't. He shouldn't be able to talk either, not with that blade through his neck. The knife trembles in his jugular as his Adam's apple bobs. There's no blood. He's not gurgling. I meet his clear, green eyes, and he smiles.

"Fipping spec!" Evan shouts, his knuckles white on the handle of the remaining knife.

A ghost. Of course Corin's a ghost. He was alive a long freakin' time ago, right? So, that means I lied. I do believe in ghosts, I saw them. The warriors, the ladies in dresses, the former leaders. All dead but here a day or so ago, talking and accepting gifts.

"I have been trying to talk to you since you came in contact with the Stone of Magic," Corin says, then yanks the knife out. Balancing the blade between his in-

dex fingers, Corin studies it. "This is Danecian silver. Expensive. Gift?"

Evan glares.

I stand frozen, a few steps from Corin, a few feet from Evan. The rectangle between us separates me from my brother. Evan moves toward the rectangle. As soon as he reaches the center, he pauses, and looks at the floor as if he sees something. "What is this?"

"Your birthright," Corin says, sliding the knife into an empty sheath on his belt. He passes me, heads to the rectangle, but stops before stepping inside it. "I'm afraid you've inherited my job, little leader."

"Who are you?" Evan asks, still looking at the floor.

"Who do you think?"

Evan raises his head, staring at Corin, face unreadable. "Why now?"

"She's back, and She's hungry, desperate," Corin says, like an instructor giving an assignment. "Things are shifting in the worlds of the gods, changing, expanding, expiring. She needs me again—you."

Evan swallows and the knife he holds disappears up one of his sleeves. He unbuttons a pocket on his thigh. Corin sucks in an audible breath as a shimmer of green light touches Evan's fingers.

"This was yours?" Evan asks, pulling the emerald out, holding it in his palm.

Corin steps back from it, but nods.

"Why did you accept?" Evan asks. "Why did you want to help Order start a war?"

Corin tosses his head back and laughs. "Start a war? You mean, continue a war. Gods fight forever. We only fight for a blink of an eye compared to them."

Evan scowls and stuffs the emerald in his pocket again. "Why?" His voice is hard.

Corin chuckles and looks off into space as if a person was standing behind Evan, a person he loves. "Because it sounded like a wonderful deal at the time. Power, glory, territory. We all wanted it. Fighting a war was fine; we did that anyway. She just gave us power to end wars."

"But the war didn't end," Evan says.

"Because I didn't finish." Corin blinks, eyes bright all of a sudden. "I was supposed to choose and I didn't. I let Her keep me from choosing."

"From choosing how the war should end?" Evan grabs Corin's wrists. "Tell me your choice. I can make it now and get it over with."

Corin's smile is melancholy and he shakes his head. "My choice wouldn't make any sense nor would it mean anything to you. You had to be there, you had to know who I was making it for and why."

"How did She—Order, right?—stop you from choosing?" I ask, and I swear they both jump, like they forgot I was there.

Corin glances at me. "I died."

My heart spasms and my mouth dries out. Oh.

"Order killed you?" Evan lets go of Corin's wrists.

Corin keeps his arms extended, like Evan's still holding his wrists, then turns them over and pushes back his gauntlet sleeves to reveal jagged vertical scars from the base of his palms to his elbows. I wanna puke.

"She didn't kill me," Corin says.

Evan backs out of the rectangle. "Your choice was to end yourself, then."

"I didn't choose anything," Corin murmurs, rubbing his left wrist.

"But...?" Evan's left hand goes to the pocket with the emerald inside.

"Your magic is strong," Corin says. "Stronger than mine ever was. There was a spell, one I couldn't do without the Stone, but you can do it naturally. You alter reality by influencing a certain state of mind."

Evan toys with the end of his braid. "Entropy?"

"Madness isn't a choice," Corin says, "when it's forced on you." He stalks to Evan, gripping his shoulders. "Don't let them win, little leader. You're not fighting people, or governments, or good or evil. Use the gifts, let the Stone amplify your magic, but never...."

The ground quakes and the temple trembles; cracks form in the columns.

Cold fear makes my teeth chatter. Energy crackles. It's different from Order's energy. Something's happening, changing.

"Never let anyone take your choices away," Corin says quickly, voice urgent. "Trust yourself and stand strong. Your choices, they'll never seem like choices; they won't be big, but they'll matter to you. And you have to make them all. You can't skip any of them. The biggest mistake we all made was not recognizing a choice, and when it's too late...."

The temple trembles again.

"What's happening?" I yell. Oranges, the smell's faint, but there, and slowly being overpowered by another odor: cinnamon and salt.

"I'm out of time," Corin says. He closes his eyes and his body begins to fade like color bleeding out of a

painting. His transparent hands are still on Evan's shoulders as he gazes into Evan's eyes. Corin's lips move, but I can't hear anything. Evan's eyes widen, the lemon and olive oil taste of his fear sharpening.

Corin pulls Evan into a hug, resting his head on my brother's shoulder. It's weird, fantastic and damn freaky, like a reflection reaching out of a haunted mirror to touch you. Corin releases Evan and walks by him, away from us, back into the shadows beyond the columns.

"W-wait!" I call, after he's completely gone from sight. The sizzling energy vanishes with him, and the ground stops moving. "Wait."

He didn't tell us enough. He didn't tell us how to get out of this. He didn't say we could just give the damn gifts back. Hell, I don't even have that stupid sapphire. I won't ever have it, because if I have to go find it or someone tries to give it to me, I just won't take it. There.

A cold breath against my neck and a tickle in the back of my mind. Heavy dread tugs on my spine. Somehow, I know I can't reject the gift. A few days ago, I made a choice.

Shit.

Heavy metal clatters against rock. I look down to see Evan's knives, the one he'd held and the one Corin took, laying on the ground at his feet. Slap, slap, slap, the sound of someone dusting their hands off.

"Damn spec," Evan mutters. He wipes his hands on his pants and paces the lengths of the rectangle. He stands on those lines like a tightrope walker over a pit of spikes. Lemons, olive oil and hot tension rattle around him. He grabs at his pocket, pulling out the emerald. "This thing." Turning it over in his palms, he studies it.

"It stays warm. It was even warm in the water."

He touches it to his cheek. "Wonder what I can do with it."

"You shouldn't do anything with it," I say, clearing my throat. "You should keep it buttoned up and forget about it."

A smirk. "Little brother, one thing you're going to learn about the world is that there's no buttoning up and forgetting about anything for long." He tosses the stone in the air and catches it. "What you don't finish, some-one else has to."

"I don't...." He doesn't know me; maybe he won't understand at all, but... "I don't care about other people."

He holds the emerald up to his face, staring at me through its facets. "A lot of people don't. Doesn't matter, a job is a job. Soon, you're going to do what I do: get it over with."

He lets his hands drop, looking at me directly in-stead of through a screen. "You're a better person than you think. I smell it in you. You wanted to help me be-fore you really knew who I was, and look what you get for it. You're not going to get to stay with our mother, you know." He snorts. "Hades and Ether, little brother, you won't even be considered a child when it counts. You'll be like me."

I lower my head.

"I don't know what's worse, leaving before you un-derstand how good your life is, or leaving after having it so good," Evan says. "But for what it's worth, thank you, Lyle."

"I'm not the only one who...."

"Thank them too, and I'll see you soon. I hope,"

Evan says.

The temple quakes again and he looks up. Four cracks on the ceiling stretch and link, making the shape of a rectangle above the burned rectangle on the floor. The cracks fatten and let in bright sunlight. Outside, double red suns blaze in an alien sky.

A breeze carries in the scent of oranges and the tang of ozone, sulfur and blood.

Evan lets out a gasping laugh, a large smile that makes him look twelve years old crossing his face. "Do you hear that?"

I strain my ears. Nothing.

"That sound. Someone's looking for me!"

"Who's...?"

"I'm here! I'm right here!" Evan yells.

He cups his hands around his mouth. "I'm h...." He retches, blood dribbling from his lips. "I'm here," he chokes and drops to his knees, clutching his left shoulder. Blood seeps through his fingers as it saturates his uniform.

I try to go to him, but steel bands wrap around my torso, squeezing the air out of my lungs, holding me back. I can't move. "E...." I can't talk.

/I'm..../

The temple, the columns, the suns, and my brother blur together, becoming abstract art. Color bleeds away, the whole scene a study of chiaroscuro. Charcoal and chalk on an ashy gray canvas. Citrus flavors disappear as I sink. I hold out my hand. Don't know what the hell it'll do for anyone, but maybe Evan will see it and reach for it. Maybe I can pull him out with me. That's a choice I'd make, but I can't.

/I'm..../

Cold floor presses against my cheek. I open my eyes to the room with no windows and a slatted wooden door.

"...sorry."

I lie there, staring at the wall, a carousel of crap rolling inside my head. If Evan dies, will it be over? We can't be the Four without him, right? Should I hope for that? Would it be wrong? My stomach clenches and I turn onto my back. The ceiling is smooth and white, no cracks.

Voices from outside are loud, feelings barge in through the door: anger, fear, excitement, fascination, scorn, hate. Thoughts trample around my walls, knocking to get in, but I'm airtight. My barriers are stronger than ever. The drugs are gone, but I'm good. Is this what that drug—what did Evan call it? Kanja water!—is this what it does? I'm crystal clear.

But how long does it last?

My stomach clenches again and I swallow bile.

Drugs and using people.

I'm sick. Who wants a sick person to be their champion? I cover my eyes with a hand, thinking, feeling. Evan said the emerald was always warm. So was the other Stone, the one that's mine. It was warm, and when I'd held it, everything was quiet, peaceful.

"I don't want it." My voice is hoarse and scratchy. Waves of warmth and well-being roll over me—the swells a brilliant, sapphire blue. Beautiful.

"I don't." I uncover my eyes as those perfect feelings are ripped out of me like rotten teeth and I'm alone, cold and empty. The ceiling's a blank page. If I had a pencil and a ladder I'd draw on it, I'd do a sketch of me

staring at nothing.

Keys jangle outside of the door and it squeaks. I keep my eyes on the blank page above me. It's waiting for me to choose something, isn't it? What fills up nothing?

Several sets of footsteps plod in my direction. Hazel eyes and a heart-shaped face hover over mine, framed by a mane of golden hair. A smooth manicured hand touches my face and the eyes turn hard and accusing as they look to someone else.

"What have you done to my son?"

26

LAWRENCE

MOM IS A WARRIOR GODDESS in khaki shorts and a T-Shirt that says: Yeah, I Said It. She's five foot seven in sneakers and kinda skinny, but the Men in Gray—because these pencil-pushers aren't cool enough to get the black suits—shrink away from her like she's a loose tigress licking her chops.

Mom, Dad, Devon, Lyle and me sit around a long table, picking at Subway sandwiches. Well, Dad's not picking, he's gobbling like he hasn't eaten all day, and knowing Mom, maybe he hasn't. He's got the look of somebody dragged out of bed at the crack of dawn. He's stubbly, his complexion's ruddy, and his blue eyes are a little bleary. He winks at me when he catches me looking at him.

Yeah, Dad's cool. He's the guy who asked me how fast I was going on my dirt bike before I wiped out and needed twenty-eight stitches in my knee and tells me I must've looked awesome. Maybe he lives vicariously through me, because he never did anything cool and cra-

zy when he was a kid.

Devon pushes his foot-long away from him with a huff and rolls his eyes at the two MIG, Men in Gray, standing guard at the door of the interrogation room they're letting us use as a cafeteria. There's a two-way mirror on one side of the room and a glass window that looks out into the heart of MIG headquarters. If I didn't know better, I'd think I was in an accounting office or something. There are rows of desks arranged in the shape of a big L, complete with dividers—cubicles. It's disappointing.

We get snatched up by the FBI, looking all bad-ass in their jackets and glasses and badges, put in the black cars, driven past wherever the FBI's cool headquarters are, and dumped with Geeks, Inc. I feel cheated. I doubt they treat the other terrorists, or suspected terrorists, this way. Not that I want to be behind bars or tortured or anything, but still. It's the principal of the situation.

"What are you thinking about Lawrie?" Dad asks with a smirk in my direction. He sits across the table from me, Devon next to him. Mom's on my right and Lyle's on the other side of her.

"Well." I open my mouth and Mom steps on my foot. "Nothing."

I shoot an innocent smile at Mom who sighs at me and reaches out to rest the back of her hand against my forehead for the fiftieth time since she got here an hour ago. I feel a lot better. I don't have a fever anymore. It broke while I was lying down on grandma's reject couch in my 'cell.'

"Are you gonna tell us what's going on out there?" Devon demands, mouth turned down into an honest to

God pout. He transforms into such a whiny brat when Mom and Dad are around, like it's gonna help him get his way.

Lyle stirs from the weird stupor he's been in since we all came together in here. "He's worried about his stupid girlfriend."

I tense, looking at Devon as a twinge of fear twists my tonsils. He cracks his knuckles but doesn't lunge at Lyle. He swallows and rubs his throat, then pulls his sandwich back to him and picks at the meat.

Mom and Dad look between the twins and share that 'parent' look, the one that drives me nuts, like they know so much about us when they don't really. For instance, they don't know that Dev and Ly tried to kill each other earlier today.

Mom clears her throat and arches a brow at Devon. "What's going on is me trying to undo your mess."

Her voice is the smooth, calm one she uses with clients. I call it her 'silky lawyer voice,' and it means she's pissed.

Devon flushes and makes a show of eating his sandwich. Dad flashes him a sympathetic look and pushes over a bag of Sour Cream and Onion Baked Lays. Devon snags the bag and studies the design like it's a Picasso.

I grin at Mom. "I still can't get over you calling the cops on us! That's hardcore. We're felons now!" I sound excited. Okay, I *am* excited. That twinge of fear from Devon and Lyle, maybe about to go psycho again, gets eaten up by 'oh hell yeah.'

Mom lets out the exasperated sigh she claims she patented just for me. Gleams of warmth and pride, mixed in with awe of my crazy, shine in her eyes for a second,

before they go quiet and serious.

"You aren't felons," she says. "You weren't arrested. You were taken into custody and questioned. Your stories coincide with other statements made this morning, absolving you of any guilt. So," she looks at Devon who's munching chips, "some hasty arrests are being reconsidered."

"Monica's free?" Chip bits fly from Devon's lips and I shield my face.

Mom and Dad share that parent look again. Dad clears his throat and flushes; Mom rolls her eyes. Oh God, I wonder if they think Monica's preggers. I bury my head in my arms on the table, holding my breath so I don't laugh.

"Your friends," Mom says, "are being released on low bail. They're only holding the three boys. The one who attacked the police."

A flash of purple light—Zeke.

"The one who confessed to masterminding the whole thing."

Electric shocks burn my arms and laughter rings in my ears—Quent.

"And the yellow boy they took from the house," Mom finishes. "Word is that those boys are going away for a while."

"Wait." I sit up straight, turning to Mom who frowns at me. She hates being interrupted. "The yellow boy they took from the house? That's Reggie. He didn't do anything bad at all. He—"

"Kidnapped you," Moms says, hazel eyes simmering. "Devon told me what happened."

Betrayal and irritation beat in my chest as I glare at

Devon. My big brother up-ends the chip bag and meets my eyes with a challenging stare.

"You jerk!" I snarl. "I told you—"

"You never would have been in that situation if it wasn't for that yellow guy!" Devon says, crumpling the chip bag.

"Yeah," I say with a dead laugh. "I'd just be...I don't know...trampled, pancaked."

Mom grabs my arm and squeezes, and I look at her. Shizz, she's pissed.

"Why do you do it, Lawrence?" she asks. "Why are you trying to kill yourself? I don't understand. What else can I give you?"

She doesn't sound frantic or hopeless, but there's a note of despair. She's this empress who always knows what to do, but never knows what to do with me.

"I'm not trying to kill myself," I say and place a hand over the one she has on my arm. Her grip is as firm as her expression. Some moms would cry or scream or tremble right now, but not my mom. She's too badass for all that. "I just...." I could tell her what Galeo said about my power or I could tell her I'm just crazy, but she knows the latter.

I shrug. "It's not your fault. I screwed up and there were some accidents. Stuff happened. That guy Reggie did right by me. He can't help it if his roommate's a psychopath."

Guilt's a wet rag being wrung in my ribcage. "Can you do something to help him? He's just a guy that wanted to win a dumb prize for his girlfriend. Damn him for trying to be normal, right? Don't blame him."

Or me. That guy running the booth started it. The

other people who jumped in the fight kept it up.

"I wanted to 'stop the hate'," I mumble.

Mom catches my chin in her free hand, looking deep into my eyes. I feel probed at the molecular level.

"And did you?" she asks, her tone not condescending or mean, just curious.

I shake my head. Reg said I helped him, but maybe I made things worse. He brought me to Quent. Quent got hyped up about what I could do. Maybe he wouldn't have gone so far if he didn't think I could quake U of H down. I don't know.

Mom lets go of my chin and my arm, and pulls me into a light hug. She rubs my back and strokes my hair like she used to when I was little. I don't want her to pull back, and I shiver when she does.

"You tried," she says. "Most people don't. I'm proud of you." She turns from me, looking at Devon and then Lyle. "I'm proud of all of you. You tried to be adults and handle business, but dammit."

Her hands curl into fists on the table. She squeezes her eyes shut as she breathes. Uh-oh, her Zen-breathing. She does this before she tells us we're on prison lockdown for six weeks.

"You should have called me immediately," she says. "You never should have tried to deal with this on your own. Look at this mess! You didn't and don't know what you're getting into, what you've done."

She trails off, Zen-breathing again.

"Guys, look," Dad says, glancing at Mom and getting a nod from her. "There are measures your mother set in place. Terms of agreement."

"Well, that's just great," Lyle drawls, standing up, making himself taller than everyone at the table, taller than Mom. "You're getting pissed at us for not knowing what was going on and trying to figure it out? This is our fault? Why didn't you tell us more? Why'd I have to get brain-bombed with all this when you knew something that could have prepared us? You think we've been having a party with this?"

"Lyle," Mom tries.

"I got dragged to hell," Lyle says, voice getting louder. "And the person I wanted to help, the reason why I'm like this right now, I'm not so sure I want to save anymore. Because if he dies, maybe I can just go home and button up and forget about all of this, though he said I can't."

Lyle backs away from us as he talks, heading for the MIGs who snap to attention and bump shoulders, blocking the exit.

"Lyle, what...?" Mom's pale.

She gets up and follows him. Devon straightens the chip bag, then rips it in half, potato flakes and onion salt dusting the table. Dad looks like he wants to get up, but he doesn't.

"Don't touch me," Lyle says to Mom. He stops in front of the MIG. "Let me out. I wanna go back to that room you had me in before."

The MIG duo gape at him.

The one on the left, with glasses and acne, reaches for his two-way radio. "Um, just a minute." He opens the door and steps out, leaving his chicken-shit partner alone with us aliens.

I resist the urge to howl. Bet the dude would scream

and run.

Mom stands a few feet behind Lyle, her shoulders straight; her head high and proud. "Come sit back down."

"Why?" Lyle asks, not looking back. His voice is tight.

"So I can tell you what I know, and what I'm going to try to do from here on out," she says. "It's time you knew what happened then."

My pulse rockets, 'gotta do something' wants to dance. Information! "Mom, you're gonna tell us about Devrik?"

She flinches and Lyle turns. His face is dark and heavy. Lyle's...I'm not used to seeing so much emotion from him. This whole time, through this whole thing with Evan, with my body being all screwy, with those drugs and Devon, he's been all over the place. Bet he's thinking it's better not to care about anything. Bet he wants to go back to being the guy girls write about on the bathroom wall.

I close my eyes. I thought Lyle wouldn't care if the world blew up and we all died. I even thought that right after I nearly drowned and Lyle pulled my water-logged ass out of the pool while everyone else just watched. Lyle was the one who brought out the family album and identified Evan by a picture. He's the one who got me to call Galeo. He's been moving this thing, talking to Evan, wanting to help him, telling Dev and me and making us help.

How could I ever think he doesn't care?

I'm a prick.

"Come back, please," Mom says, reaching out.

After a moment of Lyle staring at her hand, he takes

it. They walk back to the table. Mom's perfume wafts up my nose when she sits.

"Waaa-shoo!"

Everyone jumps, and tension is broken by a chuckle from Dad who tosses a Subway napkin my way. I blow my nose and wad up the paper, letting it fall in my lap, and then all attention goes to Mom as she takes a long sip of iced tea through her straw.

She swallows and Zen-breathes. A slow smile crosses her lips. Her eyes take on a faraway look of amusement as she looks past us, past this room.

"Devrik Lauduethe," she says, "Ricky, was a hopeless, bumbling idiot." She sighs and she's back in the room with us. She sips her tea, fingers rubbing the condensation on the side of the cup.

"We met at Disney in Florida. I had just graduated college and was on a trip with some friends. I kept running into Ricky, and," she smirks, "after a while, it started happening on purpose. He was…there was something about him that intrigued me. He was a stuck-up, bubble-brained socialite, but he made me feel different, like I could be fun and unpredictable."

I struggle with the notion of a fun and unpredictable Mom. Nope, too out there for me.

"His Visit was only supposed to last a few weeks, but he kept putting off going back," Moms says, playing with her straw. "He came to meet your grandparents. He liked sightseeing and cheese steak and being loud and obnoxious. It made me laugh. One day, he decided he wasn't going home. He quit his position, changed his name, and got a Visiting visa. We got married." She shakes her head.

"And you guys were happy?" Devon asks. "Grandma and Grandpa liked Ricky?"

Mom nods. "They adored him."

"And what about you, Dad?" Lyle asks, elbows on the table. "You dated Mom for a long time before she met Ricky. What'd you do?"

I frown at Dad. That's right. All of our relatives up north had thought Mom and Dad would get married right out of high school.

"I dated around," Dad says with a wink, "but I kept my eye on your mom and that pretty boy she paraded around town." He drags the Subway bag out from under the table and digs out a cookie. His movements are calm, measured, like all his concentration's going into that cookie.

"You know, the first time I met your big brother, he hit me with a plastic light saber right in the nuts. He was, what, three? I'd never seen him before, but looking at him then I knew he was your kid, Joey." Dad shakes his head. "He had your aim."

"I trained him well. He hit you because you called him 'Little Princess'," Mom says with a snort, humor and a hint of sadness glimmer in her eyes.

"Thought he was a girl with all that long curly hair." Dad looks at my hair and nods. He's never been a fan of me growing it past my shoulders.

"It hasn't changed much. It's really long," Lyle says softly, gazing at Mom as if sharing a secret. He kinda is. Mom hasn't seen Evan; Lyle has.

Mom breathes through her nose and looks straight ahead for a moment.

Dad smacks on chocolate chips. "Kid had good

aim, and he glared just like your mom," Dad says. "It was kinda freaky seeing such a little bugger making that face."

Mom grins and runs her thumb over the plastic cover on her cup. "Grandpa had plans for that one. Thought he'd be president one day."

My brows raise, brain whirring. So, big brother had displayed leadership potential from jump. "Did he have the Mark on his back then?" I ask.

Mom's head jerks to me, her grin fades, eyes going dark. "He had it." She sips. "When he was born, he was perfect, beautiful down to each little brown freckle on his spine. Over the years, those freckles got larger and darker, I thought they were skin tumors. A doctor removed them and they came back. When he was about four, they looked less like freckles and more like shapes and symbols. And Ricky started behaving strangely."

"He told me to keep Evan's back covered and not to talk about it anymore. He wouldn't tell me why, and then one day, a silver Rolls Royce pulled up and three men dressed in Armani suits and wearing badges got out. Ricky knew who they were before the car pulled into our driveway."

I don't know what I wanna do. I guess I wanna put my hand on her shoulder or something, but it feels corny right now. I wanna say something, but what? I can't tell her to stop, that she doesn't have to tell us anymore, because I want her to. Keep going, Mom. Ricky answered the door and what?

Mom pulls more tea through her straw. "The men in Armani were Remasian, they looked as human as Ricky, but not handsome at all. They somehow knew about Ev-

an's Mark, and said he had to go with them."

The straw makes a slurping noise.

"They took my son away and I couldn't do anything, but watch. Ricky went with him. That was the only consolation. Ricky could go because he was Remasian and a famous man's son and I wasn't. It was just over. No goodbye. No seeing them off to make sure everything was okay." She wrings her hands. Her eyes are dry. Mom doesn't cry; she gets even.

"Ricky was hopeless. He was just as bad as having another kid. He didn't know how to take care of himself, let alone a five-year-old. You guys," she looks at me, then Lyle and Devon, "had to live with Grandma and Grandpa for a little while, so I could figure things out, learn, because that was never going to happen again." Her eyes are steel. "It's never going to happen again."

Her lawyer face is back on. The lid comes off the cup and she starts crunching on the ice. "You're Earthborn, all of you. Your legal father is Frank," she nods at Dad. "He adopted you. Ricky relinquished his parental rights. You're ours, not theirs, and trying to take you from me now is a violation of interplanetary law. They'll have to take this to court, and," her smile's cold, predatory, "I don't lose."

Wow. I clap. Hell, I want to hoot and holler, but MIG in glasses comes back in looking flustered.

"Um," he stammers. He looks at his geeky partner and the two whisper for a minute. "You're being released and, uh, transferred."

"You can't release them and transfer them as well," Mom says. "Released means freed. We're going home."

Glasses Guy starts to sweat and play with his collar.

Geeky partner coughs.

"Let me say that better," Glasses Guy says. "Representatives from the Silver Allegiance of Planets issued a claim. It's been acknowledged and signed by the president of the United States. You're being released into the custody of the Inyan Ambassador SeCaeta until an envoy arrives to uh..." he chokes, looking at Mom.

Her face is hard. "I'll file a motion."

"Oh, uh...."

"Under Silver Allegiance law, I'm allowed an audience with a preceding official, and once I request it, I'm allowed the freedom of autonomy until such audience is granted." Mom puts her hands on her hips and raises her chin. "Now, as I told you before, we're going home."

Well, damn.

After sharing 'holy shizz' looks with my brothers and Dad, I hoot, holler, and "Aoooooo!"

CHAPTER **27**
EVAN

MY LUNGS BURN AS I hack up a lake of water. The rest of my body is numb. I'm too cold to shiver, too cold to think beyond how much I hurt. Niobe-va. What happened? Where am I? Wha....

Pain explodes against the side of my face. My head reels, and I open my eyes. The world around me is dark, muddy. I see shapes. Scents are dull and indistinct; everything smells the same—tangy as blood. My blood.

I'm wet. Why am I....

My heart thuds in my chest and I cough up more water, doubling over. I'm sitting? No, no I'm being held up. A large hand braces me on one side. The right. The right, because the left—

Flashes of double red suns in a green sky invade my thoughts. Green sky, green sky with two suns—Onkurus.

Weapons firing. Ground shaking. People falling—my people. Tan uniforms soaked red in blood.

The rag-staff that ripped my shoulder apart. Running. Bleeding. Telling Adonis to leave me behind.

Dying.

But I'm not dead. I'm not....

My fingers are stiff, hard to move, like I haven't moved them in days. Laughter bubbles in my burning chest—I haven't.

Pain rolls through me and I moan as I'm pulled forward, dragged across a hard surface. My stomach plummets as I fall a short distance, body hitting rough dirt and rocky terrain. The sound of a heavy chain being pulled, the slam and latch-click of a vehicle hatch.

Had I come from there? Had I been in a transport unit?

"Ayo!" A rough voice yells in my face, hot breath and warm spittle hitting my cheeks. My bones rattle as someone shakes me. "Ayo, rapi!"

Rapi—brat. Ruj—the man's speaking Ruj.

The muddy shapes of the outside world shift, blobs becoming defined, colors separating. The smooth face of a young man with dark red hair and blunt, flat features is a half-snatch away from mine. I try to jerk back, but my muscles don't obey—too cold.

The man smiles, his double rows of pointy teeth gleam like black diamonds. Diamond teeth—only Ruj generals get that honor.

My head throbs as I remember—ambush, trap.

Dying.

But I'm not—

"Greetings, little leader." The general's voice is deep. It rumbles in his chest like a growl. "Show some manners and thank the great man who has saved you."

He didn't save me. "You didn't...." I choke up more water. My voice sounds broken.

His big hands rest on my cheeks as he grins at me, his expression triumphant. "Oh, but didn't I? You were left behind. Do you know how long it's been since your people abandoned you? Onkurus has spun around four times, little one—four complete cycles. Why, they are only just now leaving to come for you, but well," he winks at me, "I found you first."

I can't think. There's something I need to remember. Something that happened.

My fingers, my right hand, stiff and achy, holds an object. It's hard and smooth, the surface slick, damp like me. And cold.

My teeth chatter as my body begins to thaw and shiver. A spark of flame kindles in my gut as my core magic tries to reignite, but it's blocked. The flame flickers out, just like before.

"Now that we're away from hallowed ground, what should I do with him?" the general asks, throwing his voice over my head and looking beyond me.

A chorus of deep, rough voices.

Broken translations flit through my mind as my comp-al implant sputters back to life.

"Kill him."

"Break him."

"Eat him."

"I like these ideas," the general says with a booming laugh. "What do you think, little one? Should I kill you? Break you? Eat you? Or keep you?"

My stomach churns at the hungry light in the general's eyes when he says 'keep you.' Smells become sharper. Over the tang of blood, there's lasic oil, fishy sweat, and un-cleaned teeth. A breeze blows and a sweet

odor washes over the bad. I inhale—and hear it. A voice.

Child of Magic.

Focus. The pool. The Stone. My brother.

My fipping little brother.

I clench the Stone in my fist as it warms in my palm.
I meet the general's yellow gaze head on, stomach still
churning at the predatory look in his eyes.

"Of course," he drawls, "if I keep you, I can't let
you possess that."

His mammoth hand dwarfs mine, squeezing my fingers over the Stone. He bellows a split second after making contact with my skin and shoves me away. The world
spirals as I fall, sprawling onto my back and staring up at
the sky, at the faces of eight, no nine, Ruj soldiers in purple and red one-piece uniforms. They train long-barreled
lasics on me and bare their white, pointed teeth.

I shiver and clench my jaw, refusing to shut my
eyes.

Will I die now?

Did I survive drowning only to be eaten by vipers?

Fear is colder than death, pricklier. It hurts like being tied and quartered. My body feels stretched to snapping point. I don't want to die.

Immolate.

What?

The Stone burns hot.

A boot's on my clenched fist. The general looms
over me, his black teeth glitter. "What importance will
the Four of Rema have, after they've become Three?"

Pressure on my fingers. The bones stress. I grit my
teeth, breathing hard. My lungs ache and wheeze, water
gurgling deep in their pockets. I don't want to die. But it

hurts too much to move, it's too cold to think.

Immolate.

"For Pan," the general murmurs like a prayer as he raises a hand. Silver flares around his wrist as the knotted chain of a thin bracelet catches in the blazing sunlight. Raven energy gathers, crackling like an electric storm around his closed hand. He smiles almost casually, like a person admiring something pleasant. Then the black crashes down toward me like a wall of darkness.

Immolate.

The Stone burns and green blazes from my palm to counteract the black. Horizontal planes of black and green phantom lights fight for dominance inches above my body. Ruj soldiers gasp and shout. Lasics hum as they charge, ready to fire.

Suddenly, my brain clears, the fear eases. The sweet nutty scent of flowering trees and the calm of the wind fill me. I understand what 'immolate' means.

My core magic ignites with the force of a flash-bomb as the Stone pulsates, feeding me magic, breaking the block that had kept me from using my power before, and stoking my inner fire until it rages.

Immolate. I weave the notes of the spell around my fire with the speed of a maestro.

I roar, spewing torrents of flame. It's endless. The crackle of the fire so loud it nearly smothers the shrieks and cries of the Ruj. They can't escape. Immolate—the curse of enchanted flames. They chase and burn until death. Enemies beware.

I've never used it before. Didn't have the power to—or the stomach.

I choke, spitting and coughing, but as soon as I get

my breath again, the Stone pushes out more energy. I bite
my lower lip, clamping my mouth shut. Heat smolders in
my mouth, but I swallow it.

Immolate.

Stop it.

I don't hear shrieking anymore. The reek of seared
flesh, charcoaled hair, and death carries, destroying the
sweet breeze. I swallow again, fire pooling in my throat
but calming.

Stop.

I breathe carefully and will my body to sit. I hurt
like an old man, bones creaking, muscles straining. I
blink away reflexive tears of pain and stare at the carnage. Men lie prone on their backs, sides, and bellies,
arms outstretched as if they'd been trying to run while
their flesh burned. Enchanted flames only take a second
to cook a body inside out.

Niobe-va.

I did this.

Stomach acid rushes up my throat. I retch and
heave bile, blood and more water into my lap. My left
arm hangs dead and useless, but my right…. I drag that
hand into my lap and turn my palm over, uncurling my
fingers and staring at the shimmering emerald.

This thing….

I shut my eyes. It saved me. I'd be dead twice over,
but….

I did this.

I let the Stone roll into my lap as I pull a blood-
sticky hand through my wet, matted hair.

What now?

There's nothing but death around me. I scorched

the land. The double suns taunt me. I…the comp-al implant is malfunctioning. I can't call anyone.

But my brother had said there would be help.

I'd thought help had come when he left me.

Silver catches my eye. The general lies a few steps from me, body black, arms spread out at his sides like he'd wanted to hug the world before falling backward. I groan as I get onto my hands and knees, the Stone tumbling into the dirt, and crawl to the general.

I pause as I near him. His chest rises and falls.

Alive.

Fear makes me shiver. Nothing survives enchanted flames.

What are you?

The bracelet on his wrist glimmers and without thinking, I reach for it, fingers grasping the cold metal… cold—how is it cold?—and I'm falling, my mind whirring, my body gone. I'm weightless and surrounded by midnight.

And then I see people, twelve shapes standing in a circle around an altar, silver and gold glinting on all of their wrists. They don't seem to notice me as they chant in a language I don't understand. The air over the altar visibly trembles and seems to fold in on itself, blue sky turning black as dimensional fabric rips. A man steps out of the portal and seats himself on top of the altar, crossing one leg over the other. He's got four eyes that are black craters in his face and lips stained with blue blood. He smiles with jagged teeth and I shudder.

I know Him.

The chanting slows, and one voice says, "Our Lord Pan."

The bracelets…and Pan.

Pan has Champions?

Niobe-va. I'm going to vomit again. Get me out of here. Let me out.

I cover my eyes and feel myself spinning, whirling, hovering and falling. I smell death again and feel the cool metal of the bracelet in my fingers. I snatch my hand back and scoot away.

Take it.

I don't want to touch it again.

Kill him.

No more.

I choose no more.

I stare at the general, watching him breathe, even as the sound of a large transport breaking through the atmosphere ruptures the quiet I'd fallen into. The ground quakes with impact. The general doesn't moan or flinch as his breathing quickens.

Voices talking, shouting.

The familiar scents of fresh water, wild fire and sweet acaigia flowers blow in the wind as I barely make out the shapes of my court, my three best friends, running toward me.

I watch them then glance over at the gray rock on the ground, tempting me to pick it back up.

Come to me.

And I crawl to it, taking it up, holding it close. It saved me twice—but look what I did with it. I should throw it away.

Adonis reaches me first, his clear gray eyes wide with fear, relief and worry. He drops to his knees beside me. Desiri comes next, she skids to a halt and turns in a

circle surveying the damage and whistling. Jalee comes last, kneeling and taking my face between her palms, her golden brown eyes drinking me in.

I wish I had words for them.

Laughter bubbles inside me. Look what I did and will probably do again. The fipping Four of Rema. My choices will save millions, hurt millions, kill millions. Yet, these people want to hold me, take me home, call me a champion.

Niobe-va.

I see Lyle's face in my mind and imagine the other two. I have no idea what they look like now. I barely remember them from childhood. They might end up hating me for making this happen to them.

Is this my fault? I didn't have to ask for help, they didn't have to try to save me. But then I wonder if any of this had been our choice at all. Corin Peredil had warned, 'Don't let Her take your choices away.' To me, he had whispered, 'Trust no god.'

I won't.

But how do I fight when it seems I have no real choices?

My head falls back as I laugh so hard I choke myself again and spit up more blood and water before passing out.

CHAPTER **28**
DEVON

"LEADER EVAN LAUDUETHE HAS BEEN secured and delivered to Rema."

I glance up at the soldier standing in the doorway and narrow my eyes. Secured and delivered, like some sort of package. "Is he okay?" My voice comes out rough. My throat's still sore from yelling at these assholes hours earlier.

I stare at the man, waiting.

The Silver Allegiance soldier's cold eyes scan the guest bedroom as if I had back-up, then come back to rest on me, sitting on the wooden floor. He seems unimpressed. I know I look like shit. It's been two hours since my brothers and I were hauled out of US legal custody and into the hands of the Silver Allegiance.

Six soldiers in two-piece black and white leather get-ups with weapons on their belts had come into the interrogation room, turned mess hall, with orders to return us to Ambassador SeCaeta's mansion. They couldn't care less what Mom had to say about it. In fact, two of

the guards held Mom and Dad back as they marched us out of the room.

I yelled until I was hot and would have swung on them, but Mom shouted after us: "Don't be stupid. I'll fix this." She was right. It would have been stupid to fight a bunch of big guys with alien weapons at the ready, so I stopped resisting and let them escort us out of the building into a long black town car.

The soldier in the doorway clears his throat and I blink back into the present. Had he spoken and I didn't notice?

"Leader Lauduethe will recover," the soldier says, his accent thick. He sounds like he's from Scandinavia. He sighs and his flat expression shifts, revealing a hint of pity.

Irritation at the look burns in my chest. "Great." And I'm happy about it. It's what we set out to do, right? At least something's happening like it should.

The guy's still watching me.

"What?" I ask.

He pulls something out of his belt and tosses it to me. I catch it in one hand. My phone. I frown at the guy. "Why are you—?"

"Contrary to what this may seem like to you," he says, "the Silver Allegiance does have your best interests in mind. You are not under arrest."

I swallow, and the man nods, closing the door and shutting me in.

Not under *real* arrest, just house arrest.

Upon our arrival, an hour earlier, Ambassador Se-Caeta had greeted us at the front door. His face grave and his walk stiff, he led us to a wing on the opposite side

of the house from Galeo's room. Lyle disappeared into
one room, Lawrie into another. We're in the same hall
now, but doors apart with armed soldiers guarding the
distance. I was the last one, walking side by side with
SeCaeta and a guard. SeCaeta opened the door to my
room and touched my shoulder before I stepped inside.

"You were warned this would happen," he said, like
a parent who hates to punish you but can't bite back an
'I told you so.'

I pull myself up off the floor, clutching my phone,
and gaze around the room. It's large with a king-sized
poster bed and big picture windows covered by drapes
that drag on the floor. A flat screen crystal TV is built into
the wall. It's probably voice-activated, and no one told
me I couldn't watch it, but I don't want noise right now.

I sit on the bed and lay my phone on my knee, un-
locking the screen and staring at my missed calls. The
two most recent are from Mom.

I swallow a lump in my throat, thinking about what
she said in the interrogation room. We were legally hers
and Dad's, and the Visitors would be breaking the law by
trying to take us. But one of the Allegiance soldiers had
explained to us that, had we been normal vulattos, we'd
have been on a plane home. It's just our luck we would
be Marked leaders of a prophecy older than dirt, which
makes us Jesus-like, and Jesus doesn't belong to anyone
but God, or a goddess in our case.

So, Mom was right, but about the wrong thing.
Though she said she'd fix it.

I want to believe her. She's mom. She can save us
from being dragged away to wherever Evan is and having to do crazy shit. She never loses. But the look in her

eyes when the soldiers had first come made my heart sink. I'd never seen her look so unsure or scared.

I take a deep breath and unlock my phone. I could call Mom back, but I think I might do something embarrassing if I talk to her right now. Maybe Lawrie and Ly got their phones back as well. I should call them, call Lyle. But what do I say? I keep hurting him.

I could barely look at him while we were with the Feds, because all I saw was that split lip I gave him. He met my eyes a few times, without looking mad or disappointed, just cool, like he'd been before he'd told me about Nisse and how his powers hurt her. God, did I mess things up with us again?

I'm such a loser.

My cell phone vibrates and I jump to my feet, nearly dropping it. The screen image is blank, unknown caller. I roll my thumb over the answer icon. "Hello?"

"Devon?" It's Monica. My breath catches.

"Oh God! Are you okay? Are you out?" My voice is high and I don't care.

"Yeah, I got home an hour ago. I'm on the house phone," Monica says. "The police let us all out. Well, not Quent or Zeke...or Reg, but the rest of us are out, even that bastard Shawn." She sounds tired.

Relief sweeps my legs out from under me and I flop back on the bed. "So, you okay?"

She sighs. "I don't know, Dev. They...there's a list of people who died. They were all in our group. Zeke killed one, but the rest.... The police did it. And there're posts on message boards and news sites that say things like: Good. We're glad they died."

"You didn't die."

"It's almost like I did. It could have been me and some racist human would say: Good."

My heart thuds. "Monica." Human, she'd said human like she was not part of them—us, I mean. But wait, am I human, really? I'm not being treated like one. I don't have rights, not human rights anyway.

"My mom's sending a message to my grandfather, the one I told you about. The Visitor. He's out there and wanted me to come to him, so I'm gonna try to go. I want to know what it's like somewhere else."

She sounds beaten down, ruined, like me. But I don't want her to feel like that. She's not a loser. She stands up for herself and what she wants. She knows who she is. She wanted me to be more. I let the phone rest on my chest after putting it on speaker, listening to her say names of people I've never met and crying for them because it didn't need to happen that way. They didn't have to die.

"Dev?" Monica's voice is rusty. "You there?"

"Yeah," I breathe, bringing the phone back to my ear and taking it off speaker.

"I'm so messed up right now," she whispers.

"I understand that," I murmur.

"I don't know what I'm doing, what I'm saying, where I'm going. I mean, you know I can't go back to school here, huh? I'm expelled." She laughs. "I know I said I wanna see my Grandpa, but living with him for real? I don't know him. Don't know what it's like out there, but there's no future for me here anymore. Nisse and Yir are getting deported, spaced."

She rambles. I listen with a gorilla on my chest. She's me. God, Monica's me right now.

"Wh-what do your parents say?" I ask. "I mean, what did they say about Quent and the school?"

Monica sniffles. "They said 'we warned you.' They asked me if I was happy, if I got what I wanted, because I never could shut up."

"Do you wish you did shut up? If you could go back, would you change anything?" She was the one who wanted me to stand up and be strong, to be a voice. If she takes it back, then does anything I'm doing matter?

I hear the sounds of bed springs creaking.

"What I wish..." Monica says suddenly, and I start, almost sitting up. "I wish I was stronger. I wish I had the power to zap Quent, to quake him and Zeke and Shawn into the ground, to melt their brains. I want your power."

Mine?

"I never want to shut up, but I'm too weak to talk. That's all yesterday proved," Monica says. "And now, I'm probably going to a place where I'll always be too weak to talk. Everyone will have power and knowledge and I'll just be the Earth kid who couldn't shut up."

"People listen to you!" I balk. "I listened!"

Silence, then a honk and a snort. Is she blowing her nose?

"Sorry," she chuckles. "So not hot, I'm so gross, but you know what?"

"What?"

"You're always hot," she says and my face burns.

Yeah, I know I'm hot, but for her to say it? It makes me wanna dig my toe into the dirt and go 'Gawsh, darn and heck.'

"You listen to me," she says, her voice still rusty, but she coughs and it becomes clear. "You can do what

I wish I could. You're strong and good, but you need a backbone."

"I've got a backbo—"

"Bull. You've got an ego," Monica says. She sounds a lot like she did in Silva's Donut shop. "You have to figure out who you are, Dev. What you want and what you stand for. You don't have time to fart around and bounce quarters off your ass anymore."

I blink. "Huh?"

"You relied on good looks and blending in to get what you needed," Monica says. "It worked for the most part, but were you happy?"

"I don't know," I say.

We're quiet. Her breath is soft and soothing over the speakers. I sound like a panting rhino in comparison. Wonder why she doesn't hang up.

"You don't have to know, babe," Monica says softly. "Being unsure is your answer."

"Babe, huh?" I grin like a fool.

"You want me to call you somethin' else?" Monica asks. "Do you want to be something else to me?"

"Uh." Gawsh, darn, and heck. "Do you wanna be my girlfriend? I know I sound lame, and I'm still in high school..." not for much longer, "and...."

"Yeah." She laughs. "I'll be your lame girlfriend. Happy?"

I know she can't see me grinning, but I don't wanna talk right now. She sniffles a little more.

"So," she murmurs, "what's happening with you?"

Wish I could say I was hijacking a plane and coming to her house. Wish I was gonna take her out and drive her around in my truck after I clean out the barf smell.

"Think I'm going to Rema soon," I say. "They're gonna crown me, or something, introduce me to a guy I don't know and make me live with him, and give me a job I can't do, but hey."

"You'll get by," Monica says.

"How do you kn—"

"Because you're strong," she says.

"Okay, but what—?"

"It's not the end of the world, Devon," Monica says. "It'll be like your parents got a divorce and your dad got custody. You'd live with him, but you'd still be able to call your mom. And when you start being awesome and traveling, you can drop in and say, hello. It's like you have tunnel vision."

She knows about my tunnel vision?

"You can't get everything you want, but maybe there's a compromise," she says.

"They didn't compromise with Evan."

"That was a long time ago." Bed springs creak again. "He was little. Your parents were young. Maybe they know what they're doing a little better now."

"My mom got totally shut down earlier," I say and tell her what happened.

Monica's quiet for my story, but when I finally finish, she chimes, "Trust your mom."

"Didn't you hear me? She looked scared."

"Maybe," Monica says. I almost hear a smirk in her voice. "But your mom's a politician and a lawyer, right?"

"Yeah," I say, not getting it.

"That means she knows how to get what she wants," Monica says. "She told you she learned from the first time."

"Yeah, and she was going with the Earthborn slant."

"But she knows you're Marked, and those Marks have probably been seen by a lot of people by now. Which means she had to know that Earthborn wouldn't cut it. Your mom's not stupid, Dev. She's playing at something."

Hope fills me. "What? You think?"

I picture Mom looking afraid when the soldiers entered, but before that she'd been calm and in control. Mom doesn't flip emotional switches that easy, and if she does, she's never shown it in her body language before. Not without a purpose.

"You're a genius," I say.

"No, you're just slow," Monica says, "but you're cute, so I'll deal with it."

I laugh so hard it hurts my stomach, but I feel better. A lot better.

"You know whatever your mom has up her sleeve won't keep you here, right?" Monica's voice is serious. "Something's gonna get worked out, you might not like it all the way, but you'll get by."

"Yeah?" I ask.

"And one good thing about fame is that I'll always know where you are," Monica says. "You'll get stronger, and you'll stand up for weak people, and I'll be glad. I'll know I was the first one to tell you to stop being a punk."

I laugh. "Maybe I'll be a Prince Charles, huh? Maybe I'll sit on my butt."

"No, not you. You're incapable of doing that, Devon Ladreth."

"Lauduethe," I practice saying it, letting the syllables roll off my tongue. Sounds weird and wrong. "Dev-

on Lauduethe."

"That name's weird," Monica says. "You should keep Ladreth."

"Ladreth's made up. Can't go by a fake name."

"Tired of being fake, huh?"

I chuckle. "I guess so."

And I mean that. I don't know what I am, might not even know what I'm not, but I need to figure out what I want. Can't do that holding back, can't do it blending in.

"I'm not weak for being scared?" I ask.

Her tickle of a laugh makes my day. "No, babe," Monica says. "If you weren't scared right now, you'd be as bat shit crazy as Zeke. You aren't nuts. You're just... normal."

"Hah, the only thing I know I'm not is normal," I say.

And man does she laugh. I hang up smiling, knowing she'll call me again tomorrow. I hope Mom really is an Oscar-worthy actress who's got something up her sleeve that's gonna keep me talking to Monica for a whole lot of tomorrows.

It's not so bad thinking about things that way. I'll have Monica, and Mom, and Dad, and strength.

I stare at the phone on my chest and pick it up again, pressing 'one' on speed dial.

It rings three times.

"Ly?" I say.

Nothing. But do I really need to say anything else? I'm sorry. He has to know that. I can't promise I won't do it again. He has to know that too. But....

"I'm gonna work on it." My temper. Everything. Because I'm strong, or I will be.

Still nothing.

"Ly?"

A breath. "Dev."

"Hey."

"I'm sorry," he whispers. He's said it before. He said it so many times after I hit him and his power strangled me. It had felt like iron chains around my throat. I couldn't break them. I thought I was gonna die. But I'm not upset about it.

"It's okay," I say. I hadn't told him that. "You wanna come over? The soldiers said we're not under arrest. We should be able to leave our rooms."

"I'm sorry," Lyle whispers again.

I sense him pulling away and it hurts. "Ly?"

"I'm working on it too," he says.

The line disconnects and I'm alone. Silence echoes around the room. I turn the TV on. The CNN logo glares at me, so I turn the TV off. Strong people don't watch and wait, they make things happen. I rise from the bed.

Lyle's across the hall. I open the door and peer out: no guards. The way's clear. Two long strides get me in front of his door, two knocks has him opening it.

He's as tall as me, almost the same face, same stance, same eyes, but what's behind his eyes is different, will always be different, and I'm supposed to know all about it. I used to know all about it.

Okay, Monica. Here's something I want.

"Ly, I want to get to know you again," I say. His brows rise and I clear my throat. "Can I come in?"

He doesn't blink, doesn't move for a minute. I hold my breath, and then he steps back, out of the doorway, clearing a path for me. I smile as I enter, nodding at him

as he closes the door behind us.
    It's beyond time to move on.

29
LYLE

PEOPLE ARE ALWAYS ON STAGE. They cry when they want to sing and dance on someone's grave. They laugh when they want to shout. They say things they'll never mean because they don't know how to mean them. Mom's an actress. She laughs at all the right times. She throws fits at opportune moments. A good mother should get over-emotional and huff and scream when others do wrong by your kids, or so the world says anyway.

Mom's the best. She knows how to play her cards. A mom who went on vacay for a week, leaving a sick kid at home, won't win much sympathy if she doesn't cry. A mom whose kids ended up on the news, burning buildings and running across state lines, loses parenting points if she doesn't go hysterical at least once. I loved seeing her on Dateline.

Dev and I sit on my bed, watching the evening news. The stuff usually bores me, but it's about us again. It's been four days since we got back to the SeCaeta mansion and three since madness exploded on every so-

cial media tool ever invented. Mom talking to reporters, Dad being interviewed and published in the papers, both of them with massive followings on FaceSpace, Vine, I-chat and Twitter. There are campaigns; half saying free us, the other half saying blast our asses to Rema.

Our school pictures are splashed over images of U of H on fire. Classmates and people from our neighborhood step into the limelight, claiming to know us. They're not shocked we're vulattos. They even seem kinda glad that there may be inhuman reasons for why we're so good-looking. Some say we cheated in school and sports with our powers. Some say we're God's gifts.

Idiots want their fifteen seconds of fame.

A new sketchpad sits on my knees. It's medium-sized and heavy. I've been drawing oranges since yesterday, ripe ones, freshly fallen, with stems and scruffy skin. A boy sleeps on the ground, surrounded by them, his long braid coiled on his chest. I shade the area beneath his eyes.

I haven't dream-walked since he was rescued.

Ambassador SeCaeta tells us Evan's doing fine, but doesn't offer to help us get in touch with him. No one talks about contact with anyone. The SeCaetas are nice people. They pity us, so they pamper us with good food and interplanetary cable with English translations. Devon's addicted to alien sports channels.

"Hey look, it's your ex-girlfriend." Devon nudges me with his elbow and points to the TV.

"Mm. Which one?" I murmur, chewing on the end of my pencil. It's the kind with no eraser. The lead tastes dull and dark on my lips.

"...should have totally known he was an alien.

Being with him is out of this world. It's like this rush of amazing-ness!" Cheerleader Heather talks with her hands—'rah, rah, rah!'—with Paul Davis standing next to her, scowling.

Can't imagine he likes being compared to me. Good. I hate his ass.

"...blew my mind!" Volleyball Gabby.

"If Mom ever had any doubts about your innocence, she knows now," Devon says with a snort. "Let me see that." He reaches for my sketchbook and I let him take it.

Dev's been really good to me these past few days. If he'd been a normal person, he'd still have black and blue marks on his neck from where I tried to strangle him. As it is, his throat is bruise-free, and with nothing to show for the attack, he acts like it never happened.

"His hair's really that long?" Devon wrinkles his nose when I nod, and sets the sketchpad down. "This whole situation...." He makes a frustrated face, one where he looks half constipated, half pissed. "I can't even eat, man. Everything tastes so good here, but I can't swallow."

He gestures to the TV. "Mom and Dad are fighting for us like hell, and it looks like they got a chance, but they're not gonna win."

I'm glad he knows. I'm tired of being the bearer of bad news. I read our future in SeCaeta's body language and careful speech as easily as reading a Dr. Seuss book. Everyone in this mansion's doing a beautiful job of sealing their thoughts, but they spring leaks all over the place. Mom impresses them, they even like her, but the Silver Allegiance slowing down the process of shipping us off is just their way of being polite. Any day

now, Ambassador SeCaeta's going to come in and give us our departure date. The only real decision to be made is who's going to see us off.

According to Mom, no one was allowed to see Evan off. But this time, maybe the Silver Allegiance will be kind enough to let Mom, Dad, and even Nikki see us to our gate. Hell, it won't even be a gate. We'll be launching from a spaceport.

"It'd be nice if we could, I don't know, maybe talk to Evan," Devon says, cracking his knuckles. "Or they could put in a call to Ricky."

"You want to talk to Ricky?" I ask.

I lie back on the bed and fold my arms under my head. I never thought about talking to our biological dad. What would I even say? Hey, nice to hear your voice. It'll be nicer to see your face—and I'm also totally lying because I don't care?

"Yeah, I guess," Devon says. He lies down too and matches my position. "You really don't?"

"I wouldn't hang up the phone."

"Do you think he wants to talk to us?" Devon asks. "From the way people describe him, maybe he's out partying or something. We could be a drag. I mean, Evan's eighteen, so Ricky just got rid of him and suddenly he's slammed with us."

I frown. "You don't know that he got rid of Evan."

"Dude, if he hadn't, do you think Evan would be where he is?" Devon asks. "I mean, Mom and Dad wouldn't let us just go off to war and not have people looking for us if we were in trouble."

"We don't know what Ricky's doing," I say. Though it's true that we haven't heard anything about him mak-

ing moves like Mom and Dad are right now. There's silence on his end, like he's dead.

"This sucks," Devon grunts. "How's your head?"

"I'm good." I smirk.

Aderyn's giving me modified dosages of the drug that mellows my telempathy. I've been lax with my shields, trusting the drugs. No horseshoes or clovers. Uncle Jonas would have loved this. I don't think he slept longer than two or three hours a night during his final year. He might have slept a little more if he'd been in a place like this. The family tried to have him committed. I remember the shouting and shattering glass. I was— am—terrified that will be me one day.

"You just saying that?" Devon asks. I feel his eyes on me.

"Probably." I turn my head, meeting his analytical gaze. "Hey, it's real cool what you're doing, but it's been years, man. I'm not ready to..." trust Devon, not all the way. He's still a big ball of confusion right now. He means well, but I've been on the bad end of his wishy-washiness too often for too long. I don't want to be hurt like that again.

Dev nods, eyes shuttered, but determination as strong as Evan's swells in him. He's not giving up. That makes me feel better.

"Hey?" He kicks me. "You ever think about you stone? Yours was blue, right?"

"It was blue." I make a fist, recalling the feel of the smooth sapphire in my hand. I feel power course through me. Power to shield my mind airtight. No drugs, no girlfriends, just....

Corin's voice. *She now has your mind. Do not let*

Her keep your mind.

"Do you want it?" Devon asks. "Sometimes, I get these craving, like I'm hungry, when I think about my stone and I want to find it."

I roll onto my side. "I don't know. Maybe I do. But those things are long lost, so who cares, right?"

"Evan found one."

"By accident," I growl. "He wasn't supposed to be there."

"But he was," Devon says lightly. "And maybe it wasn't an accident."

My body goes cold. Why the hell has that never occurred to me? Of all the places for Evan to be, and in all the places he could have stumbled into to die, it had to be there. It's too much of a coincidence.

Gooseflesh breaks out over my arms and I rub them. Something could be jerking us around, a thing that could make and take choices for and from us. What choice did Evan have but to accept the stone? Do it or die. What choice did I have but to accept? I didn't understand what was going on. Devon didn't. And since we all accepted, does Lawrie get a choice? He's the only one who hasn't dream-walked with me or seen Order.

The sound of knuckles on the door snaps me back into the real world. Devon stares at the door.

The knock again. I part my shield and reach out to feel who's outside the door. A familiar rush of manic energy greets me. Lawrie.

/Come in./

The door bursts open and Lawrie bounds in. "Mom and Dad are here! They're down in the meet and greet room talking to Gale's parents."

Devon springs up like a Pop-tart, bouncing off the bed and padding across the floor to Lawrie. "All right! Let's go!"

"Ah." Lawrie holds up both hands. "We're not supposed to know they're here yet. Saphera told me."

Galeo's sister always seems to know more about what goes on in the house than anyone else.

Devon scowls and paces around the bed. "So, we're just supposed to wait here and scratch our asses or something?"

I watch him pace 'til he makes me dizzy, then look back at Lawrie who looks brighter than he has in days. Good. I didn't like seeing him sick.

"Well, you can scratch your ass, but Gale and me came up with a way to spy on them," Lawrie says, tucking his hands in his pockets and looking like a kid who's found out where his mom hides the spare cash. "I hacked the surveillance system and we rigged his comp to give us the feed in real time."

I raise a brow. One day, Lawrie will take over the universe—and that day's coming soon. I sit up and push off the bed. Devon cracks his knuckles and glances at me before nodding to Lawrie who spins around and bows low, sweeping out his arms in an 'after you' fashion. Devon goes through the door first and I follow.

We pass a soldier on our way to Galeo's room. The woman inclines her head and doesn't ask where we're going. The six soldiers that roam the house are more like fixtures and furniture for all they move or talk. If anything busted in here trying to get us, I'm sure the soldiers would spring into action, but for anything less than that, they don't seem to care much.

We make it to Galeo's room and Lawrie throws open the door, calling, "Look who I found!"

Galeo's sitting in front of his computer. He doesn't raise his head to greet Dev or me. Ever since we scared the shit out of him, Galeo keeps his distance.

"You get the display figured out?" Lawrie asks Galeo, shoving the purple Visitor over a bit so they can share the desk chair.

"Yes," Galeo says, sounding distracted, "we should have live feed in a few seconds." He presses a few keys and scoots to the left of the computer as the screen projects 3D images.

In the room where we'd first met Galeo, sit Mom, Dad, Ambassador SeCaeta and Galeo's mom, a lean woman—she's a purple Heidi Klum clone. Mom seems at ease, wearing a short white dress with one leg folded over the other like Michelle Obama. Dad looks like a lost tourist armed with a language dictionary and a travel map as he fidgets in his slacks and button-down.

Devon and I sit on Galeo's bed and Lawrie plops down on the floor at our feet.

"...very shrewd woman, Mrs. Conway," Ambassador SeCaeta is saying, nodding his head. "Well played."

Mom smiles and a purple guy in a one-piece blue outfit walks into the room, blocking the screen for a minute, and moves back out. Now Mom, Dad and the SeCaetas hold champagne glasses with pale pink liquid inside. Dad downs his as Mom sips.

Mrs. SeCaeta swirls her drink. "I have never seen the Remasian Council so eager to come to a compromise." She smiles at Mom. "You are running for office on this planet, but I do wonder if you have set your sights

too low. Perhaps, you should be applying for an ambassadorial position. Our people would love to meet a human such as you, and we do not have a human ambassador."

Dad chokes on his drink and Mom pats his back with an amused look.

"Did I miss anything?"

We all jump and stare at the door. Saphera beams, walks in and locks the door behind her. "Honestly, Galeo, this should have been secured."

"Shut up, Saphi!" Galeo hisses and turns up the volume.

She sits down on the floor next to Lawrie and prods him with her elbow. Lawrie prods back.

"So, it is all arranged," Mrs. SeCaeta says. "You will be accompanying the children as far as Amphora where they will be released into their father's custody, and you'll be returned here. However, you will be allowed to remain in remote contact."

My stomach becomes a mass of Jell-O. We're leaving. We all knew that, but damn. There it is. And Devrik Lauduethe is going to meet us.

"And Evan, will he be there to greet us?" Mom asks.

My heart jumps with a little excitement and I sit straighter. I wonder what Evan will think of me in person. Devon scoots closer and Lawrie leans forward.

"There has been no mention of Leader Lauduethe accompanying Lord Devrik," SeCaeta says.

Disappointment throws me back into a slump.

"The Remasian Council," the ambassador continues, his voice dripping with disgust, "wanted to coronate him as the first of the Four while he was in surgery.

They have been promoting images of him being pulled from that place bloodied and torn, clutching the Stone of Magic."

"They were persuaded to wait until Leader Lauduethe recovers enough," Mrs. SeCaeta says, her lips curl like she's sucking on a lemon Warhead.

"The Stone of Magic." Mom rolls her eyes. "There's no better term? And are they even sure that's what my son found?"

Both SeCaetas look grim as they nod.

"We move into darker times," Ambassador SeCaeta says. "With those images of your son have come responses from our allies and enemies. A few border skirmishes erupted immediately and some planets seceded from the Allegiances. A few more signed territorial treaties and requested annexation. Some people think their salvation has come, and others think we have all been damned."

"What do you think?" Dad asks.

Ambassador SeCaeta sighs. "I will not let a prophecy decide my future."

Those words strike home.

"Shall we send for the children now?" Mrs. SeCaeta asks.

Mom looks eager and Dad looks less constipated.

"Quick, turn it off!" Lawrie's on his feet and at the computer helping Galeo shut down the video feed.

"Damn," Devon breathes. "So, that's it." He sounds disappointed.

"You expected more?" I ask.

He looks heavenward. "No. But that's it. They're done. We're done."

"I think your mother did an excellent job," Saphera

says, standing up. She's in a see-through yellow dress that touches the floor, but she's got on a slip underneath that covers her from breast to thigh. "I would hire her to represent me anywhere."

She puts her hands on her slim hips and I can't help but notice she's hot, hot and purple. If anyone had told me I'd ever be leering at a purple girl.... Hell, I might be leering at green and blue women in the future. Who knows what kind of aliens I'll meet and probably date. I have to get....

Wait, no. The world stops again for me. The tugging need that's chewed on my brain for so long is quiet, and I can keep it quiet. I don't have to date anymore, if I don't want to. I've got medicine to help me now.

I feel something heavy fall off my shoulders, and I'm weightless for a second. I'm free. No more Heathers or Gabbies. The world turns with Saphera as she spins, her nice butt in my face, and something stirs inside.

Well, not free, but I don't need it, and that's good enough right?

"Ly? You okay?" Devon asks.

I give him a weak smile. "Yeah." Not really, but I will be.

Devon nods at me and slides off the bed. "I'm going to my room, so it doesn't look like we were in here partying or something." He leaves.

Lawrie opens his mouth, but Saphera grabs the sleeve of his T-shirt and drags him out of the room with her. It's just Galeo and me. Galeo shifts and eyes me warily, like I'm gonna strangle him.

"Galeo?"

He blinks at me.

"Does Dr. Aderyn work for clients outside of your family?"

Galeo nods. "I'm sure he does some consulting work on the side. Why?"

I shrug. "Don't worry about it."

THE AFTERNOON AND EVENING ARE blurs of events and emotions. Mom hugged me until I thought my eyeballs would pop out of my head. Her feelings flushed through me like a river breaking through a dam. She was worried, angry and sad, all at once, but I couldn't tell it from her face or voice. After bear hugs from Mom and man-hugs from Dad, we had a private family dinner. The SeCaetas left us alone. Mom explained to us that she'd done what she could. She even thought, with more time, she could work out a way to come see us.

The SeCaetas allowed Mom and Dad to spend the night, gave them guest rooms downstairs. After midnight, Mom and Dad went to bed, Lawrie disappeared with Saphera, much to Galeo's annoyance, and Devon got on the phone with Monica.

A few minutes before 1:00 AM, I leave my room, finding the steps in the dark. I don't want anyone to see me and ask where I'm going. I've only been to the Se-Caeta's panic room/clinic once and that was a week ago. This place is a maze in the daylight, at night it's an endless labyrinth. I dip into the mind of a soldier downstairs in the kitchen and get a layout of the manor. I twist and

turn down servant corridors and take back staircases, until I reach the heavy safe-like doors of Aderyn's sanctuary.

I lean against the cool metal for a moment. The outer room is dark, the drapes pulled tight. I would be blind if not for the soldier's knowledge of the place. I network our minds like two computers in a home group, so that even with my eyes closed I see the room plain as day. I approach the vaulted door, pausing at the coded, electronic lock. The keypad is square and the buttons have alien writing on them. My fingers move over the symbols in a pattern familiar to the guard. Something inside clicks, and I push open the door.

Low lights gleam from the ceiling, casting weird shadows on the wall murals, making them disturbing instead of peaceful. I creep across the floor, passing through the make-shift lobby area. Aderyn's office is.... I tug at the soldiers's mind and see an entrance to the rear of the room. The door's splashed with the same paint as the murals and hard to see in the bad light.

I knock, wait, and then step back from the door as it swings inward.

"Ambassador, what—oh." Aderyn's eyes widen, drinking me in. This guy makes me feel naked. I scowl and push him aside so I can come in and shut the door.

"I have a proposition for you," I say, gazing around the room. It's small with light blue walls heavy with shelves covered in trinkets. Colored glass, jars of floating gooey things, 3D images of plants with bushy petals, an image of Lawrie sitting on the hull of a spaceship—no, not Lawrence. Oh man.

"Do tell." Aderyn moves behind me. Metal scrapes

the floor and I turn. He's sitting at a small metal desk, legs crossed. On the desk are glittering cylinders as wide and long as ballpoint pens. He picks one up, running his fingers along its length. He twirls it and holds it out to me. "You want more, correct?"

I nod. "A lot more."

Aderyn frowns. "You do know that long term usage of these drugs is not recommended. There are side-effects. I would prescribe psychotropic therapy for you, proper training, and..." he trails off, watching me like a specimen on a glass slide.

"I know all that. You told me, but...." How long will it take before I'm under control? I don't ever want to lose it again. There can't be another Nisse. And I don't want to die like Uncle Jonas.

"Patience is a virtue," Aderyn sings. "Yes, it could take years for you to grasp how to fully protect yourself, but only because your powers are so great. I am sure that between you and your trainers, you will come to a solution."

I swallow. "But until then, I need something. What I did before you helped me can't work anymore and I..." know how bad I can get when I crack.

Aderyn sighs and looks over his shoulder and up at the image of Devrik on the spaceship. He smiles and looks dreamy. "Hm, though it is against my better judgment, who am I to deny a son of Devrik Lauduethe."

He hands me the cylinder. "I will engineer a different cocktail, one tailored just for you, and produce enough to keep you supplied for—"

"A few months," I say. "I can call you here if I need more."

Aderyn raises a brow. "And who says I will still be here?"

What? Lousy son of a—

Aderyn purrs, "I cannot very well supply one of the Four of Rema, son of my idol, with chemicals, and stay on Earth where he can't easily access my services."

I stare at him, trying to read him, but he's put up a thicker shield. If I punch his mental wall, I can break it, but I won't do that. Not to someone who's going to help me.

"I must run another diagnostic on you. And for as long as you are under the influence of this cocktail, we will need to be in touch." Aderyn rises from his chair again. "As I said, there are side-effects to these types of chemicals, and I refuse to be the doctor who killed a son of Devrik."

His hand is on the small of my back as he pushes me toward the door.

"What a grand relationship we will have, and perhaps one day you shall introduce me to your father." He giggles as we pass through the office door, heading to one of the exam rooms.

I shuffle my feet. "Keep me stable and I'll introduce you to whoever you want."

Aderyn grins. "Lie on the table, please."

"Sure." I climb onto the slab. So, here's how it starts. Lyle Ladreth—Lauduethe—whoever the hell I am, one of the Four, heading off to do God knows what, but here's for making sure I keep a clear head.

After all, I've got a lot of choices to make, and I can't screw up.

CHAPTER 30

LAWRENCE

THIS MORNING HAS BEEN A rocket ride, almost literally, not quite yet though. The whole family—Dev, Ly, Mom, Dad, Nikki and me—got crammed in the back of an armored, silver Suburban with our Silver Allegiance guards. Then the real FBI drove us into Virginia and ferried us over to Wallops Island. Once there, our group split into three sedans. We passed several NASA owned flight facilities that ship cargo to the International Space Station and the International Outbound Transit Center.

Our final destination was the Gwyddion Elspanor Marthum Spaceport, GEMS, named after the first, official Visiting ambassador in 2012. He'd come down with his minions, said the landing spots on Earth were gross, and campaigned for SAOP to engineer a port better suited for Visiting dignitaries. He got a place constructed with the standard spread: outdoor launch pad, access ramp, storage hangars, and then added a posh clubhouse fit for a rock star. Positioned on top of steel enforced columns like something out of Roman times, the clubhouse

has huge window-walls that overlook the coastline.

Enormous saucer chairs with orange memory foam cushions are situated around a metal pedestal in the center of the room that projects the movie 'Avatar' in 3D. Headphones sit on glass tables between the orange seats. Long internet cafe tables made of polished metal are mounted to the window-walls, and flanked on one side with matching high-backed bar stools. It'd almost be cozy if not for the FBI and Silver Allegiance soldiers stationed around the room, eyes tracking our movements.

I move toward the touch screen computers built into the tables and run my fingers over a couple of the displays showing symbols and squiggles in swirling or blocky formats. At once, they merge and become the Roman alphabet.

Welcome. What would you like?

That's a loaded question.

A digital keyboard appears on screen, the letters glowing a warm blue.

I type: Give me information on Evan Lauduethe.

An image of a kid with curly blond hair hanging loose over one shoulder appears. He's smiling like someone said something really funny but he can't laugh out loud yet. His wide green eyes sparkle.

"What are you doing, Lawrie?" I smell Mom's floral perfume before she slides next to me. She inhales sharply. I gaze over at her. Her eyes are locked on Evan's image. And damn, he's like a male version of her, they even smile alike.

"You'll see him for real one day," I say, touching her hand.

Her fingers curl over mine and squeeze for a sec-

ond; she pulls away. Her eyes linger on Evan, before she clears her throat.

"How are you feeling?" she asks.

I'm tired of people asking me that. I'm fine. Haven't so much as sniffled in a week.

"I'm okay. How are you?"

"I've been better," she says with a slight smirk. "I'm not exactly looking forward to being blasted into space."

Or giving us over to Devrik Lauduethe. But I know she's not gonna say that part. That would be like admitting weakness, and Mom already did that once this month.

"...and when you come back, Melanie's supposed to go to the prom," Nikki's chirpy voice comes from nearby. I look over to see her standing on a table, Devon stands behind her. He follows as she walks the length of the table. She presses her face against the window. "You didn't move any of the Barbies around, did you?"

"Didn't touch a thing," Devon says and she beams down at him like he's Prince Charming. Dev's always been her favorite brother, and she loves telling Ly and me whenever she thinks we forget it. Maybe that's why I don't talk to her much, that and her hang-up with *My Little Ponies*.

Mom watches Nikki and Dev, a melancholy look on her face. "She doesn't understand that you won't be coming back for a while. Frank and I tried to explain, but she thinks it'll be like going to visit Grandma and Grandpa. A plane trip away, back in a few hours when needed."

Great, so we'll make a five-year-old cry. What a way to start kindergarten, huh? My big brothers are aliens. I'd

bring them to Show and Tell but they got spaced and can't come back. Maybe not can't, but who knows when we'll be back? Could be years. Maybe there'll be no more Barbie or conversations about cracked-out cartoon ponies. She could be a real person that I could talk to, but Dev'll probably still be her favorite.

I leave Mom and walk over to Dev and Nikki, offering a hand up to my little sister.

"My lady?" I ask.

She giggles, puts her tiny hand in mine and jumps off the table into my arms. She wraps her legs around my waist and hugs my neck, her cherry lollipop breath's on my ear. "I hid Princess Vanessa where you'll never find her!"

"Oh and believe me," I gaze into her eyes as she pulls back to stare at me, "I looked so hard for Princess Vanessa."

She looks so serious, probably trying to figure out if I'm lying. Her hazel eyes narrow, her long lashes lower and she pouts. She's cute. She'll grow up to be hot and I'll have to kill some guy over it. I set Nikki down and she runs right back to Dev's side.

Hmph.

Devon grabs Nikki's hands and swings her around as she laughs. They've got plenty of room, but not much time. I glance at my watch: 11:30 AM. We board the craft in thirty minutes and launch about fifteen minutes after that.

Mom touches my shoulder. "You guys are going to have to pull together and get along. I hope Evan's the kind of person who'll help you fit in. I know that Ricky will try."

"He's a nice guy like that?" I ask. I hear people talk about him being an airhead. It's not awe-inspiring.

Mom chuckles. "Yes. He's a wonderful person, but not as strong as I raised you to be. You boys will..." she frowns at me, eyes unusually soft, "...have to take care of each other. You've got some serious brains in there, kiddo, time to use them to do more than break things. I need you to look after Devon and Lyle."

I blink at her. Me? "Devon and Lyle are...."

Mom shakes her head and draws me close to her, so she can whisper. "Devon only thinks he knows what he's doing half the time. And Lyle's..." she sighs, "keep an eye on him for me."

"Why?" I ask. I glance over at Lyle sitting with Dad. Dad's got an arm around Lyle's shoulder and Lyle seems content.

"I was close to Jonas when we were little," Mom says. "Jonas was a lot like Lyle, a quiet cynic, no outside friends. I never used to worry about Lyle, because he had Dev to look out for him."

"They're getting along again," I say. Nikki's incessant giggling tells me Devon's still spinning her around.

"Hope it lasts," Mom says. I look at her. Her eyes are on Lyle and Dad. "But even so, Dev will need your help. You're stronger than him."

Ouch. "Mom, he's like the Hulk. You should see the hole he put in my wall."

Her eyes shoot hooks into me. "Hole?"

Well shizz. Just how clean did we leave the house? Dev and Ly usually straighten up pretty good, but I doubt either of them thought of that hole in the wall. Then again, Mom doesn't go in my lair. She's deemed

it condemned. Wonder what she'll do with it when I'm not there.

Homesickness hits me in the chest like a fastball.

I flashback to the conversation I had with Jeremy last night. It'd been on Skype. I'd talked to him every day since I got better. Now, all of a sudden, it's two weeks later, and who knows when I'll get to talk to him again. He'll be gone, like Mom, Dad, and Nikki.

In a few hours, all of this will be like a past life. Everything in my future will be different.

I can't lie, different excites me. Just thinking about blasting off into outer space and landing on foreign planets with folks talking alien and using translators makes 'gotta do something' crazy. I barely slept last night and woke up this morning dancing off the walls. The SeCaetas had seen us off in their front foyer. The whole family stood in a semi-circle, like a greeting line, and my family shook hands and thanked each SeCaeta.

Me? I shook Ambassador SeCaeta's hand, bowed to his wife, and hugged Galeo tight. Saphera? Not to be outdone by Galeo, she'd grabbed me in a hug that turned into an ass-kicking kiss that lasted twenty seconds. She'd tasted like peaches and vanilla bean ice cream with caramel sauce, probably her breakfast. The SeCaetas eat desserts like meals, but they'd made sure that meat, potatoes and veggies had gotten onto the table for us. I wouldn't have minded just the dessert.

An elevator door dings. Mom's hand clenches my shoulder as we look over to see the metal doors opening. A woman and man in black pants and red tunics step out. Nikki stops giggling and Devon sets her down. Lyle and Dad stand up, and Mom takes my hand like she used

to when I was a little kid. The lady and man stop paces away from us. They're brown-skinned with black hair and look to be about college-age.

"Greetings," the woman speaks first, dark doe eyes warm. Her voice is pretty and her words have a neutral accent. The top button on her tunic glitters orange as she talks. "It is an honor to be one of the first to serve you."

"I hope you are well and ready to begin your journey," the man says, his voice soft and pleasant. The top button on his shirt lights up too as he speaks.

They look like twins. The dude's pretty enough to be a girl, and the girl's hot enough to be on a magazine cover. They've both got this dewy appearance of good health. Bet Neutrogena would love to bottle some of that up and sell it for fifty dollars a pop.

"I am Erwynn and this is my brother Feswynn," the woman says. "We will attend to you for the trip. If you require anything at all, request it of us."

"This is freaky," Devon whispers, "they're like doppel-thingies." He stands on the other side of me, still holding Nikki's hand.

"Doppelgangers," I mutter. One day, when I'm bigger than him, I'm gonna smack Devon upside the head with a dictionary.

"Please follow us," Feswynn says.

We go down the elevator in two groups, my family and I with Feswynn and Erwynn in one and the soldiers in another. We walk through an underground corridor and into another elevator that lets us out in Hangar 51, home of the Han Solo and its sister ship, the much larger Princess Leia. Han Solo's a small shuttle painted jet black with icy blue flames on the nose cone and wings.

Bet when it was brand spanking new the finish was sleek and smooth. There are a few nicks from space travel but it's obvious someone's been buffing the outsides. I wanna rub my hands over it. Hell, I wanna fly it.

Princess Leia is ruby red with black flames on its nose and wings, a full-sized shuttle made to endure longer distance space travel with larger groups, designed more for comfort than speed. I'd drooled reading up on these babies; total Allegiance candy that only ferries VIPs to and from Earth.

"I wanna sit by the window!" Nikki shouts. She's up on Dad's shoulders, grinning and pointing at Princess Leia.

Aw...shizz.

"You can for a little while, baby," Dad says, voice flyaway light. He glances at Erwynn and Feswynn who wear identical frowns. "Can we come onboard just to look around? We have time for that, don't we?"

Feswynn shares a look with his sister, and then walks to the soldiers who hang back near Han Solo. I watch their lips move and heads nod. The soldiers look annoyed and Feswynn wears a bright smile that could sell every Crest White-Strip on the planet if he claimed to know what they were.

"Yes, you may board," Erwynn says before Feswynn reaches us. "Though," she dimples at Nikki, "I am afraid our chariot is the smaller vessel, my dear."

Nikki grins at Erwynn and nestles her chin in Dad's dark blond hair. "You look like a Barbie!"

Erwynn blinks. Bet she doesn't know what the hell a Barbie is, but she doesn't look offended. "Why thank you, little dear. What a precious child." She smiles at

Dad.

The Han Solo rests on double sets of thick-soled wheels like a passenger jet before take-off. An oval-shaped portal slides open near the middle of its body and a single-story staircase is rolled over by two men in collared blue shirts and khakis.

Snap, snap, snap, and the staircase is connected.

"After you." Feswynn gestures toward Han Solo then watches us intently until we start moving toward the ship.

I take the lead, Mom holding my elbow. The metal stairs ring with each step we take. When we reach the top, I take a deep breath, inhaling an interesting mixture of new car smell and Cinnamon Toast Crunch. I'm in love, pure and simple. Saphera, Taylor Swift, who? Han Solo is my soulmate.

I tug free of Mom, my sneakers crossing the threshold and sinking into plush black carpeting. The diagrams of Han Solo I studied last night churn in my head, full of pictures and labels that correspond with what I see. It's like an airplane inside, narrow and long, but there are no seats facing front in boring aisles. Instead, against the walls are black, leather couches with gleaming silver belts for security straps. The winding staircase near the back should lead up to a small second story where there's a huge mattress-like thing called a palle spread over the floor, made for people to lie down and watch the stars when the ceiling turns transparent.

I take the stairs by twos and have to duck my head to enter the star deck. The ceiling's low. There are tiny cubbies for shoes in front of the palle. I hear the clamor of other people coming aboard: heavy feet, mixed voic-

es. Han Solo shudders and a quiet hum works its way throughout the ship as it comes to life. Running lights glow a soft blue around the edges of the palle and the outlines of the shoe cubbies.

I kick off my shoes and crawl onto the soft, deep blue, almost wall-to-wall pallet. It feels like memory foam and velvet, but instead of being warm it's cool against my body as it adjusts to my weight. I flop down and roll onto my back, staring at the dark ceiling. Full lights come on, showing me a room painted black.

Soft clanging up the stairs; then Dad's head pokes over the opening. "Wow."

"Yeah. Cool, huh?" I say.

He comes the rest of the way up and stoops down to take off his shoes. He crawls onto the palle beside me and sits.

"You ready?" he asks after a beat.

I shrug. "Ready to see what it's like to travel by space shuttle? Ready to see Venus?" I smirk. "Ready to be a kingpin?"

He chuckles. "All of the above."

"Maybe." I sigh.

Dad ruffles my hair as I wait for him to say something else. I roll over to face him. He's staring at the ceiling.

"Are you okay?" I ask.

He turns his head. His eyes are bright, but he smiles. "Not really, kiddo, but so long as you guys are okay, I'll be fine."

"I'm okay." I nod. "I mean...." Did that come out bad? I don't want him to think I want to leave him or anything. "I'll miss you, and I wish—"

"I know, Lawr. Me too."

I bite my lip, listening to Dad breathe.

"I won't...." My stomach clenches. "That Ricky guy, he's not you. He's just a guy. Remember that, okay?"

Dad laughs out loud. "Your brothers said similar things. Think Dev's was the best. He said: I'll hate him if you want me to."

"Do you want him, us, to hate Ricky?" My laugh is half-hearted. I know Dad. He would never tell us to hate anyone, but I know he's gotta be jealous. I mean, what if Ricky's great, and I like him? Will he ever take the place of Dad? Will I want to call him 'dad?'

"You know the answer to that," Dad says.

"What did Lyle say?"

Dad snorts. "He told me not to worry about him liking that Ricky guy better than he likes me because it'll never happen." He shakes his head. "I believe him on that one. That brother of yours is a tough crowd."

"Not for you."

Dad grins and gestures for me to sit up. When I do, he slings an arm over my shoulder and pulls me closer to him. "I did okay by you guys, huh?"

I grunt, surprised. "Yeah, of course you did."

He kisses my temple. The last time he did that I was ten and had broken my collarbone. My eyes sting.

"I love you, Lawr."

I nod, throat tight.

"Okay." He swallows, squeezes my shoulder, and then lets his arm drop. "Come on down. I think the Doublemint twins are ready for take-off. They're smiling too much."

"They're smiling too much?" I tilt my head.

"Eh, it's a customer service thing," Dad says. "When you're ready for a customer to move on, but can't say so, you just get uncomfortably polite with them."

I raise my brows. "Is that so?"

"Yeah." Dad winks at me. "It's something you're gonna have to learn, Kingpin."

There's a lot of stuff I'm gonna have to learn.

"You're getting excited, aren't you?" Dad asks. He pokes my ribs. "Promise me you won't let anything change you."

"I promise," I say, poking him back. He hugs me tight, and I reciprocate. "I love you, Dad. You know that."

"I do."

We let go. He crawls off the pallet first; then I follow. He gets his shoes back on, but I leave mine, following him downstairs.

Erwynn and Feswynn stand near the portal leading to the cockpit wearing smiles so tight they look painful. Their eyes lock on me and their facial muscles relax.

Devon and Lyle sit on a couch with Nikki chattering between them. Devon seems attentive. Lyle looks bored.

"Well," Erwynn's voice is clear and smooth, "we have six minutes before departure. It is important that we keep to our flight schedule."

Erwynn and Feswynn bow their heads and stand together, watching us, waiting for something.

Oh!

Devon gets up and grabs Nikki's hand, pulling her off the couch. Lyle stands too. We meet in the center of the room. Dad hugs me, Devon and Lyle, then shakes our hands and turns his back to us, standing in the exit portal.

I hope he's not crying. My stomach gurgles.

"What's wrong with Daddy?" Nikki asks.

I frown at her and swallow. Devon kneels down to be at eye-level with her.

"Take care of Princess Vanessa, Nik," he says, hugging her. "And make sure Ryan is the one who asks her to prom, not Jake. Jake's a booger."

Nikki giggles. "Jake is a booger!" She pouts and pulls back from his embrace. "What's the matter?"

"Nothin'," Dev says, tweaking her nose. "You be good, 'kay?"

"Okay." She's still pouting, and Dev stands up.

Lyle hugs her next and pats her head. "See ya, brat."

"Okay." Confusion turns her pout into a frown.

I'm up next. "Uh." I scratch my head and pull her to me. She buries her head in my belly and hugs my waist. Then, she tilts her head back to look at me.

"You're just gonna visit your other daddy. Why are you so sad?"

I chuckle and rub her back. "Maybe we're gonna miss you."

"I guess," Nikki says. "But it's okay. If you start crying, your other daddy will have Mommy come get you." She smiles and it just about undoes me. What is it about little kids?

"Yeah," I mutter. She detaches herself from my waist and Mom picks her up, kissing her cheek and passing her to Dad who turns around just to take her.

Dad goes through the portal door, disappearing down the stairs.

"I didn't go upstairs, Daddy!" Nikki's voice sounds small. The door closes.

"I feel like a douche," Devon says. "What are you gonna tell her a few weeks from now?" He rubs his eyes and goes to sit on a couch. Lyle sighs and joins him.

Mom folds her arms over her chest and looks heavenward. "What I already told her, but maybe she'll understand it better when she can't see you guys."

"This sucks," Devon groans. He looks over at Lyle. "What are you thinking?"

"Doesn't matter," Lyle says. He rolls his head back on the couch and stares at the ceiling. "Nothing'll change." He talks slow, not quite slurring, but he sounds a little off.

I frown. He's still taking that stuff Aderyn gave him. Don't know when he's supposed to stop. He's been quiet, only really talking to Devon, which is new and not, and I don't know if I like it. I sit on the couch opposite the twins, studying them. Devon turns toward Lyle, nudging him and then slumps back on the couch looking vaguely content. Maybe they're having a telepathic conversation. Either way, I feel shut out.

Mom said we're gonna have to take care of each other. I've never been a part of 'Devon and Lyle.' They might be more willing to let me in, in a few days, but man, that'll be weird. And then there's Evan, a great big question mark. What if he's fun as hell, my missing link?

The leather depresses next to me. Mom sits with her legs crossed, eyes on Devon and Lyle.

"Excuse me," Erwynn says with a polite little cough. "Is everyone comfortable with their seating arrangement? The pilot would like to begin departure procedures."

"Where'd the soldiers go?" I ask.

Feswynn beams. "They are in the cockpit and the rear room. After we've broken through the atmosphere and are on our set course, you will be free to roam about the vessel. Please enjoy the amenities at your seats for now."

The Barbie twins give matching smiles and waltz to the back of the ship. What the hell is up with these guys? They're so perfet and polite it's almost scary. Could they be automatons? 'Gotta do something' sparks. Androids, terminators with living flesh, and me without a screwdriver.

"Amenities, huh?" Devon grumbles; then starts as a 3D projection rises up from the middle of the floor.

The movie 'Avatar' picks up where it'd left off in the clubhouse. The sound is soft, the images so crispy clear and lifelike I want to reach in and feel for myself. Han Solo shudders and the sound from the movie mutes as a voice comes from the ceiling and walls.

"Attention honored guests, we are preparing to leave the hangar. Please be sure that your security straps fasten properly."

The leathery seatbelt snaps around my waist and over my shoulders like a long harnesses. I click it into place with no trouble. Mom, Dev and Ly do the same.

The ship moves forward. The windows show us a view of the hangar as we roll by and then we're outdoors, sunlight pouring in. We coast along the winding path to the launch site. Han Solo jerks, making sounds similar to a rollercoaster car climbing a track. The ship tilts upward, putting us at an angle.

We're doing this. Here it comes.

"Honored guests, please prepare yourselves for

launch. You will feel some pressure and may experience some discomfort. Please remain secured until given permission to roam."

The cabin dims, tiny bulbs line the floor and exits, giving us enough light to see each other. Mom's mouth is tight, Devon's cracking his knuckles, and Lyle's eyes are closed. I laugh. This is going to be the best ride ever.

Han Solo shudders, then rumbles and rocks. The grunt and groan of metal, the sound of something huge detaching and clanking.

The engines roar and my head snaps back as the ship jolts upward, from zero to twenty thousand miles per hour. My eyeballs roll around in my head, my mouth stretches.

"Aooooooooooooo!" I howl.

I hear someone screaming. I think it's Dev. I open my eyes to see his mouth open. He's gripping the seat, knuckles white. Lyle's laughing his ass off. Mom's quiet as hell, her teeth clenched. God, we're moving fast, and only getting faster. It sounds like we're under a waterfall, feels like it too. We're swimming upstream, trying not to drown—so fast. Crazy fast.

Then *foom*. All gone. The waterfall evaporates, the pressure's not there, the sound of the movie 'Avatar' is back, and we're coasting again, only not on a path to a runway.

I look out the window to see the Earth below, all blue and green and white. I press one hand on the cool glass. Look at that. That's where I grew up. That's home, not a city, not a state, not a country, but a whole damn planet. There it goes.

My eyes burn and I blink a few times to get rid of

the feeling.

The cabin lights flicker back on, but the okay to remove our security straps isn't given. Feswynn and Erwynn glide toward our seats. Why is it all right for them to move around? I frown at them. They seem nervous; their smiles are tight.

"Before you are allowed to roam the vessel, I'm afraid we must share with you that our travel plans have been altered," Feswynn says.

"Altered how?" Mom asks, narrowing her eyes.

Feswynn and Erwynn trade glances, almost like rock-paper-scissors—you talk!

I don't feel good about this.

Feswynn actually scowls; the most normal expression I've seen on his face since I've met him. I'd believe he was human, though I know he isn't.

"We will be docking with a larger ship suited for deep, intra-space travel, instead of connecting with the Amphoran obiter. From there, we will travel on to Lenore."

"What?" Mom blinks.

"Lenore?" Devon asks. "I've heard that name before. Where's that? What is it?" He's a little green and swallowing like he's trying not to puke. He presses a fist against his lips.

"Lenore is home of the Maidens," Erwynn says. "It's said to be quite beautiful. It's an honor to be invited. No outsiders have set foot on Lenore in hundreds of cycles."

"So, why are we invited?" Lyle asks, no slur in his words and no question in his voice. He knows.

I know. My locusts return with a vengeance.

"The Maidens can translate the coordinates coded into your Marks," Feswynn says and clears his throat. "Ah...."

"Both the Nazflit and Su Coalitions have declared war," Erwynn says. "They've seized planets in Cold Zones and are attacking any Silver or Golden Allegiance vessels entering their Sectors. They've got people fighting for them that show immense power."

"We need all of our champions together," Feswynn says, looking at Devon, Lyle and me. "You have to find your Stones. Once the Maidens decode the coordinates, you'll go retrieve them."

"W-wait, we'll go to retrieve them? Us? In the middle of a war?" Devon asks, turning greener. "We can't fight. I thought we were supposed to get some kinda training."

I did too. My heart thuds against my ribs. I can't use my powers on purpose yet.

"This is ridiculous," Mom says. "You can't just throw them to the wolves—"

"Madam, if you please," Erwynn says, her voice a paragon of calm that only serves to piss Mom off more.

"No, if *you* please. You lied to us," Mom says. "The agreement, was it a joke? Did you never plan to keep it?"

"Mrs. Lauduethe—"

"Conway!" Mom snaps. "Did the Allegiance say anything that was true?"

The Barbie twins play rock-paper-scissors with their body language again.

"The agreement *was* true," Feswynn says. Damn, he must suck at rock-paper-scissors. "It was to be upheld until forty-eight Earth hours ago when war was declared.

You *are* still traveling with your sons to see them off to their next destination."

"And will Devrik be there?" Mom asks.

Feswynn shakes his head. "I don't know who will be there to greet us, but I assure you that your sons will be in good hands. Madam, we only wish to serve and protect our champions. We do have their best interests in mind."

Mom snorts. "Oh, you have interests in mind, but I won't pretend that those interests have anything to do with the well-being of my children."

I look at her, noting the glint in her eyes. That look never bodes well for anyone on the receiving end of it. Somebody's gonna pay, and I want them to. Screw them. Anger and anxiety taste like gritty baking soda-laced toothpaste in my mouth. I hate that taste as much as I hate these feelings. Mom takes my hand, squeezing my fingers. Feswynn and Erwynn take their seats at the back of the cabin again and nobody says anything else for a long time.

After what feels like hours later, a voice sounds from overhead.

"Attention honored guests, you may remove your security straps and roam the vessel. If you are experiencing motion sickness, please alert your attendants. Your comfort is important to us. Please enjoy your flight."

I un-strap and get up. Mom, Devon and Lyle stare at me, so I smile.

"I'm going upstairs." I gotta move.

Please don't let anybody want to come with me.

No one nods or says anything, so I just leave. I take the stairs slow and crawl back onto the palle. The star

deck is dark except for the blue running lights lining the
cubbies and palle. I lie on my stomach at first, staring
into the dark folds of the palle before rolling onto my
back. Slow whirling masses of space debris greet my
eyes. There are some stars and glints of far off planets.
It could be a painting. It's so dark and bright at the same
time. Amazing.

    This is where I'm going.

    The universe swirls around me. My body feels
small, weightless. 'Gotta do something' is confused. I
don't know what I want to do next, how I should feel.
But I know I don't want to cry about it. So, I keep still
and watch the world pass by until the captain calls for
everyone to return to the passenger cabin so that we can
dock with the other ship.

IEVISARA IS PROBABLY THE LENGTH and width
of two football stadiums and at least ten stories tall. I
keep my face pressed against the window as Han Solo
nears the deep space cruiser. An opening appears in the
side of the larger ship and Han Solo flies to it. We're not
docking but landing inside of Ievisara like a small plane
entering a floating hangar. Han Solo glides to a halt on
a short runway beside a smaller ship and gives several
shudders. 'Gotta do something' leaps into action as metal grinds and moans. The landing bay of Ievisara is huge
and full of people in different colored jumpsuits riding
on scooters with no wheels and walking around with 3D

screens hovering inches in front of their faces.

Some of the people have snouts and tails; some have horns and extra eyes. Some look as human as me, while others are red and blue. God, it's like Disney and Nickelodeon got together and went crazy. I gotta get out there. My knees bounce and I finger my harness, waiting for the okay to yank it off.

Soldiers wearing Allegiance uniforms scramble around Han Solo, attaching the staircase and manually opening compartments. The soldiers on the ship with us hustle out of their secured seating in the cockpit and rear and march to the hatch. It peels open and they troop down the stairs without looking back at us.

I groan and sigh, ignoring Mom's warning hand on my shoulder as we end up waiting in the passenger cabin for our luggage to be unloaded. I see one of my orange duffle bags and a cardboard box marked LAWRIE'S JUNK get tossed in a silver tube and shot up into the ceiling. Damn, we brought a lot of stuff. There'd been no limit on how much we could request from home, so we'd kinda went overboard. I think my whole lair is getting sucked up that chute.

"Honored guests, you may unclasp your security straps at this time."

I free myself from the harness and bolt for the door. 'Gotta do something' needs to explore the Ievisara. I want to dance and sing because we're in space on a freakin' King-Kong sized ship surrounded by aliens and about to go on an honest to God quest. *Final Fantasy*'s got nothing on this. My better sense, the fluttering locusts, hover in the background, but 'gotta do something' always wins in the end.

Feswynn and Erwynn are faster than me. They stand in front of the door, taking a few seconds to straighten each others' hair and clothing. I tap my foot and stare at them.

"Esteemed leaders," Erwynn says, "allow us to escort you to your first audience."

"Audience?" I ask. I glance at Mom and my brothers. "We're giving a show?"

Erwynn smiles. "We've had word that there are some individuals who are anxious to meet you."

"I don't want to meet anybody right now," Devon grumbles. He still looks nauseous and rough. His hair gel must have melted during the flight 'cause his hair's stuck to his face and there are pillow creases on his left cheek.

I bite my lip on a snicker but almost bust when Lyle snorts with laughter and ruffles Devon's hair.

Lyle snatches his hand back and curls his lip. "What the hell did you put in your hair? This is nasty!"

I shake with laughter as Lyle wipes his hand on his pants. Mom shakes her head, looking embarrassed. Devon grunts, runs his hands through his own hair, trying to fix it, and kicks Lyle.

"Boys, stop it," Mom says through her teeth. She eyeballs us. "You guys okay?"

"No," Devon huffs and kicks Lyle again when he laughs.

I study Lyle. He looks kinda glazed, worse than before. Did he take something else?

"We need to exit the ship now," Feswynn says.

The Barbie twins seem nervous again. The orange buttons on their collars flash even when they're not talking to us. What does that mean?

"Please follow," Erwynn says. She and Feswynn descend the stairs.

I shoot a quick glance at my family and then chase after Feswynn and Erwynn. The refrigerated air of Ievisara smells like stale popcorn after being in the sweet-smelling Han Solo. At the bottom of the stairs wait two Allegiance soldiers, two women, neither one of them a part of the group who'd been with us on Earth. They bow their heads and I give them a smile.

The soldiers and Feswynn and Erwynn mutter in a foreign language as Mom and my brothers join us at the bottom of the stairs. Feswynn and Erwynn look flustered. They nod a lot at whatever the soldiers are saying.

The Barbies don't seem so graceful anymore.

The soldiers say something in that other language and begin moving toward an arched door at the end of the hangar. Feswynn and Erwynn blink rapidly and gesture for us to move too. They practically jog to catch up to the soldiers.

"What the hell? They in trouble?" Devon grunts.

"They're scared," Lyle murmurs. "I think we're late."

"You can read them?" I ask.

Lyle rubs his forehead. "A little bit. Their shields are starting to fall apart."

"Come on, boys," Mom says softly. She walks after Feswynn, Erwynn and the soldiers, and after a beat, Dev, Ly and I follow too.

The hangar thrives and throbs with life energy. So many different peoples, so many skin colors, more than just red and blue, I see pink and pale yellows, scales and spots, even feathers bristling where humans might have

hair. Spicy scents of peppers and floral fragrances waft by as we pass people who turn to openly stare at us.

They have to know who we are, and I know they're curious. I would be. No one gets in our way though. We pass through the arched doorway into a wide hall with glittering purple walls and multiple doors. The soldiers stop beside the third door we approach and one of them touches a panel beside it. Lights blink and the door slides open.

The soldiers step aside; Feswynn and Erwynn copy their motion. One soldier bows deep at the waist, then sweeps an arm toward the room. "We welcome you, young lords. Please step forward."

Okay. Who the hell is on the other side of this door? Is it the entire Silver Allegiance? Is it a goddess? It's like trying to guess what's behind the curtain on a corny game show. Am I gonna win a trip to Hawaii, a car or a gag prize?

Mom squeezes my shoulders from behind, but she can't keep me from walking into the room, in fact, she gets pulled along with me. I feel like I've entered a kitchen after an oven door's been opened. It's warm on the verge of being hot. The scent of vanilla is strong but kinda nice. The room is an oval shape with couches and chairs occupied by four people; three of them stand as we enter.

One's a tall guy with black hair and shiggity, is he for real? He looks like he models Hollister for a living. Where's the portable wind machine to blow his hair? The girls stand on either side of the guy and I stare. They're hot. The one on the left is almost as tall as the guy, with coppery brown hair all down her back, and a Wonder

Woman body wrapped in a black and green jumpsuit. The other girl's smaller, my height, with thick black hair falling over her shoulders and a face to put all of Victoria's Angels to shame.

The hot trio glance back at their fourth. He gets up, almost stumbling as he moves toward us. He's several inches shorter than me and skinny, long blond hair hangs in a loose braid over one shoulder. He wears a black and green jumpsuit like the others, but it's slack in areas—too big. Large green eyes meet my gaze.

My breath catches a bit and I grin, feeling a victory dance coming on. This is the part in the movie where the hero gets a trophy; only our trophy has arms and legs.

"Evan," Mom whispers. She looks at him like a grand prize, the trip to Hawaii and the car. She pushes past me to take Evan's face in her hands. I don't know how long they stand there staring at each other, but when they finally hug I want to clap. Congratulations, Mom, you won *something*.

"I'm so sorry," Mom murmurs over and over.

She pulls back, lips parting like she wants to say more. I study Evan up close, noticing fine details: the tiny curls on his brow slightly damp with sweat, the hollows under his eyes. But then he smiles for me and his entire face lights up.

"Lawrence," he says. He hugs me next and I'm shocked to wrap my arms around lean muscle. Shizz, this guy's not as flimsy as he looks. Wonder how many people got surprise ass-whoopings thinking they could take him at first glance? I step back, gripping his shoulders. I incline my head at the feel of something hard and plastic-like under his left sleeve.

"Healing membrane. It's holding my arm together," Evan says; his words have a lilt to them. He chuckles when I snatch my hand away. "It's okay. It won't break."

But he doesn't say there's no pain.

He looks to Lyle and Devon and shifts toward them, but a soft cough in the doorway stops him. He jerks his head in the direction of the sound, and his joy at seeing us seems to evaporate.

Locusts flutter and I whip around to see two people—a very tall man with broad shoulders and an average height woman so skinny she reminds me of a stork—dressed in black tunics and pants. They enter the room as a unit. The air around them seems to freeze and the oven-like warmth of the room dies.

We all face them. Evan and the hot trio bow, and the couple stops a few feet away from us. The door to the room slides closed.

The man's eyes are almond-shaped and a blue so bright they sizzle. The woman's face is sharp and angular, her eyes black as coal. When they smile, it feels wrong, empty.

"Greetings." The man's voice is deep, an orange button clipped to his collar glows. "I am Council Theorne Vandup."

"I am Council Viveen Silaan," the woman's voice is high and sharp. A button on her collar glows as well. "We welcome you aboard the Ievisara. We are honored to be able to receive and instruct you during this part of your development."

Council?

"We are representatives from your Council of Rema," Theorne says.

The council that tells leaders what to do. The one that had sent Evan off to do their dirty work and had left him to die. I want to narrow my eyes but something about Viveen's vulture expression keeps me from doing it.

"The voyage to Amphora will take several half-spans, approximately two Earth months," Viveen says. "In that time, we will be educating you on how you are to conduct yourselves as not only leaders of Rema, but as the Four. I expect you to study hard, for time is not on your side. If you listen closely, you will learn how you are to survive to make your pre-destined choices."

Pre-destined choices? Now there's an oxymoron for you. But survival? "You'll teach us how to use our powers?" I ask.

Theorne laughs, the sound is rich—and mocking. I don't like him.

"No," Theorne says. He tilts his head toward Evan who stands off to the side now. "Your brother and his court shall handle that. We will teach you how to reign."

I stare.

"Reign over what?" Mom asks. "From what I understand, you rule Rema."

Theorne and Viveen smile at Mom and locusts clutter my windpipe. I want to tell Mom to be quiet; there's something wrong with these guys. But I can't speak.

"Don't believe everything you hear, Mrs. Conway," Viveen says, stressing Mom's last name. "Some facts are skewed to suit public opinion."

"And some facts are just right," Mom says. "How long will I get to remain with my children?" A muscle in Theorne's jaw spasms and Viveen arches a thin brow.

"Your flight will depart in the morning, Mrs. Conway," Viveen says. "We do feel horribly about our change in plans. You were probably excited to see our Devrik again. We apologize for not allowing him to join us."

Mom glares, but bites her tongue. I know she wants to say something, but she's smart. "Well," Viveen says smoothly. "We did wish to introduce ourselves, but we do not want to darken your family reunion. It is our supreme pleasure to meet you, Mrs. Conway." She offers Mom a handshake that Mom doesn't take and her thin lips part to show square white teeth.

"You."

My attention snaps to Theorne and I squirm as his electric blue eyes analyze me like a crime scene.

"You are a replica of your father, boy."

I blink.

"However, I'm sure *you'll* reach your potential," he finishes. He looks over at Evan. "We trust that you'll carry out business in a suitable manner?"

Evan's face is a perfect blank as he nods.

"Then we'll take our leave," Theorne says. He and Viveen incline their heads and turn as one, heading for the door. The coldness in the room they leave behind doesn't dissipate and we're left staring at each other as the door closes.

"Evan?" Mom asks.

Evan sighs and his face goes stern, but there's a spark of compassion in his eyes. And I think I feel it, a bond between him and me. I don't know him yet, but this guy's my brother. I wonder if Devon and Lyle feel it too. It's this bond that made me want to save him and risk my

life as it was.

In a steady voice, Evan says, "I'm going to do everything in my power to make you ready for what's next. It's not going to be fun. You're not going to like me very much. But you saved me and damned yourselves to this, and I'm going to bring you through it. I don't care what it takes."

I gulp down locusts before they fly out of my mouth. Damn, but he looks serious. That's the face of a stone cold sergeant drill master.

"We'll discuss training. Each of you needs something different and we've prepared accordingly." He looks to his trio who nod at him.

"Tomorrow morning, after..." he swallows as he looks at Mom, then continues, "after the departure, we start priming you to fight on the front lines of the biggest war since the First Champions."

Oh. Shizz.

"Um," Devon says, his voice unsteady, "I thought you all said we had two months. We can't fight a war in two months! Don't we have soldiers for that?"

Evan places a hand on Devon's arm. "You'll be a soldier."

Mom makes a choking noise and grips my hand.

"Look," I say, squeezing Mom's hand. "I know you deal with crazy all the time, being a military boss and all, but doesn't this all seem especially messed up? Two months?"

"It doesn't matter what I think," Evan says. "The choice has been made."

"But our choices are the ones that matter, right?" Lyle asks. "Pre-destined and all."

Evan smirks. "That's what the prophecy says."

But is that what it means?

Evan's smirk fades, eyes growing dark.

I don't think anyone knows what to do next, so we go through the dry motions of exchanging more hugs and greetings. Evan offers us a tour of the Ievisara. We all move like robots to an unsteady rhythm, no one smiling, no one saying anything meaningful.

And for the first time ever, 'gotta do something' doesn't want to do anything at all.

<<<<<◇>>>>>

ACKNOWLEDGMENTS

First off, I want to say thank you to my family who may think I'm a little crazy, but who also support me: Mom, Dad, and Candice. I want to thank my godmother, Joyce, and her sister, Tomilee, who believe I can do anything. Thank you to my best friend Kathleen Andrea-Liner, fellow nerd and writer, who keeps my science facts straight and whose pep talks keep my fingers on the keys. Thank you to my colleague, the fabulous poet Victor Henry, who said I must have a published book in hand before he retires in the next few years. Many thanks to Jason Jurinsky who bugs me to write even when I don't want to and offers great critique. Thank you to my friends in my online writers group, Erin Andrea and Sarah Olson, who always give me wonderful feedback. I want to give a shout out to my writing groups in Boca Raton, Florida and Monterey, California. Thank you: Janice Rocke, Colin Campbell, Trevor Lee, Beth Haymond and Cherie Rowe. Lastly, I want to give special thanks to the 48fourteen publish-

ing family. Thank you Juanita Samborski for giving this book a chance and involving me in the publishing process every step of the way. Thank you Denise DeSio for your wonderful editing job and for setting me straight on grammar rules I was always fuzzy about.

This story is my baby and without you guys my publishing dream would not be coming true. So, without exaggeration and with the upmost honesty, thank you to everyone mentioned and not mentioned, but you know who you are, on this page!

THE AUTHOR

E. Ardell spent her childhood in Houston, Texas, obsessed with anything science fiction, fantastic, paranormal or just plain weird. She loves to write stories that feature young people with extraordinary talents thrown into strange and dangerous situations. She took her obsession to the next level, earning a Master of Fine Arts from the University of Southern Maine where she specialized in young adult genre fiction. She's a big kid at heart and loves her job as a teen librarian at Monterey Public Library in Monterey, California, where she voluntarily shuts herself in rooms with hungry hordes of teenagers and runs crazy after-school programs for them. When she's not working, she's reading, writing, running writers critique groups, trying to keep up with a blog, and even writing fan fiction as her guilty pleasure.

For more about E. Ardell,
visit her at:
http://www.eardell.com/

Like her Facebook page:
https://www.facebook.com/eardell

THE THIRD GAMBIT

ORDER'S LAST PLAY

BOOK TWO

CHAPTER 1

DEVON

A LONG, CURVED BLADE SLASHES over my head. I give ground, stumbling backward and swinging my five-foot titanium staff up to catch the monster blows trying to cleave me in two. The sword leaves notches in my weapon. Sweat burns my eyes. I refuse to blink it out for fear of shutting my eyes for more than a second. I can't wipe it, because my hands are busy trying to keep this woman from killing me.

"Stop retreating!" Desiri Lilias snarls, her voice hot with venom as she rears the blade to strike again.

I jump to avoid it, boots clanking against the gray, metal floor of the ship's practice room. My arms and back ache from taking Desiri's hits. I want to attack, but when I do she kicks my legs out from under me and I end up rolling out of the way of a death blow.

"I'll stop, if you stop trying to kill me!" I shout and cringe, my voice cracks on the last word like I'm twelve instead of seventeen.

"*Fahat!* If I wanted to kill you, I wouldn't use

this!" She shakes her slasher-film-worthy weapon for emphasis, before swinging it at me again.

I dodge and trip over my own foot. My legs feel like Jell-o. This is worse than football, track and basketball training combined. In fact, I'd pay big money to be transported back to my old high school, where I hid my powers and pretended to be normal instead of combat training with a bloodthirsty battle-mage.

"She's telling the truth," a smooth voice says. I chance a look at my older brother, Evan, who sits on the sideline watching us.

I'm punished for my distraction. Pain explodes from the right side of my ribcage, and I'm airborne for a second. I crumple to the ground, staff clanging against the floor. Bright spots swim in my field of vision as I wheeze, trying to get my breath back. Damn. I think she broke one of my ribs. I make a fist and pound the floor as agony whitewashes me. My life flashes before my eyes, a pitiful life void of a senior prom and a college-aged girlfriend kissing me stupid, and I swear I see the face of God in a glowing white cloud.

Then reality smacks me harder than the blunt side of Desiri's sword. There is no one god. There are lots of them, petty and jealous, and into ruining people's lives. The memory of a goddess with four boobs, black holes for eyes and lightning for hair makes me yelp and sit up. The right side of my chest screams as I whip my head around the room, looking for Goddess Order so I can tell her: Hell no, take your stupid gift and shove it up your ass! I don't want to be anybody's leader, fight anyone's war, or have any decision of mine be the reason why a lot of people die. But it's the job I've been

cursed with, to end Order's damn war with my dumb choices. And I won't even know which choices count.

"Are you all right?" Evan calls.

My vision clears and the work room comes back into focus. It's oval-shaped and made completely of silver-colored metal, like everything else aboard the ship. Weapon racks sit against the curved walls. The ceiling is glass and the floor above it has theater seating so anyone up there can look down into the fishbowl and watch me getting my ass kicked.

I groan and cradle my ribs. I want to milk it, but everyone knows my body will heal itself in a matter of hours. I didn't used to heal this fast. I never needed to until now.

A hand rests on my shoulder and Evan kneels in front of me. The grin on his face makes him look about thirteen, though he's eighteen, older than me by eleven months, but nobody would ever guess that.

"Need a break?" he asks.

"Yeah." I needed a break two hours ago.

An annoyed growl comes from one side of the room. I look over at Desiri, who's putting her sword back on a rack.

She glowers at me. "We've still got more practice time on the schedule. I booked this room for—"

"Good!" Evan says. His voice is light and melodic. He always sounds like he's singing. "I need some exercise." He stands, stretching his right hand down to me.

I grab it, letting him help me up.

He unbuttons his green jacket and shrugs it onto the floor. He stands in a black, sleeveless tank, rolling

his left shoulder and patting the flesh-colored healing membrane encasing it from collarbone to elbow. Worry shifts through me.

"Hey, are you sure that thing's up for fighting with…" I feel Desiri's glare on my neck. I whirl and raise my hands as she comes near. I'm bigger than her, broad shoulders, muscles, and over six feet tall, but this girl scares me. She's like Starfire and Storm together, only her eyes don't glow.

"I'll go easy," Desiri purrs, eyes tracking Evan like a lion watching dinner.

He smirks and picks up my abandoned staff like it's a broomstick. The thing has to weigh over 100 pounds. It doesn't unbalance me, but my pipsqueak older brother should at least grunt. I'll never get over how friggin' strong he is. Not stronger than me, but he kicked a damn hole through one of the ship walls when someone pissed him off. No effort, just pow.

Evan spins the long staff like a baton.

"Your shoulder's not all healed up yet," I say. Not even twelve weeks ago, he'd almost died after a bad guy tried to rip his shoulder off and left him for dead on a foreign planet. There's no way that shoulder's ready for a fight.

"No," Evan says. "But I want full range of motion back, so I should exercise. Now get out of the way, unless you want to join in."

Panic flares as I shoot a look over at Desiri who's getting down a staff to match the one Evan has. Oh hell no. I scramble off the floor, my wobbly legs gaining strength as I make it to the sideline and plop down to watch.

Desiri seems to have the advantage, because she's taller with better reach, but Evan's fast and agile. He matches her blow for blow and then goes on the attack, pushing her back a few steps then striking so quick he blurs. Desiri spins and tries to kick Evan in the shins. She misses. He's behind her, next to her, in front of her, all in the blink of an eye.

He's gonna win.

Desiri smirks and breaks the staff in two. She wields the halves like something out of *Mortal Kombat*. She catches Evan's strike with one piece and stabs out with the other. Evan does a back flip and then helicopters his staff. Desiri laughs and dances out of the way. Evan grins and they circle each other like monsters in a cage.

Chills creep up my spine at how much fun they're having. I grab a nearby towel and rub the sweat off my face. These guys grew up with weapons, fighting, aliens...

No, not aliens. I gotta stop saying that. It pisses people off. But hell, months ago, before prophecies and visions, they were just aliens: Visitors. Strangers that had nothing to do with me. Months ago, I was just a really strong kid from Houston with a psychotically hyper little brother and a moody twin brother. The only thing I worried about was not being normal enough to trick my classmates into thinking I was as human as they are.

A sound like fire igniting in a hot air balloon brings my focus to the match again. I swallow. Evan's staff burns like a torch. He draws a circle of flame in the air. The ring of fire hovers in front of him. He tosses the

staff to the side with a clatter. Desiri beats her sticks together like a boy scout trying to start a fire. Sparks fly from the tips.

"Cheater," Desiri says, a Crest smile on her face.

"You never said no magic," Evan says and blows on his fire ring like a birthday candle. The flames ripple and spin toward Desiri.

Desiri's eyes widen. *"Iska!"* The flames surround her, snuffing out the fire on the ends of her double staffs. *"Gak mopi!* Encapsulate?"

"If you can't break it, I win," Evan sings-songs.

Desiri sneers and starts mouthing words. The air around her shudders and she breathes out mist like it's subzero in here. She reaches to grab the fire ring and stops, hand an inch from the flame. "Ah!" She pulls back and narrows her eyes. "Yield."

Evan sucks in a breath and the ring of fire puffs out, wisps of smoke coiling around Desiri like rope. She waves one hand and the smoke vanishes.

"Hand to hand, no magic," she says. "Right now."

Evan shakes his head. "Next time." He rolls his injured shoulder. "That staff was too heavy."

Desiri snorts and throws her weapons to the side. "Excuses." But she doesn't seem mad. She approaches Evan and corrects his technique for fighting right-handed with a long weapon.

They're so easy with each other; they've got a decade of history together. It's like Evan's related to Desiri, and not me. Guess spending two months trapped on a spaceship with the guy doesn't make up for the ten years we spent apart. I wasn't expecting to care so much, but it kinda hurts watching him goof around with

his friends the way he would have goofed around with me had we been raised on the same planet.

"I reserved the room for later on this evening," Evan says. "Rematch then?"

"No magic," Desiri says.

Evan shrugs his jacket back on and rolls his left shoulder again. Then he claps Desiri's bicep and walks over to me.

The weapon rack rattles against the wall. Desiri pulls down two long, straight swords and takes a wicked fighting stance in the middle of the floor.

Evan grimaces. "She's going to kick your ass with a vengeance during your next combat session."

"Look, I can't help it if I suck!" Frustration makes me sound like a punk. "She's like a ninja-kung fu master. I can't keep up." I'm not cut out to be a warrior.

Evan snorts. "Nobody expects you to keep up. You're a novice. But here's what she won't tell you: you're actually doing pretty good."

He kicks my leg and nods for me to stand up. I obey, legs groaning in protest. I follow him as he heads for the oval doors.

"Where're we going?" I ask.

"Upstairs," he says. "I stop into all of you guys' training sessions when I can."

We enter a bare silver corridor. The metal floor echoes under our boots. Two soldiers in tan jumpsuits round a corner, laughing and punching each other. They halt in front of us and give split-second bows at the waist. Their eyes glitter with respect as they look at Evan. Their interest dulls when it comes to me. They go back to laughing as they pass us, muttering to each

other in another language. It sounds kinda Slavic, so maybe it's Remasian. It's got the same lilt that accents Evan's otherwise perfect English.

Out of the corner of my eye, Evan smirks.

I snarl. "Are they talking about me?"

"Yes," Evan chirps.

"What the hell, man? They can't make fun of me! I'm one of their reincarnated, prophesized leaders come to save the world as they know it." There's four of us, Evan, Lyle, Lawrie and me, so we're not a Holy Trinity. "We're a Holy Quartet!" I stop and whirl around. I can't kick Desiri's ass, but if I hit one of those guys in the face they'll feel it for a month.

Evan tosses his head back and laughs. God, that noise grates on my spine. When he really gets going, he sounds like the Joker on helium.

"They like your shirt," he says, still laughing, and leaving me behind.

I scowl down at the Batman logo on my T-shirt. Nobody cares what I wear under my training clothes. But who'd have thought alien—no, Visitor—no, REMASIAN—soldiers would be into superhero junk?

"They wouldn't dare say bad things about you where I might hear it," Evan says, sounding amused. "I'd practice my wind-shear hail on them."

My boots scuff the floor as I jog to catch up to him before he reaches the Tube. I glance at him. He's got long blond curls and features that'd make old ladies pinch his cheeks and feed him cookies. I wonder how many people fall into that trap before he stomps the hell out of them. I fell into it. Thought I'd gotten a big brother I'd have to protect as much as I do my little

ones, then he punched me in the spleen for making a crack about his hair.

"You're scary man," I murmur.

He gives me a sideways smirk. "You have no idea."

The door to the Tube glows blue and slides upward. We step inside.

Evan gives a command in Remasian as the door snaps shut.

The Tube shuttle snakes through various floors and hallways, like Willy Wonka's glass elevator. The best part is that the walls are opaque, so I don't have to be scared shitless as we move.

I tap my fingers against the wall and clear my throat as Evan hums.

He glances at me. "We're a day away from landing on Lenore. When the Reading Ceremony for your Mark is over and your questing team is selected, they're going to group you with seasoned specialists. Finding your Stone will be easy. You don't have to worry so much about being really good with your powers. You just need to be good enough to protect yourself."

"It's the needing to protect myself that worries me," I mutter. "And I don't want my Stone." An image of a ruby the size of my hand flits through my thoughts: Order's gift. It calls to me and feelings of need churn in my gut. I make a fist at my side.

I. Don't. Want. It.

Evan wrinkles his nose. "And you think I want mine?"

He scratches his left palm, seemingly lost in thought. I call it Stone-Zoning. It's like his brain goes to

another dimension when the emerald he'd nearly been buried with is on his mind.

"I hate that it's onboard the ship," Evan murmurs. "I feel it under my skin, like an allergic reaction. It's poisonous."

"And we're gonna go out to find more of them," I snort, my heart a brick in my chest.

We're all gonna end up like Gollum, cracked out on the One Ring in the form of toxic gemstones. Forget power and infamy, because I can't forget that the last guys who owned those things all died bloody. Then, hundreds of years later, my brothers and me inherited their crap-jobs.

"How's the war stuff going?" I ask.

Evan's been a leader for three years and was trained to do the job for years before that. He's kept in the know when it comes to the riots and battles and death tolls. The only thing I really cared to know about is that our mom, who'd joined us on the ship for a little while, had made it back to Earth safely.

Evan sighs. "The Allegiances have lost territory and we've lost communications with two sectors. Sector Four has become pirate space. Undocumented vessels are looting Allegiance and private cargo ships." He rubs his eyes, and I notice the dark circles for the first time. "But none of that is your concern. You just—"

The shuttle rocks and the lights go out. I stagger into a wall and catch Evan as he bumps into me. Sirens blare.

"Fip," Evan breathes. A small blue and orange flame lights the shuttle. Evan's eyes widen.

A disembodied voice drifts through the walls, and

damn it all, it speaks in Remasian.

"What's it saying?" I ask. "What's wrong with the Tube?" I pound on the door.

Evan grabs my wrist and squeezes hard. "Shut up!" His militant bark practically screams: Houston, we have a problem. The mood in the shuttle shifts from inconvenienced to 'we're gonna die' in 30 seconds.

My heart pumps. "Are we under attack or something?" My voice soars.

Evan clamps a hand over my mouth. The announcement continues on in Remasian. Evan's eyes narrow.

What's it saying? Why didn't he answer me? How bad is this?

My hands shake. Is this the part in the movie where the bad guys blow us up? People don't survive being blown up in space. My knees give out. Evan sinks to the floor with me and removes his hand from my mouth.

"Breathe slower. There's a panel in the floor. I'm going to pull it out and open the trap. Stay close to me." The flame dips low to illuminate the ground. Evan's swift fingers locate a floor latch and a patch of floor opens to reveal a tablet-looking device. Evan runs a thumb over it in a series of patterns and the shuttle door trembles.

"We're between passageways," Evan mutters. "The safety won't let us open the trap. I'll have to do it."

"Between passageways?" I ask. "Like in an elevator shaft?"

Evan gives me a strange look. "Just do what I say."

"Are we under attack?" I ask, my voice a whisper.

He grabs me by the shoulders and stares me down, nose an inch from my face, eyes serious. "Yes."

Panic makes the world spin. Ohshitohshitohshit...

Evan's fingers dig into my collarbone. "We need to get to the bridge. The next Tube platform is two floors up and over. Hope you're not afraid of heights."

He lets go of me and crawls to the door, extracting a small knife from his pocket and wedging it under the metal trap. He grunts as he pulls up on the blade handle, using it as a lever. The door screeches and lifts off the floor a crack. Then, he works his fingers into the gap and tugs.

"Some help!" he snaps.

"Oh." I join him. My hands are larger than his. I can't get a decent grip, but after a minute, the door rumbles up a few feet. Good enough to crawl through. Evan's tiny flame floats out into the dark space, lighting the passageway and showing me a black hole-like drop straight down.

The shuttle quakes and the sirens blare again. Evan boosts himself out into the darkness, yelling for me to follow.

2

LAWRENCE

GLOWING STRIPS LINING THE FLOORS are the only lights in the dark corridors. The shrieking siren overhead and the pounding feet around me make my blood bubble with excitement. I laugh as I'm practically dragged after my trainer/cousin-in-law who could win an Olympic gold for running. My legs are about to fall off from trying to keep up.

Every now and again the siren stops and a lady's voice drones about damages to the ship. I've picked up some Remasian in the past few weeks: common phrases, simple sentences, lots of cuss words. I can pick out words like 'damage' and 'puncture.' I grin as adrenaline shoots through my system like an intravenous hit of Mountain Dew. I friggin' love danger. 'Gotta do something,' a crazy hormone that makes it impossible for me to stay still, is ready to bust loose. It's time to finally do something, to make up for what I couldn't do months before.

The whole place rocks and the floor lights flicker.

My sneakers lose traction as I stagger to the left then get jerked hard to my right by Adonis who never let go of my arm. Soldiers and whoever else is out in the hall around us cuss. The sounds of stumbling steps and thudding bodies echoes through the hall as the place continues to tremor. I smack into Adonis, who's slowed down. The lady on the speaker's talking again.

'Calm', 'bridge', 'leaders', 'evacuate'.

"I need to carry you." Adonis's voice is deep and passionless as ever. It's like he's eternally bored. He lets go of my arm and I feel him turn to face me.

"Wait. What? Whaa!" I'm airborne then winded as my gut smashes into Adonis's shoulder blade. He grips the backs of my knees.

And suddenly it's like I'm riding a Pegasus. I'm flying through the corridor, arms and legs bumping into random soldiers as we speed past. This isn't so bad. Just wish the lights would come back on so I can see the expressions on people's faces. Are they scared, angry, worried, pumped? Somebody else has gotta be stoked about breaking out of this training prison and getting some real action.

I've had two months of nothing but lessons on meditation and feeling the rhythms of my body from Adonis and lectures on how to behave at political functions from Council Theorne—slimy bastard. The same two months were also filled with radio silence. After Councilors Theorne and Viveen had stuffed Mom in a spaceship bound for home, they said that we had no time for distractions. I haven't spoken to Mom, Dad, my little sister, or my friends. Hope they don't think I'm dead. I mean it's not like a major interplanetary war

was declared right after I left or anything.

Adonis whips around a corner. I grunt as he slides me off his shoulders. We stand uncomfortably close, my face directly in his. Enough light shines up from the floor for me to distinguish his features. His lips are downturned and his gray eyes look black.

"What's up?" Can't be good if this guy's making facial expressions.

"I need to take you to Deck Two."

"Is it hard to get to?" I ask.

"It's five levels down from the main bridge. If I take you there, I won't be able to come back up."

"So?"

He sighs. He's not a guy who talks much, so I'm sure he's straining himself dealing with me. "The orders are to evacuate the councilors and leaders. You are to be sent out in an escape vessel surrounded by honor guard."

"You're an honor guard," I say. Well, he's one of Evan's special honor guards. People around here call them a court. I'm supposed to get a court when we land on Lenore for the Reading Ceremony. Order's Mark on my back, an involuntary tattoo that starts at the top of my neck and trails down my spine, itches like it knows I'm thinking about it.

"Evan won't follow orders and won't go to Deck Two," Adonis says. "He will go to the main bridge."

Ah. "And you want to go where he's going." Adonis doesn't seem the type to care much about anything, but he loves Evan like a brother and he's still mad guilty about Evan almost dying on his watch.

"Then let's go to the bridge!" I say with a clap.

"Pick me up again and let's run."

"It'll put you in danger," Adonis says. "If the Iev-isara cannot be salvaged and we can't defeat the attacking vessels—"

"Oh please, if this ship loses, the bad guys will come after our escape ships. What chances will those things have?" I ask. Then hum, mentally pulling up a few schematics I'd memorized. Actually escape vessels on this ship are more like pods armed with combustion canons that'd give a nuke nightmares. They'd be safer than the ship.

Adonis sighs again. "Technically, with no other superiors present, you're in charge, Leader Four. What are your orders?"

And he had to make it awkward. Leader Four—my new title. When Evan was the only leader of Rema, they'd called him Leader Lauduethe. Now, there are four Leader Lauduethes and the super creative Rema-sian Council decided on the numbering system, like they were afraid we'd name ourselves something lamer than the Four of Rema.

I bite my lip, my first order as Leader Four. "Take me to the bridge."

I sound like Captain Kirk. Energy swells inside me.

Adonis tilts his head and studies me. It's creepy. He's a weird combination of Abercrombie model and Greek statue that blinks every few hours. "All right," he says and steps toward me.

"Ah-ah, second order. Piggy-back," I say and laugh at his confused stare. "Turn around." I glomp onto his back and he catches on right away.

Adonis weaves through soldiers who'd probably part for him if they could tell who he was in the dark. He heads for the ramps that will take us up three levels. The traffic in the halls is divided; some soldiers rushing up and some down. There are three launching bays. I wonder how many soldiers are gonna go out to fight whatever's trying to blow us up.

Another thought hits me as I hang onto Adonis's shoulders. Devon and Lyle train with members of Evan's court too. Wonder if they're being taken to Deck Two or if I'm gonna see them on the bridge. Warring emotions fight it out in my stomach—excitement, because I want to see us all be awesome together; fear, because this ship really could blow up. My brothers could die. I could die.

But the fear's short-lived. 'Gotta do something' doesn't have much use for it or anxiety. Lately, though, fear and anxiety have been a little more common in my daily diet of emotions. Science says those kinds of things keep you alive, survival instincts and all. Guess something in me wants to live. Can't be mad about that.

Adonis shrugs me off. My feet clump to the ground as we near our destination, the open space of the main bridge. It's a half circle of a room that looks out into the space in front of the ship with back-up and side-view cameras. The white lights in the ceiling are on. Glittering navigation equipment spans two walls. A wide screen upfront shows us an ocean of fathomless space spotted with rapidly zigzagging red and orange patterns.

A cacophony of voices speaking in a foreign language swarms through a room buzzing with life. About

ten soldiers in tan jumpsuits with cargo pockets man multiple stations. Some gather around the various navigation boards, two strategoi stare out into the wide screen, fingers tapping the gauze-like material covering it and manipulating the zags. It's Battleship with real players in the water.

Adonis glides into the room like he owns the place. I feel like some kind of groupie beside him, though it should be the other way around. A six-foot lady with light blue skin and an inky black ponytail, so tight her eyes look squinty, plants herself in front of us. Adonis does that unnerving stare-thing of his and the lady raises her chin, matching his gaze. They're the same height and making me feel fun-sized as I lift my head to observe them.

"Mauve, why is Leader Four here?" The lady's voice is cold. An orange pin glows on the lapel of her tan jumpsuit, a translator. Most of the soldiers and crew wear them, but only a select few actually turn them on. Evan's the only person onboard, besides Lyle, Dev and me, who speaks English.

"His orders," Adonis says. He looks away from her and moves on by, glancing around the room. I smile at the lady and look around too. None of my brothers are here.

Adonis turns back to the woman. "Chelate, any word from Leader One?"

"The comp-al network has been compromised," Chelate says. "No internal messages are coming through other than what's being related on the all-net." Her hard yellow stare falls on me again. "Leader Four, I must stress your importance to society and insist that

you allow yourself to be escorted to Deck Two."

The ship rocks again, making us all stumble a few steps. Well, all of us but Adonis. Stumbling is probably too plebian for him.

"Yeah," I say to Chelate, running a hand through my tangled curls. "I'm important, I got it. But uh...."

Well, hell, what can I really do to help out? I don't know how to fly the ship or work the weapons.

"*Navai mai!*" A voice, like a pop-star calling his screaming fan-girl audience to attention, has heads turning. Evan strides onto the bridge like the boss on a mission, Devon struggling to keep up behind him. Adonis dumps me like an ugly ex and makes his way to Evan's side as Devon comes over to me.

"Hey," Dev's voice is as rough as he looks. His tan skin's flushed like he's been running laps and climbing mountains, and he's got black grease on his hands and clothes.

"Looks like you've been having fun without me." I crack and dodge the punch he aims my way. Dev's super hero strong and doesn't always pull his punches when he's mad or emo.

"Big brother had us climbing elevator shafts and kicking in doors," Dev says, eyes traveling around the room. "What are they doing?"

"Looks like they're setting attack sequences for the fighter ships," I say, staring at the wide-screen and frowning as a few of the zigzags disappear, meaning the fighter ship was no longer in service. I flinch. People are dying. Wonder if I know them—knew them. There are a lot of soldiers and crew aboard the Levisara. My memory's great, but not exactly photographic for

things that aren't awesomely nerdy. I don't remember everyone I meet.

'Gotta do something' taps its toes and I shake my head. I need to be closer. Evan and Adonis stand next to the strategoi guiding the fighters on screen. I start in their direction, but someone grabs me by my shirt collar.

I gag and turn to find Devon glaring at me.

"Have you seen Lyle?" he asks.

"No," I say. "Maybe he's on his way. Or maybe he got put in an escape vessel. That's where we're supposed to be."

"We're supposed to be escaping?" Devon frowns.

"What do you mean?"

"The instructions were for leaders, us, to evacuate. Adonis didn't think Evan would, so he wanted to come here, and hey-hey! So did I."

"That little shit!" Devon makes a fist. "He wouldn't tell me what the announcements were saying!"

I smirk. "You got played?"

Devon's face goes from really friggin' pissed to exasperated to pissed again. He growls and pantomimes choking the air in front of him, glowering in Evan's direction, but he moves no closer. It's funny. Devon would have wrestled me to the ground, he would have cussed Lyle out, but Evan, none of that. Yeah, Evan's kinda new to us, but he's not a stranger anymore. By all means, Devon should be ready to get in Evan's face about shizz not being fair to him, but I think he's scared. I chance patting Dev's shoulder. "Well, we're here now. Might as well see what's going on, huh?" I jog past him to Evan and Adonis.

New zigzags join the on-screen patterns.

"Fresh troops?" I ask, nodding at the screen.

"Yes," Evan says, sounding distracted. "Sending them out in odd intervals. A few are going to drop from Deck Seven when the escape shuttles go out. We just need to get a little closer to Madunat's pull. This force here." Evan points to a mass of zigzags, "is engaging and will hopefully draw and lead the enemy fighters out of Sector 2 and into Cold Space."

I didn't know we were already in Sector 2, the Lenoran Galaxy. "Madunat's not a populated planet, is it?" I don't remembering seeing any information about its peoples.

"It's all greenery," Evan says, "but there are a few outposts for naturalists. So the escape vessels can land safely."

"What's Cold Space?" Devon asks and I palm my forehead. I swear if it doesn't have to do with his hair or something emo, Dev's a brick of stupid.

Evan's eyes actually cross as his upper lip curls and I chuckle. At least I'm not the only one being tormented with Devon's unique brand of special right now. I groan. "Cold Space is the area within a Cold Zone. Territory not owned by a planetary allegiance or alliance." I reach up to pat Devon's spiky hair. He smacks the shizz out of my hand. My fingers throb, but that doesn't keep a smile off my face.

"What are these guys here doing?" I point to circular patterns that the strategosi seem to be ignoring. I stick my face between the two, short men controlling the fighters and receive two heated glares. I pull back. Evan points to the circular patterns. "This unit is

what is known as a home guard. They are defending this ship."

"Why so few?" I ask.

"Because this ship is meant to be a sacrifice," Evan says. "All of the important officers should be abandoning the premise. The only people left behind should be simple soldiers and crew, the last defense."

"So why are we here instead of getting out?" Devon asks and then cringes as the 'simple' soldiers in the room shoot him nasty, 'sleep with one eye open' looks. Hope none of them make it onto his quest team.

"Because I'm choosing," Evan draws out the word, "to not lose the eighty people stuck on this ship because Councilors Theorne and Viveen got twitchy. We save the Ievisara and protect Lenoran space."

Spoken like a kick-ass general. He's inches shorter than me, but I look up to Evan. Hell, I need to be like him, soon, and I'm still just learning where to start. This war isn't gonna wait for me—us, me, Devon and Lyle—to be ready. We're prophesized to end the war, Order's Endgame, and the people in charge want this war over yesterday.

'Gotta do something' gives way to a feeling of thick-bodied bugs crawling in my chest and batting their wings against my ribcage, my anxiety locusts. Thought I'd evicted these things weeks ago, but they're worse than roaches.

"Sorry," Devon grunts and gives off a kicked puppy vibe, ducking his head. A few people are still tossing him dirty looks and hissing in Remasian. In a more subdued voice, he asks, "Has anybody heard from Lyle?"

"I'm here."

I whirl around, locusts retreating at the distraction, I never stay anxious long, and wave at my older brother Lyle. He enters the room with Jalee Orcharest, another member of Evan's court, at his side. Lyle's pale, his green eyes kinda bright, like he's sick or something. He's looked like that a lot lately, less CW more HDTV that shows flaws in the complexion. If he keeps that up, people might stop accusing him and Devon of being twins.

"Lyi!" Devon sounds like a starving man being handed a twelve-pack of tacos.

Lyle and Jalee make their way to us. Lyle takes his place next to Dev and Jalee goes over to stand by Adonis. Jalee, Adonis and Evan murmur to each other in Remasian. I follow the cadence of their words and pick out some of the meanings. They're worried about how many enemy fighters are out there. And I think there's something funky going on with the enemy's shields. They're absorbing energy, when they should probably be blown to bits instead.

"You okay?" Devon asks Lyle, touching his shoulder.

Lyle takes a deep breath and massages the bridge of his nose. "Headache."

Jalee runs Lyle through psychic exercises, working on his telepathy and telekinesis. Lyle says she's a witch, literally. She does the kind of magic you see on TV, stirring up shizz in pots and carrying bags full of tiny animal bones and dirt. She teaches him about protecting his mind from outside thoughts.

"How's it going?" Devon asks, worry tainting his voice.

"I still have to take the drugs, Devon." Lyle's words are clipped.

"Oh." Devon sounds disappointed.

"Leave him alone," I snap. I don't see what the deal is about Lyle needing psychic Tylenol to help him shut outside voices down. The way I see it, he's a lot saner when he's had his candy. He'll wean off it when he gets more lessons.

"Shut the f—" Devon starts.

"Iska!" Several cusses fill the room from naviga-tion and the strategtegusi.

I look back at the screen to see a cluster of zigzags disappear from action.

Evan barks out an order in Remasian and the screen divides itself into two viewing windows. One window still shows black space filled with patterns, the other shows real-time space filled with ship debris, en-ergy residue hazy before it dissipates, and flaring out-lines of small double fighter ships.

"What model of ship is that?" Jalee asks. "Focus the image."

Evan snaps out something else in Remasian and the vid reel goes into freeze frame then zeroes in on a single ship, blowing it up until it fills the screen.

"It looks like a Manasta model," Evan says, "but look at the shape of the hull."

A blast of orange energy slams into an invisible wall around the ship. The energy shudders then gets slurped into the ship's exterior like Sunny Delight go-ing down the drain.

"Is it supposed to do that?" Devon asks. Lyle stomps on Devon's foot and Devon yowls.

I study Evan's face. His eyes are wide and his mouth is slightly open. He gives another Remasian command and the view on the screen expands again, showing more of the space battle. All of the enemy ships are sucking up the blasts from our ships like Welch's orange soda. My anxiety locusts make a comeback. If we can't stop those ships, game over.

"What about the canons on the escape vessels?" I ask. "Those things—"

"Are the same canons on the Gha squad ships," Jalee says.

"Who's the Gha squad?" I squint at the zags on the other screen. The strategosi move patterns around the board in a flurry.

"The ones getting their asses kicked," Evan mutters. "Chelate," he calls over his shoulder. "Pull up all of the latest information on Manasta models. Maybe there's an update in there about these things."

Manasta models. Mental schematics of random versions of the Ruj ships fan out in my head. What's the closest blueprint to the things on screen? Model 133479. But those are only prototypes—images and plans stolen and sold on the shiste paths. The Ruj are months away from coming up with a version that won't overheat in deep space, or so I thought.

"I know what they are!" I blurt.

All eyes are on me.

"They're those new models that haven't passed inspection yet," I say. "Guess our information was bogus. They have conversion shields that deconstruct v-wave energy and alter it into neutral fuels that the ships can absorb and get a boost from."

"All of the new canons fire v-waves," Adonis murmurs. "We don't have any older models onboard."

"Contact with Lenore is nil," one of the strategoi
says, leaving the zags for the other guy to control. His
voice sounds resigned. "But I doubt they have fighters
capable of combat with these things."

The soldiers around the navigation walls are quiet. The strategos who spoke stares at me, then looks
to Evan. I bite my lip. They're waiting for orders. My
body runs cold as I turn to Evan too. He has to decide
if we're gonna abandon ship and leave these guys to
kamikaze for us.

Evan cracks his knuckles, a nervous habit my
brothers share.

I frown, thinking about Model 1334/9. 'Gotta
do something' sparks; firecrackers replacing locusts.

"Wait-wait-wait!" I clap my hands. Oh hell yeah, I
think I got something. "Okay, all right, so those things
have converters for energy blasts. Their shields only
defend against canons and other projectile-busters that
fire energy waves."

"Which is the entirety of the weapons' systems
aboard our ships," Evan drawls, green eyes murky as
they meet mine.

"So," a smile stretches across my face, "let's not
shoot at them anymore. If there's no energy to block,
the conversion shields are just... there."

"Are you proposing we throw things at them?"
Jalee quirks a brow. This really isn't the time for me
to stare at how pretty she is. But she's like: hey, I'm
Victoria's big secret!

"Ah, uh no, maybe," I stutter, shaking my head.

"But we can—"

"Crash into them?" Adonis asks. "We have extra fighters and they don't have to be manned."

"But it's not enough," Evan says. "We've got a lot of cargo that can be jettisoned as projectiles, but we need something bigger. Something to keep them off us and Lenore. What can we use to win?"

Tick-tick-tick. I feel my brain clicking.

"Rasi-va!" Desiri stomps onto the bridge holding something that looks like a Dungeons and Dragons style mace. "Do you know how hard it is to get to this place with the Tubes down?"

"It's about time, Desiri," Jalee says, her tone dry.

"I'm only embarrassed that you beat me here, Priestess." Desiri sneers as she joins us. "Somebody give me a report."

The ship rocks and metal groans. The lights on the bridge flicker. For a few seconds, everything's black, then the power comes back on. Adonis touches Desiri's shoulder and leans toward her ear, lips moving—probably filling her in.

Tick-tick-tick. I stare at Adonis, the stoic, super-fast magic user teaching me to control elements. His specialty's water, so he's been focusing on that with me. Taking me up to the ship's reservoir and having me sit and watch the sterilized liquid swaying in its tank, breathing and feeling its cool vibes, sensing its rhythms. Water. Released in space it'd freeze hard as shigg-ity … and a mass of it the size of an Olympic swimming pool could become a block of death. "Adonis!" I shout. Everyone jumps—everyone but Adonis, because jumping is for chumps.

"I have an idea!" I look at Evan to find him gazing back at me. Do I need to ask his permission to discuss a plan/ proposal/ pipe dream?

The whole room's quiet. All attention's on me again.

Evan nods and waves a hand at me. "Talk," he says. "Fast."

The ship quakes and the lights waver. Locusts and 'gotta do something' puff up in my chest and the bean and cheese tasting soup I'd had for lunch touches the back of my throat. If these guys take me seriously, I'll be putting a military plan into action, and putting the lives of about eighty other people in my hands.

I take a deep breath, cough to clear my throat, and begin.

"I SHOULD CHARGE YOU A transportation fee," Adonis says.

I laugh. "You should be honored to carry me!" But seriously, if he charged a piggyback fee, I'd pay it. He's better than the Tube as he races through hallways and up inclines, cutting corners and taking shortcuts. We're to Reservoir Level in about 45 seconds. He drops me when we get to the thick metal door and frowns at the panel beside it.

The mounted tablet is dark, no power.

Damn. I try to recall instruction files for a manual override. "Maybe we—"

Adonis reaches out with both hands and rips the tablet from the wall. Metal shrieks and wires tumble from the hole in the silver wall. Adonis grabs the wires like he's wringing a cobra's neck and tugs. Fiber strong as steel snaps like dental floss. He tosses the tablet and wires aside, then presses the heel of his boot against the door and kicks out.

The door crashes to the ground. The floor vibrates under my feet as I stare.

Holy shiggity. Don't think I'll be pissing this guy off ever.

Adonis claps dust from his hands. "After you."

Oh yeah. "Sure." As I enter the room, I immediately notice that it's too warm. The insulated black walls of the octagon-shaped room keeps this place just under sixty degrees. Right now it feels like it's at eighty. The scent of rust spices the air. The Olympic-sized tank holds about 4.5 mega-liters of water that needs to stay tooth-numbing cold or it becomes bacteria soup. Good thing we won't need this stuff anymore.

I press my hand against the clear membrane that makes up the tank. It's slick with sweat, but the water pushing against it feels cool.

Breathe.

"Remember your rhythms," Adonis says softly. "Focus on your heartbeat."

I nod and close my eyes, forcing everything else in the room out of mind. Thump-thump. My heart pounds like a kick drum at a rave. It hypes me up. I bounce to the beat, aware of blood racing through my veins, like water.

Thump-thump.

The air fizzes with canned energy. Artificial recycled air from a machine. Its life force is dull, but it still rustles my senses. I breathe in its energy and extend my awareness. I feel the hollowness of the metal floors and walls around me. The individual elements making up the compounds within my surroundings pulse. More power for the taking, but it's like trying to pick a well-woven thread out of a heavy quilt.

A gentle murmur ghosts over my flesh. I shiver as the tingling flow of life force from pure water ripe with bubbly minerals greets me. Slowly, I open my eyes, staring at the water behind the membrane walls.

"Are you ready?" Adonis asks.

"Yeah." My voice is almost a whisper. I feel so calm; the water has no worries. It's infinite and strong.

Ly? I think my brother's name.

/You don't have to shout, Lawrie. I hear you./

Everybody hears you.

Lyle's mental voice sounds annoyed.

I jump at the sound of Evan's voice in my head and feel my connection with the water slip. Shizz. I focus on my heartbeat again. Damn, that was close, but it's freaky enough just having Lyle in my head without him linking me to various other people onboard as well.

Okay, I think. *We're about to tear the membrane and release the water. Are you sure the halls are clear?*

Everything's set. Desiri's rough voice cuts in. *Cargo Bays 3 and 15 are ready.*

Decoy ships have been released, Jalee adds.

Let it out, Evan orders. *The strategosi think they can give you a three and a half minute window. Good luck.*

I turn my head to meet Adonis's shiny gray eyes.

Let's do this!

Follow my lead. Adonis's mental voice is smooth.

He touches his hand to the membrane.

I feel the sensation of lukewarm water running over my back, though I'm not wet. The membrane trembles under my palm. I take a deep breath, energy swiveling in through my nostrils, and pull the power within the water toward me.

The liquid whirlpools and the membrane thins, straining to its popping point.

"Steady, Lawrence," Adonis says.

I'm....

The membrane bursts and over four thousand tons of water sloshes centimeters from my body, retained only by my power and Adonis's. Now I kind of know how Atlas must have felt. I feel like I'm carrying a loaded cement truck on my back.

Oh God.

/You've got this, Lawrie/ Lyle's voice is soft and assuring, a weird tone for Lyle, but it's kinda comforting. Warmth fills me. Is Lyle sending me good juju?

I pant, sweat burning my eyes and trickling down my nose. *Thanks, Ly.*

Adonis touches my shoulder.

"Let the power roll through you," he says. "Move the water like you would your legs. Guide it, but keep it behind you. And don't forget that I'm next to you."

"Y-yeah." I swallow. Thump-thump-thump-thump. My heart's in my throat as I reach for the water again, pulling it. I glimpse Adonis out of the corner of my eye,

heading for the broken door. I follow him, a small ocean rippling behind us.

"We're at three minutes," I say.

"Are you acclimated?" Adonis asks.

I hear water splashing in my ears like toddlers in a tub. I feel like I'm floating in a pool of energy, but the power caresses me. It likes me. "I got it."

Adonis moves in front of me and I glomp his back again.

Silver walls blur as Adonis flashes through the corridors. I choke a few times, breath catching in my throat. Slaps of water splash from the tidal-waving mass behind us. Metal whines as it yields to the weight of the reservoir.

Approaching Bay 12, Adonis thinks. *Lawrie, get ready to jump.*

Here comes the harder stuff: parting the sea. I nod, preparing my muscles.

Now.

I shove off Adonis's shoulders, throwing myself sideways. I rebound off a wall and my boots clump onto the damp floor. Whoa. The tough soles of my shoes squeal as I lose my balance, then right myself. I turn to the reservoir, pushing it back and watching my command slice though it like a stone in a river. There's a fork in the hall, one corridor dipping down to the lower levels while one stays on track, heading out to Bay 12.

Footsteps behind me.

"Good job guys." Evan's voice makes me yelp. I knew he'd be here, but I'd gotten so used to it being just me, Adonis, and the surging power of the tide that Evan seems alien.

"Lawrence," Adonis says as he sidesteps toward the opposite hallway, "follow my lead again. I'm going to pull half of the life force towards me. You focus on holding the pool still."

I groan as the strength of the tide divides, like an amoeba becoming two separate entities. I push as the energy tingles through my legs: stand strong, stand still. Oh shizz. I want to take a picture of this. Adonis is friggin' water-bending. He can kick an avatar's ass. The water rises up like a waterfall in reverse, funneling in his direction as he backs down the hall.

Good luck, Adonis thinks. And he's gone, taking his tide down to Flood Bay 3.

"This is going to feel strange," Evan breathes in my ear, hand on my shoulder. He sings a soft song with no words, the notes legato with mild vibrato.

My heart shudders in my chest as the pool's life force shivers in reaction to Evan's song. It's like mixing Kool-Aid into a pitcher. Evan's magic doesn't feel wrong, but it's not an original part of us—the water and me.

Don't fight me. Evan's thoughts are light. *If you do, the water won't listen and I can't help you guide it.*

Right. I'm the king. The success of Evan's magic depends on the courtesy of the elements. He has to be allowed, while I command. This is the first time since I found out I'm an elemental that I actually feel like one and it's friggin' amazing.

"Aooooooooooo!" I howl, 'gotta do something' bombs my body with excitement. Water rocks from side to side against the walls. Oh snap. I push back, reining, 'gotta do something' in.

Focus! Evan hisses.

Sorry. I take a deep breath, the tang of rust heavy in the air. Thump-thump-thump. Pull. *Do your thing.*

Big Brother:

Evan keeps a hand on my shoulder as he hums, voice rising above the crashing of the waves behind us. My heartbeat slows as some of the pulsing pressure of holding back the tide is relieved. I follow as Evan leads us into Bay 12 like a pied piper. I'm the band, he's the conductor.

Bay 12 is four stories high, a half story taller than the reservoir. Long silver beams suspend from the ceiling. They glow, illuminating the room.

I'm going to stop singing. You'll have to hold it on your own.

It's easier to hold the pool by myself since Adonis took my half, but stopping it is like restraining the ocean. I grit my teeth. My body's wet with sweat, my T-shirt and soldier cargos are glued to me.

Good. Maintain your focus.

Does he sound nervous? No, he can't. He eats bat-shit crazy danger for breakfast, lunch and snack time.

But...

I don't do this with other people. Close your eyes if you want. He hums an arrangement of notes, sounds like "Hey Diddle-Diddle." I feel a tug and let out an "oof" as Evan grabs me around the waist. My feet leave the ground; I dangle from Evan's arms as we rise.

Some water escapes my hold, leaking like bad yolk from a cracked egg. The dam's breaking.

Push. My vision's blurry. I wipe perspiration from my eyes and suck in a breath as I end up rubbing more

sweat into my eyes. The first story of the bay floods as more water ruptures my hold.

Evan speeds up the song. My ears pop as we spiral upward toward the beams. Too fast—too fast. Thump-thump-thump. My hold slips and the tidal wave crashes down. The second story floods. Water laps at my heels. I kick at it as we fly higher.

Grab a beam. Evan's voice is urgent.

I reach for one, wet fingers slipping and squeaking across the silver. I can't get a good grip—shizz—got it. My skin screams as metal cuts into my palms. I hear flesh clap against metal and look to see Evan catching hold of a beam and swinging himself up to perch on it like an acrobat. He grabs my wrist and yanks me up to sit beside him.

I gaze at the ocean beneath us completely filling out the bay. Random ship parts, crates and machinery bob in the sea, clanking against each other. Small waves crash as the water writhes.

Laughter bubbles in me and I let it rip. "We friggin' owned that piece!"

Evan smirks at me. *Jalee, Bay 12's flooded.*

Bay 3 is ready as well, Adonis thinks.

Secure yourselves. Jalee's mental voice is calm. *Inner bay doors will open in 47 wisps.*

The beam bounces as Evan stands on his toes, rapping his knuckles against the metal-patchwork ceiling. He hums off-key and I raise a brow. That's different. *I'm probing for empty space, cratch,* Evan thinks. *There's a half-level for storage up here.* Evan stops knocking, places a flat palm against a patchwork square and smiles. "Put your hand here."

"Uh," I don't have the balance that he does, but you know what? I slowly shift into a crouch and stand. Evan catches my wrist when I wobble, but lets go so I can slap my palm next to his on the ceiling.

"Can you discern the elements making up the metal?" Evan asks.

Focus. Thump-thump-thump. Breathe and extend my awareness. The metal's basically steel: carbon, sulfur, nickel, manganese, and iron glow in my mind, burning with life force. They're blended with artificial particles that are dull and cold in comparison to the naturally occurring ones. They're a bitch to work around as I shift the living elements, creating cracks in the patches.

"Twenty-eight wisps left," Evan says.

Thump-thump-thump. The fissures in the metal widen until I see the dark space above.

Evan blows on an index finger like a birthday candle and a skinny spire of fire shoots up into the dark space and becomes a mini-sphere of light. "Move your hand," Evan grunts. He makes a fist and punches the broken ceiling tiles. Fragments of steel rain down on our heads.

The beam under my feet shakes as Evan grips the jagged edges of the hole he's made and drags himself up. I watch him disappear for a second, then he's back, stretching his arms down for me to grab. He hauls me up. Ragged metal scratches my legs through the cargos, but I don't feel my skin tear. I scramble to get my legs and feet the rest of the way in as Evan scoots back.

"Fifteen wisps," he mutters. He shrugs off his black and green jacket and drapes it over our entrance

hole. The fabric barely covers the area. He runs his fingers along the edges of the jacket. I feel the frenetic
vigor of fire in his fingertips, fusing the jacket's coarse
material and flexible, metal lining to the broken floor.

*Leader One, Leader Four, Honorable Maeve, are
you in place?*—Chelate's voice.

Yes, Adonis thinks.

Do it, Evan's mental voice is weak.

*Outer bay doors opening in…*thinks Chelate.

The nightmarish roar of a tornado and a hurricane
crashing around King Kong in a rage keeps me on my
knees with my hands over my ears. The foundation rattles worse than a wooden rollercoaster with a car full of
Sumo wrestlers hitting the track at a 90-degree angle.
I'm thrown onto my side, my body rolls over the floor,
crashing into a large metal bin. My ribs cry out. I flop
onto my back, feeling the rhythm of the metal quaking beneath me. Water—the reservoir surges forward. I
close my eyes and, in my mind, see its path as it rumbles through the airlocks and out into space where it
becomes a titanic block of solid, black ice.

I sever my connection.

The storm below stops.

I pant, chest aching, body spent, soaked through
with sweat. Dammit, that felt good. I sit up; my abdominal muscles twinge like I'd done a thousand sit-ups.

Status? Evan's thought is a whisper. Concern
prickles under my ribs. He hadn't sounded so good earlier either. The little ball of fire still glows. I look for my
brother and find him hunched over his jacket.

*Herding maneuver successful. Seventy-five per-
cent of the Ruj models were destroyed by the double*

trap. Another 12 percent downed by the decoy fight-
ers—Desiri's voice. *A supplemental team from Lenore,*
Zavan Kyli models, have detained 1%, and the rest fled.

Adonis, status? Evan asks.

Clear, Adonis thinks.

"Are you okay?" I crawl to Evan. The storage level's ceiling is high enough for me to stand, but my legs
are ten ton weights. I better be ripped after this. Clark
Kent should have nothing on me.

Evan huffs like an asthmatic and clutches his left
shoulder like he's holding it together. Shizz, his arm.
With the jacket gone, the flesh-colored membrane over
his injury bleeds red.

"What can I do?" I reach him, hands hovering. I
swallow and touch his other shoulder. His skin's lava
hot. He raises his head; his eyes are glazed, but he gives
me a crooked grin.

"Good job," he pants. "Couldn't have asked for
better on your first trial."

"Th-thanks. Your arm though."

"I'll live." He closes his eyes.

/Lawrie, you guys all right?/ Lyle sounds freaked.
You're not dead, are you? Devon speaks up for the
first time.

We're okay, I think. You?

/We're good./

You two strap down on the bridge. Don't go any-
where. Evan thinks. His eyes stay closed. *Bay Door 12*
locked down?

Yes, sir, thinks Chelate.

Evan sighs.

I catch him as he slumps into me. "Whoa-whoa!"

"H-hey!" I struggle to turn him over and get him lying on his back, head in my lap.

Hey, we need a medic, I think. We're in the storage level above Bay 12.

Evan stares up at me, eyes bright. He seems pleased. *Jalee, send the battle record to the Silver and Gold Allegiance Councils. Recommend enhanced patrols of Sector 2. Desiri request for a shuttle pick-up on Madunat,* so the councilors and their honor guard can join us later.

He chuckles. "How do you feel about all that down there, little brother? What was that you said before? 'We friggin' owned that piece'?"

I laugh, hysteria and 'gotta do something' hand in hand. "Y-yeah! We were effin' awesome sauce! Batman and Nightwing with super powers! That was..."

It's what other people needed me to do for them, and I did it. I helped save eighty people. I helped protect Lenore. I did what I couldn't do back on Earth, even after I'd found out I had powers and a destiny. And this is only some of what I'll be able to do. The rest is yet to come when I'm officially Leader Four, one of Order's Champions.

Evan chuckles again, the sound hoarse and exhausted. He raises a shaky fist and I tap it with my own. I've only known this brother for a little while, but I think we're friends. It's not like with Dev and Ly, but maybe we'll get there. Especially if we keep being kickass together.

Strategos Vimraz, Evan thinks. *Resume Ievisara's course to Lenore.* He winks at me. *We've got some new leaders to get coronated.*